The Basics of Finance

T0331126

The Frank J. Fabozzi Series

The Basics of Finance

An Introduction to Financial Markets, Business Finance, and Portfolio Management

PAMELA PETERSON DRAKE
FRANK J. FABOZZI

WILEY

John Wiley & Sons, Inc.

Copyright © 2010 by John Wiley & Sons. All rights reserved.

Published by John Wiley & Sons, Inc., Hoboken, New Jersey.
Published simultaneously in Canada.

No part of this publication may be reproduced, stored in a retrieval system, or transmitted in any form or by any means, electronic, mechanical, photocopying, recording, scanning, or otherwise, except as permitted under Section 107 or 108 of the 1976 United States Copyright Act, without either the prior written permission of the Publisher, or authorization through payment of the appropriate per-copy fee to the Copyright Clearance Center, Inc., 222 Rosewood Drive, Danvers, MA 01923, (978) 750-8400, fax (978) 646-8600, or on the Web at www.copyright.com. Requests to the Publisher for permission should be addressed to the Permissions Department, John Wiley & Sons, Inc., 111 River Street, Hoboken, NJ 07030, (201) 748-6011, fax (201) 748-6008, or online at http://www.wiley.com/go/permissions.

Limit of Liability/Disclaimer of Warranty: While the publisher and author have used their best efforts in preparing this book, they make no representations or warranties with respect to the accuracy or completeness of the contents of this book and specifically disclaim any implied warranties of merchantability or fitness for a particular purpose. No warranty may be created or extended by sales representatives or written sales materials. The advice and strategies contained herein may not be suitable for your situation. You should consult with a professional where appropriate. Neither the publisher nor author shall be liable for any loss of profit or any other commercial damages, including but not limited to special, incidental, consequential, or other damages.

For general information on our other products and services or for technical support, please contact our Customer Care Department within the United States at (800) 762-2974, outside the United States at (317) 572-3993 or fax (317) 572-4002.

Wiley also publishes its books in a variety of electronic formats. Some content that appears in print may not be available in electronic books. For more information about Wiley products, visit our web site at www.wiley.com.

Library of Congress Cataloging-in-Publication Data:

Fabozzi, Frank J.
  The basics of finance : an introduction to financial markets, business finance, and portfolio management / Frank J. Fabozzi, Pamela Peterson Drake.
      p.   cm. – (Frank J. Fabozzi series ; 192)
  Includes index.
  ISBN 978-0-470-60971-2 (cloth); 978-0-470-87743-2 (ebk);
  978-0-470-87771-5 (ebk); 978-0-470-87772-2 (ebk)
  1. Finance.   I. Peterson Drake, Pamela, 1954-   II. Title.
HG173.F25 2010
332–dc22   2010010863

Printed in the United States of America.

10   9   8   7   6   5   4   3   2   1

To my husband, Randy, and my children, Ken and Erica
—P.P.D.

To my wife, Donna, and my children, Francesco,
Patricia, and Karly
—F.J.F.

Contents

Preface

An investment in knowledge pays the best interest.

—Benjamin Franklin

The purpose of this book is to provide an introduction to financial decision-making, and the framework in which these decisions are made. *The Basics of Finance* is an accessible book for those who want to gain a better understanding of this field, but lack a strong business background. In this book, we cover the essential concepts, tools, methods, and strategies in finance without delving too far into theory.

In *Basics of Finance*, we discuss financial instruments and markets, portfolio management techniques, understanding and analyzing financial statements, and corporate financial strategy, planning, and policy. We explain concepts in various areas of finance without getting too complicated.

We explore, in a basic way, topics such as cash flow analysis, asset valuation, capital budgeting, and derivatives. We also provide a solid foundation in the field of finance, which you can quickly build upon.

Along the way, we provide sample problems—Try it! problems—so that you can try out any math that we demonstrate in the chapter. We also provide end-of-chapter questions—with solutions easily accessible on our web site—that test your knowledge of the basic terms and concepts that we discuss in the chapter. Solutions to end-of-chapter problems can be downloaded by visiting www.wiley.com/go/petersonbasics. Please log in to the web site using this password: Petersonbasics123.

The Basics of Finance offers essential guidance on financial markets and institutions, business finance, portfolio management, risk management, and much more. If you're looking to learn more about finance, this is the place to start.

We thank Glen Larsen, Professor of Finance at the Kelley School of Business, Indiana University, for coauthoring with us the section on relative valuation in Chapter 19.

PAMELA PETERSON DRAKE
FRANK J. FABOZZI
May 2010

CHAPTER 1

What Is Finance?

A truly great business must have an enduring 'moat' that protects excellent returns on invested capital. The dynamics of capitalism guarantee that competitors will repeatedly assault any business 'castle' that is earning high returns. Therefore a formidable barrier such as a company's being the low cost producer (GEICO, Costco) or possessing a powerful world-wide brand (Coca-Cola, Gillette, American Express) is essential for sustained success. Business history is filled with 'Roman Candles,' companies whose moats proved illusory and were soon crossed.
— Warren Buffett, Letter to Shareholders of Berkshire Hathaway, February 2008

Finance is the application of economic principles to decision-making that involves the allocation of money under conditions of uncertainty. In other words, in finance we worry about money and we worry about the future. Investors allocate their funds among financial assets in order to accomplish their objectives, and businesses and governments raise funds by issuing claims against themselves and then use those funds for operations.

Finance provides the framework for making decisions as to how to get funds and what we should do with them once we have them. It is the financial system that provides the platform by which funds are transferred from those entities that have funds to those entities that need funds.

The foundations for finance draw from the field of economics and, for this reason, finance is often referred to as *financial economics*. For example, as you saw with the quote by Warren Buffett at the beginning of this chapter, competition is important in the valuation of a company. The ability to keep

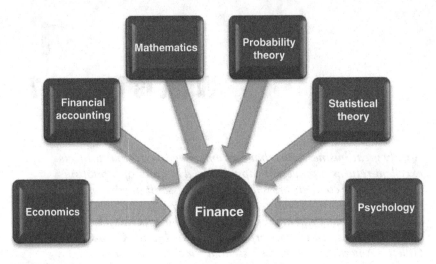

EXHIBIT 1.1   Finance and Its Relation to Other Fields

competitors at bay is valuable because it ensures that the company can continue to earn economic profits.[1]

FINANCE IS . . .

- analytical, using statistical, probability, and mathematics to solve problems.
- based on economic principles.
- uses accounting information as inputs to decision-making.
- global in perspective.
- the study of how to raise money and invest it productively.

The tools used in financial decision-making, however, draw from many areas outside of economics: financial accounting, mathematics, probability theory, statistical theory, and psychology, as we show in Exhibit 1.1.

We can think of the field of finance as comprised of three areas: capital markets and capital market theory, financial management, and investment

---

[1]*Economic profits* are earnings beyond the cost of capital used to generate those earnings. In other words, economic profits are those in excess of normal profits—those returns expected based on the investment's risk.

EXHIBIT 1.2 The Three Areas within the Field of Finance

management, as we illustrate in Exhibit 1.2. And, as this exhibit illustrates, the three areas are all intertwined, based on a common set of theories and principles. In the balance of this chapter, we discuss each of these specialty areas.

CAPITAL MARKETS AND CAPITAL MARKET THEORY

The field of *capital markets and capital market theory* focuses on the study of the financial system, the structure of interest rates, and the pricing of risky assets. The financial system of an economy consists of three components: (1) financial markets; (2) financial intermediaries; and (3) financial regulators. For this reason, we often refer to this area as *financial markets and institutions.*

Several important topics included in this specialty area of finance are the pricing efficiency of financial markets, the role and investment behavior of the players in financial markets, the best way to design and regulate financial markets, the measurement of risk, and the theory of asset pricing. The pricing efficiency of the financial markets is critical because it deals with whether investors can "beat the market." If a market is highly *price efficient,* it is extremely difficult for investors to earn returns that are greater than those expected for the investment's level of risk—that is, it is difficult for investors to beat the market. An investor who pursues an investment strategy that seeks to "beat the market" must believe that the sector of the financial market to which the strategy is applied is not highly price efficient. Such a strategy seeking to "beat the market" is called an *active strategy.* Financial theory tells us that if a capital market is efficient, the optimal strategy is not an active strategy, but rather is a *passive strategy* that seeks to match the performance of the market.

In finance, beating the market means outperforming the market by generating a return on investment beyond what is expected after adjusting for risk and transaction costs. To be able to quantitatively determine what is "expected" from an investment after adjusting for risk, it is necessary to formulate and empirically test theories about how assets are priced or, equivalently, valuing an asset to determine its fair value.

> A cow for her milk
> A hen for her eggs,
> And a stock, by heck,
> For her dividends.
>
> An orchard for fruit,
> Bees for their honey,
> And stocks, besides,
> For their dividends.
>
> —John Burr Williams
> "Evaluation of the Rule of Present Worth,"
> *Theory of Investment Value*, 1937

The fundamental principle of valuation is that the value of any financial asset is the present value of the expected cash flows. Thus, the valuation of a financial asset involves (1) estimating the expected cash flows; (2) determining the appropriate interest rate or interest rates that should be used to discount the cash flows; and (3) calculating the present value of the expected cash flows. For example, in valuing a stock, we often estimate future dividends and gauge how uncertain are these dividends. We use basic mathematics of finance to compute the present value or discounted value of cash flows. In the process of this calculation of the present value or discounted value, we must use a suitable interest rate, which we will refer to as a *discount rate*. Capital market theory provides theories that guide investors in selecting the appropriate interest rate or interest rates.

FINANCIAL MANAGEMENT

Financial management, sometimes called *business finance* or *corporate finance*, is the specialty area of finance concerned with financial decision-making within a business entity. Although financial management is often referred to as corporate finance, the principles of financial management also apply to other forms of business and to government entities. Financial managers are primarily concerned with investment decisions and financing decisions within organizations, whether that organization is a sole proprietorship, a partnership, a limited liability company, a corporation, or a governmental entity.

Regarding investment decisions, we are concerned with the use of funds—the buying, holding, or selling of all types of assets: Should a business purchase a new machine? Should a business introduce a new product line? Sell the old production facility? Acquire another business? Build a manufacturing plant? Maintain a higher level of inventory?

Financing decisions are concerned with the procuring of funds that can be used for long-term investing and financing day-to-day operations. Should financial managers use profits raised through the company's revenues or distribute those profits to the owners? Should financial managers seek money from outside of the business? A company's operations and investments can be financed from outside the business by incurring debt—such as through bank loans or the sale of bonds—or by selling ownership interests. Because each method of financing obligates the business in different ways, financing decisions are extremely important. The financing decision also involves the dividend decision, which involves how much of a company's profit should be retained and how much to distribute to owners.

A company's financial strategic plan is a framework of achieving its goal of maximizing owner's wealth. Implementing the strategic plan requires both long-term and short-term financial planning that brings together forecasts of the company's sales with financing and investment decision-making. Budgets are employed to manage the information used in this planning; performance measures are used to evaluate progress toward the strategic goals.

The *capital structure* of a company is the mixture of debt and equity that management elects to raise to finance the assets of the company. There are several economic theories about how the company should be financed and whether an optimal capital structure (that is, one that maximizes a company's value) exists.

Investment decisions made by the financial manager involve the long-term commitment of a company's scarce resources in long-term investments. We refer to these decisions as *capital budgeting decisions*. These decisions play a prominent role in determining the success of a business enterprise. Although there are capital budgeting decisions that are routine and, hence, do not alter the course or risk of a company, there are also strategic capital budgeting decisions that either affect a company's future market position in its current product lines or permit it to expand into new product lines in the future.

A financial manager must also make decisions about a company's current assets. *Current assets* are those assets that could reasonably be converted into cash within one operating cycle or one year, whichever takes longer. Current assets include cash, marketable securities, accounts receivable, and inventories, and support the long-term investment decisions of a company.

Another critical task in financial management is the *risk management* of a company. The process of risk management involves determining which risks to accept, which to neutralize, and which to transfer. The four key processes in risk management are risk:

1. Identification
2. Assessment
3. Mitigation
4. Transference

The traditional process of risk management focuses on managing the risks of only parts of the business (products, departments, or divisions), ignoring the implications for the value of the company. Today, some form of *enterprise risk management* is followed by large corporations, which is risk management applied to the company as a whole. Enterprise risk management allows management to align the risk appetite and strategies across the company, improve the quality of the company's risk response decisions, identify the risks across the company, and manage the risks across the company.

The first step in the risk management process is to acknowledge the reality of risk. Denial is a common tactic that substitutes deliberate ignorance for thoughtful planning.

—Charles Tremper

INVESTMENT MANAGEMENT

Investment management is the specialty area within finance dealing with the management of individual or institutional funds. Other terms commonly used to describe this area of finance are *asset management, portfolio management, money management,* and *wealth management.* In industry jargon, an asset manager "runs money."

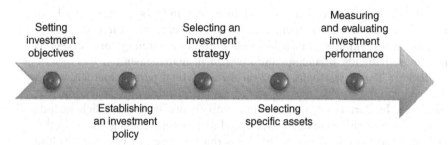

EXHIBIT 1.3   Investment Management Activities

Investment management involves five primary activities, as we detail in Exhibit 1.3. Setting investment objectives starts with a thorough analysis of what the entity or client wants to accomplish. Given the investment objectives, the investment manager develops policy guidelines, taking into consideration any client-imposed investment constraints, legal/regulatory constraints, and tax restrictions. This task begins with the decision of how to allocate assets in the portfolio (i.e., how the funds are to be allocated among the major asset classes). The *portfolio* is simply the set of investments that are managed for the benefit of the client or clients. Next, the investment manager must select a portfolio strategy that is consistent with the investment objectives and investment policy guidelines.

In general, portfolio strategies are classified as either active or passive. Selecting the specific financial assets to include in the portfolio, which is referred to as the portfolio selection problem, is the next step. The theory of portfolio selection was formulated by Harry Markowitz in 1952.[2] This theory proposes how investors can construct portfolios based on two parameters: mean return and standard deviation of returns. The latter parameter is a measure of risk. An important task is the evaluation of the performance of the asset manager. This task allows a client to determine answers to questions such as: How did the asset manager perform after adjusting for the risks associated with the active strategy employed? And, how did the asset manager achieve the reported return?

ORGANIZATION OF THIS BOOK

We have organized this book in parts to enable you to see how all the pieces in finance come together. In Part One, we provide the basic

---

[2]Harry M. Markowitz, "Portfolio Selection," *Journal of Finance* 7(1952): 77–91.

framework of the financial system and the players in this system. In Part Two, we focus on financial management, and discuss financial statements, financial decision-making within a business enterprise, strategy, and decisions including dividends, financing, and investment management.

In Part Three, we focus more on the analytical part of finance, which involves valuing assets, making investment decisions, and analyzing performance. In Part Four, we introduce you to investments, which include derivatives and risk management, as well as portfolio management. In this part, we also explain the basic methods that are used to value stocks and bonds, and some of the theories behind these valuations.

THE BOTTOM LINE

- Finance blends together economics, psychology, accounting, statistics, mathematics, and probability theory to make decisions that involve future outcomes.
- We often characterize finance as comprised of three related areas: capital markets and capital market theory, financial management, and investment management.
- Capital markets and capital market theory focus on the financial system that includes markets, intermediaries, and regulators.
- Financial management focuses on the decision-making of a business enterprise, which includes decisions related to investing in long-lived assets and financing these investments.
- Investment management deals with managing the investments of individuals and institutions.

QUESTIONS

1. What distinguishes investment management from financial management?
2. What is the role of a discount rate in decision-making?
3. What is the responsibility of the investment manager with respect to the investment portfolio?
4. Distinguish between capital budgeting and capital structure.
5. What are current assets?

6. If a market is price efficient,
   a. Can an investor "beat the market"?
   b. Which type of portfolio management—active or passive—is best?
7. What does the financing decision of a firm involve?
8. List the general steps in the risk management of a company.
9. What is enterprise risk management?
10. List the five activities of an investment manager.

The Financial System

CHAPTER 2

Financial Instruments, Markets, and Intermediaries

A strong financial system is vitally important—not for Wall Street, not for bankers, but for working Americans. When our markets work, people throughout our economy benefit—Americans seeking to buy a car or buy a home, families borrowing to pay for college, innovators borrowing on the strength of a good idea for a new product or technology, and businesses financing investments that create new jobs. And when our financial system is under stress, millions of working Americans bear the consequences. Government has a responsibility to make sure our financial system is regulated effectively. And in this area, we can do a better job. In sum, the ultimate beneficiaries from improved financial regulation are America's workers, families, and businesses—both large and small.
—Henry M. Paulson, Jr., then Secretary of the U.S. Department of the Treasury, March 31, 2008

THE FINANCIAL SYSTEM

A country's financial system consists of entities that help facilitate the flow of funds from those that have funds to invest to those who need funds to invest. Consider if you had to finance a purchase of a home by rounding up enough folks willing to lend to you. This would be challenging—and a bit awkward. In addition, this would require careful planning—and lots of paperwork—to keep track of the loan contracts, and how much you must repay and to whom. And what about the folks you borrow from? How are they going to evaluate whether they should lend to you and what interest rate they should charge you for the use of their funds?

In lending and investing situations, there is not only the awkwardness of dealing directly with the other party or parties, but there is the problem that one party has a different information set than the other. In other words, there is *information asymmetry*.

A financial system makes possible a more efficient transfer of funds by mitigating the information asymmetry problem between those with funds to invest and those needing funds. In addition to the lenders and the borrowers, the financial system has three components: (1) financial markets, where transactions take place; (2) financial intermediaries, who facilitate the transactions; and (3) regulators of financial activities, who try to make sure that everyone is playing fair. In this chapter, we look at each of these components and the motivation for their existence. Before we discuss the participants, we need to first discuss financial assets, which represent the borrowings or investments.

Financial Assets

An *asset* is any resource that we expect to provide future benefits and, hence, has economic value. We can categorize assets into two types: *tangible assets* and *intangible assets*. The value of a tangible asset depends on its physical properties. Buildings, aircraft, land, and machinery are examples of tangible assets, which we often refer to as *fixed assets*.

An intangible asset represents a legal claim to some future economic benefit or benefits. Examples of intangible assets include patents, copyrights, and trademarks. The value of an intangible asset bears no relation to the form, physical or otherwise, in which the claims are recorded. *Financial assets*, such as stocks and bonds, are also intangible assets because the future benefits come in the form of a claim to future cash flows. Another term we use for a financial asset is *financial instrument*. We often refer to certain types of financial instruments as *securities*, which include stocks and bonds.

For every financial instrument, there is a minimum of two parties. The party that has agreed to make future cash payments is the *issuer*; the party that owns the financial instrument and therefore the right to receive the payments made by the issuer is the *investor*.

Why Do We Need Financial Assets?

Financial assets serve two principal functions:

1. They allow the transference of funds from those entities that have surplus funds to invest to those who need funds to invest in tangible assets.

← FUNDS

FINANCIAL ASSETS →

EXHIBIT 2.1 The Role of the Financial Intermediary

2. They permit the transference of funds in such a way as to redistribute the unavoidable risk associated with the tangible assets' cash flow among those seeking and those providing the funds.

However, the claims held by the final wealth holders generally differ from the liabilities issued by those entities because of the activity of entities operating in financial systems—the financial intermediaries—who transform the final liabilities into different financial assets preferred by investors (see Exhibit 2.1). We discuss financial intermediaries in more detail later.

What Is the Difference between Debt and Equity?

We can classify a financial instrument by the type of claims that the investor has on the issuer. A financial instrument in which the issuer agrees to pay the investor interest, plus repay the amount borrowed, is a *debt instrument* or, simply, *debt*. A debt can be in the form of a note, bond, or loan. The issuer must pay interest payments, which are fixed contractually. In the case of a debt instrument that is required to make payments in U.S. dollars, the amount may be a fixed dollar amount or percentage of the face value of the debt, or it can vary depending upon some benchmark. The investor who lends the funds and expects interest and the repayment of the debt is a *creditor* of the issuer.

The key point is that the investor in a debt instrument can realize no more than the contractual amount. For this reason, we often refer to debt instruments as *fixed income instruments*.

MICKEY MOUSE DEBT

The Walt Disney Company bonds issued in July 1993, which mature in July 2093, pay interest at a rate of 7.55%. This means that Disney pays the investors who bought the bonds $7.55 per year for every $100 of principal value of debt they own.

In contrast to a debt obligation, an *equity instrument* specifies that the issuer pay the investor an amount based on earnings, if any, after the obligations that the issuer is required to make to the company's creditors are paid. *Common stock* and *partnership shares* are examples of equity instruments. Common stock is the ownership interest in a corporation, whereas a partnership share is an ownership interest in a partnership. We refer to any distribution of a company's earnings as *dividends*.

AN EXAMPLE OF COMMON STOCK

At the end of 2008 there were 3,032,717 shares of common stock outstanding of Proctor & Gamble, a U.S. consumer products company. At that time, financial institutions owned almost 60% of this stock. These institutions include pension funds and mutual funds. Individual investors owned the remainder of Proctor & Gamble's stock.

The stock is listed on the New York Stock Exchange with the ticker symbol PG.

Some financial instruments fall into both categories in terms of their attributes. *Preferred stock* is such a hybrid because it looks like debt because investors in this security are only entitled to receive a fixed contractual amount. Yet preferred stock is similar to equity because the payment to investors is only made after obligations to the company's creditors are satisfied.

Because preferred stockholders typically are entitled to a fixed contractual amount, we refer to preferred stock as a fixed income instrument. Hence, fixed income instruments include debt instruments and preferred stock.

Another hybrid instrument is a *convertible bond* or *convertible note*. A convertible bond or note is a debt instrument that allows the investor to convert it into shares of common stock under certain circumstances and at a specified exchange ratio.

DO YOU WANT DEBT OR STOCK?

Sirius XM Radio (ticker: SIRI) issued convertible notes in October 2004. These notes pay an interest rate of 3.25%, and can be exchanged for the common stock of Sirius XM Radio Inc. at a rate of 188.6792 shares of the company's common stock for every $1,000 principal amount of the notes.

The notes mature in 2011, so investors in these convertible notes have until that time to exchange their note for shares; otherwise, they will receive the $1,000 face value of the notes.

The classification of debt and equity is important for two legal reasons. First, in the case of a bankruptcy of the issuer, investors in debt instruments have a priority on the claim on the issuer's assets over equity investors. Second, in the United States, the tax treatment of the payments by the issuer differs depending on the type of class. Specifically, interest payments made on debt instruments are tax deductible to the issuer, whereas dividends are not.

THE ROLE OF FINANCIAL MARKETS

Investors exchange financial instruments in a financial market. The more popular term used for the exchanging of financial instruments is that they are "traded." Financial markets provide the following three major economic functions: (1) price discovery, (2) liquidity, and (3) reduced transaction costs.

Price discovery means that the interactions of buyers and sellers in a financial market determine the price of the traded asset. Equivalently, they determine the required return that participants in a financial market demand in order to buy a financial instrument. Financial markets signal how the funds available from those who want to lend or invest funds are allocated among those needing funds. This is because the motive for those seeking funds depends on the required return that investors demand.

Second, financial markets provide a forum for investors to sell a financial instrument and therefore offer investors liquidity. *Liquidity* is the presence of buyers and sellers ready to trade. This is an appealing feature when circumstances arise that either force or motivate an investor to sell a financial instrument. Without liquidity, an investor would be compelled to hold onto a financial instrument until either (1) conditions arise that allow for the disposal of the financial instrument, or (2) the issuer is contractually obligated to pay it off. For a debt instrument, that is when it matures, but for an equity instrument that does not mature—but rather, is a perpetual security—it is until the company is either voluntarily or involuntarily liquidated. All financial markets provide some form of liquidity. However, the degree of liquidity is one of the factors that characterize different financial markets.

The third economic function of a financial market is that it reduces the cost of transacting when parties want to trade a financial instrument. In general, we can classify the costs associated with transacting into two types: search costs and information costs.

Search costs in turn fall into two categories: explicit costs and implicit costs. Explicit costs include expenses to advertise one's intention to sell or purchase a financial instrument. Implicit costs include the value of time spent in locating a *counterparty*—that is, a buyer for a seller or a seller for a buyer—to the transaction. The presence of some form of organized financial market reduces search costs.

Information costs are costs associated with assessing a financial instrument's investment attributes. In a price-efficient market, prices reflect the aggregate information collected by all market participants.

THE ROLE OF FINANCIAL INTERMEDIARIES

Despite the important role of financial markets, their role in allowing the efficient allocation for those who have funds to invest and those who need funds may not always work as described earlier. As a result, financial systems have found the need for a special type of financial entity, a *financial intermediary*, when there are conditions that make it difficult for lenders or investors of funds to deal directly with borrowers of funds in financial markets. Financial intermediaries include depository institutions, nondeposit finance companies, regulated investment companies, investment banks, and insurance companies.

The role of financial intermediaries is to create more favorable transaction terms than could be realized by lenders/investors and borrowers dealing directly with each other in the financial market. Financial intermediaries accomplish this in a two-step process:

1. Obtaining funds from lenders or investors.
2. Lending or investing the funds that they borrow to those who need funds.

The funds that a financial intermediary acquires become, depending on the financial claim, either the debt of the financial intermediary or equity participants of the financial intermediary. The funds that a financial intermediary lends or invests become the asset of the financial intermediary.

Consider two examples using financial intermediaries that we will elaborate upon further:

Example 1: A Commercial Bank

A commercial bank is a type of depository institution. Everyone knows that a bank accepts deposits from individuals, corporations, and governments. These depositors are the lenders to the commercial bank. The funds received by the commercial bank become the liability of the commercial bank. In turn, as explained later, a bank lends these funds by either making loans or buying securities. The loans and securities become the assets of the commercial bank.

Example 2: A Mutual Fund

A mutual fund is one type of regulated investment company. A mutual fund accepts funds from investors who in exchange receive mutual fund shares. In turn, the mutual fund invests those funds in a portfolio of financial instruments. The mutual fund shares represent an equity interest in the portfolio of financial instruments and the financial instruments are the assets of the mutual fund.

Basically, this process allows a financial intermediary to transform financial assets that are less desirable for a large part of the investing public into other financial assets—their own liabilities—which are more widely preferred by the public. This asset transformation provides at least one of three economic functions:

1. Maturity intermediation.
2. Risk reduction via diversification.
3. Cost reduction for contracting and information processing.

We describe each of these shortly.

There are other services that financial intermediaries can provide. They include:

- Facilitating the trading of financial assets for the financial intermediary's customers through brokering arrangements.

- Facilitating the trading of financial assets by using its own capital to take the other position in a financial asset to accommodate a customer's transaction.
- Assisting in the creation of financial assets for its customers and then either distributing those financial assets to other market participants.
- Providing investment advice to customers.
- Managing the financial assets of customers.
- Providing a payment mechanism.

We now discuss the three economic functions of financial intermediaries when they transform financial assets.

Maturity Intermediation

In our example of the commercial bank, you should note two things. First, the deposits' maturity is typically short term. Banks hold deposits that are payable upon demand or have a specific maturity date, and most are less than three years. Second, the maturity of the loans made by a commercial bank may be considerably longer than three years. Think about what would happen if commercial banks did not exist in a financial system. In this scenario, borrowers would have to either (1) borrow for a shorter term in order to match the length of time lenders are willing to loan funds; or (2) locate lenders that are willing to invest for the length of the loan sought.

Now put commercial banks back into the financial system. By issuing its own financial claims, the commercial bank, in essence, transforms a longer-term asset into a shorter-term one by giving the borrower a loan for the length of time sought and the depositor—who is the lender—a financial asset for the desired investment horizon. We refer to this function of a financial intermediary a *maturity intermediation.*

The implications of maturity intermediation for financial systems are twofold. The first implication is that lenders/investors have more choices with respect to the maturity for the financial instruments in which they invest and borrowers have more alternatives for the length of their debt obligations. The second implication is that because investors are reluctant to commit funds for a long time, they require long-term borrowers to pay a higher interest rate than on short-term borrowing. However, a financial intermediary is willing to make longer-term loans, and at a lower cost to the borrower than an individual investor would because the financial intermediary can rely on successive funding sources over a long time period (although at some risk). For example, a depository institution can reasonably expect to have successive deposits to be able to fund a longer-term investment. As a result of this intermediation, the cost of longer-term borrowing is likely reduced in an economy.

Risk Reduction via Diversification

Consider the second example above of a mutual fund. Suppose that the mutual fund invests the funds received from investors in the stock of a large number of companies. By doing so, the mutual fund diversifies and reduces its risk. *Diversification* is the reduction in risk from investing in assets whose returns do not move in the same direction at the same time.

Investors with a small sum to invest would find it difficult to achieve the same degree of diversification as a mutual fund because of their lack of sufficient funds to buy shares of a large number of companies. Yet by investing in the mutual fund for the same dollar investment, investors can achieve this diversification, thereby reducing risk.

Financial intermediaries perform the economic function of diversification, transforming more risky assets into less risky ones. Though individual investors with sufficient funds can achieve diversification on their own, they may not be able to accomplish it as cost effectively as financial intermediaries. Realizing cost-effective diversification in order to reduce risk by purchasing the financial assets of a financial intermediary is an important economic benefit for financial systems.

Reducing the Costs of Contracting and Information Processing

Investors purchasing financial assets must develop skills necessary to evaluate their risk and return. After developing the necessary skills, investors can apply them in analyzing specific financial assets when contemplating their purchase or subsequent sale. Investors who want to make a loan to a consumer or business need to have the skill to write a legally enforceable contract with provisions to protect their interests. After investors make this loan, they would have to monitor the financial condition of the borrower and, if necessary, pursue legal action if the borrower violates any provisions of the loan agreement. Although some investors might enjoy devoting leisure time to this task if they had the prerequisite skill set, most find leisure time to be in short supply and want compensation for sacrificing it. The form of compensation could be a higher return obtained from an investment.

In addition to the opportunity cost of the time to process the information about the financial asset and its issuer, we must consider the cost of acquiring that information. Such costs are information-processing costs. The costs associated with writing loan agreements are *contracting costs*.

Another aspect of contracting costs is the cost of enforcing the terms of the loan agreement.

With these points in mind, consider our two examples of financial intermediaries—the commercial bank and the mutual fund. The staffs of these two financial intermediaries include investment professionals trained to analyze financial assets and manage them. In the case of loan agreements, either standardized contracts may be prepared, or legal counsel can be part of the professional staff to write contracts involving transactions that are more complex. Investment professionals monitor the activities of the borrower to assure compliance with the loan agreement's terms and, where there is any violation, take action to protect the interests of the financial intermediary.

It is clearly cost effective for financial intermediaries to maintain such staffs because investing funds is their normal business. There are economies of scale that financial intermediaries realize in contracting and processing information about financial assets because of the amount of funds that they manage.[1] These reduced costs, compared to what individual investors would have to incur to provide funds to those who need them, accrue to the benefit of (1) investors who purchase a financial claim of the financial intermediary; and (2) issuers of financial assets (a result of lower funding costs).

Regulating Financial Activities

Most governments throughout the world regulate various aspects of financial activities because they recognize the vital role played by a country's financial system. Although the degree of regulation varies from country to country, regulation takes one of four forms:

1. Disclosure regulation.
2. Financial activity regulation.
3. Regulation of financial institutions.
4. Regulation of foreign participants.

Disclosure regulation requires that any publicly traded company provide financial information and nonfinancial information on a timely basis that would be expected to affect the value of its security to actual and potential investors. Governments justify disclosure regulation by pointing out that

---

[1]*Economies of scale* are the reduction of costs per unit when the number of units produced and sold increases. In this context, this is the cost advantage an intermediary achieves when it increases the scale of its operations in contracting and processing.

the issuer has access to better information about the economic well-being of the entity than those who own or are contemplating ownership of the securities.

Economists refer to this uneven access or uneven possession of information as *asymmetric information*. In the United States, disclosure regulation is embedded in various securities acts that delegate to the Securities and Exchange Commission (SEC) the responsibility for gathering and publicizing relevant information, and for punishing those issuers who supply fraudulent or misleading data. However, disclosure regulation does not attempt to prevent the issuance of risky assets. Rather, the SEC's sole motivation is to assure that issuers supply diligent and intelligent investors with the information needed for a fair evaluation of the securities.

Rules about traders of securities and trading on financial markets comprise financial activity regulation. Probably the best example of this type of regulation is the set of rules prohibiting the trading of a security by those who, because of their privileged position in a corporation, know more about the issuer's economic prospects than the general investing public. Such individuals are insiders and include, yet are not limited to, corporate managers and members of the board of directors. Though it is not illegal for insiders to buy or sell the stock of a company in which they are considered an insider, *illegal insider trading* is the trading in a security of a company by a person who is an insider, and the trade is based on material, nonpublic information. Illegal insider trading is another problem posed by asymmetric information. The SEC is responsible for monitoring the trades that corporate officers, directors, as well as major stockholders, execute in the securities of their firms.

Another example of financial activity regulation is the set of rules imposed by the SEC regarding the structure and operations of exchanges where securities trade. The justification for such rules is that it reduces the likelihood that members of exchanges may be able, under certain circumstances, to collude and defraud the general investing public. Both the SEC and the self-regulatory organization, the Financial Industry Regulatory Authority (FINRA), are responsible for the regulation of markets and securities firms in the United States.

The SEC and the Commodity Futures Trading Commission (CFTC), another federal government entity, share responsibility for the federal regulation of trading in options, futures and other derivative instruments. *Derivative instruments* are securities whose value depends on a specified other security or asset. For example, a call option on a stock is a derivative security whose value depends on the value of the underlying stock; if the value of the stock increases, the value of the call option on the stock increases as well.

The regulation of financial institutions is a form of governmental monitoring that restricts their activities. Such regulation is justified by governments because of the vital role played by financial institutions in a country's economy.

Government regulation of foreign participants involves the imposition of restrictions on the roles that foreign firms can play in a country's internal market and the ownership or control of financial institutions. Although many countries have this form of regulation, there has been a trend to lessen these restrictions.

We list the major U.S. securities market and securities legislation in Exhibit 2.2. The current U.S. regulatory system involves an array of industry and market-focused regulators.

Though the specifics of financial regulatory reform are not determined at the time of this writing, there are several elements of reform that appear in the major proposals:

- An advanced-warning system, which would attempt to identify systemic risks before they affect the general economy.
- Increased transparency in consumer finance, mortgage brokerage, asset-baked securities, and complex securities.
- Increased transparency of credit-rating firms.
- Enhanced consumer protections.
- Increased regulation of nonbank lenders.
- Some measure to address the issue of financial institutions that may be so large that their financial distress affects the rest of the economy.

TYPES OF FINANCIAL MARKETS

Earlier we provided the general role of financial markets in a financial system. In this section, we discuss the many ways to classify financial markets.

From the perspective of a given country, we can break down a country's financial market into an internal market and an external market. The *internal market*, which we also refer to as the *national market*, is made up of two parts: the domestic market and the foreign market. The *domestic market* is where issuers domiciled in the country issue securities and where investors then trade those securities. For example, from the perspective of the United States, securities issued by Microsoft, a U.S. corporation, trade in the domestic market.

The *foreign market* is where securities of issuers not domiciled in the country are sold and traded. For example, from a U.S. perspective, the

EXHIBIT 2.2 Federal Regulation of Securities Markets in the United States

Law	Description
Securities Act of 1933	Regulates new offerings of securities to the public. It requires the filing of a registration statement containing specific information about the issuing corporation and prohibits fraudulent and deceptive practices related to security offers.
Securities and Exchange Act of 1934	Establishes the Securities and Exchange Commission (SEC) to enforce securities regulations and extends regulation to the secondary markets.
Investment Company Act of 1940	Gives the SEC regulatory authority over publicly held companies that are in the business of investing and trading in securities.
Investment Advisers Act of 1940	Requires registration of investment advisors and regulates their activities.
Federal Securities Act of 1964	Extends the regulatory authority of the SEC to include the over-the-counter securities markets.
Securities Investor Protection Act of 1970	Creates the Securities Investor Protection Corporation, which is charged with the liquidation of securities firms that are in financial trouble and which insures investors' accounts with brokerage firms.
Insider Trading Sanctions Act of 1984	Provides for treble damages to be assessed against violators of securities laws.
Insider Trading and Securities Fraud Enforcement Act of 1988	Provides preventative measures against insider trading and establishes enforcement procedures and penalties for the violation of securities laws.
Private Securities Litigation Reform Act of 1995	Limits shareholder lawsuits against companies, provides safe-harbor for forward-looking statement by companies, and provides for auditor disclosure of corporate fraud.
Securities Litigation Uniform Standards Act of 1998	Corrects the Private Securities Litigation Reform Act of 1995, reducing the ability of plaintiffs to bring securities fraud cases through state courts.
Sarbanes-Oxley Act of 2002	Wide-sweeping changes that provide reforms in corporate responsibility and financial disclosures, creates the Public Company Accounting Oversight Board, and increased penalties for accounting and corporate fraud.

securities issued by Toyota Motor Corporation trade in the foreign market. We refer to the foreign market in the United States as the "Yankee market."

The regulatory authorities where the security is issued impose the rules governing the issuance of foreign securities. For example, non–U.S. corporations that seek to issue securities in the United States must comply with U.S. securities law. A non-Japanese corporation that wants to sell its securities in Japan must comply with Japanese securities law and regulations imposed by the Japanese Ministry of Finance.

YANKEE MARKETS AND MORE ...

In Japan the foreign market is nicknamed the "Samurai market," in the United Kingdom the "Bulldog market," in the Netherlands the "Rembrandt market," and in Spain the "Matador market."

The other sector of a country's financial market is the *external market.* This is the market where securities with the following two distinguishing features are trading:

1. At issuance the securities are offered simultaneously to investors in a number of countries.
2. The securities are issued outside the jurisdiction of any single country. We also refer to the external market as the *international market*, the *offshore market*, and the *Euromarket* (despite the fact that this market is not limited to Europe).

The Money Market

The *money market* is the sector of the financial market that includes financial instruments with a maturity or redemption date one year or less at the time of issuance. Typically, money market instruments are debt instruments and include Treasury bills, commercial paper, negotiable certificates of deposit, repurchase agreements, and bankers' acceptances.[2]

Treasury bills (popularly referred to as *T-bills*) are short-term securities issued by the U.S. government; they have original maturities of four

---

[2]Under certain circumstances, we consider preferred stock as a money market instrument.

weeks, three months, or six months. T-bills carry no stated interest rate. Instead, the government sells these securities on a discounted basis. This means that the holder of a T-bill realizes a return by buying these securities for less than the maturity value and then receiving the maturity value at maturity.

Commercial paper is a promissory note—a written promise to pay—issued by a large, creditworthy corporation or a municipality. This financial instrument has an original maturity that typically ranges from one day to 270 days. The issuers of most commercial paper back up the paper with bank lines of credit, which means that a bank is standing by ready to pay the obligation if the issuer is unable to. Commercial paper may be either interest bearing or sold on a discounted basis.

Certificates of deposit (CDs) are written promises by a bank to pay a depositor. Investors can buy and sell *negotiable certificates of deposit*, which are CDs issued by large commercial banks. Negotiable CDs typically have original maturities between one month and one year and have denominations of $100,000 or more. Investors pay face value for negotiable CDs, and receive a fixed rate of interest on the CD. On the maturity date, the issuer repays the principal, plus interest.

A *Eurodollar CD* is a negotiable CD for a U.S. dollar deposit at a bank located outside the United States or in U.S. International Banking Facilities. The interest rate on Eurodollar CDs is the *London Interbank Offered Rate* (*LIBOR*), which is the rate at which major international banks are willing to offer term Eurodollar deposits to each other.

Another form of short-term borrowing is the *repurchase agreement*. To understand a repurchase agreement, we will briefly describe why companies use this instrument. There are participants in the financial system that use leverage in implementing trading strategies in the bond market. That is, the strategy involves buying bonds with borrowed funds. Rather than borrowing from a bank, a market participant can use the bonds it has acquired as collateral for a loan. Specifically, the lender will loan a certain amount of funds to an entity in need of funds using the bonds as collateral. We refer to this common lending agreement as a repurchase agreement or *repo* because it specifies that the borrower sells the bonds to the lender in exchange for proceeds and at some specified future date the borrower repurchases the bonds from the lender at a specified price. The specified price, called the repurchase price, is higher than the price at which the bonds are sold because it embodies the interest cost that the lender is charging the borrower. The interest rate in a repo is the *repo rate*. Thus, a repo is nothing more than a collateralized loan; that is, a loan backed by a specific asset. We classify it as a money market instrument because the term of a repo is typically less than one year.

Bankers' acceptances are short-term loans, usually to importers and exporters, made by banks to finance specific transactions. An acceptance is created when a draft (a promise to pay) is written by a bank's customer and the bank "accepts" it, promising to pay. The bank's acceptance of the draft is a promise to pay the face amount of the draft to whoever presents it for payment. The bank's customer then uses the draft to finance a transaction, giving this draft to the supplier in exchange for goods. Because acceptances arise from specific transactions, they are available in a wide variety of principal amounts. Typically, bankers' acceptances have maturities of less than 180 days. Bankers' acceptances are sold at a discount from their face value, and the face value is paid at maturity. The likelihood of default on bankers' acceptances is very small because acceptances are backed by both the issuing bank and the purchaser of goods.

The Capital Market

The *capital market* is the sector of the financial market where long-term financial instruments issued by corporations and governments trade. Here "long-term" refers to a financial instrument with an original maturity greater than one year and perpetual securities (those with no maturity). There are two types of capital market securities: those that represent shares of ownership interest, also called equity, issued by corporations, and those that represent indebtedness, issued by corporations and by the U.S., state, and local governments.

Earlier we described the distinction between equity and debt instruments. Equity includes common stock and preferred stock. Because common stock represents ownership of the corporation, and because the corporation has a perpetual life, common stock is a perpetual security; it has no maturity. Preferred stock also represents ownership interest in a corporation and can either have a redemption date or be perpetual.

A capital market debt obligation is a financial instrument whereby the borrower promises to repay the maturity value at a specified period of time beyond one year. We can break down these debt obligations into two categories: bank loans and debt securities. While at one time, bank loans were not considered capital market instruments, today there is a market for the trading of these debt obligations. One form of such a bank loan is a *syndicated bank loan*. This is a loan in which a group (or syndicate) of banks provides funds to the borrower. The need for a group of banks arises because the exposure in terms of the credit risk and the amount sought by a borrower may be too large for any one bank.

Debt securities include (1) bonds, (2) notes, (3) medium-term notes, and (4) asset-backed securities. The distinction between a bond and a note has to do with the number of years until the obligation matures when the issuer originally issued the security. Historically, a note is a debt security with a maturity at issuance of 10 years or less; a bond is a debt security with a maturity greater than 10 years.

The distinction between a note and a medium-term note has nothing to do with the maturity, but rather the method of issuing the security.[3] Throughout most of this book, we refer to a bond, a note, or a medium-term note as simply a bond. We will refer to the investors in any debt obligation as the *debtholder, bondholder, creditor,* or *noteholder.*

The Derivative Market

We classify financial markets in terms of cash markets and derivative markets. The *cash market,* also referred to as the *spot market,* is the market for the immediate purchase and sale of a financial instrument. In contrast, some financial instruments are contracts that specify that the contract holder has either the obligation or the choice to buy or sell something at or by some future date. The "something" that is the subject of the contract is the *underlying asset* or simply the *underlying.* The underlying can be a stock, a bond, a financial index, an interest rate, a currency, or a commodity. Such contracts derive their value from the value of the underlying; hence, we refer to these contracts as *derivative instruments,* or simply *derivatives,* and the market in which they trade is the *derivatives market.*

Derivatives instruments, or simply derivatives, include futures, forwards, options, swaps, caps, and floors. We postpone a discussion of these important financial instruments, as well as their applications in corporate finance and portfolio management, to later chapters.

The primary role of derivative instruments is to provide a transactionally efficient vehicle for protecting against various types of risk encountered by investors and issuers. Admittedly, it is difficult to see at this early stage how derivatives are useful for controlling risk in an efficient way since too often the popular press focuses on how derivatives have been misused by corporate treasurers and portfolio managers.

---

[3]This distinction between notes and bonds is not precisely true, but is consistent with common usage of the terms note and bond. In fact, notes and bonds are distinguished by whether or not there is an indenture agreement, a legal contract specifying the terms of the borrowing and any restrictions, and identifying a trustee to watch out for the debtholders' interests. A bond has an indenture agreement, whereas a note does not.

The Primary Market

When an issuer first issues a financial instrument, it is sold in the *primary market*. Companies sell new issues and thus raise new capital in this market. Therefore, it is the market whose sales generate proceeds for the issuer of the financial instrument. Issuance of securities must comply with the U.S. securities laws. The primary market consists of both a public market and a private placement market.

The public market offering of new issues typically involves the use of an investment bank. The process of investment banks bringing these securities to the public markets is *underwriting*. Another method of offering new issues is through an *auction process*. Bonds by certain entities such as municipal governments and some regulated entities are issued in this way.

There are different regulatory requirements for securities issued to the general investing public and those privately placed. The two major securities laws in the United States—the Securities Act of 1933 and the Securities Exchange Act of 1934—require that unless otherwise exempted, all securities offered to the general public must register with the SEC.

One of the exemptions set forth in the 1933 Act is for "transactions by an issuer not involving any public offering." We refer to such offerings as *private placement offerings*. Prior to 1990, buyers of privately placed securities were not permitted to sell these securities for two years after acquisition. SEC Rule 144A, approved by the SEC in 1990, eliminates the two-year holding period if certain conditions are met. As a result, the private placement market is now classified into two categories: Rule 144A offerings and non-Rule 144A (commonly referred to as *traditional private placements*).

The Secondary Market

A *secondary market* is one in which financial instruments are resold among investors. Issuers do not raise new capital in the secondary market and, therefore, the issuer of the security does not receive proceeds from the sale. Trading takes place among investors. Investors who buy and sell securities on the secondary markets may obtain the services of stockbrokers, entities who buy or sell securities for their clients.

We categorize secondary markets based on the way in which they trade, referred to as *market structure*. There are two overall market structures for trading financial instruments: order driven and quote driven.

Market structure is the mechanism by which buyers and sellers interact to determine price and quantity. In an *order-driven market structure*, buyers and sellers submit their bids through their broker, who relays these bids to a centralized location for bid-matching, and transaction execution. We also refer to an order-driven market as an *auction market*.

In a *quote-driven market structure*, intermediaries (market makers or dealers) quote the prices at which the public participants trade. *Market makers* provide a bid quote (to buy) and an offer quote (to sell), and realize revenues from the spread between these two quotes. Thus, market makers derive a profit from the spread and the turnover of their inventory of a security. There are hybrid market structures that have elements of both a quote-driven and order-driven market structure.

We can also classify secondary markets in terms of organized exchanges and over-the-counter markets. *Exchanges* are central trading locations where financial instruments trade. The financial instruments must be those listed by the organized exchange. By *listed*, we mean the financial instrument has been accepted for trading on the exchange. To be listed, the issuer must satisfy requirements set forth by the exchange.

In the case of common stock, the major organized exchange is the New York Stock Exchange (NYSE). For the common stock of a corporation to list on the NYSE, for example, it must meet minimum requirements for pretax earnings, net tangible assets, market capitalization, and number and distribution of shares publicly held. In the United States, the SEC must approve the market to qualify it as an exchange.

In contrast, an *over-the-counter market* (OTC market) is generally where unlisted financial instruments trade. For common stock, there are listed and unlisted stocks. Although there are listed bonds, bonds are typically unlisted and therefore trade over-the-counter. The same is true of loans. The foreign exchange market is an OTC market. There are listed and unlisted derivative instruments.

Market Efficiency

Investors do not like risk and they must be compensated for taking on risk—the larger the risk, the more the compensation. An important question about financial markets, which has implications for the different strategies that investors can pursue, is this: Can investors earn a return on financial assets beyond that necessary to compensate them for the risk? Economists refer to this excess compensation as an *abnormal return*. In less technical jargon, we referred to this in Chapter 1 as "beating the market." Whether this can be done in a particular financial market is an empirical question. If there is such a strategy that can generate abnormal returns, the attributes that lead one to implement such a strategy is referred to as a *market anomaly*.

We refer to how efficiently a financial market prices the assets traded in that market as *market efficiency*. A price-efficient market, or simply an *efficient market*, is a financial market where asset prices rapidly reflect all available information. This means that all available information is already impounded into an asset's price, so investors should expect to earn a return necessary to compensate them for their anticipated risk. That would seem to preclude abnormal returns. But, according to Eugene Fama, there are the following three levels of market efficiency: (1) weak-form efficient, (2) semi-strong-form efficient, and (3) strong-form efficient.[4]

In the *weak form of market efficiency*, current asset prices reflect all past prices and price movements. In other words, all worthwhile information about historical prices of the stock is already reflected in today's price; the investor cannot use that same information to predict tomorrow's price and still earn abnormal profits.[5]

In the *semi-strong form of market efficiency*, the current asset prices reflect all publicly available information. The implication is that if investors employ investment strategies based on the use of publicly available information, they cannot earn abnormal profits. This does not mean that prices change instantaneously to reflect new information, but rather that asset prices reflect this information rapidly. Empirical evidence supports the idea that the U.S. stock market is for the most part semi-strong form efficient. This, in turn, implies that careful analysis of companies that issue stocks cannot consistently produce abnormal returns.

In the *strong form of market efficiency*, asset prices reflect all public and private information. In other words, the market (which includes all investors) knows everything about all financial assets, including information that has not been released to the public. The strong form implies that investors cannot make abnormal returns from trading on inside information (discussed earlier), information that has not yet been made public. In the U.S. stock market, this form of market efficiency is not supported by empirical studies. In fact, we know from recent events that the opposite is true; gains are available from trading on inside information. Thus, the U.S. stock market, the empirical evidence suggests, is essentially semi-strong efficient but not in the strong form.

The implications for market efficiency for issuers is that if the financial markets in which they issue securities are semi-strong efficient, issuers should expect investors to pay a price for those shares that reflects their value. This also means that if new information about the issuer is revealed to the public (for example, concerning a new product), the price of the security should change to reflect that new information.

---

[4]Eugene F. Fama, "Efficient Capital Markets: A Review of Theory and Empirical Work," *Journal of Finance* 25 (1970): 383–417.

[5]Empirical evidence from the U.S. stock market suggests that in this market there is weak-form efficient. In other words, you cannot outperform ("beat") the market by using information on past stock prices.

THE BOTTOM LINE

- Financial intermediaries serve the financial system by facilitating the flow of funds from entities with funds to invest to entities seeking funds.
- Financial markets provide price discovery, provide liquidity, and reduce transactions costs in the financial system.
- Financial intermediaries not only facilitate the flow of funds in the financial system, but they also transform financial claims, providing more choices for both investors and borrowers, reducing risk through diversification, and reducing costs.
- Regulation of financial markets takes one of four forms: disclosure regulation, financial activity regulation, regulation of financial institutions, and regulation of foreign participants.
- Financial markets can be classified as follows: money markets versus capital markets, cash versus derivatives markets, primary versus secondary markets, and market structure (order driven versus quote driven).
- Market price efficiency falls into three categories (weak form, semi-strong form, and strong form), and the form of this efficiency determines whether investors can consistently earn abnormal profits.

QUESTIONS

1. What distinguishes indebtedness and equity?
2. Is preferred stock a debt or equity instrument? Explain.
3. How does a mutual fund perform its function as a financial intermediary?
4. What is meant by the term "maturity intermediation"?
5. In the United States, who are the regulators of financial markets?
6. What are examples of money market securities? Provide at least four examples.
7. What is the difference between an exchange and an over-the-counter market?
8. What are the three forms of market efficiency?
9. What distinguishes a primary market from a secondary market?
10. What distinguishes a spot market from a derivatives market?
11. What distinguishes the money market from the capital market?
12. How does the efficiency of a market affect an investor's strategy?
13. The following is an excerpt taken from a January 11, 2008, speech entitled "Monetary Policy Flexibility, Risk Management, and Financial

Disruptions" by Federal Reserve Governor Frederic S. Mishkin (www.federalreserve.gov/newsevents/speech/mishkin20080111a.htm):

> *Although financial markets and institutions deal with large volumes of information, some of this information is by nature asymmetric. . . . Historically, banks and other financial intermediaries have played a major role in reducing the asymmetry of information, partly because these firms tend to have long-term relationships with their clients.*
>
> *The continuity of this information flow is crucial to the process of price discovery. . . . During periods of financial distress, however, information flows may be disrupted and price discovery may be impaired. As a result, such episodes tend to generate greater uncertainty.*

Answer the following questions pertaining to the statement:
a. What is meant by asymmetric "information by nature"?
b. What is the problem caused by information asymmetry in financial markets?
c. How do you think banks have historically "played a major role in reducing the asymmetry of information"?
d. What is meant by "price discovery"?
e. Why is the continuity of information flow critical to the process of price discovery?

14. The following is an excerpt taken from a November 30, 2007, speech entitled "Innovation, Information, and Regulation in Financial Markets" by Federal Reserve Governor Randall S. Kroszner (www.federalreserve.gov/newsevents/speech/kroszner20071130a.htm):

> *Innovations in financial markets have created a wide range of investment opportunities that allow capital to be allocated to its most productive uses and risks to be dispersed across a wide range of market participants. Yet, as we are now seeing, innovation can also create challenges if market participants face difficulties in valuing a new instrument because they realize that they do not have the information they need or if they are uncertain about the information they do have. In such situations, price discovery and liquidity in the market for those innovative products can become impaired.*

Answer the questions pertaining to the statement:

a. What are the information costs associated with financial assets?

b. What is meant by "liquidity"?

c. Why do you think that for innovative financial products price discovery and liquidity could become impaired?

15. The following is an excerpt taken from a November 30, 2007, speech entitled "Innovation, Information, and Regulation in Financial Markets" by Federal Reserve Governor Randall S. Kroszner (www. federalreserve.gov/newsevents/speech/kroszner20071130a.htm):

> *Another consequence of information investments is a tendency towards greater standardization of many of the aspects of an instrument, which can help to increase transparency and reduce complexity.... Standardization in the terms and in the contractual rights and obligations of purchasers and sellers of the product reduces the need for market participants to engage in extensive efforts to obtain information and reduces the need to verify the information that is provided in the market through due diligence. Reduced information costs in turn lower transaction costs, thereby facilitating price discovery and enhancing market liquidity. Also, standardization can reduce legal risks because litigation over contract terms can result in case law that applies to similar situations, thus reducing uncertainty.*

Answer the following questions pertaining to the statement:

a. What does Governor Kroszner mean when he says standardization "reduces the need for market participants to engage in extensive efforts to obtain information and reduces the need to verify the information that is provided in the market through due diligence"?

b. How do "Reduced information costs in turn lower transaction costs, thereby facilitating price discovery and enhancing market liquidity"?

CHAPTER 3

The Financial System's Cast of Characters

Financial crises are extremely difficult to anticipate, and each episode of financial instability seems to have unique aspects, but two conditions are common to most such events. First, major crises usually involve financial institutions or markets that are either very large or play some critical role in the financial system. Second, the origins of most financial crises (excluding, perhaps, those attributable to natural disasters, war, and other nonfinancial events) can be traced to failures of due diligence or "market discipline" by an important group of market participants.
—Ben Bernanke, Chairman of the Federal Reserve System,
March 6, 2007

There is a large number of players in the financial system who buy and sell financial instruments. The Federal Reserve ("the Fed"), in information about the financial markets that it publishes quarterly, classifies players into sectors. We report the broadest classification in Exhibit 3.1. The purpose of this chapter is to introduce you to all these players in the financial system, which we will do using the Federal Reserve's classification by sectors.

Households and nonprofits are self explanatory, so we will focus on the other sectors.

Another way to look at the financial system is by considering how much each sector contributes to the gross domestic product (GDP). Consider the GDP components for 2008 for the United States, as we show in Exhibit 3.2. As you can see, nonfinancial businesses contribute the most to GDP.

As we discussed in Chapter 2, however, the financial sectors facilitate the flow of funds in the economy. Therefore, this sector does not produce as

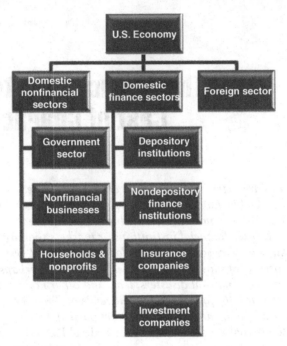

EXHIBIT 3.1 A Map of the U.S. Financial System

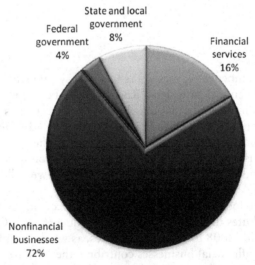

EXHIBIT 3.2 U.S. Gross Domestic Product, 2008
Data source: U.S. Census Bureau, The 2010 Statistical
Abstract, www.census.gov.

much GDP as the nonfinancial businesses, the financial sectors are important in the financing and investing activities of nonfinancial businesses.

DOMESTIC NONFINANCIAL SECTORS

The Government Sector

The government sector includes the federal government, as well as state and local government:

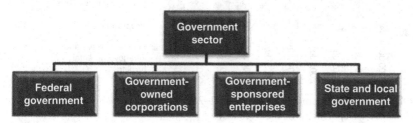

Also included in the government sectors are government–owned and government-sponsored enterprises.

The Federal Government The U.S. federal government raises funds by issuance of securities. The securities, referred to as *Treasury securities*, are issued by the U.S. Department of the Treasury through an auction process.

We show the amount of U.S. government debt over time and who owns this debt in Exhibit 3.3. Up until the most recent financial crisis, the major owners were Federal Reserve Banks and foreign investors; the latter include foreign governments. In the last few quarters in Exhibit 3.3, you see the accumulation of government debt by depository institutions.

Government-Owned Corporations The federal government has agencies that participate in the financial market by buying and selling securities. The federal government has chartered entities to provide funding for specific U.S. government projects. These entities are called *government-owned corporations*. A good example is the Tennessee Valley Authority (TVA), which was established by Congress in 1933 primarily to provide flood control, navigation, and agricultural and industrial development, and to promote the use of electric power in the Tennessee Valley region. Two other examples of government-owned corporations are the United States Postal Service and the National Railroad Passenger Corporation (more popularly known as

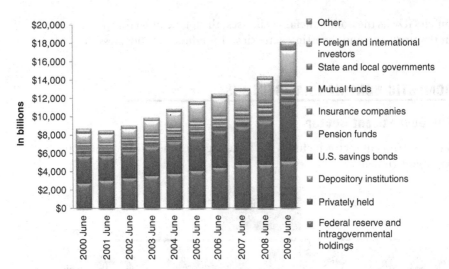

EXHIBIT 3.3 U.S. Government Debt, 2000Q2–2009Q2 (in billions)
Data source: U.S. Department of the Treasury.

Amtrak). In fact, of all the government-owned corporations, the TVA is the only one that is a frequent issuer of securities directly into the financial markets. Other government-owned corporations raise funds through the Federal Financing Bank (FFB). The FFB is authorized to purchase or sell obligations issued, sold, or guaranteed by other federal agencies.

Government-Sponsored Enterprises Another type of government-chartered entity is one that is chartered to provide support for two sectors that are viewed as critically important to the U.S. economy: housing and agricultural sectors. These entities are *government-sponsored enterprises* (GSEs), and are privately owned entities.[1] We provide a listing of GSEs in Exhibit 3.4.

There are two types of GSEs. The first is a publicly owned shareholder corporation whose stock is publicly traded. The publicly owned GSEs include the Federal National Mortgage Association, Federal Home Loan Mortgage Corporation, and Federal Agricultural Mortgage Corporation. The first two are the most well known GSEs because of the key role that they played in the housing finance market. Both Fannie Mae and Freddie Mac have similar purposes, which are to promote home ownership through

---

[1]In other countries, the term state-owned corporation is used.

EXHIBIT 3.4 U.S. GSEs

Name	Nickname	Type	Purpose
Federal Agricultural Mortgage Corporate	FAMC or Farmer Mac	Publicly owned	Agricultural
Federal Farm Credit System	FFCS	Funding entity	Agricultural
Federal Home Loan Banks	FHLB	Funding entity	Housing
Federal Home Loan Mortgage Corporation	FHLMC or Freddie Mac	Publicly owned	Housing
Federal National Mortgage Corporation	FNMA or Fannie Mae	Publicly owned	Housing

the availability of financing. They accomplish this by buying mortgages, pooling them, and selling mortgaged-backed securities to investors. Because of the financial difficulties faced by both Fannie Mae and Freddie Mac, the U.S. government took control of these two GSEs by placing them into conservatorship.[2]

The other type of GSE is a funding entity of a federally chartered bank lending system and includes the Federal Home Loan Banks and the Federal Farm Credit Banks.

Government-sponsored corporations are often confused with government-owned corporations. An important distinction is that government owned corporations do not issue stock to the public, whereas GSEs issue stock. Another distinction is that government-owned corporations are not operated for a profit, whereas GSEs are profit-oriented. Still another distinction is that the entire board of directors of a government-owned corporation is appointed by the U.S. President, whereas only five of nine directors are appointed by the President for GSEs such as Fannie Mae and Freddie Mac.[3]

State and Local Governments   State and local governments are both issuers and investors in the financial markets. In addition, these entities establish authorities and commissions that issue securities in the financial market. Examples include the New York/New Jersey Port Authority.

---

[2]The Federal Housing Finance Agency (FHFA) is the conservator of both Fannie Mae and Freddie Mac, which means that the FHFA has full power over the assets and operations of these firms.
[3]This is, of course, not considering the currently conservatorship, which gives the federal government more power in GSEs than typical.

State and local governments invest when they have excess cash due to the mismatch between the timing of tax or other revenues and when those funds have to be spent. However, the major reason why they participate as investors is due to the funds available to invest from the pension funds that they sponsor for their employees. More specifically, many state and local governments provide a defined benefit program, a form of pension where they guarantee benefits to the employees and their beneficiaries. The five largest state and local sponsors of defined pension funds (referred to as *public pension funds*) and their size, in billions of total assets as of January 26, 2009, according to *Pension & Investments* are:

California Public Employees	$213.5
California State Teachers	$147.0
New York State Common	$138.4
Florida State Board	$114.5
New York City Retirement	$ 93.2

NONFINANCIAL BUSINESSES

Nonfinancial businesses are enterprises formed by individuals and other businesses to engage in activities for a profit, where these activities are not primarily those of a financial intermediary, such as a commercial bank. These businesses issue debt and equity instruments, and they invest in financial markets.

Businesses participate as investors in the financial market by investing excess funds in the money market and, as with state and local governments, invest the funds of the defined benefit plans in which they sponsor. The largest defined benefit pension funds of businesses in the United States are those of nonfinancial corporations. According to *Pensions & Investments*, the five largest as of January 26, 2009, in terms of total asset (in billions) are:

General Motors	$91.0
AT&T	$61.9
General Electric	$50.0
IBM	$49.4
Boeing	$42.5

Some nonfinancial businesses have subsidiaries that are involved in the same activities as financial corporations. The financial subsidiaries, which we refer to as *captive finance companies*, participate in the financial market by lending funds. Examples include Ford Motor Credit (a subsidiary of Ford

Motor) and General Electric Credit Corporation (a subsidiary of General Electric).

DOMESTIC FINANCIAL SECTORS

The financial sectors include enterprises that and regulators that provide the framework for facilitating lending and borrowing. We can classify these enterprises into different sectors, depending on the type of transactions they facilitate:

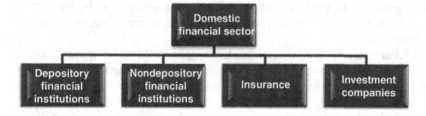

Depository Institutions

Depository institutions include commercial banks and thrifts. Thrifts include savings and loan associations, savings banks, and credit unions. As the name indicates, these entities accept deposits that represent the liabilities (i.e., debt) of the deposit-accepting institution. With the funds raised through deposits and nondeposit sources obtained by issuing debt obligations in the financial market, depository institutions make loans to various entities (businesses, consumers, and state and local governments).

Commercial banks are the largest type of depository institution and will be the focus here. A commercial bank is a financial institution that is owned by shareholders, and engages in accepting deposits and lending for a profit. A bank may be owned by a bank holding company (BHC), which is a company that owns one or more banks.

The five largest bank holding companies in the United States as of September 30, 2009, and their total assets in billions according to the Federal Reserve System, National Information Center are:

Bank of America	$2,253
J.P. Morgan Chase & Company	$2,041
Citigroup	$1,889
Wells Fargo & Company	$1,229
Goldman Sachs Group	$ 883

Bank Services   The principal services provided by commercial banks are:

1. Individual banking
2. Institutional banking
3. Global banking

Individual banking includes consumer lending, residential mortgage lending, consumer installment loans, credit card financing, automobile and boat financing, brokerage services, student loans, and individual-oriented financial investment services such as personal trust and investment services.

Institutional banking includes loans to both nonfinancial and financial business, government entities (state and local governments in the United States and foreign governments), commercial real estate financing, and leasing activities.

In global banking, commercial banks compete head-to-head with another type of financial institution—investment banking companies.[4] In the global arena, banks engage in corporate financing that involves (1) procuring of funds for a bank's customers, which can go beyond traditional bank loans to involve the underwriting of securities and providing letters of credit and other types of guarantees; and (2) financial advice on such matters as strategies for obtaining funds, corporate restructuring, divestitures, and acquisitions. Capital market and foreign exchange products and services involve transactions where the bank may act as a dealer or broker in a service.

Bank Funding   Banks are highly leveraged financial institutions, meaning that most of their funds come from borrowing.[5] One form of borrowing includes deposits. There are four types of deposit accounts issued by banks: demand deposits, savings deposits, time deposits, and money market demand accounts. *Demand deposits*, more popularly known as checking accounts, can be withdrawn upon demand and offer minimal interest. *Savings deposits* pay interest (typically below market interest rates), do not have a specific maturity, and usually can be withdrawn upon demand. *Time deposits*, more

---

[4]We discuss investment banking later, which covers a broad range of activities involving corporate financing and capital market and foreign exchange products and services.

[5]At one time, some of these activities were restricted by the Banking Act of 1933, which contained four sections (popularly referred to as the Glass-Steagall Act) barring commercial banks from certain investment banking activities. The restrictions were effectively repealed with the enactment of the Gramm-Leach-Bliley Act in November 1999, which expanded the permissible activities for banks and bank holding companies.

popularly referred to as certificates of deposit or CDs, have a fixed maturity date and pay either a fixed or floating interest rate. A *money market demand account* pays interest based on short-term interest rates.

Deposit sources other than borrowing that are available to banks are (1) borrowing by the issuance of instruments in the money and bond markets; (2) borrowing reserves in the federal funds market; and (3) borrowing from the Federal Reserve (Fed) through the discount window facility. The first source is self-explanatory. The last two require explanation.

A bank cannot invest $1 for every $1 it raises via deposit because it must maintain a specified percentage of its deposits in a noninterest-bearing account at one of the 12 Federal Reserve Banks. These specified percentages are the *reserve ratios*, and the dollar amounts based on them that are required to be kept on deposit at a Federal Reserve Bank are called *required reserves*.

The reserve ratios are established by the Federal Reserve Board and represent one of the monetary policy tools employed by the Fed. Banks satisfy these reserve requirements in each period by *actual reserves*, which are defined as the average amount of reserves held at the close of business at the Federal Reserve Bank. If actual reserves exceed required reserves, the difference is referred to as *excess reserves*. Because reserves are placed in noninterest-bearing accounts, an opportunity cost is associated with excess reserves. However, if there is shortfall, the Fed imposes penalties. Consequently, there is an incentive for banks to manage their reserves so as to satisfy reserve requirements as precisely as possible. There is a market where banks that are temporarily short of their required reserves can borrow reserves from banks with excess reserves. This market is called the *federal funds market,* and the interest rate charge to borrow funds in this market is called the *federal funds rate.*

Now let's look at how a bank can borrow at the Fed discount window. The *Fed discount window* is charged with the lending to banks to meet liquidity needs, with the Federal Reserve Bank effectively being the banker's bank. This means that the Federal Reserve Bank is the bank of last resort. If a bank is temporarily short of funds, it can borrow from the Fed at its discount window. However, borrowing at the discount window requires that the bank seeking funds put up collateral to do so. That is, the Fed is willing to make a secured or collateralized loan. The Fed establishes (and periodically changes) the types of collateral that are eligible for borrowing at the discount window. The interest rate that the Fed charges to borrow funds at the discount window is called the *discount rate*. The Fed changes this rate periodically in order to implement monetary policy.

Bank Regulation Because of their important role in financial markets, depository institutions are highly regulated and supervised by several federal and state government entities. At the federal level, supervision is undertaken by the Federal Reserve Board, the Office of the Comptroller of the Currency, and the Federal Deposit Insurance Corporation (FDIC). Banks are insured by the Bank Insurance Fund (BIF), which is administered by the Federal Deposit Insurance Corporation. Federal depository insurance began in the 1930s, and the insurance program is administered by the FDIC.

As already noted, the capital structure of banks is a highly leveraged one. That is, the ratio of equity capital to total assets is low, typically less than 8%. Consequently, there are concerns by regulators about potential insolvency resulting from the low level of capital provided by the owners. An additional concern is that the amount of equity capital is even less adequate because of potential liabilities that do not appear on the bank's balance sheet, so-called "off-balance sheet" obligations such as letters of credit and obligations on OTC derivatives. This is addressed by regulators via risk-based capital requirements.

The international organization that has established guidelines for risk-based capital requirements is the Basel Committee on Banking Supervision ("Basel Committee"). This committee is made up of banking supervisory authorities from 13 countries. By "risk-based," it is meant that the capital requirements of a bank depend on the various risks to which it is exposed.

Nondepository Financial Institutions

Nondepository financial institutions are intermediaries that do not accept deposits, but lend funds to consumers and businesses.[6] Examples of these institutions include consumer loan companies, trust companies, mortgage loan companies, credit counseling agencies, and finance companies.

Unlike depository institutions, nondepository financial institutions have been regulated only at the state level in the U.S., but there is a current discussion on increased regulation of these institutions on the national level, especially in the case of failures of large nondepository financial institutions.[7] One such failure was that of CIT Group, Inc., a commercial and consumer finance company, which filed for bankruptcy in 2009.

---

[6]Nondepository financial institutions are also referred to as nonbank financial institutions (NBFIs). The distinction of these types of companies as financial institutions was made starting with the Annuzio-Wylie Anti-Money Laundering Act of 1992, which broadened the definition of a financial institution beyond deposit accepting institutions.

[7]Chairman Ben S. Bernanke, "Financial Reform to Address Systemic Risk," March 10, 2009.

Insurance Companies

Insurance companies play an important role in an economy in that they are risk bearers or the underwriters of risk for a wide range of insurable events. Moreover, beyond their risk bearer role, insurance companies are major participants in the financial market as investors.

To understand why, we will explain the basic economics of the insurance industry. As compensation for insurance companies selling protection against the occurrence of future events, they receive one or more payments over the life of the policy. The payment that they receive is called a *premium*. Between the time that the premium is made by the policyholder to the insurance company and a claim on the insurance company is paid out (if such a claim is made), the insurance company can invest those proceeds in the financial market.

The insurance products sold by insurance companies include:

- *Life insurance.* Policies insure against death with the insurance company paying the beneficiary of the policy in the event of the death of the insured. Life policies can be for pure life insurance coverage (e.g., term life insurance) or can have an investment component (e.g., cash value life insurance).
- *Health insurance.* The risk insured is the cost of medical treatment for the insured.
- *Property and casualty insurance.* The risk insured against financial loss resulting from the damage, destruction, or loss to property of the insured property attributable to an identifiable event that is sudden, unexpected, or unusual. The major types of such insurance are (1) a residential property house and its contents and (2) automobiles.
- *Liability insurance.* The risk insured against is litigation, the risk of lawsuits against the insured resulting from the actions by the insured or others.
- *Disability insurance.* This product insures against the inability of an employed person to earn an income in either the insured's own occupation or any occupation.
- *Long-term care insurance.* This product provides long-term coverage for custodial care for those no longer able to care for themselves.
- *Structured settlements.* These policies provide for fixed guaranteed periodic payments over a long period of time, typically resulting from a settlement on a disability or other type of policy.
- *Investment-oriented products.* The products have a major investment component. They include a *guaranteed investment contract* (GIC) and *annuities.* In the case of a GIC, a life insurance company agrees that

upon the payment of a single premium, it will repay that premium plus a predetermined interest rate earned on that premium over the life of the policy.[8] While there are many forms of annuities, they all have two fundamental features: (1) whether the periodic payments begin immediately or are deferred to some future date and (2) whether the dollar amount is fixed (i.e., guaranteed dollar amount) or variable depending on the investment performance realized by the insurer.

■ *Financial guarantee insurance.* The risk insured by this product is the credit risk that the issuer of an insured bond or other financial contract will fail to make timely payment of interest and principal. A bond or other financial obligation that has such a guarantee is said to have an insurance "wrap." At one time, a large percentage of bonds issued by municipal governments were insured bonds, as well as asset-backed securities.

The leading insurance companies globally, in terms of 2008 revenues, are:[9]

Company	Country	Type of Insurance
Japan Post Holdings	Japan	Life/health
Allianz	Germany	Property/casualty
Berkshire Hathaway	United States	Property/casualty
Assicurazioni Generali	Italy	Life/health
AXA	France	Life/health

In the United States, the leading companies include Berkshire Hathaway, State Farm Insurance, and MetLife.

Investment Companies

Investment companies, also known as *asset management companies,* manage the funds of individuals, businesses, and state and local governments, and are compensated for this service by fees that they charge. The fee is tied to the amount that is managed for the client and, in some cases, to the performance of the assets managed. Some asset management companies

---

[8]Basically, a GIC is insuring that the policyholder will receive a guaranteed interest rate rather than risk that interest rates decline over the life of the policy. In the case of an annuity, the policyholder pays a single premium for the policy and the life insurance company agrees to make periodic payments over time to the policyholder.
[9]The source of this information is the Insurance Information Institute.

are subsidiaries of commercial banks, insurance companies, and investment banking companies.

The types of accounts, clients, and lines of business of asset management companies include:

- Regulated investment companies
- Exchange-traded funds
- Hedge funds
- Separately managed accounts
- Pension funds

Regulated Investment Companies *Regulated investment companies* (RICs) are financial intermediaries that sell shares to the public and invest those proceeds in a diversified portfolio of securities. Asset management companies are retained to manage the portfolio of RICs. Various U.S. securities laws regulate these entities.

There are three types of RICs managed by asset management companies: open-end funds, closed-end funds, and unit investment trusts (UITs). As you can see in Exhibit 3.5, mutual funds are the predominant form of RIC.

EXHIBIT 3.5 Assets of Regulated Investment Companies, 1995–2009 (billions)

Year	Net Assets, in Billions of Dollars		
	Mutual Funds	Closed-End Funds	Unit Investment Trusts
1995	$ 2,811	$143	$73
1996	3,526	147	72
1997	4,468	152	85
1998	5,525	156	94
1999	6,846	147	92
2000	6,965	143	74
2001	6,975	141	49
2002	6,390	159	36
2003	7,414	214	36
2004	8,107	254	37
2005	8,905	277	41
2006	10,397	298	50
2007	12,000	313	53
2008	9,601	188	29
2009	11,121	228	38

Data source: Investment Company Institute.

Each share sold represents a proportional interest in the portfolio of securities managed by the RIC on behalf of its shareholders. Additionally, the value of each share of the portfolio (not necessarily the price) is called the *net asset value* (NAV) and is computed as follows:

$$NAV = \frac{\text{Market value of portfolio} - \text{Liabilities}}{\text{Number of shares}}$$

For example, suppose that a RIC with 20 million shares outstanding has a portfolio with a market value of $430 million and liabilities of $30 million. The NAV is

$$NAV = \frac{\$430,000,000 - \$30,000,000}{20,000,000} = \$20$$

The NAV is determined only at the close of the trading day.

Mutual Funds In *open-end funds*, commonly referred to simply as *mutual funds*, the number of fund shares is not fixed. All new investments into the fund are purchased at the NAV and all redemptions (sale of the fund) redeemed from the fund are purchased at the NAV. The total number of shares in the fund increases if more investments than withdrawals are made during the day, and vice versa.

For example, assume that at the beginning of a day a mutual fund portfolio is valued at $300 million, with no liabilities, and 10 million shares outstanding. Thus, the NAV of the fund is $30. Assume that during the trading day investors deposit $5 million into the fund and withdraw $2 million, and the prices of all the securities in the portfolio remain constant. The $3 million net investment into the fund means that 100,000 shares were issued ($3 million divided by $30). After the transaction, there are 10.1 million shares and the market value of the portfolio is $303 million. Hence, the NAV is $30, unchanged from the prior day.

If, instead, the portfolio's value and the number of shares change, the NAV will change. However, at the end of day, NAV will be the same regardless of the net shares added or redeemed. In the previous example, assume that at the end of the day the portfolio's value increases to $320 million. Because new investments and withdrawals are priced at the end-of-day NAV, which is now $32, the $5 million of new investments will be credited with $5 million ÷ $32 = 156,250 shares and the $2 million redeemed will reduce the number of shares by $2 million ÷ $32 = 62,500 shares. Thus, at the end of the day the fund has 10 million + 156,250 − 62,500= 10,093,750 shares. Because the portfolio has a total value of $323 million ($320 million plus the new investment of $3 million), the end-of-day NAV is $32 and not impacted by the transactions.

Closed-End Funds   Unlike open-end funds, *closed-end funds* do not issue additional shares or redeem shares. That is, the number of fund shares is fixed at the number sold at issuance (i.e., at the time of the initial public offering). Instead, investors who want to sell their shares or investors who want to buy shares must do so in the secondary market where the shares are traded (either on an exchange or in the over-the-counter market).

Supply and demand in the market in which funds are traded determine the price of the shares of a closed-end fund. Hence, the fund share's price can trade below or above the NAV. Shares selling below NAV are said to be "trading at a discount," while shares trading above NAV are "trading at a premium." Investors who transact in closed-end fund shares must pay a brokerage commission at the time of purchase and at the time of sale.

Unit Investment Trusts   There is a third type of RIC called a *unit investment trust* (UIT). This type of RIC is assembled, but not actively managed. A unit investment trust has a finite life and a fixed portfolio of investments.

Costs to Investors   Investors in RICs bear two types of costs: (1) a shareholder fee, usually called the sales charge, which is a "one-time" charge; and (2) an annual fund operating expense, usually called the *expense ratio*, which covers the fund's expenses. The largest expense component of the expense ratio is the management fee (also called the investment advisory fees), which is an annual fee paid to the asset management company for its services.

RICs are available with different investment objectives and investing in different asset classes—stock funds, bond funds, and money market funds. There are passively managed and actively managed funds. *Passive funds* (more commonly referred to as *index funds*) are designed to replicate a market index, such as the S&P 500 stock index in the case of common stock. In contrast, with *active funds* the fund advisor attempts to outperform an index and other funds by actively trading the fund portfolio.

Exchange-Traded Funds   As an investment vehicle, open-end funds (i.e., mutual funds) are often criticized for two reasons. First, their shares are priced at, and can be transacted only at, the end-of-the-day or closing price. Specifically, transactions (i.e., purchases and sales) cannot be made at intraday prices, but only at closing prices. Second, while we did not

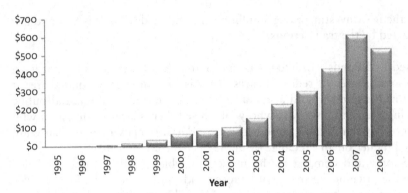

EXHIBIT 3.6 Growth of ETF Assets, 1995–2008 (billions)
Data source: Investment Company Institute.

discuss the tax treatment of open-end funds, we note that they are ineffi-cient tax vehicles. This is because withdrawals by some fund shareholders may cause taxable realized capital gains for shareholders who maintain their positions.

As a result of these two drawbacks of mutual funds, in 1993, a new investment vehicle with many of the same features of mutual funds was introduced into the U.S. financial market—*exchange-traded funds* (ETFs). This investment vehicle is similar to mutual funds but trades like stocks on an exchange. Even though they are open-end funds, ETFs are, in a sense, similar to closed-end funds, which have small premiums or discounts from their NAV. In an ETF, the investment advisor assumes responsibility for maintaining the portfolio such that it replicates the index and the index's return accurately. Because supply and demand determine the secondary mar-ket price of these shares, the exchange price may deviate slightly from the value of the portfolio and, as a result, may provide some imprecision in pricing. Deviations remain small, however, because arbitrageurs can create or redeem large blocks of shares on any day at NAV, significantly limiting the deviations.

Another advantage of ETFs in addition to being able to transact in ETFs at current prices throughout the day is the flexibility to place limit orders, stop orders, and orders to short sell and buy on margin, none of which can be done with open-end funds. With respect to taxation, ETFs overcome the disadvantages of open-end funds but we will not discuss the advantages here.

From 1995, up until 2008, there has been a steady growth in ETFs, as we show in Exhibit 3.6. There are ETFs that invest in a broad range of asset classes and new ones being introduced weekly.

Hedge Funds   The U.S. securities law does not provide a definition of the pools of investment funds run by asset managers that are referred to as *hedge funds*.[10] These entities as of this writing are not regulated.

The following is a definition of hedge funds offered by the United Kingdom's Financial Services Authority, the regulatory body of all providers of financial services in that country:[11]

> *The term can also be defined by considering the characteristics most commonly associated with hedge funds. Usually, hedge funds:*
>
> ■ *Are organised as private investment partnerships or offshore investment corporations.*
> ■ *Use a wide variety of trading strategies involving position-taking in a range of markets.*
> ■ *Employ an assortment of trading techniques and instruments, often including short-selling, derivatives, and leverage.*
> ■ *Pay performance fees to their managers.*
> ■ *Have an investor base comprising wealthy individuals and institutions and a relatively high minimum investment limit (set at US$100,000 or higher for most funds).*

This definition helps us to understand several attributes of hedge funds. First and foremost, the word "hedge" in hedge funds is misleading because it is not a characteristic of hedge funds today. Second, hedge funds use a wide range of trading strategies and techniques in an attempt to not just generate abnormal returns but rather attempt to generate stellar returns regardless of how the market moves. The strategies used by a hedge fund can include one or more of the following:

■ Leverage, which is the use of borrowed funds
■ Short selling, which is the sale of a financial instrument not owned in anticipation of a decline in that financial instrument's price
■ Derivatives to great leverage and control risk
■ Simultaneous buying and selling of related financial instruments to realize a profit from the temporary misalignment of their prices

---

[10] The term *hedge fund* was first used by *Fortune* in 1966 to describe the private investment fund of Alfred Winslow Jones. In managing the portfolio, Jones sought to "hedge" the market risk of the fund by creating a portfolio that was long and short the stock market by an equal amount.
[11] Financial Services Authority (2002, 8).

Hedge funds operate in sectors of the financial markets: cash market for stocks, bonds, and currencies, as well as in derivatives markets.

Third, in evaluating hedge funds, investors are interested in the absolute return generated by the asset manager, not the relative return. *Absolute return* is simply the return realized rather than *relative return,* which is the difference between the realized return and the return on some benchmark or index, which is quite different from the criterion used when evaluating the performance of an asset manager.

Fourth, the management fee structure for hedge funds is a combination of a fixed fee based on the market value of assets managed plus a share of the positive return. The latter is a performance-based compensation referred to as an *incentive fee.*

In the United States, hedge funds are available to accredited investors. As defined by the SEC, accredited investors include individuals with a net worth over $1 million, banks, insurance companies, and registered investment companies.[12]

Separately Managed Accounts   Instead of investing directly in stocks or bonds, or by means of alternatives such as mutual funds, ETFs, or hedge funds, asset management companies offer individual and institutional investors the opportunity to invest in a *separately managed account* (also called an *individually managed account*). In such accounts, the investments selected by the asset manager are customized to the objectives of the investor. Although separately managed accounts offer the customers of an asset management an investment vehicle that overcomes all the limitations of RICs, they are more expensive than RICs in terms of the fees charged.

Pension Funds   A pension plan fund is established for the eventual payment of retirement benefits. A *plan sponsor* is the entity that establishes the pension plan. A plan sponsor can be:

- A private business entity on behalf of its employees, called a *corporate plan* or *private plan.*
- A federal, state, and local government on behalf of its employees, called a *public plan.*
- A union on behalf of its members, called a *Taft-Hartley plan.*
- An individual, called an *individually sponsored plan.*

---

[12] Defined in Securities and Exchange Commission Rule 501 of Regulation D.

Two basic and widely used types of pension plans are defined benefit plans and defined contribution plans. In addition, a hybrid type of plan, called a cash balance plan, combines features of both pension plan types.

In a *defined benefit* (DB) *plan,* the plan sponsor agrees to make specified dollar payments to qualifying employees beginning at retirement (and some payments to beneficiaries in case of death before retirement). Effectively, the DB plan pension obligations are a debt obligation of the plan sponsor and consequently the plan sponsor assumes the risk of having insufficient funds in the plan to satisfy the regular contractual payments that must be made to currently retired employees as well as those who will retire in the future.

A plan sponsor has several options available in deciding who should manage the plan's assets. The choices are:

- *Internal management.* The plan sponsor uses its own investment staff to manage the plan's assets.
- *External management.* The plan sponsor engages the services of one or more asset management companies to manage the plan's assets.
- *Combination of internal and external management.* Some of the plan's assets are managed internally by the plan sponsor and the balance are managed by one or more asset management companies.

Asset managers who manage the assets of defined benefit plans receive compensation in the form of a management fee.

There is federal legislation that regulates pension plans—the Employee Retirement Income Security Act of 1974 (ERISA). Responsibility for administering ERISA is delegated to the Department of Labor and the Internal Revenue Service. ERISA established fiduciary standards for pension fund trustees, managers, or advisors.

In a *defined contribution* (DC) *plan,* the plan sponsor is responsible only for making specified contributions into the plan on behalf of qualifying participants with the amount that it must contribute often being either a percentage of the employee's salary and/or a percentage of the employer's profits. The plan sponsor does not guarantee any specific amount at retirement. The amount that the employee receives at retirement is not guaranteed, but instead depends on the growth (therefore, performance) of the plan assets. The plan sponsor does offer the plan participants various options as to the investment vehicles in which they may invest. Defined contribution pension plans come in several legal forms: 401(k) plans, money purchase pension plans, and *employee stock ownership plans* (ESOPs).

A hybrid pension plan is a combination of a defined benefit and defined contribution plan with the most common type being a cash balance plan. This plan defines future pension benefits, not employer contributions.

Retirement benefits are based on a fixed amount annual employer contribution and a guaranteed minimum annual investment return. Each participant's account in a cash balance plan is credited with a dollar amount
that resembles an employer contribution and is generally determined as a
percentage of pay. Each participant's account is also credited with interest
linked to some fixed or variable index such as the consumer price index
(CPI). Typically, a cash balance plan provides benefits in the form of a lump
sum distribution such as an annuity.

Investment Banks

As with commercial banks, investment banks are highly leveraged entities
that play important roles in both the primary and secondary markets. Investment banking activities include:

- Raising funds through public offerings and private placement of
  securities.
- Trading of securities.
- Mergers, acquisitions, and financial restructuring advising.
- Merchant banking.
- Securities finance and prime brokerage services.

The first role is assisting in the raising of funds by corporations, U.S.
government agencies, state and local governments, and foreign entities
(sovereigns and corporations). The second role is assisting investors who
wish to invest funds by acting as brokers or dealers in secondary market
transactions.

We can classify investment banking into two categories:

1. Companies affiliated with large financial services holding companies.
2. Companies that are independent of a large financial services holding
   company.

The large investment banks are affiliated with large commercial bank
holding companies. Examples of bank holding companies, referred to as
bank-affiliated investment banks, are Banc of America Securities (a subsidiary of Bank of America), JPMorgan Securities (a subsidiary of JPMorgan Chase), and Wachovia Securities (a subsidiary of Wells Fargo), and
Goldman Sachs.

The second category of investment banks, referred to as independent
investment banks, is a shrinking group. As of mid-2008, this group includes
Greenhill & Company and Houlihan Lokey Howard & Zukin.

Another way of classifying investment banking companies is based on the types of activities (i.e., the lines of business) in which they participate: full-service investment banks and boutique investment banks. The former are active in a wide range of investment banking activities while the latter specialize in a limited number of those activities.

In assisting entities in the raising of funds in the public market, investment bankers perform one or more of the following three functions:

- Advising the issuer on the terms and the timing of the offering.
- Underwriting.
- Distributing the issue to the public.

In their advisory role, investment bankers may be required to design a security structure that is more appealing to investors than currently available financial instruments.

The underwriting function involves the way in which the investment bank agrees to place the newly issued security in the market on behalf of the issuer. The fee earned by the investment banking company from underwriting is the difference between the price it paid to the issuer for the security and the price it reoffers the security to the public (called the *reoffering price*). This difference is referred to as the *gross spread*. There are two types of underwriting arrangements: firm commitment and best efforts. In a *firm commitment arrangement*, the investment bank purchases the newly issued security from the issuer at a fixed price and then sells the security to the public at the reoffering price. In a *best-efforts underwriting arrangement*, the investment banking firm does not buy the newly issued security from the issuer. Instead, it agrees only to use its expertise to sell the security to the public and earns the gross spread on only what it can sell.

Typically in a firm-commitment underwriting there will be several investment banks involved because of the capital commitment that must be made and the potential loss of the company's capital if the newly issued security cannot be sold to the public at a higher price than the purchase price. This is done by forming a group of companies to underwrite the issue, referred to as an *underwriting syndicate* by the lead underwriter or underwriters. The gross spread is then divided among the lead underwriter(s) and the other companies in the underwriting syndicate.

The distribution function is critical to both the issuer and the investment bank. To realize the gross spread, the entire securities issue must be sold to the public at the planned reoffering price and, depending on the size of the issue, may require a great deal of marketing effort. The members of the underwriting syndicate will sell the newly issued security to their investor client base. To increase the potential investor base, the lead underwriter(s) will often put together a *selling group*. This group includes the underwriting syndicate plus other companies not in the syndicate with the gross spread then divided among the lead underwriter(s), members of the underwriting syndicate, and members of the selling group.

Private Placement of Securities   As an alternative to issuing a new security in the public market, a company can issue a security via a private placement to a limited number of institutional investors such as insurance companies, investment companies, and pension funds. Private placement offerings are distinguished by type: non-Rule 144A offerings (traditional private placements) and Rule 144A offerings. Rule 144A offerings are underwritten by investment bankers.

Trading Securities   An obvious activity of investment banks is providing transaction services for clients. Revenue is generated on transactions in which the investment bank acts as an agent or broker in the form of a commission. In such transactions, the investment bank is not taking a position in the transaction, meaning that it is not placing its own capital at risk. In other transactions, the investment bank may act as a market maker, placing its own capital at risk. Revenue from this activity is generated through (1) the difference between the price at which the investment bank sells the security and the price paid for the securities (called the bid-ask spread); and (2) appreciation of the price of the securities held in inventory. (Obviously, if the price of the securities decline, revenue will be reduced.)

In addition to executing trades in the secondary market for clients, as well as market making in the secondary market, investment banks do proprietary trading (referred to as *prop trading*). In this activity, the investment bank's traders position some of the company's capital to bet on movements in the price of financial instruments, interest rates, or foreign exchange.

Advising in Mergers, Acquisitions, and Financial Restructuring Advising
Investment banks are active in mergers and acquisitions (M&A), leveraged buyouts (LBOs), restructuring and recapitalization of companies, and reorganization of bankrupt and troubled companies. They do so in one or more of the following ways: (1) identifying candidates for a merger or acquisition, M&A candidates; (2) advising the board of directors of acquiring companies or target companies regarding price and nonprice terms for an exchange; (3) assisting companies that are the target of an acquisition to fend off an unfriendly takeover attempt; (4) helping acquiring companies to obtain the needed funds to complete an acquisition; and (5) providing a

"fairness opinion" to the board of directors regarding a proposed merger, acquisition, or sale of assets.

Another area where investment banks advise is on a significant modification of a corporation's capital structure, operating structure, and/or corporate strategy with the objective of improving efficiency. Such modifications are referred to as *financial restructuring* of a company. This may be the result of a company seeking to avoid a bankruptcy, avoid a problem with creditors, or reorganize the company as permitted by the U.S. bankruptcy code.

The activities described above generate fee income that can either be a fixed retainer or in the case of consummating a merger or acquisition, a fee based on the size of the transaction. Thus, for most of these activities, the investment bank's capital is not at risk. However, if the investment bank provides financing for an acquisition, it does place its capital at risk. This brings us to the activity of merchant banking.

Merchant Banking The activity of merchant banking is one in which the investment bank commits its own capital as either a creditor or to take an equity stake. There are divisions or groups within an investment bank devoted to merchant banking. In the case of equity investing, this may be in the form of a series of private equity funds.

Securities, Finance, and Prime Brokerage Services There are clients of investment banks that, as part of their investment strategy, may need to either (1) borrow funds in order to purchase a security or (2) borrow securities in order to sell a security short or to cover a short sale. The standard mechanism for borrowing funds in the securities market is via a repurchase agreement (referred to as a *repo*) rather through bank borrowing. A repo is a collateralized loan where the collateral is the security purchased. Investment banks earn interest on repo transactions. A customer can borrow a security in a transaction known as a *securities lending transaction*. In such transactions, the lender of the security earns a fee for lending the securities. The activity of borrowing funds or borrowing securities is referred to as *securities finance.*

Investment banks may provide a package of services to hedge fund and large institutional investors. This package of services, referred to as *prime brokerage*, includes securities finance that we just described as well as global custody, operational support, and risk management systems.

Asset Management An investment bank may have one or more subsidiaries that manage assets for clients such as insurance companies, endowments, foundations, corporate and public pension funds, and high-net-worth individuals. These asset management divisions may also manage mutual funds and hedge funds. Asset management generates fee income based on a percentage of the assets under management.

FOREIGN INVESTORS

The sector referred to as *foreign investors* includes individuals, nonfinancial business, and financial entities that are not domiciled in the United States, as well as foreign central governments and supranationals. A foreign central bank is a monetary authority of the foreign country, such as the People's Bank of China (PBC), the European Central Bank, and the Bank of Canada. Foreign central banks participate in the U.S. financial market for two reasons. The first reason is to stabilize their currency relative to the U.S. dollar. The second reason is to purchase a financial instrument with excess funds because it is perceived to be an attractive investment vehicle.

A *supranational institution* is an international entity that is created by two or more central governments through international treaties. We can divide supranationals into two categories: multilateral development banks and others. The former are supranational financial institutions with the mandate to provide financial assistance with funds obtained from member countries to developing countries and to promote regional integration in specific geographical regions. The largest multilateral development banks are the European Investment Bank with more than $300 billion in total assets and the International Bank for Reconstruction and Development (popularly referred to as the World Bank) with more than $250 billion in total assets. The next two largest, the Inter-American Development Bank and Asian Development Bank, have less than a third of the assets of the two largest multilateral development banks.

THE BOTTOM LINE

- The financial system is comprised of financial firms, governmental entities, nonfinancial business entities, households, and nonprofit entities. The largest sector in the system consists of nonfinancial business entities.
- Government entities in the financial system include federal, state, and local governments, as well as government-owned and government-sponsored enterprises.
- The financial sector in the economy is comprised of depository institutions, nondepository financial institutions, insurance companies, and investment companies.

- The principal services provided by commercial banks are individual banking, institutional banking, and global banking.
- Insurance companies are risk bearers or are the underwriters of risk for a wide range of insurable events, and are major participants in the financial market as investors.
- Investment companies manage the funds of individuals, businesses, and state and local governments, and are compensated for this service by fees that they charge. The types of accounts, clients, and lines of business of asset management companies include regulated investment companies, exchange-traded funds, hedge funds, separately managed accounts, and pension funds.
- Investment banks play important roles in both the primary and secondary markets, and their activities include raising funds through public offerings and private placement of securities; trading of securities; advising on mergers, acquisitions, and financial restructuring; merchant banking; and securities finance and prime brokerage services.
- Foreign investors include individuals, nonfinancial business, and financial entities that are not domiciled in the United States, as well as foreign central governments and supranational institutions.

QUESTIONS

1. Who are the players in the government sector?
2. What is the distinction between a government-owned corporation and a government-sponsored enterprise?
3. What is the distinction between a depository financial institution and a nondepository bank financial institution?
4. What is an excess reserve and how is this different than required reserves?
5. List at least four different types of insurance companies.
6. What is the difference between a mutual fund and a closed-end fund?
7. If a mutual fund has a portfolio with a market value of $1 million and liabilities of $0.2 million, what is the net asset value if the fund has 0.5 million shares?
8. List two advantages, from the investor point of view, of an exchange traded fund, vis-à-vis a closed-end fund?
9. Distinguish between a defined benefit pension plan and a defined contribution plan.
10. List at least three functions of an investment bank.
11. List the major types of depository institutions.
12. How do commercial banks obtain their funds?
13. What is financial restructuring advising? Provide an example.

14. The following is an excerpt from the 2009 Annual Report of Bank of America (p. 24):

    Through our banking and various nonbanking subsidiaries throughout the United States and in selected international markets, we provide a diversified range of banking and nonbanking financial services and products through six business segments: Deposits, Global Card Services, Home Loans & Insurance, Global Banking, Global Markets and Global Wealth & Investment Management.

    a. What is meant by "Global Banking"?
    b. What is meant by "Global Wealth & Investment Management"?
15. The following excerpt if from the notes to the financial statements in the 2009 Annual Report of Bank of America (p. 147):

    The Corporation enters into trading derivatives to facilitate client transactions for proprietary trading purposes, and to manage risk exposures arising from trading assets and liabilities.

    a. What is meant by "proprietary trading"?
16. Following is an excerpt from "Merchant Banking: Past and Present" by Valentine V. Craig, published by the Federal Deposit Insurance Corporation (www.fdic.gov/bank/analytical/banking/2001sep/article2.html):

    Merchant banking has been a very lucrative—and risky— endeavor for the small number of bank holding companies and banks that have engaged in it under existing law. Recent legislation has expanded the merchant-banking activity that is permissible to commercial banks and is therefore likely to spur interest in this lucrative specialty on the part of a greater number of such institutions.

    a. What is meant by "merchant banking"?
    b. What are the risks associated with merchant banking?

PART TWO

Financial Management

CHAPTER 4

Financial Statements

Three suggestions for investors: First, beware of companies displaying weak accounting. If a company still does not expense options, or if its pension assumptions are fanciful, watch out. When managements take the low road in aspects that are visible, it is likely they are following a similar path behind the scenes. There is seldom just one cockroach in the kitchen. . . .

Second, unintelligible footnotes usually indicate untrustworthy management. If you can't understand a footnote or other managerial explanation, it's usually because the CEO doesn't want you to. Enron's descriptions of certain transactions still baffle me.

Finally, be suspicious of companies that trumpet earnings projections and growth expectations. Businesses seldom operate in a tranquil, no-surprise environment, and earnings simply don't advance smoothly (except, of course, in the offering books of investment bankers).

—Warren Buffett, Letter to Shareholders of Berkshire
Hathaway, February 21, 2003

Financial statements are summaries of the operating, financing, and investment activities of a business. Financial statements should provide information useful to both investors and creditors in making credit, investment, and other business decisions. And this usefulness means that investors and creditors can use these statements to predict, compare, and evaluate the amount, timing, and uncertainty of future cash flows. In other words, financial statements provide the information needed to assess a company's future earnings and, therefore, the cash flows expected to result from those earnings. In this chapter, we discuss the four basic financial statements: the balance sheet, the income statement, the statement of cash flows, and the statement of shareholders' equity.

ACCOUNTING PRINCIPLES: WHAT ARE THEY?

The accounting data in financial statements are prepared by the company's management according to a set of standards, referred to as *generally accepted accounting principles* (GAAP). Generally accepted accounting principles are based on the codified standards promulgated by the Financial Accounting Standards Board (FASB), as part of the *FASB Accounting Standards Codification*.[1]

The financial statements of a company whose stock is publicly traded must, by law, be audited at least annually by independent public accountants (i.e., accountants who are not employees of the company). In such an audit, the accountants examine the financial statements and the data from which these statements are prepared and attest—through the published auditor's opinion—that these statements have been prepared according to GAAP. In this case, GAAP includes not only the FASB Accounting Standards Codification, but any rules and regulations of the Securities and Exchange Commission. The auditor's opinion focuses whether the statements conform to GAAP and that there is adequate disclosure of any material change in accounting principles.

The financial statements and the auditors' findings are published in the company's annual and quarterly reports sent to shareholders and the 10-K and 10-Q filings with the Securities and Exchange Commission (SEC). Also included in the reports, among other items, is a discussion by management, entitled "Management's Discussion and Analysis of Financial Conditions and Results of Operations," which is an overview of company events. The annual reports are much more detailed and disclose more financial information than the quarterly reports.

Assumptions in Creating Financial Statements

The financial statements are created using several assumptions that affect how we use and interpret the financial data:

- **Transactions are recorded at historical cost.** Therefore, the values shown in the statements are not market or replacement values, but rather reflect the original cost (adjusted for depreciation in the case of a depreciable assets).

---

[1]Prior to Financial Accounting Standards Board Statement of Financial Accounting Standards No. 168, GAAP was a subject to a hierarchy of sources of principles, but this has been simplified, effective for companies with fiscal years ending after September 15, 2009.

- **The appropriate unit of measurement is the dollar.** While this seems logical, the effects of inflation, combined with the practice of recording values at historical cost, may cause problems in using and interpreting these values.
- **The statements are recorded for predefined periods of time.** Generally, statements are produced to cover a chosen fiscal year or quarter, with the income statement and the statement of cash flows spanning a period's time and the balance sheet and statement of shareholders' equity as of the end of the specified period. But because the end of the fiscal year is generally chosen to coincide with the low point of activity in the operating cycle, the annual balance sheet and statement of shareholders' equity may not be representative of values for the year.
- **Statements are prepared using accrual accounting and the matching principle.** Most businesses use accrual accounting, where income and revenues are matched in timing so that income is recorded in the period in which it is earned and expenses are reported in the period in which they are incurred in an attempt to generate revenues. The result of the use of accrual accounting is that reported income does not necessarily coincide with cash flows.
- **The business will continue as a going concern.** The assumption that the business enterprise will continue indefinitely justifies the appropriateness of using historical costs instead of current market values because these assets are expected to be used up over time instead of sold.
- **There is full disclosure.** Full disclosure requires providing information beyond the financial statements. The requirement that there be full disclosure means that, in addition to the accounting numbers for such accounting items as revenues, expenses, and assets, narrative and additional numerical disclosures are provided in notes accompanying the financial statements. An analysis of financial statements is, therefore, not complete without this additional information.
- **Statements are prepared assuming conservatism.** In cases in which more than one interpretation of an event is possible, statements are prepared using the most conservative interpretation.

THE BASIC FINANCIAL STATEMENTS

The basic financial statements are the balance sheet, the income statement, the statement of cash flows, and the statement of shareholders' equity. The balance sheet is a report of what the company has—assets, debt, and equity—as of the end of the fiscal quarter or year, and the income statement is a report of what the company earned during the fiscal period. The statement of cash flows is a report of the cash flows of the company over the fiscal period, whereas the statement of shareholders' equity is a reconciliation of the shareholders' equity from one fiscal year end to another.

The Balance Sheet

The *balance sheet* is a report of the assets, liabilities, and equity of a company at a point in time, generally at the end of a fiscal quarter or fiscal year. *Assets* are resources of the business enterprise, which are comprised of current or long-lived assets. How did the company finance these resources? It did so with liabilities and equity. *Liabilities* are obligations of the business enterprise that must be repaid at a future point in time, whereas *equity* is the ownership interest of the business enterprise. The relation between assets, liabilities and equity is simple, as reflected in the balance of what is owned and how it is financed, referred to as the *accounting identity*:

Assets   Assets are anything that the company owns that has a value. These assets may have a physical in existence or not. Examples of physical assets include inventory items held for sale, office furniture, and production equipment. If an asset does not have a physical existence, we refer to it as an intangible asset, such as a trademark or a patent. You cannot see or touch an intangible asset, but it still contributes value to the company.

Assets may also be current or long-term, depending on how fast the company would be able to convert them into cash. Assets are generally reported in the balance sheet in order of liquidity, with the most liquid asset listed first and the least liquid listed last.

The most liquid assets of the company are the current assets. *Current assets* are assets that can be turned into cash in one operating cycle or one year, whichever is longer. This contrasts with the noncurrent assets, which cannot be liquidated quickly.

There are different types of current assets. The typical set of current assets is the following:

- Cash, bills, and currency are assets that are equivalent to cash (e.g., bank account).
- *Marketable securities*, which are securities that can be readily sold.

- *Accounts receivable*, which are amounts due from customers arising from trade credit.
- *Inventories*, which are investments in raw materials, work-in-process, and finished goods for sale.

A company's need for current assets is dictated, in part, by its operating cycle. The *operating cycle* is the length of time it takes to turn the investment of cash into goods and services for sale back into cash in the form of collections from customers, as we display in Exhibit 4.1. The longer the operating cycle, the greater a company's need for liquidity. Most companies' operating cycle is less than or equal to one year.

Noncurrent assets comprise both physical and nonphysical assets. Plant assets are physical assets, such as buildings and equipment and are reflected in the balance sheet as gross plant and equipment and net plant and equipment. *Gross plant and equipment*, or *gross property, plant, and equipment*, is the total cost of investment in physical assets; that is, what the company originally paid for the property, plant, and equipment that it currently owns. *Net plant and equipment*, or *net property, plant, and equipment*, is the difference between gross plant and equipment and accumulated depreciation, and represents the book value of the plant and equipment assets. *Accumulated depreciation* is the sum of depreciation taken for physical assets in the company's possession.

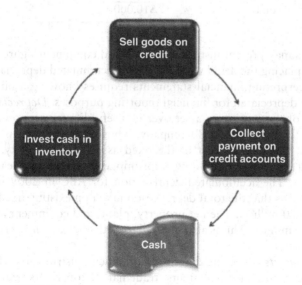

EXHIBIT 4.1 The Operating Cycle

EXHIBIT 4.2   ABC Company Balance Sheets

	December 31, 2009	December 31, 2008
Cash	$ 50	$ 100
Accounts receivable	700	600
Inventory	750	800
Total current assets	$ 1,500	$ 1,500
Gross plant and equipment	$12,000	$10,000
Accumulated depreciation	4,000	3,000
Net plant and equipment	$ 8,000	$ 7,000
Intangible assets	500	500
Total assets	$10,000	$ 9,000
Accounts payable	$ 350	$ 300
Wages payable	150	100
Total current liabilities	$ 500	$ 400
Long-term debt	$ 6,660	$ 6,660
Common stock	100	100
Additional paid-in capital	600	600
Retained earnings	2,240	1,340
Treasury stock	200	200
Accumulated other comprehensive income or loss	100	100
Shareholders' equity	2,840	1,940
Total liabilities and equity	$10,000	$ 9,000

Companies may present just the net plant and equipment figure on the balance sheet, placing the detail with respect to accumulated depreciation in a footnote. Interpreting financial statements requires knowing a bit about how assets are depreciated for financial reporting purposes. *Depreciation* is the allocation of the cost of an asset over its useful life (or economic life). In the case of the fictitious ABC Company, whose balance sheet is shown in Exhibit 4.2, the original cost of the fixed assets (i.e., property, plant, and equipment)—less any write-downs for impairment—for the year 2009 is $900 million. The accumulated depreciation for ABC in 2009 is $250 million; this means that the total depreciation taken on existing fixed assets over time is $270 million. The net property, plant, and equipment account balance is $630 million. This is also referred to as the *book value* or *carrying value* of these assets.

Intangible assets are assets that are not financial instruments, yet have no physical existence, such as patents, trademarks, copyrights, franchises, and formulae. Intangible assets may be amortized over some period, which is akin to depreciation. Keep in mind that a company may own a number of intangible assets that are not reported on the balance sheet. A company may only include an intangible asset's value on its balance sheet if (1) there are likely future benefits attributable specifically to the asset, and (2) the cost of the intangible asset can be measured.

Suppose a company has an active, ongoing investment in research and development to develop new products. It must expense what is spent on research and development each year because for a given investment in R&D does not likely meet the two criteria because it is not until much later, after the R&D expense is made, that the economic viability of the investment is determined. If, on the other hand, a company buys a patent from another company, this cost may be capitalized and then amortized over the remaining life of the patent. So when you look at a company's assets on its balance sheet, you may not be getting the complete picture of what it owns.

Liabilities We generally use the terms "liability" and "debt" as synonymous terms, though "liability" is actually a broader term, encompassing not only the explicit contracts that a company has, in terms of short-term and long-term debt obligations, but also includes obligations that are not specified in a contract, such as environmental obligations or asset retirement obligations. Liabilities may be interest-bearing, such as a bond issue, or noninterest bearing, such as amounts due to suppliers.

In the balance sheet, liabilities are presented in order of their due date and are often presented in two categories, current liabilities and long-term liabilities. *Current liabilities* are obligations due within one year or one operating cycle (whichever is longer). Current liabilities may consist of:

- *Accounts payable*, amounts due to suppliers for purchases on credit;
- Wages and salaries payable, amounts due employees;
- Current portion of long-term indebtedness; and
- Short term bank loans.

Long-term liabilities are obligations that are due beyond one year. There are different types of long-term liabilities, including:

- *Notes payables* and *bonds*, which are indebtedness (loans) in the form of securities;

- *Capital leases*, which are rental obligations that are long-term, fixed commitments;
- *Asset retirement liability*, which is the contractual or statutory obligation to retire or decommission an asset at the end of the asset's life and restore the site to required standards; and
- *Deferred taxes*, which are taxes that may have to be paid in the future that are currently not due, though they are expensed for financial reporting purposes. Deferred taxes arise from differences between accounting and tax methods (e.g., depreciation methods). [2]

Equity The equity of a company is the ownership interest. The book value of equity, which for a corporation is often referred to as shareholders' equity or stockholders' equity, is basically the amount that investors paid the company for their ownership interest, plus any earnings (or less any losses), and minus any distributions to owners. For a corporation, equity is the amount that investors paid the corporation for the stock when it was initially sold, plus or minus any earnings or losses, less any dividends paid. Keep in mind that for any company, the reported amount of equity is an accumulation over time since the company's inception (or incorporation, in the case of a corporation).

Shareholders equity is the carrying or book value of the ownership of a company. Shareholders' equity is comprised of:

- *Par value*, which is a nominal amount per share of stock (sometimes prescribed by law), or the *stated value*, which is a nominal amount per share of stock assigned for accounting purposes if the stock has no par value;
- *Additional paid-in capital*, also referred to as *capital surplus*, the amount paid for shares of stock by investors in excess of par or stated value;
- *Retained earnings*, which is the accumulation of prior and current periods' earnings and losses, less any prior or current periods' dividends; and
- *Accumulated comprehensive income or loss*, which is the total amount of income or loss that arises from transactions that result in income or losses, yet are not reported through the income statement. Items giving

---

[2]Similar to deferred tax liabilities, there is also a possibility that the company has a deferred tax asset, which is a tax benefit expected in the future. For example, if a company has net operating losses that it will likely apply against future taxable income, the deferred tax asset is the amount by which future tax bills are likely to be reduced.

rise to this income include foreign currency translation adjustments and unrealized gains or losses on available-for-sale investments.

In addition, a company that buys back its own stock from shareholders may retain this stock for use in employee stock options. The account that represents this stock is Treasury stock. This is a deduction from the other accounts to arrive at shareholders' equity.

A Note on Minority Interest   On many companies' consolidated financial statements, you will notice a balance sheet account entitled "Minority Interest" as an account in shareholders' equity. When a company owns a substantial portion of another company, accounting principles require that the company consolidate that company's financial statements into its own. Basically what happens in consolidating the financial statements is that the parent company will add the accounts of the subsidiary to its accounts (i.e., subsidiary inventory + parent inventory = consolidated inventory).[3] If the parent does not own 100% of the subsidiary's ownership interest, an account is created, referred to as *minority interest*, which reflects the amount of the subsidiary's assets *not* owned by the parent.

Prior to 2009, this account was presented between liabilities and equity on the consolidated balance sheet. However, from 2009 forward, companies are required to report this amount in shareholders' equity as equity. But is minority interest considered equity? No. Therefore, when we analyze a company's financial statement, we remove minority interest from equity. If we leave this account in equity, we will risk distorting measures of how a company finances itself.

A similar adjustment takes place on the income statement. The minority interest account on the income statement reflects the income (or loss) in proportion to the equity in the subsidiary *not* owned by the parent. Beginning with 2009 financial statements, companies are not required to subtract minority interest from their earnings, but need only disclose whether these earnings are in reported the parent company's net income.

Under the new rules, some companies may choose to report two different amounts for net income (total and parent-only), whereas other companies may simply report one net income figure and footnote the minority interest. In the former case, we would use the net income after adjusting for minority earnings. In the latter case, we need to subtract minority interest earnings from reported net income.

---

[3]There are some other adjustments that are made for inter-corporate transactions, but we won't discuss those here.

Structure of the Balance Sheet   Consider a simple balance sheet for the ABC Company shown in Exhibit 4.2 for two fiscal years. A few items to note:

- The accounting identity holds; that is, total assets are equal to the sum of the total liabilities and the total shareholders' equity.
- The asset accounts are ordered from the most liquid to the least liquid.
- The liabilities are listed in order of priority of claims, with trade creditors and employees having the best claims.

The Income Statement

The *income statement* is a summary of operating performance over a period of time (e.g., a fiscal quarter or a fiscal year). We start with the revenue of the company over a period of time and then subtract the costs and expenses related to that revenue. The bottom line of the income statement consists of the owners' earnings for the period. To arrive at this "bottom line," we need to compare revenues and expenses. We provide the basic structure of the income statement in Exhibit 4.3.

Though the structure of the income statement varies by company, the basic idea is to present the operating results first, followed by non-operating results. The *cost of sales*, also referred to as the *cost of goods sold*, is deducted from revenues, producing a gross profit; that is, a profit without considering all other general operating costs. These general operating expenses are those expenses related to the support of the general operations of the company, which includes salaries, marketing costs, and research and development. Depreciation, which is the amortized cost of physical assets, is also deducted from gross profit. The amount of the depreciation expense represents the cost of the wear and tear on the property, plant, and equipment of the company.

Once we have the operating income, we have summarized the company's performance with respect to the operations of the business. But there is generally more to the company's performance. From operating income, we deduct interest expense and add any interest income. Further, adjustments are made for any other income or cost that is not a part of the company's core business.

There are a number of other items that may appear as adjustments to arrive at net income. One of these is extraordinary items, which are defined as unusual and infrequent gains or losses. Another adjustment would be for the expense related to the write-down of an asset's value.

In the case of the ABC Company, whose income statement we provide in Exhibit 4.4, the income from operations—its core business—is $2,000 million, whereas the net income (i.e., the "bottom line") is $1,000 million.

EXHIBIT 4.3 The Basic Structure of the Income Statement

Revenues or sales	Represent the amount of goods or services sold, in terms of price paid by customers
− Cost of goods sold	The amount of goods or services sold, in terms of cost to the company
Gross profit	The difference between sales and cost of goods sold
− Selling and general administrative expenses	Salaries, administrative, marketing expenditures, etc.
Operating profit	Income from operations; earnings before interest and taxes (EBIT), operating income, and operating earnings
− Interest expense	Interest paid on debt
Income before taxes	Earnings before taxes
− Tax expense	Taxes expense for the current period
Net income	Operating profit less financing expenses (e.g., interest) and taxes
− Preferred stock dividends	Dividends paid to preferred shareholders
Earnings available to common shareholders	Net income less preferred stock dividends; residual income

Earnings Per Share Companies provide information on *earnings per share* (EPS) in their annual and quarterly financial statement information, as well as in their periodic press releases. Generally, EPS is calculated as net income divided by the number of shares outstanding. Companies must report both basic and diluted earnings per share.

EXHIBIT 4.4 The ABC Company Income Statement for the periods ending December 31, 2008 and 2009 (in millions)

Revenues or sales	$10,000
Cost of goods sold	7,000
Gross profit	$ 3,000
Selling and general administrative expenses	1,000
Operating profit	$ 2,000
Interest expense	333
Income before taxes	$ 1,667
Tax expense	667
Net income	$ 1,000

Basic earnings per share is net income (minus preferred dividends) divided by the average number of shares outstanding. *Diluted earnings per share* is net income (minus preferred dividends) divided by the number of shares outstanding considering all dilutive securities (e.g., convertible debt, options).[4] Diluted earnings per share, therefore, gives the shareholder information about the *potential* dilution of earnings. For companies with a large number of dilutive securities (e.g., stock options, convertible preferred stock, or convertible bonds), there can be a significant difference between basic and diluted EPS. You can see the effect of dilution by comparing the basic and diluted EPS.

More on Depreciation   There are different methods that can be used to allocate an asset's cost over its life. Generally, if the asset is expected to have value at the end of its economic life, the expected value, referred to as a *salvage value* (or *residual value*), is not depreciated; rather, the asset is depreciated down to its salvage value. There are different methods of depreciation that we classify as either straight-line or accelerated.

- *Straight-line depreciation* allocates the cost (less salvage value) in a uniform manner (equal amount per period) throughout the asset's life.
- *Accelerated depreciation* allocates the asset's cost (less salvage value) such that more depreciation is taken in the earlier years of the asset's life.

There are alternative accelerated methods available, including:

- *Declining balance method*, in which a *constant* rate applied to a *declining* amount (the undepreciated cost).
- *Sum-of-the-years' digits method*, in which a *declining* rate applied to the asset's *depreciable basis* and this rate is ratio of the remaining years divided by the sum of the years.[5]

Accelerated methods result in higher depreciation expenses in earlier years, relative to straight-line. As a result, accelerated methods result in lower reported earnings in earlier years, relative to straight-line, but also lower net property, plant, and equipment in earlier years as well.

Comparing companies, it is important to understand whether the companies use different methods of depreciation because the choice of depreciation method affects both the balance sheet (through the carrying

---

[4]In the case of diluted earnings per share, if the dilution potential is from convertible debt, earnings are adjusted for the interest on this convertible debt.

[5]For example, for an asset with a five year life, the first year's depreciation is 5/15, the second year's depreciation is 4/15, and so on.

value of the asset) and the income statement (through the depreciation expense).

A major source of deferred income tax liability and deferred tax assets is the accounting method used for financial reporting purposes and tax purposes. In the case of financial accounting purposes, the company chooses the method that best reflects how its assets lose value over time, though most companies use the straight-line method. However, for tax purposes the company has no choice but to use the prescribed rates of depreciation, using the *Modified Accelerated Cost Recovery System* (MACRS). For tax purposes, a company does not have discretion over the asset's depreciable life or the rate of depreciation—they must use the MACRS system.

The MACRS system does not incorporate salvage value and is based on a declining balance system. The depreciable life for tax purposes may be longer than or shorter than that used for financial reporting purposes. We provide the MACRS rates for 3, 5, 7 and 10-year assets in Exhibit 4.5.

You'll notice the fact that a 3-year asset is depreciated over four years and a 5-year asset is depreciated over six years, and so on. That is the result of using what is referred to as a *half-year convention*—using only half a year's worth of depreciation in the first year of an asset's life. This system results in a leftover amount that must still be depreciated in the last year (i.e., the fourth year in the case of a 3-year asset and the sixth year in the case of a 5-year asset).

We can compare MACRS with straight-line, using an example of an asset that costs $100,000 that has an eight-year useful life but is classified as a 7-year MACRS asset for tax purposes. If the company uses straight-line

EXHIBIT 4.5 MACRS Rates

| Year | MACRS Life, in Years | | | |
	3-year	5-year	7-year	10-year
1	33.33%	20.00%	14.29%	10.00%
2	44.44%	32.00%	24.49%	18.00%
3	14.81%	19.20%	17.49%	14.40%
4	7.41%	11.52%	12.49%	11.52%
5		11.52%	8.92%	9.22%
6		5.76%	8.92%	7.37%
7			8.92%	6.55%
8			4.46%	6.55%
9				6.55%
10				6.55%
11				3.28%

depreciation for financial reporting purposes, there will be a difference in income and tax expense for tax and financial reporting purposes.

Let's assume that the asset has no salvage value, that the company has net income before taxes and depreciation of $50,000, and that the tax rate is 30%. The amount depreciated is the same under both methods, but the annual depreciation is different:

	Depreciation Rate			Depreciation Expense	
Year	MACRS	Straight-line		MACRS	Straight-line
1	14.29%	12.50%		$ 14,286	$ 12,500
2	24.49%	12.50%		$ 24,490	$ 12,500
3	17.49%	12.50%		$ 17,493	$ 12,500
4	12.49%	12.50%		$ 12,495	$ 12,500
5	8.92%	12.50%		$ 8,925	$ 12,500
6	8.92%	12.50%		$ 8,925	$ 12,500
7	8.92%	12.50%		$ 8,925	$ 12,500
8	4.46%	12.50%		$ 4,462	$ 12,500
			Sum	$100,000	$100,000

Therefore, the difference in these methods is not the total that is depreciated, but rather the timing of the depreciation. The effects on taxable income and tax expense are also a matter of timing:

	Taxable Income		Tax Expense	
Year	MACRS	Straight-line	MACRS	Straight-line
1	$ 35,714	$ 37,500	$10,714	$11,250
2	$ 25,510	$ 37,500	$ 7,653	$11,250
3	$ 32,507	$ 37,500	$ 9,752	$11,250
4	$ 37,505	$ 37,500	$11,252	$11,250
5	$ 41,075	$ 37,500	$12,323	$11,250
6	$ 41,075	$ 37,500	$12,323	$11,250
7	$ 41,075	$ 37,500	$12,323	$11,250
8	$ 45,538	$ 37,500	$13,661	$11,250
Sum	$300,000	$300,000	$90,000	$90,000

In this example, the company would have a deferred tax liability created when MACRS tax expense is less than the straight-line tax expense, but this would reverse in later years—reducing the deferred tax liability—as the tax expense using straight-line is less than the tax expense under MACRS.

 TRY IT! MACRS DEPRECIATION

Suppose a company acquires an asset at the end of 2010 that has a cost of $20,000 and is classified as a 3-year MACRS asset. What is the depreciation expense each year?

The Statement of Cash Flows

The *statement of cash flows* is the summary of a company's cash flows, summarized by operations, investment activities, and financing activities. We provide a simplified cash flow statement in Exhibit 4.6 for the fictitious

EXHIBIT 4.6 Statement of Cash Flows for ABC Company for fiscal year ending December 31, 2009

Operating activities	
Net income	$1,000
Add: Depreciation	1,000
Subtract: increase in accounts receivable	−100
Add: Decrease in inventory	+50
Add: Increase in accounts payable	+50
Add: Increase in wages payable	+50
Cash flow from operations	$2,050
Investing activities	
Capital expenditures	−$2,000
Cash flow from investing	−$2,000
Financing activities	
Dividends paid	−$ 100
Cash flow from financing	−$ 100
Net change in cash	−$ 50

ABC Company. *Cash flow from operations* is cash flow from day-to-day operations. Cash flow from operating activities is basically net income adjusted for (1) noncash expenditures, and (2) changes in working capital accounts.

The adjustment for changes in working capital accounts is necessary to adjust net income that is determined using the accrual method to a cash flow amount. Increases in current assets and decreases in current liabilities are positive adjustments to arrive at the cash flow; decreases in current assets and increases in current liabilities are negative adjustments to arrive at the cash flow.

Cash flow for/from investing is the cash flows related to the acquisition (purchase) of plant, equipment, and other assets, as well as the proceeds from the sale of assets. *Cash flow for/from financing activities* is the cash flow from activities related to the sources of capital funds (e.g., buyback common stock, pay dividends, issue bonds). For the ABC Company, these are fairly straightforward.

Not all of the classifications required by accounting principles are consistent with the true flow for the three types of activities. For example, interest expense is a financing cash flow, yet it affects the cash flow from operating activities because it is a deduction to arrive at net income. This inconsistency is also the case for interest income and dividend income, both of which result from investing activities, but show up in the cash flow from operating activities through their contribution to net income.

The sources of a company's cash flows can reveal a great deal about the company and its prospects. For example, a financially healthy company tends to consistently generate cash flows from operations (that is, positive operating cash flows) and invests cash flows (that is, negative investing cash flows). To remain viable, a company must be able to generate funds from its operations; to grow, a company must continually make capital investments.

The change in cash flow—also called *net cash flow*—is the bottom line in the statement of cash flows and is equal to the change in the cash account as reported on the balance sheet. For the ABC Company, shown in Exhibit 4.6, the net change in cash flow is a −$50 million; this is equal to the change in the cash account from $100 million in 2008 to $50 million in 2009.

By studying the cash flows of a company over time, we can gauge a company's financial health. For example, if a company relies on external financing to support its operations (that is, reliant on cash flows from financing and not from operations) for an extended period of time, this is a warning sign of financial trouble up ahead.

TRY IT! CASH FLOW FROM OPERATIONS

Suppose a company has net income of $1 million and depreciation of $0.2 million. If the company's inventory decreased by $0.3 million and accounts receivable increased by $0.4 million, what is this company's cash flow from operations?

The Statement of Stockholders' Equity

The *statement of stockholders' equity* (also referred to as the *statement of shareholders' equity*) is a summary of the changes in the equity accounts, including information on stock options exercised, repurchases of shares, and Treasury shares. The basic structure is to include a reconciliation of the balance in each component of equity from the beginning of the fiscal year with the end of the fiscal year, detailing changes attributed to net income, dividends, purchases or sales of Treasury stock. The components are common stock, additional paid-in capital, retained earnings, and Treasury stock. For each of these components, the statement begins with the balance of each at the end of the previous fiscal period and then adjustments are shown to produce the balance at the end of the current fiscal period.

In addition, there is a reconciliation of any gains or losses that affect stockholders' equity but which do not flow through the income statement, such as foreign-currency translation adjustments and unrealized gains on investments. These items are of interest because they are part of comprehensive income, and hence income to owners, but they are not represented on the company's income statement.

HOW ARE THE STATEMENTS RELATED?

The four basic statements are the result of transactions that record each activity of the company. As a result, the financial statements are inter-related. For example,

- The change in cash, the bottom line of the statement cash flows, is equal to the change in the cash balance from the previous fiscal period to the current fiscal period.

- Net income, the bottom line of the income statement, is the starting point of the statement of cash flows, and contributes to retained earnings in the balance sheet and the statement of shareholders' equity.
- The changes in the working capital accounts are adjustments to the arrive at the cash flow from operating activities in the statement of cash flows, the changes in the asset accounts contribute to changes in cash flows from investing activities, and debt issuances and repayments, as well as issuance or repurchase of stock contribute to the change in cash flows for financing activities.

WHY BOTHER ABOUT THE FOOTNOTES?

Footnotes to the financial statements contain additional information, supplementing or explaining financial statement data. These notes are presented in both the annual report and the 10-K filing (with the SEC), though the latter usually provides a greater depth of information.

The footnotes to the financial statements provide information pertaining to:

- **The significant accounting policies and practices that the company uses.** This helps the analyst with the interpretation of the results, comparability of the results to other companies and to other years for the same company, and in assessing the quality of the reported information.
- **Income taxes.** The footnotes tell us about the company's current and deferred income taxes, breakdowns by the type of tax (e.g., federal versus state), and the effective tax rate that the company is paying.
- **Pension plans and other retirement programs.** The detail about pension plans, including the pension assets and the pension liability, is important in determining whether a company's pension plan is overfunded or underfunded.
- **Leases.** You can learn about both the capital leases, which are the long-term lease obligations that are reported on the balance sheet, and about the future commitments under operating leases, which are not reflected on the balance sheet.
- **Long-term debt.** You can find detailed information about the maturity dates and interest rates on the company's debt obligations.
- **Stock-based compensation.** You can find detailed information about stock options granted to officers and employees. This footnote also includes company's accounting method for stock-based compensation and the impact of the method on the reported results.

- **Derivative instruments.** This describes accounting policies for certain derivative instruments (financial and commodity derivative instruments), as well as the types of derivative instruments.

The phrase "the devil is in the details" applies aptly to the footnotes of a company's financial statement. Through the footnotes, a company is providing information that is crucial in analyzing a company's financial health and performance. If footnotes are vague or confusing, as they were in the case of Enron prior to the break in the scandal, the analyst must ask questions to help understand this information.

ACCOUNTING FLEXIBILITY

The generally accepted accounting principles provide some choices in the manner in which some transactions and assets are accounted. For example, a company may choose to account for inventory, and hence costs of sales, using *Last-in, First-out* (LIFO) or *First-in, First-out* (FIFO). With LIFO, the most recent costs of items inventory are used to determine cost of goods sold, whereas with FIFO the oldest costs are used. This is intentional because these principles are applied to a broad set of companies and no single set of methods offers the best representation of a company's condition or performance for all companies. Ideally, a company's management, in consultation with the accountants, chooses those accounting methods and presentations that are most appropriate for the company.

A company's management has always had the ability to manage earnings through the judicious choice of accounting methods within the GAAP framework. The company's "watchdogs" (i.e., the accountants) should keep the company's management in check. However, recent scandals have revealed that the watchdog function of the accounting companies was not working well. Additionally, some companies' management used manipulation of financial results and outright fraud to distort the financial picture.

The Sarbanes-Oxley Act of 2002 offers some comfort in terms of creating the oversight board for the auditing accounting companies. In addition, the Securities and Exchange Commission, the Financial Accounting Standards Board, and the International Accounting Standards Board are tightening some of the flexibility that companies had in the past.

U.S. ACCOUNTING VS. OUTSIDE OF THE U.S.

The generally accepted accounting standards in the United States (U.S. GAAP) differ from those used in other countries around the world. But not for long. What is happening is an international convergence of accounting standards. The first major step was the agreement in 2002 between two major standard setting bodies—the U.S.'s Financial Accounting Standards Board (FASB) and the International Accounting Standards Board (IASB)—to work together for eventual convergence of accounting principles. The second major step was the requirement of International Financial Reporting Standards (IFRS) by the European Commission, effective in 2005. The third major step is the voluntary application of IFRS by U.S. domiciled companies for fiscal years ending after December 15, 2009.[6]

IFRS are promulgated by the IASB and must be used by all publicly traded and private companies in the European Union. IFRS are also used, in varying degrees, by companies in Australia, Hong Kong, Russia, and China.

There are more similarities than differences between IFRS and U.S. GAAP. IFRS, like GAAP, uses historical cost as the main accounting convention. However, IFRS permits the revaluation of intangible assets, property, plant, and equipment, and investment property. IFRS also requires fair valuation of certain categories of financial instruments and certain biological assets. U.S. GAAP, on the other hand, prohibits revaluations except for certain categories of financial instruments, which must be carried at fair value, and goodwill, which is tested each year for impairment (that is, a loss of value).

Because there has been a long "road map" to convergence, and because many of the accounting principles issued in the past few years have been issued jointly by FASB and IASB, convergence, when it happens, should not result in a dramatic change in the financial statements of U.S. companies.

THE BOTTOM LINE

- Financial statements provide information about a company's operating performance, as well as its financial condition. These statements are prepared according to generally accepted accounting principles.
- The assumptions in preparing financial statements are that (1) transactions are recorded at historical cost, (2) the appropriate unit of measurement is the dollar, (3) statements are recorded for predefined periods

---

[6]The current "roadmap" to convergence has a 2014 target for mandatory application of IFRS to U.S. companies.

of time, (4) statements are prepared using accrual accounting and the matching principle, (5) the business will continue as a going concern, (6) there is full disclosure, and (7) if more than one interpretation of an event is possible, statements are prepared using the most conservative interpretation.

- The basic statements are the balance sheet, the income statement, the statement of cash flows, and the statement of shareholders' equity.
- There is some flexibility built into accounting principles, so it is important to understand just how much flexibility there is and how choices a company make affect the reported financial statements. For example, companies can choose among a number of methods for depreciation for financial reporting purposes, though the MACRS system is used for tax purposes.
- The footnotes to the financial statements provide information pertaining to (1) significant accounting policies and practices that the company uses, (2) income taxes, (3) pension plans and other retirement programs, (4) leases, (5) long-term debt, (6) stock-based compensation granted to officers and (7) derivative instruments.

SOLUTIONS TO TRY IT! PROBLEMS

MACRS Depreciation

Year	Rate	MACRS Depreciation
1	33.33%	$ 6,666.67
2	44.44%	$ 8,888.89
3	14.81%	$ 2,962.96
4	7.41%	$ 1,481.48
	Sum	$20,000.00

Cash Flow from Operations

Net income	$1.0
Plus depreciation	$0.2
Plus decrease in inventory	$0.3
Less increase in accounts receivable	−$0.4
Cash flow from operations	$1.1

QUESTIONS

1. What is the accounting identity?
2. List at least three of the assumptions underlying financial statements.
3. Identify at least three current asset accounts.
4. What is the operating cycle?
5. Identify three current liability accounts.
6. What are retained earnings?
7. Is the minority interest account on the balance sheet a liability, equity, or neither?
8. What is the difference between basic earnings per share and diluted earnings per share?
9. If an asset is depreciated for tax purposes using MACRS, but depreciated using straight-line depreciation for financial reporting purposes, how are deferred tax liabilities created?
10. What is the sum of the cash flows from operating activities, financing activities, and investing activities?
11. What does it mean that the financial statements are prepared based on historical cost?
12. Where can an investor find out more about deferred taxes reported in the balance sheet?
13. What follows is information from the balance sheet (in millions of dollars) for Microsoft Corporation for its 2009 fiscal year (ending June 30, 2009) with certain information intentionally deleted.

Assets		Liabilities and Stockholders' Equity	
Cash and cash equivalents	$ 6,076	Accounts payable	$ 3,324
		Short-term debt	2,000
Short-term investments	25,371	Accrued compensation	3,156
Accounts receivable	11,192	Income taxes	725
Inventories	717	Short-term unearned revenue	13,003
Deferred income taxes, current portion	2,213	Securities lending payable	1,684
		Other	3,142
Other current assets	3,711	Long-term debt	3,746
Net property and equipment	7,535	Long-term unearned revenue	1,281
		Other long-term liabilities	6,269
Equity and other investments	4,933	Stockholders' equity:	
		Common stock and paid-in capital—shares authorized 24,000; outstanding 8,908	62,382
Goodwill	12,503		
Intangible assets, net	1,759		
Deferred income taxes	279	Retained deficit, including accumulated other comprehensive income of $969	(22,824)
Other long-term assets	1,599		

Compute each of the following based on Microsoft Corporation's balance sheet:
a. Total current assets
b. Total assets
c. Total liabilities
d. Stockholders' equity
e. Total liabilities plus stockholders' equity

14. The following is a table showing the calculation of earnings per share as it appears in the 2009 financial statements of Microsoft Corporation.

In millions, except earnings per share

Year Ended June 30,	2009	2008	2007
Net income available for common shareholders (A)	$14,569	$17,681	$14,065
Weighted average outstanding shares of common stock (B)	8,945	9,328	9,742
Dilutive effect of stock-based awards	51	142	144
Common stock and common stock equivalents (C)	8,996	9,470	9,886
Earnings per share:			
Basic (A/B)	$1.63	$1.90	$1.44
Diluted (A/C)	$1.62	$1.87	$1.42

a. Why are there two earnings per share numbers reported?
b. What does "Basic" mean under "Earnings per share"?
c. What does "Diluted" mean under "Earnings per share"?
d. For all three fiscal years, both earnings per share measures in a given fiscal year are close in value. What does that suggest?

15. The following excerpt is taken from a publication of the American Institute of Certified Public Accountants (we won't give the title since it is the answer to one of the questions):

> *Great strides have been made by the FASB and the IASB to converge the content of IFRS and U.S. GAAP. The goal is that by the time the SEC allows or mandates the use of IFRS for U.S. publicly-traded companies, most or all of the key differences will have been resolved.*
>
> *Because of these ongoing convergence projects, the extent of the specific differences between IFRS and U.S. GAAP is shrinking. Yet significant differences do remain. For example IFRS does not permit Last In First Out (LIFO) as an inventory costing method.*

a. What is the FASB?
b. What is the IFRS?
c. What is meant by GAAP?

CHAPTER 5

Business Finance

*Corporate governance is about maintaining an appropriate
balance of accountability between three key players: the
corporation's owners, the directors whom the owners elect, and
the managers whom the directors select. Accountability requires
not only good transparency, but also an effective means to take
action for poor performance or bad decisions.*
—Chairman Mary L. Schapiro, U.S. Securities and Exchange
Commission, September 17, 2009

Financial management encompasses many different types of decisions. We can classify these decisions into three groups: investment decisions, financing decisions, and decisions that involve both investing and financing. Investment decisions are concerned with the use of funds—the buying, holding, or selling of all types of assets: Should we buy a new die stamping machine? Should we introduce a new product line? Sell the old production facility? Buy an existing company? Build a warehouse? Keep our cash in the bank?

Financing decisions are concerned with the acquisition of funds to be used for investing and financing day-to-day operations. Should management use the money raised through the companies' revenues? Should management seek funds from outside of the business? A company's operations and investment can be financed from outside the business by incurring debts, such as through bank loans and the sale of bonds, or by selling ownership interests. Because each method of financing obligates the business in different ways, financing decisions are very important.

Many business decisions simultaneously involve both investing and financing decisions. For example, a company may wish to acquire another company—an investment decision. However, the success of the acquisition may depend on how it is financed: by borrowing cash to meet the purchase price, by selling additional shares of stock, or by exchanging its shares of stock for the stock or assets of the company it is seeking to acquire. If management decides to borrow money, the borrowed funds must be repaid within a specified period of time. Creditors (those lending the money) generally do not share in the control of profits of the borrowing company. If, on the other hand, management decides to raise funds by selling ownership interests, these funds never have to be paid back. However, such a sale dilutes the control of (and profits accruing to) the current owners.

In this chapter, we provide an overview of financial management: the forms of business enterprise, the objectives of financial management, and the relationship between financial managers and shareholders and other stakeholders.

FORMS OF BUSINESS ENTERPRISE

Financial management is not restricted to large corporations: It is necessary in all forms and sizes of businesses. The three major forms of business organization are the sole proprietorship, the partnership, and the corporation.

These forms differ in a number of factors, of which those most important to financial decision-making are:

- Taxation
- Degree of control
- Owners' liability
- Ease of transferring ownership.
- Ability to raise additional funds.
- Longevity of the business.

We summarize the advantages and disadvantages of the major forms of business from the point of view of financial decision-making in Exhibit 5.1.

Sole Proprietorships and Partnerships

A sole proprietorship is a business entity owned by one party, and is the simplest of the forms of business:

- It is easy to form.
- The business income is taxed along with the owner's other income.
- The owner is liable for the debts of the business.
- The owner controls the decisions of the business.
- The business ends when the owner does.

EXHIBIT 5.1 Characteristics of the Basic Forms of Business

	Advantages	Disadvantages
Sole Proprietorship	1. The proprietor is the sole business decision-maker. 2. The proprietor receives all income from the business. 3. Income from the business is taxed once, at the individual taxpayer level.	1. The proprietor is liable for all debts of the business (unlimited liability). 2. The proprietorship has a limited life. 3. There is limited access to additional funds.
Partnership	1. Partners receive income according to terms in partnership agreement. 2. Income from business is taxed once as the partners' personal income. 3. Decision-making rests with the general partners only.	1. Each partner is liable for all the debts of the partnership. 2. The partnership's life is determined by agreement or the life of the partners. 3. There is limited access to additional funds.
Corporation	1. Each partner is liable for all the debts of the partnership. 2. The partnership's life is determined by agreement or the life of the partners. 3. There is limited access to additional funds.	1. Income paid to owners is subjected to double taxation. 2. Ownership and management are separated in larger organizations.

The sole proprietorship is often the starting point for a small, fledgling business. But a sole proprietorship is often limited in its access to funds beyond bank loans. Another form of business that offers additional sources of funds is the partnership.

A *partnership* is an agreement between two or more persons to operate a business. A partnership is similar to a sole proprietorship except instead of one proprietor, there is more than one. The fact that there is more than one proprietor introduces some issues: Who has a say in the day-to-day operations of the business? Who is liable (that is, financially responsible) for the debts of the business? How is the income distributed among the owners? How is the income taxed? Some of these issues are resolved with the partnership agreement; others are resolved by laws. The partnership agreement describes how profits and losses are to be shared among the partners, and it details their responsibilities in the management of the business.

Most partnerships are *general partnerships*, consisting only of general partners who participate fully in the management of the business, share in its profits and losses, and are responsible for its liabilities. Each general partner is personally and individually liable for the debts of the business, even if those debts were contracted by other partners.

A *limited partnership* consists of at least one general partner and one *limited partner*. Limited partners invest in the business, but do not participate in its management. A limited partner's share in the profits and losses of the business is limited by the partnership agreement. In addition, a limited partner is not liable for the debts incurred by the business beyond his or her initial investment.

A partnership is not taxed as a separate entity. Instead, each partner reports his or her share of the business profit or loss on his or her personal income tax return. Each partner's share is taxed as if it were from a sole proprietorship.

The life of a partnership may be limited by the partnership agreement. For example, the partners may agree that the partnership is to exist only for a specified number of years or only for the duration of a specific business transaction. The partnership must be terminated when any one of the partners dies, no matter what is specified in the partnership agreement. Partnership interests cannot be passed to heirs; at the death of any partner, the partnership is dissolved and perhaps renegotiated.

One of the drawbacks of partnerships is that a partner's interest in the business cannot be sold without the consent of the other partners. So a partner who needs to sell his or her interest because of, say, personal financial needs may not be able to do so. Still another problem involves ending a partnership and settling up, mainly because it is difficult to determine the value of the partnership and of each partner's share.

Another drawback is the partnership's limited access to new funds. Short of selling part of their own ownership interest, the partners can raise money only by borrowing from banks—and here too there is a limit to what a bank will lend a (usually small) partnership.

Corporations

A *corporation* is a legal entity created under state laws through the process of incorporation. The corporation is an organization capable of entering into contracts and carrying out business under its own name, separate from it owners. To become a corporation, state laws generally require that a company must do the following: (1) file articles of incorporation, (2) adopt a set of bylaws, and (3) form a board of directors.

The *articles of incorporation* specify the legal name of the corporation, its place of business, and the nature of its business. This certificate gives "life" to a corporation in the sense that it represents a contract between the corporation and its owners. This contract authorizes the corporation to issue units of ownership, called *shares*, and specifies the rights of the owners, the *shareholders*.

The *bylaws* are the rules of governance for the corporation. The bylaws define the rights and obligations of officers, members of the board of directors, and shareholders. In most large corporations, it is not possible for each owner to participate in monitoring the management of the business. Therefore, the owners of a corporation elect a board of directors to represent them in the major business decisions and to monitor the activities of the corporation's management. The board of directors, in turn, appoints and oversees the officers of the corporation. Directors who are also employees of the corporation are called *insider directors*; those who have no other position within the corporation are *outside directors* or *independent directors*.

The state recognizes the existence of the corporation in the corporate charter. Once created, the corporation can enter into contracts, adopt a legal name, sue or be sued, and continue in existence forever. Though owners may die, the corporation continues to live. The liability of owners is limited to the amounts they have invested in the corporation through the shares of ownership they purchased. The corporation is a taxable entity. It files its own income tax return and pays taxes on its income.

If the board of directors decides to distribute cash to the owners, that money is paid out of income left over after the corporate income tax has been paid. The amount of that cash payment, or *dividend*, must also be included in the taxable income of the owners (the shareholders). Therefore, a portion of the corporation's income (the portion paid out to owners) is subject to double taxation: once as corporate income and once as the individual owner's income.

The ownership of a corporation, also referred to as stock or equity, is represented as shares of stock. A corporation that has just a few owners who exert complete control over the decisions of the corporation is referred to as a *closely held corporation* or a *close corporation*.

A corporation whose ownership shares are sold outside of a closed group of owners is referred to as a *publicly held corporation* or a *public corporation*. Mars Inc., producer of M&M candies and other confectionery products, is a closely held corporation; Hershey Foods, also a producer of candy products among other things, is a publicly held corporation.

The shares of public corporations are freely traded in securities markets, such as the New York Stock Exchange. Hence, the ownership of a publicly held corporation is more easily transferred than the ownership of a proprietorship, a partnership, or a closely held corporation.

HOW IS INCOME DOUBLE TAXED?

Consider a corporation with $100 million of taxable income. Let's assume a simple tax system with a flat corporate tax rate is 35%. The corporation pays $35 million in taxes, and therefore has $65 million in earnings after taxes.

Now suppose that same corporation pays all of its earnings to its shareholders in the form of a cash dividend. Let's assume a simple tax system with a flat individual tax rate of 30%. Therefore, the tax the owners pay is:

$$\text{Individual income tax} = 0.3 \times \$65 \text{ million}$$
$$= \$19.5 \text{ million}$$

The total tax paid on this company's income is, effectively $35 + $19.5 million = $54.4 million. Therefore, every dollar of income of the corporation is taxed at the rate of = $54.5 million ÷ $100 million = 54.4%.

Companies whose stock is traded in public markets are required to file an initial registration statement with the Securities and Exchange Commission, a federal agency created to oversee the enforcement of U.S. securities laws. The statement provides financial statements, articles of incorporation, and descriptive information regarding the nature of the business, the debt and stock of the corporation, the officers and directors, and any individuals who own more than 10% of the stock, among other items.

 TRY IT! EFFECTIVE TAX RATE

Consider a company that generates $2 million in taxable income for a year. If the corporate tax rate is 38% and the individual shareholders' tax rate is 40%, what is the effective tax rate on the corporation's income if all of the corporation's income after tax is distributed to owners in the form of dividends?

The Limited Liability Company

A popular form of business, especially with small businesses, is the hybrid form of business, the *limited liability company* (LLC) or *a limited liability partnership* (LLP), which combine the best features of a partnership and a corporation. In 1988, the Internal Revenue Service (IRS) ruled that the LLC may be treated as a partnership for tax purposes, while retaining its limited liability for its owners. Since this ruling, every state has passed legislation permitting limited liability companies.

The LLC differs slightly from the LLP, because in the latter the partners may be liable for some, but not all, of the debts of the business. However, the distinction is subtle and most rules that apply to an LLC apply to an LLP as well. Though state laws vary slightly, in general, the owners of LLCs have limited liability. Therefore, the LLC and LLP forms represents a hybrid, with the best of both partnerships and corporations.

The owners of an LLC are referred to as members, and these owners may be individuals, partnerships, corporations, or other entities. Though there are few restrictions to who may form an LLC, banks and insurance companies are not permitted to operate as LLCs. Some types of companies that are prohibited from doing business as a corporation may be permitted to form an LLC. For example, accounting companies may operate as an LLC or an LLP, but cannot operate as a corporation.

The LLC is not considered a form of business for tax purposes, so a company formed as an LLC must file as a corporation, a partnership, or a sole proprietorship. In general, a LLP must file as a partnership. The IRS considers the LLC to be taxed as a partnership if the company has no more than two of the following characteristics: (1) limited liability, (2) centralized management, (3) free transferability of ownership interests, and (4) continuity of life. If the company has more than two of these, it will be treated as a corporation for tax purposes, subjecting the income to taxation at both the company level and the owners'.

A drawback of an LLC for tax purposes is that if the LLC has a net operating loss, the amount of the loss that is deductible for tax purposes is limited because the owners' liability is limited.

Other Forms of Business

In addition to the proprietorship, partnership, and corporate forms of business, an enterprise may be conducted using other forms of business, such as the master limited partnership, the professional corporation, and the joint venture.

A *master limited partnership* (MLP) is a partnership with limited partner ownership interests that are traded on an organized exchange. For example, more than two dozen master limited partnerships are listed on the New York Stock Exchange, including the Cedar Fair, Global Partners, and Sunoco Logistics Partners partnerships. Many of these MLPs operate in the oil and gas industry. Ownership interests, which represent a specified ownership percentage, are traded in much the same way as the shares of stock of a corporation. One difference, however, is that a corporation can raise new capital by issuing new ownership interests, whereas a master limited partnership cannot because it is not possible to sell more than a 100% interest in the partnership, yet it is possible to sell additional shares of stock in a corporation. Another difference is that the income of a master limited partnership is taxed only once, as partners' individual income.

Another variant of the corporate form of business is the professional corporation. A *professional corporation* is an organization that is formed under state law and treated as a corporation for federal tax law purposes, yet that has unlimited liability for its owners—the owners are personally liable for the debts of the corporation. Businesses that are likely to form such corporations are those that provide services and require state licensing, such as physicians', architects', and attorneys' practices since it is generally felt that it is in the public interest to hold such professionals responsible for the liabilities of the business.

A *joint venture*, which may be structured as either a partnership or as a corporation, is a business undertaken by a group of persons or entities (such as a partnership or corporation) for a specific business activity and, therefore, does not constitute a continuing relationship among the parties. For tax and other legal purposes, a joint venture partnership is treated as a partnership and a joint venture corporation is treated as a corporation.

U.S. corporations have entered into joint ventures with foreign corporations, enhancing participation and competition in the global marketplace. Joint ventures are becoming increasingly popular as a way of doing business. Participants—whether individuals, partnerships, or corporations—get together to exploit a specific business opportunity. Afterward, the venture can be dissolved. Recent alliances among communication and entertainment companies have sparked thought about what the future form of doing business will be. Some believe that what lies ahead is a virtual enterprise—a temporary alliance without all the bureaucracy of the typical corporation—that can move quickly and decisively to take advantage of profitable business opportunities.

Prevalence

The number of sole proprietorships in the U.S. is significantly larger than that of partnerships and corporations, as you can see in Exhibit 5.2 for the U.S. based on 2006 tax returns. However, the net income of corporations, which typically are larger firms than partnerships and sole proprietorships, comprises the larger portion of taxable income in the U.S.

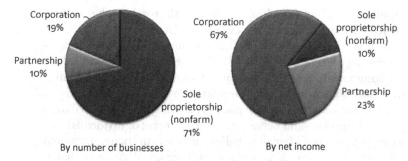

By number of businesses   By net income

EXHIBIT 5.2   Prevalence of Forms of Business, Based on Tax Returns Filed in 2006
Source of data: Statistics of Income, Internal Revenue Service.

THE OBJECTIVE OF FINANCIAL MANAGEMENT

So far we have seen that financial managers are primarily concerned with investment decisions and financing decisions within business organizations. The great majority of these decisions are made within the corporate business structure, which better accommodates growth and is responsible for over 67% of U.S. business net income.

One such issue concerns the objective of financial decision-making. What goal (or goals) do managers have in mind when they choose between financial alternatives—say, between distributing current income among shareholders and investing it to increase future income? There is actually one financial objective: the maximization of the economic well-being, or wealth, of the owners. Whenever a decision is to be made, management should choose the alternative that most increases the wealth of the owners of the business.

A Measure of Owners' Economic Well-Being

The price of a share of stock at any time, or its *market value*, represents the price that buyers in a free market are willing to pay for it. The *market value of shareholders' equity* is the value of all owners' interest in the corporation. This market value is also referred to as the stock's *market capitalization*, or simply its *market cap*. It is calculated as the product of the market value of one share of stock and the number of shares of stock outstanding:

$$\text{Market value of shareholders' equity} = \text{Market price per share of stock} \times \text{Number of shares outstanding}$$

The number of shares of stock outstanding is the total number of shares that are owned by shareholders. For example, on December 24, 2009, there were 3.81 billion Wal-Mart common shares outstanding. The price per share at the closing on that date was $53.50. Therefore, the market value of Wal-Mart's common stock is 3.81 billion × $53.60 = $204.216 billion.

Investors buy shares of stock in anticipation of future dividends and increases in the market value of the stock. How much are they willing to pay today for this future—and hence uncertain—stream of dividends? They are willing to pay exactly what they believe it is worth today, an amount that is called the *present value*, an important financial concept that we discuss in Chapter 10. The present value of a share of stock reflects the following factors:

- The uncertainty associated with receiving future payments.
- The timing of these future payments.
- Compensation for tying up funds in this investment.

The market price of a share is a measure of owners' economic well-being. Does this mean that if the share price goes up, management is doing a good job? Not necessarily. Share prices often can be influenced by factors beyond the control of management. These factors include expectations regarding the economy, returns available on alternative investments (such as bonds), and even how investors view the company and the idea of investing.

These factors influence the price of shares through their effects on expectations regarding future cash flows and investors' evaluation of those cash flows. Nonetheless, managers can still maximize the value of owners' equity, given current economic conditions and expectations. They do so by carefully considering the expected benefits, risk, and timing of the returns on proposed investments.

 TRY IT! MARKET CAPITALIZATION

The following data is available for a company at a specific point in time:

Average daily volume of shares traded	11.5 million
Book value per share	$18.27
Market price per share	$64.70
Number of shares outstanding	2.76 billion

What is the market capitalization of this company?

Financial Management and the Maximization of Owners' Wealth Financial managers are charged with the responsibility of making decisions that maximize owners' wealth. For a corporation, that responsibility translates into maximizing the value of shareholders' equity. If the market for stocks is efficient, the value of a share of stock in a corporation should reflect investors' expectations regarding the future prospects of the corporation. The value of a stock will change as investors' expectations about the future change. For financial managers' decisions to add value, the present value of the benefits resulting from decisions must outweigh the associated costs, where costs include the costs of capital.

If there is a separation of the ownership and management of a company—that is, the owners are not also the managers of the company—there are additional issues to confront. What if a decision is in the best interests of the company, but not in the best interest of the manager? How can owners ensure that managers are watching out for the owners' interests? How can owners motivate managers to make decisions that are best for the owners? We address these issues and more in the next section.

The Agency Relationship

If you are the sole owner of a business, you make the decisions that affect your own well-being. But what if you are a financial manager of a business and you are not the sole owner? In this case, you are making decisions for owners other than yourself; you, the financial manager, are an agent. An *agent* is a person who acts for—and exerts powers of—another person or group of persons. The person (or group of persons) the agent represents is referred to as the *principal*. The relationship between the agent and his or her principal is an agency relationship. There is an *agency relationship* between the managers and the shareholders of corporations.[1]

Problems with the Agency Relationship In an agency relationship, the agent is charged with the responsibility of acting for the principal. Is it possible the agent may not act in the best interest of the principal, but instead act in his or her own self-interest? Yes—because the agent has his or her own objective of maximizing personal wealth.

In a large corporation, for example, the managers may enjoy many fringe benefits, such as golf club memberships, access to private jets, and company

---

[1]The agency relationship was first described in Michael C. Jensen and William H. Meckling, "Theory of the Firm: Managerial Behavior, Agency Costs, and Ownership Structure," *Journal of Financial Economics* 3(1976): 305–360.

cars. These benefits (also called *perquisites* or *perks*) may be useful in conducting business and may help attract or retain management personnel, but there is room for abuse. What if the managers start spending more time at the golf course than at their desks? What if they use the company jets for personal travel? What if they buy company cars for their teenagers to drive? The abuse of perquisites imposes costs on the company—and ultimately on the owners of the company. There is also a possibility that managers who feel secure in their positions may not bother to expend their best efforts toward the business. This is referred to as *shirking*, and it too imposes a cost to the company.

Finally, there is the possibility that managers will act in their own self-interest, rather than in the interest of the shareholders when those interests clash. For example, management may fight the acquisition of their company by some other company, even if the acquisition would benefit shareholders. Why? In most takeovers, the management personnel of the acquired company generally lose their jobs. Envision that some company is making an offer to acquire the company that you manage. Are you happy that the acquiring company is offering the shareholders of your company more for their stock than its current market value? If you are looking out for their best interests, you should be. Are you happy about the likely prospect of losing your job? Most likely not.

Defensiveness by corporate managers in the case of takeovers, whether warranted or not, emphasizes the potential for conflict between the interests of the owners and the interests of management.[2] Defending against a takeover that would not produce a benefit for the shareholders is consistent with management's obligations. However, defending against a takeover that would produce a benefit for shareholders, but also a detriment to management (e.g., lost jobs), would be contrary to management's duty to shareholders.

Costs of the Agency Relationship   There are costs involved with any effort to minimize the potential for conflict between the principal's interest and the agent's interest. Such costs are called *agency costs*, and they are of three types: monitoring costs, bonding costs, and residual loss.

Monitoring costs are costs incurred by the principal to monitor or limit the actions of the agent. In a corporation, shareholders may require

---

[2]There was abuse by some companies during the merger mania of the 1980s. Some fought acquisition of their companies—which they labeled *hostile takeovers*—by proposing changes in the corporate charter or even lobbying for changes in state laws to discourage takeovers. Some adopted lucrative executive compensation packages—called *golden parachutes*—that were to go into effect if they lost their jobs.

managers to periodically report on their activities via audited accounting statements, which are sent to shareholders. The fees for auditing and preparing the financial statements and the management time lost in preparing such statements are monitoring costs. Another example is the implicit cost incurred when shareholders limit the decision-making power of managers. By doing so, the owners may miss profitable investment opportunities; the foregone profit is a monitoring cost.

The board of directors of a corporation has a *fiduciary duty* to shareholders; that is the legal responsibility to make decisions (or to see that decisions are made) that are in the best interests of shareholders. Part of that responsibility is to ensure that managerial decisions are also in the best interests of the shareholders. Therefore, at least part of the cost of having directors is a monitoring cost.

Bonding costs are incurred by agents to assure principals that they will act in the principal's best interest. The name comes from the agent's promise or bond to take certain actions. A manager may enter into a contract that requires him or her to stay on with the company even though another company acquires it; an implicit cost is then incurred by the manager, who foregoes other employment opportunities.

Even when monitoring and bonding devices are used, there may be some divergence between the interests of principals and those of agents. The resulting cost, called the *residual loss*, is the implicit cost that results because the principal's and the agent's interests cannot be perfectly aligned even when monitoring and bonding costs are incurred.

Motivating Managers: Executive Compensation

One way to encourage management to act in shareholders' best interests, and so minimize agency problems and costs, is through executive compensation—how top management is paid. There are several different ways to compensate executives, including:

- *Salary.* The direct payment of cash of a fixed amount per period.
- *Bonus.* A cash reward based on some performance measure, say, earnings of a division or the company.
- *Stock appreciation right.* A cash payment based on the amount by which the value of a specified number of shares has increased over a specified period of time (supposedly due to the efforts of management).
- *Performance shares.* Shares of stock given the employees, in an amount based on some measure of operating performance, such as earnings per share.
- *Stock option.* The right to buy a specified number of shares of stock in the company at a stated price—referred to as an exercise price at some

time in the future. The exercise price may be above, at, or below the current market price of the stock.

- *Restricted stock grant.* The grant of shares of stock to the employee at low or no cost, conditional on the shares not being sold for a specified time.

The salary portion of the compensation—the minimum cash payment an executive receives—must be enough to attract talented executives. But a bonus should be based on some measure of performance that is in the best interests of shareholders—not just on the past year's accounting earnings. For example, a bonus could be based on gains in market share.

The basic idea behind stock options and restricted stock grants is to make managers owners, since the incentive to consume excessive perks and to shirk are reduced if managers are also owners. As owners, managers not only share the costs of perks and shirks, but they also benefit financially when their decisions maximize the wealth of owners. Hence, the key to motivation through stock is not really the *value* of the stock, but rather *ownership* of the stock. For this reason, stock appreciation rights and performance shares, which do not involve an investment on the part of the recipients, are not effective motivators.

Stock options do work to motivate performance if they require owning the shares over a long time period; are exercisable at a price significantly *above* the current market price of the shares, thus encouraging managers to get the share price up, and require managers to tie up their own wealth in the shares. Unfortunately, executive stock option programs have not always been designed in ways to sufficiently motivate executives.

Publicly-traded companies must disclose the compensation in a table, as well as provide a discussion of key elements in the "Compensation Discussion and Analysis" portion of their SEC 10-K filing and proxy statements.[3] The table provides the investor with information on the compensation that is both cash-based and stock-based, with details on the options granted and exercised by the top paid employees. This table enables the comparison year-to-year of each of the elements of a manager's compensation.

Currently, there is a great deal of concern in some corporations because executive compensation is not linked to performance. In recent years, many U.S. companies have downsized, restructured, and laid off many employees and allowed the wages of employees who survive the cuts to stagnate. At the same time, corporations have increased the pay of top executives through both salary and lucrative stock options. If these changes lead to better value

---

[3]Rule 33-8732, August 11, 2006.

for shareholders, shouldn't the top executives be rewarded? There are two issues here. First, such a situation results in anger and disenchantment among both surviving employees and former employees. Second, the downsizing, restructuring, and lay-offs may not result in immediate (or even, eventual) increased profitability.

Owners have one more tool with which to motivate management—the threat of firing. As long as owners can fire managers, managers will be encouraged to act in the owners' interest. However, if the owners are divided or apathetic—as they might be in large corporations—or if they fail to monitor management's performance and the reaction of directors to that performance, the threat may not be credible. The removal of a few poor managers can, however, make this threat palpable.

Shareholder Wealth Maximization and Accounting "Irregularities"

There have been a number of scandals and allegations regarding the financial information that is being reported to shareholders and the market. Financial results reported in the income statements and balance sheets of some companies indicated much better performance than the true performance or much better financial condition than actual. Examples include Xerox, which was forced to restate earnings for several years because it had inflated pretax profits by $1.4 billion, Enron, which was accused of inflating earnings and hiding substantial debt, and Worldcom, which failed to properly account for $3.8 billion of expenses.

However, some companies have also encountered problems when managers understate earnings. For example, if a company's earnings are not sufficient to meet bonus targets, by understating income in one period—for example, moving expenses forward in time or delaying recognition of revenues—there is a better possibility that the company will meet the bonus targets in the following year.

Along with these financial reporting issues, the independence of the auditors and the role of financial analysts have been brought to the forefront. For example, the now-defunct public accounting company of Arthur Andersen was found guilty of obstruction of justice in 2002 for their role in the shredding of documents relating to Enron. As an example of the problems associated with financial analysts, the securities company of Merrill Lynch paid a $100 million fine for their role in hyping stocks to help win investment-banking business.[4]

It is unclear at this time the extent to which these scandals and problems were the result of simply bad decisions or due to corruption. The eagerness

---

[4]Merrill Lynch is now a part of Bank of America.

of managers to present favorable results to shareholders and the market appears to be a factor in several instances. And personal enrichment at the expense of shareholders seems to explain some cases. Whatever the motivation, chief executive officers (CEOs), chief financial officers (CFOs), and board members are being held directly accountable for financial disclosures. The Sarbanes-Oxley Act, passed in 2002, addresses these and other issues pertaining to disclosures and governance in public corporations. This Act addresses audits by independent public accountants, financial reporting and disclosures, conflicts of interest, and corporate governance at public companies. Each of the provisions of this Act can be traced to one or more scandals that occurred in the few years leading up to the passage of the Act.

The accounting scandals created an awareness of the importance of corporate governance, the importance of the independence of the public accounting auditing function, the role of financial analysts, and the responsibilities of CEOs and CFOs.

The recent economic crisis has again raised the issue of pay-for-performance as companies receiving government bailouts are scrutinized for their executive pay practices. This suggests that more reform may be necessary to insure transparency of financial information and a better linkage between pay and performance.

Shareholder Wealth Maximization and Social Responsibility   When financial managers assess a potential investment in a new product, they examine the risks and the potential benefits and costs. If the risk-adjusted benefits do not outweigh the costs, they will not invest. Similarly, managers assess current investments for the same purpose; if benefits do not continue to outweigh costs, they will not continue to invest in the product but will shift their investment elsewhere. This is consistent with the goal of shareholder wealth maximization and with the efficient allocation of resources in the economy.

Discontinuing investment in an unprofitable business, however, may mean effects on other stakeholders of the company: closing down plants, laying off workers, affecting suppliers' businesses, and, perhaps destroying an entire town that depends on the business for income. So decisions to invest or disinvest may affect great numbers of people.

THE BOTTOM LINE

- There are four primary forms of doing business: the sole proprietorship, the partnership, the corporation, and the limited liability company.

- The choice of the form of business affects the taxation of the company's income, as well as the degree of control the owners have on the company's decision-making.
- The objective of financial management is to maximize owners' wealth, which for a corporation means maximizing the value of the equity.
- When the management of the company is separated from the ownership of the company, as in the case of large corporations, there are potential problems and costs associated with the relationship between the decision-makers and the owners. The challenge is to devise a management compensation structure that sufficiently motivates management to act in owners' best interest, and which minimizes agency costs.

SOLUTIONS TO TRY IT! PROBLEMS

Effective Tax Rate

Tax on corporate income = $2 million × 0.38 = $0.76 million

Income to shareholders = $2 million − $0.76 million = $1.24 million

Tax on shareholders' income = $1.24 × 0.40 = $0.496 million

Effective tax rate = ($0.76 million + $0.496 million) ÷ $2 million = 62.8%

Market Capitalization

Market cap = 2.76 billion shares × $64.70 per share = $178.572 billion

QUESTIONS

1. What distinguishes a partnership from a corporation?
2. What is limited liability?
3. How does income get taxed twice in the case of a corporation?
4. Which forms of business have a perpetual life?
5. What are agency costs?
6. What is the objective of the financial management of a company?
7. List three types of compensation for a company's management.
8. How are options intended to align the interests of managers and owners of a corporation?
9. If a manager signs a contract with a strict provision prohibiting the manager from competing against this company if the manager leaves the company, what type of agency cost is this provision?
10. What incentive does a manager have to understate earnings?

11. What is meant by a company's market capitalization?
12. The U.S. tax code allows the creation of a taxable entity known as an S corporation. According to the Internal Revenue Service (www.irs.gov/businesses/small/article/0,,id=98263,00.html):

> *S corporations are corporations that elect to pass corporate income, losses, deductions and credit through to their shareholders for federal tax purposes. Shareholders of S corporations report the flow-through of income and losses on their personal tax returns and are assessed tax at their individual income tax rates. This allows S corporations to avoid double taxation on the corporate income. S corporations are responsible for tax on certain built-in gains and passive income.*
>
> *Corporations that do not elect to be treated as S corporations are called C corporations.*

    a. How does income get taxed twice in the case of a C corporation?
    b. The shareholders of an S corporation are still entitled to limited liability in the case of bankruptcy of the corporation. What are the advantages of being an S corporation if an entity can qualify to do so?

13. The following statement appears in "Agency Costs and Unregulated Banks: Could Depositors Protect Themselves?" by Catherine England (*Cato Journal* 7, no, 3 [Winter 1988]):

> *The agency costs literature argues that both agents and principals are aware of the potential conflicts of interest and abuses that can arise in an agency relationship. But neither group is expected to passively accept the limitations imposed by the potential problems and inefficiencies. The recognition of agency costs creates incentives for both groups to take steps to minimize and control the problem. To protect their interests, principals have reason to develop and incorporate contractual terms designed to channel the behavior of agents in desirable directions and/or to limit their ability to engage in unacceptable activities. In addition, principals setting a value on agents' services will consider the costs associated with the principal/agent relationship and reduce accordingly the compensation that would be paid to agents in a world of perfect information. Faced with the possibility of reduced compensation, agents will not only agree to*

contractual terms that reassure principals, but will also develop mechanisms that tend to make principals more confident.

a. What are agency costs?
b. What can principals do to reduce agency costs?

14. The following two statements were posted on a web site (www.inter fluidity.com) in a discussion of agency costs and leveraged investment funds. Leveraged investment funds are funds such as a hedge funds that borrow a considerable amount of money to investment in securities.

> *Limited liability creates a potential conflict of interest between investment funds and their creditors. If a fund is heavily leveraged, fund investors can reap large rewards by assuming risky positions with the understanding that if those positions go sour, a large fraction of the cost can be shifted (via actual or threatened bankruptcy) to the fund's creditors.*

a. What is meant by "limited liability"?
b. Explain whether you agree or disagree with the excerpt.

> *Like any other sort of investment manager, the interests of those who manage funds for pensions, university endowments, and charitable foundations may diverge from the interests of their diverse clientele. In particular, rational, self-interested managers may determine that pursuing peer-competitive short-term gains is wiser than carefully managing the long-term risks of fund stakeholders.*

c. What do economists call the types of costs associated with the actions described in this excerpt?
d. What is meant by "stakeholders"?

CHAPTER 6

Financial Strategy and Financial Planning

Though we are delighted with what we own, we are not pleased with our prospects for committing incoming funds. Prices are high for both businesses and stocks. That does not mean that the prices of either will fall—we have absolutely no view on that matter—but it does mean that we get relatively little in prospective earnings when we commit fresh money.

Under these circumstances, we try to exert a Ted Williams kind of discipline. In his book The Science of Hitting, *Ted explains that he carved the strike zone into 77 cells, each the size of a baseball. Swinging only at balls in his "best" cell, he knew, would allow him to bat .400; reaching for balls in his "worst" spot, the low outside corner of the strike zone, would reduce him to .230. In other words, waiting for the fat pitch would mean a trip to the Hall of Fame; swinging indiscriminately would mean a ticket to the minors.*

If they are in the strike zone at all, the business "pitches" we now see are just catching the lower outside corner. If we swing, we will be locked into low returns. But if we let all of today's balls go by, there can be no assurance that the next ones we see will be more to our liking. Perhaps the attractive prices of the past were the aberrations, not the full prices of today. Unlike Ted, we can't be called out if we resist three pitches that are barely in the strike zone; nevertheless, just standing there, day after day, with my bat on my shoulder is not my idea of fun.

—Warren Buffett, Letter to Shareholders of Berkshire Hathaway, 1997

A company's *strategic plan* is a method of achieving the goal of maximizing shareholder wealth. This strategic plan requires both long- and short-term financial planning that brings together forecasts of the company's sales with financing and investment decision making. Budgets, such as the cash budget and the production budget, are used to manage the information used in this planning, whereas performance measures, such as the balanced scorecard and economic value added, are used to evaluate progress toward the strategic goals.

A *strategy* is a direction the company intends to take to reach an objective. Once the company has its strategy, it needs a plan, in particular the strategic plan, which is the set of actions the company intends to use to follow its strategy. The investment opportunities that enable the company to follow its strategy comprise the company's *investment strategy*.

The chief financial officer (CFO), under the supervision of the board of directors, looks at the company's investment decisions and considers how to finance them. *Budgeting* is mapping out the sources and uses of funds for future periods. Budgeting requires both economic analysis (including forecasting) and accounting information. Economic analysis includes both marketing and production analysis to develop forecasts of future sales and costs. Accounting techniques are used as a measurement device: But instead of using accounting to summarize what has happened, companies use accounting to represent what the management expects to happen in the future. Therefore, budgeting involves looking forward into the future. We summarize this process in Exhibit 6.1.

Once these plans are put into effect, the management must compare what happens with what was planned. Companies use this postauditing to:

- Evaluate the performance of management.
- Analyze any deviations of actual results from planned results.
- Evaluate the planning process to determine just how good it is.

The purpose of this chapter is to explain strategic planning and how financial planning and budgeting are used in this process.

STRATEGY AND VALUE

The *strategic plan* is the path that the company intends to follow to achieve its objective, which is to put its assets to their best use, adding value. In this strategic plan is a method to make investments that will add value to the company. The way to add value is to invest in profitable projects. But

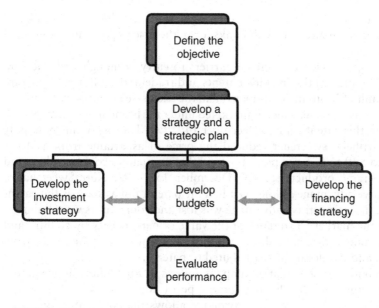

EXHIBIT 6.1   Strategy and Budgeting

where do these opportunities come from? They come from the company's comparative advantage or its competitive advantages.

Comparative and Competitive Advantages

A *comparative advantage* is the advantage one company has over others in terms of the cost of producing or distributing goods or services. For example, Wal-Mart Stores, Inc. had for years a comparative advantage over its competitors (such as Kmart) through its vast network of warehouses and its distribution system. Wal-Mart invested in a system of regional warehouses and its own trucking system. Combined with bulk purchases and a unique customer approach, Wal-Mart's comparative advantages in its warehousing and distribution systems helped it grow to be a major (and very profitable) retailer in a very short span of time. However, as with most comparative advantages, it took a few years for competitors to catch up and for Wal-Mart's advantages to disappear.

A *competitive advantage* is the advantage one company has over another because of the structure of the markets, input and output markets, in which they both operate. For example, one company may have a competitive advantage due to barriers to other companies entering the same market. This happens in the case of governmental regulations that limit the number of companies in a market, as with banks, or in the case of government-granted monopolies.

A company itself may create barriers to entry (although with the help of the government) that include patents and trademarks. NutraSweet Company, a unit of Monsanto Company, had the exclusive patent on the artificial sweetener, aspartame, which it marketed under the brand name NutraSweet. However, this patent expired December 14, 1992. The loss of the monopoly on the artificial sweetener reduced the price of aspartame from $70 per pound to $20 to $35 per pound, since other companies could produce and sell aspartame products starting December 15, 1992. NutraSweet had a competitive advantage as long as it had the patent. But as soon as the patent expired, this competitive advantage was lost and competitors were lining up to enter the market.[1] Estimates of the value of patents vary by country and industry, but studies have shown that up to one quarter of the return from research and development is attributed to patents.

The bottom line is that a company invests in something and gets more back in return only by having some type of advantage. In other words, a comparative or competitive advantage allows the company to generate economic profits—that is, profits in excess of its cost of capital. So first a management has to figure out where the company has a comparative or competitive advantage before the company's strategy can be determined.

Strategy and Adding Value

Often companies conceptualize a strategy in terms of the consumers of the company's goods and services. For example, management may have a strategy to become the world's leading producer of microcomputer chips by producing the best quality chip or by producing chips at the lowest cost, developing a cost (and price) advantage over its competitors. So management's focus is on product quality and cost. Is this strategy in conflict with maximizing owners' wealth? No.

Management must focus on the returns and risks of future cash flows to stockholders in order to add value. And management looks at a project's profitability when making decisions regarding whether to invest in it. A strategy of gaining a competitive or comparative advantage is consistent with maximizing shareholder wealth. This is because profitable projects arise when the company has a competitive or comparative advantage over other companies.

---

[1]Monsanto sold its sweetener division in 2000.

Suppose a new piece of equipment is expected to generate a return greater than what is expected for the project's risk (that is, greater than its cost of capital). But how can a company create value simply by investing in a piece of equipment? How can it maintain a competitive advantage? If investing in this equipment can create value, wouldn't the company's competitors also want this equipment? Of course—if they could use it to create value, they would surely be interested in it.

Now suppose that the company's competitors face no barriers to buying the equipment and exploiting its benefits. What will happen? The company and its competitors will compete for the equipment, bidding up its price. When does it all end? It ends when the difference between the present value of the inflows and the present value of the outflows for the equipment is zero.[2]

Suppose instead that the company has a patent on the new piece of equipment and can thus keep its competitors from exploiting the equipment's benefits. Then there would be no competition for the equipment and the company would be able to exploit it to add value.

Our acquisition decisions will be aimed at maximizing real economic benefits, not at maximizing either managerial domain or reported numbers for accounting purposes. (In the long run, managements stressing accounting appearance over economic substance usually achieve little of either.)
—Warren Buffett, Letter to Shareholders of
Berkshire Hathaway, 1981

Consider an example where trying to gain a comparative advantage went wrong. Schlitz Brewing Company attempted to reduce its costs to gain an advantage over its competitors: It reduced its labor costs and shortened the brewing cycle. Reducing costs allowed it to reduce its prices below competitors' prices. But product quality suffered—so much that Schlitz lost market share, instead of gaining it. Schlitz Brewing attempted to gain a comparative advantage, but was not true to a larger strategy to satisfy its customers—who apparently wanted quality beer more than they wanted cheap beer. And the loss of market share was reflected in Schlitz's declining stock price.[3]

---

[2]As you will see later in Chapter 13, this is when the net present value is equal to zero.

[3]The case of Schlitz Brewing is detailed in George S. Day and Liam Fahey, "Putting Strategy into Shareholder Value Analysis," *Harvard Business Review* 68 (March–April 1990): 156–162.

Value can be created only when the company has a competitive or comparative advantage. If a company analyzes a project and determines that it is profitable, the first question should be: Where did these profits come from?

Financial Planning and Budgeting

A strategy is the direction a company takes to meet its objective, whereas a strategic plan is how a company intends to go in that direction. For management, a strategic investment plan includes policies to seek out possible investments. A strategic plan also includes resource allocation. If a company intends to expand, where does it get the capital to do so? If a company requires more capital, the timing, amount, and type of capital (whether equity or debt) comprise elements of a company's financial strategic plan. These things must be planned to implement the strategy.

Financial planning allocates a company's resources to achieve its investment objectives. Financial planning is important for several reasons. First, financial planning helps managers assess the impact of a particular strategy on their company's financial position, its cash flows, its reported earnings, and its need for external financing.

By failing to prepare you are preparing to fail.

—Benjamin Franklin

Second, by formulating financial plans, management is in a better position to react to any changes in market conditions, such as slower than expected sales, or unexpected problems, such as a reduction in the supply of raw materials. By constructing a financial plan, management becomes more familiar with the sensitivity of the company's cash flows and its financing needs to changes in sales or some other factor.

Third, creating a financial plan helps management understand the trade-offs inherent in its investment and financing plans. For example, by developing a financial plan, management is better able to understand the trade-off that exists between having sufficient inventory to satisfy customer demands and the need to finance the investment in inventory.

Financial planning consists of the company's investment and financing plans. Once we know the company's investment plan, management needs to figure out when funds are needed and where they will come from. This is accomplished by developing a *budget*, which is basically the company's investment and financing plans expressed in monetary terms. A budget can represent details such as what to do with cash in excess of needs on a daily basis, or it can reflect broad statements of a company's business strategy over the next decade. Exhibit 6.2 illustrates the budgeting process.

Budgeting for the short term (less than a year) is usually referred to as *operational budgeting*; budgeting for the long term (typically three to five years ahead) is referred to as *long-run planning* or *long-term planning*. But since long-term planning depends on what is done in the short term, the operational budgeting and long-term planning are closely related.

THE BUDGETING PROCESS

The budgeting process involves putting together the financing and investment strategy in terms that allow those responsible for the financing of the company to determine what investments can be made and how these investments should be financed. In other words, budgeting pulls together decisions regarding capital budgeting, capital structure, and working capital.

Consider a company whose line of business is operating retail stores. Its store renovation plan is part of its overall strategy of regaining its share of the retail market by offering customers better quality and service. Fixing up its stores is seen as an investment strategy. The company evaluates its renovation plan using capital budgeting techniques (e.g., net present value). But the renovation program requires financing—this is where the capital structure decision comes in. If it needs more funds, where do they come from? Debt? Equity? Both? And let's not forget the working capital decisions. As the company renovates its stores, will this change its need for cash on hand? Will the renovation affect inventory needs? If the company expects to increase sales through this program, how will this affect its investment in accounts receivable? And what about short-term financing? Will it need more or less short-term financing when it renovates?

It's clearly a budget. It's got a lot of numbers in it.

—George W. Bush

While the company is undergoing a renovation program, it needs to estimate what funds it needs, in both the short and the long run. This is where cash budget and pro forma financial statements are useful. The starting point is generally a sales forecast, which is related closely to the purchasing, production, and other forecasts of the company. What are the company's expected sales in the short term? In the long term? Also, the amount that the company expects to sell affects its purchases, sales personnel, and advertising forecasts. Putting together forecasts requires cooperation among Sears's marketing, purchasing, and finance staff.

Once the company has its sales and related forecasts, the next step is a cash budget, detailing the cash inflows and outflows each period. Once the cash budget is established, pro forma balance sheet and income statements can be constructed. Following this, the company must verify that its budget is consistent with its objective and its strategies.

Budgeting generally begins four to six months prior to the end of the current fiscal period. Most companies have a set of procedures that must be followed in compiling the budget. The budget process is usually managed by either the CFO, a vice president of planning, the director of the budget, the vice president of finance, or the controller. Each division or department provides its own budgets that are then merged into a company's centralized budget by the manager of the budget.

A budget looks forward and backward. It identifies resources that the company will generate or need in the near and long term, and it serves as a measure of the current and past performance of departments, divisions, or individual managers. But management has to be careful when measuring deviations between budgeted and actual results to separately identify deviations that were controllable from deviations that were uncontrollable. For example, suppose management develops a budget expecting $10 million sales from a new product. If actual sales turn out to be $6 million, do we interpret this result as poor performance on the part of management? Maybe, maybe not: If the lower-than-expected sales are due to an unexpected downturn in the economy, probably not; but yes, if they are due to what turns out to be obviously poor management forecasts of consumer demand.

Sale Forecasting

Sales forecasts are an important part of financial planning. Inaccurate forecasts can result in shortages of inventory, inadequate short-term financing arrangements, and so on.

If a company's sales forecast misses its mark, either understating or overstating sales, there are many potential problems. Consider Nintendo, which missed its mark. This company introduced the Wii game console in November 2006, which enjoyed runaway popularity. In fact, this game console was so popular that Nintendo could not keep up with demand. It was in such demand and inventory so depleted that Nintendo was selling the game faster than they produced them.[4]

---

[4]It was not until 2009 that Nintendo's supply of Wii game consoles caught up to its demand.

Nintendo missed its mark, significantly underestimating the demand for Wii. While having a popular game console may seem like a dream for a company, this product created problems. With no Wii game consoles on store shelves, other manufacturers with gaming systems with similar (but not identical) features, were able to capture some of Nintendo's market. Also, consumers may begrudge the company for creating the demand for the game through advertising, but not having sufficient game consoles to satisfy the demand.

To predict cash flows management forecasts sales, which are uncertain because they are affected by future economic, industry, and market conditions. Nevertheless, management can usually assign meaningful degrees of uncertainty to its forecasts. Sales can be forecasted by regression analysis, market surveys, or opinions of management.

Forecasting with Regression Analysis

Regression analysis is a statistical method that enables us to fit a straight line that on average represents the best possible graphical relationship between sales and time. This best fit is called the *regression line*. One way regression analysis can be used is to simply extrapolate future sales based on the trend in past sales. Another way of using regression analysis is to look at the relation between two measures, say, sales and capital expenditures.

While regression analysis gives us what may seem to be a precise measure of the relationship among variables, there are a number of warnings that management must heed in using it:

- Using historical data to predict the future assumes that the past relationships will continue into the future, which is not always true.
- The period over which the regression is estimated may not be representative of the future. For example, data from a recessionary period of time will not tell much about a period that is predicted to be an economic boom.
- The reliability of the estimate is important: If there is a high degree of error in the estimate, the regression estimates may not be useful.
- The time period over which the regression is estimated may be too short to provide a basis for projecting long-term trends.
- The forecast of one variable may require forecasts of other variables. For example, the management may be convinced that sales are affected by gross domestic product (GDP) and use regression to analyze this relationship. But to use regression to forecast sales, management must first forecast GDP. In this case, management's forecast of sales is only as good as the forecast of GDP.

Market Surveys

Market surveys of customers can provide estimates of future revenues. In the case of Intel, for example, management would need to focus on the computer industry and, specifically, on computer, netbooks, phones, and gaming markets. For each of these markets, management would have to assess Intel's market share and also the expected sales for each market. Management should expect to learn from these market surveys:

- Product development and introductions by Intel and its competitors
- The general economic climate and the projected expenditures on computers and other electronic devices that require microprocessors

In general, management can use the company's own market survey department to survey its customers. Or it can employ outside market survey specialists.

Management Forecasts

In addition to market surveys, the company's managers may be able to provide forecasts of future sales. The experience of a company's management and their familiarity with the company's products, customers, and competitors make them reliable forecasters of future sales.

The company's own managers should have the expertise to predict the market for the goods and services and to evaluate the costs of producing and marketing them. But there are potential problems in using management forecasts. Consider the case of a manager who forecasts rosy outcomes for a new product. These forecasts may persuade the company to allocate more resources—such as a larger capital budget and additional personnel—to that manager. If these forecasts come true, the company will be glad these additional resources were allocated. But if these forecasts turned out to be too rosy, the company has unnecessarily allocated these resources.

Forecasting is an important element in planning for both the short and the long term. But forecasts are made by people. Forecasters tend to be optimistic, which usually results in rosier-than-deserved forecasts of future sales. In addition, people tend to focus on what worked in the past, so past successes carry more weight in developing forecasts than an analysis of the future. One way to avoid this is to make managers responsible for their forecasts, rewarding accurate forecasts and penalizing managers for being way off the mark.

BUDGETING

In budgeting, we bring together analyses of cash flows, projected income statements, and projected balance sheets. The cash flow analyses are most important, though the financial management staff needs to generate the income statement and balance sheet as well.

Most companies extend or receive credit, so cash flows and net income do not coincide. Typically, the finance staff must determine cash flows from accounting information on revenues and expenses. For example, combining sales projections with estimates of collections of accounts receivable results in an estimate of cash receipts.

The Cash Budget

A *cash budget* is a detailed statement of the cash inflows and outflows expected in future periods. This budget helps management identify financing and investment needs. A cash budget can also be used to compare actual cash flows against planned cash flows so that management can evaluate both management's performance and management's forecasting ability.

Cash flows come into the company from:

- Operations, such as receipts from sales and collections on accounts receivable
- The results of financing decisions, such as borrowings, sales of shares of common stock, and sales of preferred stock
- The results of investment decisions, such as sales of assets and income from marketable securities

Cash flows leave the company from:

- Operations, such as payments on accounts payable, purchases of goods, and the payment of taxes
- Financing obligations, such as the payment of dividends and interest, and the repurchase of shares of stock or the redemption of bonds
- Investments, such as the purchase of plant and equipment

As we noted before, the cash budget is driven by the sales forecast. The cash budget, by providing estimates of cash inflows and outflows, provides an estimate of the company's need for funds, requiring short- or long-term capital, or excess funds, requiring the company to invest the funds, pay down debt, or return capital to owners.

Pro Forma Financial Statements

A *pro forma balance sheet* is a projected balance sheet for a future period—a month, quarter, or year—that summarizes assets, liabilities, and equity.[5] A *pro forma income statement* is the projected income statement for a future period—a month, quarter, or year—that summarizes revenues and expenses. Together both projections help management identify the company's investment and financing needs.

PERFORMANCE EVALUATION

Planning and forecasting are important, but without some type of performance evaluation, the execution of a strategy and the accuracy of forecasting cannot be addressed. There are many performance evaluation measures and systems available. We will address two of these, economic value added and the balanced scorecard, to provide examples of how these may assist in assessing performance.

Economic Value Added

Arising from the need for better methods of evaluating performance, several consulting companies advocate performance evaluation methods that are applied to evaluate a company's performance as a whole and to evaluate specific managers' performances. These methods are, in some cases, supplanting traditional methods of measuring performance, such as the return on assets discussed in other chapters of this book. As a class, these measures are often referred to as value-based metrics or economic value–added measures. There is a cacophony of acronyms to accompany these measures, including economic value added (EVA®), market value added (MVA), cash flow return on investment (CFROI), shareholder value added (SVA), cash value added (CVA), and refined economic value added (REVA).[6]

A company's management creates value when decisions provide benefits that exceed the costs. These benefits may be received in the near or distant future. The costs include both the direct cost of the investment as well as the

---

[5]You should not confuse a pro forma financial statement with pro forma earnings that a company may announce. Pro forma earnings, in the latter context, are earnings restated using principles that are not generally accepted accounting principles.

[6]For a further discussion of these measures, see Frank J. Fabozzi and James L. Grant (eds.), *Value Based Metrics: Foundations and Practice* (Hoboken, NJ: John Wiley & Sons, 2000).

less obvious cost, the cost of capital. The cost of capital is the explicit and implicit costs associated with using investors' funds. The attention to the cost of capital sets the value-based metrics apart from traditional measures of performance such as the return on investment.

There are a number of value-added measures available. The most commonly used measures are economic value added and market value added. *Economic value added*, also referred to as *economic profit*, is the difference between operating profits and the cost of capital, where the cost of capital is expressed in dollar terms. We diagram the key elements of estimating economic value added in Exhibit 6.2.

We continue to use Economic Value Added as the basis for disciplined decision making around the use of capital. EVA is a tool that considers both financial earnings and a cost of capital in measuring performance. We look for opportunities to improve EVA because we believe there is a strong correlation between EVA improvement and creation of shareholder value.

—The Williams Companies, 2007 Annual Report

The difference between the operating profit and the cost of capital is the estimate of the company's economic value added, or economic profit. The cost of capital is the rate of return required by the suppliers of capital to the company. For a business that finances its operations or investments using both debt and equity, the cost of capital includes not only the explicit interest on the debt, but also the implicit minimum return that owners require. This

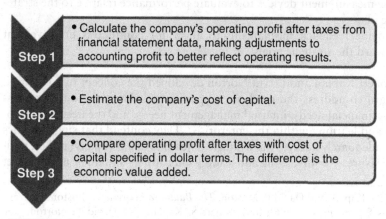

Step 1
• Calculate the company's operating profit after taxes from financial statement data, making adjustments to accounting profit to better reflect operating results.

Step 2
• Estimate the company's cost of capital.

Step 3
• Compare operating profit after taxes with cost of capital specified in dollar terms. The difference is the economic value added.

EXHIBIT 6.2 Calculating Economic Profit

minimum return to owners is necessary so that owners keep their investment capital in the company.

A measure closely related to economic profit is *market valued added.* Market value added is the difference between the company's market value and its capital. Essentially, market value added is a measure of what the company's management has been able to do with a given level of resources (the invested capital): Market value added is the difference between the market value of the company (that is, debt and equity), less the capital invested. Like economic profit, market value added is in terms of dollars and the goal of the company is to increase added value. Calculating the market value added requires comparing the market value of a company's capital with the capital invested; the difference between these two amounts is the market value added. The primary distinction between economic value added and market value added is that the latter incorporates market data in the calculation.

Balanced Scorecard

The traditional measures of a company's performance are generally historical, financial measures. With the popularity of economic value added and market value measures, many companies began to adopt forward-looking financial measures. Taking a step further, many companies are adopting the concept of a balanced scorecard. A *balanced scorecard* is a set of measures of performance that address different aspects of a company's strategic plan. A balanced scorecard is a management tool used to:

- Help put a company's strategic plan into action
- Use measurement devices to evaluate performance relative to the strategic plan
- Provide feedback mechanisms to allow for continuous improvement toward the strategic goals

Robert Kaplan and David Norton developed the concept of a balanced scorecard to address the need of companies to balance the needs of customers, financial needs, internal management needs, and the needs for innovation and learning within the enterprise.[7] They contend that single metrics do not adequately address the strategic objectives of a company; rather, multiple measures—both lagging and leading indicators—should be used to meet

---

[7]Robert S. Kaplan and David P. Norton, *The Balanced Scorecard,* (Boston: Harvard Business School Press, 1996); and Robert S. Kaplan and David P. Norton, *The Strategy-Focused Organization* (Boston: Harvard Business School Press, 2001).

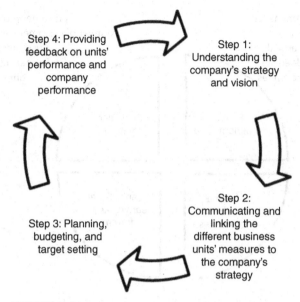

EXHIBIT 6.3 The Balanced Scorecard Process

a company's strategic goals. These measures, referred to as *key performance indicators*, include short-term and long-term measures, financial and non-financial measures, and historical and leading measures. The balanced scorecard, therefore, goes beyond the traditional financial measures of the rate of return and profitability to capture other dimensions of a company's performance and use this information to help attain the company's strategic goals.

The balanced scorecard is really a process of assessing the effectiveness of the company's strategy in meeting the company's objective, identifying measures to evaluate whether the company is meeting its short-term and long-term goals, setting targets, and then providing feedback from these measures. We illustrate this process in Exhibit 6.3. The actual balanced scorecard does not prescribe the measures to use, but rather specifies the dimensions of the company that should be considered in the system.

The developers of the balanced scorecard argue that measures and metrics used to evaluate different business units and the company should represent different dimensions of performance, including financial performance, customer relations, internal business processes, and organizational learning and growth. We illustrate these dimensions in Exhibit 6.4. However, no specific measures are prescribed; rather, the choice of measures should be tailored to the company's individual situation. The basic idea, however, is to select the key performance indicators that capture the four dimensions.

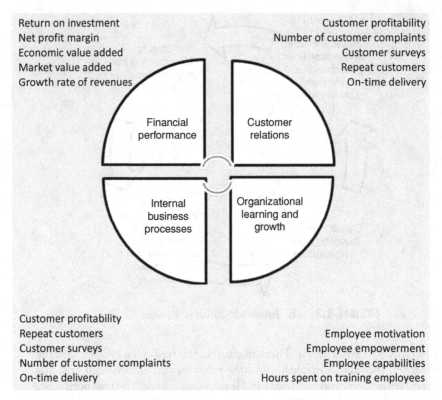

Return on investment
Net profit margin
Economic value added
Market value added
Growth rate of revenues

Customer profitability
Number of customer complaints
Customer surveys
Repeat customers
On-time delivery

Financial performance

Customer relations

Internal business processes

Organizational learning and growth

Customer profitability
Repeat customers
Customer surveys
Number of customer complaints
On-time delivery

Employee motivation
Employee empowerment
Employee capabilities
Hours spent on training employees

EXHIBIT 6.4 Possible Performance Indicators in Four Dimensions of Strategy

Within each of these dimensions, there may be any number of different measures. These measures are generally tailored to the specific business and should be consistent with the company's or unit's goals. We provide a number of possible metrics within each of these dimensions in Exhibit 6.4.

STRATEGY AND VALUE CREATION

The company's chief financial officer is in a good position to link the corporate strategy with value creation. Most surveys indicate that CFOs feel that their focus is shifting from historical assessment of performance to forward-looking tasks such as the development of strategy and decision making.

For example, a March 2006 report prepared by CFO Research Services in collaboration with Deloitte Consulting found that CFOs not only participate in the development of a company's strategy, but in many cases the

CFO is also charged with executing the strategy and measuring the company's progress toward the strategic goals.[8] The CFO role has expanded from the traditional functions—controller, financial reporting, compliance, and support—to include serving the company's strategy through financial decision making. This expansion has broadened the role from a service function to an activist function. According to an April 2005 report prepared by CFO Research Services and Booz Allen Hamilton:[9]

> *Activism—again, defined as finance in a role beyond controllership and decision support—occurs more often among survey respondents who say their finance teams have become more closely engaged with the board of directors in the last two years.*

This survey, however, indicates that those companies with closer relations with the board of directors are also companies that have greater pressure from analysts, high turnover in top management, and a need to change the company's operating model—in other words, those companies under the microscope of the business community.

It is interesting that surveys suggest an inconsistency in the CFO's role in a company's strategy and value creation.[10] The majority of CFOs feel that strategy is their top priority, yet they also feel that this is not the perception of the CFO's role among other functions within the company:

> *...found that 60% of the CFOs surveyed cite their role in the development/formulation of corporate strategy as a priority. Yet only 25% say the rest of the organization views finance as a value added function to be consulted on all important decisions.*

A 2005 survey by Financial Executives International Canada, "The Role of the CFO Today and Beyond," found that CFOs are directly accountable for financial analysis (93%), financial risk management (92.3%), forecasting and projections (87.3%), business and financial systems and reporting (82.4%), and financing and capital structure changes (79.6%). In terms of functions in which CFOs are closely involved, the top three functions are involvement in the operational risk management (70.4%), writing some or all of the strategic plan (69%), and strategic and business planning (59.9%). The results of this survey illustrate the breadth of the CFO's responsibility.

---

[8] "Different Paths to One Truth: Finance Brings Value Discipline to Strategy Execution."

[9] CFO Research Services and Booz Allen Hamilton, "The Activist CFO—Alignment with Strategy, Not Just with the Business," p. 15.

[10] Mark Frigo, *The State of Management Accounting: The Ernst & Young and IMA Survey*, Institute of Management Accounts Research Team Member, 2003, p. 7.

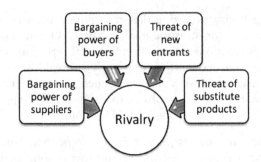

EXHIBIT 6.5   Porter's Five Forces

Sources of Value Creation

A company's strategy is a path to create value. But value cannot be created out of thin air. Value creation—that is, generating economic profit—requires identifying comparative and competitive advantages, and developing a strategy that exploits these advantages.

One way to look at these advantages is to use the framework introduced by Michael Porter.[11] He analyzed competitive structure of industries and identified five competitive forces that capture an industry's competitive rivalry, as we illustrate in Exhibit 6.5. *Porter's Five Forces* relate to the company's or industry's ability to generate economic profits. Briefly,

- The bargaining power of suppliers relates to the power of the providers of inputs—both goods and services.
- The bargaining power of buyers relates to the power of those who buy the company's goods and services.
- The threat of new entrants is related to barriers to entry into the industry.[12]
- The threat of substitutes relates to alternative goods and services the company's customers may buy.
- The competitive rivalry among existing members of the industry is affected by the number and relative size of the companies in the industry, the strategies of the companies, the differentiation among products, and the growth of the sales in the industry.

---

[11] Michael Porter, *Competitive Strategy: Techniques for Analyzing Industries and Competitors* (New York: Simon & Schuster, 1998).
[12] A barrier to entry is an impediment such as economies of scale, high initial start-up costs, cost advantages due to experience of existing participants, loyalty among customers, protections such as patents, licenses, or copyrights, or regulatory or government action that limits entrants into the industry.

EXHIBIT 6.6 Porter's Five Forces: Threats and Powers

Force	High	Low
Bargaining power of buyers	Buyers are concentrated. Suppliers have high fixed costs. Ready substitutes. Buyer could produce the good or service itself.	Many potential buyers. Buyer volume is low. Few substitutes. Buyers cannot backward integrate.
Bargaining power of suppliers	The market is dominated by a few large companies. There are no substitutes for the input. The cost of switching inputs is high. The buyers are fragmented with little buying power. The suppliers may integrate forward to capture higher prices and margins.	Many suppliers. Readily available substitutes. Low cost to switching inputs.
Threat of new entrants	Few barriers to entry. Little customer loyalty. Low capital requirements. High profits.	Significant barriers to entry. Strong customer loyalty. High learning curve. Significant capital investment.
Threat of substitutes	Little brand loyalty among customers. No close customer relations. Low costs to switching goods and services. Substitutes are lower priced.	High brand loyalty. Strong customer relations. High costs to switching goods. Substitutes are not lower priced.
Rivalry	High barriers to exit. Concentrated industry. Low barriers to entry. Large number of firms. Slow growth. Low costs for customers to switch products. High fixed costs.	Low barriers to exit. High barriers to entry. Significant product differentiation. High costs for customers to switch products.

We provide examples of how characteristics of the industries (the products, suppliers, and market structure) affect the rivalry among companies in an industry in Exhibit 6.6. For example, if buyers are concentrated, the bargaining power of buyers is high, which makes it more difficult for companies to extract economic profits. On the other hand, if there are many suppliers, the power of the suppliers is low and companies in this industry may be able to extract more economic profit.

Porter's Five Forces do not provide a magic formula for determining whether a company can create value. Rather, the purpose of the five forces is to provide a framework for thinking about the powers and threats that affect an industry's—and company's—ability to generate economic profits. The bottom line of all of this is that the ability of a company to create and maintain a comparative or competitive advantage is complex.

Porter's forces are, basically, an elaboration of the theories of economics that tell us how a company creates economic profit. Though Porter's forces may seem over simplistic in a dynamic economy, they provide a starting point for analysis of a company's ability to add value. Porter argues that an individual company may create a competitive advantage through relative cost, differentiation, and relative prices. Management, in evaluating a company's current and future performance, can use these forces and strategies to identify the company's sources of economic profit.

Management should never ignore the basic economics that lie behind value creation. If a company has a unique advantage, this can lead to value creation. If the advantage is one that can be replicated easily by others, this advantage—and hence any value creation related to it—may erode quickly. The herding behavior of companies, seeking to mimic the strategies of the better-performing companies, may result in the erosion of value from that strategy. This herding behavior therefore requires that strategic planning be dynamic and that feedback from performance evaluation is important in this planning process. Therefore, strategic planning should be a continual process that requires setting strategic objectives, developing the strategy, periodically measuring progress toward those goals, and then reevaluating the strategic objectives and strategy.

THE BOTTOM LINE

- Adding value to a company requires devising a strategy and a strategic plan to exploit the company's comparative or competitive advantages.
- An important element in financial planning for a business is forecasting revenues and expenses, and then developing the budgets.
- Evaluating a company's performance requires estimating the company's economic profit and measuring its value-added. A useful tool is to use a balanced scorecard process, which begins with the company's strategy and requires measurement and feedback of the company's performance, as well as that of the different units of the company.
- Porter's Five Forces framework is useful in identifying the degree of rivalry in an industry by focusing on the company's bargaining power

with suppliers, the buyers' bargaining power with the company, the threat of new entrants in the industry, and the threat of substitutes.

QUESTIONS

1. What is the relation between a strategy and an objective?
2. How are comparative advantages different from competitive advantages?
3. What is a strategic plan?
4. What is a financial plan, and how does it relate to a company's strategic plan?
5. What is regression analysis, and how might it assist a financial manager in planning?
6. What is a pro forma financial statement?
7. What is economic value added and why do financial managers care about this?
8. Explain what is meant by a balanced scorecard.
9. If companies in an industry have significant profits and there are no barriers to entry, how do these characteristics fit in the context of Porter's Five Forces?
10. What are sources of economic profits for a company or an industry?
11. The following is an excerpt that appeared in an article "Strategic Planning: Not Just for Big Business" published at www.smallbusinessnotes. com/planning/strategicplanning.html, sponsored by "Strategic Planning Made Easy":

> Strategic planning has become a concept that is commonly suggested as the "solution" to many business problems. Some days it appears that the chief product of many businesses is their strategic plan. Don't misunderstand me, strategic plans are wonderful when used appropriately, but they do need to be a tool of a business, not a goal unto themselves. And, most definitely, they should not be a major consumer of valuable employer/employee time.
>
> Many entrepreneurial ventures mistakenly believe that strategic planning is only for large businesses that can afford the time and personnel to develop a sound plan. However, if you are to compete in the marketplace against the "big guys," you need to learn some of their game plans—and strategic planning is a major part of any successful, large business. That does not mean that your startup needs all the bells and whistles of

the more complex plans. You can in a matter of hours sketch out a good working draft that will help keep you on course to becoming a solid competitor.

   a. How does a "strategic plan" relate to a company's objectives?
   b. Why are strategic plans considered a tool and not a solution?
12. The following excerpt is from "Integrating Strategic and Financial Planning" by Lee Ann Runy (2005), which appeared on hospitalconnect.com (www.hhnmag.com/hhnmag_app/hospitalconnect/search/article.jsp? dcrpath=HHNMAG/PubsNewsArticle/data/0506HHN_FEA_Gatefold &domain=HHNMAG):

> *Integrating strategic and financial planning is the best way for health care organizations to ensure that they are spending money wisely.... Too often, projects get approved only to be shelved because the money isn't available. And, hospitals need an accurate vision of their community and the needs and wants of their customers before embarking on costly expansions and new services.*
>
>   *It is a dynamic process: Just as budgets must be updated yearly, strategic plans must be reassessed to ensure that the organization's assumptions and projections are on track. It is important that plans remain up-to-date or the organization risks costly, unnecessary expenditures or may miss out on a good opportunity.*
>
>   *A thorough planning process incorporates strategic planning, financial and operational planning and capital allocation. "A financial plan without strategy isn't much of a plan," says Blaine O'Connell, chief financial officer at Froedert Hospital in Milwaukee. "A strategic plan without financial backing isn't much of a strategy."*

   a. What is the relationship between strategic planning and financial planning?
   b. What does financial planning involve?
   c. What do you think "operational planning" means in the excerpt?
   d. What do you think "capital allocation" means in the excerpt?
   e. Explain why you agree or disagree with the statement in the excerpt: "A financial plan without strategy isn't much of a plan."
13. *Fortune* Magazine published a 1998 interview with Peter Drucker ("Peter Drucker Takes the Long View: The Original Management Guru shares his vision of the future with *Fortune*'s Brent Schlender")

where the following appeared (money.cnn.com/magazines/fortune/
fortune_archive/1998/09/28/248706/index.htm):

> *... there is no profit unless you earn the cost of capital.
> Alfred Marshall said that in 1896, Peter Drucker said that in
> 1954 and in 1973, and now EVA (economic value added) has
> systematized this idea, thank God.*

a. What is EVA and how does it take into account the cost of capital?
b. What is the relationship between EVA and economic profit?

14. In "Using the Balanced Scorecard as a Strategic Management System"
by Robert S. Kaplan and David P. Norton (*Harvard Business Review*,
January–February 1996), the following appeared on page 2 of the
article:

> *Managers using the balanced scorecard do not have to rely on
> short-term financial measures as the sole indicators of the com-
> pany's performance. The scorecard lets them introduce four
> new management processes that, separately and in combina-
> tion, contribute to linking long-term strategic objectives with
> short-term actions.*

a. How does a balanced scorecard assist in linking objectives with actions?
b. What are the "four new management processes" mentioned in the
quote?

CHAPTER 7

Dividend and Dividend Policies

The evidence that, controlling for characteristics, firms become less likely to pay dividends says that the perceived benefits of dividends have declined through time. Some (but surely not all) of the possibilities are: (i) lower transactions costs for selling stocks for consumption purposes, in part due to an increased tendency to hold stocks via open end mutual funds; (ii) larger holdings of stock options by managers who prefer capital gains to dividends; and (iii) better corporate governance technologies (e.g., more prevalent use of stock options) that lower the benefits of dividends in controlling agency problems between stockholders and managers.

—Eugene F. Fama and Kenneth R. French,
"Disappearing Dividends: Changing Firm
Characteristics or Lower Propensity to Pay?"
Journal of Financial Economics 60 (2001): 3–43

Many corporations pay cash dividends to their shareholders despite the tax consequences of these dividends and the fact that these funds could otherwise be plowed back into the corporation for investment purposes. These dividends are often viewed as a signal of the corporation's future prosperity. Corporations may also "pay" stock dividends or split the stock, dividing the equity pie into smaller pieces, the announcement of which is often viewed as positive news by investors.

In addition to dividends, a corporation can distribute funds to shareholders other than in the form of a cash dividend. For example, a corporation may repurchase its shares from shareholders through open market purchases, tender offers, or targeted block repurchases.

The purpose of this chapter is to describe the mechanisms of providing funds to shareholders in the form of dividends, stock dividends and splits, and stock repurchases.

DIVIDENDS

A *dividend* is the cash, stock, or any type of property a corporation distributes to its shareholders. The board of directors may declare a dividend at any time, but dividends are not a legal obligation of the corporation—it is the board's choice. Unlike interest on debt securities, if a corporation does not pay a dividend, there is no violation of a contract, nor any legal recourse for shareholders.

When the board of directors declares a distribution, it specifies the amount of the distribution, the date on which the distribution is paid, and the *date of record*, which determines who has the right to the distributions. Because shares are traded frequently and it takes time to process transactions, the exchanges have devised a way of determining which investors receive the dividend: the exchanges take the record date, as specified by the board of directors, and identify the *ex-dividend date*, which is two business days prior to the record date. The ex-dividend date is often referred to simply as the *ex-date*.

Therefore, there are four key dates in a distribution:

1. The *declaration date*, which is the date the board declares the distribution.
2. The *ex-dividend date*, which is the date that determines which investors receive the dividend. Any investor who owns the stock the day before the ex-date receives the forthcoming dividend. Any investor who buys the stock on the ex-date does not receive the dividend.
3. The *date of record*, which is specified by the board of directors as the date that determines who receives the dividend.
4. The *payment date*, which is the day the distribution is made.

Most dividends are in the form of cash. Cash dividends are payments made directly to shareholders in proportion to the shares they own. When cash dividends are paid, they are paid on all outstanding shares of a class of stock.[1] A few companies pay *special dividends* or *extra dividends* occasionally—identifying these dividends apart from their regular dividends.

We usually describe the cash dividends that a company pays in terms of *dividend per share*, which we calculate as:

$$\text{Dividend per share} = \frac{\text{Cash dividends}}{\text{Number of shares outstanding}}$$

---

[1]Therefore, a corporation may pay dividends on its preferred stock, but not on its common stock.

Another way of describing cash dividends is in terms of the percentage of earnings paid out in dividends, which we refer to as the *dividend payout ratio*. We can express the dividend in terms of the proportion of earnings over a fiscal period:

$$\text{Dividend payout ratio} = \frac{\text{Cash dividends}}{\text{Earnings available to shareholders}}$$

If we take this last equation and divide both the numerator and the denominator by the number of common shares outstanding, we can rewrite the dividend payout ratio as:

$$\text{Dividend payout ratio} = \frac{\text{Dividend per share}}{\text{Earnings per share}}$$

The dividend payout ratio is the complement of the *retention ratio*, also referred to as the *plowback ratio*:

$$\text{Retention ratio} = \frac{\text{Earnings available to shareholders} - \text{Cash dividends}}{\text{Earnings available to shareholders}}$$

$$= 1 - \text{Dividend payout ratio}$$

The retention ratio is the proportion of earnings that the company retains, that is, the proportion of earnings reinvested back into the company.

We demonstrate these calculations in Exhibit 7.1, applying these calculations to Wal-Mart Stores, Inc.

EXHIBIT 7.1 The Dividends of Wal-Mart Stores, Inc.

For fiscal year 2008, Wal-Mart Stores reported the following financial results:

Earnings available to common shares	$13.400 billion
Dividends paid	$ 3.746 billion
Number of common shares outstanding	3.81 billion

Therefore, Wal-Mart Stores' dividend per share and dividend payout ratio are:

Dividend per share = $3.746 billion / $3.81 billion = $0.9832 per share
Dividend payout ratio = $3.746 billion / $13.400 billion = 27.955%

Or, in terms of dividends per share and earnings per share, we get the same result:

Dividend payout ratio = $0.9832 / $3.5171 = 27.955%

TRY IT! DIVIDENDS

Consider a company with the following information for the fiscal year:

Dividends paid	$2 million
Net income	$5 million
Number of shares outstanding	1 million

The company has no preferred stock outstanding. Complete the following:

Dividends per share [   ]
Earnings per share [   ]
Dividend payout ratio [   ]
Retention ratio [   ]

Dividend Reinvestment Plans

Many U.S. corporations allow shareholders to reinvest automatically their dividends in the shares of the corporation paying them. A *dividend reinvestment plan* (DRP or DRIP) is a program that allows shareholders to reinvest their dividends, buying additional shares of stock of the company instead of receiving the cash dividend. A DRP offers benefits to both shareholders and the corporation:

1. Shareholders buy shares without transactions costs—brokers' commissions—and at a discount from the current market price.
2. The corporation retains cash without the cost of a new stock issue.

One stickler in all this, however, is that the dividends are taxed as income before they are reinvested, even though the shareholders never see the dividend. The result is similar to a dividend cut, but with a tax consequence for the shareholders: The cash flow that would have been paid to shareholders is plowed back into the corporation.

Many corporations find high rates of participation in DRPs. If so many shareholders want to reinvest their dividends—even after considering the tax consequences—why is the corporation paying dividends? This suggests that there is some rationale, such as signaling, that compels corporations to pay dividends.

STOCK DISTRIBUTIONS

In addition to cash dividends, a corporation may provide shareholders with dividends in the form of additional shares of stock or, rarely, some types of property owned by the corporation. When dividends are not in cash, they are usually additional shares of stock. Additional shares of stock can be distributed to shareholders in two ways: paying a stock dividend and splitting the stock.

Types of Distributions

A *stock dividend* is the distribution of additional shares of stock to shareholders. Stock dividends are generally stated as a percentage of existing share holdings. If a corporation pays a stock dividend, it is not transferring anything of value to the shareholders. The assets of the corporation remain the same and each shareholder's proportionate share of ownership remains the same. All the corporation is doing is cutting its equity "pie" into more slices and at the same time cutting each shareholder's portion of that equity into more slices. So why pay a stock dividend?

A stock split is something like a stock dividend. A *stock split* splits the number of existing shares into more shares. For example, in a 2:1 split—referred to as "two for one"—each shareholder gets two shares for every one owned. If an investor owns 1,000 shares and the stock is split 2:1, the investor then owns 2,000 shares after the split. Has the portion of the investor's ownership in the company changed? No, the investor now simply owns twice as many shares—and so does every other shareholder. If the investor owned 1% of the corporation's stock before the split, the investor still owns 1% after the split.

A *reverse stock split* is similar to a stock split, but backwards: a 1:2 reverse stock split reduces the number of shares of stock such that a shareholder receives half the number of shares held before the reverse stock split. A stock split in which more shares are distributed to shareholders is sometimes referred to as a *forward stock split* to distinguish it from a reverse stock split. Similar to both the stock dividend and the stock split, there is no actual distribution or contribution made, but simply a division of the equity pie—in this case, into fewer pieces.

Stock distributions, similar to cash dividends, are a decision of the board of directors, but in this case the "payment" date is similar when the additional shares are provided to shareholders, or shares exchanged, in the case of a forward or a reverse stock split.

Reasons for Stock Distributions

There are a couple of reasons for paying dividends in the form of stock dividends. One is to provide information to the market. A company may want to communicate good news to the shareholders without paying cash. For example, if the corporation has an attractive investment opportunity and needs funds for it, paying a cash dividend doesn't make any sense—so the corporation pays a stock dividend instead. But is this an effective way of communicating good news to the shareholders? It costs very little to pay a stock dividend—just minor expenses for recordkeeping, printing, and distribution. But if it costs very little, do investors really trust it as a signal?

Another reason given for paying a stock dividend is to reduce the price of the stock. If the price of a stock is high relative to most other stocks, there may be higher costs related to investors' transactions of the stock, as in a higher broker's commission. By paying a stock dividend—which slices the equity pie into more pieces—the price of the stock should decline. Let's see how this works. Suppose an investor owns 1,000 shares, each worth $50 per share, for a total investment of $50,000. If the corporation pays the investor a 5% stock dividend, the investor then owns 1,050 shares after the dividend. Is there is any reason for your holdings to change in value? Nothing economic has gone on here—the company has the same assets, the same liabilities, and the same equity—total equity is just cut up into smaller pieces. There is no reason for the value of the portion of the equity this investor owns to change. But the price per share should decline: from $50 per share to $47.62 per share. The argument for reducing the share price only works if the market brings down the price substantially, from an unattractive trading range to a more attractive trading range in terms of reducing brokerage commissions and enabling small investors to purchase even lots of 100 shares.

So why split? Like a stock dividend, the split reduces the trading price of shares. If an investor owns 1,000 shares of the stock trading for $50 per share prior to a 2:1 split, the shares should trade for $25 per share after the split.

Aside from a minor difference in accounting, stock splits and stock dividends are essentially the same. The stock dividend requires a shift within the stockholders' equity accounts, from retained earnings to paid-in capital, for the amount of the distribution; the stock split requires only a memorandum entry. A 2:1 split has the same effect on a stock's price as a 100% stock dividend, a 1.5 to 1 split has the same effect on a stock's price as a 50% stock dividend, and so on. The basis of the accounting rules is related to the reasons behind the distribution of additional shares. If companies want to bring down their share price, they tend to declare a stock split; if companies want to communicate news, they often declare a stock dividend.

Companies tend to reverse stock split when the stock's price is extremely low, so low that they are at risk of being delisted from an exchange.[2] A low stock price is a function of how many shares are outstanding, but mostly a function of poor performance which has led to a low share price.

How can investors tell what the motivation is behind stock dividends and splits? They cannot, but they can get a general idea of how investors interpret these actions by looking at what happens to the corporation's share price when a corporation announces its decision to pay a stock dividend or split its stock, or reverse split. If the share price tends to go up when the announcement is made, the decision is probably good news; if the price tends to go down, the stock dividend is probably bad news. This is supported by evidence that indicates corporation's earnings tend to increase following stock splits and dividends.[3]

The share price of companies announcing stock distributions and forward stock splits generally increase at the time of the announcement. The stock price typically increases by 1% to 2% when the split or stock dividend is announced. When the stock dividend is distributed or the split is effected (on the ex-date), the share's price typically declines according to the amount of the distribution. Suppose a company announces a 2:1 split. Its share price may increase by 1% to 2% when this is announced, but when the shares are split, the share price will go down to approximately half of its presplit value. The most likely explanation is that this distribution is interpreted as good news—that management believes that the future prospects of the company are favorable or that the share price is more attractive to investors. We provide an example of a forward and a reverse stock split in Exhibit 7.2, using the splits and stock prices of Sun Microsystems to illustrate the price effects. As you can see in this example, the adjustment of the price is close to—but not precisely—the adjustment we expect on the basis of the amount of the split.

---

[2]A reverse stock split, especially those such as 1:300 or 1:1,000, may also be used to reduce the number of shareholders, and hence take the company private.
[3]See, for example, Maureen McNichols and Ajay Dravid, "Stock Dividends, Stock Splits, and Signaling," *Journal of Finance* 45, no. 3 (1990): 857–879.

EXHIBIT 7.2 Sun Microsystems Forward and Reverse

Sun Microsystems (ticker: JAVA) has declared numerous stock splits throughout its history, but also declared a reverse stock split. Consider two splits:

Forward split	December 6, 2000	2:1
Reverse split	November 12, 2007	1:4

The price of Sun Microsystems before and after each split:

	Two Days Before	Day Before	Split Day	Day After	Two Days After
Forward	$78.88	$91.75	$44.25	$42.81	$38.94
Reverse	$5.30	$5.14	$20.51	$21.38	$21.60

The price does not adjust solely by the split because of the influence of other market and economic events, but the adjustment is very close: the stock price is almost $1/2$ that of the presplit for the 2:1 split, and the stock price is slightly more than 4 times that presplit for the 1:4 split.

TRY IT! SPLITS AND DIVIDENDS

For each of the following cases, which is the expected share price post-split or stock dividend?

Case	Pre-Distribution Price Per Share	Number of Shares Outstanding Pre-Distribution	Distribution	Type	Expected Price Per Share	Number of Shares Outstanding Post-Split or Stock Dividend
A	$50	1 million	2:1	Forward split		
B	$20	1.5 million	1.5:1	Forward split		
C	$5	10 million	1:5	Reverse split		
D	$40	1 million	25%	Stock dividend		

DIVIDEND POLICIES

A *dividend policy* is a corporation's decision about the payment of cash dividends to shareholders. There are several basic ways of describing a corporation's dividend policy:

- No dividends.
- Constant growth in dividends per share.
- Constant payout ratio.
- Low regular dividends with periodic extra dividends.

The corporations that typically do not pay dividends are those that are generally viewed as younger, faster growing companies. For example, Microsoft Corporation was founded in 1975 and went public in 1986, but it did not pay a cash dividend until January 2003.

A common pattern of cash dividends tends to be the constant growth of dividends per share. Another pattern is the constant payout ratio. Many other companies in the food processing industry, such as Kellogg and Tootsie Roll Industries, pay dividends that are a relatively constant percentage of earnings. Some companies display both a constant dividend payout ratio and a constant growth in dividends. This type of dividend pattern is characteristic of large, mature companies that have predictable earnings growth—the dividends growth tends to mimic the earnings growth, resulting in a constant payout.

U.S. corporations that pay dividends tend to pay either constant or increasing dividends per share. Dividends tend to be lower in industries that have many profitable opportunities to invest their earnings. But as a company matures and finds fewer and fewer profitable investment opportunities, it generally pays out a greater portion of its earnings in dividends.

Many corporations are reluctant to cut dividends because the corporation's share price usually falls when a dividend reduction is announced. For example, the U.S. auto manufacturers cut dividends during the recession in the early 1990s. As earnings per share declined the automakers did not cut dividends until earnings per share were negative—and in the case of General Motors, not until it had experienced two consecutive loss years. But as earnings recovered in the mid-1990s, dividends were increased.[4]

Because investors tend to penalize companies that cut dividends, corporations tend to only raise their regular quarterly dividend when they are sure they can keep it up in the future. By giving a special or extra dividend,

---

[4]General Motors increased dividends until cutting them once again in 2006 as it incurred substantial losses.

Freeport-McMoran (ticker: FCX) is a copper and gold mining company. The company pays regular cash dividends in January, March, July, and October each year. The company also pays a supplemental dividend during periods of higher profits:

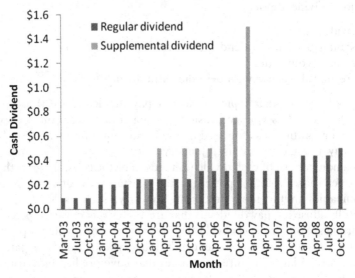

EXHIBIT 7.3 Extra Special Dividends
Data source: Freeport-McMoran Investor Center, Dividends.

the corporation is able to provide more cash to the shareholders without committing itself to paying an increased dividend each period into the future. We provide an example of special dividends in Exhibit 7.3 for the case of Freeport-McMoran, which paid special dividends, which it referred to as supplemental dividends in 2005 and 2006.

There is no general agreement whether dividends should or should not be paid. Here are several views:

- *The dividend irrelevance theory.* The payment of dividends does not affect the value of the company since the investment decision is independent of the financing decision.
- *The "bird in the hand" theory.* Investors prefer a certain dividend stream to an uncertain price appreciation.
- *The tax-preference explanation.* Due to the way in which dividends are taxed, investors should prefer the retention of funds to the payment of dividends.

- *The signaling explanation*. Dividends provide a way for the management to inform investors about the company's future prospects.
- *The agency explanation*. The payment of dividends forces the company to seek more external financing, which subjects the company to the scrutiny of investors.

The Dividend Irrelevance Theory

The dividend irrelevance argument was developed by Merton Miller and Franco Modigliani.[5] Basically, the argument is that if there is a *perfect capital market*—no taxes, no transactions costs, no costs related to issuing new securities, and no costs of sending or receiving information—the value of the corporation is unaffected by payment of dividends.

How can this be? Suppose investment decisions are fixed—that is, the company will invest in certain projects regardless how they are financed. The value of the corporation is the present value of all future cash flows of the company—which depend on the investment decisions that management makes, *not* on how these investments are financed. If the investment decision is fixed, whether a corporation pays a dividend or not does not affect the value of the corporation.

A corporation raises additional funds either through earnings or by selling securities—sufficient to meet its investment decisions and its dividend decision. The dividend decision therefore affects only the financing decision—how much capital the company has to raise to fulfill its investment decisions.

The Miller and Modigliani argument implies that the dividend decision is a residual decision: If the company has no profitable investments to undertake, the company can pay out funds that would have gone to investments to shareholders. And whether or not the company pays dividends is of no consequence to the value of the company. In other words, dividends are irrelevant.

But companies don't exist in a perfect world with a perfect capital market. Are the imperfections (taxes, transactions costs, etc.) enough to alter the conclusions of Miller and Modigliani? It isn't clear.

The "Bird in the Hand" Theory

A popular view is that dividends represent a sure thing relative to share price appreciation. The return to shareholders is comprised of two parts: the

---

[5]Merton Miller and Franco Modigliani, "Dividend Policy, Growth and the Valuation of Shares," *Journal of Business* 34 (1961): 411–433.

return from dividends—the *dividend yield*—and the return from the change in the share price—the *capital yield*. Corporations generate earnings and can either pay them out in cash dividends or reinvest earnings in profitable investments, increasing the value of the stock and, hence, share price.

Once a dividend is paid, it is a certain cash flow. Shareholders can cash their quarterly dividend checks and reinvest the funds. But an increase in share price is not a sure thing. It only becomes a sure thing when the share's price increases over the price the shareholder paid and he or she sells the shares.

We can observe that prices of dividend-paying stocks are less volatile than nondividend-paying stocks. But are dividend-paying stocks less risky because they pay dividends? Or are less risky companies more likely to pay dividends? Most of the evidence supports the latter. Companies that have greater risk—business risk, financial risk, or both—tend to pay little or no dividends. In other words, companies whose cash flows are more variable tend to avoid large dividend commitments that they could not satisfy during periods of poorer financial performance.

A bird in the hand's worth two fleeing by.

—Scottish proverb

The Tax-Preference Explanation

If dividend income is taxed at the same rates as capital gain income, investors may prefer capital gains because of the time value of money: capital gains are only taxed when realized—that is, when the investor sells the stock—whereas dividend income is taxed when received. If, on the other hand, dividend income is taxed at rates higher than that applied to capital gain income, investors should prefer stock price appreciation to dividend income because of both the time value of money and the lower rates.

Historically, capital gain income in the United States has been taxed at rates lower than that applied to dividend income for individual investors. However, the current situation for individuals is that dividend income and capital gain income are taxed at the same rates. Even with the same rates applied to income, capital gain income is still preferred because the tax on any stock appreciation is deferred until the stock is sold—which can be many years into the future.

But the tax impact is different for different types of shareholders. A corporation receiving a dividend from another corporation may take a *dividends received deduction*—a deduction of a large portion of the dividend income.[6] The dividends received deduction ranges from 70% to 100%, depending on the ownership relation between the two corporations. Therefore, corporations pay taxes on a small portion of their dividend income, mitigating some, and perhaps all of double taxation on corporate income distributed to other corporations. Still other shareholders may not even be taxed on dividend income. For example, a pension fund beneficiary does not pay taxes on the dividend income it gets from its investments (these earnings are eventually taxed when the pension is paid out to the employee after retirement).

Even if dividend income were taxed at rates higher than that of capital gains, investors could take investment actions that affect this difference. First, investors that have high marginal tax rates may gravitate toward stocks that pay little or no dividends. This means the shareholders of dividend paying stocks have lower marginal tax rates. This is referred to as a *tax clientele*—investors who choose stocks on the basis of the taxes they have to pay. Second, investors with high marginal tax rates can use legitimate investment strategies—such as borrowing to buy stock and using the deduction from the interest payments on the loan to offset the dividend income in order to reduce the tax impact of dividends.

The Signaling Explanation

Companies that pay dividends seem to maintain a relatively stable dividend, either in terms of a constant or growing dividend payout ratio or in terms of a constant or growing dividend per share. And when companies change their dividend—either increasing or reducing ("cutting") the dividend—the price of the company's shares seems to be affected: When a dividend is increased, the price of the company's shares typically goes up; when a dividend is cut, the price usually goes down. This reaction is attributed to investors' perception of the meaning of the dividend change: Increases are good news, decreases are bad news.

The board of directors is likely to have some information that investors do not have, a change in dividend may be a way for the board to signal this private information. Because most boards of directors are aware that when dividends are lowered, the price of a share usually falls, most investors do not expect boards to increase a dividend unless they thought the company

---

[6]In other words, the dividends are included in income, but then the receiving corporation takes a large deduction.

could maintain it into the future. Realizing this, investors may view a dividend increase as the board's increased confidence in the future operating performance of the company.

The Agency Explanation

The relation between the owners and the managers of a company is an agency relationship: The owners are the principals and the managers are the agents. Management is charged with acting in the best interests of the owners. Nevertheless, there are possibilities for conflicts between the interests of the two.

If the company pays a dividend, the company may be forced to raise new capital outside of the company—that is, issue new securities instead of using internally generated capital—subjecting them to the scrutiny of equity research analysts and other investors. This extra scrutiny helps reduce the possibility that managers will not work in the best interests of the shareholders. But issuing new securities is not costless. There are costs of issuing new securities—flotation costs. In "agency theory-speak," these costs are part of monitoring costs—incurred to help monitor the managers' behavior and insure behavior is consistent with shareholder wealth maximization.

The payment of dividends also reduces the amount of free cash flow under control of management. *Free cash flow* is the cash in excess of the cash needed to finance profitable investment opportunities. A profitable investment opportunity is any investment that provides the company with a return greater than what shareholders could get elsewhere on their money—that is, a return greater than the shareholders' opportunity cost.

Because free cash flow is the cash flow left over after all profitable projects are undertaken, the only projects left are the unprofitable ones. Should free cash be reinvested in the unprofitable investments or paid out to shareholders? Of course if boards make decisions consistent with shareholder wealth maximization, any free cash flow should be paid out to shareholders since—by the definition of a profitable investment opportunity—the shareholders could get a better return investing the funds they receive.

If the company pays a dividend, funds are paid out to shareholders. If the company needs additional funds, it could be raised by issuing new securities; in this event, shareholders wishing to reinvest the funds received as dividends in the company could buy these new securities. One view of the role of dividends is that the payment of dividends therefore reduces the cash flow in the hands of management, reducing the possibility that managers will invest funds in unprofitable investment opportunities.

To Pay or Not to Pay Dividends

We can figure out reasons why a company should or should not pay dividends, but not why they actually do or do not—this is the "dividend puzzle" coined by Fischer Black.[7] But we do know from looking at dividends and the market's reaction to dividend actions that:

- If a company increases its dividends or pays a dividend for the first time, this is viewed as good news—its share price increases.
- If a company decreases its dividend or omits it completely, this is viewed as bad news—its share price declines.

That is why corporations must be aware of the relation between dividends and the value of the common stock in establishing or changing dividend policy.

STOCK REPURCHASES

Corporations have repurchased their common stock from their shareholders. A corporation repurchasing its own shares is effectively paying a cash dividend, with one important difference: taxes. Cash dividends are ordinary taxable income to the shareholder. A company's repurchase of shares, on the other hand, results in a capital gain or loss for the shareholder, depending on the price paid when they were originally purchased. If the shares are repurchased at a higher price, the difference may be taxed as capital gains, which may be taxed at rates lower than ordinary income.

Methods of Repurchasing Stock

The company may repurchase its own stock by any of three methods: (1) a tender offer, (2) open market purchases, and (3) a targeted block repurchase. A *tender offer* is an offer made to all shareholders, with a specified deadline and a specified number of shares the corporation is willing to buy back. The tender offer may be a fixed price offer, where the corporation specifies the price it is willing to pay and solicits purchases of shares of stock at that price.

---

[7]Fischer Black, "The Dividend Puzzle," *Journal of Portfolio Management* 2 (1976): 5–8.

A tender offer may also be conducted as a *Dutch auction* in which the corporation specifies a minimum and a maximum price, soliciting bids from shareholders for any price within this range at which they are willing to sell their shares. After the corporation receives these bids, they pay all tendering shareholders the maximum price sufficient to buy back the number of shares they want. A Dutch auction reduces the chance that the company pays a price higher than needed to acquire the shares. Dutch auctions are gaining in popularity relative to fixed-price offers.

Biogen, a biotechnology company, announced a Dutch auction tender offer in May 2007 for shares of its common stock. In Exhibit 7.4, the offer was for up to 57 million shares of stock, at a price not less than $47 per share and not more than $53 per share. Biogen accepted 56,424,155 shares at $53 per share, or 16.4% of its shares outstanding at the time of the offer.

A corporation may also buy back shares directly in the open market. This involves buying the shares through a broker. A corporation that wants to buy shares may have to spread its purchases over time so as not to drive the share's price up temporarily by buying large numbers of shares.

The third method of repurchasing stock is to buy it from a specific shareholder. This involves direct negotiation between the corporation and the shareholder. This method is referred to as a *targeted block repurchase*, since there is a specific shareholder (the "target") and there are a large number of shares (a "block") to be purchased at one time. Targeted block repurchases, also referred to as "greenmail," were used in the 1980s to fight corporate takeovers.

Reasons to Repurchase Stock

Corporations repurchase their stock for a number of reasons. First, a repurchase is a way to distribute cash to shareholders at a lower cost to both the company and the shareholders than dividends. If capital gains are taxed at rates lower than ordinary income, which until recently has been the case with U.S. tax law, repurchasing is a lower cost way of distributing cash. However, since shareholders have different tax rates—especially when comparing corporate shareholders with individual shareholders—the benefit is mixed. The reason is that some shareholders' income is tax-free (e.g., pension funds), some shareholders are only taxed on a portion of dividends (e.g., corporations receiving dividends from other corporations), and some shareholders are taxed on the full amount of dividends (e.g., individual taxpayers).

Another reason to repurchase stock is to increase earnings per share. A company that repurchases its shares increases its earnings per share simply because there are fewer shares outstanding after the repurchase. But there are two problems with this motive. First, cash is paid to the shareholders, so less cash is available for the corporation to reinvest in profitable projects. Second, because there are fewer shares, the earnings pie is sliced in fewer pieces, resulting in higher earnings per share. The individual "slices" are bigger, but the pie itself remains the same size.

Looking at how share prices respond to gimmicks that manipulate earnings, there is evidence that a company cannot fool the market by playing an earnings-per-share game. The market can see through the earnings per share to what is really happening and that the company will have less cash to invest.

Still another reason for stock repurchase is that it could tilt the debt-equity ratio so as to increase the value of the company. By buying back stock—thereby reducing equity—the company's assets are financed to a greater degree by debt. Does this seem wrong? It's not. To see this, suppose a corporation has a balance sheet consisting of assets of $100 million, liabilities of $50 million, and $50 million of equity. That is, the corporation has financed 50% of its assets with debt, and 50% with equity. If this corporation uses $20 million of its assets to buy back stock worth $20 million, its balance sheet will have assets of $80 million financed by $50 million of liabilities and $30 million of equity. It now finances 62.5% of its assets with debt and 37.5% with equity.

If financing the company with more debt is good—that is, the benefits from deducting interest on debt outweigh the cost of increasing the risk of bankruptcy—repurchasing stock may increase the value of the company. But there is the flip-side to this argument: Financing the company with more debt may be bad if the risk of financial distress—difficulty paying legal obligations—outweighs the benefits from tax deductibility of interest. So, repurchasing shares from this perspective would have to be judged on a case-by-case basis to determine if it's beneficial or detrimental.

One more reason for a stock repurchase is that it reduces total dividend payments—without seeming to. If the corporation cuts down on the number of shares outstanding, the corporation can still pay the same amount of dividends *per share*, but the *total* dividend payments are reduced. If the shares are correctly valued in the market (there is no reason to believe otherwise), the payment for the repurchased shares equals the reduction in the value of the company—and the remaining shares are worth the same as they were before.

Some argue that a repurchase is a signal about future prospects. That is, by buying back the shares, the management is communicating to investors that the company is generating sufficient cash to be able to buy back shares.

But does this make sense? Not really. If the company has profitable investment opportunities, the cash could be used to finance these investments, instead of paying it out to the shareholders.

A stock repurchase may also reduce agency costs by reducing the amount of cash the management has on hand. Similar to the argument suggested for dividend payments, repurchasing shares reduces the amount of free cash flow and, therefore, reduces the possibility that management will invest it unprofitably. Many companies use stock buybacks to mitigate the dilution resulting from executive stock options, as well as to shore up their stock price.

Repurchasing shares tends to shrink the company: Cash is paid out and the value of the company is smaller. Can repurchasing shares be consistent with wealth maximization? Yes. If the best use of funds is to pay them out to shareholders, repurchasing shares maximizes shareholders' wealth. If the company has no profitable investment opportunities, it is better for a company to shrink by paying funds to the shareholders than to shrink by investing in lousy investments.

So how does the market react to a company's intention to repurchase shares? A number of studies have looked at how the market reacts to such announcements. In general, the share price goes up when a company announces it is going to repurchase its own shares. It is difficult to identify the reason the market reacts favorably to such announcements since so many other things are happening at the same time. By piecing bits of evidence together, however, we see that it is likely that investors view the announcement of a repurchase as good news—a signal of good things to come.

THE BOTTOM LINE

- Companies may distribute funds to owners in the form of periodic cash dividends. A company's board of directors decides on the amount and timing of dividends.
- Companies may make stock dividends or split the stock. Though not an event that results in any economic value to owners, investors often interpret the decision to pay a stock dividend or to split the stock as conveying information about the company's future prospects.
- There are several theories related to why companies pay dividends, including the dividend irrelevance theory, the bird-in-the-hand theory, the tax-preference theory, signaling theory, and agency theory.

- As an alternative to paying dividends, a company may choose to distribute funds to shareholders by repurchasing its own stock from shareholders, either through a tender offer, open market purchases, or a block repurchase.

SOLUTIONS TO TRY IT! PROBLEMS

Dividends

Dividends per share	$2
Earnings per share	$5
Dividend payout ratio	40%
Retention ratio	60%

Stock Distributions

Case	Expected Price Per Share Post-Distribution	Number of Shares Outstanding Post-Distribution
A	$25.00	2 million
B	$13.33	2.25 million
C	$25.00	2 million
D	$32.00	1.25 million

QUESTIONS

1. Distinguish between the dividend payout ratio and the dividend per share.
2. If a company has a dividend payout ratio of 80%, what is the company's retention ratio?
3. If a company has a dividend per share of $2 and earnings per share of $8, which is the company's dividend payout ratio?
4. What are the benefits from the perspective of a shareholder of a dividend reinvestment plan?
5. What is the difference between a stock dividend and a stock split?
6. Why would a company want to use a reverse stock split?
7. If a company splits its stock, what is the expected effect on the stock's share price?

8. Why might a company "pay" as a stock dividend?
9. List the three possible explanations for why companies pay cash dividends.
10. Identify three different methods that a company can use to repurchase its own stock from investors.
11. Complete the following table:

Stock	Price Per Share Before Distribution	Number of Shares Outstanding Before the Distribution	Distribution	Expected Price Per Share After the Distribution	Number of Shares Outstanding After the Distribution
ABC	$20	1 million	2:1		
DEF	$40	0.5 million	1:5		
GHI	$25	2 million	2.5:1		

12. Suppose a company with net income of $200 million and 3 million shares outstanding pays $50 million in cash dividends.
    a. What is the dividend payout ratio?
    b. What is the dividend per share?
13. If a company's stock has a dividend per share of $2 and earnings per share of $5, what is the company's retention ratio?
14. The following is from the 2008 Annual Report of Philips Company regarding its dividend policy (www.annualreport2008.philips.com/pages/investor_information/dividend_policy.asp)

> Our aim is to sustainably grow our dividend over time. Philips' present dividend policy is based on an annual pay-out ratio of 40 to 50% of continuing net income.

What does this mean?
15. The following excerpts are taken from "Dividend Policy Determinants: An Investigation of the Influences of Stakeholder Theory" by Mark E. Holder, Frederick W. Langrehr, and J. Lawrence Hexter, published in the Autumn 1998 issue of Financial Management:

> There is considerable debate on how dividend policy affects firm value. Some researchers believe that dividends increase shareholder wealth..., others believe that dividends are irrelevant..., and still others believe that dividends decrease shareholder wealth.

a. What are the arguments in support of the dividend policy increasing shareholder wealth?
b. What are the arguments in support of the irrelevance of dividend policy?
c. What are the arguments in support of the dividend policy decreasing shareholder wealth?

> *One group of financial theorists . . . provides a hypothesis for dividend policy irrelevance. This group bases its theory on the assumptions of 1) perfect capital markets . . . ; 2) rational behavior on the part of participants in the market, valuing securities based on the discounted value of future cash flows accruing to investors; 3) certainty about the investment policy of the firm and complete knowledge of these cash flows; and 4) managers that act as perfect agents of the shareholders.*

d. What is meant by a perfect capital market?
e. What is assumed about the company's investment policy?
f. What is meant by "managers that act as perfect agents of the shareholders"?

CHAPTER 8

The Corporate Financing Decision

How much does the company owe, and how much does it own?
Debt versus equity. It's just the kind of thing a loan officer would
want to know about you in deciding if you are a good credit risk.
A normal corporate balance sheet has two sides. On the left side
are the assets (inventories, receivables, plant and equipment, etc.).
The right side shows how the assets are financed. One quick way
to determine the financial strength of a company is to compare the
equity to the debt on the right side of the balance sheet.
—Peter Lynch with John Rothchild, *One Up on Wall Street*
(New York: Penguin Books, 1989), p. 201

A business invests in new plant and equipment to generate additional revenues and income—the basis for its growth. One way to pay for investments is to generate capital from the company's operations. Earnings generated by the company belong to the owners and can either be paid to them—in the form of cash dividends—or plowed back into the company.

The owners' investment in the company is referred to as *owners' equity* or, simply, *equity*. If earnings are plowed back into the company, the owners expect it to be invested in projects that will enhance the value of the company and, hence, enhance the value of their equity. But earnings may not be sufficient to support all profitable investment opportunities. In that case management is faced with a decision: Forego profitable investment opportunities or raise additional capital. New capital can be raised by either borrowing or selling additional ownership interests or both. We refer to the mix of debt and equity that a company uses as its *capital structure*.

The decision about how the company should be financed, whether with debt or equity, is referred to as the *capital structure decision*. In this chapter, we discuss the capital structure decision. There are different theories about how the company should be financed and we review these theories in this chapter.

DEBT VS. EQUITY

The capital structure of a company is some mix of the three sources of capital: debt, internally generated equity, and new equity. But what is the right mixture? The best capital structure depends on several factors. If a company finances its activities with debt, the creditors expect the interest and principal—fixed, legal commitments—to be paid back as promised. Failure to pay may result in legal actions by the creditors. If the company finances its activities with equity, the owners expect a return in terms of cash dividends, an appreciation of the value of the equity interest or, as is most likely, some combination of both.

Suppose a company borrows $100 million and promises to repay the $100 million plus $5 million in one year. Consider what may happen when the $100 is invested:

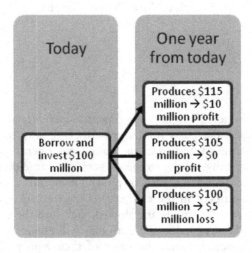

So, if the company reinvests the funds and generates more than the $100 million + $5 million = $105 million, the company keeps all the profits. But if the project generates $105 million or less, the lender still gets her or his $5 million—but there is nothing left for the company's owners. This is the basic idea behind *financial leverage*—the use of financing that has fixed, but limited payments.

If the company has abundant earnings, the owners reap all that remains of the earnings after the creditors have been paid. If earnings are low, the creditors still must be paid what they are due, leaving the owners nothing out of the earnings. Failure to pay interest or principal as promised may result in financial distress. *Financial distress* is the condition where a company makes decisions under pressure to satisfy its legal obligations to its creditors. These decisions may not be in the best interests of the owners of the company.

With equity financing there is no obligation. Though the company may choose to distribute funds to the owners in the form of cash dividends, there is no legal requirement to do so. Furthermore, interest paid on debt is deductible for tax purposes, whereas dividend payments are not tax deductible.

One measure of the extent debt is used to finance a company is the *debt ratio*, the ratio of debt to equity:

$$\text{Debt ratio} = \frac{\text{Debt}}{\text{Equity}}$$

This is relative measure of debt to equity. The greater the debt ratio, the greater is the use of debt for financing operations relative to equity financing. Another measure is the *debt-to-assets ratio,* which is the extent to which the assets of the company are financed with debt:

$$\text{Debt-to-assets ratio} = \frac{\text{Debt}}{\text{Total assets}}$$

This is the proportion of debt in a company's capital structure, measured using the book, or carrying value of the debt and assets.

It is often useful to focus on the long-term capital of a company when evaluating the capital structure of a company, looking at the interest-bearing debt of the company in comparison with the company's equity or with its capital. The *capital* of a company is the sum of its interest-bearing debt and its equity. The debt ratio can be restated as the ratio of the interest-bearing debt of the company to the company's equity:

$$\text{Debt-equity ratio} = \frac{\text{Interest-bearing debt}}{\text{Equity}}$$

and the debt-to-assets can be restated as the proportion of interest-bearing debt of the company's capital:

$$\text{Debt-equity ratio} = \frac{\text{Interest-bearing debt}}{\text{Total capital}}$$

By focusing on the long-term capital, the working capital decisions of a company that affect current liabilities such as accounts payable, are removed from this analysis.

The equity component of all of these ratios is often stated in book, or carrying value terms. However, when taking a markets perspective of the company's capital structure, it is often useful to compare debt capital with the market value of equity. In this latter formulation, for example, the total capital of the company is the sum of the market value of interest-bearing debt and the market value of equity.

If market values of debt and equity are the most useful for decision-making, should management ignore book values? No, because book values are relevant in decision-making also. For example, bond covenants are often specified in terms of book values or ratios of book values. As another example, dividends are distinguished from the return of capital based on the availability of the book value of retained earnings. Therefore, though the focus is primarily on the market values of capital, management must also keep an eye on the book value of debt and equity as well.

There is a tendency for companies in some sectors and industries to use more debt than others. We can make some generalizations about differences in capital structures across sectors:

- Companies that are more reliant upon research and development for new products and technology—for example, pharmaceutical companies—tend to have lower debt-to-asset ratios than companies without such research and development needs.
- Companies that require a relatively heavy investment in fixed assets tend to have lower debt-to-asset ratios.

Considering these generalizations and other observations related to differing capital structures, why do some industries tend to have companies with higher debt ratios than other industries? By examining the role of financial leveraging, financial distress, and taxes, we can explain some of the variation in debt ratios among industries. And by analyzing these factors, we can explain how the company's value may be affected by its capital structure.

Capital Structure and Financial Leverage

Debt and equity financing create different types of obligations for the company. Debt financing obligates the company to pay creditors interest and principal—usually a fixed amount—when promised. If the company earns more than necessary to meet its debt payments, it can either distribute the surplus to the owners or reinvest. Equity financing does not obligate the company to distribute earnings. The company may pay dividends or repurchase stock from the owners, but there is no obligation to do so.

Creditors have better memories than debtors.

—Benjamin Franklin

The fixed and limited nature of the debt obligation affects the risk of the earnings to the owners. We illustrate the effect on earnings using three different companies, each with a different capital structure:

- Company NL, with no debt
- Company L, with some debt
- Company LL, with lots of debt

Let's assume that each company has $100 million in assets. Company NL finances these assets completely with equity. Company L finances its assets with 25% debt and 75% equity, while Company LL finances its assets with 75% debt and 25% equity:

In Millions	Company NL	Company L	Company LL
Assets	$100	$100	$100
Debt	$ 0	$ 25	$ 75
Equity	$100	$ 75	$ 25

The leverage ratios of these companies are therefore:

	Company NL	Company L	Company LL
Debt-equity	0%	33%	300%
Debt-to-assets	0%	25%	75%

Let's further assume that the companies have identical operating earnings, $10 million, and that any debt has an interest rate of 5%.[1] Operating earnings are the income from the operations of the business (that is, revenues less cost of goods sold and operating expenses), but before any outlays to the

---

[1]Assuming that the interest rate on debt is the same, no matter the leverage, this will at least help illustrate the immediate issues.

providers of capital, such as interest on debt and dividends to owners. Let's also assume, for right now, that there are no taxes on income. Therefore, the net income of these companies is:

	Company NL	Company L	Company LL
Operating earnings	$10.00	$10.00	$10.00
Interest on debt	0.00	2.25	3.75
Net income	$10.00	$ 8.75	$ 6.25

And the return on assets and return on equity for each are:

	Company NL	Company L	Company LL
Return on assets	10.00%	8.75%	6.25%
Return on equity	10.00%	11.67%	25.00%

The return on assets is the ratio of the company's net income to its total assets, whereas the return on equity is the ratio of the company's net income to owners' equity.

Company LL has the highest return on equity, though the lowest return on assets. This is because Company LL pays the higher interest on debt, which lowers net income and hence produces the lower return on assets, but has the lowest amount of equity, so when the lower income is compared to the lower shareholders' equity, Company LL has the highest return to shareholders.

Now let's assume that operating earnings are, instead, $4 million. In this case:

	Company NL	Company L	Company LL
Operating earnings	$4.00	$4.00	$4.00
Interest on debt	$0.00	$1.25	$3.75
Net income	$4.00	$2.75	$0.25

And the returns are:

	Company NL	Company L	Company LL
Return on assets	4.00%	2.75%	0.25%
Return on equity	4.00%	3.67%	1.00%

In this case, Company LL has the lowest net income and the lowest returns.

When you combine ignorance and leverage, you get some pretty interesting results.

—Warren Buffett

This example illustrates the role of debt financing on the risk associated with earnings: the greater the use of debt vis-à-vis equity, the greater the risk associated with earnings to owners. Or, using the leverage terminology, the greater the degree of financial leverage, the greater the financial risk. The effect of financial risk in addition to the operating risk magnifies the risk to the owners.

Comparing the results of each of the three companies provides information on the effects of using debt financing. As more debt is used in the capital structure, the greater the "swing" in returns, as we show in Exhibit 8.1 for a range of operating earnings for Companies NL, L, and LL.

An interesting exercise is to see at which level of earnings the returns are the same for two or more different types of financing. In our example, when operating earnings are $5 million, the returns on equity for Company NL,

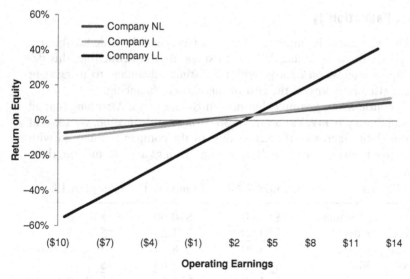

EXHIBIT 8.1   Returns to Equity for Company NL, Company L, and Company LL, Ignoring Taxes and Assuming Interest on Debt of 5%

Company L, and Company LL are the same at 5%. Therefore, the break-even operating earnings for these companies—before we consider taxes and assuming that the interest on debt is the same across companies—is $5 million.

 TRY IT! RETURNS WITH LEVERAGE

Suppose we have another company, Company SL, that has the same interest rate on debt as Company L in our example. If we assume that there are no taxes, complete the following if Company SL has a capital structure of $50 million debt and $50 equity:

In Millions	
Operating earnings	$5.00
Interest on debt	
Net income	
Return on assets	
Return on equity	

Interest Deductibility

In the United States, the interest a business pays on debt is deductible for tax purposes. Because dividends paid on stock are not deductible, this deductibility of interest on debt provides a distinct advantage to using debt because it effectively lowers the cost of this form of financing.

Let's continue our example, but now introduce taxes. Assuming that all three companies pay taxes at a rate of 30% on taxable income, we see that this deductibility increases the net income of the companies financed with debt, relative to the no-tax case. If operating earnings are $10 million, then:

In Millions	Company NL	Company L	Company LL
Operating earnings	$10.00	$10.00	$10.00
Interest on debt	$ 0.00	$ 1.25	$ 3.75
Taxable income	$10.00	$ 8.75	$ 6.25
Taxes at 30%	$ 3.00	$ 2.63	$ 1.88
Net income	$ 7.00	$ 6.13	$ 4.38
Return on assets	7.00%	6.13%	4.38%
Return on equity	7.00%	8.17%	17.50%

And if operating earnings are $4 million, then:

In Millions	Company NL	Company L	Company LL
Operating earnings	$4.00	$4.00	$4.00
Interest on debt	$0.00	$1.25	$3.75
Taxable income	$4.00	$2.75	$0.25
Taxes at 30%	$1.20	$0.83	$0.08
Net income	$2.80	$1.93	$0.18
Return on assets	2.80%	1.93%	0.18%
Return on equity	2.80%	2.57%	0.70%

The deductibility of interest represents a form of a government subsidy of financing activities. By allowing interest to be deducted from taxable income, the government is sharing the company's cost of debt. Who benefits from this tax deductibility? The owners.

An interesting element introduced into the capital structure decision is the reduction of taxes due to the payment of interest on debt. We refer to the benefit from interest deductibility as the *interest tax shield,* because the interest expense shields income from taxation. The tax shield from interest deductibility is

$$\text{Interest tax shield} = \text{Tax rate} \times \text{Interest expense}$$

Company L has $25 million of 5% debt and is subject to a tax of 30% on net income, the tax shield is

$$\text{Tax shield} = 0.30 \, (\$25 \times 0.05) = 0.30 \times \$1.25 = \$0.375 \text{ million}$$

A $1.25 million interest expense means that $1.25 million of income is not taxed at 30%, saving the company $0.375 million. Company LL, with more debt, has a tax shield of the following:

$$\text{Tax shield} = 0.30 \, (\$75 \times 0.05) = 0.30 \times \$3.75 = \$1.125 \text{ million}$$

Recognizing that the interest expense is the interest rate on the debt, r_d, multiplied by the face value of debt the tax shield for a company is

$$\text{Tax shield} = \text{Tax rate} \times \text{Interest rate} \times \text{Face value of debt}$$

We should specify that the tax rate is the *marginal tax rate*—the tax rate on the next dollar of income.

How does this tax shield affect the value of the company? The tax shield reduces the net income of the company that goes to pay taxes. And because management is concerned with how interest protects income from taxation, the focus should be on how it shields taxable income beyond the income that is shielded by all other tax deductible expenses. As long as the company can use these tax shields—that is, it generates income that interest reduces—the tax shield is valuable to owners.

 TRY IT! RETURNS WITH LEVERAGE AND TAXES

Suppose we have another company, Company SL, that has the same interest rate on debt as Company L in our example. If we assume a tax rate of 30%, complete the following if Company SL has a capital structure of $50 million debt and $50 equity:

In Millions	
Operating earnings	$5.00
Interest on debt	
Taxable income	
Taxes	
Net income	
Return on assets	
Return on equity	

FINANCIAL LEVERAGE AND RISK

The use of financial leverage (that is, the use of debt in financing a company) increases the range of possible outcomes for owners of the company. As we saw previously, the use of debt financing, relative to equity financing, increases both the upside and downside potential earnings for owners. In other words, financial leverage increases the risk to owners. Now that we understand the basics of leverage, let's quantify its effect on the risk of earnings to owners.

Another way to view the choice of financing is to calculate the degree of financial leverage, denoted by DFL, which is the ratio of operating earnings to earnings after deducting interest:

$$DFL = \frac{\text{Operating earnings}}{\text{Operating earnings} - \text{Interest}}$$

Calculating the DFL for the three companies at different levels of operating earnings, we see the differences in DFL among the three companies, with Company LL having the highest degree of financial leverage:

Operating Earnings in Millions	DFL		
	Company NL	Company L	Company LL
$4	1.00	1.45	16.00
$5	1.00	1.33	4.00
$6	1.00	1.26	2.67
$7	1.00	1.22	2.15
$8	1.00	1.19	1.88
$9	1.00	1.16	1.71
$10	1.00	1.14	1.60

The interpretation of the DFL is similar to any elasticity measure: If the DFL is 4, this means a 1% change in operating earnings will produce a $1\% \times 4 = 4\%$ change in earnings to owners.

Equity owners can reap most of the rewards through financial leverage when their company does well. But they may suffer a downside when the company does poorly. What happens if earnings are so low that it cannot cover interest payments? Interest must be paid no matter how low the earnings. How does a company obtain money with which to pay interest when earnings are insufficient?

- By reducing the assets in some way, such as using working capital needed for operations or selling buildings or equipment
- By taking on more debt obligations
- By issuing more shares of stock

Whichever the company chooses, the burden ultimately falls upon the owners.

Leverage and Financial Flexibility

The use of debt also reduces a company's financial flexibility. A company with debt capacity that is unused, sometimes referred to as *financial slack*, is more prepared to take advantage of investment opportunities in the future. This ability to exploit these future, strategic options is valuable and, hence, taking on debt increases the risk that the company may not be sufficiently nimble to act on valuable opportunities.

There is evidence that suggests that companies that have more cash flow volatility tend to build up more financial slack and, hence, their investments are not as sensitive to their ability to generate cash flows internally. Rather, the financial slack allows them to exploit investment opportunities without relying on recent internally generated cash flows.

In the context of the effect of leverage on risk, this means that companies that tend to have highly volatile operating earnings may want to maintain some level of financial flexibility by not taking on significant leverage in the form of debt financing.

Governance Value of Debt Financing

A company's use of debt financing may provide additional monitoring of a company's management and decisions, reducing agency costs. Agency costs are the costs that arise from the separation of the management and the ownership of a company, which is particularly acute in large corporations. These costs are the costs necessary to resolve the agency problem that may exist between management and ownership of the company and may include the cost of monitoring company management. These costs include the costs associated with the board of directors and providing financial information to shareholders and other investors.

An agency problem that may arise in a company is how effectively a company uses its cash flows. The free cash flow of a company is, basically, its cash flow less any capital expenditures and dividends. One theory that has been widely regarded is that by using debt financing, the company reduces its free cash flows and, therefore, it must reenter the debt market to raise new capital.[2] It is argued that this benefits the company in two ways. First, there are fewer resources under control of management and less chance of wasting these resources in unprofitable investments. Second, the continual dependence of the debt market for capital imposes a monitoring or governance discipline on the company that would not have been there otherwise.

If we assume that there are no direct or indirect costs to financial distress, the cost of capital for the company should be the same, no matter the method of financing. If the operating earnings are $7.14 million, which produces a return on equity of 5% for Company NL (that is, net income divided by equity) and the cost of capital is 5%, the debt adds to the value of equity, benefitting owners, as we show in Exhibit 8.2.

---

[2]Michael C. Jensen, "Agency Cost of Free Cash Flow, Corporate Finance, and Takeovers," *American Economic Review* 76 (1986): 323–329.

EXHIBIT 8.2 Value Added by the Tax Deductibility of Debt

In Millions	Company NL	Company L	Company LL
Operating income	$7.14	$7.14	$7.14
Interest expense	0.00	1.25	3.75
Taxable income	$7.14	$5.89	$3.39
Taxes at 30%	2.14	1.77	1.02
Income to owners	$5.00	$4.13	$2.38
Income to the government	$2.14	$1.77	$1.02
Income to creditors	0.00	1.25	3.75
Income to owners	5.00	4.13	2.38
Income to all	$7.14	$7.14	$7.14
Value to creditors	$0.00	$25.00	$75.00
Value to owners	100.00	82.50	47.50
Value of company	$100.00	$107.50	$122.50
Capital contributed by:			
Creditors	$0.00	$25.00	$75.00
Owners	100.00	75.00	25.00
Total contributed capital	$100.00	$100.00	$100.00
Value added by the tax deductibility of debt	$0.00	$7.50	$22.50
Return on equity	5.00%	5.50%	9.50%

A few notes about what we show in Exhibit 8.2:

1. The income to owners is less at this return on equity if the company has more debt, but the capital contributed by owners is less if debt financing is used.
2. The income to the government is less as more debt is used because more income is shielded from taxation.
3. The value to creditors is the face amount of the debt, whereas the value to owners is today's value of the income to owners, valued as a perpetuity (that is, income divided by the cost of equity, 5%).
4. The owners reap the benefits from the use of debt, with more value-added as more debt is used.
5. The owners have a greater return on their investment, as measured by the return on equity, the more debt financing in relation to equity.

FINANCIAL DISTRESS

A company that has difficulty making payments to its creditors is in financial distress. Not all companies in financial distress ultimately enter into the legal status of bankruptcy. However, extreme financial distress may very well lead to bankruptcy.[3]

The Role of Limited Liability

Limited liability limits owners' liability for obligations to the amount of their original investment in the shares of stock. Limited liability for owners of some forms of business creates a valuable right and an interesting incentive for shareholders. This valuable right is the right to default on obligations to creditors—that is, the right not to pay creditors. Because the most shareholders can lose is their investment, there is an incentive for the company to take on very risky projects: If the projects turn out well, the company pays creditors only what it owes and keeps the remainder and if the projects turn out poorly, it pays creditors what it owes—if there is anything left.

The fact that owners with limited liability can lose only their initial investment—the amount they paid for their shares—creates an incentive for owners to take on riskier projects than if they had unlimited liability: They have little to lose and much to gain. Owners of a company with limited liability have an incentive to take on risky projects since they can only lose their investment in the company. But they can benefit substantially if the payoff on the investment is high. You can see this by looking back at Exhibit 8.2. The return on equity for Company LL is much more than that of Company NL.[4]

For companies whose owners have limited liability, the more the assets are financed with debt, the greater the incentive to take on risky projects, leaving creditors "holding the bag" if the projects turn out to be unprofitable. This is a problem for it poses a conflict of interest between shareholders' interests and creditors' interests. The investment decisions are made by management (who represent the shareholders) and, because of limited liability, there is an incentive for management to select riskier projects that may harm creditors who have entrusted their funds (by lending them) to the company.

---

[3]While bankruptcy is often a result of financial difficulties arising from problems in paying creditors, some bankruptcy filings are made prior to distress when a large claim is made on assets (for example, class action liability suit).

[4]As long as the return on equity is above the break-even point, the return on the levered company is greater than the return on the nonlevered company. Below that break-even point is where the advantage of limited liability lies.

The right to default is a *call option*: The owners have the option to buy back the entire company by paying off the creditors at the face value of their debt. As with other types of options, the option is more valuable, the riskier the cash flows. However, creditors are aware of this and demand a higher return on debt (and hence a higher cost to the company). Jensen and Meckling analyze the agency problems associated with limited liability.[5] They argue that creditors are aware of the incentives the company has to take on riskier projects. Creditors will demand a higher return and may also require protective provisions in the loan contract. The result is that shareholders ultimately bear a higher cost of debt.

Costs of Financial Distress

The costs related to financial distress without legal bankruptcy can take different forms. For example, to meet creditors' demands, a company takes on projects expected to provide a quick payback. In doing so, the financial manager may choose a project that decreases owners' wealth or may forgo a profitable project.

Another cost of financial distress is the cost associated with lost sales. If a company is having financial difficulty, potential customers may shy away from its products because they may perceive the company unable to provide maintenance, replacement parts, and warranties. Lost sales due to customer concerns represent a cost of financial distress—an opportunity cost, something of value (sales) that the company would have had if it were not in financial difficulty.

Still another example of a cost of financial distress is the cost associated with suppliers. If there is concern over the company's ability to meet its obligations to creditors, suppliers may be unwilling to extend trade credit or may extend trade credit only at unfavorable terms. Also, suppliers may be unwilling to enter into long-term contracts to supply goods or materials. This increases the uncertainty that the company will be able to obtain these items in the future and raises the costs of renegotiating contracts.

Bankruptcy and Bankruptcy Costs   When a company is having difficulty paying its debts, there is a possibility that creditors will foreclose (that is, demand payment) on loans, causing the company to sell assets that could impair or cease the company's operations. But if some creditors force payment,

[5]Michael C. Jensen and William H. Meckling, "Theory of the Firm: Managerial Behavior, Agency Costs, and Ownership Structure," *Journal of Financial Economics* 3 (1976): 305–360.

this may disadvantage other creditors. So what has developed is an orderly way of dealing with the process of the company paying its creditors—the process is called *bankruptcy*.

Bankruptcy in the United States is governed by the Bankruptcy Code, which is found under U.S. Code Title 11. A company may be reorganized under Chapter 11 of this Code, resulting in a restructuring of its claims, or liquidated under Chapter 7.

Chapter 11 bankruptcy provides the troubled company with protection from its creditors while it tries to overcome its financial difficulties. A company that files bankruptcy under Chapter 11 continues operations during the process of sorting out which of its creditors get paid and how much. On the other hand, a company that files under bankruptcy Chapter 7, under the management of a trustee, terminates its operations, sells its assets, and distributes the proceeds to creditors and owners.

We can classify *bankruptcy costs* into direct and indirect costs. Direct costs include the legal, administrative, and accounting costs associated with the filing for bankruptcy and the administration of bankruptcy. The indirect costs of bankruptcy are more difficult to evaluate. Operating a company while in bankruptcy is difficult, since there are often delays in making decisions, creditors may not agree on the operations of the company, and the objectives of creditors may be at variance with the objective of efficient operation of the company.

Another indirect cost of bankruptcy is the loss in value of certain assets. If the company has assets that are intangible or for which there are valuable growth opportunities or options, it is less likely to borrow because the loss of value in the case of financial distress is greater than, say, a company with marketable assets. Because many intangible assets derive their value from the continuing operations of the company, the disruption of operations during bankruptcy may change the value of the company. The extent to which the value of a business enterprise depends on intangibles varies among industries and among companies; so the potential loss in value from financial distress varies as well. For example, a drug company may experience a greater disruption in its business activities, than say, a steel manufacturer, since much of the value of the drug company may be derived from the research and development that leads to new products.

Financial Distress and Capital Structure   The relationship between financial distress and capital structure is simple: As more debt financing is used, fixed legal obligations increase (interest and principal payments), and the ability of the company to satisfy these increasing fixed payments decreases. Therefore, as more debt financing is used, the probability of financial distress and then bankruptcy increases.

For a given decrease in operating earnings, a company that uses debt to a greater extent in its capital structure (that is, a company that uses more financial leverage), has a greater risk of not being able to satisfy the debt obligations and increases the risk of earnings to owners.

Another factor to consider in assessing the probability of financial distress is the business risk of the company. As discussed earlier, the business risk interacts with the financial risk to affect the risk of the company.

Management's concern in assessing the effect of financial distress on the value of the company is the present value of the expected costs of financial distress. And the present value depends on the probability of financial distress: The greater the probability of financial distress, the greater the expected costs of financial distress.

The present value of the costs of financial distress increases with the increasing relative use of debt financing because the probability of financial distress increases with increases with financial leverage. In other words, as the debt ratio increases, the present value of the costs of financial distress increases, lessening some of the value gained from the use of tax deductibility of interest expense.

Management does not know the precise manner in which the probability of distress increases as the debt-to-equity ratio increases. Yet, it is reasonable to think that as the company increases its use of debt, relative to equity, in financing its operations and assets:

- The likelihood of distress increases.
- The benefit from the tax deductibility of interest increases.
- The present value of the cost of financial distress increases.

THE COST OF CAPITAL

The capital structure of a company is intertwined with the company's cost of capital. The *cost of capital* is the return that must be provided for the use of an investor's funds. If the funds are borrowed, the cost is related to the interest that must be paid on the loan. If the funds are equity, the cost is the return that investors expect, both from the stock's price appreciation and dividends. The cost of capital is a *marginal* concept. That is, the cost of capital is the cost associated with raising one more dollar of capital.

There are two reasons for determining a corporation's cost of capital. First, the cost of capital is often used as a starting point (a benchmark) for determining the cost of capital for a specific project. Often in capital budgeting decisions, the company's cost of capital is adjusted upward or downward depending on whether the project's risk is more than or less than the company's typical project. Second, many of a company's projects have risk similar to the risk of the company as a whole. So the cost of capital of the company is a reasonable approximation for the cost of capital of one of its projects that are under consideration for investment.

A company's cost of capital is the cost of its long-term sources of funds: debt, preferred stock, and common stock. And the cost of each source reflects the risk of the assets the company invests in. A company that invests in assets having little risk will be able to bear lower costs of capital than a company that invests in assets having a high risk. Moreover, the cost of each source of funds reflects the hierarchy of the risk associated with its seniority over the other sources. For a given company, the cost of funds raised through debt is less than the cost of funds from preferred stock which, in turn, is less than the cost of funds from common stock. This is because creditors have seniority over preferred shareholders, who have seniority over common shareholders. If there are difficulties in meeting obligations, the creditors receive their promised interest and principal before the preferred shareholders who, in turn, receive their promised dividends before the common shareholders.

For a given company, debt is less risky than preferred stock, which is less risky than common stock. Therefore, preferred shareholders require a greater return than the creditors and common shareholders require a greater return than preferred shareholders. Figuring out the cost of capital requires us to determine the cost of each source of capital the company expects to use, along with the relative amounts of each source of capital the company expects to raise. Putting together all these pieces, the company can then estimate the marginal cost of raising additional capital.

We estimate the company's cost of capital in three steps:

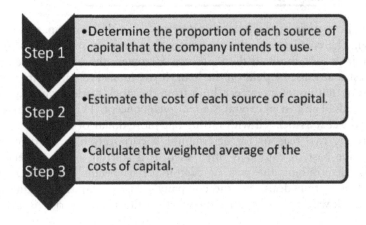

Step 1
- Determine the proportion of each source of capital that the company intends to use.

Step 2
- Estimate the cost of each source of capital.

Step 3
- Calculate the weighted average of the costs of capital.

We estimate the proportion of each source of capital using the company's target capital structure. We do not use book values of capital from the balance sheet because these are historical costs and may not represent how the company intends to raise new capital.

In calculating the cost of each financing source, we estimate the cost of raising additional capital from each source; in other words, their marginal costs. The cost of debt is the after-tax cost of debt, which we can estimate by using current yields on the company's debt, multiplied by one minus the company's marginal tax rate. If r_d is the marginal cost of debt before adjusting for taxes and t is the marginal tax rate, then the after-tax cost of debt, r_d^*, is

$$r_d^* = r_d \times (1 - t)$$

Why adjust for taxes? Because interest on debt is deductible for tax purposes, so the cost of the debt is not the current yield, but rather the yield adjusted for the tax deductibility of interest.

We can estimate the cost of preferred stock by using current yields on the company's preferred stock, if applicable. However, the cost of equity is by far much more difficult to estimate. There are several models available for estimating the cost of equity, including the dividend valuation model and the capital asset pricing model. What is critical to understand is that these different models can generate significantly different estimates for the cost of common stock and, as a result, the estimated cost of capital will be highly sensitive to the model selected.

In the case of both preferred stock and common stock, there is no adjustment for taxes because the distributions to shareholders are paid out of after-tax dollars. In other words, dividends paid on stock are not tax deductible.

The last step is to weight the cost of each source of funding by the proportion of that source in the target capital structure. This weighted average represents the marginal cost of raising an additional $1 of new capital. See Exhibit 8.3.

As a company adjusts its capital structure, its cost of capital also changes. Up to a point, using more debt relative to equity will lower the cost of capital because the after-tax cost of debt is less than the cost of equity. There is some point, however, when the likelihood and, hence, cost of financial distress increases and may in fact outweigh the benefit from taxes. After this point—wherever this may be—the cost of both debt and equity increases because both are much riskier.

Therefore, the trade-off theory of capital structure dictates that as the company uses more debt relative to equity, the value of the company is

EXHIBIT 8.3 Example of the Cost of Capital Calculation

Consider a company with the following information:

Source of Capital	Target Capital Structure Proportions	Pretax Costs of Capital
Debt	40%	5%
Preferred stock	10%	6%
Common stock	50%	12%

What is this company's cost of capital if the company's marginal tax rate is 40%?

Solution
The after-tax cost of debt is $5\% \times (1 - 0.40) = 3\%$. Therefore, the weighted average of the costs of capital is 7.8%:

$$\text{Cost of capital} = (40\% \times 3\%) + (10\% \times 6\%) + (50\% \times 12\%) = 7.8\%$$

This means that for every $1 the company plans to obtain from financing, the cost is 7.8%.

---

enhanced from the benefit of the interest tax shields. But the theory also states that there is some point at which the likelihood of financial distress increases such that there is an ever-increasing likelihood of bankruptcy.[6] Therefore:

- The value of the company declines as more and more debt is used, relative to equity.
- The cost of capital increases because the costs of the different sources of capital increase.

Though the trade-off theory simplifies the world too much, it gives the management an idea of the trade-offs involved. Introduce the value of financial flexibility and the governance value of debt, and management has the key inputs to consider in the capital structure decision.

---

[6]This is why we noted earlier in the chapter that we assumed that the interest on debt was the same for Company L and for Company LL, even though this was not realistic. Because of the increased likelihood of distress, Company LL's cost of debt should be higher than that of Company L.

TRY IT! COST OF CAPITAL

Consider a company with the following information:

Source of Capital	Target Capital Structure Proportions	Pretax Costs of Capital
Debt	25%	6.5%
Common stock	75%	10%

If the company's marginal tax rate is 40%, what is the company's cost of capital?

OPTIMAL CAPITAL STRUCTURE: THEORY AND PRACTICE

Management can try to evaluate whether there is a capital structure that maximizes the value of the company. This capital structure, if it exists, is referred to as the *optimal capital structure*. However, even if the company's optimal capital structure cannot be determined precisely, management should understand that there is an economic benefit from the tax deductibility of taxes, but eventually this benefit may be reduced by the costs of financial distress.

Looking at the financing behavior of companies in conjunction with their dividend and investment opportunities, we can make several observations:

- Companies prefer using internally generated capital (retained earnings) to externally raised funds (issuing equity or debt).
- Companies try to avoid sudden changes in dividends.
- When internally generated funds are greater than needed for investment opportunities, companies pay off debt or invest in marketable securities.
- When internally generated funds are less than needed for investment opportunities, companies use existing cash balances or sell off marketable securities.
- If companies need to raise capital externally, they issue the safest security first; for example, debt is issued before preferred stock, which is issued before common equity.

The trade-off among taxes and the costs of financial distress leads to the belief that there is some optimal capital structure, such that the value of the company is maximized. Yet it is difficult to reconcile this with some observations in practice. Why?

One possible explanation is that the trade-off analysis is incomplete. We didn't consider the relative costs of raising funds from debt and equity. Because there are no out-of-pocket costs to raising internally generated funds (retained earnings), it may be preferred to debt and to externally raised funds. Because the cost of issuing debt is less than the cost of raising a similar amount from issuing common stock (typically flotation costs of 2.2% versus 7.1%), debt may be preferred to issuing stock.

Another explanation for the differences between what we observe and what we believe should exist is that companies may wish to build up financial slack, in the form of cash, marketable securities, or unused debt capacity, to avoid the high cost of issuing new equity.

Still another explanation is that management may be concerned about the signal given to investors when equity is issued. It has been observed that the announcement of a new common stock issue is viewed as a negative signal, since the announcement is accompanied by a drop in the value of the equity of the company. It is also observed that the announcement of the issuance of debt does not affect the market value of equity. Therefore, management must consider the effect that the new security announcement may have on the value of equity and therefore may shy away from issuing new equity.

The concern over the relative costs of debt and equity and the concern over the interpretation by investors of the announcement of equity financing leads to a preferred ordering, or *pecking order,* of sources of capital: first internal equity, then debt, then preferred stock, then external equity (new common stock). A result of this preferred ordering is that companies prefer to build up funds, in the form of cash and marketable securities, so as not to be forced to issue equity at times when internal equity (that is, retained earnings) is inadequate to meet new profitable investment opportunities.[7]

Modigliani-Miller Theory of Capital Structure

Franco Modigliani and Merton Miller provide a theory of capital structure that is a framework for the discussion of the factors most important in a company's capital structure decision: taxes, financial distress, and risk. Though

---

[7]For a more complete discussion of the pecking order explanation, especially the role of asymmetric information, see Stewart C. Myers, "The Capital Structure Puzzle," *Midland Corporate Finance Journal* 3 (1985): 65–76.

this theory does not give a prescription for capital structure decisions, it does offer a method of examining the role of these important factors that provide the financial manager with the basic decision-making tools in analyzing the capital structure decision. Within their theory, Modigliani and Miller demonstrate that without taxes and costs of financial distress, the capital structure decision is irrelevant to the value of the company.

The capital structure decision becomes value-relevant when taxes are introduced into the situation, such that an interest tax shield from the tax deductibility of interest on debt obligations encourages the use of debt because this shield becomes a source of value. Financial distress becomes relevant because costs associated distress mitigate the benefits of debt in the capital structure, offsetting or partially offsetting the benefit from interest deductibility. The value of a company—meaning the value of all its assets—is equal to the sum of its liabilities and its equity (the ownership interest). Does the way we finance the company's assets affect the value of the company and hence the value of its owners' equity? Yes. How does it affect the value of the company?

M&M Irrelevance Proposition   Franco Modigliani and Merton Miller developed the basic framework for the analysis of capital structure and how taxes affect the value of the company.[8] The essence of this framework is that what matters in the value of the company is the company's operating cash flows and the uncertainty associated with these cash flows.

Modigliani and Miller (M&M) reasoned that if the following conditions hold, the value of the company is not affected by its capital structure:

Condition 1: Individuals and corporations can borrow and lend at the same terms (referred to as *equal access*).

Condition 2: There is no tax advantage associated with debt financing vis-à-vis to equity financing.

Condition 3: Debt and equity trade in a market where assets that are substitutes for one another, they trade at the same price.

Under the first condition, individuals can borrow and lend on the same terms as the business entities. Therefore, if individuals are seeking a given level of risk they can either: (1) borrow or lend on their own, or (2) invest in a business that borrows or lends. In other words, if an individual investor

---

[8]Franco Modigliani and Merton H. Miller, "The Cost of Capital, Corporation Finance, and the Theory of Investment," *American Economic Review* 48 (1958): 261–297.

wants to increase the risk of the investment, the investor could choose to invest in a company that uses debt to finance its assets. Or the individual could invest in a company with no financial leverage and take out a personal loan—increasing the investor's own financial leverage.

The second condition isolates the effect of financial leverage. If deducting interest from earnings is allowed in the analysis, it would be difficult to figure out what effect financial leverage itself has on the value of the company. M&M relax this later, but at this point assume no tax advantage exists between debt or equity securities—either for the company or the investor.

The third condition ensures that assets are priced according to their risk and return characteristics. This condition establishes what is referred to as a perfect capital market: If assets are traded in a perfect market, the value of assets with the same risk and return characteristics trade for the same price.

Under these conditions, the value of a company is the same, no matter how it chooses to finance itself. The *total* cash flow to owners and creditors is the same and the value of the company is the present value of the company's operating cash flows in perpetuity.

M&M show that in the simplified world without taxes or costs of distress, the value of the company depends on the cash flows of the company, not on how the company's cash flows are divided between creditors and owners. An implication of the M&M analysis is that the use of debt financing increases the risk of the future cash flows to owners and, therefore, increases the discount rate investors use to value these future earnings. M&M reason that the effect that the increased expected cash flows has on the value of equity is just offset by the increased discount rate applied to these riskier earnings, keeping the cost of capital the same no matter the capital structure.

M&M with Tax Deductibility of Interest Paid on Debt   M&M's second proposition is that when interest on debt is deducted in determining taxable income, but dividends are not, the value of the company is enhanced because of this tax deductibility of interest. When Modigliani and Miller introduce the tax deductibility of interest into the framework, the use of debt has a distinct advantage over financing with stock. The deductibility of interest represents a form of a government subsidy of financing activities; the government is sharing the company's cost of debt. We refer to the benefit from interest deductibility as the *interest tax shield* because the interest expense shields income from taxation. The tax shield from interest deductibility is the amount by which taxes are reduced by the deduction for interest.

If there are no costs associated with financial distress, then the value of the company increases with ever-increasing use of debt financing because of the value enhancement from the use of the interest tax shield. Further, if there are no costs to financial distress, the cost of capital for the company decreases with ever-increasing use of debt financing because the after-tax cost of debt affects the cost of capital for the company as a whole such that the increased use of the debt reduces the cost of capital.

Is there a limit to how much debt a company can take on? As long as there are no costs to financial distress, the only limit is the existence of at least a small percentage of equity in the capital structure.[9]

Capital Structure Theory and Costs to Financial Distress If the debt burden is too much, the company may experience financial distress, resulting in an increasing cost of capital: At some point, the value of the company declines and the cost of capital increases with increasing use of debt financing. Financial distress results in both direct and indirect costs including legal costs, opportunity costs for projects, and the effect of distress on the relationship with customers and suppliers.

At some capital structure, these costs begin to offset the benefit of the interest deductibility of debt. The optimal capital structure is the point at which the value of the company is maximized. Up until the optimal capital structure, the benefits from the tax deductibility of interest outweigh the cost of financial distress. When the amount of financial leverage exceeds the optimal capital structure, the benefits from the tax deductibility of interest are outweighed by the cost of financial distress. Because of the relation between the value of the company and the cost of capital, the capital structure that maximizes the value of the company is the same capital structure that minimizes the cost of capital.

The problem is that we cannot determine beforehand what the optimal capital structure is for a given company. The theory is not prescriptive in terms of identifying this precise point. What we can observe is when a company takes on too much debt and distress occurs. The optimal capital structure depends, in large part, on the business risk of the company: the greater the business risk of the company, the sooner this optimal capital structure is reached.

So what good is the theory of capital structure if financial managers cannot determine the optimal capital structure? The M&M theory, along with subsequent, related theories and evidence, provides a framework for decision making:

- There is a benefit to taking on debt—to a point.
- The cost of capital of a company decreases with ever-increasing use of debt financing—to a point.

---

[9]In theory and in practicality, there always must be some equity in a company, even if it is very little.

- The optimal capital structure depends on the risk associated with the company's operating cash flows.

Current Capital Structure Theory and Practice The M&M theory offers a trade-off model of capital structure: some balance exists between the present value of the interest tax shields and the present value of the costs of financial distress. We simply cannot determine, based on this theory, where this point is for a given company.

Since M&M introduced their theory of capital structure in a series of articles, there have been many other considerations offered by researchers, including:

- Agency costs that may complicate the maximization of shareholders' wealth.[10]
- Asymmetric information and signaling that result in a pecking order of financing choices.[11]
- Nonfinancial stakeholder issues that may affect the costs of financial distress.[12]

These additional considerations complicate the analysis, but do not replace the fundamental concept that there is a trade-off between the benefits of debt and the costs of having too much debt.

THE BOTTOM LINE

- A company may finance its business operations by raising funds internally, through retained earnings, issuing stock, or borrowing.
- Using borrowed funds, as compared to using equity, as a source of financing increases the risk to owners at the same time potentially enhancing the returns to owners through a leveraging effect.
- A way to view the choice of financing is to calculate the degree of financial leverage, which is the ratio of operating earnings to earnings after deducting interest.

---

[10]Jensen and Meckling, "Theory of the Firm: Managerial Behavior, Agency Costs, and Ownership Structure."
[11]Myers, "The Capital Structure Puzzle"; and Stewart C. Myers and N. S. Majluf, "Corporate Financing and Investment Decisions when Firms Have Information Investors Do Not Have," *Journal of Financial Economics* 13 (1984): 187–221.
[12]Mark Grinblatt and Sheridan Titman, *Financial Markets and Corporate Strategy* (Boston: Irwin/McGraw-Hill, 2002).

- Failure to pay interest or principal as promised may result in financial distress, the condition where a company makes decisions under pressure to satisfy its legal obligations to its creditors. These decisions may not be in the best interests of the owners of the company. The costs related to financial distress without legal bankruptcy can take different forms.

- The use of debt also reduces a company's financial flexibility. The management of a company that has financial slack (i.e., debt capacity that is unused) is more prepared to take advantage of investment opportunities in the future.

- The use of debt may enhance the value of equity because owners do not have to share income with creditors beyond the required interest payment on the debt, while owners benefit from the tax subsidy provided to companies that use debt financing. There may be a point, however, when amount of financing from debt becomes too much, and the company becomes distressed and may end up in bankruptcy.

- Though theory identifies the benefits of debt and the potential financial distress when a company takes on too much debt, we cannot tell at what point a company has taken on too much debt—until it becomes distressed.

- The cost of capital of a company is affected by the mix of debt and equity financing: the cost of capital is reduced as the company takes on more debt, but only to a point—after which it rises as the company encounters costs of financial distress that outweigh the tax advantages of debt.

- Management can try to evaluate whether there is an optimal capital structure (i.e., a capital structure that maximizes the value of the company). However, even if the company's optimal capital structure cannot be determined precisely, management should understand that there is an economic benefit from the tax deductibility of taxes, but eventually this benefit may be reduced by the costs of financial distress.

- The Modigliani Miller theory of capital structure provides a framework for the discussion of the factors most important in a company's capital structure decision: taxes, financial distress, and risk. Though this theory does not give a prescription for capital structure decisions, it does offer a method of examining the role of these important factors that aid management with the basic decision-making tools in analyzing the capital structure decision.

- According to the Modigliani-Miller theory of capital structure, in the absence of taxes and costs of financial distress, the capital structure decision is irrelevant to the value of the company. The capital structure decision becomes relevant when taxes are introduced into the analysis, such that an interest tax shield from the tax deductibility of interest on debt obligations encourages the use of debt because this shield becomes a source of value.

SOLUTIONS TO TRY IT! PROBLEMS

Returns with Leverage

In Millions

Operating earnings	$5.00
Interest on debt	$2.50
Net income	$2.50
Return on assets	2.5%
Return on equity	5.0%

Returns with Leverage and Taxes

In Millions

Operating earnings	$5.00
Interest on debt	$2.50
Taxable income	$2.50
Taxes at 40%	$1.00
Net income	$1.50
Return on assets	1.5%
Return on equity	3.0%

Cost of Capital

Source of Capital	Target Capital Structure Proportions	Pretax Costs of Capital	Costs of Capital	Weight x Cost
Debt	25%	6.5%	3.9%	0.975%
Common stock	75%	10%	10%	7.500%
	100%		Cost of capital =	8.475%

QUESTIONS

1. Briefly explain the role of financial leverage in affecting returns on equity.
2. What is an interest tax shield, and how does this affect the value of a company?
3. If a company's marginal tax rate were to increase, what is the effect on the interest tax shield from the company's debt?
4. If a company has a degree of financial leverage of 2.0, what is the expected effect of a 2% increase in operating earnings to the earnings to owners?
5. How may using debt financing increase the governance of a company?
6. Explain how limited liability may affect the capital structure decisions of a corporation.
7. If there are costs associated with financial distress, how may this affect the capital structure decision of a company?
8. Why do we adjust for taxes in determining the cost of debt, but not for the costs of preferred stock and common stock?
9. What is traded off in the trade-off theory of capital structure?
10. What is the relation between a company's operating risk and its optimal capital structure?
11. What is meant by the pecking order theory of capital structure?
12. What are the implications of the Modigliani-Miller theory of capital structure when the assumption of no corporate taxes is not valid?
13. Consider three financing alternatives:
    Alternative A: Finance solely with equity
    Alternative B: Finance using 50% debt, 50% equity
    Alternative C: Finance solely with debt
    a. Which of the three alternatives involves the greatest financial leverage?
    b. Which of the three alternatives involves the least financial leverage?
14. List the potential costs associated with financial distress.
15. List the potential direct and indirect costs associated with bankruptcy.
16. Regarding financial slack:
    a. What is it?
    b. How is slack created?
    c. Why do companies wish to have financial slack?

CHAPTER 9

Financial Risk Management

But innovation is more than a new method. It is a new view of the universe, as one of risk rather than of chance or of certainty. It is a new view of man's role in the universe; he creates order by taking risks. And this means that innovation, rather than being an assertion of human power, is an acceptance of human responsibility.

—Peter F. Drucker, *Landmarks of Tomorrow*
(New York: Harper Colophon Books, 1959)

All companies face a variety of risks. Scandals such as Enron, WorldCom, Tyco, and Adelphia, the tragic events such as 9/11, and the economic downturn associated with the U.S. subprime mortgage crisis have reinforced the need of companies to manage risk. Moreover, risk management should not be an after-thought, but instead should be a key element of any investment or financing decision.

In this chapter we discuss the four key processes in financial risk management: risk identification, risk assessment, risk mitigation, and risk transferring. The process of risk management involves determining which risks to accept, which to neutralize, and which to transfer.

THE DEFINITION OF RISK

There is no shortage of definitions for risk. We often refer to *risk* as the uncertainty regarding what may happen in the future. In some definitions, risk is distinguished from uncertainty, such that risk is uncertainty that can be quantified.

In everyday parlance, risk is often viewed as something that is negative, such as a danger, a hazard, or a loss. But we know that some risks lead to economic gains, while others have purely negative consequences. For example, the purchase of a lottery ticket involves an action that results in the risk of the loss equal to the cost of the ticket, but potentially has a substantial monetary reward. In contrast, the risk of death or injury from a random shooting is purely a negative consequence.

In the corporate world, accepting risks is necessary to obtain a competitive advantage and generate a profit. Introducing a new product or expanding production facilities involves both return and risk. When a company is exposed to an event that can cause a shortfall in a targeted financial measure or value, this is *financial risk*. The financial measure or value could be earnings per share, return on equity, or cash flows, to name some of the important ones. Financial risks include market risk, credit risk, market liquidity risk, operational risk, and legal risk.

The word "risk" is derived from the Italian verb *riscare*, which means "to dare." Business entities therefore "dare to" generate profits by taking advantage of the opportunistic side of risk.

We can classify risks as *core risks* and *noncore risks*. The distinction is important in the management of risk. In attempting to generate a return on invested funds that exceeds the risk-free interest rate, a company must bear risk. The core risks are those risks that the company is in the business to bear and the term *business risk* is used to describe this risk.

In contrast to core risk, risks that are incidental to the operations of a business are *noncore risks*. To understand the difference, consider the risk associated with the uncertainty about the price of electricity. For a company that produces and sells electricity, the risk that the price of electricity that it supplies may decline is a core risk. However, for a manufacturing company that uses electricity to operate its plants, the price risk associated with electricity (i.e., the price increasing) is a noncore risk. Yet changing the circumstances could result in a different classification. For example, suppose that the company producing and selling electricity is doing so on a fixed-price contract for the next three years. In this case, the price risk associated with electricity is a non core risk.

Sustainability Risk

In the past, the management of risks that a company faces has focused on its business and financial risks. The business risks include the *sales risk*—driven by competition and demand—and *operating risks*, affected by the structure of operating costs. The financial risks relate to the use of debt in the company's capital structure.

Take calculated risk. That is quite different from being rash.

—George Patton

In the past two decades there has been a broadening of the perception of risk to extend traditional business and financial risks to the complete spectrum of risk that a company faces that includes social and environmental responsibilities. This broad spectrum of risk is *sustainability risk*. For example, the social responsibilities of a company include labor and human rights, working conditions, training, governance, and ethics, whereas the environmental responsibilities include recycling and waste management, oversight, reporting, and resource use. Without effective management of these risks, a business risks the potential damages from boycotts, shareholder actions, lawsuits, and additional regulations.

The concept of sustainability has slowly gained prominence in the past two decades as investors, regulators, and companies grappled with the effects of corporate scandals, catastrophes, and tragedies. Many began to question whether the objective of the company as shareholder wealth maximization is too simplistic. In other words, the question arises as to whether a company is valued considering not only its financial performance, but its environmental and social responsibility records as well. There is no definitive empirical evidence that the environmental and social dimensions of a company affect its value, but there is anecdotal evidence that investors may consider these dimensions.

As the issue of sustainability has grown in prominence, there has also been a surge of measures of companies' sustainability risk, including the Institutional Shareholders Services Sustainability Risk Reports and the Deloitte Sustainability Reporting Scorecard. In addition, indexes, including the Dow Jones Sustainability Indexes (DJSI) and the FTSE4Good indexes, have been created that track the performance of companies focusing on sustainability. Further, many companies are now reporting their sustainability risk and risk management efforts to investors. For example, some companies now report on sustainability using the framework provided by the Global Reporting Initiative (GRI), though others develop their own reporting frameworks. Though GRI and other measures are still evolving, there is increasing pressure for some form of reporting on these risks.

A lot of people approach risk as if it's the enemy when it's really fortune's accomplice.

—Sting, in a quote from an essay Sting wrote entitled "Risk: Let Your Soul Be Your Bookie" that appears in Sarah Ban Breathnach and Michael Segell, *A Man's Journey to Simple Abundance* (New York: Scribner, 2000)

ENTERPRISE RISK MANAGEMENT

The traditional process of risk management focuses on managing the risks of only parts of the business (products, departments, or divisions), ignoring the implications for the value of the company. The organization of a risk management process focusing on only parts of a business is referred to as a *silo structure*. What is needed is a process that management can employ to effectively handle uncertainty and evaluate how the risks and opportunities that a company faces can either create, destroy, or preserve a company's value. This process should allow management to:

- Align the risk appetite and strategies across the company.
- Improve the quality of the company's risk-response decisions.
- Identify the risks across the company.
- Manage the risks across the company.

This process is *enterprise risk management* (ERM).

A company's internal controls provide a mechanism for mitigating risks, and increase the likelihood that a company will achieve its financial objective. As we will explain, ERM goes beyond internal controls in three significant ways. First, when establishing its strategy for the company, ERM requires that the board consider risks. Second, ERM requires that the board identify what level of risk it is willing to accept. Finally, ERM requires that risk management decisions be made throughout the company in a manner consistent with the risk policy established.

Definitions of ERM

Enterprise risk management is an ongoing process that provides a structured means for reducing the adverse consequences of big surprises due to natural catastrophes, terrorism, changes in the economic, political, and legal environments, tax litigation, failure of the company's corporate governance, and product and financial market volatility. In fact, Moody's states that the ultimate objective of a company's risk management organization should be to make sure that there are no major surprises that place the company in peril.[1] Second, the starting point for an effective ERM system is at the board level. This means that corporate governance is a critical element.

DEFINITIONS OF ENTERPRISE RISK MANAGEMENT

The most popular definition is proposed by the Committee of Sponsoring Organizations of the Treadway Commission (COSO):

> *"a process, effected by an entity's board of directors, management and other personnel, applied in strategy setting and across the enterprise, designed to identify potential events that may affect the entity, and manage risk to be within its risk appetite, to provide reasonable assurance regarding the achievement of entity objectives."*[*]

The Casualty Actuarial Society (CAS) provides a broader definition of ERM:

> *"the discipline by which an organization in any industry assesses, controls, exploits, finances, and monitors risk from all sources for the purposes of increasing the organization's short- and long-term value to its stakeholders."*[**]

---

[*]Committee of Sponsoring Organizations of the Treadway Commission, *Enterprise Risk Management—Integrated Framework Executive Summary* (September 2004), p. 8.
[**]Casualty Actuarial Society, Overview of Enterprise Risk Management (May 2003).

The term "enterprise" can have different meanings within ERM.[2] One is that ERM is linked to strategic planning and organizational objectives of the

---

[1]Moody's, "Risk Management Assessments," *Moody's Research Methodology* (July 2004).
[2]As the Society of Actuaries (SOA) points out, there are two main definitions [Society of Actuaries, *Enterprise Risk Management Specialty Guide* (May 2006), p. 9].

business enterprise. The second definition is in terms of *modern portfolio theory* (MPT) that we describe in Chapter 16. In this theory, formulated by Harry Markowitz, the focus is on the risk of the portfolio and not the individual securities comprising the portfolio.[3] In other words, the enterprise is a portfolio in this context. This leads to the conclusion that it is not the stand-alone risk of an individual security that is relevant but only the contribution of that as asset makes to a portfolio's risk.

A portfolio manager can use the basic ideas from MPT to create efficient portfolios, assembling a portfolio that offers the maximum expected return for a given level of risk. The portfolio manager's task is to select one of these efficient portfolios given the manager's or client's risk appetite. The manager can use derivatives instruments that we describe in Chapter 14 to alter the risk profile of a portfolio and can use risk budgeting to decide how to allocate risk. In the context of ERM, the enterprise is viewed as a "portfolio of risks." It is not stand-alone risk that is key, but the risk to the entire company. The risk profile can be altered using derivative instruments as well as other risk transfer products and strategies discussed later in this chapter.

ERM Process

There is no fixed formula for developing an ERM system, but rather some general principles that provide guidance. This is because there is considerable variation in company size, organizational structures (centralized versus decentralized, for example), and types of risk faced in different industries. So, although different internal controls vary from company to company, the underlying principles do not. In the literature, there are several proposals for the ERM process.

The four risk objectives of ERM are the following:[4]

1. *Strategic.* Supporting the corporation's strategic goals (i.e., high-level goals).
2. *Operations.* Achieving performance goals and taking measures to safeguard against loss through operational efficiency.
3. *Reporting.* Providing reliable financial and operational data and reports internally and externally.
4. *Compliance.* Complying with laws and regulations at all levels (local, state, national, and in other countries where the company operates).

---

[3]Harry M. Markowitz, "Portfolio Selection," *Journal of Finance* 7(1952): 77–91.
[4]These are from the Committee of Sponsoring Organizations (COSO) framework.

While there are common risks shared by all companies and there are risks unique to some companies, the building blocks for the ERM process are common to all companies.

Basically, ERM is chiefly concerned with

- evaluating the company's risk processes and risk controls, and
- identifying and quantifying risk exposures.

ERM is broader in its scope than traditional risk management, which focuses on products, departments, or divisions practiced within a silo structure. In ERM, all the risks of a company are treated as a portfolio of risks and managed on a portfolio or company level. That is, the risk context is the company, not individual products, departments, or divisions.

For example, suppose that a company has a target minimum earnings figure established either by its own financial plan or based on Wall Street analysts' consensus earnings. ERM can be used to identify the threats to the company of hitting that target. Once those risks are identified and prioritized, management can examine the potential shortfall that may occur and decide how to reduce the likelihood that there will be a shortfall using some risk transfer strategies.

Themes of ERM

There are four themes in enterprise risk management, as we detail in Exhibit 9.1.[5]

The *risk control* process involves identifying, evaluating, monitoring, and managing risk. The process of reflecting risk and risk capital in strategic options from which a corporation can select is called *strategic risk management*. This process requires adjusting for risk in valuing investments, making investment decisions, and evaluating an investment's performance.

Catastrophic events are extreme events that could threaten the survival of a company. *Catastrophic risk management* involves planning so as to minimize the impact of potential catastrophic events and having in place an early warning system that, if possible, could identify a potential disaster.

In catastrophic control, several analyses provide information. For example, trend analysis can identify any patterns suggesting potential emergence of catastrophes, and stress testing can show the impact of a catastrophe on the financial condition and reputation of the company. Once we have an understanding regarding the possible scenarios, we can plan for

---

[5]The four themes are proposed by the *Enterprise Risk Management Specialty Guide*, pp. 26–38.

Risk control	Strategic risk management	Catastrophic control	Risk management culture
• Identify risks • Evaluate risks • Monitor risks • Set risk limits • Avoid certain risks • Offset certain risks • Transfer risks • Review and evaluate new investments	• Estimate economic capital • Value investments • Make investment decisions • Evaluate performance	• Perform trend analysis • Perform stress testing • Plan for contingencies • Evaluate risk transfer	• Identify best risk management practices • Develop supporting documentation • Communicate • Reinforce through education and training

EXHIBIT 9.1 The Four Themes of Enterprise Risk Management

contingencies, prepare communication strategies for stakeholders, and consider effectiveness and cost to transfer risk.

The Society of Actuaries (SOA) defines a *risk management culture* as an environment in which the entity has an approach to dealing with risks, and that this approach is part of the entity's culture. Hence, when a risk event occurs, a plan is in place for dealing with this risk.[6]

> Reports that say something hasn't happened are always interesting to me because, as we know, there are known knowns; there are things we know we know. We also know there are known unknowns; that is to say, we know there are some things we do not know. But there are also unknown unknowns—the ones we don't know we don't know.
> —Donald Rumsfeld, U.S. Secretary of Defense
> (Press Conference, Brussels, Belgium, June 6, 2002)

This culture requires that the entity identify and measure risks, and examine best practices in the management of risk. In addition, the risk management culture requires that the entity develop a system of documenting risk and risk management and communicating risk management policies and practices to stakeholders. Further, a risk management culture should educate all employees or other decision-makers in risk management and provide training regarding risk management. This education and training reinforces the importance of risk management.

---

[6]Exhibit 9.1 is a summary of the description of the themes of risk management provided by *Enterprise Risk Management Specialty Guide*, p. 26–28.

Specifying an Entity's Risk Policy

The implementation of an ERM policy requires that the amount of risk that a company is willing to accept be specified. Corporations through their board set the boundaries as to how much risk the company is prepared to accept. Often in referring to risk, the terms *risk appetite* and *risk tolerance* are used interchangeably. However, there is a subtle distinction between the two concepts.

Basically, the company's risk appetite is the amount of risk exposure that the entity decides it is willing to accept or retain.[7] When the risk exposure of the entity exceeds the risk tolerance threshold, risk management processes kick into return the exposure level back within the accepted range.

Once an entity has implemented a risk policy of the company, it is important to communicate it to stakeholders. For a corporation, this is through the management discussion and analysis section required in SEC filings (8-K and 10-K), press releases, communications with rating agencies, and investor meetings. Now that the credit rating services are incorporating ERM measures into the credit rating process, it is more important than ever for companies to pay attention to the company's ERM system and to communicate this system to stakeholders.

MANAGING RISKS

A company's *risk retention decision* is how it elects to manage an identified risk. This decision is more than a risk management decision, it is also a financing decision. The choices are:

- Retain
- Neutralize
- Transfer

Of course, each identified risk faced by the company can be treated in a different way. For each of the three choices—retention, neutralization, and transfer of risk—there are in turn two further decisions as to how they can be handled.

Retained Risk and Risk Finance

The decision by a company of which identified risks to retain is based on an economic analysis of the expected benefits versus expected costs associated with bearing that particular risk. The aggregate of all the risks across the

---

[7]*Enterprise Risk Management—Integrated Framework Executive Summary*, p. 2.

company that it has elected to bear is called its *retained risk*. Because if a retained risk is realized it will adversely impact the company's earnings and cash flows, a company must decide to fund or not fund a retained risk.

An *unfunded retained risk* is a retained risk for which potential losses are not financed until they occur. In contrast, a *funded retained risk* is a retained risk for which an appropriate amount is set aside up front (either as cash or an identified source for raising funds) to absorb the potential loss. For example, with respect to corporate taxes, management may decide to hold as cash reserves all or a portion of the potential adverse outcome of litigation with tax authorities. This management of retained risk is referred to as *risk finance*.

Risk Neutralization

If a company elects not to retain an identified risk, it can either neutralize the risk or transfer the risk. *Risk neutralization* is a risk management policy whereby a company acts on its own to mitigate the outcome of an expected loss from an identified risk without transferring that risk to a third party. This can involve reducing the likelihood of the identified risk occurring or reducing the severity of the loss should the identified risk be realized. Risk neutralization management for some risks may be a natural outcome of the business or financial factors affecting the company.

Consider an example involving a business risk. Suppose that a company projects an annual loss of $30 million to $50 million from returns due to product defects, and this amount is material relative to its profitability. A company can introduce improved production processes to reduce the upper range of the potential loss.

As an example involving a financial factor, a U.S. multinational company will typically have cash inflows and outflows in the same currency such as the euro. As a result, there is currency risk—the risk that the exchange rate moves adversely to the company's exposure in that currency. But this risk has offsetting tendencies if there are both cash inflows and outflows in the same currency. Assuming the currency is the euro, the cash inflows are exposed to a depreciation of the euro relative to the U.S. dollar; the cash outflows are exposed to an appreciation of the euro relative to the U.S. dollar. If the company projects future cash inflows over a certain time period of €50 million and a cash outflow over the same period of €40 million, the company's net currency exposure is a €10 million cash inflow. That is, €40 million exposure is hedged naturally.

Risk Transfer

For certain identifiable risks, the company may decide to transfer the risk from shareholders to a third party. This can be done either by entering into a contract with a counterparty willing to take on the risk the company seeks to transfer, or by embedding that risk in a structured financial transaction, thereby transferring it to bond investors willing to accept that risk.

There are various forms of *risk transfer management*. The vehicles or instruments for transferring risk include traditional insurance, derivatives, alternative risk transfer, and structured finance.

Traditional Insurance   The oldest form of risk transfer vehicle is insurance. An insurance policy is a contract whereby an insurance company agrees to make a payment to the insured if a defined adverse event is triggered. The insured receives the protection by paying a specified amount periodically, called the *insurance premium*.

The contract can be a valued contract or unvalued contract. In a *valued contract*, the policy specifies the agreed value of the property insured. With the exception of life insurance contracts purchased by companies, valued contracts are not commonly used as a form of risk transfer. There are exceptions, of course, such as an art museum insuring valuable works of art with the amount fixed at the time of negotiation of the contract to avoid needing an appraisal of the artwork after the insured event is triggered.

In an *unvalued contract*, also called a *contract of indemnity*, the value of the insured property is not fixed. Rather, there may be a maximum amount payable, yet the payment is contingent on the actual amount of the insured's loss resulting from the trigger event. A contract of indemnity is the typical type of contract used in risk transfer.

Derivatives   As will be explained in Chapter 14, there are capital market products available to transfer risks that are not readily insurable by an insurance company. Such risks include risks associated with a rise in the price of a commodity purchased as an input, a decline in a commodity price of a product the company sells, a rise in the cost of borrowing funds, and an adverse exchange-rate movement. *Derivate instruments*, which are capital market instruments, can be used to provide such protection. These instruments include futures contracts, forward contracts, option contracts, swap agreements, and cap and floor agreements.

There have been shareholder concerns about the use of derivative instruments by companies. This concern arises from major losses resulting from positions in derivative instruments. However, an investigation of the reason for major losses would show that the losses were not due to derivatives per se, but the improper use of them by management that either was ignorant about the risks associated with using derivative instruments or sought to use them in a speculative manner rather than as a means for managing risk.

MISHAPS IN RISK MANAGEMENT THROUGH DERIVATIVES

- Procter & Gamble lost $195.5 million in an interest rate swap in 1994, but its obligation to pay this to Bankers Trust was forgiven in a settlement.

- Amaranth Advisors, a hedge fund, lost $6.4 billion in 2006 in futures contracts on natural gas.

- Over several years, American International Group sold credit default swaps. When the credit quality of many bonds deteriorated as the economy entered into a recession, AIG's selling of swaps resulted in its losing more than $18 billion in 2008.

Alternative Risk Transfer

Alternative risk transfer (ART), also known as *structured insurance*, provides unique ways to transfer the increasingly complex risks faced by corporations that cannot be handled by traditional insurance and has led to the growth in the use of this form of risk transfer. These products combine elements of traditional insurance and capital market instruments to create highly sophisticated risk transfer strategies tailored for a corporate client's specific needs and liability structure that traditional insurance cannot handle.[8] For this reason, ART is sometimes referred to as "insurance-based investment banking."

An example of one type of ART is an *insurance-linked note* (ILN). This type of ART has been primarily used by life insurers and property and casualty insurers to bypass the conventional reinsurance market and synthetically reinsure against losses by tapping the capital markets. Basically, an ILN is a means for securitizing insurance risk and is typically referred to as *catastrophe-linked bonds* or simply *cat bonds*.

The first use of catastrophe-linked bonds in corporate risk management by a noninsurance company was by the owner-operator of Tokyo Disneyland, Oriental Land Co. Rather than obtain traditional insurance against

---

[8]For a detailed discussion of ART, see Christopher L. Culp, *Structured Finance and Insurance: The ART of Managing Capital and Risk* (Hoboken, NJ: John Wiley & Sons, 2006) and Erik Banks, *Alternative Risk Transfer: Integrated Risk Management Through Insurance, Reinsurance and the Capital Markets* (Hoboken, NJ: John Wiley & Sons, 2004).

earthquake damage for the park, it issued a $200 million cat bond in 1999. Three years later, Vivendi Universal obtained protection for earthquake damage for its studios (Universal Studios) in California by issuing a $175 million cat bond with a maturity of 3.5 years.

Whereas catastrophe-linked bonds have primarily been used for perils such as earthquakes and hurricanes, corporations are using them in other ways. For example, the risk to the lessor (i.e., the owner of the leased equipment) in a leasing transaction is that the value of the leased equipment when the lease terminates (the residual value) is below its expected value when the lease was negotiated.

CASE IN POINT: CAT BONDS

Toyota Motor Credit Corp. was concerned that the 260,000 1998 motor vehicles (cars and light-duty trucks) it leased to customers would decline in value if the used-car market weakened. To protect itself, Toyota issued a cat bond that provided protection for itself against a loss in market value of the fleet of leased motor vehicles.

Structured Finance *Structured finance* involves the creation of nontraditional-type securities with risk and return profiles targeted to certain types of investors. Structured finance includes asset securitization, structured notes, and leasing.

THE BOTTOM LINE

- Financial risk management involves identifying and measuring risk, as well as determining how much, if any, risk to retain.
- We can categorize risks as core risks and noncore risks. The core risks are business risks, those risks that the company is in the business to bear. Noncore risks are risks that are incidental to the operations of a business.
- Sustainability risk is the extension of traditional business and financial risks to the complete spectrum of risk that a company faces that includes social and environmental responsibilities.
- Enterprise risk management is the holistic approach to risk management, where risk is managed from the perspective of the entire entity or portfolio.

- An entity can decide whether to retain risk, neutralize it, or transfer it to another party.
- Retained risks are the aggregate of all the risks across the company that a company's management has elected to bear. Because management decides to fund or not fund a retained risk, management of retained risk is referred to as risk finance.
- Risk neutralization is a risk management policy whereby a company acts on its own to mitigate the outcome of an expected loss from an identified risk without transferring that risk to a third party.
- Risk transfer management involves transferring certain identifiable risks from shareholders to a third party either by entering into a contract with a counterparty willing to take on the risk the company seeks to transfer or by embedding that risk in a structured financial transaction.

QUESTIONS

1. What is the difference between core and no-core risk?
2. How does the theory of portfolio risk relate to enterprise risk management?
3. What is meant by sustainability risk?
4. What are the three choices available to management for dealing with risk?
5. What distinguishes an unfunded from a funded retained risk?
6. What is the function of an insurance-linked note for risk management?
7. What methods can a company use to transfer risk?
8. How does a core risk differ from a non core risk?
9. How can derivatives be used in risk management?
10. What is a cat bond and how can it be used to manage risk?
11. The following "Company Overview" of AIG Risk Finance was described on the Internet (investing.businessweek.com/research/stocks/private/snapshot.asp?privcapId=11673577):

    AIG Risk Finance designs and implements risk financing solutions. The company offers structured insurance, exotic buyouts, and unconventional life programs.... AIG Risk Finance operates as a subsidiary of American International Group, Inc.

    a. What is meant by "structured insurance"?
    b. What is an alternative name for structured insurance?
    c. Give two examples of structured insurance.

Valuation and Analytical Tools

CHAPTER 10

The Math of Finance

*The price then that the borrower has to pay for the loan of capital,
and which he regards as interest, is from the point of view of the
lender more properly to be regarded as profits: for it includes
insurance against risks which are often very heavy, and earnings of
arrangement for the task, which is often very arduous, of keeping
those risks as small as possible. Variations in the nature of these
risks and of the task of management will of course occasion
corresponding variations in the gross interest—so called that is
paid of the use of money.*
—Alfred Marshall, *Principles of Economics: Volume 2*
(London: MacMillan & Co., 1890), p. 623

Investment decisions made by financial managers, to acquire capital assets
such as plant and equipment, and asset managers, to acquire securities
such as stocks and bonds, require the valuation of investments and the
determination of yields on investments. The concept that must be understood
to determine the value of an investment, the yield on an investment, and
the cost of funds is the time value of money. This simple mathematical
concept allows financial and asset managers to translate future cash flows
to a value in the present, translate a value today into a value at some future
point in time, and calculate the yield on an investment. The time-value-of-
money mathematics allows an evaluation and comparison of investments
and financing arrangements and is the subject of this chapter.

WHY THE TIME VALUE OF MONEY?

The notion that money has a time value is one of the most basic concepts
in investment analysis. Making decisions today regarding future cash flows

requires understanding that the value of money does not remain the same throughout time.

A dollar today is worth less than a dollar at some future for two reasons:

Reason 1: Cash flows occurring at different times have different values relative to any one point in time.

One dollar one year from now is not as valuable as one dollar today. After all, you can invest a dollar today and earn interest so that the value it grows to next year is greater than the one dollar today. This means we have to take into account the *time value of money* to quantify the relation between cash flows at different points in time.

Reason 2: Cash flows are uncertain.

Expected cash flows may not materialize. Uncertainty stems from the nature of forecasts of the timing and the amount of cash flows. We do not know for certain when, whether, or how much cash flows will be in the future. This uncertainty regarding future cash flows must somehow be taken into account in assessing the value of an investment.

Translating a current value into its equivalent future value is *compounding*. Translating a future cash flow or value into its equivalent value in a prior period is *discounting*. In this chapter, we outline the basic mathematical techniques of compounding and discounting.

Suppose someone wants to borrow $100 today and promises to pay back the amount borrowed in one month. Would the repayment of only the $100 be fair? Probably not. There are two things to consider. First, if the lender didn't lend the $100, what could he or she have done with it? Second, is there a chance that the borrower may not pay back the loan? So, when considering lending money, we must consider the opportunity cost (that is, what could have been earned or enjoyed), as well as the uncertainty associated with getting the money back as promised.

Let's say that someone is willing to lend the money, but that they require repayment of the $100 plus some compensation for the opportunity cost and any uncertainty the loan will be repaid as promised. Then:

- the amount of the loan, the $100, is the principal; and
- the compensation required for allowing someone else to use the $100 is the interest.

Looking at this same situation from the perspective of time and value, the amount that you are willing to lend today is the loan's present value. The amount that you require to be paid at the end of the loan period is the loan's future value. Therefore, the future period's value is comprised of two parts:

$$
\begin{array}{ccccc}
\begin{array}{c}\text{Amount paid at the}\\ \text{end of the loan}\\ \downarrow\end{array} & & \begin{array}{c}\text{Principal}\\ \downarrow\end{array} & & \begin{array}{c}\text{Interest}\\ \downarrow\end{array}\\
\text{Future value} & = & \text{Present value} & + & \text{Interest}
\end{array}
$$

or, using notation,

$$FV \quad = \quad PV \quad + \quad (i \times PV)$$

If you would know the value of money, go and try to borrow some.

—Benjamin Franklin

The interest is compensation for the use of funds for the period of the loan. It consists of:

1. compensation for the length of time the money is borrowed; and
2. compensation for the risk that the amount borrowed will not be repaid exactly as set forth in the loan agreement.

CALCULATING THE FUTURE VALUE

Suppose you deposit $1,000 into a savings account at the Safe Savings Bank and you are promised 5% interest per period. At the end of one period, you would have $1,050. This $1,050 consists of the return of your principal amount of the investment (the $1,000) and the interest or return on your investment (the $50). Let's label these values:

- $1,000 is the value today, the present value, PV.
- $1,050 is the value at the end of one period, the future value, FV.
- 5% is the rate interest is earned in one period, the interest rate, i.

To get to the future value from the present value:

$$
\begin{array}{rll}
FV & = PV & + \text{ Interest}\\
FV & = PV & + PV \times i\\
FV & = PV & \times (1 + i)\\
\$1,050 & = \$1,000 & \times (1.05)
\end{array}
$$

If the $50 interest is withdrawn at the end of the period, the principal is left to earn interest at the 5% rate. Whenever you do this, you earn *simple interest*. It is simple because it repeats itself in exactly the same way from one period to the next as long as you take out the interest at the end of each period and the principal remains the same.

Time is money.

—Benjamin Franklin

If, on the other hand, both the principal and the interest are left on deposit at the Safe Savings Bank, the balance earns interest on the previously paid interest, referred to as *compound interest*. Earning interest on interest is called compounding because the balance at any time is a combination of the principal, interest on principal, and *interest on accumulated interest* (or simply, *interest on interest*).

If you compound interest for one more period in our example, the original $1,000 grows to $1,052.50:

$$
\begin{aligned}
FV &= \text{Principal} &&+ \text{First period interest} + \text{Second period interest} \\
&= PV &&+ PV \times i &&&+ [PV(1+i)] \times i \\
&= \$1,000.00 + (\$1,000.00 \times 0.05) + (\$1,050.00 \times 0.05) \\
&= \$1,000.00 + 50.00 &&+ 52.50 \\
&= \$1,052.50
\end{aligned}
$$

The present value of the investment is $1,000, theinterest earned over two years is $52.50, and the future value of the investment after two years is $1,052.50. If this were simple interest, the future value would be $1,050. Therefore, the interest on interest—the results of compounding—is $2.50.

We can use some shorthand to represent the FV at the end of two periods:

$$FV = PV(1+i)^2$$

The balance in the account two years from now, $1,052.50, is comprised of three parts:

- The principal, $1,000.
- Interest on principal: $50 in the first period plus $50 in the second period.
- Interest on interest: 5% of the first period's interest, or $0.05 \times \$50 = \$2.50$.

To determine the future value with compound interest for more than two periods, we follow along the same lines:

$$FV = PV(1 + i)^N \tag{10.1}$$

The value of N is the number of compounding periods, where a compounding period is the unit of time after which interest is paid at the rate i. A period may be any length of time: a minute, a day, a month, or a year. The important thing is to be consistent through the calculations. The term "$(1 + i)^N$" is the *compound factor*, and it is the rate of exchange between present dollars and future dollars, n compounding periods into the future.

The entire essence of America is the hope to first make money—then make money with money—then make lots of money with lots of money.

—Paul Erdman

Equation (10.1) is the foundation of financial mathematics. It relates a value at one point in time to a value at another point in time, considering the compounding of interest.

We show the relation between present and future values for a principal of $1,000 and interest of 5% per period through 10 compounding periods in Exhibit 10.1. For example, the value of $1,000, earning interest at 5% per period, is $1,628.89, which is 10 periods into the future:

$$FV = \$1,000(1 + 0.05)^{10} = \$1,000(1.62898) = \$1,628.89$$

After ten years, there will be $1,628.89 in the account, consisting of:

- The principal, $1,000;
- Interest on the principal of $1,000: $50 per period for 10 periods or $500; and
- Interest on interest totaling $128.89.

If you left the money in the bank, after 50 years you would have:

$$FV = \$1,000(1 + 0.05)^{50} = \$11,467.40$$

If this were simple interest instead of compound interest, the balance after 50 years would be: $1,000 + [50 \times \$1,000 \times 0.05] = \$3,500$. In other words, the $11,467.40 − 3,500 = $7,967.40. This is the power of compounding.

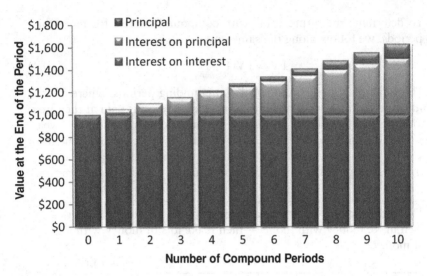

EXHIBIT 10.1 The Future Value of $1,000 Invested for 10 Years in an Account That Pays 10% Compounded Interest per Year

We can use financial calculators, scientific calculators with financial functions, or spreadsheets to solve most any financial problem. Consider the problem of calculating the future value of $1,000 at 5% for 10 years:

Hewlett-Packard 10B	Texas Instruments 83/84	Microsoft Excel
1000 +/− PV	N = 10	=FV(.05,10,0,−1000)
10 N	I% = 5	
5 I/YR	PV = −1000	
PV	*Place cursor at* FV = *and then* SOLVE	

A few notes about entering the data into the calculator or spreadsheet:

1. You need to change the sign of the present value to negative, reflecting the investment (negative cash flow).
2. You enter interest rates as whole values form when using the financial functions within a calculator, but enter these in decimal form if using the math functions of a calculation or the financial functions of a spreadsheet.

3. If you are using the financial function of a scientific calculator, you need to first enter this function. In the case of the Texas Instruments 83 or 84 calculator, for example, this is done through APPS >Finance>TVM Solver.
4. If you are using a spreadsheet function, you must enter a 0 in place of an unused argument.[1]

EXAMPLE 10.1: GUARANTEED INVESTMENT CONTRACTS

A common investment product of a life insurance company is a guaranteed investment contract (GIC). With this investment, an insurance company guarantees a specified interest rate for a period of years. Suppose that the life insurance company agrees to pay 6% annually for a five-year GIC and the amount invested by the policyholder is $10 million.

The amount of the liability (that is, the amount this life insurance company has agreed to pay the GIC policyholder) is the future value of $10 million when invested at 6% interest for five years:

$$PV = \$10,000,000, \; i = 6\%, \; \text{and } N = 5,$$

so that the future value is

$$FV = \$10,000,000(1 + 0.06)^5 = \$13,382,256$$

 TRY IT! FUTURE VALUE

If you deposit $100 in a saving account that pays 2% interest per year, compounded annually, how much will you have in the account at the end of

a. five years?
b. 10 years?
c. 20 years?

---

[1]For example, the FV function has the following arguments: interest rate, number of periods, payment, and present value. Because this last problem does not involve any periodic payments, we used a zero for that argument.

Growth Rates and Returns

We can express the change in the value of the savings balance as a growth rate. A *growth rate* is the rate at which a value appreciates (a positive growth) or depreciates (a negative growth) over time. Our $1,000 grew at a rate of 5% per year over the 10-year period to $1,628.89. The average annual growth rate of our investment of $1,000 is 5%—the value of the savings account balance increased 5% per year.

We could also express the appreciation in our savings balance in terms of a return. A *return* is the income on an investment, generally stated as a change in the value of the investment over each period divided by the amount at the investment at the beginning of the period. We could also say that our investment of $1,000 provides an average annual return of 5% per year. The average annual return is not calculated by taking the change in value over the entire 10-year period ($1,629.89 − $1,000) and dividing it by $1,000. This would produce an *arithmetic average return* of 62.889% over the 10-year period, or 6.2889% per year. But the arithmetic average ignores the process of compounding, so this is not the correct annual return.

The correct way of calculating the average annual return is to use a *geometric average return*:

$$\text{Geometric average return} = \sqrt[N]{\frac{FV}{PV}} - 1 \qquad (10.2)$$

which is a rearrangement of equation (10.1). Using the values from the example,

$$\text{Geometric average return} = \sqrt[10]{\frac{\$1,628.89}{\$1,000.00}} - 1 = 5\%$$

Therefore, the annual return on the investment as the *compound average annual return* or the *true return*—is 5% per year.

Hewlett-Packard 10B	Texas Instruments 83/84	Microsoft Excel
1000 +/− PV	N = 10	=RATE(10,0,−1000,1628.89)
10 N	PV = −1000	
1628.89 FV	FV = 1628.89	
I/YR	*Place cursor at*	
	I% = and then	
	SOLVE	

TRY IT! GROWTH RATES

Suppose you invest $2,000 today and you double your money after five years. What is the annual growth rate on your investment?

Compounding More Than Once per Year

An investment may pay interest more than one time per year. For example, interest may be paid semiannually, quarterly, monthly, weekly, or daily, even though the stated rate is quoted on an annual basis. If the interest is stated as, say, 4% per year, compounded semiannually, the nominal rate—often referred to as the *annual percentage rate* (APR)—is 4%.

Suppose we invest $10,000 in an account that pays interest stated at a rate of 4% per year, with interest compounded quarterly. How much will we have after five years if we do not make any withdrawals? We can approach problems when compounding is more frequent than once per year using two different methods:

Method 1: Convert the information into compounding periods and solve

The inputs:

$PV = \$10,000$

$N = 5 \times 4 = 20$

$i = 4\% \div 4 = 1\%$

Solve for FV:

$FV = \$10,000 \, (1 + 0.01)^{20} = \$12,201.90$

Method 2: Convert the APR into an effective annual rate and solve

The inputs:

$PV = \$10,000$

$N = 5$

$i = (1 + 0.01)^4 - 1 = 4.0604\%$

Solve for FV:

$FV = \$10,000 \, (1 + 0.040601)^5 = \$12,201.90$

Both methods will get you to the correct answer. In Method 1, you need to adjust both the number of periods and the rate. In Method 2, you need to first calculate the effective annual rate, in this case 4.0601%, before calculating the future value.

Compounding frequency	Compound period	Rate per compound period	Number of compound periods in 10 years	Future value
Annual	1 year	8%	10	$215.89
Semiannual	6 months	4%	20	$219.11
Quarterly	3 months	2%	40	$220.80
Monthly	1 month	0.67%	120	$221.96

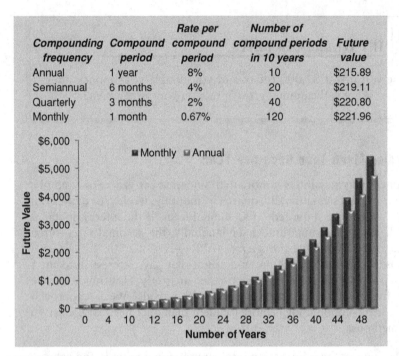

EXHIBIT 10.2 Value of $100 Invested in the Account That Pays 8% Interest per Year for 10 Years for Different Frequencies of Compounding

The frequency of compounding matters. To see how this works, let's use an example of a deposit of $100 in an account that pays interest at a rate of 8% per year, with interest compounded for different compounding frequencies. How much is in the account after, say, 10 years depends on the compounding frequency, as we show in Exhibit 10.2. At the end of ten years, the difference in the future values between annual and monthly compounding is a little more than $6. After 50 years, the difference is $5,388 – 4,690 = $698.

EXAMPLE 10.2: QUARTERLY COMPOUNDING

Suppose we invest $200,000 in an investment that pays 4% interest per year, compounded quarterly. What will be the future value of this investment at the end of 10 years?

Solution:

The given information is:

$$i = 4\%/4 = 1\% \text{ and } N = 10 \times 4 = 40 \text{ quarters.}$$

Therefore, $FV = \$200,000(1 + 0.01)^{40} = \$297,772.75$

 TRY IT! MORE GROWTH RATES

Complete the following table, calculating the annual growth rate for each investment.

Present Value	Future Value	Number of Years	Growth Rate
$1	$3	6	☐
$1,000	$2,000	9	☐
$500	$600	7	☐
$1	$1.50	4	☐

Continuous Compounding

The extreme frequency of compounding is *continuous compounding*—interest is compounded instantaneously. The factor for compounding continuously for one year is e^{APR}, where e is $2.71828\ldots$, the base of the natural logarithm. And the factor for compounding continuously for two years is $e^{APR} \times e^{APR}$ or e^{2APR}. The future value of an amount that is compounded continuously for N years is

$$FV = PVe^{N(APR)} \tag{10.3}$$

where APR is the annual percentage rate and $e^{N(APR)}$ is the compound factor.

If $1,000 is deposited in an account for five years, with interest of 12% per year, compounded continuously,

$$FV = \$1,000\,e^{5(0.12)}$$
$$= \$1,000(e^{0.60})$$
$$= \$1,000 \times 1.82212$$
$$= \$1,822.12$$

Comparing this future value with that if interest is compounded annually at 12% per year for five years, $1,000 $(1 + 0.12)^5 = \$1,762.34$, we see the effects of this extreme frequency of compounding.

This process of growing proportionately, at every instant, to the magnitude at that instant, some people call a logarithmic rate of growing. Unit logarithmic rate of growth is that rate which in unit time will cause 1 to grow to 2.718281.

It might also be called the organic rate of growing: because it is characteristic of organic growth (in certain circumstances) that the increment of the organism in a given time is proportional to the magnitude of the organism itself.

—Silvanus P. Thompson, *Calculus Made Easy*
(London: MacMillan and Co. Limited, 1914), p. 140

 TRY IT! FREQUENCY OF COMPOUNDING

If you deposit $100 in a saving account today that pays 2% interest per year, how much will you have in the account at the end of 10 years if interest is compounded:

a. annually?
b. quarterly?
c. continuously?

Multiple Rates

In our discussion thus far, we have assumed that the investment will earn the same periodic interest rate, i. We can extend the calculation of a future value to allow for different interest rates or growth rates for different periods.

Suppose an investment of $10,000 pays 5% during the first year and 4% during the second year. At the end of the first period, the value of the investment is $10,000 (1 + 0.05), or $10,500. During the second period, this $10,500 earns interest at 4%. Therefore, the future value of this $10,000 at the end of the second period is

$$FV = \$10,000\,(1 + 0.05)\,(1 + 0.4) = \$10,920$$

We can write this more generally as:

$$FV = PV(1 + i_1)(1 + i_2)(1 + i_3)\ldots(1 + i_N) \tag{10.4}$$

where i_N is the interest rate for period N.

EXAMPLE 10.3: DIFFERENT INTEREST RATES FOR DIFFERENT PERIODS

Consider a $50,000 investment in a one-year bank *certificate of deposit* (CD) today and rolled over annually for the next two years into one-year CDs. The future value of the $50,000 investment will depend on the one-year CD rate each time the funds are rolled over. Assume that the one-year CD rate today is 5% and that it is expected that the one-year CD rate one year from now will be 6%, and the one-year CD rate two years from now will be 6.5%.

  a. What is the future value of this investment at the end of three years?
  b. What is the average annual return on your CD investment?

Solution

  a. $FV = \$50,000(1 + 0.05)(1 + 0.06)(1 + 0.065) = \$59,267.25$

  b. $i = \sqrt[3]{\dfrac{\$59,267.25}{\$50,000}} - 1 = 5.8315\%$

CALCULATING A PRESENT VALUE

Now that we understand how to compute future values, let's work the process in reverse. Suppose that for borrowing a specific amount of money today, the Trustworthy Company promises to pay lenders $5,000 two years from today. How much should the lenders be willing to lend Trustworthy in exchange for this promise? This dilemma is different than calculating a future value. Here we are given the future value and have to calculate the present value. But we can use the same basic idea from the future value problems to solve present value problems.

If you can earn 5% on other investments that have the same amount of uncertainty as the $5,000 Trustworthy promises to pay, then:

- The future value, $FV = \$5,000$.
- The number of compounding periods, $N = 2$.
- The interest rate, $i = 5\%$.

We also know the basic relation between the present and future values:

$$FV = PV(1 + i)^N$$

Substituting the known values into this equation:

$$\$5,000 = PV(1 + 0.05)^2$$

To determine how much you are willing to lend now, PV, to get $5,000 one year from now, FV, requires solving this equation for the unknown present value:

$$FV = PV(1 + i)^N$$
$$\$5,000 = PV(1 + 0.05)^2$$

Therefore, you would be willing to lend $4,535.15 to receive $5,000 one year from today if your opportunity cost is 5%. We can check our work by reworking the problem from the reverse perspective. Suppose you invested $4,535.15 for two years and it earned 5% per year. What is the value of this investment at the end of the year?

We know: $PV = \$4,535.15.25$, $N = 5\%$ or 0.05, and $i = 2$. Therefore, the future value is $5,000:

$$FV = PV(1 + i)^N = \$4,535.15(1 + 0.05)^2 = \$5,000.00$$

Compounding translates a value in one point in time into a value at some future point in time. The opposite process translates future values into present values: Discounting translates a value back in time. From the basic valuation equation,

$$FV = PV(1 + i)^N$$

we divide both sides by $(1 + i)^N$ and exchange sides to get the present value,

$$PV = \frac{FV}{(1 + i)^N} = FV\left(\frac{1}{1 + i}\right)^N = FV\left[\frac{1}{(1 + i)^N}\right] \qquad (10.5)$$

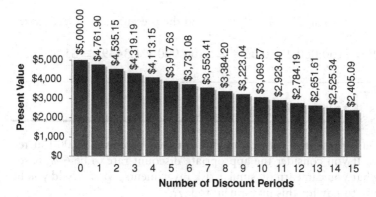

EXHIBIT 10.3 Present Value of $5,000 for 0 to 15 Periods, at a Discount Rate of 5% per Period

In the right-most form, the term in square brackets is referred to as the *discount factor* since it is used to translate a future value to its equivalent present value. We can restate our problem as:

$$PV = \frac{\$5,000}{(1+0.05)^2} = \$5,000 \left[\frac{1}{(1+0.05)^2} \right] = \$5,000 \times 0.90703$$
$$= \$4,535.15,$$

where the discount factor is 0.90703. We provide the present value of $5,000 for discount periods ranging from 0 to 15 in Exhibit 10.3.

We can also calculate this present using a calculator or a spreadsheet. Consider the present value of the $5,000 at 5% for ten years:

Hewlett-Packard 10B	Texas Instruments 83/84	Microsoft Excel
5000 FV	N = 10	=PV(.05,10,0,5000)
10 N	FV = 5000	
5 I/YR	I% = 5	
PV	Place cursor at I% = and then SOLVE	

If the frequency of compounding is greater than once a year, we make adjustments to the rate per period and the number of periods as we did in compounding. For example, if the future value five years from today is $100,000 and the interest is 6% per year, compounded semiannually,

$i = 6\% \div 2 = 3\%$, $N = 5 \times 2 = 10$, and the present value is $134,392:

$$PV = \$100{,}000(1 + 0.03)^{10} = \$100{,}000 \times 1.34392 = \$134{,}392$$

TRY IT! PRESENT VALUE

You are presented with an investment that promises $1,000 in ten years. If you consider the appropriate discount rate to be 6%, based on what you can earn on similar risk investments, what would you be willing to pay for this investment today?

EXAMPLE 10.4: MEETING A SAVINGS GOAL

Suppose that the goal is to have $75,000 in an account by the end of four years. And suppose that interest on this account is paid at a rate of 5% per year, compounded semiannually. How much must be deposited in the account today to reach this goal?

Solution

We are given $FV = \$75{,}000$, $i = 5\% \times 2 = 2.5\%$ per six months, and $N = 4 \times 2 = 8$ six-month periods. Therefore, the amount of the required deposit is:

$$PV = \frac{\$75{,}000}{(1 + 0.025)^8} = \$61{,}555.99$$

DETERMINING THE UNKNOWN INTEREST RATE

As we saw earlier in our discussion of growth rates, we can rearrange the basic equation to solve for i:

$$i = \sqrt[N]{\frac{FV}{PV}} - 1$$

which is the same as:

$$i = (FV/PV)^{1/N} - 1$$

As an example, suppose that the value of an investment today is $2,000 and the expected value of the investment in five years $3,000. What is the annual rate of appreciation in value of this investment over the five-year period?

$$i = \sqrt[5]{\frac{\$3,000}{\$2,000}} - 1 = 8.447\%$$

There are many applications in finance where it is necessary to determine the rate of change in values over a period of time. If values are increasing over time, we refer to the rate of change as the growth rate. To make comparisons easier, we usually specify the growth rate as a rate per year.

EXAMPLE 10.5: INTEREST RATES

Consider the growth rate of dividends for General Electric. General Electric pays dividends each year. In 1996, for example, General Electric paid dividends of $0.317 per share of its common stock, whereas in 2006 the company paid $1.03 in dividends per share in 2006.

Solution

This represents a growth rate of 12.507%:

$$i = \sqrt[10]{\frac{\$1.03}{\$0.317}} - 1 = 12.507\%$$

THE TIME VALUE OF A SERIES OF CASH FLOWS

Applications in finance may require determining the present or future value of a series of cash flows rather than simply a single cash flow. The principles of determining the future value or present value of a series of cash flows are the same as for a single cash flow, yet the math becomes a bit more cumbersome.

Suppose that the following deposits are made in a Thrifty Savings and Loan account paying 5% interest, compounded annually:

Period	End of Period Cash Flow
0	$1,000
1	$2,000
2	$1,500

What is the balance in the savings account at the end of the second year if there are no withdrawals and interest is paid annually?

Let's simplify any problem like this by referring to today as the end of period 0, and identifying the end of the first and each successive period as 1, 2, 3, and so on. Represent each end-of-period cash flow as CF with a subscript specifying the period to which it corresponds. Thus, CF_0 is a cash flow today, CF_{10} is a cash flow at the end of period 10, and CF_{25} is a cash flow at the end of period 25, and so on. In our example, CF_0 is $1,000, CF_1 is $2,000, and CF_2 is $1,500.

Representing the information in our example using cash flow and period notation:

$$FV = CF_0(1+i)^2 + CF_1(1+i)^1 + CF_2(1+i)^0$$

It is important to get the compounding correct. For example, there is no compounding of the cash flow that occurs at the end of the second period to arrive at a future value at the end of the second period. Hence, the factor is $(1+i)^0 = 1$.

We can represent these cash flows in a time line in Exhibit 10.4 to help graphically depict and sort out each cash flow in a series. From this example, you can see that the future value of the entire series is the sum of each of the

EXHIBIT 10.4 Time Line for the Future Value of a Series of Uneven Cash Flows Deposited to Earn 5% Compound Interest per Period

0	1	2
$1,000.00	$2,000.00	$1,500.00
	↳ $2,000 (1 + 0.05) =	2,100.00
↳ $1,000.00 (1 + 0.05)^2 =		1,102.50
		$4,702.50

compounded cash flows comprising the series. In much the same way, we can determine the future value of a series comprising any number of cash flows. And if we need to, we can determine the future value of a number of cash flows before the end of the series.

To determine the present value of a series of future cash flows, each cash flow is discounted back to the present, where we designate the beginning of the first period, today, as 0. As an example, consider the Thrifty Savings & Loan problem from a different angle. Instead of calculating what the deposits and the interest on these deposits will be worth in the future, let's calculate the present value of the deposits. The present value is what these future deposits are worth today.

Suppose you are promised the following cash flows:

Period	Cash Flow	End of Period Cash Flow
0	CF_0	$1,000
1	CF_1	$2,000
2	CF_2	$1,500

What is the present value of these cash flows—that is, at the end of period 0—if the discount rate is 5%? We would use the same method that we used in the previous problem—just backwards. We show this in Exhibit 10.5. As you can see in this exhibit, we don't discount the cash flow that occurs today. We discount the first period's cash flow one period, and discount the second period's cash flow two periods.

EXHIBIT 10.5 Time Line for the Present Value of a Series of Uneven Cash Flows Deposited to Earn 5% Compounded Interest per Period

0	1	2
$1,000.00	$2,000.00	$1,500.00
1,904.76	$\dfrac{\$2,000}{(1+0.05)}$ ⏎	
1,360.54		$\dfrac{\$1,500}{(1+0.05)^2}$ ⏎
$4,265.30		

You may also notice a relation between the future value that we calculated in Exhibit 10.4 and the present value that we calculated in Exhibit 10.5, with both examples using the same set of cash flows and same interest rate—just going in different directions:

$$\$4,265.30\,(1 + 0.05)^2 = \$4,702.50$$

Gettin' Fancy

We can represent the future value of a series of cash flows as:

$$FV = \sum_{t=0}^{N} CF_t(1 + i)^{N-t} \tag{10.6}$$

This, simply, means that the future value of a series of cash flows is the sum of the future value of each cash flow, where each of the future value considers the amount of the cash flow and the number of compounding period. Therefore, if there are 10 periods, the cash flow from occurring at the end of the sixth period, CF_6, would have interest compounded $N - t = 10 - 6 = 4$ periods, and the cash flow occurring at the end of the tenth period would not have any compounding.

And, likewise, we can represent the present value of a series using summation notation as:

$$PV = \sum_{t=0}^{N} \frac{CF_t}{(1 + i)^t} \tag{10.7}$$

with a similar explanation. For example, the cash flow occurring at the end of the fifth period is discounted five periods at the discount rate of i.

Multiple Rates

In our illustrations thus far, we have used one interest rate to compute the present value of all cash flows in a series. However, there is no reason that one interest rate must be used. For example, suppose that the cash flow is the same as used earlier: $1,000 today, $2,000 at the end of period 1, and $1,500 at the end of period 2. Now, instead of assuming that a 5% interest rate can be earned if a sum is invested today until the end of period 1 and the end of period 2, it is assumed that an amount invested today for one period can earn 5% but an amount invested today for two periods can earn 6%.

In this case, the calculation of the present value of the cash flow at the end of period 1 (the $2,000) is obtained in the same way as before: computing the present value using an interest rate of 5%. However, we

EXHIBIT 10.6 Time Line for the Present Value of a Series of Uneven Cash Flows Deposited to Earn 5% Compounded Interest per Period

0	1	2
|	|	|
|	|	|
$1,000.00	$2,000.00	$1,500.00
1,904.76	$\dfrac{\$2,000}{(1+0.05)}$ ↙	
1,334.99		$\dfrac{\$1,500}{(1+0.06)^2}$ ↙
$4,239.75		

must calculate the present value for the cash flow at the end of period 2 (the $1,500) using an interest rate of 6%. We depict the present value calculation in Exhibit 10.6. As expected, the present value of the cash flows is less than a 5% interest rate is assumed to be earned for two periods ($4,239.75 versus $4,265.39).

Although in many illustrations and applications throughout this book we will assume a single interest rate for determining the present value of a series of cash flows, in many real-world applications multiple interest rates are used. This is because in real-world financial markets the interest rate that can be earned depends on the amount of time the investment is expected to be outstanding. Typically, there is a positive relationship between interest rates and the length of time the investment must be held. The relationship between interest rates on investments and the length of time the investment must be held is called the yield curve.

The formula for the present value of a series of cash flows when there is a different interest rate is a simple modification of the single interest rate case. In the formula, i is replaced by i with a subscript to denote the period, i_t. That is,

$$PV = \sum_{t=0}^{N} \frac{CF_t}{(1+i_t)^t}$$

ANNUITIES

There are valuation problems that require us to evaluate a series of level cash flows—each cash flow is the same amount as the others—received at regular intervals. Let's suppose you expect to deposit $2,000 at the end of

EXHIBIT 10.7 Time Line for a Series of Even Cash Flows Deposited to Earn 5% Interest per Period

A: Future Value

0	1	2	3	4
	$2,000.00	$2,000.00	$2,000.00	$2,000.00
				2,100.00
				2,205.00
				2,315.25
				$8,620.25

B: Present Value

0	1	2	3	4
	$2,000.00	$2,000.00	$2,000.00	$2,000.00
$1,904.76				
1,814.06				
1,727.68				
1,645.40				
$7,091.90				

each of the next four years in an account earning 8% compounded interest. How much will you have available at the end of the fourth year?

As we just did for the future value of a series of uneven cash flows, we can calculate the future value (as of the end of the fourth year) of each $2,000 deposit, compounding interest at 5%, as we show in Exhibit 10.7. The future value of this series is $8,620.25. Modifying the future value of a series equation to reflect that all of the cash flows are the same,

$$FV = \sum_{t=0}^{N} CF(1+i)^{N-t} = CF \sum_{t=0}^{N} (1+i)^{N-t} \qquad (10.8)$$

A series of cash flows of equal amount, occurring at even intervals is referred to as an *annuity*. Determining the value of an annuity, whether compounding or discounting, is simpler than valuing uneven cash flows.

Consider the same series of $2,000 for four periods, but calculate the present value of the series. We show this calculation in Panel B of Exhibit 10.7. The present value of this series is $7,091.90.

EXAMPLE 10.6: FUTURE VALUE OF AN ANNUITY

Suppose you wish to determine the future value of a series of deposits of $1,000, deposited each year in the No Fault Vault Bank for five years, with the first deposit made at the end of the first year. If the NFV Bank pays 5% interest on the balance in the account at the end of each year and no withdrawals are made, what is the balance in the account at the end of the five years?

Solution

In equation form,

$$FV = \$1,000 \sum_{t=1}^{5} (1 + 0.05)^{N-t} = \$1,000(5.5263) = \$5,525.63$$

Summing the individual future values:

Cash Flow	Amount	Future Value
CF_1	$1,000	$1,215.51
CF_2	$1,000	1,157.63
CF_3	$1,000	1,102.50
CF_4	$1,000	1,050.00
CF_5	$1,000	1.000.00
	Total	$5,525.63

Calculator and spreadsheet inputs:

Periodic payment = PMT = 1,000

i = 5% (input as 5 for calculator, 0.05 for spreadsheet)

N = 5

Solve for FV

As we did with the future value of an even series, we can simplify the equation for the present value of a series of level cash flows beginning after one period as:

$$PV = \sum_{t=0}^{N} \frac{CF}{(1+i)^t} = CF \sum_{t=0}^{N} \frac{1}{(1+i)^t} \qquad (10.9)$$

EXHIBIT 10.8 Time Line for a Series of Even Cash Flows Deposited to Earn 4% Interest per Period

A: Future Value of the Ordinary Annuity

0	1	2	3	4
	$500.00	$500.00	$500.00	$500.00
			↪	520.00
		↪		540.80
	↪			562.43
				$2,123.23

B: Future Value of the Annuity Due

0	1	2	3	4
$500.00	$500.00	$500.00	$500.00	
			↪	$520.00
		↪		540.80
	↪			562.43
				584.93
				$2,208.16

Another way of looking at this is that the present value of an annuity is equal to the amount of one cash flow multiplied by the sum of the discount factors.

If the cash flows occur at the end of each period (that is, the first cash flow occurs one period from today), we refer to this as an *ordinary annuity*. The two examples that we provide in Exhibit 10.8 are both ordinary annuities.

EXAMPLE 10.7: PRESENT VALUE OF AN ANNUITY

Consider a five-payment annuity, with payments of $500 at the end of each of the next five years.

a. If the appropriate discount rate is 4%, what is the present value of this annuity?
b. If the appropriate discount rate is 5%, what is the present value of this annuity?

Solution

  a. Given: $PMT = \$500; i = 4\%; N = 5$. Solve for PV. $PV = \$2,225.91$
  b. Given: $PMT = \$500, i = 4\%, N = 5$. Solve for PV. $PV = \$2,164.74$

Note: The higher the discount rate, the lower the present value of the annuity.

Equations (10.8) and (10.9) are the valuation—future and present value—formulas for an ordinary annuity. An ordinary annuity is therefore a special form of annuity, where the first cash flow occurs at the end of the first period.

This annuity short-cut is built into financial calculators and spreadsheet functions. For example, in the case of the present value of the four-payment ordinary annuity of $2,000 at 5%:

Hewlett-Packard 10B	Texas Instruments 83/84	Microsoft Excel
2000 PMT	N = 4	=PV(.05,4,2000,0)
4 N	I% = 5	
5 I/YR	PMT = 2000	
PV	FV = 0	
	Place cursor at PV = *and then* SOLVE	

Valuing a Perpetuity

There are some circumstances where cash flows are expected to continue forever. For example, a corporation may promise to pay dividends on preferred stock forever, or, a company may issue a bond that pays interest every six months, forever. How do you value these cash flow streams? Recall that when we calculated the present value of an annuity, we took the amount of one cash flow and multiplied it by the sum of the discount factors that corresponded to the interest rate and number of payments. But what if the number of payments extends forever—into infinity?

A series of cash flows that occur at regular intervals, forever, is a *perpetuity*. Valuing a perpetual cash flow stream is just like valuing an ordinary annuity, but the N is replaced by ∞:

$$PV = CF \sum_{t=1}^{\infty} \left(\frac{1}{1+i} \right)^t$$

As the number of discounting periods approaches infinity, the summation approaches $1/i$, so:

$$PV = \frac{CF}{i} \tag{10.10}$$

Suppose you are considering an investment that promises to pay $100 each period forever, and the interest rate you can earn on alternative investments of similar risk is 5% per period. What are you willing to pay today for this investment?

$$PV = \frac{\$100}{0.05} = \$2,000$$

Therefore, you would be willing to pay $2,000 today for this investment to receive, in return, the promise of $100 each period forever.

EXAMPLE 10.8: PERPETUITY

Suppose that you are given the opportunity to purchase an investment for $5,000 that promises to pay $50 at the end of every period forever. What is the periodic interest per period—the return—associated with this investment?

Solution

We know that the present value is $PV = \$5,000$ and the periodic, perpetual payment is $CF = \$50$. Inserting these values into the formula for the present value of a perpetuity,

$$\$5,000 = \frac{\$50}{i}$$

Solving for i, $CF = \$50$, $i = 0.01$ or 1%. Therefore, an investment of $5,000 that generates $50 per period provides 1% compounded interest per period.

Valuing an Annuity Due

In the ordinary annuity cash flow analysis, we assume that cash flows occur at the end of each period. However, there is another fairly common cash flow pattern in which level cash flows occur at regular intervals, but the first cash flow occurs immediately. This pattern of cash flows is called an *annuity due*. For example, if you win the Mega Millions grand prize, you will receive your winnings in 20 installments (after taxes, of course). The 20 installments are paid out annually, beginning immediately. The lottery winnings are therefore an annuity due.

Like the cash flows we have considered thus far, the future value of an annuity due can be determined by calculating the future value of each cash flow and summing them. And, the present value of an annuity due is determined in the same way as a present value of any stream of cash flows.

Let's consider first an example of the future value of an annuity due, comparing the values of an ordinary annuity and an annuity due, each comprising four cash flows of $500, compounded at the interest rate of 4% per period. We show the calculation of the future value of both the ordinary annuity and the annuity due at the end of three periods in Exhibit 10.8. You will notice that the future value of the annuity due is $1 + i$ multiplied by the future value of the ordinary annuity. This is because each cash flow earns interest for one more periods in the case of the annuity due.

The present value of the annuity due is calculated in a similar manner, adjusting the ordinary annuity formula for the different number of discount periods. Because the cash flows in the annuity due situation are each discounted one less period than the corresponding cash flows in the ordinary annuity, the present value of the annuity due is greater than the present value of the ordinary annuity for an equivalent amount and number of cash flows. We show this in Exhibit 10.9 for the same four-payment, $500 annuity, but this time we compare the present value of the ordinary annuity with the present value of the annuity due.

You will notice that there is one more period of discounting for each cash flow in the ordinary annuity, as compared to the annuity due. Therefore, the present value of the annuity due is equal to the present value of the ordinary annuity multiplied by $1 + i$; that is, $1,814.95 $(1 + 0.04) =$ $1,887.55.

Calculating the value of an annuity due using a calculator or a spreadsheet is similar to that of the ordinary annuity, but with one small difference. With calculators, you need to change the mode to the "due" or "begin" mode. For example, when calculating the present value of the four-payment, $500 annuity with the HP10B calculator,

EXHIBIT 10.9 Time Line for a Series of Even Cash Flows Deposited to Earn 4% Interest per Period

A: Present Value of the Ordinary Annuity

0	1	2	3	4
	$500.00	$500.00	$500.00	$500.00
$480.77				
462.28				
444.50				
427.40				
$1,814.95				

B: Present Value of the Annuity Due

0	1	2	3	4
$500.00	$500.00	$500.00	$500.00	
480.77				
462.28				
444.50				
$1,887.55				

Ordinary Annuity	Annuity Due
PMT = 500	PMT = 500
i = 4	i = 4
N = 4	N = 4
END mode	BEG mode

Using spreadsheets, the only difference is the last argument in the function (0 or nothing for an ordinary annuity, 1 for an annuity due):

Ordinary Annuity	Annuity Due
=PV(0.04,4,500,0,0)	=PV(0.04,4,500,0,1)

Valuing a Deferred Annuity

A *deferred annuity* has a stream of cash flows of equal amounts at regular periods starting at some time after the end of the first period. When we calculated the present value of an annuity, we brought a series of cash flows back to the beginning of the first period—or, equivalently the end of the period 0. With a deferred annuity, we determine the present value of the ordinary annuity and then discount this present value to an earlier period.

Suppose you want to deposit an amount today in an account such that you can withdraw $100 per year for three years, with the first withdrawal occurring three years from today. We diagram this set of cash flows in Panel A of Exhibit 10.9.

We can solve this problem in two steps:

Step 1: Solve for the present value of the withdrawals.

Step 2: Discount this present value to the present.

The first step requires determining the present value of a three-cash-flow ordinary annuity of $100. This calculation provides the present value as of the end of the second year (one period prior to the first withdrawal), using an ordinary annuity. Based on this calculation (present value of an ordinary annuity, $N = 3$, $i = 5\%$, $PMT = \$100$), you need $272.32 in the account at the end of the second period in order to satisfy the three withdrawals. We show this in Panel B of Exhibit 10.9.[2]

The next step is to determine how much you need to deposit today to meet the savings goal of $272.32 at the end of the second year. The $272.32 is the future value, $N = 2$, and $i = 5\%$. Therefore, you need to deposit $247.01 today so that you will have $272.32 in two years, so that you can then begin to make withdrawals starting at the end of the third year. We show this in Panel C of Exhibit 10.9.

We can check our work by looking at the balance in the account at the end of each period, as we show in Panel D of Exhibit 10.9. If we have performed the calculations correctly, we should end up with a zero balance at the time of the last $100 withdrawal. Remember, the funds left in the account earn 5%. Therefore, for example, in the third period, you begin with $272.33 in the account. The account balance earns 5% or $13.62 of interest during the third year. This brings the balance in the account to

---

[2]We could have also solved this problem using an annuity due in the first step, which would mean that we would discount the value from the first step three periods instead of two.

$272.33 + 13.62 = \$285.95$. Once we remove the $100, the balance at the end of the third year is $185.95.

EXAMPLE 10.9: DEFERRED ANNUITY

Suppose you want to retire and be able to withdraw $40,000 per year each year for twenty years after your retirement. If you plan to stop deposits in your retirement account ten years prior to retirement, what is the balance that you must have in your retirement account ten years before you retire if you can earn 4% per year on your retirement investments?

Solution

Balance in the account one year before retirement is the present value of an ordinary annuity with:

$PMT = \$40,000$
$N = 20$
$i = 4\%$
Solve for PV. $PV_{\text{one year before retirement}} = \$543,613.05$

Balance needed ten years before retirement:

$$PV_{10 \text{ years before retirement}} = PV_{\text{one year before retirement}} \div (1 + 0.04)^9$$
$$= \$381,935.32$$

Deferred annuity problems can become more complex, such as determining a set of payments needed for some future goal. However, all deferred annuity problems can be solved easily by breaking down the problem into steps.[3]

LOAN AMORTIZATION

If an amount is loaned and then repaid in installments, we say that the loan is amortized. Therefore, *loan amortization* is the process of calculating

---

[3]Unfortunately, there are no calculator functions or spreadsheet functions that perform deferred annuity calculations specifically, because there are so many variations possible on how these are designed.

the loan payments that amortize the loaned amount. We can determine the amount of the loan payments once we know the frequency of payments, the interest rate, and the number of payments.

Consider a loan of $100,000. If the loan is repaid in four annual installments (at the end of each year) and the interest rate is 6% per year. The first thing we need to do is to calculate the amount of each payment. In other words, we need to solve for *CF*:

$$\$100,000 = \sum_{t=1}^{4} \frac{CF}{(1 + 0.06)^t}$$

We want to solve for the loan payment, that is, the amount of the annuity. The calculator and spreadsheet inputs for this calculation are:

$$PV = 100,000$$
$$i = 6\%$$
$$N = 4$$

and then solve for *PMT*. This is the *CF*, the loan payment.

The loan payment is $28,859.15. We can calculate the amount of interest and principal repayment associated with each loan payment using a loan amortization schedule, as we show in Panel A of Exhibit 10.10.

The loan payments are determined such that after the last payment is made there is no loan balance outstanding. Thus, the loan is referred to as a *fully amortizing loan*. You can see this in Panel B of Exhibit 10.3. Even though the loan payment each year is the same, the proportion of interest and principal differs with each payment: the interest is 5% of the principal amount of the loan that remains at the beginning of the period, whereas the principal repaid with each payment is the difference between the payment and the interest. As the payments are made, the remainder is applied to repayment of the principal. This is the scheduled principal repayment or the *amortization*. As the principal remaining on the loan declines, less interest is paid with each payment.

Loan amortization works the same whether this is a mortgage loan to purchase a home, a term loan, or any other loan such as an automobile loan in which the interest paid is determined on the basis of the remaining amount of the loan. You can modify the calculation of the loan amortization to suit different principal repayments, such as additional lump-sum payments, known as *balloon payments*. See Exhibit 10.11.

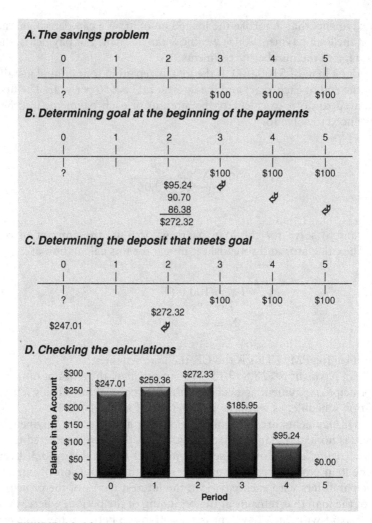

A. The savings problem

B. Determining goal at the beginning of the payments

C. Determining the deposit that meets goal

D. Checking the calculations

EXHIBIT 10.10 Deferred Annuity Time Lines for a Three-Period, $100 Annuity with the First Cash Flow Deferred Three Periods

INTEREST RATES AND YIELDS

Calculating the present or future value of a lump-sum or set of cash flows requires information on the timing of cash flows and the compound or discount rate. However, there are many applications in which we are presented with values and cash flows, and wish to calculate the yield or implied

A. Amortization of the loan

Year	Beginning balance of the loan outstanding	Payment	Interest = 6% × beginning balance of the loan	Principal repaid with payment = payment − interest	Remaining principal = beginning balance − principal repaid
1	$100,000.00	$28,859.15	$6,000.00	$22,859.15	$77,140.85
2	$77,140.85	$28,859.15	$4,628.45	$24,230.70	$52,910.15
3	$52,910.15	$28,859.15	$3,174.61	$25,684.54	$27,225.61
4	$27,225.61	$28,859.15	$1,633.54	$27,225.61	$0.00

B. Payoff of loan

EXHIBIT 10.11 Loan Amortization of a Four-Year $100,000 Loan, with an Interest Rate of 6%

interest rate associated with these values and cash flows. By calculating the yield or implied interest rate, we can then compare investment or financing opportunities.

Annual Percentage Rate vs. Effective Annual Rate

A common problem in finance is comparing alternative financing or investment opportunities when the interest rates are specified in a way that makes it difficult to compare terms. The Truth in Savings Act of 1991 requires institutions to provide the annual percentage yield for savings accounts. As a result of this law, consumers can compare the yields on different savings arrangements. But this law does not apply beyond savings accounts. One investment may pay 10% interest compounded semiannually, whereas another investment may pay 9% interest compounded daily. One financing arrangement may require interest compounding quarterly, whereas another may require interest compounding monthly.

Want to compare investments or financing with different frequencies of compounding? We must first translate the stated interest rates into a common basis. There are two ways to convert interest rates stated over different time intervals so that they have a common basis: the annual percentage rate and the effective annual interest rate.

One obvious way to represent rates stated in various time intervals on a common basis is to express them in the same unit of time—so we annualize them. The annualized rate is the product of the stated rate of interest per compound period and the number of compounding periods in a year. Let i be the rate of interest per period and n be the number of compounding periods in a year. The annualized rate, which is as we indicated earlier in this chapter also referred to as the nominal interest rate or the annual percentage rate (APR), is

$$APR = i \times n \tag{10.11}$$

Another way of converting stated interest rates to a common basis is the effective rate of interest. The *effective annual rate (EAR)* is the true economic return for a given time period because it takes into account the compounding of interest. We also refer to this rate as the *effective rate of interest*. The formula is

$$EAR = (1 + i)n - 1 \tag{10.12}$$

Let's look how the EAR is affected by the compounding. Suppose that the Safe Savings and Loan promises to pay 2% interest on accounts, compounded annually. Because interest is paid once, at the end of the year, the effective annual return, EAR, is 2%. If the 2% interest is paid on a semi-annual basis—1% every six months—the effective annual return is larger than 2% since interest is earned on the 1% interest earned at the end of the first six months. In this case, to calculate the EAR, the interest rate per compounding period—six months—is 0.01 (that is, $0.02 \div 2$) and the number of compounding periods in an annual period is 2:

$$EAR = (1 + 0.01)^2 - 1 = 1.0201 - 1 = 0.0201 \text{ or } 2.01\%$$

In the case of continuous compounding, the EAR is simply:

$$EAR_{\text{continuous compounding}} = e^{APR} - 1 \tag{10.13}$$

Extending this example to the case of quarterly compounding and continuous compounding with a nominal interest rate of 2%, we first calculate the interest rate per period, i, and the number of compounding periods in a year, n:

Frequency of Compounding	Calculation	Effective Annual Rate
Annual	$(1 + 0.02)^1 - 1$	2.00%
Semiannual	$(1 + 0.01)^2 - 1$	2.01%
Quarterly	$(1 + 0.005)^4 - 1$	2.02%
Continuous	$e^{0.02} - 1$	2.02%

Figuring out the effective annual rate is useful when comparing interest rates for different investments. It doesn't make sense to compare the APRs for different investments having a different frequency of compounding within a year. But since many investments have returns stated in terms of APRs, we need to understand how to work with them.

To illustrate how to calculate effective annual rates, consider the rates offered by two banks, Bank A and Bank B. Bank A offers 4.2% compounded semiannually and Bank B other offers 4.158% compounded continuously. We can compare these rates using the *EAR*s. Which bank offers the highest interest rate? The effective annual rate for Bank A is $(1 + 0.021)^2 - 1 = 4.2441\%$. The effective annual rate for Bank B is $e^{0.04158} - 1 = 4.2457\%$. Therefore, Bank B offers a slightly higher interest rate.

Yields on Investments

Suppose an investment opportunity requires an investor to put up $10,000 million and offers cash inflows of $4,000 after one year and $7,000 after two years. The return on this investment, or *yield*, is the interest rate that equates the present values of the $4,000 and $7,000 cash inflows to equal the present value of the $1 million cash outflow. This yield is also referred to as the *internal rate of return (IRR)* and is calculated as the rate that solves the following:

$$\$10,000 = \frac{\$4,000}{(1 + IRR)^1} + \frac{\$7,000}{(1 + IRR)^2}$$

Unfortunately, there is no direct mathematical solution (that is, closed-form solution) for the *IRR*, but rather we must use an iterative procedure. Fortunately, financial calculators and financial software ease our burden in this calculation. The *IRR* that solves this equation is 6.023%. In other words, if you invest $10,000 today and receive $4,000 in one year and $7,000 in two years, the return on your investment is 6.023%.

Another way of looking at this same yield is to consider that an investment's *IRR* is the interest rate that makes the present value of all expected future cash flows—both the cash outflows for the investment and the subsequent inflows—equal to zero. We can represent the IRR as the rate that solves

$$\$0 = \sum_{t=0}^{N} \frac{CF_t}{(1 + IRR)^t}$$

We can use a calculator or a spreadsheet to solve for *IRR*. To do this, however, we must enter the series of cash flows in a manner that can be used with the appropriate function. Consider the problem with the present value of $10,000 and cash flows of $4,000 and $7,000. The financial routines require that the cash flows be entered in chronological order, and then the IRR function be used with these cash flows.[4]

Hewlett-Packard 10B	Texas Instruments 83/84	Microsoft Excel	
10000 +/− CFj	{4000,7000} →		A
4000 CFj	STO L1	1	− 10000
7000 CFj	IRR(− 10000,L1)	2	4000
IRR		3	7000
		4	= IRR(A1:A3)

EXAMPLE 10.10: CALCULATING A YIELD

Suppose an investment of $1 million produces no cash flow in the first year but cash flows of $200,000, $300,000, and $900,000 two, three, and four years from now, respectively. What is the return on this investment?

---

[4]If there is no cash flow for a given period, both the calculators and the spreadsheets require you to enter a zero in place of that cash flow; failing to do so will result in an incorrect *IRR*.

Solution

The *IRR* for this investment is the interest rate that solves:

$$\$1,000,000 = \frac{\$200,000}{(1 + IRR)^2} + \frac{\$300,000}{(1 + IRR)^3} + \frac{\$900,000}{(1 + IRR)^4}$$

The return is 10.172%.

We can use this approach to calculate the yield on any type of investment, as long as we know the cash flows—both positive and negative—and the timing of these flows. Consider the case of the yield to maturity on a bond. Most bonds pay interest semiannually—that is, every six months. Therefore, when calculating the yield on a bond, we must consider the timing of the cash flows to be such that the discount period is six months.

 TRY IT! THE YIELD ON AN INVESTMENT

Suppose you invest $1,000 today in an investment that promises you $1,000 in two years and $10,000 in three years. What is the *IRR* on this investment?

EXAMPLE 10.11: CALCULATING THE YIELD ON A BOND

Consider a bond that has a current price of 90; that is, if the par value of the bond is $1,000, the bond's price is 90% of $1,000 or $900. And suppose that this bond has five years remaining to maturity and an 8% coupon rate. With five years remaining to maturity, the bond has 10 six-month periods remaining.

(continued)

(Continued)

Solution

With a coupon rate of 8%, this means that the cash flows for interest is $40 every six months. For a given bond, we therefore have the following information:

Present value = $900

Number of periods to maturity = 10

Cash flow every six months = $40

Additional cash flow at maturity = $1,000

The six-month yield, r_d, is the discount rate that solves:

$$\$900 = \left[\sum_{t=1}^{10} \frac{\$40}{(1 + r_d)^t} \right] + \frac{\$1,000}{(1 + r_d)^{10}}$$

Using a calculator or spreadsheet, we calculate the six-month yield as 5.315% [PV = $900; N = '10; PMT = $40; FV = $1,000]. Bond yields are generally stated on the basis of an annualized yield, referred to as the *yield to maturity* on a bond-equivalent basis. This measure is analogous to the *APR* with semiannual compounding. Therefore, yield to maturity is 10.63%.

THE BOTTOM LINE

- The time value of money is one of the foundation concepts and tools in financial and investment management.
- Using compound interest, we can estimate a value of in the future; using discounting, we can translate a future value into a value today—a present value.
- It is important to consider the type of interest—compounding vs. simple—and the frequency of compounding in determining a present value of a future value.
- The time value of money mathematics can be used to determine the present value or future value of a lump-sum amount or of a series of cash flows, the growth rate of values, the number of periods of interest to meet a goal, or to simply amortize a loan.

■ Given the cost of an investment and its cash flows, we can calculate the yield or implied interest rate. By calculating the yield or implied interest rate, we can then compare investment or financing opportunities. The yield or internal rate of return on an investment is the interest rate at which the present value of the cash flows equals the initial investment outlay.

SOLUTIONS TO TRY IT! PROBLEMS

Future Value

a. $FV = \$100 \ (1 + 0.02)^5 = \$110.41$
b. $FV = \$100 \ (1 + 0.02)^{10} = \$121.90$
c. $FV = \$100 \ (1 + 0.02)^{20} = \$148.59$

Growth Rates

$PV = \$2,000; FV = \$4,000; N = 5$ Solve for i. $i = 14.87\%$

More Growth Rates

Present Value	Future Value	Number of Periods	Growth Rate
$1	$3	6	20.094%
$1000	$2000	9	8.006%
$500	$600	7	2.639%
$1	$1.50	4	10.668%

Frequency of Compounding

a. $\$100 \ (1 + 0.02)^{10} = \$121.899$
b. $\$100 \ (1 + 0.005)^{40} = \$122.079$
c. $\$100 \ e^{0.2} = \$122.140$

Present Value

$PV = \$1,000 \div (1 + 0.06)10 = \$558.39$

The Yield on an Investment

Cash flows are $-\$10,000, \$0, \$1,000$ and $\$10,000$. The yield is 3.332%

QUESTIONS

1. What is the relationship between compounding and discounting of a lump-sum?
2. Complete the following: "The larger the interest rate, the_____ (larger/smaller) the future value of a value today."
3. Holding everything else the same, what is the effect of using a higher discount rate to discount a future value to the present?
4. If you invest the same amount in each of three accounts today, which account produces the highest future value if the annual percentage rate is the same? Account A: annual compounding, Account B: quarterly compounding, Account C: continuous compounding.
5. What distinguishes an ordinary annuity from an annuity due?
6. What distinguishes an ordinary annuity from a deferred annuity?
7. If a cash flow is the same amount each period, *ad infinitum*, how do we value the present value of this series of cash flows?
8. Which is most appropriate to use in describing the annual growth of the value of an investment: the arithmetic average growth rate or the geometric average growth rate? Why?
9. How can we break down the valuation of a deferred annuity into manageable parts for computation purposes?
10. Which has the highest present value if the payments and number of payments are identical, an ordinary annuity or an annuity due?
11. If you are offered two investments, one that pays 5% simple interest per year and one that pays 5% compound interest per year, which would you choose? Why?
12. Consider a borrowing arrangement in which the annual percentage rate (APR) is 8%.
    a. Under what conditions does the effective annual rate of interest (EAR) differ from the APR of 8%?
    b. As the frequency of compounding increases within the annual period, what happens to the relationship between the EAR and the APR?
13. Suppose you deposit $1,000 in an account with an APR of 4%, with compounding quarterly.
    a. After 10 years, what is the balance in the account if you make no withdrawals?
    b. After 10 years, how much interest on interest did you earn?
14. Suppose you are promised $10,000 five years from today. If the appropriate discount rate is 6%, what is this $10,000 worth to you today?

15. Suppose you buy a car today and finance $10,000 of its cost at an APR of 3%, with payments made monthly.
    a. If you finance the car for 24 months, what is the amount of your monthly car payment?
    b. If you finance the car for 36 months, what is the amount of your monthly car payment?

CHAPTER 11

Financial Ratio Analysis

A man who keeps all his property in the form of cash and government bonds has comparatively little to worry or think about; but on the other hand, he is not using his resources productively. As the same man proceeds with the development of some business enterprise, he puts more and more of his capital into the various forms of tangible and intangible assets which are required for the upbuilding of the business. Presently, if he is not careful, he may find himself short of cash and unable to meet his obligations, although he may be earning good profits.

The same tendency is present everywhere. The executives who are managing the financial affairs of a company cannot assist in making the business profitable merely by piling up unnecessary cash resources. They must be prepared to venture out into the main current of business affairs along with their associates. And as they venture farther and farther, the danger increases that their financial craft may be swept out of their control. It requires constant watchfulness and sound knowledge to steer a middle course between excessive caution on the one side and rashness in financial management on the other.

—William H. Lough, *Business Finance*
(New York: The Ronald Press Company, 1919), p. 500

Financial analysis involves the selection, evaluation, and interpretation of financial data and other pertinent information to assist in evaluating the operating performance and financial condition of a company. The information that is available for analysis includes economic, market, and financial information. But some of the most important financial data are provided by the company in its annual and quarterly financial statements.

The operating performance of a company is a measure of how well a company has used its resources to produce a return on its investment. The financial condition of a company is a measure of its ability to satisfy its obligations, such as the payment of interest on its debt in a timely manner. An investor has many tools available in the analysis of financial information. These tools include financial ratio analysis and cash flow analysis. Cash flows provide a way of transforming net income based on an accrual system to a more comparable basis. Additionally, cash flows are essential ingredients in valuation because the value of a company today is the present value of its expected future cash flows. Therefore, understanding past and current cash flows may help in forecasting future cash flows and, hence, determine the value of the company. Moreover, understanding cash flow allows the assessment of the ability of a company to maintain current dividends and its current capital expenditure policy without relying on external financing.

In this chapter and the next, we describe and illustrate the basic tools of financial analysis. In this chapter, our focus is on financial ratio analysis. In the next chapter, we cover cash flow analysis.

CLASSIFYING FINANCIAL RATIOS

A financial ratio is a comparison between one bit of financial information and another. Consider the ratio of current assets to current liabilities, which we refer to as the *current ratio*. This ratio is a comparison between assets that can be readily turned into cash—current assets—and the obligations that are due in the near future—current liabilities. A current ratio of 2, or 2:1, means that we have twice as much in current assets as we need to satisfy obligations due in the near future.

We can classify ratios according to the way they are constructed and the financial characteristic they are describing. For example, we will see that the current ratio is constructed as a coverage ratio (i.e., the ratio of current assets—available funds—to current liabilities, i.e., the obligation) that we use to describe a company's liquidity (its ability to meet its immediate needs). We can also classify ratios according to the dimension of the company's performance or condition. For example, a current ratio provides information on a company's liquidity, whereas a turnover ratio provides information on the effectiveness to which the company puts its asset to use.

There are as many different financial ratios as there are possible combinations of items appearing on the income statement, balance sheet, and statement of cash flows. We can classify ratios according to the financial characteristic that they capture.

When we assess a company's operating performance, a concern is whether the company is applying its assets in an efficient and profitable manner. When an investor assesses a company's financial condition, a concern is whether the company is able to meet its financial obligations. The investor can use financial ratios to evaluate five aspects of operating performance and financial condition:

1. Liquidity
2. Profitability
3. Activity
4. Financial leverage
5. Return on investment

There are several ratios reflecting each of the five aspects of a company's operating performance and financial condition. We apply these ratios to the Exemplar Corporation, whose balance sheets, income statements, and statement of cash flows for two years we show in Exhibits 11.1, 11.2, and

EXHIBIT 11.1 Exemplar Corporation's Balance Sheets

	As of		
In Millions	Dec. 31, 20X2	Dec. 31, 20X1	Dec. 31, 20X0
Cash and cash equivalents	$110	$105	$100
Accounts receivable	200	250	175
Inventory	490	510	500
Total current assets	$800	$865	$775
Gross property, plant, and equipment	1,200	1,100	1,000
Accumulated depreciation	400	300	200
Net property, plant, and equipment	800	800	$800
Intangible assets	50	50	50
Goodwill	75	75	75
Total assets	$1,725	$1,790	$1,700
Accounts payable	$100	$90	$100
Current portion of long-term debt	30	25	20
Total current liabilities	$130	$115	$120
Long-term debt	163	319	$300
Common stock	$20	$20	$20
Paid-in capital in excess of par	100	100	100
Retained earnings	1,332	1,256	1,170
Treasury stock	20	20	10
Shareholders' equity	$1,432	$1,356	$1,280
Total liabilities and equity	$1,725	$1,790	$1,700

EXHIBIT 11.2 Exemplar Corporation's Income Statements

	For the Year Ending	
In Millions	Dec. 31, 20X2	Dec. 31, 20X1
Revenues	$2,000	$1,900
Cost of goods sold	1,600	1,500
Gross profit	$400	$400
Selling, general, and administrative expenses	200	180
Earnings before interest and taxes	$200	$220
Interest expense	17	16
Earnings before taxes	$183	$204
Taxes	73	82
Net income	$110	$122

11.3, respectively. We refer to the most recent fiscal year for which financial statements are available, FY20X2, as the "current year." The "prior year" is the fiscal year prior to the current year.

The ratios we introduce here are by no means the only ones that can be formed using financial data, though they are some of the more commonly

EXHIBIT 11.3 Exemplar Corporation's Statement of Cash Flows

	For the Year Ending	
In Millions	Dec. 31, 20X2	Dec. 31, 20X1
Net income	$110	$122
Add: depreciation expense	100	100
Changes in working capital accounts		
Accounts receivable	50	−75
Inventory	20	−10
Accounts payable	10	−10
Cash flow for/from operations	$290	$127
Capital expenditures	−$100	−$100
Sale of property, plant and equipment	0	0
Cash flow for/from investment	−$100	−$100
Borrowings	$0	$25
Repayments of debt	−152	0
Dividends	33	37
Repurchase of stock	0	10
Cash flow for/ from financing	−$185	−$22
Change in cash	$5	$5

used. Further, when we form a ratio using a balance sheet account, such as inventory, we are simplifying things a bit because in applying these ratios to evaluate a company's performance we could more appropriately use an average of that balance sheet account through the year in some cases, rather than the year-end value. However, our primary purpose in this chapter is to establish the basic concepts, definitions, and calculations in financial ratio analysis before getting too technical.

LIQUIDITY

Liquidity reflects the ability of a company to meet its short-term obligations using those assets that are most readily converted into cash. Assets that may be converted into cash in a short period of time are referred to as liquid assets; they are listed in financial statements as current assets. We often refer to current assets as *working capital*, because they represent the resources needed for the day-to-day operations of the company's long-term capital investments. Current assets are used to satisfy short-term obligations, or current liabilities. The amount by which current assets exceed current liabilities is referred to as the *net working capital*.

Operating Cycle

How much liquidity a company needs depends on its operating cycle. The *operating cycle* is the duration from the time cash is invested in goods and services to the time that investment produces cash.

What does the operating cycle have to do with liquidity? The longer the operating cycle, the more current assets are needed (relative to current liabilities) since it takes longer to convert inventories and receivables into cash. In other words, the longer the operating cycle, the greater the amount of net working capital required.

We can estimate the operating cycle for Exemplar Corporation for the current year using the balance sheet and income statement data. The number of days Exemplar ties up funds in inventory is determined by the total amount of money represented in inventory and the average day's cost of goods sold. The current investment in inventory—that is, the money "tied up" in inventory—is the ending balance of inventory on the balance sheet. The *average day's cost of goods sold* is the cost of goods sold on an average day in the year, which can be estimated by dividing the cost of goods sold (which is found on the income statement) by the number of days in the year:

$$\text{Average day's cost of goods sold} = \frac{\text{Cost of goods sold}}{365} \quad (11.1)$$

Exemplar's average day's cost of goods sold for FY20X2 is $1,600 ÷ 265 = $4.384 million per day.

Exemplar has $490 million of inventory on hand at the end of the year. How many days' worth of goods sold is this? One way to look at this is to imagine that Exemplar stopped buying more raw materials and just finished producing whatever was on hand in inventory, using available raw materials and work-in-process. How long would it take Exemplar to run out of inventory?

We compute the *days sales in inventory* (DSI), also known as the *number of days of inventory*, by calculating the ratio of the amount of inventory on hand (in dollars) to the average day's cost of goods sold (in dollars per day):

$$\text{Days sales in inventory (DSI)} = \frac{\text{Inventory}}{\text{Average day's cost of goods sold}} \quad (11.2)$$

For Exemplar, the DSI is $490 million ÷ $4.384 million = 111.78 days. In other words, Exemplar has approximately 112 days of goods on hand at the end of the current year. If sales continued at the same price, it would take Exemplar 112 days to run out of inventory.

We can extend the same logic for calculating the number of days between a sale—when an account receivable is created—and the time it is collected in cash. If we assume that Exemplar sells all goods on credit, we can first calculate the average credit sales per day and then calculate how many days' worth of credit sales are represented by the ending balance of receivables.

The *average credit sales per day* are the ratio of credit sales to the number of days in a year:

$$\text{Average credit sales per day} = \frac{\text{Credit sales}}{365} \quad (11.3)$$

If all of its sales are on credit, Exemplar generates $2,000 million ÷ 365 = $5.479 million of credit sales per day. The *days sales outstanding* (DSO), also known as the *number of days of credit*, in this ending balance is calculated by taking the ratio of the balance in the accounts receivable account to the credit sales per day:

$$\text{Days sales outstanding (DSO)} = \frac{\text{Accounts receivable}}{\text{Average credit sales per day}} \quad (11.4)$$

With an ending balance of accounts receivable of $200 million and assuming all sales are on credit, Exemplar's DSO for FY20X2 is $200 million ÷ $5,479 million = 36.5 days.

If the ending balance of receivables at the end of the year is representative of the receivables on any day throughout the year, then it takes, on average, approximately 36.5 days to collect the accounts receivable.

The operating cycle is the sum of the days sales in inventory and the days sales outstanding:

$$\text{Operating cycle} = \text{DSI} + \text{DSO} \tag{11.5}$$

Using what we have determined for the inventory cycle and cash cycle, we see that for Exemplar the operating cycle is $111.78 + 36.5 = 148.281$ days.

We also need to look at the liabilities on the balance sheet to see how long it takes a company to pay its short-term obligations. We can apply the same logic to accounts payable as we did to accounts receivable and inventories. How long does it take a company, on average, to go from creating a payable (buying on credit) to paying for it in cash?

First, we need to determine the amount of an average day's purchases on credit. However, purchases are not identified on the financial statements, but instead we must infer this amount from accounts in both the income statement and the balance sheet. If we assume all the Exemplar purchases are made on credit and there was no change in the level of inventory, the total purchases for the year would be the cost of goods sold less any amounts included in cost of goods sold that are not purchases, such as depreciation. Because we do not have a breakdown on the company's cost of goods sold showing how much was paid for in cash and how much was on credit, we will assume that the following relationship holds for Exemplar:

$$\begin{array}{l}\text{Beginning} \\ \text{inventory}\end{array} + \text{Purchases} = \left(\begin{array}{l}\text{Cost of} \\ \text{goods sold}\end{array} - \text{Depreciation}\right) + \begin{array}{l}\text{Ending} \\ \text{inventory}\end{array}$$

$$\tag{11.6}$$

For Exemplar in FY20X2, we infer purchases of $1,480 million. Therefore, the purchases per day are

$$\text{Average purchases per day} = \frac{\text{Annual purchases}}{365} \tag{11.7}$$

which for Exemplar are $4.055 million.

The *days payables outstanding* (DPO), also known as the *number of days of purchases*, represented in the ending balance in accounts payable is calculated as the ratio of the balance in the accounts payable account to the average day's purchases:

$$\text{Days payables outstanding (DPO)} = \frac{\text{Accounts payable}}{\text{Average purchases per day}} \quad (11.8)$$

For Exemplar in the current year, the DPO is \$100 million ÷ \$4.055 million = 24.662 days. This means that on average Exemplar takes approximately 25 days to pay out cash for a purchase.

The operating cycle is how long it takes to convert an investment in cash back into cash (by way of inventory and accounts receivable). The number of days of payables tells us how long it takes to pay on purchases made to create the inventory. If we put these two pieces of information together, we can see how long, on net, we tie up cash. The difference between the operating cycle and the number of days of purchases is the *cash conversion cycle* (CCC), also known as the *net operating cycle*:

$$\text{Cash conversion cycle} = \text{DSI} + \text{DSO} - \text{DPO} \quad (11.9)$$

For Exemplar's FY20X2,

$$\text{Cash conversion cycle} = 11.781 + 36.500 - 24.662 = 123.619 \text{ days}$$

The cash conversion cycle is how long it takes for the company to get cash back from its investments in inventory and accounts receivable, considering that purchases may be made on credit. By not paying for purchases immediately (that is, using trade credit), the company reduces its liquidity needs. Therefore, the longer the net operating cycle, the greater the required liquidity.

 TRY IT! THE OPERATING CYCLE

Complete the following using Exemplar Corporation's FY20X1 financial statements:

Days sales outstanding	
Days sales in inventory	
Days purchases outstanding	
Operating cycle	
Cash conversion cycle	

Measures of Liquidity

We can describe a company's ability to meet its current obligations in several ways. We can form the current ratio, which is one of the most commonly used measures of liquidity:

$$\text{Current ratio} = \frac{\text{Current assets}}{\text{Current liabilities}} \qquad (11.10)$$

The current ratio is an indication of how many times the company can cover its current liabilities, using its current assets. Exemplar's current ratio for FY20X2 is $800 million ÷ $130 = 6.154 times.

Another liquidity measure is the quick ratio, which is similar to the current ratio, except we remove the least liquid of the current assets from the numerator:

$$\text{Quick ratio} = \frac{\text{Current assets} - \text{Inventory}}{\text{Current liabilities}} \qquad (11.11)$$

The two-for-one ratio of quick assets to current liabilities does not have to be explained in detail because its use is so general in statement analysis. It is the first step toward establishing a student in proportions. Its adoption as a test resulted from the certain knowledge, acquired by bitter experience, that a shrinkage might easily occur in asset, but rarely in liabilities.

—Robert Morris Associates, Financial Statements,
An Explanation in Brief of a New System for Their
Analysis from the Standpoint of the Credit Grantor
and Business Executive, 1921

By leaving out the least liquid asset, the quick ratio provides a more conservative view of liquidity. The quick ratio is also known as the *acid test ratio*. For Exemplar in the current year, the quick ratio is 2.385 times.

Still another way to measure the company's ability to satisfy short-term obligations is the *net working capital-to-sales ratio,* which compares net working capital (current assets less current liabilities) with sales:

$$\text{Net working capital to sales} = \frac{\text{Net working capital}}{\text{Revenues}} \qquad (11.12)$$

This ratio tells us the "cushion" available to meet short-term obligations relative to sales. Consider two companies with identical working capital of $100,000, but one has sales of $500,000 and the other sales of $1,000,000.

If they have identical operating cycles, this means that the company with the greater sales has more funds flowing in and out of its current asset investments (inventories and receivables). The company with more funds flowing in and out needs a larger cushion to protect itself in case of a disruption in the cycle, such as a labor strike or unexpected delays in customer payments. The longer the operating cycle, the more of a cushion (i.e., net working capital) a company needs for a given level of sales.

For Exemplar Corporation, the net working capital to sales ratio for FY20X2 is

$$\text{Net working capital to sales} = \frac{\$800 \text{ million} - 130 \text{ million}}{\$2,000 \text{ million}} = 0.335$$

The ratio of 0.335 tells us that for every dollar of sales, Exemplar has 33.5 cents of net working capital to support it.

Given the measures of time related to the current accounts—the operating cycle and the cash conversion cycle—and the three measures of liquidity—current ratio, quick ratio, and net working capital-to-sales ratio—we know the following about Exemplar Corporation's ability to meet its short-term obligations:

- Inventory is less liquid than accounts receivable (comparing days of inventory with days of credit).
- Current assets are greater than needed to satisfy current liabilities in a year (from the current ratio).
- The quick ratio tells us that Exemplar can meet its short-term obligations even without resorting to selling inventory.
- The net working capital "cushion" is 33.5 cents for every dollar of sales (from the net working capital-to-sales ratio.)

Unfortunately, these liquidity ratios don't provide us with answers to the following questions:

- How liquid are the accounts receivable? How much of the accounts receivable will be collectible? Whereas we know it takes, on average, 36.5 days to collect, we do not know how much will never be collected.
- What is the nature of the current liabilities? How much of current liabilities consists of items that recur (such as accounts payable and wages payable) each period and how much consists of occasional items (such as income taxes payable)?
- Are there any unrecorded liabilities (such as operating leases) that are not included in current liabilities?

TRY IT! LIQUIDITY RATIOS

Complete the following using Exemplar Corporation's FY20X1 financial statements:

Current ratio	
Quick ratio	
Net working capital to sales	

PROFITABILITY RATIOS

Liquidity ratios indicate a company's ability to meet its immediate obligations. Now we extend the analysis by adding *profitability ratios*, which help the investor gauge how well a company is managing its expenses. *Profit margin ratios* compare components of income with sales. They give the investor an idea of which factors make up a company's income and are usually expressed as a portion of each dollar of sales. For example, the profit margin ratios we discuss here differ only in the numerator. It is in the numerator that we can evaluate performance for different aspects of the business.

For example, suppose the investor wants to evaluate how well production facilities are managed. The investor would focus on gross profit (revenues less cost of goods sold), a measure of income that is the direct result of production management. Comparing gross profit with sales produces the *gross profit margin:*

$$\text{Gross profit margin} = \frac{\text{Gross profit}}{\text{Revenues}} \qquad (11.13)$$

This ratio tells us the portion of each dollar of sales that remains after deducting production expenses. For Exemplar Corporation for the current year,

$$\text{Gross profit margin} = \frac{\$400 \text{ million}}{\$2,000 \text{ million}} = 20\%$$

For each dollar of revenues, the company's gross profit is 35 cents. Looking at sales and cost of goods sold, we can see that the gross profit margin is affected by:

- Changes in sales volume, which affect cost of goods sold and sales.
- Changes in sales price, which affect revenues.
- Changes in the cost of production, which affect cost of goods sold.

Any change in gross profit margin from one period to the next is caused by one or more of those three factors. Similarly, differences in gross margin ratios among companies are the result of differences in those factors.

To evaluate operating performance, we need to consider operating expenses in addition to the cost of goods sold. To do this, remove operating expenses (e.g., selling and general administrative expenses) from gross profit, leaving operating profit, also referred to as *earnings before interest and taxes*. Therefore, the *operating profit margin* is

$$\text{Operating profit margin} = \frac{\text{Operating profit}}{\text{Revenues}} \qquad (11.14)$$

For Exemplar in the current year, the operating profit margin is 10%. Therefore, for each dollar of revenues, Exemplar has 10 cents of operating income. The operating profit margin is affected by the same factors as gross profit margin, plus operating expenses.

Both the gross profit margin and the operating profit margin reflect a company's operating performance. But they do not consider how these operations have been financed. To evaluate both operating and financing decisions, the investor must compare net income (that is, earnings after deducting interest and taxes) with revenues. The result is the *net profit margin*:

$$\text{Net profit margin} = \frac{\text{Net profit}}{\text{Revenues}} \qquad (11.15)$$

The net profit margin is the net income generated from each dollar of revenues; it considers financing costs that the operating profit margin does not consider. For Exemplar for the current year, the net profit margin is 5.484%. In other words, for every dollar of revenues, Exemplar generates 5.484 cents in net profits.

The profitability ratios indicate the following about the operating per-formance of Exemplar for FY20X2:

- Each dollar of revenues contributes 20 cents to gross profit and 10 cents to operating profit.
- Every dollar of revenues contributes 5.484 cents to owners' earnings.
- By comparing the 20 cents operating profit margin with the 5.484 cents net profit margin, we see that Exemplar has a little more than 14 cents of financing costs for every dollar of revenues.

What these ratios do not indicate about profitability is the sensitivity of gross, operating, and net profit margins to changes in the sales price and changes in the volume of sales.

Looking at the profitability ratios for one company for one period gives the investor very little information that can be used to make judgments regarding future profitability. Nor do these ratios provide the investor any information about why current profitability is what it is. We need more information to make these kinds of judgments, particularly regarding the future profitability of the company. For that, turn to activity ratios, which are measures of how well assets are being used.

 TRY IT! PROFITABILITY RATIOS

Complete the following using Exemplar Corporation's FY20X1 finan-cial statements:

Gross profit margin	
Operating profit margin	
Net profit margin	

ACTIVITY RATIOS

We use *activity ratios*—for the most part, turnover ratios—to evaluate the benefits produced by specific assets, such as inventory or accounts receivable, or to evaluate the benefits produced by the totality of the company's assets.

Inventory management

The *inventory turnover ratio* is a measure of how quickly a company has used inventory to generate the goods and services that are sold. The inventory turnover is the ratio of the cost of goods sold to inventory:

$$\text{Inventory turnover} = \frac{\text{Cost of goods sold}}{\text{Inventory}} \qquad (11.16)$$

For Exemplar for the current year, the inventory turnover is 3.265 times. This ratio indicates that Exemplar turns over its inventory 3.265 times per year. On average, cash is invested in inventory, goods and services are produced, and these goods and services are sold 3.265 times a year. Looking back to the number of days of inventory, we see that this turnover measure is consistent with the results of that calculation: There are 111.78 calendar days of inventory on hand at the end of the year; dividing 365 days by 111.78 days, we find that inventory cycles through (that is, from cash to sales) 3.265 times a year.

Accounts Receivable Management

In much the same way inventory turnover can be evaluated, an investor can evaluate a company's management of its accounts receivable and its credit policy. The *accounts receivable turnover* ratio is a measure of how effectively a company is using credit extended to customers. The reason for extending credit is to increase sales. The downside to extending credit is the possibility of default—customers not paying when promised. The benefit obtained from extending credit is referred to as net credit sales—sales on credit less returns and refunds.

$$\text{Accounts receivable turnover} = \frac{\text{Credit sales}}{\text{Accounts receivable}} \qquad (11.17)$$

Looking at the Exemplar Corporation income statement, we see an entry for revenues, but we do not know how much of the amount stated is on credit. In the case of evaluating a company, an investor would have an estimate of the amount of credit sales. Let us assume that the entire sales amount represents net credit sales. For Exemplar for the current year, the accounts receivable turnover is $2,000 million ÷ $200 million = 10 times. Therefore, 10 times in the year there is, on average, a cycle that begins with a sale on credit and finishes with the receipt of cash for that sale.

The number of times accounts receivable cycle through the year is consistent with the days sales outstanding (36.5 days) that we calculated earlier—accounts receivable turn over 10 times during the year, and the average number of days of sales in the accounts receivable balance is 365 days ÷ 10 times = 36.5 days.

Overall Asset Management

The inventory and accounts receivable turnover ratios reflect the benefits obtained from the use of specific assets (inventory and accounts receivable). For a more general picture of the productivity of the company, an investor can compare the sales during a period with the total assets that generated these revenues.

One way is with the *total asset turnover ratio*, or simply the *asset turnover*, which is how many times during the year the value of a company's total assets is generated in revenues:

$$\text{Total asset turnover} = \frac{\text{Revenues}}{\text{Total assets}} \qquad (11.18)$$

For Exemplar in the current year, the total asset turnover is $2,000 million ÷ $1,175 = 1.159 times.

The turnover ratio of 1.159 indicated that in the current year, every dollar invested in total assets generates $1.159 of revenues. Because total assets include both tangible and intangible assets, this turnover indicates how efficiently all assets were used.

From these ratios the investor can determine that:

- Inventory flows in and out almost 3.3 times a year (from the inventory turnover ratio).
- Accounts receivable are collected in cash, on average, 36.5 days after a sale (from the number of days of credit). In other words, accounts receivable flow in and out almost 10 times during the year (from the accounts receivable turnover ratio).

But what these ratios do not indicate about the company's use of its assets:

- The sales not made because credit policies are too stringent.
- How much of credit sales is not collectible.
- Which assets contribute most to the total asset turnover.

TRY IT! ACTIVITY RATIOS

Complete the following using Exemplar Corporation's FY20X1 financial statements:

	Turnover	Number of days	Product of the turnover and the number of days
Inventory			
Accounts receivable			

FINANCIAL LEVERAGE

A company can finance its assets with equity or with debt. Financing with debt legally obligates the company to pay interest and to repay the principal as promised. Equity financing does not obligate the company to pay anything because dividends are paid at the discretion of the board of directors. There is always some risk, which we refer to as *business risk*, inherent in any business enterprise. But how a company chooses to finance its operations—the particular mix of debt and equity—may add financial risk on top of business risk. *Financial risk* is risk associated with a company's ability to satisfy its debt obligations, and is often measured using the extent to which debt financing is used relative to equity.

We use financial leverage ratios to assess how much financial risk the company has taken on. There are two types of financial leverage ratios: component percentages and coverage ratios. Component percentages compare a company's debt with either its total capital (debt plus equity) or its equity capital. Coverage ratios reflect a company's ability to satisfy fixed financing obligations, such as interest, principal repayment, or lease payments.

Component Percentage Ratios

A ratio that indicates the proportion of assets financed with debt is the *debt-to-assets ratio*, which compares total liabilities (Short-term debt + Long-term debt) with total assets:

$$\text{Debt to assets} = \frac{\text{Debt}}{\text{Total assets}} \qquad (11.19)$$

For Exemplar in the current year, the debt to assets is 16.959%. This ratio indicates that 16.959% of the company's assets are financed with debt (both short term and long term).

Another way to look at the financial risk is in terms of the use of debt relative to the use of equity. The *debt-to-equity ratio*, or simply the *debt-equity ratio*, is a measure how the company finances its operations with debt relative to the book value of its shareholders' equity:

$$\text{Debt to equity} = \frac{\text{Debt}}{\text{Shareholders' equity}} \qquad (11.20)$$

Shareholders' equity is the book value, or carrying value, of shareholders' equity as reported on the company's balance sheet. For Exemplar for FY20X2, the debt to equity ratio is ($130 million + 163 million) ÷ $1,432 million or 0.204. For every one dollar of book value of shareholders' equity, Exemplar uses 20.4 cents of debt.

Both of these ratios can be stated in terms of total debt, as above, or in terms of long-term debt or even simply interest-bearing debt. And it is not always clear in which form—total, long-term debt, or interest-bearing—the ratio is calculated. Additionally, it is often the case that the current portion of long-term debt is excluded in the calculation of the long-term versions of these debt ratios.

One problem with using a financial ratio based on the book value of equity to analyze financial risk is that there is seldom a strong relationship between the book value and market value of a stock. The distortion in values on the balance sheet is obvious by looking at the book value of equity and comparing it with the market value of equity. The book value of equity consists of:

- The proceeds to the company of all the stock issues since it was first incorporated, less any stock repurchased by the company.
- The accumulative earnings of the company, less any dividends, since it was first incorporated.

The book value of equity generally does not give a true picture of the investment of shareholders in the company because:

- Earnings are recorded according to accounting principles, which may not reflect the true economics of transactions.
- Due to inflation, the earnings and proceeds from stock issued in the past do not reflect today's values.

In other words, the book value often understates the value of shareholders' equity.

The market value of equity, on the other hand, is the value of equity as perceived by investors. It is what investors are willing to pay. So why bother with book value? For two reasons: First, if the company is not publicly traded, it is easier to obtain the book value than the market value of a company's securities. Second, many financial services report ratios using book value rather than market value. However, you can easily restate any of the ratios presented in this chapter that use the book value of equity using the market value of equity.

Coverage Ratios

The ratios that compare debt to equity or debt to assets indicate the amount of financial leverage, which enables an investor to assess the financial condition of a company. Another way of looking at the financial condition and the amount of financial leverage used by the company is to see how well it can handle the financial burdens associated with its debt or other fixed commitments.

One measure of a company's ability to handle financial burdens is the *interest coverage ratio*, also referred to as the *times interest-covered ratio*. This ratio tells us how well the company can cover or meet the interest payments associated with debt. The ratio compares the funds available to pay interest (that is, earnings before interest and taxes) with the interest expense:

$$\text{Interest coverage ratio} = \frac{\text{EBIT}}{\text{Interest expense}} \qquad (11.21)$$

The greater the interest coverage ratio, the better able the company is to pay its interest expense. For Exemplar for the current year, the interest coverage ratio is $200 million ÷ $17 million = 11.617 times. An interest coverage ratio of 11.617 times means that the company's earnings before interest and taxes are 11.617 times greater than its interest payments.

The interest coverage ratio provides information about a company's ability to cover the interest related to its debt financing. However, there are other costs that do not arise from debt but that nevertheless must be considered in the same way we consider the cost of debt in a company's financial obligations. For example, lease payments are fixed costs incurred in financing operations. Like interest payments, they represent legal obligations. We could also consider another fixed charge, such as preferred stock dividends, which the company must pay before a company pays any common stock dividends.[1]

Up to now, we considered earnings before interest and taxes as funds available to meet fixed financial charges. EBIT includes noncash items such as depreciation and amortization. If an investor is trying to compare funds available to meet obligations, a better measure of available funds is cash flow from operations, as reported in the statement of cash flows. A ratio that considers cash flows from operations as funds available to cover interest payments is referred to as the *cash flow interest coverage ratio:*

$$\frac{\text{Cash flow}}{\text{interest coverage}} = \frac{\dfrac{\text{Cash flow}}{\text{from operations}} + \text{Interest} + \text{Taxes}}{\text{Interest}} \quad (11.22)$$

We take the amount of cash flow from operations that is in the statement of cash flows is net of interest and taxes. Therefore, we must add back interest and taxes to cash flow from operations to arrive at the cash flow amount before interest and taxes in order to determine the cash flow available to cover interest payments.

For Exemplar for the current year, the cash flow interest coverage is

$$\frac{\text{Cash flow}}{\text{interest coverage}} = \frac{\$290 \text{ million} + 17 \text{ million} + 73 \text{ million}}{\$17 \text{ million}} = 22.565$$

This coverage ratio indicates that, in terms of cash flows, Exemplar has 22.565 times more cash than is needed to pay its interest. This is a better picture of interest coverage than the 11.617 times reflected by EBIT. Why the difference? Because cash flow considers not just the accounting income, but noncash items as well. In the case of Exemplar, depreciation is a noncash charge that reduced EBIT but not cash flow from operations—it is added back to net income to arrive at cash flow from operations.

These ratios indicate that Exemplar uses its financial leverage as follows:

- Assets are 17% financed with debt, measured using book values.
- Long-term debt is approximately 20% of equity.

---

[1]When we alter the interest coverage ratio to consider these other fixed obligations, we alter the numerator as well to restate it to reflect the funds available to cover these obligations.

These ratios do not indicate:

- What other fixed, legal commitments the company has that we cannot see by simply looking at the balance sheet (for example, operating leases).
- What the intentions of management are regarding taking on more debt as the existing debt matures.

TRY IT! FINANCIAL LEVERAGE RATIOS

Complete the following using Exemplar Corporation's FY20X1 financial statements:

Debt to assets	
Debt to equity	
Interest coverage ratio	
Cash flow interest coverage	

RETURN ON INVESTMENT

Return-on-investment ratios compare measures of benefits, such as earnings or net income, with measures of investment. For example, if an investor wants to evaluate how well the company uses its assets in its operations, he could calculate the return on assets—sometimes called the *basic earning power ratio*—as the ratio of earnings before interest and taxes (also known as operating earnings) to total assets:

$$\text{Basic earning power} = \frac{\text{Earnings before interest and taxes}}{\text{Total assets}} \qquad (11.23)$$

For Exemplar Corporation, for the current year, the basic earning power ratio is \$110 million ÷ \$1,725 million = 11.594%. This means that for every dollar invested in assets, Exemplar earned about 11.6 cents in the current year. This measure deals with earnings from operations; it does not consider how these operations are financed.

Another return-on-assets ratio uses net income—operating earnings less interest and taxes—instead of earnings before interest and taxes. This is the more commonly used return on assets ratio:

$$\text{Return on assets} = \frac{\text{Net income}}{\text{Total assets}} \qquad (11.24)$$

For Exemplar in the current year, the return on assets is $110 million ÷ $1,725 million = 6.358%.

Thus, without taking into consideration how assets are financed, the return on assets for Exemplar is 11.594%. Taking into consideration how assets are financed, the return on assets is 6.358%. The difference is due to Exemplar financing part of its total assets with debt, incurring interest of $17 million in the current year.

If we look at Exemplar's liabilities and equities, we see that the assets are financed by both liabilities and equity. Investors may not be interested in the return the company gets from its total investment (debt plus equity), but rather shareholders are interested in the return the company can generate on their investment. The *return on equity* is the ratio of the net income shareholders receive to their equity in the stock:

$$\text{Return on equity} = \frac{\text{Net income}}{\text{Shareholders' equity}} \qquad (11.25)$$

For Exemplar Corporation, there is only one type of shareholder: common. For the current year, the return on equity is $110 million ÷ $1,725 million = 7.656%.

THE DUPONT SYSTEM

The returns-on-investment ratios provide a "bottom line" on the performance of a company, but do not tell us anything about the "why" behind this performance. For an understanding of the "why," an investor must dig a bit deeper into the financial statements. A method that is useful in examining the source of performance is the DuPont system.

The *DuPont system* is a method of breaking down return ratios into their components to determine which areas are responsible for a company's performance. To see how it is used, let us take a closer look at the first definition of the basic earning power in equation (11.23). We can break down this ratio into its components: profit margin and activity. We do this by relating both the numerator and the denominator to sales activity. Divide both the numerator and the denominator of the basic earning power ratio by revenues, which produces

$$\text{Basic earning power} = \frac{\text{EBIT}}{\text{Revenues}} \times \frac{\text{Revenues}}{\text{Total assets}}$$

In other words, the earning power of the company is related to profitability (in this case, operating profit or EBIT) and a measure of activity (Total asset turnover = Revenues/Total assets):

$$\text{Basic earning power} = \frac{\text{Operating}}{\text{profit margin}} \times \frac{\text{Total asset}}{\text{turnover}}$$

Therefore, when analyzing a change in the company's basic earning power, an investor could look at this breakdown to see the change in its components: operating profit margin and total asset turnover.

Let's look at the return on assets of Exemplar for the two years. Its returns on assets were 20% in the prior year and 18.18% in the current year. We can decompose the company's returns on assets for the two years to obtain:

$$\text{FY20X2: } 11.594\% = \frac{\$200}{\$2,000} \times \frac{\$2,000}{\$1,725} = 10\% \times 1.1594$$

$$\text{FY20X1: } 12.291\% = \frac{\$180}{\$1,090} \times \frac{\$1,900}{\$1,790} = 11.579\% \times 1.0615$$

We see that operating profit margin declined over the two years, yet asset turnover improved slightly. Therefore, the decline in the return-on-assets is attributable to lower profit margins.

We can break down the return on assets and the return on equity into components in a similar manner. Expanding equation (11.24),

$$\text{Return on assets} = \frac{\text{Net income}}{\text{Revenues}} \times \frac{\text{Revenues}}{\text{Total assets}} = \frac{\text{Net profit}}{\text{margin}} \times \frac{\text{Total asset}}{\text{turnover}}$$

Recognizing the accounting relationship between operating profit and net income, and letting EBT = EBIT − interest, then

$$\frac{\text{Net income}}{\text{Revenues}} = \frac{\text{EBIT}}{\text{Revenues}} \times \frac{\text{EBT}}{\text{EBIT}} \times (1 - \text{Tax rate})$$

and, therefore,

$$\text{Return on assets} = \frac{\text{EBIT}}{\text{Revenues}} \times \frac{\text{EBT}}{\text{EBIT}} \times (1 - \text{Tax rate}) \times \frac{\text{Revenues}}{\text{Total assets}}$$

In other words, the return on assets is:

- Positively related to the operating profit margin, EBIT/Revenues.
- Negatively related to the amount of interest, relative to earnings (the greater the interest, the lower is EBT/EBIT.
- Negatively related to the tax rate.
- Positively related to the asset turnover.

The breakdown of a return-on-equity ratio from equation (11.25) requires a bit more decomposition because instead of total assets as the denominator, the denominator in the return is shareholders' equity. Because activity ratios reflect the use of all of the assets, not just the proportion financed by equity, we need to adjust the activity ratio by the proportion that assets are financed by equity (i.e., the ratio of the book value of shareholders' equity to total assets):

$$\text{Return on equity} = \frac{\text{Net income}}{\text{Total assets}} \times \frac{\text{Total assets}}{\text{Shareholders' equity}}$$

Identifying the ratio of total assets to shareholders' equity as the equity multiplier, which captures the company's financial leverage, we can rephrase return on equity as

$$\text{Return on equity} = \text{Return on assets} \times \text{Equity multiplier}$$

If we substitute the breakdown of the return on assets into this equation for the return on equity, we have

$$\begin{aligned} \text{Return on} \\ \text{equity} \end{aligned} = \left[\frac{\text{EBIT}}{\text{Revenues}} \times \frac{\text{EBT}}{\text{EBIT}} \times (1 - \text{Tax rate}) \times \frac{\text{Revenues}}{\text{Total assets}} \right]$$
$$\times \frac{\text{Total assets}}{\text{Shareholders' equity}}$$

In other words, the return on equity is a function of operating profit, the company's interest burden, the tax rate, asset utilization, and financial leverage. Applying this to Exemplar for FY20X2,

$$\text{Return on equity} = 0.010 \times 0.914 \times (1 - 0.4) \times 1.159 \times 1.204 = 7.656\%$$

TRY IT! BREAKING DOWN THE RETURN ON EQUITY

Complete the following using Exemplar Corporation's FY20X1 financial statements:

Return on equity	
Basic earning power ratio	
Operating profit margin	
EBT/EBIT	
Tax rate	
Equity multiplier	

COMMON-SIZE ANALYSIS

An investor can evaluate a company's operating performance and financial condition through ratios that relate various items of information contained in the financial statements. Another way to analyze a company is to look at its financial data more comprehensively.

Common-size analysis is a method of analysis in which the components of a financial statement are compared. In the vertical common-size analysis, each financial statement item is compared to a benchmark item for that same year. The first step in this form of common-size analysis is to break down a financial statement—either the balance sheet or the income statement—into its parts. The next step is to calculate the proportion that each item represents relative to some benchmark. In the case of a vertical common size analysis of the balance sheet, the benchmark is total assets; in the case of the income statement, the benchmark is revenues.

Another form of common-size analysis is *horizontal common-size analysis*, in which we use either an income statement or a balance sheet in a fiscal year and compare accounts to the corresponding items in another year.

Let us see how it works by doing some common-size financial analysis for the Exemplar Corporation. In the income statement, as with the balance sheet, the items may be restated as a proportion of sales; this statement is referred to as the common-size income statement. We provide the

EXHIBIT 11.4 Exemplar Corporation's Vertical Common-Size Income Statements

	For Year Ending	
	Dec. 31, 20X2	Dec. 31, 20X1
Revenues	100%	100%
Cost of goods sold	80%	79%
Gross profit	20%	21%
Selling, general, and administrative expenses	10%	9%
Earnings before interest and taxes	10%	12%
Interest expense	1%	1%
Earnings before taxes	9%	11%
Taxes	4%	4%
Net income	5%	6%

common-size income statements for Exemplar for the two years in Exhibit 11.4. For the current year, the major costs are associated with goods sold (80%). Looking at gross profit, EBIT, and net income, these proportions are the profit margins we calculated earlier. Using the common-size income statement, we learn about the profitability of different aspects of the company's business. Again, the picture is not yet complete. For a more complete picture, the investor must look at trends over time and make comparisons with other companies in the same industry.

We restate the company's balance sheet in Exhibit 11.5. This statement does not look precisely like the balance sheet we have seen before. Nevertheless, the data are the same but reorganized. Each item in the original balance sheet has been restated as a proportion of total assets for that year. Hence, we refer to this as the *common-size balance sheet*.

In this common-size balance sheet, we see, for example, that in the current year cash is 6% of total assets. The largest investment is in plant and equipment, which comprises 46% of total assets. On the liabilities side, current liabilities are 8% of liabilities and equity. Using the common-size balance sheet, we can see, in very general terms, how Exemplar has raised capital and where this capital has been invested. As with financial ratios, however, the picture is not complete until trends are examined and compared with those of other companies in the same industry.

We provide a horizontal common-size analysis for Exemplar's balance sheet in Exhibit 11.6. In this analysis, we see that current and total assets have declined since FY20X1, the company is using less long-term debt, and equity has increased. If we wanted to look at relative trends, we could carry this out over 5 or 10 fiscal periods.

EXHIBIT 11.5 Exemplar Corporation's Vertical Common-Size Balance Sheets

	As of	
	Dec. 31, 20X2	Dec. 31, 20X1
Cash and cash equivalents	6%	6%
Accounts receivable	12%	14%
Inventory	28%	28%
Total current assets	46%	48%
Gross property, plant, and equipment	70%	61%
Accumulated depreciation	23%	17%
Net property, plant, and equipment	46%	45%
Intangible assets	3%	3%
Goodwill	4%	4%
Total assets	100%	100%
Accounts payable	6%	5%
Current portion of long-term debt	2%	1%
Total current liabilities	8%	6%
Long-term debt	9%	18%
Common stock	1%	1%
Paid-in capital in excess of par	6%	6%
Retained earnings	77%	70%
Treasury stock	1%	1%
Shareholders' equity	83%	76%
Total liabilities and equity	100%	100%

Note: Each account is divided by total assets. For example, FY20X2 inventory of $490 million, divided by total assets of $1,725, results in 28.41%.

USING FINANCIAL RATIO ANALYSIS

Financial analysis provides information concerning a company's operating performance and financial condition. This information is useful for an investor in evaluating the performance of the company as a whole, as well as of divisions, products, and subsidiaries. An investor must also be aware that financial analysis is also used by investors and investors to gauge the financial performance of the company.

But financial ratio analysis cannot tell the whole story and must be interpreted and used with care. Financial ratios are useful but, as noted in the discussion of each ratio, there is information that the ratios do not reveal. For example, in calculating inventory turnover we need to assume that the inventory shown on the balance sheet is representative of inventory

EXHIBIT 11.6 Exemplar Corporation's Horizontal Common-Size Analysis Balance Sheet (*base year is fiscal year 20X1*)

	Dec. 31, 20X2	Dec. 31, 20X1
Cash and cash equivalents	105%	100%
Accounts receivable	80%	100%
Inventory	96%	100%
Total current assets	92%	100%
Gross property, plant, and equipment	109%	100%
Accumulated depreciation	133%	100%
Net property, plant, and equipment	100%	100%
Intangible assets	100%	100%
Goodwill	100%	100%
Total assets	96%	100%
Accounts payable	111%	100%
Current portion of long-term debt	120%	100%
Total current liabilities	113%	100%
Long-term debt	51%	100%
Common stock	100%	100%
Paid-in capital in excess of par	100%	100%
Retained earnings	106%	100%
Treasury stock	100%	100%
Shareholders' equity	106%	100%
Total liabilities and equity	96%	100%

Note: Each account in Y20X2 is divided by the account's value in FY20X1. For example, the FY20X2 inventory divided by FY20X1 inventory, $490 million ÷ 510 million, is 96.08%.

throughout the year. Another example is in the calculation of accounts receivable turnover. We assumed that all sales were on credit. If we are on the outside looking in—that is, evaluating a company based on its financial statements only, such as the case of a financial investor or investor—and, therefore, do not have data on credit sales, assumptions must be made that may or may not be correct.

In addition, there are other areas of concern that an investor should be aware of in using financial ratios:

- Limitations in the accounting data used to construct the ratios.
- Selection of an appropriate benchmark company or companies for comparison purposes.
- Interpretation of the ratios.

- Pitfalls in forecasting future operating performance and financial condition based on past trends.

THE BOTTOM LINE

- Financial ratios are useful in evaluating the operating performance and financial condition of a company. With ratios, we can examine a company's liquidity, profitability, and efficiency in putting its assets to use, as well as its ability to meet it debt obligations.
- Liquidity reflects the ability of a company to meet its short-term obligations using those assets that are most readily converted into cash. Two of the most commonly used liquidity ratios are the current ratio and the quick ratio.
- Profitability ratios help investors gauge how well a company is managing its expenses. Profit margin ratios compare components of income with sales.
- Activity ratios help investors and analysts evaluate the benefits produced by specific assets, such as inventory or accounts receivable, or evaluate the benefits produced by the totality of the company's assets. For the most part, activity ratios are turnover ratios.
- Financial leverage ratios aid investors and analysts in assessing the exposure of the company to financial risk. There are two types of financial leverage ratios: component percentages and coverage ratios.
- Return-on-investment ratios provide investors and analysts with a way to compare measures of benefits, such as earnings or net income, with measures of investment.
- We can break down overall performance measures, such as the return on assets, into components using the DuPont system. This breakdown is useful in examining the drivers to changes in returns.
- We can use common-size analysis to examine relative changes in accounts over time, either using horizontal analysis or vertical analysis.

SOLUTIONS TO TRY IT! PROBLEMS

The Operating Cycle

Days sales outstanding	124.1
Days sales in inventory	48.026
Days purchases outstanding	23.298
Operating cycle	172.126
Cash conversion cycle	148.828

Liquidity Ratios

Current ratio	7.522
Quick ratio	3.087
Net working capital to sales	0.395

Profitability Ratios

Gross profit margin	21.053%
Operating profit margin	11.579%
Net profit margin	6.442%

Activity Ratios

	Turnover	Number of Days	Product of the Turnover and the Number of Days
Inventory	2.941	124.100	365
Accounts receivable	7.600	48.036	365

Financial Leverage Ratios

Debt to assets	24.264%
Debt to equity	0.320
Interest coverage ratio	13.75
Cash flow interest coverage	8.963

Breaking Down the Return on Equity

Return on equity	9.029%
Basic earning power ratio	12.291%
Operating profit margin	11.579%
EBT/EBIT	0.927
Tax rate	40%
Equity multiplier	1.320

QUESTIONS

1. What is the relation between a company's current ratio and its quick ratio?
2. What is the relation between the cash conversion cycle and a company's need for liquidity?

3. Can a company's cash conversion cycle ever be negative? Explain.
4. What is the relation between a company's inventory turnover and the number of days' inventory?
5. If a company has a return on assets of 10% and a net profit margin of 5%, what is the company's total asset turnover?
6. If a company has a debt-to-assets ratio of 35%, what is the company's debt-to-equity ratio?
7. If a company's use of debt financing increases, as compared to equity financing, what would you expect to find in terms of a change in return on equity if the company's return on assets remains the same?
8. If a company has no debt in its balance sheet, what is the relation between the return on assets and the return on equity?
9. When would you want to use the basic earning power to compare companies instead of the return on assets?
10. If a company has a return on assets of 10% and has a debt-to-assets ratio of 50%, what is the company's return on equity?
11. Suppose you calculate the following ratios for two companies, A and B.

	Company A	Company B
Current ratio	2.0	2.0
Quick ratio	1.0	1.5

What can you say about the relative investment in inventory?
12. Suppose you are comparing two companies that are in the same line of business. Company C has an operating cycle of 40 days, and Company D has an operating cycle of 60 days. Company C has a current ratio of 3, and Company D has a current ratio of 2.5. Comment on the liquidity of the two companies. Which company has more risk of not satisfying its near-term obligations? Why?
13. Suppose you calculate a return on fixed assets of 20% for 2008 and 15% for 2009 for a company. Explain how you would use the DuPont system to further investigate this change in the return on fixed assets.
14. In examining the trend of returns on assets over a 20-year period for a company, you find that the returns have been declining gradually over this period. What information would you look at to further explain this trend?

15. Data for the Lubbock Corporation is provided as follows:

Lubbock Corporation
Balance Sheet
As of December 31, 2009 (in millions)

Cash	$ 100	Accounts payable	$ 300
Marketable securities	300	Other current liabilities	200
Accounts receivable	600	Long-term debt	500
Inventory	1,000	Common stock	2,000
Net plant and equipment	4,000	Retained earnings	3,000
Total assets	$6,000	Total liabilities and equity	$6,000

Lubbock Corporation
Income Statement
For Year Ending December 31, 2009 (in millions)

Sales	$12,000
Cost of goods sold*	10,800
Gross profit	$1,200
Administration expenses	150
Earnings before interest and taxes	$1,050
Interest expense	50
Earnings before taxes	$1,000
Taxes	400
Net income	$ 600

*Includes depreciation of $800.

Calculate the following ratios for the Lubbock Corporation:
a. Current ratio
b. Quick ratio
c. Inventory turnover ratio
d. Total asset turnover ratio
e. Gross profit margin
f. Operating profit margin
g. Net profit margin
h. Debt-to-assets ratio
i. Debt-to-equity ratio
j. Return on assets (basic earning power)
k. Return on equity
16. Consider two companies, each with a return on assets of 10%. Company X has a return on equity of 15%, and Company Y has a return on equity of 20%. Which company uses more financial leverage? Explain.

17. Construct the common size balance sheet for Grisham Company for 2009:

Balance Sheet (in millions)

Cash	$50	Current liabilities	$30
Accounts receivable	30	Long-term debt	90
Inventory	80	Equity	240
Plant and equipment	200		
Total assets	$360	Total liabilities and equity	$360

CHAPTER 12

Cash Flow Analysis

Driven by the downturn, CFOs and treasurers are increasingly switching their companies' financial yardsticks from earnings to cash. As a result, they're tracking the flow of cash into and out of every nook and cranny of their companies' operations. And the cash-management buzzword of the day is visibility.

—David M. Katz, "The New Cash Managers,"
CFO Magazine, November 23, 2009

One of the key financial measures that an investor should understand is the company's cash flow. This is because the cash flow aids in assessing the ability of the company to satisfy its contractual obligations and maintain current dividends and current capital expenditure policy without relying on external financing. Moreover, an investor must understand why this measure is important for external parties, specifically stock analysts covering the company. The reason is that the basic valuation principle is that the value of a company today is the present value of its expected future cash flows. In this chapter, we discuss cash flow analysis.

DIFFICULTIES WITH MEASURING CASH FLOW

Cash flow is the flow of funds within a company during a period of time. The primary difficulty with measuring a cash flow is that it is a flow: Cash flows into the company (i.e., cash inflows) and cash flows out of the company (i.e., cash outflows). At any point in time, there is a stock of cash on hand, but the stock of cash on hand varies among companies because of the size of the company, the cash demands of the business, and a company's management of working capital. So what is cash flow? Is it the total amount of cash flowing into the company during a period? Is it the total amount of cash flowing out of the company during a period? Is it the net of the cash inflows and outflows for a period? Well, there is no specific definition of cash flow—and that's probably why there is so much confusion regarding the measurement of cash flow. Ideally, a measure of the company's operating performance that is comparable among companies is needed—something other than net income.

A simple, yet crude method of calculating cash flow requires simply adding noncash expenses (e.g., depreciation and amortization) to the reported net income amount to arrive at cash flow:

$$\text{Cash flow (Definition 1)} = \text{Net income} + \text{Depreciation and amortization} \tag{12.1}$$

Consider the example of the Exemplar Corporation, whose balance sheet, income statement, and statement of cash flows we present in Exhibits 12.1, 12.2, and 12.3, respectively. The simplest cash flow estimate, which we refer to as Definition 1, is:

	Net income	$110
Plus	Depreciation	100
Equals	Cash flow (Definition 1)	$210

This amount is not really a cash flow, but simply earnings before depreciation and amortization. Is this a cash flow that we should use in valuing a company? Though not a cash flow, this estimated cash flow does allow a quick comparison of income across companies that may use different depreciation methods and depreciable lives.

The problem with this measure is that it ignores the many other sources and uses of cash during the period. Consider the sale of goods for credit. This transaction generates sales for the period. Sales and the accompanying cost of goods sold are reflected in the period's net income and the estimated cash flow amount. However, until the account receivable is collected, there is no cash from this transaction. If collection does not occur until the next period, there is a misalignment of the income and cash flow arising from this transaction. Therefore, the simple estimated cash flow ignores some cash flows that, for many companies, are significant.

Another estimate of cash flow that is simple to calculate is *earnings before interest, taxes, depreciation, and amortization* (EBITDA):

$$\frac{\text{Cash flow}}{\text{(Definition 2)}} = \frac{\text{Earnings before}}{\text{interest and taxes}} + \frac{\text{Depreciation}}{\text{and amortization}} \tag{12.2}$$

EXHIBIT 12.1 Exemplar Corporation's Balance Sheets

In Millions	As of		
	Dec. 31, 20X2	Dec. 31, 20X1	Dec. 31, 20X0
Cash and cash equivalents	$110	$105	$100
Accounts receivable	200	250	175
Inventory	490	510	500
Total current assets	$800	$865	$775
Gross property, plant, and equipment	1,200	1,100	1,000
Accumulated depreciation	400	300	200
Net property, plant, and equipment	$800	$800	$800
Intangible assets	50	50	50
Goodwill	75	75	75
Total assets	$1,725	$1,790	$1,700
Accounts payable	$100	$90	$100
Current portion of long-term debt	30	25	20
Total current liabilities	$130	$115	$120
Long-term debt	163	319	300
Common stock	20	20	20
Paid-in capital in excess of par	100	100	100
Retained earnings	1,332	1,256	1,170
Treasury stock	20	20	10
Shareholders' equity	$1,432	$1,356	$1,280
Total liabilities and equity	$1,725	$1,790	$1,700

For Exemplar's 20X2 fiscal year:

	Earnings before interest and taxes	$200
PLUS	Depreciation and amortization	100
EQUALS	Cash flow (Definition 2): EBITDA	$300

However, this measure suffers from the same accrual-accounting bias as the previous measure, which may result in the omission of significant cash flows. Additionally, EBITDA does not consider interest and taxes, which may also be substantial cash outflows for some companies.

These two rough estimates of cash flows are used in practice not only for their simplicity, but because they experienced widespread use prior to the disclosure of more detailed information in the statement of cash flows.

EXHIBIT 12.2 Exemplar Corporation's Income Statements

	For the Year Ending	
In Millions	Dec. 31, 20X2	Dec. 31, 20X1
Revenues	$2,000	$1,900
Cost of goods sold	1,600	1,500
Gross profit	$400	$400
Selling, general, and administrative expenses	200	180
Earnings before interest and taxes	$200	$220
Interest expense	17	16
Earnings before taxes	$183	$204
Taxes	73	82
Net income	$110	$122

EXHIBIT 12.3 Exemplar Corporation's Statements of Cash Flows

	For the Year Ending	
In Millions	Dec. 31, 20X2	Dec. 31, 20X1
Operations		
Net income	$110	$122
Add: depreciation expense	100	100
Changes in working capital accounts		
Accounts receivable	50	−75
Inventory	20	−10
Accounts payable	10	−10
Cash flow for/from operations	$290	$127
Investments		
Capital expenditures	−$100	−$100
Sale of property, plant, and equipment	0	0
Cash flow for/from investment	−$100	−$100
Financing		
Borrowings	$0	$25
Repayments of debt	−152	0
Dividends	−33	−37
Repurchase of stock	0	−10
Cash flow for/from financing	−$185	−$23
Change in cash	$5	$5

Currently, the measures of cash flow are wide-ranging, including the simplistic cash flow measures, measures developed from the statement of cash flows, and measures that seek to capture the theoretical concept of *free cash flow.*

Cash Flows and the Statement of Cash Flows

Prior to the adoption of the statement of cash flows, the information regarding cash flows was quite limited. The first statement that addressed the issue of cash flows was the statement of financial position, which was required starting in 1971. This statement was quite limited, requiring an analysis of the sources and uses of funds in a variety of formats. In its earlier years of adoption, most companies provided this information using what is referred to as the *working capital concept*—a presentation of working capital provided and applied during the period. Over time, many companies began presenting this information using the cash concept, which is a most detailed presentation of the cash flows provided by operations, investing, and financing activities.

Consistent with the cash concept format of the funds flow statement, the statement of cash flows is now a required financial statement. The requirement that companies provide a statement of cash flows applies to fiscal years after 1987.[1] This statement requires the company to classify cash flows into three categories, based on the activity: operating, investing, and financing. Cash flows are summarized by activity and within activity by type (e.g., asset dispositions are reported separately from asset acquisitions). We have highlighted the activities in the statement we show in Exhibit 12.3: operations, investments, and financing.

CASH FLOWS FROM AND FOR

The statement of cash flow provides information on three activities: operations, investments, and financing. The cash flows are usually indicated as "from" if the cash flows are positive for that activity, and "for" if the cash flow is negative—that is, cash flows out of the company.

(continued)

---

[1]Statement of Financial Accounting Standards No. 95, "Statement of Cash Flows."

(*Continued*)

However, in some financial statements, the cash flow may simply be reported as "from," no matter the sign—positive or negative—the cash flow. The key is to look at the summed amount for the activity: positive means that funds have flowed to the company and negative means that funds have flowed from the company.

You may also see variations in the name of the summation. For example, you may see for operations, "Cash flow from operations" or "Cash flow from operating activities."

The reporting company may report the cash flows from operating activities on the statement of cash flows using either the *direct method*—reporting all cash inflows and outflows—or the indirect method—starting with net income and making adjustments for depreciation and other noncash expenses and for changes in working capital accounts. Though the direct method is recommended, it is also the most burdensome for the reporting company to prepare. Most companies report cash flows from operations using the indirect method. The indirect method has the advantage of providing the financial statement user with a reconciliation of the company's net income with the change in cash. The indirect method produces a cash flow from operations that is similar to the estimated cash flow measure discussed previously, yet it encompasses the changes in working capital accounts that the simple measure does not.

The cash flow from operations is our third definition of cash flow:

$$\begin{array}{l} \text{Cash flow} \\ \text{(Definition 3)} \end{array} = \begin{array}{l} \text{Net} \\ \text{income} \end{array} + \begin{array}{l} \text{Depreciation} \\ \text{and amortization} \end{array} - \begin{array}{l} \text{Increase in} \\ \text{working capital} \end{array} \quad (12.3)$$

From Exhibit 12.3, we see that Exemplar's cash flow from operations is $290 million in FY20X2:

	Net income	$110
PLUS	Depreciation expense	100
PLUS	Increase in working capital accounts	80
EQUALS	Cash flow (Definition 3)	$290

The classification of cash flows into the three types of activities provides useful information that can be used by an analyst to see, for example, whether the company is generating sufficient cash flows from operations to sustain its current rate of growth. However, the classification of particular items is not necessarily as useful as it could be. Consider some of the classifications:

- Cash flows related to interest expense are classified in operations, though they are clearly financing cash flows.[2]
- Income taxes are classified as operating cash flows, though taxes are affected by financing (e.g., deduction for interest expense paid on debt) and investment activities (e.g., the reduction of taxes from tax credits on investment activities).
- Interest income and dividends received are classified as operating cash flows, though these flows are a result of investment activities.

Whether these items have a significant effect on the analysis depends on the particular company's situation. Exemplar, for example, has no interest and dividend income, and its interest expense of $17 million is not large relative to its earnings before interest and taxes ($200 million). However, for some companies and some operations, these are significant.

Looking at the relation among the three cash flows in the statement provides a sense of the activities of the company. A young, fast-growing company may have negative cash flows from operations, yet positive cash flows from financing activities (i.e., operations may be financed in large part with external financing). As a company grows, it may rely to a lesser extent on external financing. The typical, mature company generates cash from operations and reinvests part or all of it back into the company. Therefore, cash flow related to operations is positive (i.e., a source of cash) and cash flow related to investing activities is negative (i.e., a use of cash). As a company matures, it may seek less financing externally and may even use cash to reduce its reliance on external financing (e.g., repay debts).

Another variation in the estimation of cash flow is the discretionary cash flow.[3] Starting with the first definition of cash flow, we adjust for changes in working capital to arrive at an operating cash flow. From this, we subtract

---

[2]The interest expense is deducted from earnings before interest and taxes, and, therefore, affects the net income and cash flow from operations.

[3]This is based on the cash flow definition promoted by Martin Fridson in *Financial Statement Analysis: A Practitioner's Guide* (New York: John Wiley & Son, 1995). This definition results from reformatting the statement of cash flows to remove the nondiscretionary cash flows.

the capital expenditures to arrive at our fourth definition of cash flow, the discretionary cash flow:

$$\text{Cash flow (Definition 4)} = \text{Net income} + \text{Depreciation and amortization} - \text{Increase in working capital} - \text{Capital expenditures}$$

$$(12.4)$$

The cash flows related to financing are then provided, resulting in a bottom-line cash flow. By restructuring the statement of cash flows in this way, it can be seen how much flexibility the company has when it must make business decisions that may adversely impact the long-run financial health of the enterprise. We show this restated cash flow statement in Exhibit 12.4.

For example, consider a company with a basic cash flow of $800 million and operating cash flow of $500 million. Suppose that this company pays dividends of $130 million and that its capital expenditure is $300 million. The discretionary cash flow for this company is $200 million found by subtracting the $300 million capital expenditure from the operating cash flow of $500 million. This means that even after maintaining a dividend payment of $130 million, its cash flow is positive. Notice that asset sales and other investing activity, which are considered "Other investing activities," are not needed to generate cash to meet the dividend payments because these items are subtracted after accounting for the dividend payments. In fact, if this company planned to increase its capital expenditures, this breakdown

EXHIBIT 12.4 Reformatted Cash Flow Statement, Highlighting the Exemplar Corporation's Financial Flexibility

		For the Year Ending	
		Dec. 31, 20X2	Dec. 31, 20X1
	Net income	$110	$122
PLUS	Depreciation expense	100	100
	Cash flow (Definition 1)	$210	$222
LESS	Increase in working capital	−80	95
	Operating cash flow (Definition 3)	$290	$127
LESS	Capital expenditures	100	100
	Discretionary cash flow (Definition 4)	$190	$27
LESS	Dividends	33	37
LESS	Other investing activities	0	0
	Cash flow before financing	$157	−$10
PLUS	Borrowings	0	24
LESS	Repayments of debt	152	0
LESS	Repurchase of stock	0	10
	Change in cash	$5	$4

of cash flows into discretionary and nondiscretionary can be used to assess how much that expansion can be before affecting dividends or increasing financing needs.

Though we can classify a company based on the sources and uses of cash flows, more data is needed to put this information in perspective. What is the trend in the sources and uses of cash flows? What market, industry, or company-specific events affect the company's cash flows? How does the company being analyzed compare with other companies in the same industry in terms of the sources and uses of funds?

TRY IT! CALCULATING CASH FLOWS

Calculate the cash flow using each of the four definitions and Exemplar's FY20X1 financial information:

Cash flow (Definition 1)	
Cash flow (Definition 2)	
Cash flow (Definition 3)	
Cash flow (Definition 4)	

FREE CASH FLOW

Cash flows without any adjustment may be misleading because they do not reflect the cash outflows that are necessary for the future existence of a company. An alternative measure, free cash flow, was developed by Michael Jensen in his theoretical analysis of agency costs and corporate takeovers.[4] In theory, *free cash flow* is the cash flow left over after the company funds all positive net present value projects. Positive net present value projects are those capital investment projects for which the present value of expected future cash flows exceeds the present value of project outlays, all discounted at the cost of capital.[5] In other words, free cash flow

---

[4]Michael C. Jensen, "Agency Costs of Free Cash Flow, Corporate Finance, and Takeovers," *American Economic Review* 76 (1985): 323–329.
[5]The *cost of capital* is the cost to the company of funds from creditors and shareholders. The cost of capital is basically a hurdle: If a project returns more than its cost of capital, it is a profitable project spent on low-return exploration and

is the cash flow of the company, less capital expenditures necessary to stay in business (i.e., replacing facilities as necessary) and grow at the expected rate (which requires increases in working capital).

The theory of free cash flow was developed by Jensen to explain behaviors of companies that could not be explained by existing economic theories. Jensen observed that companies that generate free cash flow should disgorge that cash rather than invest the funds in less profitable investments. There are many ways in which companies can disgorge this excess cash flow, including the payment of cash dividends, the repurchase of stock, and debt issuance in exchange for stock. The debt-for-stock exchange, for example, increases the company's leverage and future debt obligations, obligating the future use of excess cash flow. If a company does not disgorge this free cash flow, there is the possibility that another company—a company whose cash flows are less than its profitable investment opportunities or a company that is willing to purchase and lever-up the company—will attempt to acquire the free-cash-flow-laden company.

As a case in point, Jensen observed that the oil industry illustrates the case of wasting resources: The free cash flows generated in the 1980s were spent on low-return exploration and development, and on poor diversification attempts through acquisitions. He argues that these companies would have been better off paying these excess cash flows to shareholders through share repurchases or exchanges with debt.

By itself, the fact that a company generates free cash flow is neither good nor bad. What the company does with this free cash flow is what is important. And this is where it is important to measure the free cash flow as that cash flow in excess of profitable investment opportunities. Consider the simple numerical exercise with the Winner Company and the Loser Company:

	Winner Company	Loser Company
Cash flow before capital expenditures	$1,000	$1,000
Capital expenditures, positive net present value projects	750	250
Capital expenditures, negative net present value projects	0	500
Cash flow	$250	$250
Free cash flow	$250	$750

---

development and on poor diversification attempts through acquisitions. Jensen argues that these companies would have been better off paying these excess cash flows to shareholders through share repurchases or exchanges with debt.

These two companies have identical cash flows and the same total capital expenditures. However, the Winner Company spends only on projects that add value (in terms of positive net present value projects), whereas the Loser Company spends on both profitable projects and wasteful projects. The Winner Company has a lower free cash flow than the Loser Company, indicating that they are using the generated cash flows in a more profitable manner. The lesson is that the existence of a high level of free cash flow is not necessarily good—it may simply suggest that the company is either a very good takeover target or the company has the potential for investing in unprofitable investments. Positive free cash flow may be good or bad news; likewise, negative free cash flow may be good or bad news:

Free Cash Flow	Good News	Bad News
+	Generating substantial operating cash flows, beyond those necessary for profitable projects.	Generating more cash flows than it needs for profitable projects and may waste these cash flows on unprofitable projects.
−	Has more profitable projects than it has operating cash flows and must rely on external financing to fund these projects.	Unable to generate sufficient operating cash flows to satisfy its investment needs for future growth.

Therefore, once the free cash flow is calculated, other information (e.g., trends in profitability) must be considered to evaluate the operating performance and financial condition of the company.

Calculating Free Cash Flow

There is some confusion when this theoretical concept is applied to actual companies. The primary difficulty is that the amount of capital expenditures necessary to maintain the business at its current rate of growth is generally not known; companies do not report this item and may not even be able to determine how much of a period's capital expenditures are attributed to maintenance and how much are attributed to expansion.

One approach is to estimate free cash flow by assuming that all capital expenditures are necessary for the maintenance of the current growth of the company. Though there is little justification in using all expenditures, this is a practical solution to an impractical calculation. This assumption allows us to estimate free cash flows using published financial statements.

Another issue in the calculation is defining what is truly "free" cash flow. Generally we think of "free" cash flow as what is left over after all necessary financing expenditures are paid; this means that free cash flow is after interest on debt is paid. Others calculate free cash flow before such financing expenditures, others calculate free cash flow after interest, and still others calculate free cash flow after both interest and dividends (assuming that dividends are a commitment, though not a legal commitment).

There is no one correct method of calculating free cash flow and different analysts may arrive at different estimates of free cash flow for a company. The problem is that it is impossible to measure free cash flow as dictated by the theory, so many methods have arisen to calculate this cash flow. A simple method is to start with the cash flow from operations and then deduct capital expenditures:

$$\text{Free cash flow (Definition 1)} = \text{Cash flow from operations} - \text{Capital expendiures} \qquad (12.5)$$

This is the same as the discretionary cash flow, our fourth definition of cash flow that we discussed previously. For Exemplar in FY20X2:

	Cash flow from operations	$290
LESS	Capital expenditures	100
EQUALS	Free cash flow (Definition 1)	$190

Another estimate of free cash flow is to adjust the cash flow from operations for the after-tax interest, adding this amount back to arrive at an adjusted cash flow from operations. We make this adjustment because we want to estimate how much free cash flow is available to both bondholders and equity owners:[6]

$$\text{Free cash flow (Definition 2)} = \text{Cash flow from operations} - \text{Adjusted interest} - \text{Capital expenditures} \qquad (12.6)$$

---

[6]This definition is similar to still another definition of free cash flow, *net free cash flow*, which adjusts for both interest expenses, but only deducts cash taxes, not the sum of deferred taxes and cash taxes as represented by the tax expense on a company's income statement.

We often refer to this calculation of free cash flow as the *free cash flow to the firm* (FCFF) because it is the flow available to the suppliers of capital.

Exemplar's interest expense is $17 million and its tax rate is 40%. Making an adjustment for the after-tax interest and financing expenses, $17 million $(1 - 0.4) = \$10.2$ million (which we round to $10 million for simplicity in our example), we have another measure of free cash flow:

	Cash flow from operations	$290
Plus	Adjusted interest	10
	Adjusted cash flow from operations	$300
Less	Capital expenditures	100
Equals	Free cash flow, FCFF (Definition 2)	$200

Still another free cash flow is a cash flow that adjusts for the net borrowings of the company. The basic idea is that if we want to focus on the funds available to the owners, we need to consider not only the capital expenditures, which reduce cash flow available to owners, but also funds raised through borrowing, which are available to owners.

$$\frac{\text{Free cash flow}}{\text{(Definition 3)}} = \frac{\text{Cash flow}}{\text{from operations}} - \frac{\text{Capital}}{\text{expenditures}} + \text{Borrowings} - \frac{\text{Debt}}{\text{repayments}}$$

$$(12.7)$$

This free cash flow definition begins with cash flow from operations, removes capital expenditures, adds new borrowings, and subtracts debt repayments:

	Cash flow from operations	$290
Less	Capital expenditures	100
Plus	Borrowings	0
Less	Debt repayments	152
Equals	Free cash flow, FCFE (Definition 3)	$ 38

Based on this third definition of free cash flow, Exemplar has free cash flow available to spend for FY20X2 of $38 million. We refer to this definition of free cash flow as the *free cash flow to equity*, FCFE, because it is the cash flow available for the company's owners.

TRY IT! CALCULATING FREE CASH FLOWS

Calculate the free cash flow using each of the three definitions and Exemplar's FY20X1 financial information:

Free cash flow (Definition 1)	
Free cash flow (Definition 2)	
Free cash flow (Definition 3)	

USEFULNESS OF CASH FLOWS ANALYSIS

The usefulness of cash flows for financial analysis depends on whether cash flows provide unique information or provide information in a manner that is more accessible or convenient for the analyst. The cash flow information provided in the statement of cash flows, for example, is not necessarily unique because most, if not all, of the information is available through analysis of the balance sheet and income statement. What the statement does provide is a classification scheme that presents information in a manner that is easier to use and, perhaps, more illustrative of the company's financial position.

An analysis of cash flows and the sources of cash flows can reveal the following information:

- *The sources of financing the company's capital spending.* Does the company generate internally (i.e., from operations) a portion or all of the funds needed for its investment activities? If a company cannot generate cash flow from operations, this may indicate problems up ahead. Reliance on external financing (e.g., equity or debt issuance) may indicate a company's inability to sustain itself over time.
- *The company's dependence on borrowing.* Does the company rely heavily on borrowing that may result in difficulty in satisfying future debt service?
- *The quality of earnings.* Large and growing differences between income and cash flows suggest a low quality of earnings.

KRISPY KREME: NOT SO SWEET

Krispy Kreme, a wholesaler and retailer of doughnuts, grew rapidly after its initial public offering (IPO) in 2000. Income grew as Krispy Kreme increased the number of retail stores, but the tide in income turned in the 2004 fiscal year and losses continued thereafter:

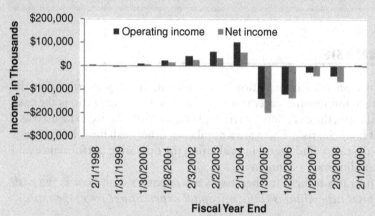

Krispy Kreme's growth after its IPO was financed by both operating activities and external financing, as evident from its cash flows:

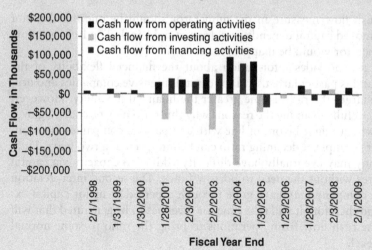

(continued)

(Continued)

As you can see, approximately half of the funds to support its rapid growth came from financing, in particular debt financing. This resulted in problems as the company's debt burden became almost three times its equity as revenue growth slowed by the 2005 fiscal year.

RATIO ANALYSIS

One use of cash flow information is in ratio analysis, primarily with the balance sheet and income statement information. One such ratio is the cash flow–based ratio, the cash flow interest coverage ratio, which can be used as a measure of financial risk. There are a number of other cash flow–based ratios that an analyst may find useful in evaluating the operating performance and financial condition of a company.

A useful ratio to help further assess a company's cash flow is the *cash flow to capital expenditures ratio*, or *capital expenditures coverage ratio*:

$$\text{Cash flow to capital expenditures} = \frac{\text{Cash flow}}{\text{Capital expenditures}} \qquad (12.8)$$

The cash flow measure in the numerator should be one that has not already removed capital expenditures; for example, including free cash flow in the numerator would be inappropriate.

This ratio provides information about the financial flexibility of the company and is particularly useful for capital-intensive companies and utilities.[7] The larger the ratio is, the greater the financial flexibility. However, one must carefully examine the reasons why this ratio may be changing over time and why it might be out of line with comparable companies in the industry. For example, a declining ratio can be interpreted in two ways. First, the company may eventually have difficulty adding to capacity via capital expenditures without the need to borrow funds. The second interpretation is that the company may have gone through a period of major capital expansion and therefore it will take time for revenues to be generated that will increase the cash flow from operations to bring the ratio to some normal long-run level.

---

[7]Fridson, *Financial Statement Analysis: A Practitioner's Guide*, 173.

Another useful cash flow ratio is the *cash flow to debt ratio*:

$$\text{Cash flow to debt} = \frac{\text{Cash flow}}{\text{Debt}} \qquad (12.9)$$

where debt can be represented as total debt, long-term debt, or a debt measure that captures a specific range of maturity (e.g., debt maturing in five years). This ratio gives a measure of a company's ability to meet maturing debt obligations. A more specific formulation of this ratio is Fitch's *CFAR* ratio, which compares a company's three-year average net free cash flow to its maturing debt over the next five years. By comparing the company's average net free cash flow to the expected obligations in the near term (i.e., five years), this ratio provides information on the company's credit quality.

Using Cash Flow Information

The analysis of cash flows provides information that can be used along with other financial data to help assess the financial condition of a company. Consider the cash-flow-to-capital-expenditures and the cash-flow-to-debt ratios calculated using the different measures of cash flow for Exemplar Corporation for the 20X2 fiscal year:

	Cash Flow to Debt Ratio	Cash Flow to Capital Expenditures
Cash flow (Definition 1)	0.717	2.224
Cash flow (Definition 2)	1.025	3.200
Cash flow (Definition 3)	0.990	1.274
Cash flow (Definition 4)	0.648	0.274
Free cash flow (Definition 1)	0.648	0.274
Free cash flow (Definition 2)	0.683	0.370
Free cash flow (Definition 3)	0.129	0.520

The cash flow to capital expenditures ratio ranges from 0.274 to 3.2, whereas the cash flow to debt ratio ranges from 0.129 to 1.025. As you can see, it is important to understand the differences among the cash flow measures, especially when interpreting cash flows and ratios involving cash flows.

CASH FLOW MATTERS

James Largay and Clyde Stickney analyzed the financial statements of W. T. Grant during the 1966–1974 period preceding its bankruptcy in 1975 and ultimate liquidation.[8] They noted that financial indicators such as profitability ratios, turnover ratios, and liquidity ratios showed some downward trends, but provided no definite clues to the company's impending bankruptcy.

A study of cash flows from operations, however, revealed that the company's operations were causing an increasing drain on cash, rather than providing cash. This necessitated an increased use of external financing, the required interest payments on which exacerbated the cash flow drain. Cash flow analysis clearly was a valuable tool in this case since W. T. Grant had been running a negative cash flow from operations for years.

[8]James A. Largay and Clyde P. Stickney, "Cash Flows, Ratio Analysis and the W. T. Grant Company Bankruptcy," *Financial Analysts Journal* 36 (1980): 51–54.

THE BOTTOM LINE

- Cash flow analysis is important because a company's sustainability depends on its ability to generate cash flows. There are alternative measures of cash flow, including cash flow from operations and free cash flow.
- A company's free cash flow is the cash flow it generates in excess of what is needed for its capital expenditures.
- We can examine sources and uses of cash flows to gauge a company's ability to finance its own operations. Especially useful in this task is the cash flows from operating activities, financing activities, and investing activities that a company reports on its statement of cash flows. We can also use cash flow financial ratios to evaluate a company's performance and condition.
- Free cash flow is a company's cash flow that remains after making capital investments that maintain the company's current rate of growth. It is not possible to calculate free cash flow precisely, resulting in many different variations in calculations of this measure.

SOLUTIONS TO TRY IT! PROBLEMS

Calculating Cash Flows

Cash flow (Definition 1)	$222
Cash flow (Definition 2)	$320
Cash flow (Definition 3)	$127
Cash flow (Definition 4)	$ 27

Calculating Free Cash Flows

Free cash flow (Definition 1)	$27
Free cash flow (Definition 2)	$37
Free cash flow (Definition 3)	$52

QUESTIONS

1. Why is depreciation added back to net income to arrive at cash flow?
2. Why do we adjust net income for changes in working capital accounts?
3. If a company has cash flow from operations of $3 million, depreciation and amortization of $2 million, and its working capital accounts did not change from the previous period, what its net income for this period?
4. How does the statement of cash flows relate to the balance sheet?
5. How does the statement of cash flows relate to the income statement?
6. Is it possible for a company to have a net loss for a period, yet still have a positive cash flow?
7. What distinguishes the free cash flow of a firm from its cash flow from operations?
8. What is the relation between EBITDA and cash flow from operations?
9. How can a negative free cash flow be considered good news?
10. How can a positive free cash flow be considered bad news?
11. Consider the Austin Company, which has a free cash flow to equity of $100 million, and free cash flow to the firm of $125 million. If the Austin Company had interest after tax of $10 million, what is the amount of net borrowing for the Austin Company for this period?
12. Suppose the cash flow from operations of the Knoxville Company is $200 million and the company had capital expenditures of $50 million during this period. If Knoxville has no debt in its capital structure, what is its cash flow to the firm? What is its cash flow to equity?

13. Suppose Provo, Inc., had net income of $30 million for the most recent fiscal period. If its depreciation and amortization for the period is $3 million and its cash flow from operations is $35 million, what is its change in working capital for this most recent fiscal period?
14. Using the data in this chapter for the Exemplar Company for fiscal year 20X2 and the cash flow from operations as the measure of cash flow (cash flow definition 3), calculate the:
    a. Cash flow to capital expenditures ratio.
    b. Cash flow to debt ratio.

CHAPTER 13

Capital Budgeting

*The general principle is, therefore, that out of the various
income-streams at the disposal of the capitalist, he chooses the
most advantageous, or more fully expressed, the one which,
compared with any other, offers advantages which, reckoned in
present estimation at the given rate of interest, outweigh the
disadvantages; and this is evidently merely a new formulation of
the original principle that the use chosen will be that which has the
maximum present value at the given rate of interest.*
— Irving Fisher, *The Rate of Interest: Its Nature,
Determination and Relation to Economic Phenomena*
(New York: MacMillan Company, 1907), p. 152

Capital budgeting decisions involve the long-term commitment of a company's scarce resources in long-term investments. These decisions play a prominent role in determining whether a company will be successful. The commitment of funds to a particular capital project can be enormous and may be irreversible. Whereas some capital budgeting decisions are routine decisions that do not change the course or risk of a company, there are strategic capital budgeting decisions that will either have an impact on the company's future market position in its current product lines or permit it to expand into a new product line in the future.

The company's capital investment decision may be comprised of a number of distinct decisions, each referred to as a *project*. A capital project is a set of assets that are contingent on one another and are considered together. For example, suppose a company is considering the production of a new product. This capital project requires the company to acquire land, build facilities, and purchase production equipment. And this project may also require the company to increase its investment in its working capital—inventory, cash, or accounts receivable. *Working capital* is the collection of assets needed for day-to-day operations that support a company's long-term investments.

There are several techniques that are used in practice to evaluate capital budgeting proposals. Evaluating whether a company should invest in a capital project requires an analysis of whether the project adds value to the company. In this chapter we cover the capital budgeting decision. First, we explain the capital budgeting process and the classification of investment projects. Second, we show how to estimate the expected change to a company's future cash flow as a result of a capital investment decision. As will become apparent, estimating cash flow is an imprecise art at best. Finally, we look at the techniques used to evaluate capital budgeting projects.

INVESTMENT DECISIONS AND OWNERS' WEALTH

Managers must evaluate a number of factors in making investment decisions. Not only does the financial manager need to estimate how much the company's future cash flows will change if it invests in a project, but the manager must also evaluate the uncertainty associated with these future cash flows.

The value of the company today is the present value of all its future cash flows. But we need to understand better where these future cash flows come from. They come from assets that are already in place, which are the assets accumulated as a result of all past investment decisions, and future investment opportunities.

The value of a company is therefore the present value of the company's future cash flows, where these future cash flows include the cash flows from all assets in place and the cash flows from future investment opportunities. These future cash flows are discounted at a rate that represents investors' assessments of the uncertainty that these cash flows will flow in the amounts and when expected. As you can see, we need to evaluate the risk of these future cash flows in order to understand the risk of any investment opportunity on the value of the company.

Cash flow risk comes from two basic sources:

1. **Sales risk.** The degree of uncertainty related to the number of units that will be sold and the price of the good or service.
2. **Operating risk.** The degree of uncertainty concerning operating cash flows that arises from the particular mix of fixed and variable operating costs.

Sales risk is related to the economy and the market in which the company's goods and services are sold. *Operating risk*, for the most part, is determined by the product or service that the company provides and is related to the sensitivity of operating cash flows to changes in sales. We refer to the combination of these two risks as *business risk*.

A project's business risk is reflected in the discount rate, which is the rate of return required to compensate the suppliers of capital (bondholders and owners) for the amount of risk they bear. From the perspective of investors, the discount rate is the *required rate of return* (RRR). From the company's perspective, the discount rate is the *cost of capital*—what it costs the company to raise a dollar of new capital. The cost of capital and the required rate of return are the same concept, but from different perspectives: the cost of capital is generally from the perspective of the business enterprise, whereas the required rate of return is from the perspective of the suppliers of capital, the creditors and owners. Therefore, we will use the terms interchangeably in our study of capital budgeting. In the context of evaluating capital projects, the cost of capital is the cost of raising new capital appropriate for the risk of the project; hence, the cost of capital is project-specific.

For example, suppose a company invests in a new project, Project X. How does the Project X affect the company's value?

- If Project X generates cash flows that just compensate the suppliers of capital for the risk they bear on this project (that is, it earns the cost of capital), the value of the company does not change.
- If Project X generates cash flows greater than needed to compensate them for the risk they take on, it earns more than the cost of capital, increasing the value of the company.
- If Project X generates cash flows *less* than needed, it earns less than the cost of capital, decreasing the value of the company.

How do we know whether the cash flows are more than or less than needed to compensate for the risk that they will indeed need? If we discount all the cash flows at the cost of capital, we can assess how this project affects the present value of the company. If the expected change in the value of the company from an investment is:

- Positive, the project returns more than the cost of capital, and therefore it adds value to the company.
- Negative, the project returns less than the cost of capital, and therefore it reduces the value of the company.
- Zero, the project returns the cost of capital, and therefore it does not affect the value of the company.

Capital budgeting is the process of identifying and selecting investments in long-lived assets; that is, selecting assets expected to produce benefits over more than one year.

THE CAPITAL BUDGETING PROCESS

Because a company must continually evaluate possible investments, capital budgeting is an ongoing process. However, before a company begins thinking about capital budgeting, it must first determine its corporate strategy—its broad set of objectives for future investment. For example, the Walt Disney Company has stated that its objective is to "be one of the world's leading producers and providers of entertainment and information, using its portfolio of brands to differentiate its content, services, and consumer products."

How does a company achieve its corporate strategy? This is accomplished by making investments in long-lived assets that maximize owners' wealth. Selecting these projects is what capital budgeting is all about.

Stages in the Capital Budgeting Process

Though every company has its own set of procedures and processes for capital budgeting, we can generalize the process as consisting of five stages, as we illustrate in Exhibit 13.1.

Stage 1: Investment Screening and Selection
> Projects consistent with the corporate strategy are identified by production, marketing, and research and development management of the company. Once identified, projects are evaluated and screened

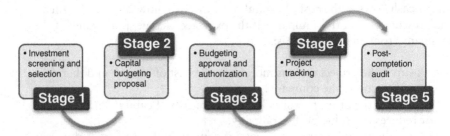

EXHIBIT 13.1   The Capital Budgeting Process

by estimating how they affect the future cash flows of the company and, hence, the value of the company.

Stage 2: Capital Budgeting Proposal

A capital budget is proposed for the projects surviving the screening and selection process. The budget lists the recommended projects and the dollar amount of investment needed for each. This proposal may start as an estimate of expected revenues and costs, but as the project analysis is refined, data from marketing, purchasing, engineering, accounting, and finance functions are put together.

Stage 3: Budgeting Approval and Authorization

Projects included in the capital budget are authorized, allowing further fact gathering and analysis, and approved, allowing expenditures for the projects. In some companies, the projects are authorized and approved at the same time. In others, a project must first be authorized, requiring more research before it can be formally approved. Formal authorization and approval procedures are typically used on larger expenditures; smaller expenditures are at the discretion of management.

Stage 4: Project Tracking

After a project is approved, work on it begins. The manager reports periodically on its expenditures, as well as on any revenues associated with it. This is referred to as *project tracking*, the communication link between the decision makers and the operating management of the company. For example, tracking can identify cost over-runs and uncover the need for more marketing research.

Stage 5: Post-completion Audit

No matter the number of stages in a company's capital budgeting process, most companies include some form of *post-completion audit* that involves a comparison of the actual cash from operations of the project with the estimated cash flow used to justify the project. There are two reasons why the post-completion audit is beneficial. First, many companies find that the knowledge that a post-completion audit will be undertaken causes project proposers to be more careful before endorsing a project. Second, it will help senior management identify proposers who are consistently optimistic or pessimistic with respect to cash flow estimates. Senior management will then be in a better position to evaluate the bias that may be expected when a particular individual or group proposes a project.

Classifying Investment Projects

Financial decision-makers may classify projects in different ways, based on the projects' useful life, risk, or dependence on other projects. Classifying projects may help the decision-maker in terms of estimating the cash flows of the projects and the methods used to analyze the projects. We take a brief look at the different ways projects may be classified.

Classifying by Economic Life An investment generally provides benefits over a limited period of time, referred to as its *economic life.* The economic life or useful life of an asset is determined by factors including physical deterioration, obsolescence, and the degree of competition in the market for a product.

The economic life is an estimate of the length of time that the asset will provide benefits to the company. After its useful life, the revenues generated by the asset tend to decline rapidly and its expenses tend to increase.

Typically, an investment requires expenditures up front—immediately —and provides benefits in the form of cash flows received in the future. If benefits are received only within the current period—within one year of making the investment—we refer to the Project X as a short-term investment. If these benefits are received beyond the current period, we refer to the Project X as a long-term project and refer to the expenditure as a capital expenditure.

Any project representing an investment may comprise one or more assets. For example, a new product may require investment in production equipment, a building, and transportation equipment—all making up the bundle of assets comprising the project we are evaluating. Short-term investment decisions involve, primarily, investments in current assets: cash, marketable securities, accounts receivable, and inventory. The objective of investing in short-term assets is the same as long-term assets: maximizing owners' wealth. Nevertheless, we consider them separately for two practical reasons:

1. Decisions about long-term assets are based on projections of cash flows far into the future and require us to consider the time value of money.
2. Long-term assets do not figure into the daily operating needs of the company.

Decisions regarding short-term investments, or current assets, are concerned with day-to-day operations. And a company needs some level of current assets to act as a cushion in case of unusually poor operating periods, when cash flows from operations are less than expected.

Classifying by Risk   Suppose you are faced with two investments, A and B, each promising a $100 cash inflow 10 years from today. If A is riskier than B, what are they worth to you today? If you do not like risk, you would consider A less valuable than B because the chance of getting the $100 in 10 years is less for A than for B. Therefore, valuing a project requires considering the risk associated with its future cash flows.

The project's risk of return can be classified according to the nature of the project represented by the investment:

- *Replacement projects:* investments in the replacement of existing equipment or facilities.
- *Expansion projects:* investments in projects that broaden existing product lines and existing markets.
- *New products and markets:* projects that involve introducing a new product or entering into a new market.
- *Mandated projects:* projects required by government laws or agency rules.

Replacement projects include the maintenance of existing assets to continue the current level of operating activity. Projects that reduce costs, such as replacing older technology with newer technology or improving the efficiency of equipment or personnel, are also considered replacement projects.

To evaluate replacement projects we need to compare the value of the company with the replacement asset to the value of the company without that same replacement asset. What we're really doing in this comparison is looking at opportunity costs: what cash flows would have been if the company had stayed with the old asset.

There's little risk in the cash flows from replacement projects. The company is simply replacing equipment or buildings already operating and producing cash flows. And the company typically has experience in managing similar new equipment.

Expansion projects are intended to enlarge a company's established product or market. There is little risk associated with expansion projects. The reason: A company with a history of experience in a product or market can estimate future cash flows with more certainty when considering expansion than when introducing a new product outside its existing product line.

Investment projects that involve introducing new products or entering into new markets are riskier than the replacement and expansion projects. That's because the company has little or no management experience in the new product or market. Hence, there is more uncertainty about the future cash flows from investments in new product or new market projects.

A company is forced or coerced into its *mandated projects*. These are government mandated projects typically found in "heavy" industries, such as utilities, transportation, and chemicals, all industries requiring a large portion of their assets in production activities. Government agencies, such as the Occupational Safety and Health Administration (OSHA) or the Environmental Protection Agency (EPA), may impose requirements that companies install specific equipment or alter their activities, such as how they dispose of waste or remediate property.

Classifying by Dependence on Other Projects   In addition to considering the future cash flows generated by project, a company must consider how it affects the assets already in place—the results of previous project decisions—as well as other projects that may be undertaken. Projects can be classified as follows according to the degree of dependence with other projects: independent projects, mutually exclusive projects, contingent projects, and complementary projects.

An *independent project* is one whose cash flows are not related to the cash flows of any other project. In other words, accepting or rejecting an independent project does not affect the acceptance or rejection of other projects. An independent project can be evaluated strictly on the effect it will have on the value of a company without having to consider how it affects the company's other investment opportunities, and vice versa.

Projects are *mutually exclusive projects* if the acceptance of one precludes the acceptance of other projects. There are some situations where it is technically impossible to take on more than one project. For example, suppose a manufacturer is considering whether to replace its production facilities with more modern equipment. The company may solicit bids among the different manufacturers of this equipment. The decision consists of comparing two choices:

1. Keeping its existing production facilities, or
2. Replacing the facilities with the modern equipment of one manufacturer.

Because the company cannot use more than one production facility, it must evaluate each bid and determine the most attractive one. The alternative production facilities are mutually exclusive projects: the company can accept only one bid. The alternatives of keeping existing facilities or replacing them are also mutually exclusive projects. The company cannot keep the existing facilities and replace them!

Contingent projects are dependent on the acceptance of another project. For example, toy and video-game tie-in agreements with movies are dependent on the movie coming to the market. Or, as another example, the manufacturer of an automobile part, such as a specifically-designed electric window, is contingent on the sale of the automobile.

Another form of dependence is found in *complementary projects*. Projects are complementary projects if the investment in one enhances the cash flows of one or more other projects. Consider a manufacturer of personal computer equipment. The sale of computers that have video-gaming capabilities may spur sales of video-games or video-game controls.

DETERMINING CASH FLOWS FROM INVESTMENTS

A company invests only to make its owners "better off," meaning increasing the value of their ownership interest. A company will have cash flows in the future from its past investment decisions. When it invests in new assets, it expects the future cash flows to be greater than without this new investment. Otherwise it doesn't make sense to make this investment. The difference between the cash flows of the company with the investment project and the cash flows of the company without the investment project—both over the same period of time—is referred to as the project's *incremental cash flows*.

To evaluate an investment, we'll have to look at how it will change the future cash flows of the company. In other words, we examine how much the value of the company changes as a result of the investment. The change in a company's value as a result of a new investment is the difference between its benefits and its costs:

Change in the value of the company = Project's benefits − Project's costs

A more useful way of evaluating the change in the value is the breakdown the project's cash flows into two components:

1. The present value of the cash flows from the project's operating activities (revenues and operating expenses), referred to as the project's *operating cash flows* (OCF); and
2. The present value of the investment cash flows, which are the expenditures needed to acquire the project's assets and any cash flows from disposing the project's assets.

or,

Change in the value of the company = Present value of the change in operating cash flows + Present value of investment cash flows

The present value of a project's operating cash flows is typically positive (indicating predominantly cash inflows) and the present value of the investment cash flows is typically negative (indicating predominantly cash outflows).

Investment Cash Flows

When we consider the cash flows of an investment we must also consider all the cash flows associated with acquiring and disposing of assets in the investment. An investment may comprise:

- one asset or many assets;
- an asset purchased and another sold; and
- cash outlays that occur at the beginning of the project or spread over several years.

Let's first become familiar with cash flows related to acquiring assets; then we'll look at cash flows related to disposing assets.

Asset Acquisition In acquiring any asset, there are three cash flows to consider:

1. The cost of the asset,
2. Set-up expenditures, including shipping and installation; and
3. Any tax credit.

The tax credit may be an investment tax credit or a special credit—such as a credit for a pollution control device—depending on the tax law. The cash flow associated with acquiring an asset is:

Cash flow from acquiring assets = Cost + Set-up expenditures + Tax credit.

Suppose the company buys equipment that costs $100,000 and it costs $10,000 to install. If the company is eligible for a 10% tax-credit on this equipment (that is, 10% of the total cost of buying and installing the equipment), the change in the company's cash flow from acquiring the asset is $99,000:

$$\begin{array}{l} \text{Cash flow from} \\ \text{acquiring assets} \end{array} = -\$100,000 - 10,000 + 0.10\,(\$100,000 + 10,000)$$
$$= -\$100,000 - 10,000 + \$11,000$$
$$= -\$99,000$$

The cash outflow is −$99,000 when this asset is acquired: −$110,000 to buy and install the equipment and $11,000 in from the reduction in taxes.

What about expenditures made in the past for assets or research that would be used in the project we're evaluating? Suppose the company spent $1,000,000 over the past three years developing a new type of toothpaste. Should the company consider this $1,000,000 spent on research and development when deciding whether to produce this new project we are considering? No! These expenses have already been made and do not affect how the new product changes the future cash flows of the company. We refer to this $1,000,000 as a sunk cost and do not consider it in the analysis of our new project. Whether or not the company goes ahead with this new product, this $1,000,000 has been spent. A *sunk cost* is any cost that has already been incurred that does not affect future cash flows of the company.

Let's consider another example. Suppose the company owns a building that is currently empty. Let's say the company suddenly has an opportunity to use it for the production of a new product. Is the cost of the building relevant to the new product decision? The cost of the building itself is a sunk cost because it was an expenditure made as part of some previous investment decision. The cost of the building does not affect the decision to go ahead with the new product.

Suppose the company is using the building in some way producing cash (i.e., renting it) and the new project is going to take over the entire building. The cash flows given up represent opportunity costs that must be included in the analysis of the new project. However, these forgone cash flows are not asset acquisition cash flows. Because they represent operating cash flows that could have occurred, but will not because of the new project, they must be considered part of the project's future operating cash flows. Further, if we incur costs in renovating the building to manufacture the new product, the renovation costs are relevant and should be included in our asset acquisition cash flows.

EXAMPLE 13.1: INITIAL CASH FLOW

Suppose a company spends $1 million on research and development of a new drug. The cost to buy the necessary equipment to produce and distribute the drug is $2.5 million. Working capital is expected to increase by $250,000 when the company embarks on the new product. What is the initial cash flow for this project?

(continued)

(Continued)

Solution

Cash Flow

Cost of equipment	−$2,500,000
Increase in working capital	−250,000
Initial cash flow	−$2,750,000

Asset Disposition Many new investments require getting rid of old assets. At the end of the useful life of an asset, the company may be able to sell it or may have to pay someone to haul it away. If the company is making a decision that involves replacing an existing asset, the cash flow from disposing of the old asset must be included because it is a cash flow relevant to the acquisition of the new asset.

If the company disposes of an asset, whether at the end of its useful life or when it is replaced, we must consider two types of cash flows:

1. what you receive or pay in disposing of the asset; and
2. any tax consequences resulting from the disposal.

or

$$\text{Cash flow from disposing assets} = \text{Proceeds or payment from disposing assets} - \text{Taxes from disposing assets}$$

The proceeds are what you expect to sell the asset for if you can get someone to buy it. If the company must pay for the disposal of the asset, this cost is a cash outflow.

Consider the investment in a dry cleaner. The current owner may want to leave the business (retire, whatever), selling the dry cleaning business to another dry cleaner proprietor. But if a buyer cannot be found because of lack of buyers in the area, the current owner may be required to mitigate the site for any environmental damage from the solvents. Thus, a cost is incurred at the end of the asset's life.

The tax consequences are a bit more complicated. Taxes depend on:

- the expected sales price, and
- the book value of the asset for tax purposes at the time of disposition.

If a company sells the asset for more than its book value but less than its original cost, the difference between the sales price and the book value is a gain, taxable at ordinary tax rates. If a company sells the asset for more than its original cost, then the gain is broken into two parts:

1. *Capital gain:* the difference between the sales price and the original cost; and
2. *Recapture of depreciation:* the difference between the original cost and the book value.

The capital gain is the benefit from the appreciation in the value of the asset and may be taxed at special rates, depending on the tax law at the time of sale. The recapture of depreciation represents the amount by which the company has over-depreciated the asset during its life. This means that more depreciation has been deducted from income (reducing taxes) than necessary to reflect the usage of the asset. The recapture portion is taxed at the ordinary tax rates, since this excess depreciation taken all these years has reduced taxable income.

If a company sells an asset for less than its book value, the result is a capital loss. In this case, the asset's value has decreased by more than the amount taken for depreciation for tax purposes. A capital loss is given special tax treatment:

- If there are capital gains in the same tax year as the capital loss, they are combined, so that the capital loss reduces the taxes paid on capital gains, and
- If there are no capital gains to offset against the capital loss, the capital loss is used to reduce ordinary taxable income.

The benefit from a loss on the sale of an asset is the amount by which taxes are reduced. The reduction in taxable income is referred to as a tax shield, since the loss shields some income from taxation. If the company has a loss of $1,000 on the sale of an asset and has a tax rate of 40%, this means that its taxable income is $1,000 less and its taxes are $400 less than they would have been without the sale of the asset.

We summarize the breakdown of gains on sales of assets in Exhibit 13.2. The key is to compare the sales price of the asset with its original cost and book value.

Suppose you are evaluating an asset that costs $10,000 that you expect to sell in five years. Suppose further that the book value of the asset for tax purposes will be $3,000 after five years and that the company's tax rate is 40%. What are the expected cash flows from disposing this asset? If you

EXHIBIT 13.2   Gains and Losses on Sales

expect the company to sell the asset for $8,000 in five years, $10,000 − 3,000 = $7,000 of the asset's cost will be depreciated, yet the asset lost only $10,000 − 8,000 = $2,000 in value. Therefore, the company has *over-depreciated* the asset by $5,000. Because this over-depreciation represents deductions to be taken on the company's tax returns over the five years that don't reflect the actual depreciation in value (the asset doesn't lose $7,000 in value, only $2,000), this $5,000 is taxed at ordinary tax rates. If the company's tax rate is 40%, the tax is 40% × $5,000, or $2,000.

The cash flow from disposition is the sum of the direct cash flow (someone pays us for the asset or the company pays someone to dispose of it) and the tax consequences. In this example, the cash flow is the $8,000 we expect someone to pay the company for the asset, less the $2,000 in taxes we expect the company to pay, or $6,000 cash inflow.

Suppose instead that you expect the company to sell this asset in five years for $12,000. Again, the asset is over-depreciated by $7,000. In fact, the asset is not expected to depreciate, but rather appreciate over the five years. The $7,000 in depreciation is recaptured after five years and taxed at ordinary rates: 40% of $7,000, or $2,800. The $2,000 capital gain is the appreciation in the value of the asset and may be taxed at special rates. If the tax rate on capital gain income is 30%, you expect the company to pay 30% of $2,000, or $600 in taxes on this gain. Selling the asset in five years for $12,000 therefore results in an expected cash inflow of $12,000 − 2,800 − 600 = $8,600.

Suppose you expect the company to sell the asset in five years for $1,000. If the company can reduce its ordinary taxable income by the amount of the capital loss, $3,000 − 1,000 = $2,000, our tax will be 40% of $2,000, or $800 because of this loss. We refer to this reduction in the taxes as a tax shield, since the loss "shields" $2,000 of income from taxes. Combining the $800 tax reduction with the cash flow from selling the asset, the $1,000, gives the company a cash inflow of $1,800.

Let's also not forget about disposing of any existing assets. Suppose the company bought equipment 10 years ago and at that time expected to be able to sell fifteen years later for $10,000. If the company decides today to replace this equipment, it must consider what it is giving up by not disposing of an asset as planned. If the company does not replace the equipment today, it would continue to depreciate it for five more years and then sell it for $10,000; if the company replaces the equipment today, it would not have five more years' depreciation on the replaced equipment and it would not have $10,000 in five years (but perhaps some other amount today). This $10,000 in five years, less any taxes, is a forgone cash flow that we must figure into the investment cash flows. Also, the depreciation the company would have had on the replaced asset must be considered in analyzing the replacement asset's operating cash flows.

 TRY IT! DISPOSITION CASH FLOWS, USING STRAIGHT-LINE

Consider equipment that is bought for $500,000. Suppose it is depreciated over four years at a straight-line rate of 25% per year. At the end of two years, the equipment is sold for $100,000. What is the cash flow effect of this sale? Assume a 35% tax rate.

Operating Cash Flows

In the simplest form of investment, there will be a cash outflow when the asset is acquired and there may be either a cash inflow or an outflow at the end of its economic life. In most cases these are not the only cash flows—the investment may result in changes in revenues, expenditures, taxes, and working capital. These are operating cash flows because they result directly from the operating activities—the day-to-day activities of the company.

What we are after here are estimates of operating cash flows. We cannot know for certain what these cash flows will be in the future, but we must attempt to estimate them. What is the basis for these estimates? We base them on marketing research, engineering analyses, operations research, analysis of our competitors—and our managerial experience.

The key in the analysis of operating cash flows is to determine the incremental cash flows: "How are the cash flows of the company expected to change when the new project is undertaken?"

Change in Revenues Suppose we are a food processor considering a new investment in a line of frozen dinner products. If we introduce a new ready-to-eat dinner product that is not frozen, our marketing research will indicate how much we should expect to sell. But where do these new product sales come from? Some may come from consumers who do not already buy frozen dinner products. But some of the not-frozen dinner product sales may come from consumers who choose to buy the not-frozen dinner product instead of frozen dinners. It would be nice if these consumers are giving up buying our competitors' frozen dinners. Yet some of them may be giving up buying our frozen dinners. So, when we introduce a new product, we are really interested in how it changes the sales of the entire company (that is, the incremental sales), rather than the sales of the new product alone.

We also need to consider any foregone revenues—opportunity costs—related to our investment. Suppose our company owns a building currently being rented to another company. If we are considering terminating that rental agreement so we can use the building for a new project, we need to consider the foregone rent—what we would have earned from the building. Therefore, the revenues from the new project are really only the additional revenues—the revenues from the new project minus the revenue we could have earned from renting the building.

So, when a company undertakes a new project, the financial managers want to know how it changes the company's total revenues, not merely the new product's revenues.

Change in Expenses When a company takes on a new project, all the costs associated with it change the company's expenses. If the investment involves changing the sales of an existing product, we need an estimate the change in unit sales. Once we have an estimate in how sales may change, we can develop an estimate of the additional costs of producing the additional number of units by consulting with production management. And, we will want an estimate of how the product's inventory may change when production and sales of the product change.

If the investment involves changes in the costs of production, we compare the costs without this investment with the costs with this investment. For example, if the investment is the replacement of an assembly line machine with a more efficient machine, we need to estimate the change in the company's overall production costs such as electricity, labor, materials, and management costs.

A new investment may change not only production costs but also operating costs, such as rental payments and administration costs. Changes in operating costs as a result of a new investment must be considered as part of the changes in the company's expenses. Increasing cash expenses are cash outflows, and decreasing cash expenses are cash inflows.

Change in Taxes Taxes figure into the operating cash flows in two ways. First, if revenues and expenses change, taxable income and, therefore, taxes change. That means we need to estimate the change in taxable income resulting from the changes in revenues and expenses resulting from a new project to determine the effect of taxes on the company. Second, the deduction for depreciation reduces taxes. Depreciation itself is not a cash flow. But depreciation reduces the taxes that must be paid, shielding income from taxation. The tax shield from depreciation is like a cash inflow.

Suppose a company is considering a new product that is expected to generate additional sales of $200,000 and increase expenses by $150,000. If the company's tax rate is 40%, considering only the change in sales and expenses, taxes go up by $50,000 × 40% or $20,000. This means that the company is expected to pay $20,000 more in taxes because of the increase in revenues and expenses.

Let's change this around and consider that the product will generate $200,000 in revenues and $250,000 in expenses. Considering only the change in revenues and expenses, if the tax rate is 40%, taxes go down by $50,000 × 40%, or $20,000. This means that we reduce our taxes by $20,000, which is like having a cash inflow of $20,000 from taxes.

Now, consider depreciation. When a company buys an asset that produces income, the tax laws allow it to depreciate the asset, reducing taxable income by a specified percentage of the asset's cost each year. By reducing taxable income, the company is reducing its taxes. The reduction in taxes is like a cash inflow since it reduces the company's cash outflow to the government.

Suppose a company has taxable income of $50,000 before depreciation and a flat tax rate of 40%. If the company is allowed to deduct depreciation of $10,000, how has this changed the taxes it pays?

	Without Depreciation	With Depreciation
Taxable income	$50,000	$40,000
Tax rate	× 0.40	× 0.40
Taxes	$20,000	$16,000

Depreciation reduces the company's tax-related cash outflow by $20,000 − 16,000 = $4,000 or, equivalently, by $10,000 × 40% = $4,000.

A reduction is an outflow (taxes in this case) is an inflow. We refer to the effect depreciation has on taxes as the *depreciation tax shield.*

Depreciation itself is not a cash flow. But in determining cash flows, we are concerned with the effect depreciation has on our taxes—and we all know that taxes are a cash outflow. Because depreciation reduces taxable income, depreciation reduces the tax outflow, which amounts to a cash inflow.

For tax purposes, companies use accelerated depreciation; specifically, the rates specified under the *Modified Accelerated Cost Recovery System* (MACRS) or straight-line. An accelerated method is preferred in most situations because it results in larger deductions sooner in the asset's life than using straight-line depreciation. Therefore, accelerated depreciation, if available, is preferable to straight-line due to the time value of money. We provide the MACRS depreciation rates in Exhibit 13.3. Depreciable assets are classified by type and the set of rates for that class prescribed by the U.S. Tax Code. For example, a truck is classified as a 5-year MACRS asset, so the rates associated with the 5-year column in Exhibit 13.3 are applied against the cost of the asset.

Suppose you have an asset that costs $100,000 and is considered a 3-year MACRS asset. What is the depreciation expense for tax purposes each year? What is the depreciation tax shield each year? If you keep the asset for five years and the tax rate is 35%,

Year	Depreciation Expense $100,000 × MACRS Rate	Ending Book Value Original Cost—Accumulated Depreciation	Depreciation Tax Shield Depreciation × 35%
1	$33,330	$66,670	$11,666
2	$44,450	$22,220	$15,558
3	$14,810	$7,410	$5,184
4	$7,410	$0	$2,594
5	$0	$0	$0

Under the present tax code, assets are depreciated to a zero book value. *Salvage value*—what we expect the asset to be worth at the end of its life—is not considered in calculating depreciation. So is salvage value totally irrelevant to the analysis? No. Salvage value is our best guess today of what the asset will be worth at the end of its useful life, sometime in the future. In other words, salvage value is our estimate of how much we can get when we

EXHIBIT 13.3 MACRS Depreciation Rates

Year	3-Year	5-Year	7-Year	10-Year	15-Year
1	33.33%	20.00%	14.29%	10.00%	5.00%
2	44.45	32.00	24.49	18.00	9.50
3	14.81	19.20	17.49	14.40	8.55
4	7.41	11.52	12.49	11.52	7.70
5		11.52	8.93	9.22	6.93
6		5.76	8.92	7.37	6.23
7			8.93	6.55	5.90
8			4.46	6.55	5.90
9				6.56	5.91
10				6.55	5.90
11				3.28	5.91
12					5.90
13					5.91
14					5.90
15					5.91
16					2.95

dispose of the asset. Just remember you can't use it to figure depreciation for tax purposes.

Let's look at another depreciation example, this time considering the effect of replacing an asset has on the depreciation tax shield cash flow. Suppose you are replacing a machine that you bought five years ago for $75,000. You were depreciating this old machine using straight-line depreciation over 10 years, or $7,500 depreciation per year. If you replace it with a new machine that costs $50,000 and is depreciated over five years, or $10,000 each year, how does the change in depreciation affect the cash flows if the company's tax rate is 30%? We can calculate the effect two ways:

1. We can compare the depreciation and related tax shield from the old and the new machines. The depreciation tax shield on the old machine is 30% of $7,500, or $2,250. The depreciation tax shield on the new machine is 30% of $10,000, or $3,000. Therefore, the change in the cash flow from depreciation is $3,000 − $2,250 = $750.
2. We can calculate the change in depreciation and calculate the tax shield related to the change in depreciation. The change in depreciation is $10,000 − 7,500 = $2,500. The change in the depreciation tax shield is 30% of $2,500, or $750.

TRY IT! ASSET DISPOSITION CASH FLOWS, USING MACRS

Consider equipment that is bought for $500,000. Suppose it is depreciated as a three-year MACRS asset. At the end of two years, the equipment is sold for $100,000. What is the cash flow effect of this sale? Assume a 35% tax rate.

Change in Working Capital

Working capital consists of short-term assets, also referred to as current assets, which support the day-to-day operating activity of the business. Net working capital is the difference between current assets and current liabilities. Net working capital is what would be left over if the company had to pay off its current obligations using its current assets. The adjustment we make for changes in net working capital is attributable to two sources:

1. a change in current asset accounts for transactions or precautionary needs; and
2. the use of the accrual method of accounting.

An investment may increase the company's level of operations, resulting in an increase in the net working capital needed (also considered transactions needs). If the investment is to produce a new product, the company may have to invest more in inventory (raw materials, work-in-process, and finished goods). If to increase sales means extending more credit, then the company's accounts receivable will increase. If the investment requires maintaining a higher cash balance to handle the increased level of transactions, the company will need more cash. If the investment makes the company's production facilities more efficient, it may be able to reduce the level of inventory.

Because of an increase in the level of transactions, the company may want to keep more cash and inventory on hand for precautionary purposes. That is because as the level of operations increase, the effect of any fluctuations in demand for goods and services may increase, requiring the company to keep additional cash and inventory "just in case." The company may increase working capital as a precaution because if there is greater variability of cash and inventory, a greater safety cushion will be needed. On the other hand, if a project enables the company to be more efficient or lowers costs, it may lower its investment in cash, marketable securities, or inventory, releasing funds for investment elsewhere in the company.

We also use the change in working capital to adjust accounting income (revenues less expenses) to a cash basis because cash flow is ultimately what we are valuing, not accounting numbers. But since we generally have only the accounting numbers to work from, we use this information, making adjustments to arrive at cash.

To see how this works, let's look at the cash flow from sales. Not every dollar of sales is collected in the year of sale. Customers may pay some time after the sale. Using information from the accounts receivable department about how payments are collected, we can determine the change in the cash flows from revenues. Suppose we expect sales in the first year to increase by $20,000 per month and it typically takes customers thirty days to pay. The change in cash flows from sales in the first year is $20,000 × 11 = $220,000—not $20,000 × 12 = $240,000. The way we adjust for this difference between what is sold and what is collected in cash is to keep track of the change in working capital, which is the change in accounts receivable in this case. An increase in working capital is used to adjust revenues downward to calculate cash flow:

Change in revenues	$240,000
Less: Increase in accounts receivable	20,000
Change in cash inflow from sales	$220,000

On the other side of the balance sheet, if the company is increasing its purchases of raw materials and incurring more production costs, such as labor, the company may increase its level of short-term liabilities, such as accounts payable and salary and wages payable.

Suppose expenses for materials and supplies are forecasted at $10,000 per month for the first year and it takes the company thirty days to pay. Expenses for the first year are $10,000 × 12 = $120,000, yet cash outflow for these expenses is only $10,000 × 11 = $110,000 since the company does not pay the last month's expenses until the following year. Accounts payable increases by $10,000, representing one month of expenses. The increase in net working capital (increase in accounts payable ⇨ increases current liabilities ⇨ increases net working capital) reduces the cost of goods sold to give us the cash outflow from expenses:

Cost of goods sold	$120,000
Less: increase in accounts payable	10,000
Change in cash flow from expenses	$110,000

A new project may result in either:

- an increase in net working capital;
- a decrease in net working capital; or
- no change in net working capital.

CLASSIFYING WORKING CAPITAL CHANGES

In many applications, we can arbitrarily classify the change in working capital as either investment cash flows or operating cash flows. And the classification doesn't really matter since it's the bottom line, the net cash flows, that matter. How we classify the change in working capital doesn't affect a project's attractiveness.

Further, working capital may change at the beginning of the project and at any point during the life of the project. For example, as a new product is introduced, sales may be terrific in the first few years, requiring an increase in cash, accounts receivable, and inventory to support these increased sales. But all of this requires an increase in working capital—a cash outflow.

But later sales may fall off as competitors enter the market. As sales and production fall off, the need for the increased cash, accounts receivable, and inventory falls off also. As cash, accounts receivable, and inventory are reduced, there is a cash inflow in the form of the reduction in the funds that become available for other uses within the company.

A change in net working capital can be thought of specifically as part of the initial investment—the amount necessary to get the project going. Or it can be considered generally as part of operating activity—the day-to-day business of the company. So where do we classify the cash flow associated with net working capital? With the asset acquisition and disposition represented in the new project or with the operating cash flows?

If a project requires a change in the company's net working capital accounts that persists for the duration of the project—say, an increase in inventory levels starting at the time of the investment—we tend to classify the change as part of the acquisition costs at the beginning of the project and as part of disposition proceeds at the end of project. If, on the other hand, the change in net working capital is due to the fact that accrual accounting does not coincide with cash flows, we tend to classify the change is part of the operating cash flows.

Putting It All Together Here's what we need to put together to calculate the change in the company's operating cash flows related to a new investment we are considering:

- Changes in revenues and expenses;
- Cash flow from changes in taxes from changes in revenues and expenses;
- Cash flow from changes in cash flows from depreciation tax shields; and
- Changes in net working capital.

There are many ways of compiling the component cash flow changes to arrive at the change in operating cash flow. We will start by first calculating taxable income, making adjustments for changes in taxes, non cash expenses, and net working capital to arrive at operating cash flow.

Suppose you are evaluating a project that is expected to increase sales by $200,000 and expenses by $150,000. Accounts receivable are expected to increase by $20,000 and accounts payable are expected to increase by $5,000, but no changes in cash or inventory are expected. Further, suppose the project's assets will have a $10,000 depreciation expense for tax purposes. If the tax rate is 40%, what is the operating cash flow from this project?

	Change in sales	$200,000
Less	Change in expenses	150,000
Less	Change in depreciation	10,000
Equals	Change in taxable income	$40,000
Less	Taxes	16,000
Equals	Change in income after taxes	$24,000
Plus	Depreciation	10,000
Less	Increase in working capital	15,000
Equals	Change in operating cash flow	$19,000

So that we can mathematically represent how to calculate the change in operating cash flows for a project, let's use the symbol "Δ" to indicate "change in":

ΔOCF = change in operating cash flow;

ΔR = change in revenues;

ΔE = change in expenses;

ΔD = change in depreciation;

t = tax rate; and

ΔNWC = change in working capital

The change in the operating cash flow is:

$$\Delta OCF = (\Delta R - \Delta E - \Delta D)(1 - t) + \Delta D - \Delta NWC$$

We can also write this as:

$$\Delta OCF = (\Delta R - \Delta E)(1 - t) + \Delta Dt - \Delta NWC$$

Applying these equations to the previous example,

$\Delta OCF = (\Delta R - \Delta E - \Delta D) \times (1 - t) + \Delta D - \Delta NWC$
$\Delta OCF = (\$200,000 - 150,000 - 10,000) \times (1 - 0.40) + \$10,000$
$\qquad - \$15,000$
$\Delta OCF = \$19,000$

or, using the rearrangement of the equation,

$\Delta OCF = (\Delta R - \Delta E)(1 - t) + \Delta Dt - \Delta NWC$
$\Delta OCF = (\$200,000 - 150,000) \times (1 - 0.40) + (\$10,000 \times 0.40)$
$\qquad - \$15,000$
$\Delta OCF = \$19,000.$

Let's look at one more example for the calculation of operating cash flows. Suppose you are evaluating modern equipment which you expect will reduce expenses by $100,000 during the first year. And, since the new equipment is more efficient, you can reduce the level of inventory by $20,000 during the first year. The old machine cost $200,000 and was depreciated using straight-line over 10 years, with five years remaining. The new machine cost $300,000 and will be depreciated using straight-line over 10 years. If the company's tax rate is 30%, what is the expected operating cash flow in the first year? Let's identify the components:

ΔR	$= \$0$	The new machine does not affect revenues.
ΔE	$= -\$100,000$	The new machine reduces expenses that will reduce taxes and increase cash flows.
ΔD	$= +10,000$	The new machine increases the depreciation expense from $20,000 to $30,000.
ΔNWC	$= -\$20,000$	The company can reduce its investment in inventory releasing funds to be invested elsewhere.
t	$= 30\%$	

The operating cash flow from the first year is therefore:

$$\Delta OCF = (\Delta R - \Delta E - \Delta D) \times (1 - t) + \Delta D - \Delta NWC$$
$$\Delta OCF = (\$100,000 - 10,000) \times (1 - 0.30) + \$10,000 - \$20,000$$
$$\Delta OCF = \$63,000 + \$10,000 + \$20,000$$
$$\Delta OCF = \$93,000$$

EXAMPLE 13.2: CHANGE IN DEPRECIATION

Suppose the Inter.Com Company is evaluating its depreciation methods on a new piece of equipment that costs $100,000. And suppose the equipment can be depreciated using straight-line over five years or treating it as a 3-year MACRS asset. What is the difference in the cash flows associated with depreciation under these two methods in the second year if its marginal tax rate is 40%?

Solution

Difference in depreciation = $20,000 - 44,450 = $24,450

Tax shield of difference = 0.40 × $24,450 = $9,780

 ## TRY IT! CHANGE IN EXPENSES

If a project is expected to increase costs by $50,000 per year and the tax rate of the company is 40%, what is the net cash flow from the change in costs?

Net Cash Flows By now we should know that an investment's cash flows consist of: (1) cash flows related to acquiring and disposing the assets represented in the investment, and (2) how it affects cash flows related to operations. To evaluate any investment project, we must consider both to determine whether or not the company is better off with or without it.

The sum of the cash flows from asset acquisition and disposition and from operations is the *net cash flows* (NCF). And this sum is calculated for each period. In each period, we add the cash flow from asset acquisition and disposition and the cash flow from operations. For a given period,

Net cash flow = Investment cash flow + Change in operating cash flow

The analysis of the cash flows of investment projects can become quite complex. But by working through any problem systematically, line-by-line, you will be able to sort out the information and focus on those items that determine cash flows.

A Comprehensive Example

The Acme.Com Company is evaluating replacing its production equipment that produces anvils. The current equipment was purchased 10 years ago at a cost of $1.5 million. Acme depreciated its current equipment using MACRS, considering the equipment to be a 5-year MACRS asset. If they sell the current equipment, they estimate that they can get $100,000.

The new equipment would cost $2.5 million and would be depreciated as a 5-year MACRS asset. The new equipment would not affect sales, but would result in a costs savings of $400,000 each year of the asset's 10-year useful life.

At the end of its 10-year life, Acme estimates that it can sell the equipment for $30,000. Also, because the new equipment would be more efficient, Acme would have less work-in-process anvils, reducing inventory needs initially by $20,000. Acme's marginal tax rate is 40%. Assume that the equipment purchase (and sale of the old equipment) occurs at the end of Year 0 and that the first year of operating this equipment is Year 1 and the last year of operating the equipment is Year 10.

From this scenario, we can pick out pieces of information that we need in our analysis:

- Book value of existing equipment = $0
- Sale of current equipment = $100,000 cash inflow
- Tax on sale of current equipment = $40,000 cash outflow
- Initial outlay for new = $2,500,000 cash outflow
- $\Delta R = \$0$
- $\Delta E = \$400,000$ each year
- $\Delta WC = -\$20,000$ cash outflow initially
- $\Delta WC = \$20,000$ cash inflow at the end of project

The depreciation on the new equipment, based on MACRS rates, is:

Year	Calculation	Depreciation expense
1	0.2000 × $2,500,000	$500,000
2	0.3200 × $2,500,000	$800,000
3	0.1920 × $2,500,000	$480,000
4	0.1152 × $2,500,000	$288,000
5	0.1152 × $2,500,000	$288,000
6	0.0576 × $2,500,000	$144,000

There is no depreciation expense after Year 6.

We provide the cash flow calculations in Exhibit 13.4. The net cash flow initially is negative, but then is positive for each year thereafter.

Simplifications   To actually analyze a project's cash flows, we need to make several simplifications:

- We assume that cash flows into or out of the company at certain points in time, typically at the end of the year, although we realize a project's cash flows into and out of the company at irregular intervals.
- We assume that the assets are purchased and put to work immediately.
- By combining inflows and outflows in each period, we are assuming that all inflows and outflows in a given period have the same risk.

Because there are so many flows to consider, we focus on flows within a period (say a year), assuming they all occur at the end of the period. We assume this to reduce the number of things we have to keep track of. Whether or not this assumption matters depends on: (1) the difference between the actual time of cash flow and whether we assume it flows at the end of the period (that is, a flow on January 2 is 364 days from December 31, but a flow on December 30 is only one day from December 31), and (2) the opportunity cost of funds. Also, assuming that cash flows occur at specific points in time simplifies the financial mathematics we use in valuing these cash flows.

CAPITAL BUDGETING TECHNIQUES

The estimation of the net cash flows of a project is an important step in the capital budgeting decision, but making a capital budgeting decision requires analyzing these cash flows to determine whether the project should be undertaken.

EXHIBIT 13.4 Acme.com Cash Flow Analysis

Year	0	1	2	3	4	5	6	7	8	9	10
Initial payment	-$2,500,000										
Sale of new	100,000										$30,000
Tax on sale of new	-40,000										-12,000
Change in working capital	20,000										-20,000
Investment cash flows	-$2,420,000										-$2,000
Change in revenues		$0	$0	$0	$0	$0	$0	$0	$0	$0	$0
Change in expenses		-400,000	-400,000	-400,000	-400,000	-400,000	-400,000	-400,000	-400,000	-400,000	-400,000
Change in depreciation		500,000	800,000	480,000	288,000	288,000	144,000	$0	$0	$0	$0
Change in taxable income		-$100,000	-$400,000	-$80,000	$112,000	$112,000	$256,000	$400,000	$400,000	$400,000	$400,000
Change in taxes		-40,000	-160,000	-32,000	44,800	44,800	102,400	160,000	160,000	160,000	160,000
Change in after-tax income		-$60,000	-$240,000	-$48,000	$67,200	$67,200	$153,600	$240,000	$240,000	$240,000	$240,000
Change in depreciation		500,000	800,000	480,000	288,000	288,000	144,000	0	0	0	0
Change in operating cash flows		$440,000	$560,000	$432,000	$355,200	$355,200	$297,600	$240,000	$240,000	$240,000	$240,000
Net cash flow	-$2,420,000	$440,000	$560,000	$432,000	$355,200	$355,200	$297,600	$240,000	$240,000	$240,000	$238,000

The value of a company today is the present value of all its future cash flows. These future cash flows come from assets that are already in place and from future investment opportunities. The value of the company today is the present value of these future cash flows, discounted at a rate that represents investors' assessments of the uncertainty that they will flow in the amounts and when expected.

The degree of uncertainty, or risk, of a project is reflected in the project's cost of capital. The cost of capital is what the company must pay for the funds to finance its investment.

Given estimates of incremental cash flows for a project and given a cost of capital that reflects the project's risk, we look at alternative techniques that are used to select projects. For now all we need to understand about a project's risk is that we can incorporate risk in either of two ways: (1) we can discount future cash flows using a higher discount rate, the greater the cash flow's risk, or (2) we can require a higher annual return on a project, the greater the risk of its cash flows.

Evaluation Techniques

We look at six techniques that are commonly used by companies to evaluating investments in long-term assets:

1. Payback period
2. Discounted payback period
3. Net present value
4. Profitability index
5. Internal rate of return
6. Modified internal rate of return

We are interested in how well each technique discriminates among the different projects, steering us toward the projects that maximize owners' wealth. An evaluation technique should:

- Consider all the future incremental cash flows from the project
- Consider the time value of money
- Consider the uncertainty associated with future cash flows
- Have an objective criterion by which to select a project

Projects selected using a technique that satisfies all four criteria will, under most general conditions, maximize owners' wealth.

EXHIBIT 13.5 Estimated Cash Flows for Project One and Project Two

	End of Period Cash Flows	
Year	Project One	Project Two
20X1	−$100,000	−$100,000
20X2	$0	$30,000
20X3	$0	$30,000
20X4	$0	$30,000
20X5	$140,000	$30,000

In addition to judging whether each technique satisfies these criteria, we will also look at which ones can be used in special situations, such as when a dollar limit is placed on the capital budget.

We use two projects, Project One and Project Two, to illustrate the techniques. We show the cash flows related to each project in Exhibit 13.5. Can you tell by looking at the cash flows for Project One whether or not it enhances wealth? Or, can you tell by just looking at Projects One and Two which one is better? Perhaps with some projects you may think you can pick out which one is better simply by gut feeling or eyeballing the cash flows. But why do it that way when there are precise methods to evaluate investments by their cash flows?

Payback Period

The *payback period* for a project is the time from the initial cash outflow to invest in it until the time when its cash inflows add up to the initial cash outflow. In other words, how long it takes to get your money back. The payback period is also referred to as the *payoff period* or the *capital recovery period*. If you invest $10,000 today and are promised $5,000 one year from today and $5,000 two years from today, the payback period is two years—it takes two years to get your $10,000 back.

How long does it take to get your $100,000 from Project One back? The payback period for Project One is four years:

Year	Project One Cash Flows	Accumulated Project One Cash Flows
20X1	−$100,000	−$100,000
20X2	$0	−$100,000
20X3	$0	−$100,000
20X4	$0	−$100,000
20X5	$130,000	$30,000

325

By the end of 20X4, the full $100,000 is not paid back, but by 20X5, the accumulated cash flow is positive. Therefore, the payback period for Project One is four years.

The payback period for Project Two is also four years. It is not until the end of 20X5 that the $100,000 original investment (and more) is paid back: At the end of the third year, 20X4, all but $10,000 is paid back, but at the end of 20X5, the entire $100,000 is paid back.

We have assumed that the cash flows are received at the end of the year. So we always arrive at a payback period in terms of a whole number of years. If we assume that the cash flows are received, say, uniformly, such as monthly or weekly, throughout the year, we arrive at a payback period in terms of years and fractions of years. If the company receives cash flows uniformly throughout the year, the payback period for Project Two is $3^2/_3$ years. Our assumption of end-of-period cash flows may be unrealistic, but it is convenient to use this assumption to demonstrate how to use the various evaluation techniques. Using this assumption, the payback for both Project One and Project Two is four years. We will continue to use this end-of-period assumption throughout the coverage of capital budgeting techniques.

Is Project One or Two more attractive? A shorter payback period is better than a longer payback period. Yet there is no clear-cut rule for how short is better. If we assume that all cash flows occur at the end of the year, Project One provides the same payback as Project Two. Therefore, we do not know in this particular case whether quicker is better.

In addition to having no well-defined decision criteria, payback period analysis favors investments with "front-loaded" cash flows: an investment looks better in terms of the payback period the sooner its cash flows are received no matter what its later cash flows look like. Payback period analysis is a type of "break-even" measure. It tends to provide a measure of the economic life of the investment in terms of its payback period. The more likely the life exceeds the payback period, the more attractive the investment. The economic life beyond the payback period is referred to as the *post-payback duration*. If post-payback duration is zero, the investment is worthless, no matter how short the payback. This is because the sum of the future cash flows is no greater than the initial investment outlay. And since these future cash flows are really worth less today than in the future, a zero post-payback duration means that the present value of the future cash flows is less than the project's initial investment.

The payback method should only be used as a coarse initial screen of investment projects. But it can be a useful indicator of some things. Because a dollar of cash flow in the early years is worth more than a dollar of cash flow in later years, the payback period method provides a simple, yet crude measure of the liquidity of the investment.

The payback period also offers some indication on the risk of the investment. In industries where equipment becomes obsolete rapidly or where there are very competitive conditions, investments with earlier payback are more valuable. That's because cash flows farther into the future are more uncertain and therefore have lower present value. In the personal computer industry, for example, the fierce competition and rapidly changing technology requires investment in projects that have a payback of less than one year since there is no expectation of project benefits beyond one year.

Because the payback method doesn't tell us the particular payback period that maximizes wealth, we cannot use it as the primary decision tool for the investment in long-lived assets.

Discounted Payback Period

The *discounted payback period* is the time needed to pay back the original investment in terms of discounted future cash flows. Therefore, we must discount each cash flow to the beginning of the project; the discounted payback period is the length of time it takes these accumulated cash flows to become positive.

Each cash flow is discounted back to the beginning of project at a rate that reflects both the time value of money and the uncertainty of the future cash flows. This rate is the cost of capital—the return required by the suppliers of capital (creditors and owners) to compensate them for time value of money and the risk associated with the investment. The more uncertain the future cash flows, the greater the cost of capital.

We discount an uncertain future cash flow to the present at some rate that reflects the degree of uncertainty associated with this future cash flow. The more uncertain, the less the cash flow is worth today—this means that a higher discount rate is used to translate it into a value today. This discount rate is a rate that reflects the opportunity cost of funds. We refer to this opportunity cost as the cost of capital.

We don't want to do anything that doesn't create more than a dollar's worth of value for every dollar expended. And we'll do the best we can.

—Warren Buffett, Presentation to the Wharton School, 2008

Returning to Project One and Project Two, suppose that each has a cost of capital of 5%. The first step in determining the discounted payback period is to discount each year's cash flow to the beginning of the investment (the end of the year 20X1) at the cost of capital:

Project One

Year	Cash Flows	Discounted Cash Flows	Accumulated Discounted Cash Flows
20X1	−$100,000	−$100,000	−$100,000
20X2	$0	$0	−$100,000
20X3	$0	$0	−$100,000
20X4	$0	$0	−$100,000
20X5	$130,000	$106,951	$6,951

Project Two

Year	Cash Flows	Discounted Cash Flows	Accumulated Discounted Cash Flows
20X1	−$100,000	−$100,000	−$100,000
20X2	$30,000	$28,571	−$71,429
20X3	$30,000	$27,211	−$44,218
20X4	$30,000	$25,915	−$18,303
20X5	$30,000	$24,681	$6,379

How long does it take for each investment's discounted cash flows to pay back its $100,000 investment? The discounted payback period for both Projects One and Two is four years.

It appears that the shorter the payback period, the better, whether using discounted or non discounted cash flows. But how short is better? We don't know. All we know is that an investment "breaks-even" in terms of discounted cash flows at the discounted payback period—the point in time when the accumulated discounted cash flows equal the amount of the investment.

If a project never pays back in terms of the discounted payback period, we know that this project is not acceptable. Using the length of the discounted payback as a basis for selecting investments that do payback, in terms of discounted cash flow, we cannot distinguish Projects One and Two. Both have a discounted payback period of four years. But we've ignored some valuable cash flows for both investments, those beyond what is necessary for recovering the initial cash outflow.

Net Present Value

If offered an investment that costs $1,000 today and promises to pay you $1,200 two years from today, and if your opportunity cost for projects of similar risk is 5%, would you make this investment? To determine whether or not this is a good investment you need to compare your $1,000 investment with the $1,200 cash flow you expect in two years. Because you determine that a discount rate of 5% reflects the degree of uncertainty associated with the $1,200 expected in two years, today it is worth:

$$\text{Present value of \$1,200 to be received in 2 years} = \frac{\$1,200}{(1 + 0.05)^2}$$

$$= \$1,088.44$$

By investing $1,000, today you are getting in return, a promise of a cash flow in the future that is worth $1,088.44 today. You increase your wealth by $88.44, which we refer to as the net present value.

The *net present value* (NPV) is the present value of all expected cash flows. The word "net" in this term indicates that we consider all cash flows—both positive and negative. We can represent the net present value using summation notation, where t indicates any particular period, CF_t represents the cash flow at the end of period t, i represents the cost of capital, and N the number of periods comprising the economic life of the investment:

$$NPV = \sum_{t=0}^{N} \frac{CF_t}{(1 + i)^t} \tag{13.1}$$

Cash inflows are positive values of CF_t and cash outflows are negative values of CF_t. For any given period t, we collect all the cash flows (positive and negative) and net them together. To make things a bit easier to track, let's just refer to cash flows as inflows or outflows, and not specifically identify them as operating or investment cash flows.

Take another look at Projects One and Two. Using a 5% cost of capital, the net present values are $6,951 and $6,379, respectively:

Project One

Year	Cash Flows	Discounted Cash Flows
20X1	−$100,000	−$100,000
20X2	$0	0
20X3	$0	0
20X4	$0	0
20X5	$130,000	106,951
Net present value =		$6,951

Project Two

Year	Cash Flows	Discounted Cash Flows
20X1	−$100,000	−$100,000
20X2	$30,000	28,571
20X3	$30,000	27,211
20X4	$30,000	25,915
20X5	$30,000	24,681
Net present value =		$6,379

These values should look familiar because we used these discounted cash flows in the discounted payback period. The NPV for Project One indicates that if we invest in this project, we expect to increase the value of the company by $6,951. Calculated in a similar manner, the net present value of Project Two is $6,379.

We can use a financial calculator to solve for the NPV, keying in the cash flows in order. We can also use Microsoft Excel's NPV function to solve for the net present value:

TI-83/84	HP10B	Microsoft Excel	
{0,0,0,130000}	100000+/−		
STO *listname*	CF$_j$	**A**	**B**
NPV(5,−100000,*listname*)	0 CF$_j$	1 Year	Project One
	0 CF$_j$	2 20X1	−$100,000
	0 CF$_j$	3 20X2	$0
	130000CF$_j$	4 20X3	$0
	5 i/YR	5 20X4	$0
	NPV	6 20X5	$130,000
			=NPV(.1,B3:B6)+B2

Net Present Value Decision Rule A positive net present value means that the investment increases the value of the company—the return is more than sufficient to compensate for the required return of the investment. Another way of stating this is that a project that has a positive net present value is profitable in an economic sense.[1]

---

[1]This does not mean, however, that the project is profitable in terms of financial accounting.

A negative net present value means that the investment decreases the value of the company—the return is less than the cost of capital. A zero net present value means that the return just equals the return required by owners to compensate them for the degree of uncertainty of the investment's future cash flows and the time value of money. Therefore,

If...	this means that the investment is expected...	and you should...
NPV > $0	to increase shareholder wealth	accept the project.
NPV < $0	to decrease shareholder wealth	reject the project.
NPV = $0	not to change shareholder wealth	be indifferent between accepting or rejecting the project.

Project One is expected to increase the value of the company by $6,951, whereas Project Two is expected to add $6,379 in value. If these are independent investments, both should be taken on because both increase the value of the company. If Projects One and Two are mutually exclusive, such that the only choice is either One or Two, Project One is preferred since it has the greater NPV.

The Investment Profile   We may want to see how sensitive is our decision to accept a project to changes in our cost of capital. We can see this sensitivity in how a project's net present value changes as the discount rate changes by looking at a project's *investment profile*, also referred to as the *net present value profile*. The investment profile is a graphical depiction of the relation between the net present value of a project and the discount rate: the profile shows the net present value of a project for each discount rate, within some range.

We provide the net present value profile for the two projects in Exhibit 13.6 for discount rates from 0% to 20%. The NPV for Project One is positive for discount rates from 0% to 6.779%, and negative for discount rates higher than 6.779%. The 6.779% is the internal rate of return; that is, the discount rate at which the net present value is equal to $0. Therefore, Project One increases owners' wealth if the cost of capital on this project is less than 6.779%, and decreases owners' wealth if the cost of capital on this project is greater than 6.779%.

If the discount rate is less than 5.361%, Project One adds more value than Project Two, but if the discount rate is more than 5.361% but less

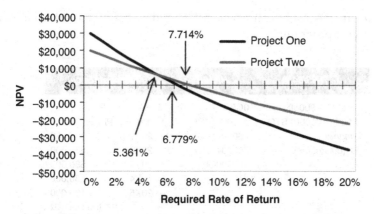

EXHIBIT 13.6   The Investment Profiles of Projects One and Two

than 7.714%, Project Two increases wealth more than Project One. If the discount rate is greater than 7.714%, we should invest in neither project because both would decrease wealth. The 5.361% is the *cross-over discount rate* which produces identical NPVs for the two projects. If the discount rate is 5.361%, the net present value of both investments is $5,492.

Solving for the Cross-Over Rate   For Projects One and Two, the cross-over rate is the rate that causes the net present value of the two investments to be equal. Basically, this boils down to a simple approach: calculate the differences in the cash flows and then solve for the internal rate of return of these differences.

Year	Project One	Project Two	Difference
20X1	−$100,000	−$100,000	$0
20X2	$0	$30,000	−$30,000
20X3	$0	$30,000	−$30,000
20X4	$0	$30,000	−$30,000
20X5	$130,000	$30,000	$100,000

The internal rate of return of these differences is the cross-over rate, or 5.361%. Does it matter which project's cash flows you deduct from the other? Not at all—just be consistent each period. Using a financial calculator or spreadsheet program:

TI-83/84	HP10B	Microsoft Excel		
{−30000, −30000,	0CF_j		A	B
−30000,100000} STO	30000+/− CF_j	1	Year	Project Two
listname	30000+/− CF_j	2	20X1	$0
IRR(0,listname)	30000+/− CF_j	3	20X2	$30,000
	100000CF_j	4	20X3	$30,000
	IRR	5	20X4	$30,000
		6	20X5	$100,000
				=NPV(.1,B3:B6)+B2

Profitability Index

The *profitability index* uses some of the same information we used for the net present value, but it is stated in terms of an index. Whereas the net present value is:

$$NPV = \sum_{t=0}^{N} \frac{CF_t}{(1+i)^t}$$

The profitability index, *PI*, is:

$$PI = \sum_{t=0}^{N} \frac{\dfrac{CIF_t}{(1+i)^t}}{\dfrac{COF_t}{(1+i)^t}} \qquad (13.2)$$

where CIF and COF are cash inflows and cash outflows, respectively.

For Project One, the profitability index is:

$$PI_{\text{Project One}} = \frac{\$106,951}{\$100,000} = 1.06951$$

The index value is greater than one, which means that the investment produces more in terms of benefits than costs. The decision rule for the profitability index is therefore depends on the PI relative to 1.0:

If . . .	this means that the investment is expected to . . .	and you should . . .
PI > 1.0	increase shareholder wealth	accept the project.
PI < 1.0	decrease shareholder wealth	reject the project.
PI = 1.0	not to change shareholder wealth	be indifferent between accepting or rejecting the project.

The profitability index for Project Two is 1.06379. Therefore, both projects are acceptable according to the profitability index criteria.

There is no direct solution for PI on your calculator; what you need to do is calculate the present value of all the cash inflows and then divide this value by the present value of the cash outflows. In the case of Project One, there is only one cash out flow and it is already in present value terms (i.e., it occurs at the end of 20X1).

 TRY IT! NPV AND PI

Consider a project that requires a $10,000 cash outlay and provides $5,000 after one year and $7,000 after three years. If the cost of capital of this project is 10%, what is the net present value and profitability of this project?

Internal Rate of Return

Suppose you are offered an investment opportunity that requires you to put up $1,000 and has an expected cash inflow of $1,200 after two years. The return on this investment is the discount rate that causes the present values of the $1,200 cash inflow to equal the present value of the $1,000 cash outflow:

$$\$1,000 = \frac{\$1,200}{(1 + IRR)^2}$$

Another way to look at this is to consider the investment's cash flows discounted at a rate of 5%. The NPV of this project if the discount rate is 5% (the IRR in this example), is positive, $88.44. Therefore, we know that the rate that causes the NPV to be zero is greater than 5%. If we apply a

10% discount rate, the NPV is −$8.26. Therefore, we know that the IRR is between 5% and 10%, and closer to 10%.

An investment's *internal rate of return* (IRR) is the discount rate that makes the present value of all expected future cash flows equal to zero. We can represent the IRR as the rate that solves:

$$\$0 = \sum_{t=0}^{N} \frac{CF_t}{(1 + \text{IRR})^t} \tag{13.3}$$

The IRR for the investment of $1,000 that produces $1,200 two years later is 9.545%.

Returning once again to Projects One and Two, the IRR of Project One is 6.951% and the IRR of Project Two is 7.714%. As you may recall from our discussion of the investment profiles, these are the discount rates at which each project crosses the horizontal axis (i.e., NPV = $0).

We can use a financial calculator or a spreadsheet program to solve for the IRR. For example, for Project One,

TI-83/84	HP10B	Microsoft Excel	
{0,0,0,130000}	−100000+/−		A	B
STO *listname*	CFⱼ	1	Year	Project One
IRR(−100000,	0 CFⱼ	2	20X1	−$100,000
listname)	0 CFⱼ	3	20X2	$0
	0 CFⱼ	4	20X3	$0
	130000CFⱼ	5	20X4	$0
	IRR	6	20X5	$130,000
				=IRR(B2:B6)

The internal rate of return is a yield—what we earn, on average, per year. How do we use it to decide which investment, if any, to choose? Let's revisit Investments A and B and the IRRs we just calculated for each. If, for similar risk investments, owners earn 10% per year, then both A and B are attractive. They both yield more than the rate owners require for the level of risk of these two investments:

Project	IRR	Required Rate of Return
One	6.779%	5%
Two	7.714%	5%

The decision rule for the internal rate of return is to invest in a project if it provides a return greater than the cost of capital. The cost of capital, in the context of the IRR, is a hurdle rate—the minimum acceptable rate of return. For independent projects and situations in which there is no capital rationing, we compare the IRR with the required rate of return, RRR:

If...	this means that the investment is expected to...	and you should...
IRR > RRR	increase shareholder wealth	accept the project.
IRR < RRR	decrease shareholder wealth	reject the project.
IRR = RRR	not change shareholder wealth	be indifferent between accepting or rejecting the project.

What if we were forced to choose between Projects One and Two because they are mutually exclusive? Project Two has a higher IRR than Project One—so at first glance we might want to accept Project Two. What about the NPV of One and Two? What does the NPV tell us to do? If we choose on the basis of the higher IRR, we go with Project Two. If we choose the project with the higher NPV when the cost of capital is 5%, we go with Project One. Which is correct? Choosing the project with the higher net present value is consistent with maximizing owners' wealth. Why? Because if the cost of capital is 5%, we would calculate different NPVs and come to a different conclusion, as you can see from the investment profiles in Exhibit 13.6.

When evaluating mutually exclusive projects, the one with the highest IRR may not be the one with the best NPV. The IRR may give a different decision than NPV when evaluating mutually exclusive projects because of the built-in assumptions with these methods:

- NPV assumes cash flows reinvested at the cost of capital.
- IRR assumes cash flows reinvested at the internal rate of return.

These assumptions may cause different decisions in choosing among mutually exclusive projects when:

- the timing of the cash flows is different among the projects,
- there are scale differences (that is, very different cash flow amounts), or
- the projects have different useful lives.

THE TROUBLE WITH IRR

"How large is the potential impact of a flawed reinvestment-rate assumption? Managers at one large industrial company approved 23 major capital projects over five years on the basis of IRRs that averaged 77%. Recently, however, when we conducted an analysis with the reinvestment rate adjusted to the company's cost of capital, the true average return fell to just 16%. The order of the most attractive projects also changed considerably. The top-ranked project based on IRR dropped to the tenth-most-attractive project. Most striking, the company's highest-rated projects—showing IRRs of 800, 150, and 130%—dropped to just 15, 23, and 22%, respectively, once a realistic reinvestment rate was considered. Unfortunately, these investment decisions had already been made."

The McKinsey Quarterly, McKinsey & Co., October 20, 2004.

With respect to the role of the timing of cash flows in choosing between two projects: Project Two's cash flows are received sooner than Project One's. Part of the return on either is from the reinvestment of its cash inflows. And, in the case of Project Two, there is more return from the reinvestment of cash inflows. The question is "What do you do with the cash inflows when you get them?" We generally assume that if you receive cash inflows, you'll reinvest those cash flows in other assets.

With respect to the reinvestment rate assumption in choosing between these projects, suppose we can reasonably expect to earn only the cost of capital on our investments. Then for projects with an IRR above the cost of capital we would be overstating the return on the investment using the IRR.

The bottom line? If we evaluate projects on the basis of their IRR, we may select one that does not maximize value.

With respect to the NPV method: if the best we can do is reinvest cash flows at the cost of capital, the NPV assumes the more reasonable rate (the cost of capital). If the reinvestment rate is assumed to be the project's cost of capital, we would evaluate projects on the basis of the NPV and select the one that maximizes owners' wealth.

But what if there is capital rationing? Suppose Projects One and Two are *independent projects*. Projects are independent if that the acceptance of one does not prevent the acceptance of the other. And suppose the capital budget is limited to $100,000. We are therefore forced to choose between Projects

One and Two. If we select the one with the highest IRR, we choose Project Two. But Two is expected to increase wealth less than Project One. Ranking and selecting investments on the basis of their IRRs may not maximize wealth.

The source of the problem in the case of capital rationing is that the IRR is a percentage, not a dollar amount. Because of this, we cannot determine how to distribute the capital budget to maximize wealth because the investment or group of investments producing the highest yield does not mean they are the ones that produce the greatest wealth.

The typical project usually involves only one large negative cash flow initially, followed by a series of future positive flows. But that's not always the case. Suppose you are involved in a project that uses environmentally sensitive chemicals. It may cost you a great deal to dispose of them. And that will mean a negative cash flow at the end of the project.

Suppose we are considering a project that has cash flows as follows:

Period	End of Period Cash Flow
0	−$1,010
1	+2,400
2	−1,400

What is this project's IRR? One possible solution is IRR = 2.85%, yet another possible solution is IRR = 34.78%, as we show in Exhibit 13.7.

Remember that the IRR is the discount rate that causes the NPV to be zero. In terms of this graph, this means that the IRR is the discount rate where the NPV is $0, the point at which the present value changes sign—from positive to negative or from negative to positive.

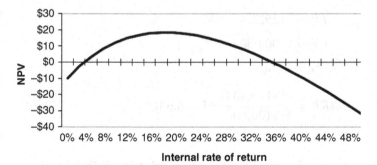

EXHIBIT 13.7   The Case of Multiple IRRs

TRY IT! IRR

Consider a project that requires a $1,000 outlay and provides $1,000 in one year and $200 in two years. What is the IRR of this project?

Modified Internal Rate of Return

When we use the internal rate of return method, we are assuming that any cash inflows are reinvested at the investment's internal rate of return. Consider Project One. The IRR is 10.17188%. If we take each of the cash inflows from Project Two and reinvest them at 5%, we will have $129,304 at the end of 20X5:

Year	Project Two Cash Flows	Future Value of Cash Inflows
20X1	−$100,000	
20X2	$30,000	$34,729
20X3	$30,000	33,075
20X4	$30,000	31,500
20X5	$30,000	30,000
	Terminal value	$129,304

The $129,304 is the project's *terminal value*.[2] The terminal value is how much the company has from this investment if all proceeds are reinvested at the IRR. When the terminal value is used, the return calculated is the *modified internal rate of return (MIRR)*. The MIRR for Project Two using the terminal value as the future value we have:

$$FV = \$129,304$$

$$PV = \$100,000$$

$$N = 4 \text{ years}$$

$$MIRR = \sqrt[4]{\frac{\$129,304}{\$100,000}} - 1 = 6.636\%$$

---

[2]For example, the 2008 cash flow of $200,000 is reinvested at 10.17188% for two periods (that is, for 2009 and 2010), or $200,000 $(1 + 0.1017188)^2 = \$242,756.88$.

In other words, by investing $1,000,000 at the end of 20X1 and receiving $129,304 produces an average annual return of 6.636%, which is the project's internal rate of return.

The MIRR is the return on the project assuming reinvestment of the cash flows at a specified rate. Consider Project One if the reinvestment rate is 6%:

Year	Project Two Cash Flows	Future Value of Cash Inflows
20X1	−$100,000	
20X2	$30,000	$34,729
20X3	$30,000	33,075
20X4	$30,000	31,500
20X5	$30,000	30,000
	Terminal value	$131,238

If the reinvestment rate is 6%, the MIRR is 7.032%: If we, instead, reinvest Project Two's cash flows at Project Two's IRR, 7.714%, we calculate the MIRR to be 7.714%.

The MIRR is therefore a function of both the reinvestment rate and the pattern of cash flows, with higher the reinvestment rates leading to greater MIRRs:

If...	this means that the investment is expected to...	and you should...
MIRR > RRR	return more than required	accept the project.
MIRR < RRR	return less than required	reject the project.
MIRR = RRR	return what is required	be indifferent between accepting or rejecting the project.

You can see this in Exhibit 13.8, where the *MIRR*s of both Project One and Project Two are plotted for different reinvestment rates. Project Two's MIRR is sensitive to the reinvestment rate; Project One's MIRR is the same as its IRR because it has a single cash inflow at the end of the life of the project.

Issues to Consider

Scale differences—differences in the amount of the cash flows—between projects can lead to conflicting investment decisions among the discounted cash flow techniques. Consider two projects, Project Big and Project Little. Each has a required rate of return of 5% per year with the following cash flows:

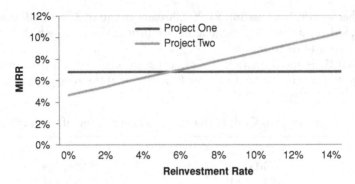

EXHIBIT 13.8 MIRRs for Project One and Project Two

End of Period	Project Big Cash Flows	Project Little Cash Flows
0	$1,000,000	$1.00
1	+ 400,000	+ 0.40
2	+ 400,000	+ 0.40
3	+ 400,000	+ 0.50

Applying the discounted cash flow techniques to each project, and assuming reinvestment at the required rate of return for the MIRR, we see that selecting the project with the higher profitability index, internal rate of return, or modified internal rate of return will result in selecting the project that adds the least value:

Technique	Project Big	Project Little
NPV	$89,299	$0.1757
PI	1.0893	1.1757
IRR	9.7010%	13.7789%
MIRR	8.0368%	10.8203%

We already have seen that when selecting between mutually exclusive projects, we should use the NPV instead of the IRR. Now, considering scale differences, we add another precaution: When selecting among projects of different scales, the profitability index and the modified internal rate of return may lead to an incorrect decision.

Suppose a company is subject to capital rationing—say a limit of $1,000,000—and Big and Little are independent projects. Which project should the company choose? The company can only choose one—spend $1 or $1,000,000, but not $1,000,001. If you go strictly by the PI, IRR, or MIRR criteria, the company would choose Project Little. But is this the better project? Again, the techniques that ignore the scale of the investment—PI, IRR, and MIRR—may lead to an incorrect decision.

Comparing Techniques

If we are dealing with mutually exclusive projects, the NPV method leads us to invest in projects that maximize wealth, that is, capital budgeting decisions consistent with owners' wealth maximization. If we are dealing with a limit on the capital budget, the NPV and PI methods lead us to invest in the set of projects that maximize wealth.

We summarize the advantages and disadvantages of each of the techniques for evaluating investments in Exhibit 13.9. We see in this table that the discounted cash flow techniques are preferred to the non discounted cash flow techniques. The discounted cash flow techniques—NPV, PI, IRR, MIRR—are preferable since they consider (1) all cash flows, (2) the time value of money, and (3) the risk of future cash flows. The discounted cash flow techniques are also useful because we can apply objective decision criteria—criteria we can actually use that tells us when a project increases wealth and when it does not.

We also see in this table that not all of the discounted cash flow techniques are right for every situation. There are questions we need to ask when evaluating a project, and the answers determine the appropriate technique is the one to use for that investment:

- Are the projects mutually exclusive or independent?
- Are the projects subject to capital rationing?
- Are the projects of the same risk?
- Are the projects of the same scale of investment?

Here are some simple rules:

1. If projects are independent and not subject to capital rationing, we can evaluate them and determine the ones that maximize wealth based on any of the discounted cash flow techniques.
2. If the projects are mutually exclusive, have the same investment outlay, and have the same risk, we must use only the NPV or the MIRR techniques to determine the projects that maximize wealth.
3. If projects are mutually exclusive and are of different risks or are of different scales, NPV is preferred over MIRR.

If the capital budget is limited, we can use either the NPV or the PI. We must be careful, however, not to select projects on the basis of their NPV (that is, ranking on NPV and selecting the highest NPV projects), but rather how we can maximize the NPV of the total capital budget.

EXHIBIT 13.9 Advantages and Disadvantages of the Capital Budgeting Techniques

---

Payback Period

Advantages

1. Simple to compute.
2. Provides some information on the risk of the investment.
3. Provides a crude measure of liquidity.

Disadvantages

1. No concrete decision criteria to indicate whether an investment increases the company's value.
2. Ignores cash flows beyond the payback period, the time value of money, and the risk of future cash flows.

Discounted Payback Period

Advantages

1. Considers the time value of money.
2. Considers the project's cash flows' risk through the cost of capital.

Disadvantages

1. No concrete decision criteria that indicate whether the investment increases the company's value.
2. Requires an estimate of the cost of capital in order to calculate the payback.
3. Ignores cash flows beyond the discounted payback period.

Net Present Value

Advantages

1. Indicates whether the investment is expected to increase the company's value.
2. Considers all the cash flows, the time value of money, and the risk of future cash flows.

Disadvantages

1. Requires an estimate of the cost of capital in order to calculate the net present value.
2. Expressed in terms of dollars.

Profitability Index

Advantages

1. Tells whether an investment increases the company's value.
2. Considers all cash flows of the project, the time value of money, and future cash flows' risk.
3. Useful in ranking and selecting projects when capital is rationed.

Disadvantages

1. Requires an estimate of the cost of capital in order to calculate the profitability index.
2. May not give the correct decision when used to compare mutually exclusive projects.

EXHIBIT 13.9 (*Continued*)

Internal Rate of Return

Advantages

1. Tells whether an investment increases the company's value.
2. Considers all cash flows of the project, the time value of money, and future cash flows' risk.

Disadvantages

1. Requires an estimate of the cost of capital in order to make a decision.
2. May not give the value-maximizing decision when used to compare mutually exclusive projects.
3. May not give the value-maximizing decision when used to choose projects when there is capital rationing.
4. Cannot be used in situations in which the sign of the cash flows of a project change more than once during the project's life.

Modified Internal Rate of Return

Advantages

1. Indicates whether an investment is expected to increase the company's value.
2. Considers all cash flows of the project, the time value of money, and future cash flows' risk.

Disadvantages

1. Requires an estimate of the cost of capital in order to make a decision.
2. May not give the value-maximizing decision when used to compare mutually exclusive projects or when there is capital rationing.

 TRY IT! ACME.COM

Using the cash flows of the Acme.com project that we provide in Exhibit 13.4, calculate:

1. Payback period,
2. Discounted payback period,
3. Net present value,
4. Profitability index,
5. Internal rate of return, and
6. Modified internal rate of return.

Assume a required rate of return of 6% and a reinvestment rate of 6%.

THE BOTTOM LINE

- Capital budgeting involves allocating capital among long-lived investment projects. Capital budgeting requires estimating the incremental cash flows that the project is expected to generate, and then applying techniques such as the net present value or the internal rate of return to evaluate the cash flows and determine whether the investment in the project is consistent with maximizing owners' wealth.
- The key to evaluating cash flows is to identify how the company's cash flows change if the investment is made. This requires estimating cash flows pertaining to the acquisition and eventual disposal of the capital project assets, as well as the change in the company's operating cash flows.
- The methods available to evaluate a capital project include the payback period, the discounted payback period, the net present value, the profitability index, the internal rate of return, and the modified internal rate of return.
- The preferred method of evaluating capital projects in the net present value method, though in certain circumstances we would arrive at the same decision using other methods, such as the internal rate of return.

SOLUTIONS TO TRY IT! PROBLEMS

Disposition Cash Flows, Using Straight-Line

Book value (BV) at the time of sale = $500,000 × (1 − 0.25 − 0.25)
= $250,000

Loss = $100,000 − 250,000 = −$150,000
Tax benefit = 0.35 × $150,000 = $52,500
CF = $100,000 + 52,500 = $152,500

Disposition Cash Flows, Using MACRS

Book value (BV) at the time of sale = $500,000 × (1 − 0.3333 − 0.4445)
= $111,100

Loss = $100,000 − 111,100 = −$11,000
Tax benefit = 0.35 × $11,100 = $3,885
CF = $100,000 + 3,885 = $103,885

Change in Expenses

$$\text{Cash flow} = -\$50{,}000 + 20{,}000 = -\$30{,}000$$

NPV & PI

$$\text{NPV} = -\$195.34$$
$$\text{PI} = 0.9805$$

IRR

$$\text{IRR} = 17.082\%$$

Acme.com

Payback period	6 years
Discounted payback period	9 years
Net present value	$197,928
Profitability index	1.082
Internal rate of return	8.009%
Modified internal rate of return	6.8412%

QUESTIONS

1. If a project does not affect a company's revenues, but reduces its costs, how can this affect the value of the company?
2. What is a depreciation tax shield, and how does this affect a capital budgeting decision?
3. If a company is making an investment decision to use a facility that is currently idle, how does the cost of this facility enter into the decision?
4. If a capital project has a positive net present value, does it pay back in terms of discounted cash flows? Explain.
5. If a company sells an asset for less than its original cost, but more than its book value, how is that gain classified and taxed?
6. If a company chooses to use straight-line depreciation instead of MACRS depreciation for an asset, how does this decision affect the profitability of the project?
7. If a company is deciding between two projects, and can only select one of the two projects, what evaluation techniques should this company use in the analysis of these projects?

8. Suppose, when evaluating two mutually exclusive projects, the company makes the value-maximizing decision to select the one with the lower internal rate of return. What does this tell you regarding the relation between the discount rate and the cross-over rate?

9. When selecting capital projects and there is a limit to the capital budget, which evaluation techniques are appropriate to use?

10. The net present value method and the internal rate of return method may produce different decisions when selecting among mutually exclusive projects. What is the source of this conflict?

11. Classify each of the following projects for a toy manufacturer into one of the three categories: replacement, new product or market, or mandated, by checking the appropriate box:

	Replacement	New Product or Market	Mandated
Opening a retail outlet	☐	☐	☐
Introducing a new line of dolls	☐	☐	☐
Introducing a new action figure in an existing line of action figures	☐	☐	☐
Adding pollution control equipment to avoid environmental fines	☐	☐	☐
Computerizing the doll molding equipment	☐	☐	☐
Introducing a child's version of an existing adult board game	☐	☐	☐

12. A shoe manufacturer is considering introducing a new line of boots. When evaluating the incremental revenues from this new line, what should be considered?

13. The Pittsburgh Steel Company is considering two different wire soldering machines. Machine 1 has an initial cost of $100,000, costs $20,000 to set up, and is expected to be sold for $20,000 after 10 years. Machine 2 has an initial cost of $80,000, costs $30,000 to set up, and is expected to be sold for $10,000 after 10 years. Both machines would be depreciated over 10 years using straight-line depreciation. The company Pittsburgh has a tax rate of 35%.

   a. What are the cash flows related to the acquisition of each machine?
   b. What are the cash flows related to the disposition of each machine?

14. The president of Fly-by-Night Airlines has asked you to evaluate the proposed acquisition of a new jet. The jet's price is $40 million, and it is classified in the 10-year MACRS class. The purchase of the jet would require an increase in net working capital of $200,000. The jet would increase the firm's before-tax revenues by $20 million per year, but would also increase operating costs by $5 million per year. The jet is expected to be used for three years and then sold for $25 million. The firm's marginal tax rate is 40%.

    a. What is the amount of the investment outlay required at the beginning of the project?

    b. What is the amount of the operating cash flow each year?

    c. What is the amount of the nonoperating cash flow in the third year?

    d. What is the amount of the net cash flow for each year?

15. Suppose you calculate a project's net present value to be $10 million. What does this mean?

16. Suppose you calculate a project's profitability index to be 1.3. What does this mean?

17. Suppose you calculate a project's net present value to be $30 million. If the required outlay for this project is $100 million, what is the project's profitability index?

18. You are evaluating an investment project with the following cash flows:

Period	Cash Flow
0	−$100,000
1	35,000
2	35,000
3	35,000
4	35,000

Calculate the following:

    a. Payback period

    b. Discounted payback period, assuming a 10% cost of capital

    c. Discounted payback period, assuming a 16% cost of capital

    d. Net present value, assuming a 10% cost of capital

    e. Net present value, assuming a 16% cost of capital

    f. Profitability index, assuming a 10% cost of capital

    g. Profitability index, assuming a 16% cost of capital

    h. Internal rate of return

    i. Modified internal rate of return, assuming reinvestment at 0%

    j. Modified internal rate of return, assuming reinvestment at 10%

19. Suppose you are evaluating two mutually exclusive projects, Thing 1 and Thing 2, with the following cash flows:

	End-of-Year Cash Flows	
Year	Thing 1	Thing 2
0	−$10,000	−$10,000
1	3,293	0
2	3,293	0
3	3,293	0
4	3,293	14,641

   a. If the cost of capital on both projects is 5%, which project, if any, would you choose? Why?

   b. If the cost of capital on both projects is 8%, which project, if any, would you choose? Why?

   c. If the cost of capital on both projects is 11%, which project, if any, would you choose? Why?

   d. If the cost of capital on both projects is 14%, which project, if any, would you choose? Why?

   e. At what discount rate would you be indifferent when choosing between Thing 1 and Thing 2?

   f. On the same graph, draw the investment profiles of Thing 1 and Thing 2, indicating the following items:
- Cross-over discount rate
- NPV of Thing 1 if the cost of capital is 5%
- NPV of Thing 2 if the cost of capital is 5%
- IRR of Thing 1
- IRR of Thing 2

CHAPTER 14

Derivatives for Controlling Risk

SARBANES: "Warren Buffett has warned us that derivatives are time bombs, both for the parties that deal in them and the economic system. The Financial Times *has said so far, there has been no explosion, but the risks of this fast growing market remain real. How do you respond to these concerns?"*

BERNANKE: "I am more sanguine about derivatives than the position you have just suggested. I think, generally speaking, they are very valuable. They provide methods by which risks can be shared, sliced, and diced, and given to those most willing to bear them. They add, I believe, to the flexibility of the financial system in many different ways. With respect to their safety, derivatives, for the most part, are traded among very sophisticated financial institutions and individuals who have considerable incentive to understand them and to use them properly. The Federal Reserve's responsibility is to make sure that the institutions it regulates have good systems and good procedures for ensuring that their derivatives portfolios are well managed and do not create excessive risk in their institutions."

—Interchange between Senator Paul Sarbanes and Federal
Reserve Bank Chairman Ben Bernanke,
Senate Banking Committee hearing, November 2005

Derivative instruments play an important role in financial markets as well as commodity markets by allowing market participants to control their exposure to different types of risk. In this chapter, we describe four types of derivative contracts:

1. Futures,
2. Forwards,

3. Options, and
4. Swaps.

As we discuss these derivatives, you will likely begin to see the common threads among them. First, these instruments derive their value from another security or asset, which we refer to as the *underlying asset*, or simply as the *underlying*. Second, the value of a derivative is dependent not only on the value of the underlying, but also on the features of the derivative itself.

Derivatives are like prescription drugs. They can be beneficial when used appropriately, but they may be habit-forming and carry the risk of unpleasant side effects.
                                         —David Litvack, *Risk*, April 2006, p. 20

FUTURES AND FORWARD CONTRACTS

Futures and forward contracts are contracts between a buyer and a seller for the future delivery, at a specified point in time, of a specified commodity, security, or other asset. Futures contracts are standardized agreements as to the delivery date (or month) and quality of the deliverable, and are traded on organized exchanges. A forward contract differs in that it is usually non-standardized (that is, the terms of each contract are negotiated individually between buyer and seller). We will first look at futures contracts, and then focus on forward contracts.

Futures Contracts

A *futures contract* is a legal agreement between a buyer and a seller in which:

- The buyer agrees to take delivery of something at a specified price at the end of a designated period of time.
- The seller agrees to make delivery of something at a specified price at the end of a designated period of time.

Of course, no one buys or sells anything when entering into a futures contract. Rather, those who enter into a contract agree to buy or sell a specific amount of a specific item at a specified future date. When we speak of the "buyer" or the "seller" of a contract, we are simply adopting the jargon of the futures market, which refers to parties of the contract in terms of the future obligation they are committed to.

Let's look closely at the key elements of this contract. The price at which the parties agree to transact in the future is the *futures price*. The designated date at which the parties must transact is the *settlement date* or *delivery date.* The "something" that the parties agree to exchange is the underlying. We refer to the party on the opposite side of the transaction as the *counterparty.* Therefore, the buyer is the counterparty of the seller, and the seller is the counterparty to the buyer.

To illustrate, suppose a futures contract is traded on an exchange where the underlying to be bought or sold is asset XYZ, and the settlement is three months from now. Assume further that Bert buys this futures contract, and Ernie sells this futures contract, and the price at which they agree to transact in the future is $100. Then $100 is the futures price. At the settlement date, Ernie will deliver asset XYZ to Bert. Bert will give Ernie $100, the futures price.

When an investor takes a position in the market by buying a futures contract (or agreeing to buy at the future date), the investor is said to be in a *long position* or to be *long futures.* If, instead, the investor's opening position is the sale of a futures contract (which means the contractual obligation to sell something in the future), the investor is said to be in a *short position* or *short futures.*

The buyer of a futures contract realizes a profit if the futures price increases; the seller of a futures contract realizes a profit if the futures price decreases. For example, suppose that one month after Bert and Ernie take their positions in the futures contract, the futures price of asset XYZ increases to $120. Bert, the buyer of the futures contract, could then sell the futures contract and realize a profit of $20. Effectively, at the settlement date, he has agreed to buy asset XYZ for $100 and has agreed to sell asset XYZ for $120. Ernie, the seller of the futures contract, will realize a loss of $20.

If the futures price falls to $40 and Ernie buys back the contract at $40, he realizes a profit of $60 because he agreed to sell asset XYZ for $100 and now can buy it for $40. Bert would realize a loss of $60. Thus, if the futures price decreases, the buyer of the futures contract realizes a loss while the seller of the futures contract realizes a profit:

	Price of Underlying at Settlement Is $120		Price of Underlying at Settlement Is $60	
	Bert	Ernie	Bert	Ernie
Sell the underlying	$120	$100	$60	$100
Buy the underlying	100	120	100	60
Profit or loss	$20	−$20	−$40	$40

Liquidating a Position Most financial futures contracts have settlement dates in the months of March, June, September, or December. This means that at a predetermined time in the settlement month, the contract stops trading, and a price is determined by the exchange for settlement of the contract. For example, on January 4, 200X, suppose Bert buys and Ernie sells a futures contract that settles on the third Friday of March of 200X. Then, on that date, Bert and Ernie must perform—Bert agreeing to buy asset XYZ at $100, and Ernie agreeing to sell asset XYZ at $100. The exchange will determine a settlement price for the futures contract for that specific date. For example, if the exchange determines a settlement price of $130, then Bert has agreed to buy asset XYZ for $100 but can settle the position for $130, thereby realizing a profit of $30. Ernie would realize a loss of $30.

Instead of Bert or Ernie entering into a futures contract on January 4, 200X that settles in March, they could have selected a settlement in June, September, or December. The contract with the closest settlement date is called the *nearby futures contract*. The *next futures contract* is the one that settles just after the nearby contract. The contract farthest away in time from settlement is called the *most distant futures contract*.

A party to a futures contract has two choices regarding the liquidation of the position. First, the position can be liquidated prior to the settlement date. For this purpose, the party must take an offsetting position in the same contract. For the buyer of a futures contract, this means selling the same number of identical futures contracts; for the seller of a futures contract, this means buying the same number of identical futures contracts. An identical contract means the contract for the same underlying and the same settlement date. So, for example, if Bert buys one futures contract for asset XYZ with settlement in March 200X on January 4, 200X, and wants to liquidate a position on February 14, 200X, he can sell one futures contract for asset XYZ with settlement in March 200X. Similarly, if Ernie sells one futures contract for asset XYZ with settlement in March 200X on January 4, 200X, and wants to liquidate a position on February 22, 200X, he can buy one futures contract for asset XYZ with settlement in March 200X. A futures contract on asset XYZ that settles in June 200X is not the same contract as a futures contract on asset XYZ that settles in March 200X.

The alternative is to wait until the settlement date. At that time, the party purchasing a futures contract accepts delivery of the underlying; the party that sells a futures contract liquidates the position by delivering the underlying at the agreed upon price. For some futures contracts that we shall describe later in later chapters, settlement is made in cash only. Such contracts are referred to as *cash settlement contracts*.

A useful statistic for measuring the liquidity of a contract is the number of contracts that have been entered into but not yet liquidated. This figure is called the contract's *open interest*. An exchange reports an open interest figure for every futures contracts traded on the exchange.

The Role of the Clearinghouse Associated with every futures exchange is a clearinghouse, which performs several functions. One of these functions is to guarantee that the two parties to the transaction will perform. Because of the clearinghouse, the two parties need not worry about the financial strength and integrity of the other party taking the opposite side of the contract. After initial execution of an order, the relationship between the two parties ends. The clearinghouse interposes itself as the buyer for every sale and as the seller for every purchase. Thus, the two parties are then free to liquidate their positions without involving the other party in the original contract, and without worry that the other party may default.

Margin Requirements When a position is first taken in a futures contract, the investor must deposit a minimum dollar amount per contract as specified by the exchange. This amount, called *initial margin,* is required as a deposit for the contract. The initial margin may be in the form of an interest-bearing security, such as a U.S. Treasury bill. The initial margin is placed in an account, and the amount in this account is referred to as the *investor's equity.* As the price of the futures contract fluctuates each trading day, the value of the investor's equity in the position changes.

At the end of each trading day, the exchange determines the "settlement price" for the futures contract. The settlement price is different from the closing price, which is the price of the security in the final trade of the day (whenever that trade occurred during the day). By contrast, the settlement price is that value the exchange considers to be representative of trading at the end of the day. The exchange uses the settlement price to mark to market the investor's position, so that any gain or loss from the position is quickly reflected in the investor's equity account.

A *maintenance margin* is the minimum level (specified by the exchange) by which an investor's equity position may fall as a result of unfavorable price movements before the investor is required to deposit additional margin. The maintenance margin requirement is a dollar amount that is less than the initial margin requirement. It sets the floor that the investor's equity account can fall to before the investor is required to furnish additional margin. The additional margin deposited, called *variation margin,* is an amount necessary to bring the equity in the account back to its initial margin level. Unlike initial margin, variation margin must be in cash, not interest-bearing instruments. Any excess margin in the account may be withdrawn by the investor. If a party to a futures contract who is required to deposit a variation margin fails to do so within 24 hours, the futures position is liquidated by the clearinghouse.[1]

Regarding the variation margin, we should note two things: First, the variation margin must be cash. Second, the amount of variation margin required is the amount to bring the equity up to the initial margin, not the maintenance margin.

Leveraging When taking a position in a futures contract, a party need not put up the entire amount of the investment. Instead, the exchange requires that only the initial margin be invested. To see the crucial consequences of this fact, suppose Bert has $100 and wants to invest in asset XYZ because he believes its price will appreciate. If asset XYZ is selling for $100, he can buy one unit of the asset in the cash market, the market where goods are delivered upon purchase. His payoff will then be based on the price action of one unit of asset XYZ.

Suppose that the exchange where the futures contract for asset XYZ is traded requires an initial margin of only 5%, which in this case would be $5. Then Bert can purchase 20 contracts with his $100 investment. (This example ignores the fact that Bert may need funds for variation margin.) His payoff will then depend on the price action of 20 units of asset XYZ. Thus, he can leverage the use of his funds. (The degree of leverage equals 1/margin rate. In this case, the degree of leverage equals 1/0.05, or 20.) While the degree of leverage available in the futures market varies from contract to contract, as the initial margin requirement varies, the leverage attainable is considerably greater than in the cash market.

At first, the leverage available in the futures market may suggest that the market benefits only those who want to speculate on price movements. This is not true. As we shall see, futures markets can be used to reduce

---

[1]Although there are initial and maintenance margin requirements for buying securities on margin, the concept of margin differs for securities and futures. When securities are acquired on margin, the difference between the price of the security and the initial margin is borrowed from the broker. The security purchased serves as collateral for the loan, and the investor pays interest. For futures contracts, the initial margin, in effect, serves as "good-faith" money, an indication that the investor will satisfy the obligation of the contract. Normally, no money is borrowed by the investor.

price risk. Without the leverage possible in futures transactions, the cost of reducing price risk using futures would be too high for many market participants.

Forward Contracts

A *forward contract*, just like a futures contract, is an agreement for the future delivery of the underlying at a specified price at the end of a designated period of time. Unlike futures, there is no clearinghouse, and secondary markets are often nonexistent or extremely thin. A forward contract is an over-the-counter instrument.

Because there is no clearinghouse that guarantees the performance of a counterparty in a forward contract, the parties to a forward contract are exposed to *counterparty risk,* the risk that the other party to the transaction will fail to perform. Futures contracts are marked to market at the end of each trading day, while forward contracts usually are not. Consequently, futures contracts are subject to interim cash flows because additional margin may be required in the case of adverse price movements or because cash may be withdrawn in the case of favorable price movements. A forward contract may or may not be marked to market. Where the counterparties are two high-credit-quality entities, the two parties may agree not to mark positions to market. However, if one or both of the parties are concerned with the counterparty risk of the other, then positions may be marked to market. Thus, when a forward contract is marked to market, there are interim cash flows just as with a futures contract. When a forward contract is not marked to market, then there are no interim cash flows.

Other than these differences, what we said about futures contracts applies to forward contracts too.

The Basics of Pricing Futures and Forward Contracts When using derivatives, a market participant should understand the basic principles of how they are valued. While there are many models that have been proposed for valuing financial instruments that trade in the cash (spot) market, the valuation of all derivative models are based on arbitrage arguments. Basically, this involves developing a strategy or a trade wherein a package consisting of a position in the underlying (that is, the underlying asset or instrument for the derivative contract) and borrowing or lending so as to generate the same cash flow profile as the derivative. The value of the package is then equal to the theoretical price of the derivative. If the market price of the derivative deviates from the theoretical price, then the actions of arbitrageurs will drive the market price of the derivative toward its theoretical price until the arbitrage opportunity is eliminated.

In developing a strategy to capture any mispricing, certain assumptions are made. When these assumptions are not satisfied in the real world, the theoretical price can only be approximated. Moreover, a close examination of the underlying assumptions necessary to derive the theoretical price indicates how a pricing formula must be modified to value specific contracts.

Here we describe how futures and forward are valued. The pricing of futures and forward contracts is similar. If the underlying asset for both contracts is the same, the difference in pricing is due to differences in features of the contract that must be dealt with by the pricing model.

We illustrate the basic model for pricing futures contract. By "basic," we mean that we are extrapolating from the nuisances of the underlying for a specific contract. The issues associated with applying the basic pricing model to some of the more popular futures contracts are not described here. Moreover, while the model described here is said to be a model for pricing futures, technically, it is a model for pricing forward contracts with no mark-to-market requirements.

Rather than deriving the formula algebraically, we demonstrate the basic pricing model using an example. We make the following six assumptions for a futures contract that has no initial and variation margin:

1. The price of Asset U in the cash market is $100.
2. There is a known cash flow for Asset U over the life of the futures contract.
3. The cash flow for Asset U is $8 per year paid quarterly ($2 per quarter).
4. The next quarterly payment is exactly three months from now.
5. The futures contract requires delivery three months from now.
6. The current three-month interest rate at which funds can be lent or borrowed is 4% per year.

The objective is to determine what the futures price of this contract should be. To do so, suppose that the futures price in the market is $105. Let's see if that is the correct price. We can check this by implementing the following simple strategy:

- Sell the futures contract at $105.
- Purchase Asset U in the cash market for $100.
- Borrow $100 for three months at 4% per year ($1 per quarter).

The purchase of Asset U is accomplished with the borrowed funds. Hence, this strategy does not involve any initial cash outlay. At the end of three months, the following occurs:

- $2 is received from holding Asset U.
- Asset U is delivered to settle the futures contract.
- The loan is repaid.

This strategy results in the following outcome, indicating what happens now and later (that is, three months from now):

Now		Later	
Action	**Cash Flow**	**Action**	**Cash Flow**
Sell futures	$0	Pay off loan	−$100
Borrow $100	100	Interest on loan	−1
Buy Asset U	−100	Deliver Asset U	105
		Receive payment	2
Cash flow	$0	Cash flow	$6

The profit of $6 from this strategy is guaranteed regardless of what the cash price of Asset U is three months from now. This is because in the preceding analysis of the outcome of the strategy, the cash price of Asset U three months from now never enters the analysis. Moreover, this profit is generated with no investment outlay; the funds needed to acquire Asset U are borrowed when the strategy is executed. In financial terms, the profit in the strategy we have just illustrated arises from a riskless arbitrage between the price of Asset U in the cash market and the price of Asset U in the futures market.

In a well-functioning market, arbitrageurs who could realize this riskless profit for a zero investment would implement the strategy described above. By selling the futures and buying Asset U in order to implement the strategy, this would force the futures price down so that at some price for the futures contract, the arbitrage profit is eliminated.

This strategy that resulted in the capturing of the arbitrage profit is referred to as a *cash-and-carry trade*. The reason for this name is that implementation of the strategy involves borrowing cash to purchase the underlying and "carrying" that underlying to the settlement date of the futures contract.

From the cash-and-carry trade we see that the futures price cannot be $105. Suppose instead that the futures price is $95 rather than $105. Let's try the following strategy to see if that price can be sustained in the market:

- Buy the futures contract at $95.
- Sell (short) Asset U for $100.
- Invest (lend) $100 for three months at 1% per year.

We assume once again that in this strategy there is no initial margin and variation margin for the futures contract. In addition, we assume that there is no cost to selling the asset short and lending the money. Given these assumptions, there is no initial cash outlay for the strategy just as with the cash-and-carry trade.

This strategy produces the following now and later, at the end of three months:

Now		Later	
Action	Cash Flow	Action	Cash Flow
Buy futures	$0	Receive loan repayment	$100
Lend $100	−100	Receive interest on loan	1
Sell Asset U	+100	Buy Asset U to cover short sale	−95
		Make payment	−2
Cash flow	$0	Cash flow	$4

As with the cash-and-carry trade, the $4 profit from this strategy is a riskless arbitrage profit. This strategy requires no initial cash outlay, but will generate a profit whatever the price of Asset U is in the cash market at the settlement date. In real-world markets, this opportunity would lead arbitrageurs to buy the futures contract and short Asset U. The implementation of this strategy would be to raise the futures price until the arbitrage profit disappeared.

This strategy to capture the arbitrage profit is known as a *reverse cash-and-carry trade*. That is, with this strategy, the underlying is sold short and the proceeds received from the short sale are invested.

We can see that the futures price cannot be $95 or $105. What is the theoretical futures price given the assumptions in our illustration? As we show in Exhibit 14.1, if the futures price is $99 there is no opportunity for an arbitrage profit. That is, neither the cash-and-carry trade nor the reverse cash-and-carry trade generates an arbitrage profit.

EXHIBIT 14.1 Cash Flow When There Is a No-Arbitrage Futures Price

Cash and Carry Cash Flows if the Futures Price Is $99

Now		Later	
Action	Cash Flow	Action	Cash Flow
Sell futures	$0	Pay off loan	−$100
Borrow $100	100	Interest on loan	−1
Buy Asset U	−100	Deliver Asset U	99
		Receive payment	2
Cash flow	$0	Cash flow	$0

Reverse Cash and Carry Cash Flow if the Futures Price Is $99

Now		Later	
Action	Cash Flow	Action	Cash Flow
Buy futures	$0	Receive loan repayment	$100
Sell Asset U	+100	Receive interest on loan	1
Lend $100	−100	Buy Asset U to cover short sale	−99
		Make payment	−2
Cash flow	$0	Cash flow	$0

In general, the formula for determining the theoretical price given the assumptions of the model is:

$$\text{Theoretical futures price} = \text{Cash market price} + \left[\text{Cash market price} \times \left(\text{Financing cost} - \text{Cash yield} \right) \right]$$

$$(14.1)$$

In the formula given by equation (14.1), "Financing cost" is the interest rate to borrow funds and "Cash yield" is the payment received from investing in the asset as a percentage of the cash price. In our illustration, the financing cost is 1% and the cash yield is 2%.

In our illustration, because the cash price of Asset U is $100, the theoretical futures price is:

$$\$100 + [\$100 \times (1\% - 2\%)] = \$99$$

The future price can be above or below the cash price depending on the difference between the financing cost and cash yield. The difference between these rates is the *net financing cost*. A more commonly used term for the net financing cost is the *cost of carry*, or, simply, *carry*. *Positive carry* means that the cash yield exceeds the financing cost.[2] *Negative carry* means that the financing cost exceeds the cash yield. As a result,

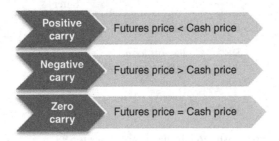

Positive carry	Futures price < Cash price
Negative carry	Futures price > Cash price
Zero carry	Futures price = Cash price

Note that at the settlement date of the futures contract, the futures price must equal the cash market price. The reason is that a futures contract with no time left until delivery is equivalent to a cash market transaction. Thus, as the delivery date approaches, the futures price converges to the cash market price. This fact is evident from the formula for the theoretical futures price given by equation (14.1). The financing cost approaches zero as the delivery date approaches. Similarly, the yield that can be earned by holding the underlying approaches zero. Hence, the cost of carry approaches zero, and the futures price approaches the cash market price.

TRY IT! FUTURES

Suppose you borrow $1,000 at 8% per year so that you can use this money to buy Asset W. You also sell a futures contract on Asset W, with delivery in one year.

1. What type of transaction is this?
2. Is this a profitable transaction if the futures price is $1,010?

A Closer Look at the Theoretical Futures Price   In deriving theoretical futures price using the arbitrage argument, we made several assumptions. These assumptions, as well as the differences in contract specifications, result

---

[2]Note that while the difference between the financing cost and the cash yield is a negative value, carry is said to be positive.

in the futures price in the market deviating from the theoretical futures price as given by equation (14.1). It may be possible to incorporate these institutional and contract specification differences into the formula for the theoretical futures price. In general, however, because it is often too difficult to allow for these differences in building a model for the theoretical futures price, the end result is that one can develop bands or boundaries for the theoretical futures price. So long as the futures price in the market remains within the band, no arbitrage opportunity is possible.

There are some institutional and contract specification differences that cause prices to deviate from the theoretical futures price, as given by the basic pricing model:

- *Interim cash flows.* In the derivation of a basic pricing model, we assume that no interim cash flows arise because of changes in futures prices (that is, there is no variation margin). As noted earlier, in the absence of initial and variation margins, the theoretical price for the contract is technically the theoretical price for a forward contract that is not marked to market, rather than a futures contract.

  In addition, the model assumes implicitly that any dividends or coupon interest payments are paid at the settlement date of the futures contract rather than at any time between initiation of the cash position and settlement of the futures contract. However, we know that the underlying for financial futures contracts (such as stock index futures contracts and bond futures contracts) do have interim cash flows.

- *Differences in borrowing and lending rates.* In the formula for the theoretical futures price, it is assumed in the cash-and-carry trade and the reverse cash-and-carry trade that the borrowing rate and lending rate are equal. Typically, however, the borrowing rate is higher than the lending rate. The impact of this inequality is that there is a band of futures prices; within this band, there are no arbitrage opportunities.

- *Transaction costs.* The two strategies to exploit any price discrepancies between the cash market and theoretical price for the futures contract require the arbitrageur to incur transaction costs. In real-world financial markets, the costs of entering into and closing the cash position, as well as round-trip transaction costs for the futures contract, affect the futures price. As in the case of differential borrowing and lending rates, transaction costs widen the bands for the theoretical futures price.

- *Short selling.* The reverse cash-and-strategy trade requires the short selling of the underlying. It is assumed in this strategy that the proceeds from the short sale are received and reinvested. In practice, for individual investors, the proceeds are not received, and, in fact, the individual investor is required to deposit margin (securities margin and not futures margin) to short sell.

For institutional investors, the underlying may be borrowed, but there is a cost to borrowing. This cost of borrowing can be incorporated into the model by reducing the cash yield on the underlying. For strategies applied to stock index futures, a short sale of the components stocks in the index means that all stocks in the index must be sold simultaneously. This may be difficult to do and, therefore, would widen the band for the theoretical future price.

- *Deliverable is a basket of securities.* Some futures contracts have as the underlying a basket of assets or an index, rather than a single asset. Stock index futures are the most obvious example.

Using Futures and Forward Contracts

As we explained, futures and forward contracts can be used for leverage. It is the misuse of these contracts, indeed the misuse of all derivatives described in this chapter, by corporate treasurers and investment managers for speculative purposes (i.e., betting on something occurring) that is often discussed in the media. But derivatives provide a means for controlling risk, as the illustrations to follow will make clear. The focus of the media is on those cases of misusing derivatives, not on how participants in the financial market have used derivatives to successfully protect against major losses due to adverse movements in prices, foreign exchange, or interest rates.

It is important to note that futures and forward contracts are *risk-sharing instruments*. This means that both parties to the transaction are sharing the risk associated with the underlying. So if the underlying is, say, a commodity such as wheat, then both parties to a trade are exposed to the price risk of wheat. One party will be exposed to the price of wheat declining (the long position) and the other party will be exposed to the price of wheat increasing (the short position).

Let's continue with the wheat example for our first application. Consider the economic exposure to price risk by a farmer who grows wheat and a food manufacturer that uses wheat to create its products. The farmer is exposed to the risk that the price of wheat will decline by the time the wheat is brought to market. The food manufacturer is exposed to the risk that the price of wheat will increase in the future and therefore the cost of one of its major inputs will increase. If both the farmer and the food manufacturer wanted to basically eliminate their respective exposures to the price risk associated with wheat, they can do so by using futures contracts. The farmer could lock in a future price for wheat by buying a futures contract; the food manufacturer could lock in a future price for wheat by selling a futures contract. Thus, each party has shifted the undesired price risk to the other party. Notice that neither party will benefit if there is favorable price movement for wheat. That is, if the price of wheat rises in the future, the farmer cannot benefit; if the price of wheat declines in the future, the food manufacturer cannot benefit.

The same situation applies to entities that have exposure to changes in a foreign currency. The price of a foreign currency is given by the exchange rate between two currencies. Suppose the two currencies are the U.S. dollar and the euro. A U.S. manufacturer that sells products in France and is paid in euros by the French customer is concerned that the value of the euro will decline (i.e., depreciate) relative to the U.S. dollar. In contrast, another U.S. manufacturer who buys material from a firm in Spain and must pay for that material in euros is concerned that the euro will increase (i.e., appreciate) relative to the U.S. dollar. To protect against the adverse fluctuation of the currency, the two U.S. manufacturing firms can take the appropriate position in foreign exchange futures or forward contracts.

As our final application, suppose a corporate treasurer knows that $200 million must be borrowed six months from now. The concern that the corporate treasurer has is that in the future interest rates may rise, making the cost of borrowing more expensive. Suppose that the portfolio manager of a pension fund knows that six months from now there will be $200 million in cash inflows to invest and plans to invest that sum in bonds. The risk faced by the portfolio manager is that interest rates will decline and therefore the portfolio will earn a lower interest rate on the funds invested six months from now. Again, both the corporate treasurer and the portfolio manager are exposed to an unfavorable movement in something; that something in this case is interest rates. But once again what is an adverse movement to one party is a favorable one to the other party. To protect against an adverse movement in interest rates, there are interest rate futures contracts that the two parties can employ.

OPTIONS

We now turn to another derivative instrument, an option contract. An *option* is a contract in which the option seller grants the option buyer the right to enter into a transaction with the seller to either buy or sell an underlying asset at a specified price on or before a specified date.

Basic Features of Options

An investor who buys an option has the choice of exercising it—that is, buying the underlying asset—or not. Unlike a futures contract, the investor in an option can simply not do anything, letting the option expire. The option seller grants this right in exchange for a certain amount of money, which is the *option premium* or *option price*. The option seller is the *option writer*, while the option buyer is the *option holder*.

The specified price that the option buyer may buy or sell the underlying is the *strike price* or *exercise price* which is fixed in the option contract. The specified date is the expiration date.

The asset that is the subject of the option is the underlying, and the underlying can be an individual stock, a stock index, a bond, or even another derivative instrument, such as a futures contract. The option writer can grant the option holder one of two rights. If the right is to purchase the underlying, the option is a *call option*. If the right is to sell the underlying, the option is a *put option*.

We can categorize an option according to when it may be exercised by the buyer. This is the exercise style. A *European option* can only be exercised at the expiration date of the contract. An *American option*, in contrast, can be exercised any time on or before the expiration date. An option that can be exercised before the expiration date, but only on specified dates is called a *Bermuda option* or an *Atlantic option*.

The terms of the exchange are represented by the contract unit and are standardized for most contracts. The option holder enters into the contract with an opening transaction. Subsequently, the option holder then has the choice to exercise or to sell the option. The sale of an existing option by the holder is a *closing sale*.

Let's use an illustration to demonstrate the fundamental option contract. Suppose that Jack buys a call option for $3 (the option price) with the following terms:

Feature	Specification
Underlying	One unit of asset ABC
Exercise price	$100
Expiration date	3 months from now
Exercise style	American

At any time up to and including the expiration date, Jack can decide to buy from the writer of this option one unit of asset ABC, for which he will pay a price of $100. If it is not beneficial for Jack to exercise the option, he will not; we'll explain shortly how he decides when it will be beneficial. Whether Jack exercises the option or not, the $3 he paid for it will be kept by the option writer.

If Jack buys a put option rather than a call option, then he would be able to sell asset ABC to the option writer for a price of $100. Like the call option, he will only exercise the put option if it is beneficial to do so.

The maximum amount that an option buyer can lose is the option price. The maximum profit that the option writer can realize is the option price. The option buyer has substantial upside return potential, while the option writer has substantial downside risk. We'll investigate the risk/reward relationship for option positions later in this chapter.

Options, like other financial instruments, may be traded either on an organized exchange or in the over-the-counter (OTC) market. The advantages of an exchange-traded option are as follows. First, the exercise price and expiration date of the contract are standardized. Second, as in the case of futures contracts, the direct link between buyer and seller is severed after the order is executed because of the interchangeability of exchange-traded options. The clearinghouse associated with the exchange where the option trades performs the same function in the options market that it does in the futures market. Finally, the transactions costs are lower for exchange-traded options than for OTC options.

The higher cost of an OTC option reflects the cost of customizing the option for the many situations where a corporation seeking to use an option to manage risk needs to have a tailor-made option because the standardized exchange-traded option does not satisfy its objectives. Some commercial and investment and banking firms act as principals as well as brokers in the OTC options market. OTC options are sometimes referred to as *dealer options*. While an OTC option is less liquid than an exchange-traded option, this is typically not of concern to the user of such an option.

Differences Between Options and Futures Contracts

Notice that, unlike in a futures contract, one party to an option contract is not obligated to transact—specifically, the option buyer has the right but not the obligation to transact. The option writer does have the obligation to perform. This is different than in the case of a futures contract where both buyer and seller are obligated to perform.[3]

Consequently, the risk/reward characteristics of the two contracts are also different. In the case of a futures contract, the buyer of the contract realizes a dollar-for-dollar gain when the price of the futures contract increases and suffers a dollar-for-dollar loss when the price of the futures

---

[3]Of course, a futures buyer does not pay the seller to accept the obligation, while an option buyer pays the seller the option price.

contract drops. The opposite occurs for the seller of a futures contract. Because of this relationship, futures are referred to as having a "linear payoff."

Options do not provide this symmetric risk/reward relationship. The most that the buyer of an option can lose is the option price. While the buyer of an option retains all the potential benefits, the gain is always reduced by the amount of the option price. The maximum profit that the writer may realize is the option price; this is offset against substantial downside risk. Because of this characteristic, options are referred to as having a *nonlinear payoff*.

The difference in the type of payoff between futures and options is extremely important because market participants can use futures to protect against symmetric risk and options to protect against asymmetric risk.

Risk and Return of Options

Here we illustrate the risk and return characteristics of the four basic option positions—buying a call option, selling a call option, buying a put option, and selling a put option. The illustrations assume that each option position is held to the expiration date and not exercised early. Also, to simplify the illustrations, we ignore transactions costs.

Buying Call Options   The purchase of a call option creates a position referred to as a *long call position*. To illustrate this position, assume that there is a call option on Asset X that expires in one month and has an exercise price of $60. The option price is $2. What is the profit or loss for the investor who purchases this call option and holds it to the expiration date?

The profit and loss from the strategy will depend on the price of Asset X at the expiration date. A number of outcomes are possible.[4] We

---

[4]In addition, the illustrations do not address the cost of financing the purchase of the option price or the opportunity cost of investing the option price. Specifically, the buyer of an option must pay the seller the option price at the time the option is purchased. Thus, the buyer must finance the purchase price of the option or, assuming the purchase price does not have to be borrowed, the buyer loses the income that can be earned by investing the amount of the option price until the option is sold or exercised. In contrast, assuming that the seller does not have to use the option price as margin for the short position or can use an interest-earning asset as security, the seller has the opportunity to earn income from the proceeds of the option sale.

provide the detail calculations for prices of Asset X between $58 and $65:

Price of Asset X	Exercise?	Calculation	Option Buyer Profit or Loss
$58	No		−$2
$59	No		−$2
$60	No		−$2
$61	Yes	$61 − 60 − 2 =	−$1
$62	Yes	$62 − 60 − 2 =	$0
$63	Yes	$63 − 60 − 2 =	$1
$64	Yes	$64 − 60 − 2 =	$2
$65	Yes	$65 − 60 − 2 =	$3

- If the price of Asset X at the expiration date is less than or equal to $60 (the option price), the investor will not exercise the option.

  It would be foolish to pay the option writer $60 when Asset X can be purchased in the market at a lower price. In this case, the option buyer loses the entire option price of $2.
- If Asset X's price is more than $60 the option buyer will exercise the option.
- If less than $62 at the expiration date, the option buyer will exercise the option. By exercising, the option buyer can purchase Asset X for $60 (the exercise price) and sell it in the market for the higher price.
- If Asset X's price at the expiration date is equal to $62 the investor breaks even, realizing a gain of $2 that offsets the cost of the option, $2.
- If Asset X's price at the expiration date is more than $62, the investor will exercise the option and realize a profit.

Writing (Selling) Call Options   The writer of a call option is said to be in a *short call position.* To illustrate the option seller's (i.e., writer's) position, we use the same call option we used to illustrate buying a call option. The profit and loss profile of the short call position (that is, the position of the call option writer) is the mirror image of the profit and loss profile of the long call position (the position of the call option buyer). Consider the profit or loss for the option writer for prices of Asset X between $58 and $65:

Price of Asset X	Will the Option Buyer Exercise?	Calculation	Option Writer Profit or Loss
$58	No		$2
$59	No		$2
$60	No		$2
$61	Yes	$60 − 61 + 2 =	$1
$62	Yes	$60 − 62 + 2 =	$0
$63	Yes	$60 − 63 + 2 =	−$1
$64	Yes	$60 − 64 + 2 =	−$2
$65	Yes	$60 − 65 + 2 =	−$3

Consequently, the maximum profit that the short call position can produce is the option price. The maximum loss is not limited because it is the highest price reached by Asset X on or before the expiration date, less the option price; this price can be indefinitely high.

We provide a graph of the profit/loss profile for both the option buyer and the option writer for this option in Exhibit 14.2 for prices of the underlying from $40 to $70. As you can see in this graph, That is, the profit of the short call position for any given price for Asset X at the expiration date is the same as the loss of the long call position.

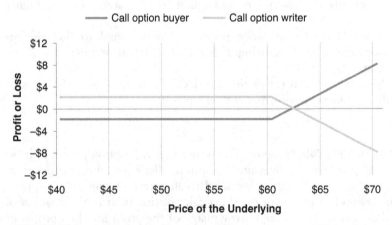

EXHIBIT 14.2   Profit or Loss for the Call Option Buyer and Writer for an Option with an Exercise Price of $60 and a Call Premium of $2

TRY IT! THE PAYOFF FROM A CALL OPTION

Suppose you buy a call option with an exercise price of $50, paying an option premium of $3. If the underlying stock's price is $60 at the time you exercise this option, what is your profit on this option?

Buying Put Options   The buying of a put option creates a financial position referred to as a *long put position*. To illustrate this position, we assume a hypothetical put option on one unit of Asset Y with one month to maturity and an exercise price of $100. Assume the put option is selling for $3. The profit or loss for this position at the expiration date depends on the market price of Asset Y. Consider the possible outcomes for the put option buyer for prices of Asset Y from $93 to $103:

Price of Asset Y	Exercise?	Calculation	Option Buyer Profit or Loss
$93	Yes	$100 − 93 − 3 =	$4
$94	Yes	$100 − 94 − 3 =	$3
$95	Yes	$100 − 95 − 3 =	$2
$96	Yes	$100 − 96 − 3 =	$1
$97	Yes	$100 − 97 − 3 =	$0
$98	Yes	$100 − 98 − 3 =	−$1
$99	Yes	$100 − 99 − 3 =	−$2
$100	No		−$3
$101	No		−$3
$102	No		−$3
$103	No		−$3

- If Asset Y's price is greater than $100, the buyer of the put option will not exercise it because exercising would mean selling.
- If the price of Asset Y at expiration is equal to $100, the buyer of the put option will not exercise it, leaving the put buyer with a loss equal to the option price of $3.
- Any price for Asset Y that is less than $100 but greater than $97 will result in a loss; exercising the put option, however, limits the loss to less than the option price of $2.
- At a $97 price for Asset Y at the expiration date, the put buyer will break even. The investor will realize a gain of $3 by selling Asset Y

to the writer of the option for $100, offsetting the cost of the option, the $3.

■ If Asset Y's price is below $97 at the expiration date, the long put position (the put buyer) will realize a profit.

Writing (Selling) Put Options   Writing a put option creates a position referred to as a *short put position*. The profit and loss profile for a short put option is the mirror image of the long put option. The maximum profit from this position is the option price. The theoretical maximum loss can be substantial should the price of the underlying fall; at the extreme, if the price were to fall all the way to zero, the loss would be as large as the exercise price less the option price.

In the case of the option on Asset Y, with an exercise price of $100 and an option premium of $3:

Price of Asset Y	Exercise?	Calculation	Option Writer Profit or Loss
$93	Yes	$100 − 93 − 3 =	−$4
$94	Yes	$100 − 94 − 3 =	−$3
$95	Yes	$100 − 95 − 3 =	−$2
$96	Yes	$100 − 96 − 3 =	−$1
$97	Yes	$100 − 97 − 3 =	$0
$98	Yes	$100 − 98 − 3 =	+$1
$99	Yes	$100 − 99 − 3 =	+$2
$100	No		+$3
$101	No		+$3
$102	No		+$3
$103	No		+$3

We provide the profit and loss profile for the long put position in graphical form in Exhibit 14.3. As with all long option positions, the loss is limited to the option premium paid by the investor. The profit potential, however, is substantial: The theoretical maximum profit is generated if Asset Y's price falls to zero. Contrast this profit potential with that of the buyer of a call option. The theoretical maximum profit for a call buyer cannot be determined beforehand because it depends on the highest price that can be reached by Asset Y before or at the option expiration date.

To summarize, buying calls or selling puts allows the investor to gain if the price of the underlying rises. Selling calls and buying puts allows the investor to gain if the price of the underlying falls.

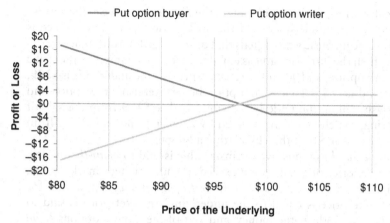

EXHIBIT 14.3 Profit or Loss for the Put Option Buyer and Writer for an Option with an Exercise Price of $100 and a $3 Option Premium

TRY IT! THE PAYOFF FROM A PUT OPTION

Suppose you buy a put option with an exercise price of $50, paying an option premium of $3. If the underlying stock's price is $48 at the time you exercise this option, what is your profit or loss on this option?

Basic Components of the Option Price

The option price is a reflection of the option's *intrinsic value* and any additional amount over its intrinsic value. The premium over intrinsic value is often referred to as the *time premium*.

As with futures and forward contracts, the theoretical price of an option is also derived from arguments based on arbitrage. However, the pricing of options is not as simple as the pricing of futures and forward contracts. The theoretical price of an option is made up of two components: the intrinsic value and a premium over intrinsic value.

The *intrinsic value* is the option's economic value if it is exercised immediately. If no positive economic value would result from exercising immediately, the intrinsic value is zero. An option's intrinsic value is easy to compute given the price of the underlying and the strike price.

For a call option, the intrinsic value is the difference between the current market price of the underlying and the strike price. If that difference is positive, then the intrinsic value equals that difference; if the difference is zero or negative, then the intrinsic value is equal to zero. For example, if the strike price for a call option is $100 and the current price of the underlying is $109, the intrinsic value is $9. That is, an option buyer exercising the option and simultaneously selling the underlying would realize $109 from the sale of the underlying, which would be covered by acquiring the underlying from the option writer for $100, thereby netting a $9 gain.

An option that has a positive intrinsic value is said to be *in-the-money*. When the strike price of a call option exceeds the underlying's market price, it has no intrinsic value and is said to be *out-of-the-money*. An option for which the strike price is equal to the underlying's market price is said to be *at-the-money*. Both at-the-money and out-of-the-money options have intrinsic values of zero because it is not profitable to exercise them. Our call option with a strike price of $100 would be:

- in the money when the market price of the underlying is more than $100;
- out of the money when the market price of the underlying is less than $100; and
- at the money when the market price of the underlying is $100.

For a put option, the intrinsic value is equal to the amount by which the underlying's market price is below the strike price. For example, if the strike price of a put option is $100 and the market price of the underlying is $95, the intrinsic value is $5. That is, the buyer of the put option who simultaneously buys the underlying and exercises the put option will net $5 by exercising. The underlying will be sold to the writer for $100 and purchased in the market for $95. With a strike price of $100, the put option would be (1) in the money when the underlying's market price is less than $100; (2) out of the money when the underlying's market price exceeds $100; and (3) at the money when the underlying's market price is equal to $100.

The time premium of an option, also referred to as the *time value of the option*, is the amount by which the option's market price exceeds its intrinsic value. It is the expectation of the option buyer that at some time prior to the expiration date changes in the market price of the underlying will increase the value of the rights conveyed by the option. Because of this expectation, the option buyer is willing to pay a premium above the intrinsic value. For example, if the price of a call option with a strike price of $100 is $12 when the underlying's market price is $104, the time premium of this option is $8 ($12 minus its intrinsic value of $4). Had the underlying's market price been $95 instead of $104, the time premium of this option would be the entire $12 because the option has no intrinsic value. All other things being equal, the time premium of an option will increase with the amount of time remaining to expiration.

An option buyer has two ways to realize the value of an option position. The first way is by exercising the option. The second way is to sell the option in the market. In the first example above, selling the call for $12 is preferable to exercising, because the exercise will realize only $4 (the intrinsic value), but the sale will realize $12. As this example shows, exercise causes the immediate loss of any time premium. It is important to note that there are circumstances under which an option may be exercised prior to the expiration date. These circumstances depend on whether the total proceeds at the expiration date would be greater by holding the option or exercising and reinvesting any received cash proceeds until the expiration date.

Factors That Influence an Option's Price   The factors that affect the price of an option include:

1. Market price of the underlying.
2. Strike price of the option.
3. Time to expiration of the option.
4. Expected volatility of the underlying over the life of the option.
5. Short-term, risk-free interest rate over the life of the option.
6. Anticipated cash payments on the underlying over the life of the option.

The impact of each of these factors may depend on whether (1) the option is a call or a put, and (2) the option is an American option or a European option. We summarize these factors in Exhibit 14.4 and how each of the six factors listed above affects the price of a put and call option. Here, we briefly explain why the factors have the particular effects.

- *Market price of the underlying asset.* The option price will change as the price of the underlying changes. For a call option, as the underlying's price increases (all other factors being constant), the option price increases. The opposite holds for a put option: As the price of the underlying increases, the price of a put option decreases.
- *Strike price.* The strike price is fixed for the life of the option. All other factors being equal, the lower the strike price, the higher the price for a call option. For put options, the higher the strike price, the higher the option price.
- *Time to expiration of the option.* After the expiration date, an option has no value. All other factors being equal, the longer the time to

EXHIBIT 14.4   Summary of Factors that Affect the Price of an Option

Factor	Effect of an Increase of a Factor on the ...	
	Call Option Price	Put Option Price
Market price of the underlying	↑	↓
Strike price of the option	↓	↑
Time to expiration of the option	↑	↑
Expected volatility of the underlying over the life of the option	↑	↑
Short-term, risk-free interest rate over the life of the option	↑	↓
Anticipated cash payments on the underlying over the life of the option	↓	↑

expiration of the option, the higher the option price. This is because, as the time to expiration decreases, less time remains for the underlying's price to rise (for a call buyer) or fall (for a put buyer), and therefore the probability of a favorable price movement decreases. Consequently, as the time remaining until expiration decreases, the option price approaches its intrinsic value.

- *Expected volatility of the underlying over the life of the option.* All other factors being equal, the greater the expected volatility (as measured by the standard deviation or variance) of the underlying, the more the option buyer would be willing to pay for the option, and the more an option writer would demand for it. This occurs because the greater the expected volatility, the greater the probability that the movement of the underlying will change so as to benefit the option buyer at some time before expiration.

- *Short-term, risk-free interest rate over the life of the option.* Buying the underlying requires an investment of funds. Buying an option on the same quantity of the underlying makes the difference between the underlying's price and the option price available for investment at an interest rate at least as high as the risk-free rate. Consequently, all other factors being constant, the higher the short-term, risk-free interest rate, the greater the cost of buying the underlying and carrying it to the expiration date of the call option. Hence, the higher the short-term, risk-free interest rate, the more attractive the call option will be relative to the direct purchase of the underlying. As a result, the higher the short-term, risk-free interest rate, the greater the price of a call option.

■ *Anticipated cash payments on the underlying over the life of the option.* Cash payments on the underlying tend to decrease the price of a call option because the cash payments make it more attractive to hold the underlying than to hold the option. For put options, cash payments on the underlying tend to increase the price.

Option Pricing Models Earlier in this chapter, we explained how the theoretical price of a futures contract and forward contract is determined based on arbitrage arguments. An option pricing model uses a set of assumptions and arbitrage arguments to derive a theoretical price for an option. Deriving a theoretical option price is much more complicated than deriving a theoretical futures or forward price because the option price depends on the expected volatility of the underlying over the life of the option.

Several models have been developed to determine the theoretical price of an option. The most popular one was developed by Fischer Black and Myron Scholes for valuing European call options on common stock.[5] Because of the technical nature of this model, we describe it in the appendix to this chapter.

Using Options

Unlike futures and forward contracts, which are risk-sharing instruments, options are *insurance-type instruments*. The buyer of the option pays the seller/writer of the option the option price to obtain the desired protection. This is the reason the option price is often referred to as the option premium, the term used in the insurance industry for the cost of buying insurance. Because an option contract obligates only the seller and not the buyer to perform, a party that buys an option can benefit from a favorable movement in the underlying. Recall that when we discussed the use of futures and forward contracts, that was not an attribute of those instruments.

Let's look at how the wheat farmer and the food manufacturer in our earlier discussion on the applications of futures and forward contracts could have used options. To protect against a decline in the price of wheat, the farmer could purchase a put option on wheat. The minimum price at which the farmer could then sell wheat is the exercise price of the option. However,

---

[5]Fischer Black and Myron Scholes, "Pricing of Options and Corporate Liabilities," *Journal of Political Economy* 81(1973): 637–654.

since the farmer must pay the option price, the effective sale price for wheat by buying the option is the exercise price reduced by the cost of the option. Notice that this is the downside price risk for the farmer. The farmer will benefit from an increase in the price of wheat, but that upside is reduced by the cost of the option.

The food manufacturer can buy a call option on wheat. By doing so, the food manufacturer knows that it will not have to pay more for wheat than the exercise price. Since the food manufacturer must pay the option premium, the effective maximum price that the food manufacturer will have to pay for wheat is the sum of the exercise price and the cost of the option. Should the price of wheat decline, the food manufacturer can benefit, but the savings from the price decline are reduced by the cost of the option.

SWAPS

A *swap* is an agreement whereby two parties (called *counterparties*) agree to exchange periodic payments. The dollar amount of the payments exchanged is based on some predetermined dollar principal, which is called the *notional principal amount* or simply *notional amount*. The dollar amount each counterparty pays to the other is the agreed-upon periodic rate multiplied by the notional amount. The only dollars exchanged between the parties are the agreed-upon payments, not the notional amount.

A swap is an over-the-counter contract. Hence, the counterparties to a swap are exposed to counterparty risk.

We look at four types of swaps—interest rate swaps, currency swaps, commodity swaps, and credit default swaps—that are the most common swaps used by businesses. We illustrate these types of swaps in this section.

Interest Rate Swap

In an *interest rate swap*, the counterparties swap payments in the same currency based on an interest rate. For example, one of the counterparties can pay a fixed interest rate and the other party a floating interest rate. The floating interest rate is commonly referred to as the *reference rate*.

For example, suppose the counterparties to a swap agreement are Farm Equip Corporation (a manufacturing firm) and PNC Bank. The notional amount of this swap is $100 million and the term of the swap is five years. Every year for the next five years, Farm Equip Corporation agrees to pay PNC Bank 8% per year, while PNC Bank agrees to pay Farm Equip Corporation the one-year LIBOR as the reference rate. This means that every year, Farm Equip Corporation will pay $8 million (8% times $100 million) to PNC Bank. The amount PNC Bank will pay Farm Equip Corporation depends on LIBOR. For example, one-year LIBOR is 6%, PNC Bank will pay Farm Equip Corporation $6 million (6% times $100 million).

The best advice may be this: treat exotic derivatives like powerful medicines, large doses of which can be harmful. Use them in moderation, for a particular purpose (such as risk management) and only after having read the instructions on the bottle.

—Philippe Jorion, *Bad Bets Gone Bad*
(New York: Academic Press, 1995), p. 57

Taking this a step further, if the LIBOR is 6%,

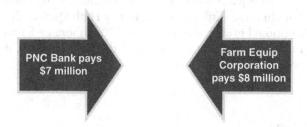

Only the net cash flow is actually exchanged, so in this case Farm Equip pays $1 million to PNC Bank. If, instead, the LIBOR is 9%,

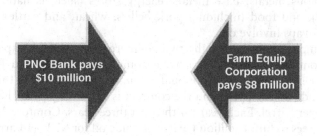

In this case the net cash flow is $2 million, paid from PNC to Farm Equip Corporation.

Why use an interest rate swap? Though we'll discuss this later in the book when we discuss how a company finances itself, the motivation relates to the costs of financing, and whether the financing is fixed (such as the commitment that Farm Equip has made) or floating (such as the commitment that PNC Bank has made).

Currency Swaps

In a *currency swap*, two parties agree to swap payments based on different currencies. Companies use currency swaps to raise funds outside of their home currency and then swap the payments into their home currency. This allows a corporation with operations outside their home country to eliminate currency risk (i.e., unfavorable exchange rate or currency movements) when borrowing outside of its domestic currency.

To illustrate a currency swap, suppose there are two counterparties: High Quality Electronics Corporation (a U.S. manufacturing firm) and Citibank. The notional amount is $100 million and its Swiss franc (CHF) equivalent. At the time the contract was entered into, $100 million was equal to CHF 127 million. And suppose the swap term is eight years. Every year for the next eight years the U.S. manufacturing firm agrees to pay Citibank Swiss francs equal to 5% of the Swiss franc notional amount, or CHF 6.35 million. In turn, Citibank agrees to pay High Quality Electronics 7% of the U.S. notional principal amount of $100 million, or $7 million. If the exchange rate between the U.S. dollar and the CHF changes, the value of what is exchanged changes.

Commodity Swaps

In a *commodity swap*, the exchange of payments by the counterparties is based on the value of a particular physical commodity. Physical commodities include precious metals, base metals, energy stores (such as natural gas or crude oil), and food (including pork bellies, wheat, and cattle). Most commodity swaps involve oil.

For example, suppose that the two counterparties to this swap agreement are Comfort Airlines Company, a commercial airline, and Prebon Energy (an energy broker). The notional amount of the contract is 1 million barrels of crude oil each year and the contract is for three years. The swap price is $19 per barrel. Each year for the next three years, Comfort Airlines Company agrees to buy 1 million barrels of crude oil for $19 per barrel. So, each year Comfort Airlines Company pays $19 million to Prebon Energy ($19 per barrel times 1 million barrels) and receives 1 million barrels of crude oil.

The motive for Comfort Airlines of using the commodity swap is that it allows the company to lock in a price for 1 million barrels of crude oil at $19 per barrel regardless of how high crude oil's price increases over the next three years.

Credit Default Swaps

A *credit default swap* (CDS) is an OTC derivative that permits the buying and selling of credit protection against particular types of events that can adversely affect the credit quality of a bond such as the default of the borrower. Although it is referred to as a "swap," it does not follow the general characteristics of a swap described earlier. There are two parties: the *credit protection buyer* and *credit protection seller*. Over the life of the CDS, the protection buyer agrees to pay the protection seller a payment at specified dates to insure against the impairment of the debt of a *reference entity* due to a credit-related event.

The reference entity is a specific issuer, say, Ford Motor Company. The specific credit-related events are identified in the contract that will trigger a payment by the credit protection seller to the credit protection buyer are referred to as *credit events*. If a credit event does occur, the credit protection buyer only makes a payment up to the credit event date and makes no further payment. At this time, the protection buyer is obligated to fulfill its obligation. The contract will call for the protection seller to compensate for the loss in the value of the debt obligation. The specific method for compensating the protection buyer is not important at this time for this brief description of this derivative contract.

THE BOTTOM LINE

- Derivatives are contracts whose value depends on some other asset. Derivatives include futures contracts, forward contracts, options, and swaps.
- The traditional purpose of derivative instruments is to provide an important opportunity to manage against the risk of adverse future price, exchange rate, or interest rate movements.
- Futures contracts are creations of exchanges, which require initial margin from parties. Each day positions are marked to market. Additional margin is required if the equity in the position falls below the maintenance margin. The clearinghouse guarantees that the parties to the futures contract will satisfy their obligations.
- A forward contract differs in several important ways from a futures contract. In contrast to a futures contract, the parties to a forward contract are exposed to the risk that the other party to the contract will fail to perform. The positions of the parties may not necessarily marked to market, so in such cases there are no interim cash flows associated

with a forward contract. Finally, unwinding a position in a forward contract may be difficult.

- Both futures and forward contracts are risk-sharing instruments, allowing a party to control risk by locking in a future value but giving up the opportunity to benefit from a favorable movement in the value of the underlying.
- An option grants the buyer of the option the right either to buy from (in the case of a call option) or to sell to (in the case of a put option) the seller (writer) of the option the underlying at the exercise (strike) price by the option's expiration date. The price that the option buyer pays to the writer of the option is the option price or option premium.
- The most popular model used to determine the fair market value of an option is the Black-Scholes option pricing model.
- The buyer of an option cannot realize a loss greater than the option price, and has all the upside potential. By contrast, the maximum gain that the writer (seller) of an option can realize is the option price; the writer is exposed to all the downside risk.
- Unlike futures and forward contracts that are risk-sharing instruments, options are insurance-type contracts. The buyer of the option pays the option price to obtain protection against adverse movements in the value of the underlying but maintains the upside potential (reduced by the cost of the option).
- The option price consists of two components: the intrinsic value and the time premium. The intrinsic value is the economic value of the option if it is exercised immediately (except that if there is no positive economic value that will result from exercising immediately, then the intrinsic value is zero). The time premium is the amount by which the option price exceeds the intrinsic value.
- Swap contracts allow for the exchange of a set of cash flows, and can be based on interest rates, currency exchange rates, commodity prices, or credit protection.

APPENDIX: BLACK-SCHOLES OPTION PRICING MODEL

In the chapter, we explained the basic factors that affect the value of an option, also referred to as the option price. The option price is a reflection of the option's intrinsic value and any additional amount over its intrinsic value, called the time premium. In this appendix, we explain how the theoretical price of a non-dividend-paying European call option can be determined using a well-known financial model, the *Black-Scholes option pricing model.* We do not provide the details with respect to how the model was derived by its developers. Rather, we will set forth the basics of the model. Recall that a European option is one that cannot be exercised prior to the expiration date.

Basically, the idea behind the arbitrage argument in deriving the option pricing model is that if the payoff from owning a call option can be replicated by (1) purchasing the stock underlying the call option; and (2) borrowing funds, then the price of the option will be (at most) the cost of creating the payoff replicating strategy.

By imposing certain assumptions (to be discussed later) and using arbitrage arguments, the Black-Scholes option pricing model computes the fair (or theoretical) price of a European call option on a non-dividend-paying stock with the following equation:

$$C = S N(d_1) - Xe^{-rt} N(d_2) \qquad (14A.1)$$

where:
$$d_1 = \frac{\ln\left(S/X\right) + \left(r + 0.5s^2\right)t}{s\sqrt{t}};$$

$d_2 = d_1 - s\sqrt{t}$;
$\ln$ = Natural logarithm;
C = Call option price;
S = Price of the underlying asset;
X = Strike price;
r = Short-term risk-free rate;
e = 2.718 (the natural antilog of 1);
t = Time remaining to the expiration date, as a fraction of a year;
s = Standard deviation of the value of the underlying asset; and
$N(.)$ = Cumulative probability density.[6]

Notice that five of the factors that we indicated in the chapter that influence the price of an option are included in the formula. Anticipated cash dividends are not included because the model is for a non-dividend-paying stock. In the Black-Scholes option pricing model, the direction of the influence of each of these factors is the same as stated in the chapter. Four of the factors—strike price, price of underlying asset, time to expiration, and risk-free rate—are easily observed. The standard deviation of the price of the underlying asset must be estimated.

---

[6] We obtain the value for $N(.)$ from a normal distribution function that is tabulated in most statistics textbooks or from spreadsheets that have this built-in function.

The option price derived from the Black-Scholes option pricing model is "fair" in the sense that if any other price existed, it would be possible to earn riskless arbitrage profits by taking an offsetting position in the underlying asset. That is, if the price of the call option in the market is higher than that derived from the Black-Scholes option pricing model, an investor could sell the call option and buy a certain quantity of the underlying asset. If the reverse is true, that is, the market price of the call option is less than the "fair" price derived from the model, the investor could buy the call option and sell short a certain amount of the underlying asset. This process of hedging by taking a position in the underlying asset allows the investor to lock in the riskless arbitrage profit.

To illustrate the Black-Scholes option pricing formula, assume the following values:

Stock price	=	S =	$47
Strike price	=	X =	$45
Risk-free rate of interest	=	r =	10%
Time remaining to expiration	=	t =	183 days ÷ 365 days = 0.5
Expected price volatility	=	s =	25%

Substituting these values into the Black-Scholes option pricing model, we get

$$d_1 = \frac{\ln\left(^{47}/_{45}\right) + \left(0.1 + \left(0.5 \times 0.25^2\right)\right)0.5}{0.25\sqrt{0.5}} = 0.6172$$

and

$$d_2 = 0.6172 - 0.25\sqrt{0.5} = 0.4404$$

From a normal distribution table,

$$N(0.6172) = 0.7315 \text{ and } N(0.4404) = 0.6702$$

Substituting these values into equation (14A.1),

$$C = (\$47 \times 0.7315) - \$45(e^{-(0.10 \times 0.5 \times 0.6702)}) = \$5.69$$

Therefore, the value of the call option is $5.69.

Let's look at what happens to the theoretical option price if the expected price volatility is 40% rather than 25%. Then

From a normal distribution table,

$$N(0.4719) = 0.6815 \text{ and } N(0.1891) = 0.5750$$

Then

$$C = (\$47 \times 0.6815) - \$45(e^{-(0.10 \times 0.5 \times 0.5750)}) = \$7.42$$

Notice that the higher the assumed expected price volatility of the underlying asset, the higher the price of a call option.

In Exhibit 14.5A, we show the option value as calculated from the Black-Scholes option pricing model for different assumptions concerning the standard deviation (Panel A), the time remaining to expiration (Panel B), and the risk-free rate of interest (Panel C). Notice that the option price varies directly with all three variables. That is,

- the higher the volatility, the higher the option price;
- the longer the time remaining to expiration, the higher the option price;
- the higher the risk-free rate, the higher the option price.

All of this agrees with what we stated in this chapter about the effect of a change in one of the factors on the price of a call option.

The Black-Scholes option pricing model assumes that the call option is a European call option. Because the model is for a non-dividend-paying stock, early exercise of an option will not be economical because by selling rather than exercising the call option, the option holder can recoup the option's time premium.

SOLUTIONS TO TRY IT! PROBLEMS

Futures

1. Cash and carry
2. $2

	Now		Later	
Action	Cash Flow	Action	Cash Flow
Sell futures	$0	Pay off loan	−$1,000
Borrow	1,000	Interest on loan	−8
Buy Asset U	−1,000	Deliver Asset U	1,010
Cash flow	$0	Cash flow	$2

A. Changes in the standard deviation, all else held constant

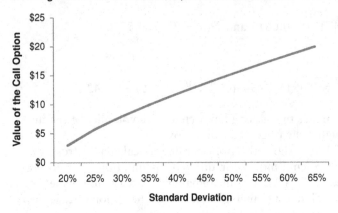

B. Changes in the time to expiration, all else held constant

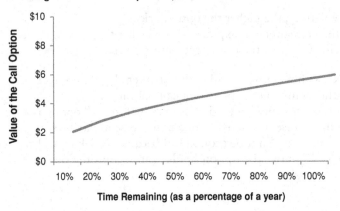

C. Changes in the risk-free rate of interest, all else held constant

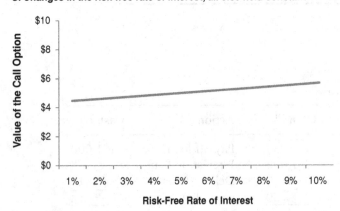

EXHIBIT 14.5 The Value of an Option Based on the Black-Scholes Model

The payoff from a call option
    Profit = $60 − 50 − 3 = $7
The payoff from a put option
    Loss = $50 − 48 − 3 = −$1

QUESTIONS

1. What is the difference between a cash and carry trade and a reverse cash and carry trade?
2. If there is no arbitrage opportunity, what is the expected profit from a cash and carry in futures?
3. What is the difference between forwards and futures?
4. If a call option's exercise price is $100 and the underlying is currently $90, is this option in, at, or out of the money?
5. If the payoff of a call option at a specified price is $5, what is the payoff for the call writer at that price?
6. What is the relation between the time to expiration and the value of a:
   a. call option?
   b. put option?
7. What is the relation between the volatility of the price of the underlying and the value of a:
   a. call option?
   b. put option?
8. If you believe that a stock's price will fall over the next few months, what option transaction are you most likely to use?
9. If you believe that a stock's price will fall over the next few months, what option transactions are you most likely to use?
10. What is the transaction that involves one party agreeing to pay a fixed interest rate, based on a notional amount, and the other party agreeing to pay interest that is pegged to some reference rate?
11. The following appears in the 2000 10-K of International Business Machines:

> *The company employs a number of strategies to manage these risks, including the use of derivative financial instruments. Derivatives involve the risk of non-performance by the counterparty.*

Explain what is meant in the last sentence of this quotation.

12. A manufacturer of furniture is concerned that the price of lumber will increase over the next three months. Explain how the manufacturer can protect against a rise in the price of lumber using lumber futures contracts.

13. The chief financial officer of the corporation you work for recently told you that he had a strong preference to use forward contracts rather than futures contracts to hedge: "You can get contracts tailor-made to suit your needs."
    a. Comment on the CFO's statement.
    b. What other factors influence the decision to use futures or forward contracts?

14. What is the difference between a put option and a call option?

15. What distinguishes an American option from a European option?

16. "There's no real difference between options and futures. Both are tools for controlling risk, and both are derivative products. It's just that with options you have to pay an option price, while futures require no up-front payment except for a good-faith margin. I can't understand why anyone would use options." Do you agree with this statement?

17. The treasurer of the KSiR Corporation is attempting to manage risks using options.
    a. What option strategy can the treasurer take to protect against a rise in the cost of one of the company's inputs in the production process, assuming that there is an option available?
    b. What option strategy can the treasurer take to protect against a decline in the selling price of one of the company's products assuming that there is an option available?

18. How does the price of an option and the exercise price affect the payoff from an option.

19. Suppose that the price of the underlying is $40 and that the option price is $5.
    a. If the exercise price for a put option is $42, what are the intrinsic value and the time premium for this option?
    b. If the exercise price for a call option is $50, what are the intrinsic value and the time premium for this option?

20. Orono Bank and the Portland Manufacturing Corp. enter into the following seven-year swap with a notional amount of $75 million and the following terms: Every year for the next seven years, Orono Bank agrees to pay Portland Manufacturing 7% per year and receive LIBOR from Portland Manufacturing.
    a. What type of swap is this?
    b. In the first year payments are to be exchanged, suppose that LIBOR is 4%. What is the amount of the payment that the two parties must make to each other?

Investment Management

Investment Management

Investors, who cannot or who will not take the trouble to comprehend the laws that govern stock transactions, must be content with a very moderate return. They may, if they choose, learn the character of the risks, and understand the conditions of success, by the exercise of ordinary intelligence. No Prospero's wand is needed in order to avoid failure; but only common sense and common prudence, such as all may cultivate.

On the other hand, there are no short and sure cuts to success. It does not come by wishing and waiting for it. The proper means must be used, likely opportunities turned to advantage, and a careful judgment must be exercised. If it be thought that in one or two transactions of five or ten thousand each a great fortune will be instantly secured, there is certain to be a speedy process of disillusioning. Neither can it be expected that every venture will prove lucrative. "The best laid schemes o' mice an' men gang aft agley." No mechanism is so automatically perfect in it working as to be free from all risk of friction. It is the same with investments. However carefully made, it sometimes happens that unexpected complications arise, such as no foresight could have anticipated or guarded against. Yet the law of averages is certain to operate, as is the case with accidents, with fires, and with every business.

—William Hickman Smith Aubrey, *Stock Exchange
Investments: Their History; Practice; and Results*, 4th ed.
(London: Simpkin, Marshall, Hamilton Kent & Co. Ltd., 1897),
pp. 210–211

A *portfolio*, simply put, is a group of investments. These investments may include cash, common stocks, bonds, and real estate, among other assets, and are managed for a specific objective or purpose.

Investment management—which is also known as *portfolio management, asset management,* and *money management*—is the process of managing a portfolio. Accordingly, the individual who manages a portfolio of investments is referred to as an *investment manager,* a *portfolio manager,* an *asset manager,* or a *money manager.* In industry jargon, an investment manager "runs money." To be effective, the investment manager must understand the various investment vehicles, the way these investment vehicles are valued, and the various strategies to select the investment vehicles to include in a portfolio to accomplish the investment objectives. The purpose of this chapter is to describe the process of investment management, which can be applied to institutional investors or individual investors.

We illustrate the investment management process in Exhibit 15.1. Though the process begins with setting the investment objective, it is really a cyclical process where performance evaluation may result in feedback, affecting changes to the objectives, policies, strategies, and composition of the portfolio.

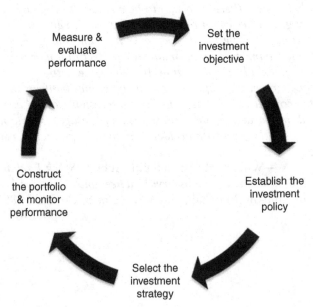

EXHIBIT 15.1   The Investment Management Process

SETTING INVESTMENT OBJECTIVES

Setting investment objectives starts with a thorough analysis of the investment objectives of the entity whose funds are being managed. These entities can be classified as individual investors and institutional investors. Within each of these broad classifications is a wide range of investment objectives.

The objectives of an individual investor may be to accumulate funds to purchase a home or other major acquisition, to have sufficient funds to be able to retire at a specified age, or to accumulate funds to pay for college tuition for children. An individual investor may engage the services of a financial advisor/consultant in establishing investment objectives.

Institutional investors include:

- Pension funds.
- Depository institutions (commercial banks, savings and loan associations, and credit unions).
- Insurance companies (life companies, property and casualty companies, and health companies).
- Regulated investment companies (mutual funds and closed-end funds).
- Hedge funds.
- Endowments and foundations.
- Treasury departments of corporations, municipal governments, and government agencies.

No matter the investor, the first step in the investment process is the same: Set an objective for the portfolio.

Classification of Investment Objectives

In general, we can classify the investment objectives of investors into the following two broad categories:

- Liability-driven objectives.
- Nonliability-driven objectives.

A liability in this context is a cash outlay that must be made at a specific future date in order to satisfy the contractual terms of an obligation. For example, a pension fund manager is concerned with both the amount and timing of liabilities when managing a plan that has a defined benefit because the portfolio must produce cash flows to meet payments promised to retirees in a timely way. Similarly, an individual may manage their investments to meet specific a retirement objective or college tuition.

A portfolio managed for a nonliability objective is not seeking a particular cash flow stream, but rather is managed to meet a return or risk objective. An example of an institutional investor that is not driven by liabilities is a mutual fund.

Some institutional investors may have accounts that have both nonliability-driven objectives and liability-driven objectives. For example, a life insurance company may have obligations that are fixed in amount, such as a guaranteed investment contract (GIC), and variable, as with a variable annuity account. With a variable annuity account, an investor makes either a single payment or a series of payments to the life insurance company and, in turn, the life insurance company invests the payments received and makes payments to the investor at some future date. The payments that the life insurance company makes depend on the performance of the insurance company's asset manager. While the life insurance company does have a liability, it does not guarantee any specific dollar payment.

Benchmark

Regardless of the type of investment objective, we need to establish a benchmark to evaluate the performance of an asset manager. A *benchmark* is a portfolio or index that is used for comparison purposes in evaluating a portfolio's performance. The benchmark should be similar to the investor's investment objective in terms of the:

- Asset class or classes in the portfolio.
- Risk objective of the portfolio.
- Sensitivity to economic factors.

In some cases, determining a benchmark is fairly simple—and in other cases, not. For example, in the case of a liability-driven objective, the benchmark is typically an interest rate target, where that interest rate is expected to satisfy the needed cash flow stream. In the case of a nonliability-driven objective, the benchmark is typically the asset class in which the assets are invested. For example, benchmarks for equity portfolios are often indexes, such as the S&P 500 index.

There may not always be a readily available benchmark for a specific investment objective, so it may be necessary to develop a customized benchmark. The bottom line, however, is that the benchmark serves as a basis of comparison for the performance of the portfolio.

ESTABLISHING AN INVESTMENT POLICY

The second major activity in the investment management process is establishing policy guidelines to satisfy the investment objectives. Setting policy begins with the asset allocation decision. The asset allocation decision addresses the question: How should the portfolio's investments be distributed among the major asset classes? In other words, what should be the mix of assets in the portfolio?

Asset Allocation

The term *asset allocation* means different things to different people and in different contexts. We can divide asset allocation into three types:

1. Policy asset allocation.
2. Dynamic asset allocation.
3. Tactical asset allocation.[1]

We can loosely characterize *policy asset allocation* as a long-term asset allocation decision, in which the investor seeks an appropriate long-term asset mix that represents the risk and return consistent with the investment objective, seeking the greatest possible return for the appropriate level of risk. Investors often use the mean-variance portfolio allocation model in determining the policy asset allocation. The strategies that offer the greatest prospects for strong long-term rewards to accomplish the investment objectives tend to be inherently risky strategies. The strategies that offer the greatest safety tend to offer only modest return opportunities. Policy asset allocation is the balancing of these conflicting goals.

In *dynamic asset allocation,* the asset mix is mechanistically shifted in response to changing market conditions. Once the policy asset allocation has been established, the investor can turn attention to the possibility of active departures from the normal asset mix established by policy. That is, suppose that the long-run asset mix is established by the policy allocation as 60% equities and 40% bonds. In dynamic asset allocation, a departure from this mix may be allowed under certain circumstances. If a decision to deviate from this mix is based upon rigorous objective measures of value, we refer to this as *tactical asset allocation.* Tactical asset allocation, however, is not a single, clearly defined strategy.

---

[1]Based on Robert D. Arnott and Frank J. Fabozzi, "The Many Dimensions of the Asset Allocation Decision," in *Active Asset Allocation,* ed. Robert D. Arnott and Frank J. Fabozzi, 3–8 (Chicago: Probus, 1992).

Tactical asset allocation broadly refers to active strategies that seek to enhance performance by opportunistically shifting the asset mix of a portfolio in response to the changing patterns of reward available in the capital markets. Notably, tactical asset allocation tends to refer to disciplined processes for evaluating prospective rates of return on various asset classes and establishing an asset allocation response intended to capture higher rewards.

Many variations and nuances are involved in building a tactical allocation process. One of the problems in reviewing the concepts of asset allocation is that the same terms are often used for different concepts. The term "dynamic asset allocation" has been used to refer to the long-term policy decision and to intermediate-term efforts to strategically position the portfolio to benefit from major market moves, as well as to refer to aggressive tactical strategies. As an investor's risk expectations and tolerance for risk change, the normal or policy asset allocation may change.

A good portfolio is more than a long list of goods stocks and bonds. It is a balanced whole, providing the investor with protections and opportunities with respect to a wide range of contingencies.
—Harry M. Markowitz, *Portfolio Selection: Efficient Diversification of Investments* (New York: John Wiley & Sons, 1959)

Asset Classes

We can classify investable investments into four major asset classes based on the type and risk associated with the investments' cash flows and value, legal and regulation issues, and sensitivity to economic influences:

1. Common stocks
2. Bonds
3. Cash equivalents
4. Real estate

Based on this way of defining an asset class, the correlation between the returns of different asset classes would be low.

We can extend the four major asset classes to create other asset classes. For example, we can expand four major asset classes separating foreign securities from domestic securities, as we show in Exhibit 15.2. Common stocks are the ownership interests in a corporation, whereas bonds are

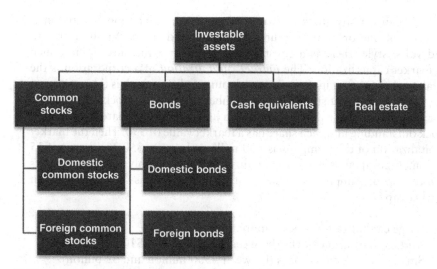

EXHIBIT 15.2 Investable Assets and Traditional Asset Classes

indebtedness of an entity. Cash equivalents are liquid, low-risk investments that can be, by definition, converted quickly into cash. Cash equivalents include Treasury bills, certificates of deposit, and money market accounts. Real estate investments include physical property, as well as interests in real estate, such as through real estate investment trusts. Our focus in this chapter is on common stocks and bonds because these represent the predominant asset classes in most individual and institutional portfolios.

Common Stock Style Categories In the early 1970s, academic studies found that there were categories of stocks that had similar characteristics and performance patterns. Moreover, the returns of these stock categories performed differently than did those of other categories of stocks. That is, the returns of stocks within a category were highly correlated, and the returns between categories of stocks were relatively uncorrelated. In the latter half of the 1970s, other studies suggested that an even simpler categorization by size, produced different performance patterns.

Practitioners began to view these categories or clusters of stocks with similar performance as a style of investing. Today, the notion of an *equity investment style* is widely accepted in the investment community. We can see the acceptance of equity style investing from the proliferation of style indexes published by several vendors that serve as benchmarks for portfolios managed according to different styles.

We can classify stocks by style in many ways. The most common is in terms of one or more measures of growth and value. Within a growth and value style, there is a substyle based on some measure of size, such as market capitalization. The *market capitalization* of a corporation is the total market value of its common stock outstanding, which is the product of the price per share of stock and the number of shares of stock outstanding. For example, suppose that a corporation has 500 million shares of common stock outstanding and each share has a market value of $50. Then the market capitalization of this company is 500 million shares × $50 per share = $25 billion. A company's market capitalization is commonly referred to as its *market cap* or, simply, *cap*. The most plain-vanilla classification based on market cap is:

- Large capitalization stocks (more than $10 billion).
- Mid-capitalization stocks (between $2 billion and $10 billion).
- Small capitalization stocks (between $300 million and $2 billion).

Other categories include mega-cap stocks (more than $200 billion), micro-cap stocks (between $50 million and $300 million), and nano-cap stocks (less than $50 million).

We can explain the motivation for the value/growth–style categories in terms of the most commonly used measure for classifying stocks as growth or value—the price-to-book value per share (P/B) ratio. First, consider that earnings growth increases the book value per share in (the denominator of P/B). Second, assuming no change in the P/B ratio, a stock's price will increase if earnings grow (affecting the numerator of P/B).

An investment manager who is growth-oriented is concerned with earnings growth, and seeks those stocks from a universe of stocks that have higher relative earnings growth. The growth manager's risks are that growth in earnings does not materialize and/or that the P/B ratio decline. An investment manager who is value-oriented is concerned with the price rather than with the future earnings growth. Value stocks within a universe of stocks are viewed as "cheap" in terms of their P/B ratio. By cheap we mean that the P/B ratio is low relative to that of the universe of stocks. The expectation of the manager who follows a value style is that the P/B ratio returns to some normal level and, thus, even with book value per share constant, the price will rise. The risk is that the P/B ratio does not increase.

We can classify on the basis of whether the issuer is domestic or foreign. Because the correlation of returns of stocks other nondomestic companies may not be highly correlated with those of the domestic corporations, there are opportunities to increase diversification within the common stock asset class on the basis of the domicile of the issuing company.

Bond Investment Categories We can classify bonds different ways. One way to classify bonds is to classify bonds by the issuer:

- Government bonds
- Municipal bonds
- Corporate bonds
- Asset-backed bonds

Government bonds are bonds issued by a country's central government. In the United States, these bonds are U.S. Treasury bonds that are indebtedness with maturities beyond one year. Municipal bonds are issued by state and local governments. Corporate bonds, as the name implies, are issued by corporations. Asset-backed securities are issued by dealers who pool assets together, such as residential mortgages, commercial mortgages, and issue claims that are backed by these assets.

We can also classify bonds by whether they are issued by a domestic issuer or by a nondomestic, or foreign issuer. We can further classify the foreign issuers by the development of the financial markets, into either developed markets or emerging markets. Emerging markets are those in countries that (1) have economies that are in transition but have started implementing political, economic, and financial market reforms in order to participate in the global capital market; (2) may expose investors to significant price volatility attributable to political risk and the unstable value of their currency; and (3) have a short period over which their financial markets have operated.

We provide a classification of bond investments in Exhibit 15.3. Though other classification schemes exist, this provides you with one possible way of looking at bond investments.

Alternative Asset Classes With the exception of real estate, all of the asset classes we have identified above are referred to as *traditional asset classes*. Other investments are *nontraditional asset classes* or *alternative asset classes*. These include hedge funds, private equity, and commodities.

Hedge funds are pools of investments, in which these investments are wide-ranging. Because of their typically high-risk nature, the investment in hedge funds is limited to professional investors and wealthy investors. Private equity investments are investments that provide the long-term equity base of a company that is not listed on any exchange and consequently does not have the ability to raise capital in the public stock market. Commodity investments are investments in the actual commodity or contracts based on commodities ranging from agricultural products (such as corn, pork bellies, and orange juice) to precious metals (such as gold and silver).

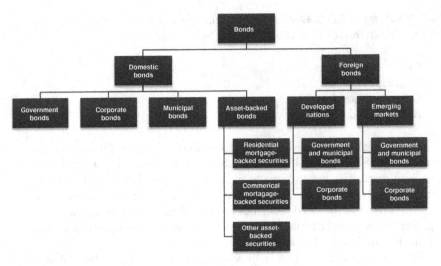

EXHIBIT 15.3   Classification of Bond Investments

Investment Factors

In the development of an investment policy, client constraints, regulatory constraints, and taxes must be considered.

Client-Imposed Constraints   Examples of client-imposed constraints are restrictions that specify the types of securities that a manager may invest and concentration limits on how much or little may be invested in a particular asset class or in a particular issuer. Where the objective is to meet the performance of a particular market or customized benchmark, there may be a restriction as to the degree to which the manager may deviate from some key characteristics of the benchmark.

Regulatory Constraints   Regulatory constraints involve constraints on the asset classes that are permissible and concentration limits on investments. Moreover, in making the asset allocation decision, the investment manager must consider any risk-based capital requirements, which are present in portfolios managed for banking and insurance institutions. The amount of statutory capital required for banking and insurance companies is related to the quality of the assets in which the institution has invested.[2] As an example of another type of regulatory constraint, regulated investment management companies face restrictions on the amount of leverage they employ.[3]

Tax Considerations Tax considerations are important for several reasons. First, certain institutional investors such as pension funds, endowments, and foundations are exempt from federal income taxation. Consequently, the asset classes in which they invest will not be those that are tax-advantaged investments. Second, there are tax factors that must be incorporated into the investment policy. For example, while a pension fund might be tax-exempt, there may be certain assets or the use of some investment vehicles in which it invests whose earnings may be taxed.

Selecting a Portfolio Strategy

Another major activity in the investment management process is selecting a portfolio strategy consistent with the investment objectives and investment policy guidelines of the client or institution. Portfolio strategies may be active or passive strategies, or some blend of the two.

An *active portfolio strategy* uses available information and forecasting techniques to seek a better performance than a portfolio that is simply diversified broadly. Essential to all active strategies are expectations about the factors that have been found to influence the performance of an asset class. In the case of active common stock strategies, this may include forecasts of future earnings, dividends, or price-earnings ratios. With actively managed bond portfolios, expectations may involve forecasts of future interest rates and sector spreads. Active portfolio strategies involving foreign securities may require forecasts of local interest rates and exchange rates.

A *passive portfolio strategy* involves minimal expectations input, and instead relies on diversification to match the performance of some market index. In effect, a passive strategy assumes that the marketplace efficiently reflects all available information in the price paid for securities.

Between these extremes of active and passive strategies, several strategies have sprung up that have elements of both. For example, the core of a portfolio may be passively managed with the balance actively managed.

---

[2]*Statutory capital* is the amount of equity and equivalents that a company must have to meet minimum regulatory standards. Risk-based capital standards specify that the amount of capital needed as a minimum is based on the riskiness of the assets of the company.

[3]Leverage in this context is borrowing funds in order to make investments.

A useful way of thinking about active versus passive management is in terms of the three activities performed by the manager:

1. Portfolio construction (deciding on the stocks to buy and sell).
2. Trading of securities.
3. Portfolio monitoring.

Generally, active managers devote the majority of their time to portfolio construction. In contrast, passive strategies managers devote less time to this activity.

With bond investments, there are several strategies classified as *structured portfolio strategies* that are a type of liability-driven strategy. A structured portfolio strategy is one in which a portfolio is designed to achieve the performance of some predetermined liabilities that must be paid out. These strategies are frequently used when trying to match the funds received from an investment portfolio to the future liabilities that must be paid and are therefore *liability-driven strategies*.

Given the choice among active and passive management, which should be selected? The answer depends on the:

1. Client's or money manager's view of how "price-efficient" the market is.
2. Client's risk tolerance.
3. Nature of the client's liabilities.

As we discussed in Chapter 1, market price efficiency is how difficult it would be to earn a greater return than passive management after adjusting for the risk associated with a strategy and the transaction costs associated with implementing that strategy.

CONSTRUCTING AND MONITORING A PORTFOLIO

Once a portfolio strategy is selected, the investment manager must select the assets to be included in the portfolio. The investment management process includes:

- Producing realistic and reasonable return expectations and forecasts.
- Constructing an efficient portfolio.
- Monitoring, controlling, and managing risk exposure.
- Managing trades and transaction costs.

In seeking to produce realistic and reasonable return expectations, the investment manager has several analytical tools available. An active portfolio manager seeks to identify mispriced securities or market sectors. This information is then used as inputs to construct an efficient portfolio. An *efficient portfolio* is a portfolio that offers the greatest expected return for a given level of risk or, equivalently, the lowest risk for a given expected return.

Once a portfolio is constructed, the investment manager must monitor the portfolio to determine how the portfolio's risk exposure may have changed given prevailing market conditions and information about the assets in the portfolio. The current portfolio may no longer be efficient and, as a result, the investment manager is likely to rebalance the portfolio in order to produce an efficient portfolio.

Transaction costs affect performance. The investment manager must consider transactions costs not only in the initial construction of the portfolio, but when the portfolio is rebalanced.

MEASURING AND EVALUATING PERFORMANCE

The measurement and evaluation of investment performance involves two activities. The first activity is performance measurement which involves properly calculating the return realized by an investment manager over some time interval, referred to as the *evaluation period*. The second activity is performance evaluation, which is concerned with determining whether the investment manager added value by outperforming the established benchmark.

Measuring Performance

The starting point for evaluating the performance of an asset manager is measuring return. This might seem quite simple, but several practical issues make the task complex because we must take into account any cash distributions made from a portfolio during the evaluation period.

Alternative Return Measures The dollar return realized on a portfolio for any evaluation period (i.e., a year, month, or week) is equal to the sum of:

1. The difference between the market value of the portfolio at the end of the evaluation period and the market value at the beginning of the evaluation period.
2. Any capital or income distributions from the portfolio to a client or beneficiary of the portfolio.

The *rate of return*, or simply *return*, expresses the dollar return in terms of the amount of the market value at the beginning of the evaluation period.

Thus, the return can be viewed as the amount (expressed as a fraction of the initial portfolio value) that can be withdrawn at the end of the evaluation period while maintaining the initial market value of the portfolio intact.

We can express the portfolio's return as

$$R_p = \frac{V_1 - V_0 + D}{V_0} \tag{15.1}$$

where: R_p is the return on the portfolio.
   V_1 is the market value of the portfolio at the end of the evaluation period.
   V_0 is the market value of the portfolio at the beginning of the evaluation period.
   D is the cash distribution from the portfolio, if any, during the evaluation period.

EXAMPLE 15.1: RETURN FOR A PERIOD

Consider a portfolio that begins the quarter with a market value of $3 million, distributes $0.1 million to investors, and ends the quarter with a market value of $3.2 million. What is the return on this portfolio for this quarter?

Solution

$$R_p = \frac{\$3.2 \text{ million} + 3.0 \text{ million} + 0.1 \text{ million}}{\$3.0 \text{ million}}$$

When calculating the return on a portfolio in this manner we are making three assumptions:

1. All cash inflows from dividends and interest during the evaluation period are reinvested into the portfolio.
2. If there are distributions from the portfolio, they either occur at the end of the evaluation period or are held in the form of cash until the end of the evaluation period.
3. There are no cash contributions made after the start of the evaluation period.

TRY IT! RETURN FOR A PERIOD

What is the return for each of the following periods?

Period	Value at the Beginning Period	Dividend	Value at the End of the Period
1	$10	$1	$9
2	$100	$5	$101
3	$1,000	$5	$1,100

Thus, while we can determine the return calculation for a portfolio using equation (15.1) for an evaluation period of any length of time (such as one day, one month, or five years), from a practical point of view the assumptions of this approach limit its application. Not only does the violation of the assumptions make it difficult to compare the returns of two money managers over some evaluation period, but it is also not useful for evaluating performance over different periods.

The way to handle these practical issues is to calculate the return for a short unit of time such as a month or a quarter. We call the return so calculated the *subperiod return*. To get the return for the evaluation period, the subperiod returns are then averaged. So, for example, if the evaluation period is one year, and we calculate 12 monthly returns, the monthly returns are the subperiod returns and we average these to get the one-year return. If we want a three-year return, and we have available 12 quarterly returns, the quarterly returns are the subperiod returns, and we average these to get the three-year return. For comparability with other investments, we will then want to convert this three-year return into an annual return. For now, let's focus on calculating the subperiod return.

We can calculate an average of the subperiod returns using one of three methodologies:

1. The arithmetic average rate of return
2. The time-weighted rate of return
3. The dollar-weighted return

We demonstrate and compare these averages using the following example of the ABC Portfolio, with dollar amounts in millions:

End of Quarter	Beginning Value	Ending Value	Return for the Quarter
Q1	$1.0	$1.5	50%
Q2	$1.5	$1.0	–33%
Q3	$1.0	$1.5	50%
Q4	$1.5	$1.0	–33%

Assume that there are no contributions to, nor withdrawals from, this portfolio over these four quarters. What is the average quarterly return for the ABC Portfolio?

Arithmetic Average Rate of Return   The *arithmetic average rate of return*, R_a, is an unweighted average of the subperiod returns:

$$R_a = \frac{R_1 + R_2 + R_3 + \cdots R_n}{n} = \frac{\sum_{t=1}^{n} R_t}{n}$$

where: R_a is the arithmetic average return,
          R_t is the return for period t,
          n is the number of periods.

In our example, the arithmetic average quarterly return for the ABC portfolio is

$$R_a = \frac{0.5 - 0.333 - 0.5 - 0.333}{4} = 8.333\%$$

This illustrates a major problem with using the arithmetic average rate of return. To see this problem, consider that there were no contributions to or cash withdrawals from this portfolio, and the portfolio's value at the end of the four quarters is exactly what it was to begin with. Yet the arithmetic average rate of return is 8.333%. Not a bad return, considering that the portfolio's value did not change. But think about this number. The portfolio's initial market value was $1 million. Its market value at the end of four quarters is $1 million. The return over this four-month evaluation period is zero. Yet the arithmetic rate of return says it is 8.333%. Now you can see why we do not use the arithmetic average in evaluating investment performance.

Time-Weighted Rate of Return The *time-weighted rate of return* measures the compounded rate of growth of the initial portfolio market value during the evaluation period, assuming that all cash distributions are reinvested in the portfolio. We also refer to this return as the *geometric mean return* because it is computed by taking the geometric average of the portfolio subperiod returns. The time-weighted rate of return, R_{TW}, is

$$R_{TW} = \sqrt[4]{\prod_{t=1}^{n} (1 + R_t)}$$

In our example, the quarterly average time-weighted return is zero for the ABC portfolio:

$$R_p = \sqrt[4]{(1 + R_1)(1 + R_2)(1 + R_3)(1 + R_4)} - 1$$

$$R_p = \sqrt[4]{(1.50)(0.667)(1.5)(0.667)} - 1 = 0\%$$

EXAMPLE 15.2: TIME-WEIGHTED RATE OF RETURN

Consider portfolio returns of –10%, 20%, and 5% in July, August, and September, respectively. What is the time-weighted monthly rate of return?

Solution

$$R_{TW} = \{[1 + (-0.10)] \, (1 + 0.20) \, (1 + 0.05)\}^{1/3} - 1$$
$$= [(0.90) \, (1.20) \, (1.05)]^{1/3} - 1$$
$$= 0.043 \text{ or } 4.3\%$$

In other words, $1 invested in the portfolio at the beginning of July would have grown at a rate of 4.3% per month during the three-month evaluation period.

In general, the arithmetic and time-weighted average returns produce different values for the portfolio return. This is because in the arithmetic average rate of return calculation we assume that the amount invested is maintained (through additions or withdrawals) at its initial portfolio market value. In our example, the portfolio value changes each quarter. The time-weighted return, on the other hand, is the return on a portfolio that varies in size because of the assumption that all proceeds are reinvested.

Dollar-Weighted Rate of Return The *dollar-weighted rate of return*, or the *money-weighted rate of return*, is the rate of interest rate equates the present value of the cash flows from all the subperiods in the evaluation period, including the terminal market value of the portfolio, to the initial market value of the portfolio. The cash flow for each subperiod reflects the difference between the cash inflows due to investment income (i.e., dividends and interest) and to contributions made by the client to the portfolio and the cash outflows reflecting distributions to the client. Notice that it is not necessary to know the market value of the portfolio for each subperiod to determine the dollar-weighted rate of return.

The dollar-weighted rate of return is simply an internal rate of return calculation. The dollar-weighted return, R_{DW}, solves the following:

$$V_0 = \sum_{t=1}^{n} \frac{CF_t}{(1 + R_{DW})^t} + \frac{V_n}{(1 + R_{DW})^n}$$

where: CF_t is the cash flow for the portfolio (cash inflows minus cash outflows) for subperiod t.

V_0 is the initial value of the portfolio.

V_n is the ending value of the portfolio.

EXAMPLE 15.3: DOLLAR-WEIGHTED RATE OF RETURN

Consider a portfolio with a market value of $100,000 at the beginning of July, capital withdrawals of $5,000 at the end of months July, August, and September, no cash inflows from the client in any month, and a market value at the end of September of $110,000. What is the dollar-weighted monthly rate of return?

Solution

$$\$100,000 = \frac{\$5,000}{(1 + R_{DW})^1} + \frac{\$5,000}{(1 + R_{DW})^2} + \frac{\$115,000}{(1 + R_{DW})^3}$$

In terms of a financial calculator or a spreadsheet, the cash flows are:

$CF_0 = -\$100,000$
$CF_1 = \$5,000$
$CF_2 = \$5,000$
$CF_3 = \$115,000$

The dollar-weighted return, calculated using a financial calculator or a spreadsheet, is 8.078%.

In the case of the ABC Portfolio, $V_n = V_0$, so the dollar-weighted average quarterly return, R_{DW}, is 0%:

$$\$1.0 = \frac{\$1.0}{(1 + R_{DW})^4}$$

The dollar-weighted rate of return and the time-weighted rate of return produce the same result if no withdrawals or contributions over the evaluation period, and if all of the portfolio's cash inflows from dividends and interest are reinvested. Therefore, for the ABC Portfolio, the time-weighted and dollar-weighted average quarterly returns are the same, 0%.

The problem with the dollar-weighted rate of return is that it is affected by factors that are beyond the control of the investment manager. Specifically, any contributions made by the client or withdrawals that the client requires affect the calculated dollar-weighted rate of return. This makes it difficult to compare the performance of two money managers or between a portfolio and its benchmark. To see how this works, consider the following investment cash flows for the DEF Portfolio, which are similar to the earlier problem, but the investor invests an additional $1 million at the end of the second quarter and there are two distributions, one at the end of the third quarter and one at the end of the fourth quarter:

Cash Flows

Quarter	Beginning Value	Change in Market Value	Cash Contributions	Cash Withdrawals	Ending Value
Q1	$1.0	$0.5			$1.5
Q2	$1.5	−$0.5	$1.0		$2.0
Q3	$2.0	$0.5		$0.5	$2.0
Q4	$2.0	−$0.5		$1.0	$0.5

The time-weighted average quarterly return for the DEF Portfolio is 17.02%:

End of Quarter	Calculation	Return
Q1	$0.5/$1.0	50.0%
Q2	(−$0.5)/$1.5	−33.3%
Q3	($0.5 + 0.5)/$2.0	50.0%
Q4	−($0.5 + 1)/$2.0	25.0%
Average	(1 + 0.5)(1 − 0.333)(1 + 0.5)(1 + 0.25)	17.02%

Each quarter's return requires comparing the change in value and any withdrawals with the value of the portfolio at the beginning of the quarter.

The dollar-weighted average quarterly return for the DEF Portfolio is 0%:

End of Quarter	Type of Cash Flow	Cash Flows
Q1	Initial investment	−$1.0
Q2	Contribution	−$1.0
Q3	Withdrawal	+$0.5
Q4	Withdrawal, plus ending value	+$1.5

We summarize the advantages and disadvantages of each method in Exhibit 15.4. In general, we use the time-weighted average when we are focusing on evaluating the portfolio manager, because this average is not

EXHIBIT 15.4 Advantages and Disadvantages to Alternative Rate of Return Calculations

Type of Average	Advantages	Disadvantages
Arithmetic average	Easy to calculate	Ignores compounding
Time weighted	Not sensitive to cash contributions and distributions Considers compounding of returns through time	Requires the market value at the end of each subperiod
Dollar weighted	Makes intuitive sense as an internal rate of return No need to know value of portfolio in each subperiod	Distorted if there are cash contributions or distributions Requires iterative process to solve

affected by cash inflows and outflows of the portfolio that are often outside of the portfolio manager's control. The time-weighted return, however, requires the market value of the investment at the end of each period. The dollar-weighted average provides the average return on all funds invested in the portfolio, which provides a good measure of the portfolio's performance if the portfolio manager has control over cash inflows and outflows of the portfolio.

 TRY IT! RETURNS

Consider a portfolio with a market value of $10 million at the beginning of January, capital withdrawals of $1 million at the end of months January, February, and March, no cash inflows from the client in any month, and a market value at the end of September of $9 million.

   a. What is the time-weighted monthly return on this portfolio?
   b. What is the dollar-weighted monthly return on this portfolio?

Evaluating Performance

A performance measure does not answer two questions:

1. How did the asset manager perform after adjusting for the risk associated with the active strategy employed?
2. How did the asset manager achieve the reported return?

The answers to these two questions are critical in assessing how well or how poorly the asset manager performed relative to some benchmark. In answering the first question, we must consider risk so that we can then judge whether the performance was acceptable in the face of the risk.

The answer to the second question tells us whether the asset manager, in fact, achieved a return by following the anticipated strategy. While a client would expect that any superior return accomplished is a result of a stated strategy, this may not always be the case.

We briefly describe methodologies for adjusting returns for risk so you can analyze the return of a portfolio to uncover the reasons why a return was realized. We refer to this analysis as *performance evaluation.*

Single-Index Performance Evaluation Measures In the 1960s, several single-index measures were used to evaluate the relative performance of money managers. These measures of performance evaluation did not specify how or why a money manager may have outperformed or underperformed a benchmark. The three measures, or indexes, are the Treynor index, the Sharpe index, and the Jensen index.[4] All three measures assume that there is a linear relationship between the portfolio's return and the return on some broad-based market index.

Performance Attribution Models   In broad terms, we can explain an actively managed portfolio's return performance by three types of actions of the investment manager. The first is actively managing a portfolio to capitalize on factors expected to perform better than other factors. The second is actively managing a portfolio to take advantage of anticipated movements in the market. For example, the manager of a common stock portfolio can increase the portfolio's beta when the market is expected to increase, and decrease it when the market is expected to decline. The third is actively managing the portfolio by buying securities that are believed to be undervalued, and selling (or shorting) securities that are believed to be overvalued.

Attribution models evaluate the performance of a portfolio, attributing a portfolio's performance to style and selection. One of the key elements of such models is to explain why a portfolio's performance differed from that of its benchmark. If the portfolio's return differed from the benchmark, was this due to asset allocation (that is, how much is allocated to each class)? How much is due to the particular investment selection within the asset classes?

THE BOTTOM LINE

- The investment management process begins with the setting of investment objectives, and then process with setting a policy, selecting a strategy, constructing a portfolio, and then evaluating the performance of the portfolio in the context of the investment objectives.
- The investment objectives of investors fall into two broad categories: liability-driven objectives and non-liability-driven objectives. A benchmark is needed to evaluate the performance of an asset manager.
- The asset allocation decision involves determining how the portfolio's investments should be distributed among the major asset classes. The three different types of asset allocation decisions are policy asset allocation, dynamic asset allocation, and tactical asset allocation.

---

[4]Jack Treynor, "How to Rate Management of Investment Funds," *Harvard Business Review* 44 (1965): 63–75; William F. Sharpe, "Mutual Fund Performance," *Journal of Business* 34 (1966): 119–138; and, Michael C. Jensen, "The Performance of Mutual Funds in the Period 1945–1964," *Journal of Finance* 23 (1968): 389–416.

- Investable investments are classified into asset classes based on the type and risk associated with the investments' cash flows and value, legal and regulatory issues, and sensitivity to economic influences. The four major asset classes are common stocks, bonds, cash equivalents, and real estate. To create other asset classes, the four major asset classes can be extended by, for example, separating foreign securities from domestic securities. There are nontraditional asset classes (such as hedge funds) that are referred to as alternative asset classes.
- In formulating an investment policy, client constraints, regulatory constraints, and taxes must be considered.
- Portfolio strategies may be active or passive strategies, or some blend of the two. An active portfolio strategy uses available information and forecasting techniques to seek a better performance than a portfolio that is simply diversified broadly. A passive portfolio strategy involves minimal expectations input, and instead relies on diversification to match the performance of some market index.
- The selection of the specific assets to be included in a portfolio after the portfolio strategy is selected involves producing realistic and reasonable return expectations and forecasts; constructing an efficient portfolio; monitoring, controlling; managing risk exposure; and managing trades and transaction costs. An efficient portfolio is a portfolio that offers the greatest expected return for a given level of risk or, equivalently, the lowest risk for a given expected return.
- The measurement and evaluation of investment performance involves performance measurement (i.e., properly calculating the return realized by an investment manager over the evaluation period) and performance evaluation (i.e., determining whether the investment manager added value by outperforming the established benchmark).
- Evaluating the performance of an investment portfolio requires estimating returns, adjusting for risk, and comparing the portfolio's performance against a benchmark portfolio's performance.

SOLUTIONS TO TRY IT! PROBLEMS

Return for a Period

Period	Solution
1	$R = \dfrac{\$9 + 1 - 10}{\$10} = 0\%$
2	$R = \dfrac{\$101 + 5 - 100}{\$100} = 6\%$
3	$R = \dfrac{\$1{,}100 + 5 - 1{,}000}{\$1{,}000} = 10.5\%$

Returns

a. $R_{TW} = [(1 + 0.10)(1 + 0.10)(1 + 0.00)]^{1/3} - 1 = 1.21^{1/3} - 1 = 6.56\%$

b. $\$10 = \dfrac{\$1}{(1 + R_{DW})^1} + \dfrac{\$1}{(1 + R_{DW})^1} + \dfrac{\$1 + 9}{(1 + R_{DW})^1}; \ R_{DW} = 6.886\%$

QUESTIONS

1. What are the four major asset classes?
2. Distinguish between policy asset allocation and dynamic asset allocation.
3. What is meant by "market cap," and how does this affect common stock portfolio decisions?
4. What distinguishes a passive portfolio strategy from an active portfolio strategy?
5. How does price efficiency influence the decision to pursue an active or passive portfolio strategy?
6. What is the primary problem with the arithmetic average rate of return in evaluating a portfolio's performance?
7. If you want to evaluate the performance of a portfolio manager, which would be more appropriate to use in calculating subperiod returns: the dollar-weighted average or the time-weighted average? Why?
8. Consider a portfolio that has a value of $5 at the beginning of January, with returns of –5%, 10%, and 10% in January, February, and March, respectively. If there are no cash contributions or withdrawals during the three months, what is the time-weighted average monthly rate of return?
9. Consider a portfolio that has a value of $5 at the beginning of January, with returns of –5%, 10%, and 10% in January, February, and March, respectively. If there are no cash contributions or withdrawals during the three months, what is the money-weighted average monthly rate of return?
10. What is the purpose of a performance attribution model?
11. In terms of the price-to-book (P/B) ratio, why are value stocks generally considered those with low P/B ratios?
12. Comment on the following statements:
    a. "All one needs to know about a portfolio manager's ability is to compare the return on the portfolio to the return on the benchmark."
    b. "By looking at the difference between the portfolio return and the return on a benchmark, one can determine how a portfolio manager was able to outperform or underperform a benchmark."

   c. "In establishing an investment policy, investors should ignore any liabilities and just select a market index that they want to outperform."

13. What type of constraints may a client impose on a portfolio manager?
14. If an investment in stock has a value of $3,000 at the beginning of the year and $3,500 at the end of the year, and paid a dividend of $250 at the end of the year, what is the return on the stock for the year?
15. Consider an investment with the following returns:

Year	Return
1	5%
2	−3%
3	4%
4	5%

What is the time-weighted annual return for this investment for the four-year period?

CHAPTER 16

The Theory of Portfolio Selection

*Throughout most of the history of stock markets—about
200 years in the United States and even longer in some European
countries—it never occurred to anyone to define risk with a
number. Stocks were risky and some were riskier than others, and
people let it go at that. Risk was in the gut, not in the numbers.
For aggressive investors, the goal was simply to maximize return;
the faint-hearted were content with savings accounts and
high-grade long-term bonds.*
—Peter L. Bernstein, *Against the Gods: The Remarkable Story
of Risk* (New York: John Wiley & Sons, 1996), p. 247

In this chapter and the next, we set forth theories that are the underpinnings for the management of portfolios: portfolio theory and capital market theory. Portfolio theory deals with the selection of portfolios that maximize expected returns consistent with individually acceptable levels of risk. Using quantitative models and historical data, portfolio theory defines "expected portfolio returns" and "acceptable levels of portfolio risk," and shows how to construct an optimal portfolio. Capital market theory deals with the effects of investor decisions on security prices. More specifically, it shows the relationship that should exist between security returns and risk if investors constructed portfolios as indicated by portfolio theory. Together, portfolio and capital market theories provide a framework to specify and measure investment risk and to develop relationships between expected security return and risk (and hence between risk and required return on an investment).

The goal of portfolio selection is the construction of portfolios that maximize expected returns consistent with individually acceptable levels of risk. Using both historical data and investor expectations of future returns, portfolio selection uses modeling techniques to quantify "expected portfolio returns" and "acceptable levels of portfolio risk," and provides methods to select an optimal portfolio. The theory allows investment managers to quantify the investment risk and expected return of a portfolio, providing an objective complement to the subjective art of investment management. More importantly, whereas at one time the focus of portfolio management used to be the risk of individual assets, the theory of portfolio selection has shifted the focus to the risk of the entire portfolio. This theory shows that it is possible to combine risky assets and produce a portfolio whose expected return reflects its components, but with the potential for considerably lower risk. In other words, it is possible to construct a portfolio whose risk is less than the sum of all its individual parts.

In this chapter, we present the theory of portfolio selection as formulated by Harry Markowitz.[1] This theory is also referred to as *mean-variance portfolio analysis* or simply *mean-variance analysis*. We also take a brief look at behavioral finance, and how the theories formulated by proponents of this field of finance relate to investor choices.

SOME BASIC CONCEPTS

Portfolio theory draws on concepts from two fields: financial economic theory and probability and statistical theory. This section presents the concepts from financial economic theory we use in portfolio theory. While many of the concepts presented here have a more technical or rigorous definition, the purpose is to keep the explanations simple and intuitive so the reader can appreciate the importance and contribution of these concepts to the development of modern portfolio theory.

Utility Function and Indifference Curves

In life there are many situations where entities (i.e., individuals and firms) face two or more choices. The economic "theory of choice" uses the concept of a utility function to describe the way entities make decisions when faced with a set of choices. A *utility function* assigns a numeric value to all possible choices faced by the entity. The higher the value of a particular choice, the greater the utility derived from that choice. The choice that is selected is the one that results in the maximum utility given a set of (budget) constraints faced by the entity.

---

[1] Harry M. Markowitz, "Portfolio Selection," *Journal of Finance* 7 (1952): 77–91.

In portfolio theory too, entities are faced with a set of choices. Different portfolios have different levels of expected return and risk. Also, the higher the level of expected return is, the larger the risk. Entities are faced with the decision of choosing a portfolio from the set of all possible risk–return combinations: where return is a desirable that increases the level of utility, and risk is an undesirable that decreases the level of utility. Therefore, entities obtain different levels of utility from different risk-return combinations. The utility obtained from any possible risk–return combination is expressed by the utility function. Put simply, the utility function expresses the preferences of entities over perceived risk and expected return combinations.

A utility function can be expressed in graphical form by a set of indifference curves. In Exhibit 16.1, we show indifference curves labeled u_1, u_2, and u_3. By convention, the horizontal axis measures risk and the vertical axis measures expected return. Each curve represents a set of portfolios with different combinations of risk and return. All the points on a given indifference curve indicate combinations of risk and expected return that will give the same level of utility to a given investor. For example, on utility curve u_1, there are two points, U and U', with U having a higher expected return than U', but also having a higher risk. Because the two points lie on the same indifference curve, the investor has an equal preference for (or is indifferent to) the two points, or, for that matter, any point on the curve. The (positive) slope of an indifference curve reflects the fact that, to obtain the same level

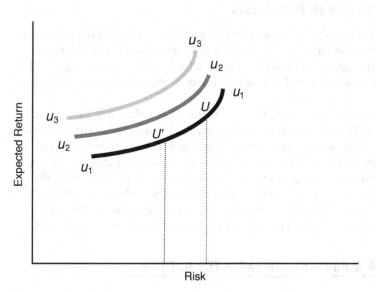

EXHIBIT 16.1 Utility Functions and Indifference Curves

of utility, the investor requires a higher expected return in order to accept higher risk.

For the three indifference curves shown in Exhibit 16.1, the utility the investor receives is greater the further the indifference curve is from the horizontal axis, because that curve represents a higher level of return at every level of risk. Thus, for the three indifference curves shown in the exhibit, u_3 has the highest utility and u_1 the lowest.

Efficient Portfolios and the Optimal Portfolio

Portfolios that provide the largest possible expected return for given levels of risk are called *efficient portfolios*. To construct an efficient portfolio, it is necessary to make some assumption about how investors behave when making investment decisions. One reasonable assumption is that investors are *risk averse*. A risk-averse investor is an investor who, when faced with choosing between two investments with the same expected return but two different risks, prefers the one with the lower risk.

In selecting portfolios, an investor seeks to maximize the expected portfolio return given his tolerance for risk. Alternatively stated, an investor seeks to minimize the risk that he is exposed to given some target expected return. Given a choice from the set of efficient portfolios, an *optimal portfolio* is the one that is most preferred by the investor.

Risky Assets vs. Risk-Free Assets

A risky asset is one for which the return that will be realized in the future is uncertain. Common stock is considered a risky asset because of the uncertainty about the future dividends and price when the investor wants to sell the stock. The same is true for bonds because of the risk the issuer might default.

There are assets, however, for which the return that will be realized in the future is known with certainty today. Such assets are referred to as *risk-free* or *riskless assets*. The risk-free asset is commonly defined as a short-term obligation of the U.S. government. For example, if an investor buys a U.S. government security that matures in one year and plans to hold that security for one year, then there is no uncertainty about the return that will be realized. The investor knows that in one year, the maturity date of the security, the government will pay a predetermined amount to retire the debt.

ESTIMATING A PORTFOLIO'S EXPECTED RETURN

We are now ready to define and measure the actual and expected return of a risky asset and a portfolio of risky assets.

For a Single-Period Portfolio Return

The actual return on a portfolio of assets over some specific time period is a weighted average of the returns on the individual assets in the portfolio, and is straightforward to calculate using the following:

$$R_p = w_1 R_1 + w_2 R_2 + \cdots + w_G R_G \qquad (16.1)$$

where: R_p is the rate of return on the portfolio over the period,
R_g is the rate of return on asset g over the period,
w_g is the weight of asset g in the portfolio (i.e., market value of asset g is a proportion of the market value of the total portfolio) at the beginning of the period, and
G is the number of assets in the portfolio.

In shorthand notation, we can express equation (16.1) as

$$R_p = \sum_{g=1}^{G} w_g R_g \qquad (16.2)$$

In equation (16.2), the return on a portfolio, R_p, of G assets is equal to the sum over the products of the individual assets' weights in the portfolio and their respective return. The portfolio return R_p is sometimes called the *holding period return* or the *ex post return*.

For example, consider the following portfolio consisting of three assets:

Asset	Market Value at the Beginning of the Holding Period	Holding Period Return
1	$6 million	12%
2	8 million	10%
3	11 million	5%
Total	$25 million	

Restating this, using the proportion of the total market value for each asset:

Asset	Proportion of Portfolio's Market Value	Holding Period Return
1	$6 million ÷ $25 million = 24%	12%
2	$8 million ÷ $25 million = 32%	10%
3	$11 million ÷ $25 million = 44%	5%

Notice that the sum of the weights is equal to 1. Substituting into equation (16.1), we get the holding period portfolio return,

$$R_p = (0.24 \times 0.12) + (0.32 \times 0.10) + (0.44 \times 0.05) = 8.28\%$$

The holding period portfolio return is 8.28%. Therefore, the growth in the portfolio's value in monetary terms over the holding period is $25 million $\times$ 0.0828 = $2.07 million.

For a Portfolio of Risky Assets

In equation (16.1), we show how to calculate the actual return of a portfolio over some specific time period. In portfolio management, the investor also wants to know the expected (or anticipated) return from a portfolio of risky assets. In other words, the *ex ante return*. The expected portfolio return is the weighted average of the expected return of each asset in the portfolio. The weight assigned to the expected return of each asset is the percentage of the market value of the asset to the total market value of the portfolio. That is,

$$E(R_p) = w_1 E(R_1) + w_2 E(R_2) + \cdots + w_G E(R_G) \tag{16.3}$$

The $E(\ )$ signifies expectations, and $E(R_p)$ is the expected portfolio return over some specific time period.

We calculate the expected return, $E(R_i)$, on a risky asset i as follows. First, we specify the probability distribution for the possible rates of return we expect to occur in the future period. A *probability distribution* is a function that assigns a probability of occurrence to all possible outcomes for a random variable. Given the probability distribution, the expected value of a random variable is simply the weighted average of the possible outcomes, where the weight is the probability associated with the possible outcome.

In our case, the random variable is the uncertain return of asset i. Having specified a probability distribution for the possible rates of return, the expected value of the rate of return for asset i is the weighted average of the possible outcomes. Finally, rather than use the term "expected value of the return of an asset," we simply use the term "expected return." Mathematically, the expected return of asset i is expressed as

$$E(R_i) = p_1 R_1 + p_2 R_2 + \cdots + p_N R_N \tag{16.4}$$

where: R_n is the nth possible rate of return for asset i.
$\quad\quad\quad p_n$ is the probability of attaining the rate of return n for asset i.
$\quad\quad\quad N$ is the number of possible outcomes for the rate of return.

EXHIBIT 16.2 Probability Distribution for the Return for Asset XYZ and Asset ABC

Possible Outcome	Return on Asset XYZ	Return on Asset ABC	Probability of Occurrence	Return on Asset XYZ × Probability	Return on Asset ABC × Probability
1	12%	21%	18%	0.0216	0.0378
2	10	14	24	0.0240	0.0336
3	8	9	29	0.0232	0.0261
4	4	4	16	0.0064	0.0064
5	−4	−3	13	−0.0052	−0.0039
Total			100%	0.0700	0.1000
Expected return				7%	10%

In Exhibit 16.2 we provide the probability distribution for two hypothetical assets, Asset XYZ and Asset ABC. The expected return for Asset XYZ is 7% and the expected return for Asset ABC is 10%.

TRY IT! EXPECTED RETURN

What is the expected return for Asset Three and for Asset Four, given the following probability distributions?

Possible Outcome	Probability of Occurrence	Return on Asset Three	Return on Asset Four
1	25%	12%	21%
2	45%	10%	14%
3	30%	8%	9%

MEASURING PORTFOLIO RISK

The dictionary defines risk as "hazard, peril, exposure to loss or injury." With respect to investments, investors have used a variety of definitions to describe risk. Markowitz quantified the concept of risk using the well-known statistical measures of variances and covariances. He defined the risk of a portfolio as the sum of the variances of the investments and covariances among the investments. The notion of introducing the covariances among returns of the investments in the portfolio to measure the risk of a portfolio forever changed how the investment community thought about the concept of risk.

Variance and Standard Deviation as a Measure of Risk

The *variance of a random variable* is a measure of the dispersion or variability of the possible outcomes around the expected value.[2] In the case of an asset's return, the variance is a measure of the dispersion of the possible rate of return outcomes around the expected return.

The equation for the variance of the expected return for asset i, denoted $\sigma^2(R_i)$, is

$$\sigma^2(R_i) = p_1(r_1 - E(R_i))^2 + p_2(r_2 - E(R_i))^2 + \cdots + p_N(r_N - E(R_i))^2$$

(16.5)

assuming N possible outcomes. This can also be expressed as

$$\sigma^2(R_i) = \sum_{n=1}^{N} p_n(r_n - E(R_i))^2$$

The variance associated with a distribution of returns measures the compactness with which the distribution is clustered around the mean or expected return. Markowitz argued that this variance is equivalent to the uncertainty or riskiness of the investment. If an asset is riskless, it has an expected return dispersion of zero. In other words, the return (which is also the expected return in this case) is certain, or guaranteed.

Because the variance is in squared units, it is common to see the variance converted to the standard deviation, σ, by taking the positive square root of the variance:

$$\sigma(R_i) = \sqrt{\sigma^2(R_i)}$$

We provide the calculation of the standard deviation of the distribution of the returns on Asset XYZ using this formula in Exhibit 16.3(Panel A).

Because expected return and variance are the only two parameters that investors are assumed to consider in making investment decisions, we often refer to the Markowitz formulation of portfolio theory as a *two-parameter*

---

[2]The expected value is the weighted mean of the probability distribution, where the probabilities are the weights.

EXHIBIT 16.3 Standard Deviation of the Distribution of Returns for Asset XYZ and Asset ABC

A. Asset XYZ

Possible Outcome	Return Less Expected Return	Square of Deviation	Probability x Squared Deviation
1	0.0500	0.0025	0.0005
2	0.0300	0.0009	0.0002
3	0.0100	0.0001	0.0000
4	−0.0300	0.0009	0.0001
5	−0.1100	0.0121	0.0016
		Variance =	0.0024
		Standard deviation =	4.90%

B. Asset ABC

Possible Outcome	Return Less Expected Return	Square of Deviation	Probability x Squared Deviation
1	0.1100	0.0121	0.0022
2	0.0400	0.0016	0.0004
3	−0.0100	0.0001	0.0000
4	−0.0600	0.0036	0.0006
5	−0.1300	0.0169	0.0022
		Variance =	0.0054
		Standard deviation =	7.32%

model or *mean-variance analysis*. There have been models that propose including additional measures of a return distribution into the portfolio selection model.

 TRY IT! STANDARD DEVIATION OF A DISTRIBUTION

What is the standard deviation of the following distribution of returns for Asset Five and Asset Six?

Possible Outcome	Probability of Occurrence	Return on Asset Five	Return on Asset Six
1	25%	20%	25%
2	50%	10%	5%
3	25%	−5%	−15%

Measuring the Portfolio Risk of a Two-Asset Portfolio

In equation (16.5), we provide the variance for an individual asset's return. The variance of a portfolio consisting of two assets is a little more difficult to calculate. It depends not only on the variance of the two assets, but also upon how closely the returns of one asset track those of the other asset. The formula for the variance of the portfolio is

$$\sigma^2(R_p) = w_i^2\sigma_i^2 + w_i^2\sigma_i^2 + 2w_iw_j \, \text{cov}(R_i, R_j) \tag{16.6}$$

where $\text{cov}(R_i,R_j)$ is the covariance between the return for assets i and j. In other words, the variance of the portfolio return is the sum of the squared weighted variances of the two assets, plus two times the weighted covariance between the two assets. We can generalize this equation to the case where more than two assets are in the portfolio.

Covariance

Like the variance, the *covariance* has a precise mathematical translation. Its practical meaning is the degree to which the returns on two assets *covary* or change together. In fact, the covariance is just a generalized concept of the variance applied to multiple assets. A positive covariance between two assets means that the returns on two assets tend to move or change in the same direction, while a negative covariance means the returns tend to move in opposite directions. The covariance between any two assets i and j is computed using the following formula:

$$\begin{aligned}\text{cov}(R_i, R_j) = {} & p_1\left[(r_{i1} - E\,(R_i))\,(r_{j1} - ER_j)\right] \\ & + p_2\left[(r_{i2} - E\,(R_i))\,(r_{j2} - ER_j)\right] + \cdots \\ & + p_N\left[(r_{iN} - E\,(R_i))\,(r_{jN} - ER_j)\right]\end{aligned} \tag{16.7}$$

where: r_{in} is the nth possible rate of return for asset i.

r_{jn} is the nth possible rate of return for asset j.

p_n is the probability of attaining the rate of return n for assets i and j.

N is the number of possible outcomes for the rate of return.

The *correlation* between the returns for assets i and j, denoted by $\rho_{i,j}$ is the covariance of the two assets divided by the product of their standard deviations:

$$\rho_{i,j} = \frac{\text{cov}(R_i, R_j)}{\sigma_i\sigma_j} \tag{16.8}$$

EXHIBIT 16.4 Calculation of Covariance and Correlation between Assets i and j

Possible Outcome	Probability	Deviation for Asset XYZ $(r_{iXYZ} - E(R_{XYZ}))$	Deviation for Asset ABC $(r_{iABC} - E(R_{ABC}))$	Product of the Deviations and Probability
1	18%	0.0500	0.1100	0.0010
2	24%	0.0300	0.0400	0.0003
3	29%	0.0100	−0.0100	0.0000
4	16%	−0.0300	−0.0600	0.0003
5	13%	−0.1100	−0.1300	0.0019
			Covariance =	0.0034
			Correlation =	0.9441

The correlation coefficient can have values ranging from +1.0, denoting perfect comovement in the same direction, to –1.0, denoting perfect co-movement in the opposite direction. Because standard deviations are always positive, the correlation can only be negative if the covariance is a negative number. A correlation of zero implies that the returns are uncorrelated.

The correlation and the covariance are conceptually similar terms, yet scaled differently. The correlation between two random variables is the covariance divided by the product of their standard deviations. Because the correlation is a standardized number (i.e., it has been corrected for differences in the standard deviation of the returns), the correlation is comparable across different assets.

The correlation between the returns for Asset XYZ and Asset ABC is 0.9441. We provide the details of this calculation in Exhibit 16.4.

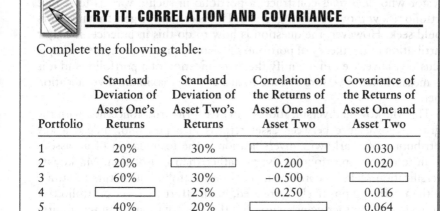

TRY IT! CORRELATION AND COVARIANCE

Complete the following table:

Portfolio	Standard Deviation of Asset One's Returns	Standard Deviation of Asset Two's Returns	Correlation of the Returns of Asset One and Asset Two	Covariance of the Returns of Asset One and Asset Two
1	20%	30%	[ ]	0.030
2	20%	[ ]	0.200	0.020
3	60%	30%	−0.500	[ ]
4	[ ]	25%	0.250	0.016
5	40%	20%	[ ]	0.064

Measuring the Risk of a Portfolio Comprised of More than Two Assets

So far we have defined the risk of a portfolio consisting of two assets. The extension to three assets—i, j, and k—is as follows:

$$\sigma^2\left(R_p\right) = w_i^2\sigma^2\left(R_i\right) + w_j^2\sigma^2\left(R_j\right) + w_k^2\sigma^2\left(R_k\right) + 2w_i w_j \ \text{cov}(R_i R_j)$$

$$+2w_i w_k \ \text{cov}(R_i R_k) + 2w_j w_k \ \text{cov}(R_j R_k) \tag{16.9}$$

In words, equation (16.9) states that the variance of the portfolio return is the sum of the squared weighted variances of the individual assets plus two times the sum of the weighted pairwise covariances of the assets. In general, for a portfolio with G assets, the portfolio variance is given by

$$\sigma^2\left(R_p\right) = \sum_{g=1}^{G}\sum_{h=1}^{G} w_g w_h \ \text{cov}(R_g R_h) \tag{16.10}$$

In equation (16.10), the terms for which $h = g$ results in the variances of the G assets, and the terms for which $h \neq g$ results in all possible pairwise covariances amongst the G assets. Therefore, equation (16.10) is shorthand notation for the sum of all G variances and the possible covariances amongst the G assets.

PORTFOLIO DIVERSIFICATION

Often, one hears investors talking about diversifying their portfolio. An investor who *diversifies* constructs a portfolio in such a way as to reduce portfolio risk without sacrificing return. This is certainly a goal that investors should seek. However, the question is how to do this in practice. A major contribution of the theory of portfolio selection is that by using the concepts discussed above, we can quantify the diversification of a portfolio, and it is this measure that investors can use to achieve the maximum diversification benefits.

The Markowitz diversification strategy is primarily concerned with the degree of covariance between asset returns in a portfolio. Indeed a key contribution of Markowitz diversification is the formulation of an asset's risk in terms of a portfolio of assets, rather than in isolation. Markowitz diversification seeks to combine assets in a portfolio with returns that are less than perfectly positively correlated, in an effort to lower portfolio risk (variance) without sacrificing return. It is the concern for maintaining return, while lowering risk through an analysis of the covariance between asset returns, that separates Markowitz diversification from a naive approach to diversification and makes it more effective.

We illustrate Markowitz diversification and the importance of asset correlations with a simple two-asset portfolio example. To do this, we first show the general relationship between the risk of a two-asset portfolio and the correlation of returns of the component assets. Then we look at the effects on portfolio risk of combining assets with different correlations.

Portfolio Risk and Correlation

In our two-asset portfolio, assume that Asset C and D are available with expected returns and standard deviations of:

Asset	$E(R)$	$\sigma(R)$
Asset C	12%	30%
Asset D	18%	40%

If an equal 50% weighting is assigned to both Asset C and D, the expected portfolio return using equation (16.1) is 15% and the variance of the return on the two-asset portfolio from equation (16.6) is

$$\sigma^2(R_p) = [0.5^2 \times 0.3^2] + [0.5^2 \times 0.4^2] + [2 \times 0.5^2 \times 0.5^2 \times \text{cov}(R_C, R_D)]$$

Using the relation between the covariance and the standard deviations of the two securities from equation (16.8),

$$\rho_{C,D} = \frac{\text{cov}(R_C, R_D)}{\sigma_C \sigma_D} \qquad (16.11)$$

so

$$\text{cov}(R_C, R_D) = \sigma(R_C)\,\sigma(R_D)\rho(R_C, R_D)$$

Because $\sigma(R_C) = 30\%$ and $\sigma(R_D) = 40\%$, then

$$\text{cov}(R_C, R_D) = (30\% \times 40\%)\,\rho(R_C, R_D) = 0.12\,\rho(R_C, R_D)$$

Substituting into the expression for $\sigma^2(R_p)$, we get

$$\sigma^2(R_p) = [0.5^2 \times 0.3^2] + [0.5^2 \times 0.4^2] + [2 \times 0.5 \times 0.5 \times 0.12\,\rho(R_C, R_D)]$$

Therefore,

$$\sigma^2(R_p) = 0.0225 + 0.04 + 0.06\,\rho(R_C, R_D)$$

Multiplying and taking the square root of the variance gives

$$\sigma(R_p) = \sqrt{0.0625 + (0.06\,\rho(R_C\,R_D))}$$

Let's look at our two-asset portfolio with different correlations between the returns of the component assets. Specifically, consider the following three cases for $\rho(R_C, R_D)$: +1.0, 0, and −1.0. Substituting into equation (16.11) for these three cases of $\rho(R_C, R_D)$, we get the following:

Correlation	$E(R_p)$	$\sigma(R_p)$
+1.0	15%	35%
0.0	15%	25%
−1.0	15%	5%

As the correlation between the expected returns on Asset C and Asset D decreases from +1.0 to 0.0 to −1.0, the standard deviation of the expected portfolio return also decreases from 35% to 5%. However, the expected portfolio return remains 15% for each case.

This is an example of Markowitz diversification. The principle of Markowitz diversification is that as the correlation between the returns for assets that are combined in a portfolio decreases, so does the variance (hence the standard deviation) of the return for the portfolio.

In choosing a portfolio, investors should seek broad diversification. Further, they should understand that equities—and corporate bonds also—involve risk; that markets inevitably fluctuate, and the portfolio should be such that they are willing to ride out the bad as well as the good times.

—Harry Markowitz, October 7, 2008

CHOOSING A PORTFOLIO OF RISKY ASSETS

Diversification in the manner suggested by Markowitz leads to the construction of portfolios that have the highest expected return at a given level of risk. We refer to such portfolios as *efficient portfolios*. In order to construct efficient portfolios, the theory makes some basic assumptions about asset selection behavior by investors. The assumptions are as follows:

1. The only two parameters that affect an investor's decision are the expected return and the variance. (That is, investors make decisions using the two-parameter model formulated by Markowitz.)
2. Investors are risk averse. That is, when faced with two investments with the same expected return but two different risks, investors will prefer the one with the lower risk.
3. All investors seek to achieve the highest expected return at a given level of risk.
4. All investors have the same expectations regarding expected return, variance, and covariances for all risky assets. This assumption is referred to as the *homogeneous expectations assumption*.
5. All investors have a common one-period investment horizon.

Constructing Efficient Portfolios

The technique of constructing efficient portfolios from large groups of assets requires a massive number of calculations. For a portfolio of just 50 securities, there are 1,224 covariances that must be calculated. For 100 securities, there are 4,950. Furthermore, in order to solve for the portfolio that minimizes risk for each level of return, a mathematical technique called *quadratic programming* must be used. A discussion of this technique is beyond the scope of this chapter. However, it is possible to illustrate the general idea of the construction of efficient portfolios by referring again to the simple two-asset portfolio consisting of Assets C and D.

Recall that for these two assets,

$$E(R_C) = 12\% \quad \text{and} \quad \sigma(R_C) = 30\%$$

$$E(R_D) = 18\% \quad \text{and} \quad \sigma(R_D) = 40\%$$

Now further assume that $\rho(R_C, R_D) = -0.5$. We provide the expected portfolio return and standard deviation for five different portfolios made up of varying proportions of C and D in Exhibit 16.5. As you can see in Panel A of Exhibit 16.5, the mix of 50–50 for C and D in the portfolio results in the lowest standard deviation of the five mixes. In Panel B of Exhibit 16.5, we show the portfolio standard deviation for a wider range of mixes of Asset C and D, you can see that the portfolio's standard deviation is lowest around 60% Asset C and 40% Asset D.

A. Portfolio standard deviation for five different mixes of Asset C and Asset D

Mix	Weight of C	Weight of D	Expected return	Variance	Standard deviation
1	100%	0%	12.00%	0.09000	30.00%
2	75%	25%	13.50%	0.03813	19.53%
3	50%	50%	15.00%	0.03250	18.03%
4	25%	75%	16.50%	0.07313	27.04%
5	0%	100%	18.00%	0.16000	40.00%

B. Portfolio standard deviation for weights of Asset C from 100% to 0%

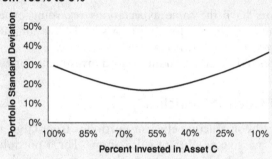

EXHIBIT 16.5   Portfolio Expected Return and Standard Deviation for a Portfolio Comprised of Asset C and D

Feasible and Efficient Portfolios

A *feasible portfolio* is any portfolio that an investor can construct given the assets available. The five portfolios presented in Exhibit 16.5 are all feasible portfolios. The collection of all feasible portfolios is called the *feasible set of portfolios*. With only two assets, the feasible set of portfolios is graphed as a curve that represents those combinations of risk and expected return that are attainable by constructing portfolios from all possible combinations of the two assets. In Panel B of Exhibit 16.5, we show the feasible set of portfolios for all combinations of assets C and D.

In contrast to a feasible portfolio, an efficient portfolio is one that gives the highest expected return of all feasible portfolios with the same risk. An efficient portfolio is also said to be a *mean-variance efficient portfolio*. Thus, for each level of risk there is an efficient portfolio. The collection of all efficient portfolios is called the *efficient set*.

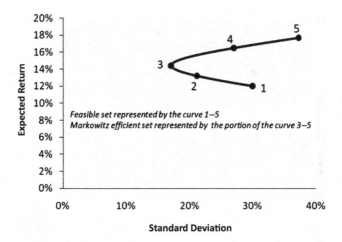

EXHIBIT 16.6   Efficient Portfolios with Assets C and D

We provide the efficient set for the feasible set presented in Exhibit 16.6. Efficient portfolios are the combinations of Assets C and D that result in the risk–return combinations on the curve from Portfolio 3 to 5. These portfolios offer the highest expected return at a given level of risk. Notice that Portfolios 1 and 2 are not included in the efficient set. This is because there is at least one portfolio in the efficient set (for example, Portfolio 3) that has a higher expected return and lower risk than both of them.

We can also see that Portfolio 4 has a higher expected return and lower risk than Portfolio 1. In fact, the whole curve section 1–3 is not efficient. For any given risk-return combination on this curve section, there is a combination (on the curve section 3–5) that has the same risk and a higher return, or the same return and a lower risk, or both. In other words, for any portfolio that results in the return-risk combination on the curve section 1–3 (excluding Portfolio 3), there exists a portfolio that dominates it by having the same return and lower risk, or the same risk and a higher return, or a lower risk and a higher return. For example, Portfolio 4 dominates Portfolio 1, and Portfolio 3 dominates both Portfolio 1 and 2.

In Exhibit 16.7 we illustrate the feasible and efficient sets when there are more than two assets. In this case, the feasible set is not a curve, but rather an area. This is because, unlike the two-asset case, it is possible to create asset portfolios that result in risk–return combinations that not only result in combinations that lie on the curve I–II–III, but all combinations that lie in the shaded area. However, the efficient set is given by the curve II–III. It is easily seen that all the portfolios on the efficient set dominate the portfolios in the shaded area.

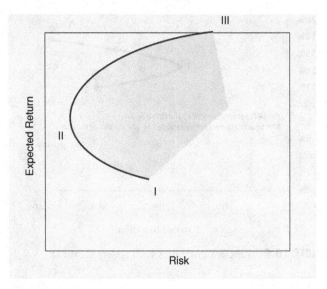

EXHIBIT 16.7   Feasible and Efficient Portfolios with More
Than Two Assets

We sometimes refer to the efficient set of portfolios as the *efficient frontier*, because graphically all the efficient portfolios lie on the boundary of the set of feasible portfolios that have the maximum return for a given level of risk. Any risk–return combination above the efficient frontier cannot be achieved, while risk–return combinations of the portfolios that make up the efficient frontier dominate those that lie below the efficient frontier.

Choosing the Optimal Portfolio in the Efficient Set

Now that we have constructed the efficient set of portfolios, the next step is to determine the optimal portfolio.

Because all portfolios on the efficient frontier provide the greatest possible return at their level of risk, an investor or entity will want to hold one of the portfolios on the efficient frontier. Notice that the portfolios on the efficient frontier represent trade-offs in terms of risk and return. Moving from left to right on the efficient frontier, the risk increases, but so does the expected return. The question is which one of those portfolios should an investor hold? The best portfolio to hold of all those on the efficient frontier is the *optimal portfolio*.

Intuitively, the optimal portfolio should depend on the investor's preference over different risk-return trade-offs. As explained earlier, this preference can be expressed in terms of a utility function.

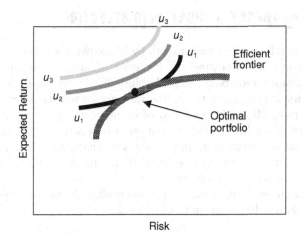

EXHIBIT 16.8 Selecting the Optimal Portfolio

We drew the three indifference curves representing a utility function and the efficient frontier in Exhibit 16.8, drawn on the same diagram. An indifference curve indicates the combinations of risk and expected return that give the same level of utility. Moreover, the farther the indifference curve from the horizontal axis, the higher the utility.

From Exhibit 16.8, we can determine the optimal portfolio for the investor with these indifference curves. Remember that the investor wants to get to the highest indifference curve achievable given the efficient frontier. Given that requirement, the optimal portfolio is represented by the point where an indifference curve is tangent to the efficient frontier. In Exhibit 16.8, that is the portfolio.

Consequently, for the investor's preferences over risk and return as determined by the shape of the indifference curves represented in Exhibit 16.8. If this investor prefers more return and less risk, the optimal portfolio is as indicated in Exhibit 16.8: at the point of tangency of the efficient frontier and utility curve u_2. If this investor had a different preference for expected risk and return, there would have been a different optimal portfolio.

At this point in our discussion, a natural question is how to estimate an investor's utility function so that the indifference curves and, hence, the optimal portfolio can be determined. Unfortunately, there is little guidance about how to construct one. In general, economists have not been successful in estimating utility functions. The inability to estimate utility functions does not mean that the theory is flawed. What it does mean is that once an investor constructs the efficient frontier, the investor will subjectively determine that efficient portfolio is appropriate given his or her tolerance to risk.

ISSUES IN THE THEORY OF PORTFOLIO SELECTION

The theory of portfolio selection set forth by Markowitz was based on some modeling assumptions regarding the behavior of investors when making investment decisions and about the probability distribution of the return on assets that made it acceptable to use the variance or standard deviation as a measure of risk. Moreover, in terms of implementation of the portfolio selection model that relied on the estimation of inputs from historical data, no consideration was given to the implications of what happens if a portfolio manager misestimates the inputs required by the model: expected returns, variances, and covariances of returns.

In this section, we look at the issues surrounding the theory of portfolio selection and the implementation of the model.

Alternative Risk Measures for Portfolio Selection

If the return distribution is normally distributed, then the variance is a useful measure of risk. The normal distribution is a symmetric distribution so outcomes above and below the expected value are equally likely. However, there are both empirical studies of real-world financial markets as well as theoretical arguments that suggest that we should reject the normal distribution assumption.[3]

Markowitz considered the problems associated with using the variance of returns as a measure of investment risk. In fact, he recognized that an alternative to the variance is the semivariance. The *semivariance* is similar to the variance except that in the calculation no consideration is given to returns above the expected return. Portfolio selection could be recast in terms of mean-semivariance. However, if the return distribution is symmetric, Markowitz argues that both the variance and the semivariance produce similar decisions, and that, further, the variance is a more familiar statistic than the semivariance.[4,5]

---

[3] For a review of the empirical evidence, see Svetlozar T. Rachev, Christian Menn, and Frank J. Fabozzi, *Fat-Tailed and Skewed Asset Return Distributions: Implications for Risk Management, Portfolio Selection, and Option Pricing* (Hoboken, NJ: John Wiley & Sons, 2005).

[4] Harry M. Markowitz, *Portfolio Selection: Efficient Diversification of Investment* (New York: John Wiley & Sons, 1959), 190, 193–194.

[5] The mean and the variance are the first two moments of a probability distribution. The third moment is a measure of skewness and the fourth moment is a measure of kurtosis. A generalization of the mean-variance framework that incorporates higher moments, such as skewness and kurtosis, has been developed. Because of the technical complexity of these models, we do not discuss them here.

There is debate on the best risk measures to use for optimizing an investor's portfolio. According to the literature on portfolio theory, two disjointed categories of risk measures can be defined: dispersion measures and safety-risk measures. We describe some of the most well-known dispersion measures and safety-first measures next.

VARIANCE VS. SEMIVARIANCE

The variance of a probability distribution, σ^2, is

$$\sigma^2 = \sum_{n=1}^{N} p_n(x_n - E(x))^2$$

The semivariance, σ_S^2, is calculated using only those observations below the expected value:

$$\sigma_S^2 = \sum_{for\ n\ if\ x_n < E(x)}^{N} p_n(x_n - E(x))^2$$

Dispersion Measures The variance or standard deviation (more technically referred to as the *mean-standard deviation*) is a dispersion measure. There are several different measures of dispersion available. The most commonly used measure (and easiest to understand) is the mean-absolute deviation.

The *mean-absolute deviation* (MAD) dispersion measure is based on the absolute value of the deviations from the mean rather than the squared deviations as in the case of the mean-standard deviation. Whereas the variance is affected by outliers, especially because of the squaring of deviations from the mean, the MAD is less affected by outliers.

Safety-First Risk Measures Many suggest *safety-first rules* as a criterion for decision making under uncertainty.[6] In these models, a subsistence, a

---

[6]See, among others, Andrew D. Roy, "Safety-First and the Holding of Assets," *Econometrica* 20 (1952): 431–449; Lester G. Tesler, "Safety First and Hedging," *Review of Economic Studies* 23 (1955/1956): 1–16; Vijay S. Bawa, "Admissible Portfolio for All Individuals," *Journal of Finance* 31 (1976): 1169–1183; and Vijay S. Bawa, "Safety-First Stochastic Dominance and Optimal Portfolio Choice," *Journal of Financial and Quantitative Analysis* 13 (1978): 255–271.

benchmark, or a disaster level of returns is identified. The objective is the maximization of the probability that the returns are above the benchmark. Thus, most of the safety-first risk measures proposed in the literature are linked to the benchmark-based approach.

Some of the most well-known safety-first risk measures proposed in the literature are:

- Classical safety-first
- Value at risk
- Conditional value at risk/expected tail loss
- Lower partial moment

In the *classical safety-first* portfolio choice problem, the risk measure is the probability of loss or, more generally, the probability of portfolio return less than some specified value.[7] In terms of implementation, generally, this approach requires solving a much more complex optimization problem to find the optimal portfolios in contrast to the mean-variance model.

Probably the most well-known downside risk measure is *value at risk* (VaR). This measure is related to the percentiles of loss distributions, and measures the predicted maximum loss at a specified probability level (for example, 95%) over a certain time horizon (for example, 10 days). The main characteristic of VaR is that of synthesizing in a single value the possible losses that could occur with a given probability in a given temporal horizon. This feature, together with the very intuitive concept of maximum probable loss, allows investors to figure out how risky a portfolio or trading position is. There are various ways to calculate the VaR of a security or a portfolio but a discussion of these methodologies is beyond the scope of this book.

Despite the advantages cited for VaR as a measure of risk, it does have several theoretical limitations. Specifically, it ignores returns beyond the VaR (i.e., it does not consider the concentration of returns in the tails beyond VaR). To overcome these limitations and problems, the *conditional value at risk* (CVaR) has been suggested as an alternative risk measure. CVaR, which we also refer to as the *expected shortfall* or *expected tail loss*, measures the expected value of portfolio returns, given that the VaR has been exceeded.

A natural extension of semivariance is the *lower partial moment risk measure*.[8] This measure, also called *downside risk*, depends on two

---

[7]See Roy, "Safety-First and the Holding of Assets."
[8]See Bawa, "Admissible Portfolio for All Individuals"; and Peter C. Fishburn, "Mean-risk Analysis with Risk Associated with Below-Target Returns," *American Economic Review* 67 (1977): 116–126.

parameters: (1) a power index, which is a proxy for the investor's degree of risk aversion; and (2) the target rate of return, which is the minimum return that must be earned.

Though the mathematics of these measures are complex, the bottom line is that measures exist that investors can use in addition to the mean-variance analysis to assist in the construction of a portfolio.

Robust Portfolio Optimization   Despite the influence and theoretical impact of modern portfolio theory, today—almost 60 years after Markowitz's seminal work—full risk–return optimization at the asset level is primarily done only at the more quantitatively-oriented asset management firms. The availability of quantitative tools is not the issue—today's optimization technology is mature and much more user-friendly than it was at the time Markowitz first proposed the theory of portfolio selection—yet many asset managers avoid using the quantitative portfolio allocation framework altogether.

A major reason for the reluctance of portfolio managers to apply quantitative risk–return optimization is that they have observed that it may be unreliable in practice. Specifically, mean-variance optimization (or any measure of risk for that matter) is very sensitive to changes in the inputs. In the case of mean-variance optimization, such inputs include the expected return, the variance of each asset, and the asset covariance between each pair of assets.

While it can be difficult to make accurate estimates of these inputs, estimation errors in the forecasts significantly affect the resulting portfolio weights. As a result, the optimal portfolios generated by the mean-variance analysis generally have extreme or counterintuitive weights for some assets.[9] Such examples, however, are not necessarily a sign that the theory of portfolio selection is flawed; rather that, when used in practice, the mean-variance analysis as presented by Markowitz has to be modified in order to achieve reliability, stability, and robustness with respect to model and estimation errors.

It goes without saying that advances in the mathematical and physical sciences have had a major impact upon finance. In particular, mathematical areas such as probability theory, statistics, econometrics, operations research, and mathematical analysis have provided the necessary tools and discipline for the development of modern financial economics. Substantial

---

[9]See Michael J. Best and Robert R. Grauer, "On the Sensitivity of Mean-Variance Efficient Portfolios to Changes in Asset Means: Some Analytical and Computational Results," *Review of Financial Studies* 4 (1991): 315–342; Mark Broadie, "Computing Efficient Frontiers Using Estimated Parameters," *Annals of Operations Research* 45 (1993): 21–58; and Vijay K. Chopra and William T. Ziemba, "The Effects of Errors in Means, Variances, and Covariances on Optimal Portfolio Choice," *Journal of Portfolio Management* 19 (1993): 6–11.

advances in the areas of robust estimation and robust optimization were made during the 1990s, and have proven to be of great importance for the practical applicability and reliability of portfolio management and optimization.

Any statistical estimate is subject to error—estimation error. A robust estimation is a statistical estimation technique that is less sensitive to outliers in the data. For example, in practice, it is undesirable that one or a few extreme returns have a large impact on the estimation of the average return of a stock. Nowadays, statistical techniques such as Bayesian analysis and robust statistics are more commonplace in asset management. Taking it one step further, practitioners are starting to incorporate the uncertainty introduced by estimation errors directly into the optimization process. This is very different from traditional mean-variance analysis, where one solves the portfolio optimization problem as a problem with deterministic inputs (i.e., inputs that are assumed to be known with certainty), without taking the estimation errors into account. In particular, the statistical precision of individual estimates is explicitly incorporated into the portfolio allocation process. Providing this benefit is the underlying goal of robust portfolio optimization.

BEHAVIORAL FINANCE AND PORTFOLIO THEORY

In building economic models, financial economists make assumptions about the behavior of those who make investment decisions in financial markets. We refer to these entities as *economic agents*. More specifically, they make assumptions about how economic agents make investment choices in selecting assets to include in their portfolio.

The underlying economic theory that financial economists draw upon in formulating various theories of choice is utility theory. There are concerns with the reliance on such theories. Prominent economists, such as John Maynard Keynes, have argued that investor psychology affects security prices. Support for this view came in the late 1970 when two psychologists, Daniel Kahneman and Amos Tversky, demonstrated that the actions of economic agents in making investment decisions under uncertainty are inconsistent with the assumptions made by financial economists in formulating financial theories.[10]

Based on numerous experiments, Kahneman and Tversky attacked utility theory and presented their own view as to how investors made choices

---

[10]See Daniel Kahneman and Amos Tversky, "Advances in Prospect Theory: Cumulative Representation of Uncertainty," *Journal of Risk and Uncertainty* 5 (1992): 297–323.

under uncertainty that they called *prospect theory*. Prospect theory focuses on decision-making under uncertainty, describing behavior as involving a heuristic.[11] First, individuals consider the possible investments and decide which ones are similar and which ones are different. Second, individuals evaluate the possible outcomes and probabilities, selecting the investment based on decision weighting, such that these weights do not necessarily relate to probabilities. An important contribution of the work of Kahneman and Tversky is that they argue that individuals behave differently regarding gains and losses. This is in contrast to the mean-variance theories that use variance, which assumes investors view gains and losses as symmetric.

Other attacks on the assumptions of traditional financial theory drawing from the field of psychology lead to the specialized field in finance known as behavioral finance.[12] Behavioral finance looks at how psychology affects investor decisions and the implications not only for the theory of portfolio selection, but in deriving a theory about asset pricing.

The foundations of behavioral finance have the following three behavioral themes:[13]

Theme 1: When making investment decisions, investors make errors because they rely on rules of thumb.

Theme 2: Investors are influenced by form as well as substance in making investment decisions.

Theme 3: Prices in the financial market are affected by errors and decision frames.

---

[11]"Prospect theory" does not relate to prospecting. As related by Peter Bernstein in his book *Against the Gods: The Remarkable Story of Risk* (New York: John Wiley & Sons, 1996), Kahneman states, "We just wanted a name that people would notice and remember."

[12]For a further discussion of behavioral finance, see the following chapters in Frank J. Fabozzi (ed.), *Handbook of Finance*, vol. 2 (Hoboken, NJ: John Wiley & Sons, 2008): Meir Statman, Chapter 9, "What Is Behavioral Finance"; Jarrod W. Wilcox, Chapter 8, "Behavioral Finance"; Victor Ricciardi, Chapter 10, "The Psychology of Risk: The Behavioral Finance Perspective"; and Frank J. Fabozzi (ed.), *Handbook of Finance*, vol. 2 (Hoboken, NJ: John Wiley & Sons, 2008): Victor Ricciardi, Chapter 2, "Risk: Traditional Finance versus Behavioral Finance."

[13]These themes are from Hersh Shefrin, *Beyond Greed and Fear: Understanding Behavioral Finance and the Psychology of Investing* (New York: Oxford University Press, 2002) and are based on Daniel Kahneman, Paul Slovic, and Amos Tversky, *Judgment under Uncertainty: Heuristics and Biases* (New York: Cambridge University Press, 1982).

Behavioral Finance Theme 1 involves the concept of *heuristics*. Heuristics are rules of thumb or guides that individuals will pursue to reduce the time required to make a decision. For example, in planning for retirement, a rule of thumb that has been suggested for having sufficient funds to retire is to invest 10% of annual pretax income. As for what to invest into reach that retirement goal (that is, the allocation among asset classes), a rule of thumb that has been suggested is that the percentage that an investor should allocate to bonds should be determined by subtracting that investor's age from 100. So, for example, a 45-year old individual should invest 55% of his or her retirement funds in bonds.

Although there are circumstances where heuristics can work fairly well, studies in the field of psychology suggest that heuristics can lead to systematic biases in decision making. This systematic bias is referred to by psychologists as *cognitive biases*. In the context of finance, these biases lead to errors in making investment decisions, or *heuristic-driven biases*.[14] Contrast this with the assumption made in the theory of portfolio selection that all investors estimate the mean and variance of every asset return and based on those estimates construct an optimal portfolio for each level of risk (i.e., the efficient frontier).

EXAMPLES OF COGNITIVE BIASES

- *Anchoring.* The tendency for an individual to focus either on a past reference or on a specific piece of information, without considering the complete set of information.
- *Bandwagon effect.* The tendency of individuals to go along with what others are doing.
- *Confirmation bias.* The interpretation or seeking of information that supports oneself or confirms a hypothesis.
- *Disposition effect.* The tendency of investors to hold on to assets that have declined in value, yet sell assets that have increased in value.
- *Framing.* Making decisions considering the manner or presentation of the situation.

---

[14]Shefrin, *Beyond Greed and Fear: Understanding Behavioral Finance and the Psychology of Investing.*

- *Gamblers' fallacy.* The belief that probabilities in the future are affected by past events.
- *Negative bias.* The tendency for individuals to focus more on the negative than positive.
- *Overconfidence bias.* The tendency to exaggerate one's own ability to judge the value of an asset.
- *Self-serving bias.* Interpretation of information that puts oneself in a better light.

Behavioral Finance Theme 2 involves the concept of *framing*. This term deals with the way in which a situation or choice is presented to an investor. Behavioral finance theorists argue that the framing of investment choices can result in significantly different assessments by an investor as to the risk and return of each choice and, therefore, the ultimate decision made.[15]

Behavioral Finance Theme 3 recognizes that not all participants in markets are rational and that occasional mispricing may occur due to this irrationality. This irrationality may stem from cognitive biases such as over-confidence and herding, and may result in a divergence between an asset's price, as observed in the market, and an asset's intrinsic value.

Behavioral theories may explain what we observe that may not be consistent with traditional theories of finance, but it also helps explain why investors make the choices they do based on risk aversion.

THE BOTTOM LINE

- Combining assets in a portfolio whose returns are not perfectly, positively correlated with one another can reduce the risk of the portfolio through diversification. Diversification allows an entity to reduce risk, to a point, without necessarily sacrificing return.
- Given the set of all possible combinations of assets that we can form, there will be some portfolios that are better than others in terms of risk and return. The efficient frontier is the set of portfolios that have the highest return for a given level of risk or, equivalently, the lowest risk for a given return.

---

[15] See Amos Tversky and Daniel Kahneman, "The Framing of Decisions and the Psychology of Choice," *Science* 211 (1961): 453–458; and Amos Tversky and Daniel Kahneman, "Rational Choice and the Framing of Decisions," *Journal of Business* 59 (1986): S251–S278.

- For a given investor, the portfolio that is best from those on the efficient frontier depends on the investor's individual preference for return and dislike for risk.
- Though portfolio theory focuses on the portfolio's variance and standard deviation as measures of risk, there are alternative measures of risk that focus on the downside risk, including the mean absolute deviation, semivariance, and value at risk.
- Behavioral finance uses the analysis of cognitive biases of individuals to explain observed market behavior, some of which may not be consistent with the traditional view of the rational investor.

SOLUTIONS TO TRY IT! PROBLEMS

Correlation and Covariance

Portfolio	Standard Deviation of Asset One's Returns	Standard Deviation of Asset Two's Returns	Correlation of the Returns of Asset One and Asset Two	Covariance of the Returns of Asset One and Asset Two
1	20%	30%	0.500	0.030
2	20%	50%	0.200	0.020
3	60%	30%	−0.500	−0.090
4	25%	25%	0.250	0.016
5	40%	20%	0.800	0.064

Expected Return

Possible Outcome	Probability of Occurrence	Return on Asset Three	Return on Asset Four	Return on Asset Three × Probability	Return on Asset Four × Probability
1	25%	12%	21%	0.0300	0.0525
2	45%	10%	14%	0.0450	0.0630
3	30%	8%	9%	0.0240	0.0270
Total	100%			0.0990	0.1425

Expected return on Asset Three = 9.9%

Expected return on Asset Four = 14.25%

Standard Deviation of a Distribution

Asset Five

Possible Outcome	Return Less Expected Return	Return Less Expected Return Squared	Probability x Squared Deviation
1	0.2000	0.2000	0.2000
2	0.2000	0.2000	0.2000
3	0.2000	0.2000	0.2000
		Variance =	0.0080
		Standard deviation =	8.93%

Asset Six

Possible Outcome	Return Less Expected Return	Return Less Expected Return Squared	Probability x Squared Deviation
1	0.2000	0.0400	0.0100
2	0.0000	0.0000	0.0000
3	−0.2000	0.0400	0.0100
		Variance =	0.0200
		Standard deviation =	14.14%

QUESTIONS

1. What is meant by a utility function?
2. If two assets' returns are positively correlated, what is the covariance between the returns of these two assets?
3. What is the relation between the correlation between and among assets and diversification?
4. How does an efficient portfolio relate to a feasible portfolio?
5. What information does the semivariance convey?
6. What is a safety-first rule?
7. What is prospect theory?
8. What is meant by framing and how may this affect an investor's decision making?
9. Identify three safety-first methods.
10. What is a cognitive bias and how might it affect investors' decision making?

11. The covariance of returns on Asset A and Asset B are negative.
    a. What does this tell us about the correlation coefficient for their returns?
    b. If we form a portfolio comprised of Asset A and Asset B, what is the relation between the portfolio's risk and the risks of Asset A and Asset B considered separately?
12. Consider the following stocks and their expected returns and standard deviations:

Stock	Expected Return	Standard Deviation
A	10%	14%
B	10%	13%
C	12%	12%
D	12%	14%

    a. Between Stock A and Stock B, which would a risk-averse investor prefer? Explain.
    b. Between Stock C and Stock D, which would a risk-averse investor prefer? Explain.
    c. Between Stock B and Stock C, which would a risk-averse investor prefer? Explain.
13. If the economy recovers next year, analysts expect Stock X's return for the year to be 20%; if the economy does not recover, analysts expect Stock X's return for the year to be −5%. If there is a 40% chance that the economy will recover and a 60% that it will not, what is:
    a. The expected return on Stock X for next year?
    b. The standard deviation of the return on Stock X for next year?
14. If the economy recovers next year, analysts expect Stock Y's return for the year to be 15%; if the economy does not recover, analysts expect Stock Y's return for the year to be −15%. If there is a 50% chance that the economy will recover, and a 50% that it will not, what is:
    a. The expected return on Stock Y for next year?
    b. The standard deviation of the return on Stock Y for next year?
15. Consider a portfolio comprised of two securities, M and N. The correlation of the returns on these securities is 0.25. And suppose that these securities have different standard deviations. Explain how different combinations of these two securities can result in different estimates for portfolio risks.

CHAPTER 17

Asset Pricing Theory

There are two key messages in CAPM, if you get down to the bedrock. One is that a broadly diversified market-like portfolio is a very good thing to think about. That gave rise to the notion of the index fund. That is an important message, as strange and heretical as it seemed when we first started.

The other message is that to get a higher expected return, you have got to accept a higher beta value. There is also a broader version. What kind of risk do you expect to get rewarded for in the long term? Answer: the risk of doing badly in bad times. If there is a reward for bearing risk, it almost has to be that. Otherwise, the world makes no sense at all. The premium for bearing risk is related to the risk that just when you need it, you are going to be poor. If that kind of risk is not rewarded, then there is no reason to believe that there is a risk premium for stocks as opposed to putting your money in the bank. In the CAPM world, beta is the measure of how badly you do in bad times—high beta securities or portfolios are going to really tank if the market goes down.

—William F. Sharpe, "The Gurus,"
CFO Magazine, January 2000

Asset pricing theory seeks to describe the relationship between risk and expected return. Although we refer to asset pricing models in this chapter, what we mean is the expected return investors require given the risk associated with an investment. The two most well-known equilibrium asset pricing models are the capital asset pricing model and the arbitrage pricing theory model. In this chapter, we describe these two models.

CHARACTERISTICS OF AN ASSET PRICING MODEL

In well-functioning capital markets, an investor should be rewarded for accepting the various risks associated with investing in an asset. We often refer to risks as "risk factors" or "factors." We can express an *asset pricing model* in general terms based on risk factors as follows:

$$E(R_i) = f(F_1, F_2, F_3, \ldots F_N) \tag{17.1}$$

where: $E(R_i)$ is the expected return for asset i.
        F_k is the risk factor k.
        N is the number of risk factors.

In other words, the expected return on an asset is the function of N risk factors. The trick is to determine what the risk factors are and to specify the precise relationship between expected return and the risk factors.

We can fine-tune the asset pricing model given by equation (17.1) by thinking about the minimum expected return we would want from investing in an asset. Securities issued by the U.S. Department of the Treasury offer a known return if held over some period of time. The expected return offered on such securities is the risk-free return or the risk-free rate because we believe these securities to have no default risk. By investing in an asset other than such securities, investors will demand a premium over the risk-free rate. That is, the expected return that an investor will require is:

$$E(R_i) = R_f + \text{Risk premium}$$

where R_f is the risk-free rate.

The "risk premium," or additional return expected over the risk-free rate, depends on the risk factors associated with investing in the asset. Thus, we can rewrite the general form of the asset pricing model given by equation (17.1) as:

$$E(R_i) = R_f + f(F_1, F_2, F_3, \ldots F_N) \tag{17.2}$$

We can divide risk factors into two general categories. The first category is risk factors that cannot be reduced with diversification. That is, no matter what the investor does, the investor cannot eliminate these risk factors. We refer to these risk factors as *systematic risk factors* or *nondiversifiable risk factors*. The second category is risk factors that can be eliminated through diversification. These risk factors are unique to the asset and are referred to as *unsystematic risk factors* or *diversifiable risk factors*.

SYSTEMATIC RISK VS. SYSTEMIC RISK

The recent financial crisis has elevated the use of the word systemic. Systemic risk should not be confused with systematic risk:

- *Systemic risk* is risk that is inherent within an entire economy or organism and generally refers to the risk that the economy or organism may collapse.
- *Systematic risk* is the risk that cannot be diversified away.

THE CAPITAL ASSET PRICING MODEL

The first asset pricing model, the *capital asset pricing model* (CAPM), was derived from economic theory formulated by the individual works of William Sharpe, John Lintner, Jack Treynor, and Jan Mossin.[1] The CAPM has only one systematic risk factor—the risk of the overall movement of the market, which we refer to as *market risk*. So, in the CAPM, market risk and systematic risk are interchangeable terms. Market risk means the risk associated with holding a portfolio consisting of all assets; that is, the market portfolio. In the market portfolio, an asset is held in proportion to its market value. For example, if the total market value of all assets is $X and the market value of asset j is $Y, then asset j comprises $Y \div $X of the market portfolio.

---

[1]William F. Sharpe, "Capital Asset Prices," *Journal of Finance* 19 (1964): 425–442; John Lintner, "The Valuation of Risk Assets and the Selection of Risky Investments in Stock Portfolio and Capital Budgets," *Review of Economics and Statistics* 47 (1965): 13–37; Jack L. Treynor, "Toward a Theory of Market Value of Risky Assets," unpublished manuscript, 1962; and Jan Mossin, "Equilibrium in Capital Asset Market," *Econometrica* 34 (1965): 768–783.

In the CAPM, the expected return on asset i is

$$E(R_i) = R_f + \beta_i[E(R_M) - R_f] \qquad (17.3)$$

where: $E(R_M)$ is the expected return on the market portfolio.
β_i is the measures of systematic risk of asset i relative to the market portfolio.

What does this tell us about the expected returns? The expected return for an asset i, according to the CAPM, is equal to the risk-free rate plus a risk premium. The risk premium is $\beta_i[E(R_M) - R_f]$. Another way of looking at this is that the risk premium on the market portfolio is $E(R_M) - R_f$, and we use β_i to adjust this for the systematic risk of asset i.

Beta, β_i, is a measure of the sensitivity of the return of asset i to the return of the market portfolio. Therefore,

$\beta_i = 1.0$ The asset or portfolio has the same quantity of risk as the market portfolio.
$\beta_i > 1.0$ The asset or portfolio has more market risk than the market portfolio.
$\beta_i < 1.0$ The asset or portfolio has less market risk than the market portfolio.

The second component of the risk premium in the CAPM is the difference between the expected return on the market portfolio, $E(R_M)$, and the risk-free rate. It measures the potential reward for taking on the risk of the market above what can earned by investing in an asset that offers a risk-free rate.

Taken together, the risk premium is a product of the quantity of market risk (as measured by beta, β_i) and the potential compensation of taking on market risk, $E(R_M) - R_f$.

Let's use some values for beta to see if all of this makes sense. Suppose that a portfolio has a beta of zero. That is, the return for this portfolio has no market risk. Substituting zero for β_i in the CAPM given by equation (17.3), the expected return is equal to the risk-free rate. This makes sense since a portfolio that has no market risk should have an expected return equal to the risk-free rate.

Consider a portfolio that has a beta of 1. This portfolio has the same market risk as the market portfolio. Substituting 1 for β_i in the CAPM given by equation (17.3), the expected return is equal to that of the market portfolio. Again, this is what one should expect for the return of this portfolio since it has the same market risk exposure as the market portfolio.

If a portfolio has greater market risk than the market portfolio, beta will be greater than 1 and the expected return will be greater than that of the market portfolio. If a portfolio has less market risk than the market portfolio, beta will be less than 1 and the expected return will be less than that of the market portfolio.

Assumptions of the CAPM

The CAPM is an abstraction of real world capital markets and, as such, is based on some assumptions. These assumptions simplify matters a great deal, and some of them may even seem unrealistic. However, these assumptions make the CAPM more tractable from a mathematical standpoint. The CAPM assumptions are as follows:

Assumption 1: Investors make investment decisions based on the expected return and variance of returns and subscribe to the Markowitz method of portfolio diversification.

Assumption 2: Investors are rational and risk averse.

Assumption 3: Investors all invest for the same period of time.

Assumption 4: Investors have the same expectations about the expected return and variance of all assets.

Assumption 5: There is a risk-free asset and investors can borrow and lend any amount at the risk-free rate.

Assumption 6: Capital markets are completely competitive and frictionless.

The first four assumptions deal with the way investors make decisions. The last two assumptions relate to characteristics of the capital market. These assumptions require further explanation. Many of these assumptions have been challenged resulting in modifications of the CAPM. Behavioral finance is highly critical of these assumptions, resulting in the formulation of a different CAPM theory that we describe later.

Let's look at Assumption 1. Recall from the theory of portfolio selection that Harry Markowitz formulated a framework for constructing a portfolio that maximizes expected returns consistent with individually acceptable levels of risk.[2] The measure of risk that Markowitz proposed is the variance or standard deviation of the return of an asset. In this framework, investors make decisions based on expected returns and the variance of returns.

---

[2]Harry M. Markowitz, "Portfolio Selection," *Journal of Finance* 7 (1952): 77–91.

The expected return for an asset's return is typically estimated from the historical mean of an asset's return over some time period. Consequently, the terms "expected return" and "mean return" are often used interchangeably. For this reason, the theory of portfolio selection is often referred to as mean-variance portfolio analysis or simply mean-variance analysis. The focus of portfolio selection is not on the risk of individual securities but the risk of the portfolio. This theory shows that it is possible to combine risky assets to produce a portfolio whose expected return reflects its components, but with considerably lower risk. In other words, it is possible to construct a portfolio whose risk is smaller than the sum of all its individual parts.

Assumption 2 indicates that in order to accept greater risk, investors must be compensated by the opportunity of realizing a higher return. We refer to the behavior of such investors as being *risk averse*. What this means is that if an investor faces a choice between two portfolios with the same expected return, the investor will select the portfolio with the lower risk.

Assumption 3 states that all investors make investment decisions over some single-period investment horizon. The theory does not specify how long that period is (i.e., six months, one year, two years, and so on). In reality, the investment decision process is more complex than that, with many investors having more than one investment horizon. Nonetheless, the assumption of a one-period investment horizon is necessary to simplify the mathematics of the theory.

Assumption 4 states that investors have the same expectations with respect to the inputs that are used to derive efficient portfolios: asset returns, variances, and correlations/covariances. The assumption allows investors to compute the efficient frontier, which is the set of portfolios with the best risk–return combination. We refer to Assumption 4 as the "homogeneous expectations assumption."

Assumption 5 is important in deriving the CAPM because it allows for a risk-free asset, and unlimited borrowing and lending at this risk-free rate. This is because efficient portfolios are created for portfolios consisting of risky assets. In the CAPM, we assume not only that there is a risk-free asset, but that an investor can borrow funds at the same interest rate paid on a risk-free asset. This is a common assumption in many economic models developed in finance despite the fact it is well understood in reality that there is a different rate at which investors can borrow and lend funds.

Finally, Assumption 6 specifies that the capital market is perfectly competitive. In general, this means the number of buyers and sellers is sufficiently large, and all investors are small enough relative to the market so that no individual investor can influence an asset's price. Consequently, all investors are price takers, and the market price is determined where there is equality

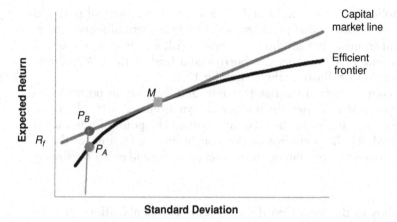

EXHIBIT 17.1 The CAPM and the Efficient Frontier

of supply and demand. In addition, according to this assumption, there are no transaction costs or impediments that interfere with the supply of and demand for an asset.[3]

In economic modeling, the model is modified by relaxing one or more of the assumptions. There are several extensions and modifications of the CAPM, but we will not review them here. No matter the extension or modification, however, the basic implications are unchanged: investors are only rewarded for taking on systematic risk and the only systematic risk is market risk.

The Capital Market Line

To derive the CAPM, we begin with the efficient frontier from the theory of portfolio selection, which we show in Exhibit 17.1. Every point on the efficient frontier is derived as explained earlier and is the maximum portfolio return for a given level of risk. In the figure, risk is measured on the horizontal axis by the standard deviation of the portfolio's return, which is the square root of the variance.

In the efficient frontier, there is no consideration of a risk-free asset. In the absence of a risk-free rate, we can construct efficient portfolios based

---

[3]Economists refer to these various costs and impediments as "frictions." The costs associated with frictions generally result in buyers paying more than in the absence of frictions and sellers receiving less.

on a portfolio's expected return and variance, with the optimal portfolio being the one portfolio that is tangent to the investor's indifference curve. The efficient frontier changes, however, once a risk-free asset is introduced and we assume that investors can borrow and lend at the risk-free rate (Assumption 6). We illustrate this in Exhibit 17.1.

Every combination of the risk-free asset and the efficient portfolio denoted by point M is shown on the line drawn from the vertical axis at the risk-free rate tangent to the efficient frontier. The point of tangency is denoted by M. All the portfolios on the straight line are feasible for the investor to construct by combining the market portfolio and either borrowing or lending.

- Portfolios to the left of portfolio M represent combinations of risky assets and the risk-free asset.
- Portfolios to the right of M include purchases of risky assets made with funds borrowed at the risk-free rate. Such a portfolio is called a *leveraged portfolio* because it involves the use of borrowed funds.

The line from the risk-free rate that is tangent to portfolio M is called the *capital market line* (CML).

Let's compare a portfolio on the CML to a portfolio on the efficient frontier with the same risk. For example, compare portfolio P_A, which is on the efficient frontier, with portfolio P_B, which is on the CML and, therefore, is comprised of some combination of the risk-free asset and the efficient portfolio M. Notice that for the same risk, the expected return is greater for P_B than for P_A. By Assumption 2, a risk-averse investor will prefer P_B to P_A. That is, P_B will dominate P_A. In fact, this is true for all but one portfolio on the CML: portfolio M, the market portfolio.

Once we introduce the risk-free asset into the mix, we can now say that an investor will select a portfolio on the CML that represents a combination of borrowing or lending at the risk-free rate and the efficient portfolio M. The particular efficient portfolio on the CML that the investor selects depends on the investor's risk preference. This can be seen in Exhibit 17.2, which is similar to Exhibit 17.1, but we have added the investor's indifference curves. The investor selects the portfolio on the CML that is tangent to the highest indifference curve, u_2 in the exhibit. Notice that without the risk-free asset, an investor could only get to u_1, which is the indifference curve that is tangent to the efficient frontier. Thus, the opportunity to borrow or lend at the risk-free rate results in a capital market where risk-averse investors will prefer to hold portfolios consisting of combinations of the risk-free asset and some portfolio M on the efficient frontier.

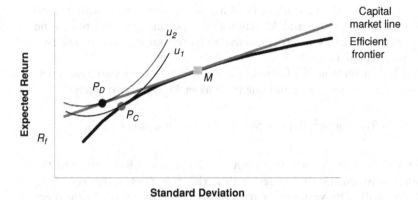

EXHIBIT 17.2 The CAPM and Utility Curves

Based on the model assumptions, we can use a bit of algebra to derive the formula for the CML. Based on the assumption of homogeneous expectations (Assumption 4), all investors can create an efficient portfolio consisting of w_f, placed in the risk-free asset, and w_M in portfolio M, where w represents the corresponding percentage weight of the portfolio allocated to each asset. We will refer to portfolio M as the risky asset. Therefore,

$$w_f + w_M = 1$$

or

$$w_f = 1 - w_M$$

The expected return is equal to the weighted average of the expected return of the two assets. Therefore, the expected portfolio return, $E(R_p)$, is

$$E(R_p) = w_f R_f + w_M E(R_M)$$

We know that $w_f = 1 - w_M$, so we can rewrite $E(R_p)$ as

$$E(R_p) = (1 - w_M)R_f + w_M E(R_M)$$

Based on the model assumptions and a bit of algebra,

$$E(R_p) = R_f + w_M[E(R_M) - R_f] \tag{17.4}$$

where w represents the percentage (weight) of the portfolio allocated to an asset with the subscript f and M denoting the percentage allocated to the risk-free asset and risky asset, respectively. Note that the sum of the two weights must equal 1.

Now let's determine the formula for the variance for a two-asset portfolio, with the risk-free asset and one risky asset M as the two assets:

$$\sigma^2(R_p) = w_f^2\sigma^2(R_f) + w_f^2\sigma^2(R_M) + 2w_f\,w_M\,cov(R_f R_M)$$

The variance of the risk-free asset is zero (i.e., $\sigma^2(R_f) = 0$), and the covariance between the risky asset and the risk-free asset is also zero (i.e., $cov(R_f R_M) = 0$). The variance of the risk-free asset is zero because there is no possible variation in the return since the future return is known. The covariance between the risk-free asset and the risky asset is zero because the risk-free asset has no variability.

The variance of the portfolio consisting of the risk-free asset and risky asset is then:

$$\sigma^2\left(R_p\right) = w_f^2\sigma^2\left(R_M\right)$$

In other words, the variance of the portfolio is represented by the weighted variance of the risky asset M.

We can solve for the weight of the risky asset M by substituting standard deviations for variances. Because the standard deviation of the portfolio $(\sigma(R_p))$ is the square root of the variance, we can write the standard deviation of the portfolio consisting of the risk-free asset and the risky asset M as

$$\sigma(R_p) = w_M\sigma(R_M)$$

and, therefore,

$$w_M = \frac{\sigma(R_p)}{\sigma(R_M)}$$

If we substitute the above result for w_M in equation (17.4) and rearrange terms we get the CML:

$$E(R_p) = R_f + \left[\frac{E(R_M) - R_f}{\sigma(R_M)}\right]\sigma\left(R_p\right) \qquad (17.5)$$

What Is Portfolio *M*?

Now that we know that risky asset *M* is pivotal to the CML, what is risky asset *M*? That is, how does an investor select risky asset *M*? It has been proven by financial theorists that risky asset *M* is not a single asset but rather a portfolio consisting of all assets available to investors, with each asset held in proportion to its market value relative to the total market value of all assets.[4] That is, portfolio *M* is the market portfolio described earlier. So, rather than referring to risky asset *M* as the market portfolio, we often simply refer to this portfolio as the market.

The Risk Premium in the Capital Market Line

With homogeneous expectations, $\sigma(R_M)$ and $\sigma(R_p)$ are the market's consensus for the expected return distributions for portfolio *M* and portfolio *p*. The risk premium for the CML is

$$\frac{E(R_M - R_f)}{\sigma(R_M)}\sigma(R_p)$$

Let's examine the economic meaning of the risk premium. The numerator of the first term, $E(R_M) - R_f$, is the expected return from investing in the market beyond the risk-free return. It is a measure of the reward for holding the risky market portfolio rather than the risk-free asset. The denominator, $\sigma(R_M)$, is the market risk of the market portfolio. Thus, the first term, $E(R_M - R_f)/\sigma(R_M)$, is the measure the reward per unit of market risk. Because the CML represents the return offered to compensate for a perceived level of risk, each point on the CML is a balanced market condition, or equilibrium. The slope of the CML (that is, the first term) determines the additional return needed to compensate for a unit change in risk. That is why we refer to the slope of the CML as the equilibrium market price of risk.

Therefore, along the CML, the expected return on a portfolio is equal to the risk-free rate, plus a risk premium equal to the market price of risk (as measured by the reward per unit of market risk), multiplied by the quantity of risk for the portfolio (as measured by the standard deviation of the portfolio). That is,

$$E(R_p) = R_f + (\text{Market price of risk} \times \text{Quantity of risk})$$

---

[4]Eugene F. Fama, "Efficient Capital Markets: A Review of Theory and Empirical Work," *Journal of Finance* 25 (1970): 383–417.

Systematic and Unsystematic Risk

Now we know that a risk-averse investor who makes decisions based on expected return and variance should construct an efficient portfolio using a combination of the market portfolio and the risk-free rate. The combinations are identified by the CML.

We can fine-tune our thinking about the risk associated with an asset, using the pricing model developed by William Sharpe.[5] Specifically, we can show that the appropriate risk that investors should be compensated for accepting is not the variance of an asset's return but some other quantity. In order to do this, let's take a closer look at risk.

We can do this by looking at the variance of the portfolio. The variance of the market portfolio containing N assets is equal to

$$
\begin{aligned}
\sigma^2(R_M) = {}& w_{1,M} \, \text{cov}(R_1, R_M) + w_{2,M} \, \text{cov}(R_2, R_M) \\
& + w_{3,M} \, \text{cov}(R_3, R_M) + \cdots + w_{N,M} \, \text{cov}(R_N, R_M)
\end{aligned}
\tag{17.6}
$$

where $w_{i,M}$ is equal to the proportion invested in asset i in the market portfolio. Notice that the portfolio variance does not depend on the variance of the assets comprising the market portfolio, but rather their covariance with the market portfolio.

Sharpe defines the degree to which an asset covaries with the market portfolio as the asset's systematic risk. More specifically, he defines systematic risk as the portion of an asset's variability that can be attributed to a common factor. Systematic risk is the minimum level of risk that can be obtained for a portfolio by means of diversification across a large number of randomly chosen assets. As such, systematic risk is that which results from general market and economic conditions that cannot be diversified away.

Sharpe defines the portion of an asset's variability that can be diversified away as *nonsystematic risk*. This is the risk that is unique to an asset.

SYSTEMATIC AND UNSYSTEMATIC RISK

Systematic Risk Is also Known as:	Unsystematic Risk Is also Known as:
Market risk	Diversifiable risk
Undiversifiable risk	Unique risk
Nondiversifiable risk	Residual risk
	Company-specific risk

---

[5]Sharpe, "Capital Asset Prices."

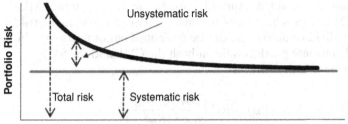

EXHIBIT 17.3 Components of Portfolio Risk

Consequently, total risk (as measured by the variance) can be partitioned into systematic risk as measured by the covariance of asset i's return with the market portfolio's return and nonsystematic risk. The relevant risk for decision-making purposes is the systematic risk.

We illustrate how diversification reduces nonsystematic risk for portfolios in Exhibit 17.3. The vertical axis shows the variance of the portfolio return. The variance of the portfolio return represents the total risk for the portfolio (that is, systematic plus nonsystematic). The horizontal axis shows the number of holdings of different assets (e.g., the number of common stock held of different issuers). As you can see, as the number of asset holdings increases, the level of nonsystematic risk is almost completely eliminated (that is, diversified away). Studies of different asset classes support this. For example, for common stock, several studies suggest that a portfolio size of about 20 randomly-selected companies will completely eliminate nonsystematic risk leaving only systematic risk.[6]

The Security Market Line

The CML represents an equilibrium condition in which the expected return on a portfolio of assets is a linear function of the expected return of the market portfolio. Individual assets do not fall on the CML. For individual assets, we expect the following to hold:

$$E(R_i) = R_f + \frac{E(R_M) - R_f}{\sigma^2(R_M)} \text{cov}(R_i, R_M) \qquad (17.7)$$

This is the *security market line* (SML).

---

[6]Wayne H. Wagner and Shiela C. Lau, "The Effect of Diversification on Risks," *Financial Analysts Journal* 27 (1971): 48–53.

In equilibrium, the expected return of individual assets lies on the SML, but not on the CML. This is because of the high degree of nonsystematic risk that remains in individual assets that can be diversified out of portfolios. In equilibrium, only efficient portfolios lie on both the CML and the SML.

We can also express the SML as

$$E(R_i) = R_f + \left(E(R_M) - R_f\right)\left[\frac{\text{cov}(R_i, R_M)}{\sigma^2(R_M)}\right] \tag{17.8}$$

How can we estimate the ratio in equation (17.8) for each asset? We can do so empirically using return data for the market portfolio and the return on the asset. The empirical analogue for equation (17.8) is

$$r_{it} - R_f = \alpha_i + \beta_i(r_{Mt} - r_{ft}) + \varepsilon_{it} \tag{17.9}$$

where ε_{it} is the error term, and β_i is the estimate of $\text{cov}(R_i, R_M)/\sigma^2(R_M)$. Equation (17.8) is the *characteristic line*.

Substituting β_i into the SML given by equation (17.8) gives the beta version of the SML:

$$E(R_i) = R_f + \beta_i(E(R_M) - R_f) \tag{17.10}$$

This is the CAPM form given by equation (17.3). This equation states that, given the assumptions of the CAPM, the expected return on an individual asset is a positive, linear function of its index of systematic risk as measured by beta. The higher the beta, the higher the expected return.

EXAMPLE 17.1

Suppose the risk-free asset's rate of return is 2% and you forecast a return on the market portfolio of 8%. If the beta for some asset x is 1.2, what is the expected return on asset x?

Solution

$$E(R_i) = R_f + \beta_i(E(R_M) - R_f)$$
$$E(R_i) = 0.02 + 1.2(0.08 - 0.02) = 9.2\%$$

An investor pursuing an active portfolio strategy searches for under-priced assets to purchase or retain and overpriced assets to sell or avoid (if held in the current portfolio, or sold short if permitted). If an investor believes that the CAPM is the correct asset pricing model, the investor can use the SML to identify mispriced securities.

- An asset is perceived to be underpriced (that is, undervalued) if the "expected" return projected by the investor is greater than the return stipulated by the SML.
- An asset is perceived to be overpriced (that is, overvalued), if the ex-pected return projected by the investor is less than the return stipulated by the SML.

Said another way, if the expected return of an asset plots above the SML, the asset is underpriced; if it plots below the SML, it is overpriced.

TRY IT! EXPECTED RETURNS

Complete the following table:

Asset	Return on the Risk-Free Asset	Expected Return on the Market	Beta	Expected Return on the Asset
1	1.0%	10.0%	⬜	10.00%
2	2.0%	⬜	0.8	10.80%
3	⬜	8.0%	1.3	9.65%
4	3.0%	9.0%	0.9	⬜

Tests of the CAPM

Now, that's the theory. The question is whether or not the theory is sup-ported by empirical evidence. There has been a large number of academic papers written on the subject, with researchers in almost all studies using common stock to test the theory. These papers cover not only the empirical evidence, but the challenges to testing the theory.

Let's start with the empirical evidence. There are two important results of the empirical tests of the CAPM that question its validity. First, it has been found that stocks with low betas have exhibited higher returns than the

CAPM predicts and stocks with high betas have been found to have lower returns than the CAPM predicts. Second, market risk is not the only risk factor priced by the market. Several studies have discovered other factors that explain stock returns.

While on the empirical level there are serious questions raised about the CAPM, there is an important paper challenging the validity of these empirical studies. Richard Roll demonstrates that the CAPM is not testable until the exact composition of the "true" market portfolio is known, and the only valid test of the CAPM is to observe whether the ex ante true market portfolio is mean-variance efficient.[7] As a result of his work, Roll argues that there will never be an unambiguous test of the CAPM. He does not say that the CAPM is invalid. Rather, Roll says that there is likely to be no unambiguous way to test the CAPM and its implications due to the fact that we cannot observe the true, theoretical market portfolio and its characteristics.

Criticisms of the CAPM

There have been attacks on the CAPM from those who believe that this cornerstone theory of finance is on shaky grounds. The three major attacks are

Attack 1: The use of the standard deviation or variance as a measure of risk does not capture what is observed in financial markets regarding the probability distribution of asset returns.

Attack 2: The behavioral assumptions of the CAPM do not reflect the way investors make portfolio decisions in the real world.

Attack 3: There is evidence that there is more than one risk factor that affects asset returns.

Attack 1 is essentially a criticism of an assumption that the return distribution for asset returns follows a normal distribution. Attack 2 is the criticism of proponents of behavioral finance theory who, as explained in the previous chapter, have attacked economic theories based on observing how economic agents such as investors actually go about making decisions. Finally, an alternative economic theory of asset pricing, such as the arbitrage pricing model, is based on more than one factor. One such model is the subject of the next section.

---

[7]Richard R. Roll, "A Critique of the Asset Pricing Theory's Tests," *Journal of Financial Economic* 4 (1977): 129–176.

THE ARBITRAGE PRICING THEORY MODEL

Stephen Ross developed an alternative to the equilibrium asset-pricing model just discussed, an asset-pricing model based purely on arbitrage arguments.[8] The model, called the *arbitrage pricing theory* (APT) *model*, postulates that an asset's expected return is influenced by a variety of risk factors, as opposed to just market risk as suggested by the CAPM. According to the APT model, the return on an asset is linearly related to a number of risk factors. However, the APT model does not specify what these risk factors are, but in the model the relationship between asset returns and the risk factors is linear. Moreover, in the APT model, unsystematic risk can be eliminated so that an investor is only compensated for accepting the systematic risk factors.

The Arbitrage Principle

The APT relies on arbitrage arguments, but what is arbitrage? In its simple form, arbitrage is the simultaneous buying and selling of an asset at two different prices in two different markets. The arbitrageur profits without risk by buying cheaply in one market and simultaneously selling at the higher price in the other market. However, such opportunities are rare in financial markets. In fact, a single arbitrageur with unlimited ability to sell short could correct a mispricing condition by financing purchases in the underpriced market with proceeds of short sales in the overpriced market.[9] This means that any arbitrage opportunities are short-lived.

Less obvious arbitrage opportunities exist in situations where a package of assets can produce a payoff (that is, expected return) identical to an asset that is priced differently. This arbitrage relies on a fundamental principle of finance, the *law of one price*, which states that a given asset must have the same price regardless of the means by which one goes about creating that asset. The law of one price implies that if an investor can synthetically create the payoff of an asset using a package of assets, the price of the package and the price of the asset whose payoff it replicates must be equal. When a situation is discovered whereby the price of the package of assets differs from that of an asset with the same payoff, rational investors will trade these assets in such a way as to restore price equilibrium.

The APT assumes that this arbitrage mechanism is possible, and is founded on the fact that an arbitrage transaction does not expose the

---

[8]Stephen A. Ross, "The Arbitrage Theory of Capital Asset Pricing," *Journal of Economic Theory* 13 (1976): 343–362.
[9]Short selling means selling an asset that is not owned in anticipation of a price decline.

investor to any adverse movement in the market price of the assets in the transaction. For example, let us consider how we can produce an arbitrage opportunity involving the three assets A, B, and C. These assets can be purchased today at the prices shown, and can each produce only one of two payoffs (referred to as State 1 and State 2) a year from now:

Asset	Price	Payoff in State 1	Payoff in State 2
A	$70	$50	$100
B	60	30	120
C	80	38	112

While it is not obvious from the data presented her, an investor can construct a portfolio consisting of assets A and B that will have the identical return as asset C in both State 1 and State 2. Let w_A and w_B be the proportion of assets A and B, respectively, in the portfolio. We can specify the payoff (that is, the terminal value of the portfolio) under the two states as:

$$\text{If State 1 occurs: Payoff} = \$50w_A + \$30w_B$$
$$\text{If State 2 occurs: Payoff} = \$100w_A + \$120w_B$$

Can we create a portfolio consisting of assets A and B that will reproduce the payoff of C regardless of the state that occurs one year from now? Yes. Here is how: For either condition (State 1 and State 2), we set the expected payoff of the portfolio equal to the expected payoff for C, as follows:

$$\text{State 1: Payoff} = \$50w_A + \$30w_B = \$38$$
$$\text{State 2: Payoff} = \$100w_A + \$120w_B = \$112$$

Because the proportions invested in the two assets must sum to one, we also know that $w_A + w_B = 1$.

If we solve for the weights for w_A and w_B that would simultaneously satisfy the preceding equations, we would find that the portfolio should have 40% in asset A (that is, $w_A = 0.4$) and 60% in asset B (that is, $w_B = 0.6$). The cost of that portfolio will be equal to:

$$\text{Cost of the portfolio with } w_A \text{ of 0.4 and } w_B \text{ of 0.6} = (0.4 \times \$70) + (0.6 \times \$60) = \$64$$

Our portfolio (that is, package of assets) comprised of assets A and B has the same payoff in State 1 and State 2 as the payoff of asset C. The cost of asset C is $80, whereas the cost of the portfolio is only $64. This is an arbitrage opportunity that can be exploited by buying assets A and B in the proportions given and shorting (selling) asset C.

For example, suppose that we invest $1 million to create the portfolio with assets A and B. The $1 million is obtained by selling short asset C. The proceeds from the short sale of asset C provide the funds to purchase assets A and B. Thus, there would be no cash outlay by the investor. The payoffs for States 1 and 2 are:

Asset	Investment	Payoff in State 1	Payoff in State 2
A	$ 400,000	$ 285,715	$ 571,429
B	600,000	300,000	1,200,000
C	−1,000,000	−475,000	−1,400,000
Total	$ 0	$ 110,715	$ 371,429

In either State 1 or 2, the investor profits without risk. The APT model assumes that such an opportunity would be quickly eliminated by the marketplace.

APT Model Formulation

The APT model postulates that an asset's expected return is influenced by a variety of risk factors, as opposed to just market risk in the case of the CAPM. That is, the APT model asserts that the return on an asset is linearly related to H "factors." The APT does not specify what these factors are, but it is assumed that the relationship between asset returns and the factors is linear. Specifically, the APT model asserts that the rate of return on asset i is given by the following relationship:

$$R_i = E(R_i) + \beta_{i,1} F_1 + \beta_{i,2} F_2 + \cdots + \beta_{i,H} F_H + e_i$$

where:
    R_i = the rate of return on asset i
    $E(R_i)$ = the expected return on asset i
    F_h = the hth factor that is common to the returns of all assets
        $(h = 1, \ldots, H)$
    $\beta_{i,h}$ = the sensitivity of the ith asset to the hth factor
    e_i = the unsystematic return for asset i

For equilibrium to exist, the following conditions must be satisfied: Using no additional funds (wealth) and without increasing risk, it should not be possible, on average, to create a portfolio to increase return. In essence, this condition states that there is no so-called money machine available in the market.

Ross derived the following relationship, which is what is referred to as the APT model:

$$E(R_i) = R_f + \beta_{i,F1}[E(R_{F1}) - R_f] + \beta_{i,F2}[E(R_{F2}) - R_f] + \cdots$$
$$+ \beta_{i,FH}[E(R_{FH}) - R_f]$$

where $[E(R_{Fj}) - R_f]$ is the excess return of the jth systematic risk factor over the risk-free rate, and can be thought of as the price (or risk premium) for the jth systematic risk factor. The derivation of the APT model is much more mathematically complicated than deriving the CAPM, so we will not provide the details here.

The APT model asserts that investors want to be compensated for all the risk factors that systematically affect the return of an asset. The compensation is the sum of the products of each risk factor's systematic risk $(\beta_{i,Fh})$, and the risk premium assigned to it by the financial market $[E(R_{Fh}) - R_f]$. As in the case of the CAPM, an investor is not compensated for accepting unsystematic risk. However, the CAPM states that systematic risk is market risk, while the APT model does not specify the systematic risks.

Supporters of the APT model argue that it has several major advantages over the CAPM. First, it makes less restrictive assumptions about investor preferences toward risk and return. As explained earlier, the CAPM theory assumes investors trade off between risk and return solely on the basis of the expected returns and standard deviations of prospective investments. The APT model, in contrast, simply requires some rather unobtrusive bounds be placed on potential investor utility functions. Second, no assumptions are made about the distribution of asset returns. Finally, because the APT model does not rely on the identification of the true market portfolio, the theory is potentially testable.

Multifactor Risk Models in Practice

The APT model provides theoretical support for an asset pricing model where there is more than one risk factor. Consequently, we refer to these models as *multifactor risk models*. These models provide the tools for quantifying the risk profile of a portfolio relative to a benchmark, for constructing a portfolio relative to a benchmark, and for controlling risk. There are two types of multifactor risk models used in both equity and bond portfolio management: statistical factor models and fundamental factor models.

In a *statistical factor model*, historical and cross-sectional data on stock returns are tossed into a statistical model. The goal of the statistical model is to best explain the observed stock returns with factors that are linear return combinations and uncorrelated with each other. For example, suppose that you compute the monthly returns for 5,000 companies for 10 years. The goal of the statistical analysis is to produce factors that best explain the variance of the observed stock returns. For example, suppose that there are six factors that do this. These factors are statistical artifacts. The objective in a statistical factor model then becomes to determine the economic meaning of each of these statistically derived factors. Because of the problem of interpretation, it is difficult to use the factors from a statistical factor model for valuation, portfolio construction, and risk control. Instead, practitioners prefer the next model described, which allows an asset manager to prespecify meaningful factors and thus produce a more intuitive model.

Fundamental factor models use company and industry attributes and market data as raw descriptors. Examples of raw descriptors in equity factor models are price/earnings ratios, book/price ratios, estimated economic growth, and stock trading activity. The inputs into a fundamental factor model are stock returns and the raw descriptors about a company. Those fundamental variables about a company that are pervasive in explaining stock returns are then the raw descriptors retained in the model. Using cross-sectional analysis, the sensitivity of a stock's return to a raw descriptor can be estimated.

SOME PRINCIPLES TO TAKE AWAY

In this chapter we have covered the two principal models associated with asset pricing theory. We have emphasized the assumptions and their critical role in the development of these theories. While you may understand the topics covered, you may still be uncomfortable about where we have progressed in financial theory, given the lack of theoretical and empirical support for the CAPM or the difficulty of identifying the factors in the APT model. You're not alone. A good number of practitioners and academics feel uncomfortable with these models, particularly the CAPM.

Nevertheless, what is comforting is that there are several general principles of investing that are derived from these theories that very few would question. They are:

- Investing has two dimensions, risk and return. Therefore, focusing only on the actual return without looking at the risk that has to be accepted to achieve that return is inappropriate.
- It is also inappropriate to look at the risk of an individual asset when deciding whether it should be included in a portfolio. What is important

is how the inclusion of an asset into a portfolio will affect the risk of the portfolio.

- Whether investors consider one risk or a thousand risks, risk can be divided into two general categories: systematic risks that cannot be eliminated by diversification, and unsystematic risks that can be diversified away.
- Investors should be compensated only for accepting systematic risks. Thus, it is critical in formulating an investment strategy to identify the systematic risks.

THE BOTTOM LINE

- Asset pricing involves determining the expected return investors require in order to invest in risky assets. The two most well-known equilibrium pricing models are the capital asset pricing model developed in the 1960s and the arbitrage pricing theory model developed in the mid-1970s.
- The risks associated with assets and portfolios can be divided into systematic risk and unsystematic risk. The latter risks can be eliminated by diversification; the former risks cannot be eliminated by diversifying.
- In deriving the CAPM, assumptions are made. A key assumption is that investors make investment decisions in accordance with the theory of portfolio selection as formulated by Markowitz. The goal of portfolio selection is the construction of portfolios that maximize expected returns consistent with individually acceptable levels of risk.
- In the theory of portfolio selection, risk is measured by the variance (or standard deviation) and evaluated considering the expected return, and hence this is often referred to as mean-variance analysis. The CAPM formalizes the relationship that should exist between asset returns and risk if investors behave in a hypothesized manner. Together, the theory of portfolio selection and CAPM provide a framework to specify and measure investment risk, and to develop relationships between expected asset return and risk (and hence between risk and required return on an investment).
- The CAPM asserts that the only risk that is priced by rational investors is systematic risk, because that risk cannot be eliminated by diversification. Essentially, the CAPM says that the expected return of an asset or a portfolio is equal to the rate on a risk-free security asset plus a risk premium. The risk premium in the CAPM is the product of the quantity of risk as measured by beta multiplied by the market price of risk. An asset or portfolio's beta is an index of the systematic risk of the asset.

- There have been numerous empirical tests of the CAPM, and, in general, these have failed to fully support the theory. However, these studies have been criticized because of the difficulty of identifying the true market portfolio. Further, such tests are not likely to appear soon, if at all, according to financial theorists.
- The arbitrage pricing theory model is developed purely from arbitrage arguments. The theory postulates that the expected return on an asset or a portfolio is influenced by several risk factors. Proponents of the APT model cite its less restrictive assumptions as a feature that makes it more appealing than the CAPM. Moreover, testing the APT model does not require identification of the true market portfolio.
- Despite the fact that the two major asset pricing theories—CAPM and APT—are controversial or may be difficult to implement in practice, there are several principles of investing that are not controversial that can be taken away from these theories and applied in formulating portfolio management strategies.

SOLUTIONS TO TRY IT! PROBLEMS

Expected Returns

Asset	Return on the Risk-Free Asset	Expected Return on the Market	Beta	Expected Return on the Asset
1	1.0%	10.0%	1.0	10.00%
2	2.0%	13.0%	0.8	10.80%
3	2.5%	8.0%	1.3	9.65%
4	3.0%	9.0%	0.9	8.40%

QUESTIONS

1. What is diversifiable risk?
2. What is the role of diversification in the capital asset pricing model?
3. If investors are risk averse, which would they prefer: a stock with an expected return of 5% with a beta of 1.2 or a stock with an expected return of 6% with a beta of 1.3? Explain.
4. If a stock has both diversifiable risk and nondiversifiable risk, which, if any, of these risks are considered in the pricing of the asset?

5. In the context of the CAPM, what is the term represented by $E(R_M) - R_f$?
6. Explain what beta represents in terms of asset pricing.
7. If asset A's beta is greater than asset B's beta, does this mean that asset A has more risk than asset B? Explain.
8. What is the difference between the security market line and the capital market line?
9. If a stock's return and risk are such that this would plot above the security market line, is this stock overpriced or underpriced?
10. Suppose you expected the return on the market to be 10% and the return on the risk-free asset to be 2%. If you are considering a stock with a beta of 1.2, what is the expected return on this stock according to the security market line?
11. How should an investor construct an efficient portfolio in the presence of a risk-free asset?
12. What is the theoretical problem inherent in verifying the CAPM empirically?
13. Why is the CAPM's assumption that investors can borrow and lend at the risk-free rate questionable?
14. What is meant by the "homogeneous assumption" in the CAPM?
15. What is meant by the law of one price, and what does it imply about a package of securities and a given security that have the same payoff?
16. What are the fundamental principles underlying the APT model?
17. What are the advantages of the APT model relative to the CAPM?
18. What are the difficulties of applying the arbitrage pricing theory model in practice?
19. Indicate why you agree or disagree with the following statements:
    a. "As a percentage of the total risk, the unsystematic risk of a diversified portfolio is greater than that of an individual asset."
    b. "An investor should be compensated for accepting unsystematic risk."
20. "In the CAPM, investors should be compensated for accepting systematic risk; for the APT model, investors are rewarded for accepting both systematic risk and unsystematic risk." Do you agree with this statement?

CHAPTER 18

The Structure of Interest Rates

Some discussion of the arithmetic of longer-term yields provides a useful perspective on recent developments in bond markets. The ten-year Treasury yield, for example, can be viewed as a weighted average of the current one-year rate and nine one-year forward rates, with the weights depending on the coupon yield of the security. [E]ach of these forward rates can be split further into (1) a portion equal to the one-year spot rate that market participants currently expect to prevail at the corresponding date in the future, and (2) a portion that reflects additional compensation to the bondholder for the risk of holding longer-dated instruments.

Current and near-term forward rates are particularly sensitive to monetary policy actions, which directly affect spot short-term interest rates and strongly influence market expectations of where spot rates are likely to stand in the next year or two.
— Ben S., Bernanke, Chairman of the Federal Reserve,
Speech before the Economic Club of New York,
New York, March 20, 2006

A casual examination of the financial pages of a journal would be enough to convey the idea that nobody talks about an "interest rate." There are interest rates reported for borrowing money and investing. These rates are not randomly determined; that is, there are factors that systematically determine how interest rates on different types of loans and debt instruments vary from each other. We refer to this as the *structure of interest rates* and we discuss the factors that affect this structure in this chapter.

THE BASE INTEREST RATE

The securities issued by the U.S. Department of the Treasury, popularly referred to as Treasury securities or simply Treasuries, are backed by the full faith and credit of the U.S. government. At the time of this writing, market participants throughout the world view U.S. Treasuries as being free of default risk, although there is the possibility that unwise economic policy by the U.S. government may alter that perception. While historically Treasury securities have served as the benchmark interest rates throughout the U.S. economy as well as in international capital markets, there are other important interest rate benchmarks used by market participants that we will discuss later.

The *base interest rate* is the sum of the real interest rate and the rate of inflation. This is the interest rate appropriate for an investment with no default risk. A factor that is important in determining the level of interest rates is the expected rate of inflation. That is, we can express the base interest rate as:

Base interest rate = Real interest rate + Expected rate of inflation

The *real interest rate* is the rate that would exist in the economy in the absence of inflation.

The Risk Premium

Debt instruments not issued or backed by the full faith and credit of the U.S. government are available in the market at an interest rate or yield that is different from an otherwise comparable maturity Treasury security. We refer to the difference between the interest rate offered on a non-Treasury security and a comparable maturity Treasury security as the *spread*. For example, if the yield on a five-year non-Treasury security is 5.4% and the yield on a 10-year Treasury security is 4%, the spread is said to be 1.4%. Rather than referring to the spread in percentage terms, such as 1.4%, market participants refer to the spread in terms of basis points. A basis point is equal to 0.01%. Consequently, 1% is equal to 100 basis points. In our example, the spread of 1.4% is equal to 140 basis points.

The spread exists because of the additional risk or risks to which an investor is exposed by investing in a security that is not issued by the U.S. government. Consequently, the spread is referred to as a *risk premium*. Thus, we can express the interest rate offered on a non-Treasury security with the same maturity as a Treasury security as:

Interest rate = Base interest rate + Spread

or, equivalently,

$$\text{Interest rate} = \text{Base interest rate} + \text{Risk premium}$$

While the spread or risk premium is typically positive, there are factors that can cause the risk premium to be negative. The general factors that affect the risk premium between a non-Treasury security and a Treasury security with the same maturity are:

- The market's perception of the credit risk of the non-Treasury security.
- Any features provided of the non-Treasury security that make it attractive or unattractive to investors.
- The tax treatment of the interest income from the non-Treasury security.
- The expected liquidity of the non-Treasury issue.

Risk Premium Due to Default Risk

Default risk refers to the risk that the issuer of a debt obligation may be unable to make timely payment of interest or the principal amount when it is due. Most market participants gauge default risk in terms of the credit rating assigned by the three major commercial rating companies: (1) Moody's Investors Service, (2) Standard & Poor's Corporation, and (3) Fitch Ratings. These companies, referred to as *rating agencies*, perform credit analyses of issuers and issues and express their conclusions by a system of ratings.

We summarize the rating systems used by the three major services in Exhibit 18.1. These are the major rating classes, though the rating services

S&P and Fitch	Moody's		
AAA	Aaa	High quality	Investment grade
AA	Aa		
A	A		
BBB	Baa		
BB	Ba	Non-investment grade	
B	B		
C	C		

EXHIBIT 18.1   Credit Ratings

breakdown some of these classes to provide more information. For example, Moody's uses 1, 2, or 3 to provide a narrower credit quality breakdown within each class; S&P and Fitch use plus and minus signs for the same purpose.

In all rating systems the term *high grade* means low credit risk or, conversely, high probability of future payments. Bonds rated AAA (or Aaa) through BBB (or Baa) are considered *investment grade bonds*. Issues that carry a rating below the top four categories are referred to as *noninvestment-grade bonds*, or more popularly as *high-yield bonds* or *junk bonds*.

The spread or risk premium between Treasury securities and non-Treasury securities, which are identical in all respects except for credit rating, is the *credit spread*. For example, on August 5, 2008, finance.yahoo.com reported (based on information supplied by ValuBond) that the five-year Treasury yield was 3.29%. The yield and credit spreads on five-year corporate bonds rated AAA, AA, and A were:

Rating	Yield August 5, 2008	Credit Spread in Basis Points
AAA rated	5.01%	172
AA rated	5.50%	221
A rated	5.78%	249

Note that the lower the credit rating, the higher the credit spread.

 TRY IT! CREDIT SPREADS

Complete the following table when the yield on a similar-maturity Treasury bond is 3.73%:

Rated Bond	Yield	Credit Spread
AAA rated	4.92%	[ ]
AA rated	5.43%	[ ]
A rated	5.90%	[ ]
BBB rated	6.32%	[ ]

Inclusion of Attractive and Unattractive Provisions

The terms of the loan agreement may contain provisions that make the debt instrument more or less attractive compared to other debt instruments that do not have such provisions. When there is a provision attractive to an investor, the spread decreases relative to a Treasury security of the same maturity. The opposite occurs when there is an unattractive provision: The spread increases relative to a comparable-maturity Treasury security.

The three most common features found in bond issues are the:

1. Call provision,
2. Put provision, and
3. Conversion provision.

A bond may have one of more of these features—or none of these features.

A *call provision* grants the issuer the right to retire the bond issue prior to the scheduled maturity date. A bond issue that contains such a provision is a *callable bond*. The inclusion of a call provision benefits the issuer by allowing it to replace that bond issue with a lower interest cost bond issue should interest rates in the market decline. Effectively, a call provision allows the issuer to alter the maturity of the bond issue. A call provision is an unattractive feature for the investor (i.e., the bondholder) because the bondholder will not only be uncertain about maturity, but faces the risk that the issuer will exercise the call provision when interest rates have declined below the interest rate on the bond issue. As a result, the bondholder must reinvest the proceeds received when the bond issue is called into another bond issue paying a lower interest rate. This risk associated with a callable bond is *reinvestment risk*. For this reason, investors require compensation for accepting reinvestment risk and they receive this compensation in the form of a higher spread or risk premium.

A bond issue with a *put provision* grants the bondholder the right to sell the issue back to the issuer at par value on designated dates. A bond that contains this provision is a *putable bond*. Unlike a call provision, a put provision is an advantage to the bondholder. The reason is that if interest rates rise after the issuance of the bond, the price of the bond will decline. The put provision allows that bondholder to sell the bond back to the issuer, avoiding a market value loss on the bond and allowing the bondholder to reinvest the proceeds from the sale of the bond at a higher interest rate. Hence, a bond issue that contains a put provision will sell in the market at a lower spread than an otherwise comparable-maturity Treasury security.

A *conversion provision* grants the bondholder the right to exchange the bond issue for a specified number of shares of common stock. A bond with this provision is a *convertible bond*. The conversion provision allows the bondholder the opportunity to benefit from a favorable movement in the price of the stock into which it can exchange the bond. Hence, the conversion provision results in a lower spread relative to a comparable-maturity Treasury issue. For example, the provision may specify that the bond may be exchanged into 50 shares of the common stock of the issue. The investor then compares the value of the bond as a bond with the value converted into the common stock.

The three provisions we have described are, effectively, options. Unlike a traded option, such as a stock option, these provisions are referred to as *embedded options* because they are options embedded in a bond issue.

EXAMPLE 18.1: CALLABLE DEBT

Kellogg Co. issued $1.1 of callable debentures in 2001 that mature April 1, 2031. The debentures are callable by Kellogg at par value. Therefore, Kellogg has a call option on these debentures: it can buy these debentures back from the investors at 100% of the principal amount, plus accrued interest.

Taxability of Interest

The U.S. federal tax code specifies that interest income is taxable at the federal income tax level unless otherwise exempted. The federal tax code specifically exempts the interest income from qualified municipal bond issues from taxation at the federal level. Municipal bonds are securities issued by state and local governments and by their creations, such as "authorities" and special districts. The tax-exempt feature of municipal bonds is an attractive feature to an investor because it reduces taxes and, therefore, the spread is often such that the municipal bond issue sells in the market at a lower interest rate than a comparable-maturity bond issue.

For example, on August 5, 2008 finance.yahoo.com reported (based on information supplied by ValuBond) that the five-year Treasury yield was 3.29% and the yield on five-year municipal bonds was as follows: AAA-rated bonds 2.95%, AA rated bonds 3.04%, and A rated bonds 3.27%.

When comparing the yield on a municipal bond issue to that of the yield on a comparable-maturity Treasury issue, the market convention is not to compute the basis point difference (i.e., the spread) between the two bond issues. Instead, the market convention is to compute the ratio of the yield of a municipal bond issue to the yield of a comparable-maturity Treasury security. The resulting ratio is the *municipal yield ratio* or the *muni-Treasury yield ratio*:

Rating	Yield August 5, 2008	Muni-Treasury Yield Ratio
AAA rated	2.95%	0.90
AA rated	3.04%	0.92
A rated	3.27%	0.99

In selecting between a taxable bond (such as a corporate bond) and a municipal bond with the same maturity and credit rating, an investor can calculate the yield that must be offered on a taxable bond issue to give the same after-tax yield as a municipal bond issue. This yield measure is called the *equivalent taxable yield* and is determined as follows:

$$\text{Equivalent taxable yield} = \frac{\text{Tax-exempt yield}}{(1 - \text{Marginal tax rate})}$$

For example, suppose an investor is considering the purchase of an AA rated five-year municipal bond on August 5, 2008 offering a yield of 3.04% (the tax-exempt yield). Then

$$\text{Equivalent taxable yield} = \frac{0.0304}{(1 - 0.35)} = 4.677\%$$

That is, for an investor in the 35% marginal tax bracket, a taxable bond with a 4.677% yield would provide the equivalent of a 3.04% tax-exempt yield.

 TRY IT! EQUIVALENT TAXABLE YIELD

Complete the following table:

Tax-Exempt Yield	Marginal Tax Rate	Equivalent Taxable Yield
5%	40%	[ ]
4%	45%	[ ]
6%	30%	[ ]

Expected Liquidity of a Bond Issue

When an investor wants to sell a particular bond issue, he or she is concerned whether the price that can be obtained from the sale will be close to the "true" value of the issue. For example, if recent trades in the market for a particular bond issue have been between 87.25 and 87.75 and market conditions have not changed, an investor would expect to sell the bond somewhere in the 87.25 to 87.75 range.

The concern that the investor has when contemplating the purchase of a particular bond issue is that he or she will have to sell it below its true value where the true value is indicated by recent transactions. This risk is referred to as *liquidity risk*. The greater the liquidity risk that investors perceive there is with a particular bond issue, the greater the spread or risk premium relative to a comparable-maturity Treasury security. The reason is that Treasury securities are the most liquid securities in the world.

THE TERM STRUCTURE OF INTEREST RATES

The price of a debt instrument will fluctuate over its life as yields in the market change. The price volatility of a bond depends on its maturity, among other things. Holding all other factors constant, the longer the maturity of a bond the greater is the price volatility resulting from a change in market interest rates. The spread between any two maturities in a sector of a market is the *maturity spread*. Although we can calculate this spread for any sector of the market, it is most commonly calculated for the Treasury sector.

The relationship between the yields on comparable securities but different maturities is the *term structure of interest rates*. Again, the primary focus is the Treasury market. The graphic that depicts the relationship between the yields on Treasury securities with different maturities is known as the *yield curve* and, therefore, we also refer to the maturity spread as the *yield curve spread*.

We show three hypothetical Treasury yield curves in Exhibit 18.2. Though we have observed all three types in the U.S., the predominant type is the upward sloping yield curve.

The Treasury yield curve plays the role as a benchmark for setting yields in many other sectors of the debt market. However, a Treasury yield curve based on observed yields on the Treasury market is an unsatisfactory measure of the relation between required yield and maturity. The key reason is that securities with the same maturity may actually provide different yields. Hence, it is necessary to develop more accurate and reliable estimates of the Treasury yield curve. Specifically, the key is to estimate the theoretical

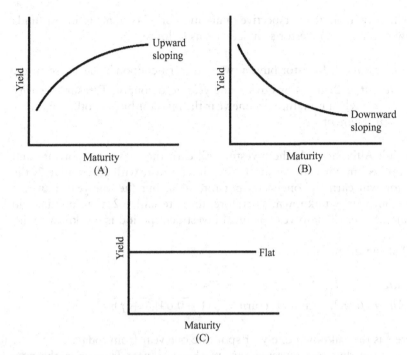

EXHIBIT 18.2 Three Observed Shapes for the Yield Curve

interest rate that the U.S. Treasury would have to pay assuming that the security it issued is a zero-coupon security. Due its complexity, we will not explain how this is done. However, at this point all that is necessary to know is that there are procedures for estimating the theoretical interest rate or yield that the U.S. Treasury would have to pay for bonds with different maturities. These interest rates are referred to as the *Treasury spot rates.*

We can obtain valuable information for market participants from the Treasury spot rates. These rates are *forward rates.* Let's see how we obtain these rates and then we will discuss theories about what determines forward rates.

Forward Rates

Consider the following two Treasury spot rates: the spot rate for a zero-coupon Treasury security maturing in one year is 4% and the spot rate for a zero-coupon Treasury security maturing in two years is 5%. Let's look at this situation from the perspective of an investor who wants to invest funds for two years. The investor's choices are as follows:

Alternative 1. Investor buys a two-year zero-coupon Treasury security.

Alternative 2. Investor buys a one-year zero-coupon Treasury security and when it matures in one year the investor buys another one-year instrument.

With Alternative 1, the investor will earn the two-year spot rate and that rate is known with certainty: 5%. In contrast, with Alternative 2, the investor will earn the one-year spot rate, 4%, but the one-year spot one year from now is unknown. Therefore, for Alternative 2, the rate that will be earned over the two-year planned investment period is not known with certainty.[1]

Putting the numbers to this,

Alternative 1:   Annual return = 5%

Alternative 2:   Annual return = $\sqrt{(1 + 0.04)(1 + f)}$

where f is the unknown one-year spot rate one year from today.

Suppose that this investor expects that one year from now the one-year spot rate will be higher than it is today. The investor might then feel Alternative 2 would be the better investment. However, this is not necessarily true. To understand why it is necessary to know what the forward rate is, let's continue with our illustration.

The investor will be indifferent to the two alternatives if they produce the same total dollars over the two-year investment horizon. Given the two-year spot rate, there is some spot rate on a one-year zero-coupon Treasury security one year from now that will make the investor indifferent between the two alternatives.

We can determine the value of f given the two-year spot rate and the one-year spot rate by solving for the rate f such that the investment in

---

[1]Alternative 2 uses the calculation of the geometric mean return. For two periods, with r_1 the rate in the first period and r_2 the expected rate in the second period, the two-year rate is the average annual return over the two periods, which is the square root of $(1 + r_1)(1 + r_2)$, or two-year rate = $\sqrt[2]{(1 + r_1)(1 + r_2)}$. Therefore, in Alternative 2 we solve for the one-year rate expected one year from now based on the two-year return and the one-year return in the first period.

the two-year security at 5% is equivalent to an investment in a one-year investment at 4% and a subsequent one-year investment at the rate f:

$$(1 + 0.05)^2 = (1 + 0.04)(1 + f)$$

Using a bit of algebra to solve for f,

$$(1 + f) = \frac{(1 + 0.05)^2}{(1 + 0.04)}$$
$$f = 6.01\%$$

We can check our work to see if both alternatives provide the same number of dollars at the end of the two-year investment horizon:

- *Alternative 1:* If an investor placed $100 in the two-year zero-coupon Treasury security earning 5%, the total dollars that at the end of two years is $100 × (1.05)^2 = $110.25.
- *Alternative 2:* The proceeds from investing in the one-year Treasury security at 4% generates $104 at the end of the first year. Investing this for the next period at 6.01% produces an end of period value of $104 × (1+ 0.0601) = $110.25.

Here is how we use this forward rate of 6.01%. If the one-year spot rate one year from now is less than 6.01%, then the total dollars at the end of two years would be higher by investing in the two-year zero-coupon Treasury security (Alternative 1). If the one-year spot rate one year from now is greater than 6.01%, then the total dollars at the end of two years would be higher by investing in a one-year zero-coupon Treasury security and reinvesting the proceeds one year from now at the one-year spot rate at that time (Alternative 2). Of course, if the one-year spot rate one year from now is 6.01%, the two alternatives give the same total dollars at the end of two years.

Now that we have the forward rate, f, in which we are interested and we know how that rate can be used, let's return to the question that we posed at the outset. Suppose the investor expects that one year from now, the one-year spot rate one year from now will be 5.5%. That is, the investor expects the one-year spot rate one year from now will be higher than its current level. Should the investor select Alternative 2 because the one-year spot rate one year from now is expected to be higher? The answer is no, because this produces a value less than investing at 5% for two years:

Investment value
at the end of two years $= \$100 \times 1.40 \times 1.055 = \$109.72$

In this example, if the spot rate in the second year is less than 6.01%, then Alternative 1 is the better alternative. If this investor expects a rate of 5.5%, then he or she should select Alternative 1 despite the fact that he or she expects the one-year spot rate to be higher next year than it is today.

This is a somewhat surprising result for some investors. But the reason for this is that the market prices its expectations of future interest rates into the rates offered on investments with different maturities. This is why knowing forward rates is critical. Some market participants believe that the forward rate is the market's consensus of future interest rates.

Similarly, borrowers need to understand what is meant by a forward rate. For example, suppose a borrower must choose between a two-year loan and a series of two one-year loans. If the forward rate is less than the borrower's expectations of one-year rates one year from now, the borrower will be better off with a two-year loan. If, instead, the borrower's expectations are that the one-year rate one year from now will be less than the forward rate, the borrower will be better off by choosing a series of two one-year loans.

In practice, a company's treasurer needs to know both forward rates and future spreads. A company often pays the Treasury rate (i.e., the benchmark) plus a spread on its borrowings, so understanding current and future rates is critical.

A natural question about forward rates is how well they do at predicting future interest rates. Studies have demonstrated that forward rates do not do a good job in predicting future interest rates. Then, why the big deal about understanding forward rates? The reason, as we demonstrated in our illustration of how to select between two alternative investments, is that the forward rates indicate how an investor's and borrower's expectations must differ from the market consensus, as measured by forward rates, in order to make the correct decision.

In our illustration, the one-year forward rate may not be realized. That is irrelevant. The fact is that the one-year forward rate indicated to the investor that if expectations about the one-year rate one month from now are less than 6.01%, the investor would be better off with Alternative 1.

For this reason, as well as others explained later, some market participants do not refer to forward rates as being market consensus rates. Instead, they refer to forward rates as *hedgeable rates*. For example, by investing in the two-year Treasury security, the investor was able to hedge the one-year rate one year from now. Similarly, a corporation issuing a two-year security is hedging the one-year rate one year from now.

 TRY IT! FORWARD RATES

Complete the following table for the one-year rate one year from now that would make the investor indifferent between the two-year zero-coupon security and two, successive one-year zero-coupon securities:

Case	2-Year Spot Rate	1-Year Spot Rate	One-Year Rate One Year from Now
A	5.00%	4.25%	☐
B	2.25%	1.75%	☐
C	3.00%	2.75%	☐
D	4.00%	3.80%	☐

Determinants of the Shape of the Term Structure

At a given point in time, if we plot the term structure—the yield to maturity, or the spot rate, at successive maturities against maturity—we would observe one of the three shapes we show in Exhibit 18.2.

In Exhibit 18.3, we show a yield curve where the yield increases with maturity. This type of yield curve is an *upward-sloping yield curve* or a *positively sloped yield curve*. We provide four examples of upward-sloping yield curves in Panel A of Exhibit 18.4.

We distinguish upward sloping yield curves based on the steepness of the yield curve. The steepness of the yield curve is typically measured in terms of the maturity spread between long-term and short-term yields. While there are many maturity candidates to proxy for long-term and short-term yields, many market participants use the maturity spreads between the 30-year yield and six-month yield. Consider the upward sloping curves in Exhibit 18.3 for June 12, 1991 and January 1, 2010. The spread between the 30-year and six-month yields are 248 basis points and 461 basis points, respectively. Therefore, we would conclude that the yield curve in January 2010 is steeper than that of June 1991.

In practice, we refer to a Treasury positively sloped yield curve whose maturity spread as measured by the 30-year yields and six-month yields as

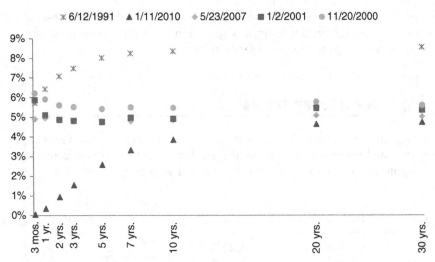

EXHIBIT 18.3 Four Observed Actual Yield Curves
Source: U.S. Treasury.

a normal yield curve when the spread is 300 basis points or less. The yield curve on June 12, 1991 is therefore a normal yield curve. When the maturity spread is more than 300 basis points, the yield curve is said to be a steep yield curve. The yield curve on January 11, 2010 is a steep yield curve.

We also provide two examples of downward-sloping or *inverted yield curves*, where yields in general decline as maturity increases: November 20, 2000 and January 2, 2001. There have not been many instances in the recent history of the U.S. Treasury market where the yield curve exhibited this characteristic. We provide additional examples in Exhibit 18.4, Panel B. The most notable is on August 14, 1981, when Treasury yields were at a historic high. The yield on the two-year Treasury was 16.91% and declined for each subsequent maturity until it reached 13.95% for the 30-year maturity.

We also show a *flat yield curve* from May 23, 2007 in Exhibit 18.3. For a flat yield curve, the yields are not identical for each maturity; rather, the yields for all maturities are similar. You can see additional examples of this type of yield curve in Panel C of Exhibit 18.4.

A variant of the flat yield curve is one in which the yield on short-term and long-term Treasuries are similar but the yield on intermediate-term Treasuries are much lower than the six-month and 30-year yields. Such a yield curve is referred to as a *humped yield curve*. We provide examples of humped yield curves in Panel D of Exhibit 18.4.

EXHIBIT 18.4 Examples of Actual Yield Curves

A: Upward sloping

Day	3 mos.	6 mos.	1 yr.	2 yrs.	3 yrs.	5 yrs.	7 yrs.	10 yrs.	20 yrs.	30 yrs.	Spread
04/15/1992	3.70%	3.84%	4.14%	5.22%	5.77%	6.66%	7.02%	7.37%	NA	7.87%	403 bp
02/05/2010	0.03	0.10	0.17	0.31	0.77	1.28	2.23	3.00	4.36	4.51	441 bp

B: Downward sloping

Day	3 mos.	6 mos.	1 yr.	2 yrs.	3 yrs.	5 yrs.	7 yrs.	10 yrs.	20 yrs.	30 yrs.	Spread
02/21/2007	5.18%	5.16%	5.05%	4.82%	4.74%	4.68%	4.68%	4.69%	4.90%	4.79%	−37 bp
01/19/2007	6.33	6.15	6.46	6.4	6.31	6.35	6.16	6.29	5.92	6.33	18 bp

C: Flat

Day	3 mos.	6 mos.	1 yr.	2 yrs.	3 yrs.	5 yrs.	7 yrs.	10 yrs.	20 yrs.	30 yrs.	Spread
01/03/1990	7.89%	7.94%	7.85%	7.94%	7.96%	7.92%	8.04%	7.99%	NA	8.04%	10 bp
05/23/2007	4.91	5.01	4.96	4.85	4.79	4.79	4.80	4.86	5.09	5.01	0 bp

D: Humped

Day	3 mos.	6 mos.	1 yr.	2 yrs.	3 yrs.	5 yrs.	7 yrs.	10 yrs.	20 yrs.	30 yrs.	Spread
11/24/2000	6.34%	6.12%	5.86%	5.84%	5.63%	5.70%	5.63%	5.86%	5.67%	6.34%	22 bp
01/02/2000	5.87	5.58	5.11	4.87	4.82	4.76	4.97	4.92	5.46	5.35	−23 bp

Note:
1. NA indicates no securities with that maturity for that date
2. The spread is the difference in basis points between the 30-year maturity and the 6-month maturity.
Source: U.S. Treasury.

TERM STRUCTURE OF INTEREST RATES THEORIES

There are two major economic theories that have evolved to account for the observed shapes of the yield curve: the *expectations theory* and the *market segmentation theory*.

Expectations Theories

There are two forms of the expectations theory: pure expectations theory and biased expectations theory. Both theories share a hypothesis about the behavior of short-term forward rates and also assume that the forward rates in current long-term bonds are closely related to the market's expectations about future short-term rates.

The two theories differ, however, on whether or not other factors also affect forward rates, and how. The *pure expectations theory* postulates that no systematic factors other than expected future short-term rates affect forward rates; the *biased expectations theory* asserts that there are other factors.

Pure Expectations Theory   According to the pure expectations theory, the forward rates exclusively represent the expected future rates. Thus, the entire term structure at a given time reflects the market's current expectations of the family of future short-term rates. Under this view, an upward-sloping yield curve indicates that the market expects short-term rates to rise throughout the relevant future. Similarly, a flat term structure reflects an expectation that future short-term rates will be mostly constant, while a falling term structure must reflect an expectation that future short rates will decline steadily.

A major shortcoming of the pure expectations theory is that it ignores the risks inherent in investing in debt instruments. If forward rates were perfect predictors of future interest rates, then the future prices of bonds would be known with certainty. The return over any investment period would be certain and independent of the maturity of the debt instrument initially acquired and of the time at which the investor needed to liquidate the debt instrument. However, with uncertainty about future interest rates and hence about future prices of bonds, these debt instruments become risky investments in the sense that the return over some investment horizon is unknown.

Similarly, from a borrower's perspective, the cost of borrowing for any required period of financing would be certain and independent of the maturity of the debt instrument if the rate at which the borrower must refinance debt in the future is known. But with uncertainty about future interest rates, the cost of borrowing is uncertain if the borrower must refinance at some time over the period in which the funds are initially needed.

Biased Expectations Theory Biased expectations theories take into account the shortcomings of the pure expectations theory. The two theories are the liquidity theory and the preferred habitat theory.

According to the *liquidity theory*, the forward rates will not be an unbiased estimate of the market's expectations of future interest rates because they embody a premium to compensate for risk; this risk premium is a *liquidity premium*. Therefore, an upward-sloping yield curve may reflect expectations that future interest rates will either rise, fall, or remain the same, but with a liquidity premium increasing fast enough with maturity so as to produce an upward-sloping yield curve.

The *preferred habitat theory* also adopts the view that the term structure reflects the expectation of the future path of interest rates as well as a risk premium. However, the preferred habitat theory rejects the assertion that the risk premium must rise uniformly with maturity. Instead, proponents of the preferred habitat theory say that the latter conclusion could be accepted if all investors intend to liquidate their investment at the first possible date, while all borrowers are eager to borrow long. However, this is an assumption that can be rejected for a number of reasons. The argument is that different financial institutions have different investment horizons and have a preference for the maturities in which they invest. The preference is based on the maturity of their liabilities. To induce a financial institution out of that maturity sector, a premium must be paid. Thus, the forward rates include a liquidity premium and compensation for investors to move out of their preferred maturity sector. Consequently, forward rates do not reflect the market's consensus of future interest rates.

Market Segmentation Theory

The *market segmentation theory* also recognizes that investors have preferred habitats dictated by saving and investment flows. This theory also proposes that the major reason for the shape of the yield curve lies in asset/liability management constraints (either regulatory or self-imposed) and/or creditors restricting their lending or borrowers restricting their financing to specific maturity sectors.

The market segmentation theory differs from the preferred habitat theory because the market segmentation theory assumes that neither investors nor borrowers are willing to shift from one maturity sector to another to take advantage of opportunities arising from differences between expectations and forward rates. Thus, according to the market segmentation theory, the shape of the yield curve is determined by the supply of and the demand for securities within each maturity sector.

SWAP RATE YIELD CURVE

Another benchmark interest rate that is used by global investors is the swap rate. As explained in Chapter 14, in a generic interest rate swap the parties exchange interest payments on specified dates: One party pays interest based on a fixed rate and the other party based on a floating rate over the life of the swap. In a typical swap the floating rate is based on a reference rate and the reference rate is typically LIBOR. The fixed interest rate that is paid by the fixed rate counterparty is the *swap rate*.

The relationship between the swap rate and maturity of a swap is the *swap rate yield curve*, or more commonly the *swap curve*. Because the reference rate is typically LIBOR, the swap curve is also called the *LIBOR curve*.

The swap curve is used as a benchmark in many countries outside the United States. Unlike a country's government bond yield curve, however, the swap curve is not a default-free yield curve. Instead, it reflects the credit risk of the counterparty to an interest rate swap. Because the counterparty to an interest rate swap is typically a bank-related entity, the swap curve reflects the average credit risk of representative banks that provide interest rate swaps. More specifically, a swap curve is viewed as the *interbank yield curve*. It is also referred to as the *AA rated yield curve* because the banks that borrow money from each other at LIBOR have credit ratings of Aa/AA or above.

We see the effect of this credit risk when we compare the yield curve based on U.S. Treasuries with the swap rate curve. For example, consider the rates for August 22, 2008:

	1 yr.	2 yrs.	3 yrs.	4 yrs.	5 yrs.	7 yrs.	10 yrs.	30 yrs.
Yield curve, U.S. Treasuries	2.15%	2.35%	2.62%	NA	3.07%	3.39%	3.82%	4.44%
Swap curve	3.05%	3.38%	3.73%	3.95%	4.10%	4.36%	4.58%	4.92%
Spread in basis points	90	103	111	NA	103	97	76	48

The spread between these two curves ranges from 48 basis points for 30-year yield to 111 basis points for three-year yield.

There are reasons why investors prefer to use a country's swap curve if it available than a country's yield curve obtained from its government bonds.[2]

THE BOTTOM LINE

- In financial markets there is not one interest rate but rather a structure of interest rates that is affected by various risk factors and tax factors. Because a security's value depends, in part, on the expected yield or rate of return investors want, the structure of interest rates affects the value of a security.
- The base interest rate is the sum of the real interest rate and the expected rate of inflation. Because securities issued by the U.S. Department of the Treasury are backed by the full faith and credit of the U.S. government, the interest rate on these securities is viewed as the base interest rate.
- An interest rate reflects the base interest rate and risk. The risk premium is measured using the spread on the yields between a risky security and that of a similar-maturity risk-free security, such as a U.S. Treasury security. Factors that affect the risk premium include the market's perception of the credit risk of the non-Treasury security, any features of the non-Treasury security that make it attractive or unattractive to investors, and the expected liquidity of the non-Treasury issue.
- The term structure of interest rates is the relationship between the yields on comparable securities but different maturities. The yield curve is the graphic that depicts this relationship. The yield curve spread measures the difference in the yield between two maturities. Historically, the yield curve is normally upward sloping, reflecting higher yields for longer-term securities, though flat, humped, and downward sloping yield curves have been observed.
- Forward rates can be extrapolated from the term structure of interest rates to provide valuable information for borrowing strategies and investing strategies. A forward rate is the rate for a future time period. Although market participants often state that forward rates are the market's consensus of future rates, the most useful way to think of these rates is as rates that can be locked in today (that is, hedgeable rates).
- There are two main theories that seek to explain the shape of the yield curve: expectations theory and market segmentation theory. There are

---

[2]For more information, see Uri Ron, "A Practical Guide to Swap Curve Construction," in Frank J. Fabozzi (ed.), *Interest Rate, Term Structure, and Valuation Modeling* (Hoboken, NJ: John Wiley & Sons, 2002).

two forms of the expectations theory: pure expectations theory and biased expectations theory. The theories seek to explain the behavior of short-term forward rates and also assume that the forward rates in current long-term bonds are closely related to the market's expectations about future short-term rates. The two theories as to the extent that factors other than the market's expectations theory, also affect forward rates, and how. According to the pure expectations there are no systematic factors other than expected future short-term rates that affect forward rates; the biased expectations theory asserts that there are other factors such as liquidity (liquidity theory) and the preferred maturity sector of investors (preferred habitat theory). The market segmentation theory assumes that neither investors nor borrowers are willing to shift from one maturity sector to another to take advantage of opportunities arising from differences between expectations and forward rates.

- Another benchmark interest rate used by global investors is the swap rate. The relationship between the swap rate and maturity of a swap is the swap rate yield curve or swap curve. These rates do not reflect default-free rates but rather reflect the average risk of banks that are involved in interest rate swaps.

SOLUTIONS TO TRY IT! PROBLEMS

Credit Spreads

Rated Bond	Yield	Credit Spread
AAA rated	4.92%	119
AA rated	5.43%	170
A rated	5.90%	217
BBB rated	6.32%	259

Equivalent Taxable Yields

Tax-Exempt Yield	Marginal Tax Rate	Equivalent Taxable Yield
5%	40%	8.33%
4%	45%	7.27%
6%	30%	8.57%

Forward Rates

Case	2-Year Rate	1-Year Rate	One-Year Spot Rate One Year from Now
A	5.00%	4.25%	5.76%
B	2.25%	1.75%	2.75%
C	3.00%	2.75%	3.25%
D	4.00%	3.80%	4.20%

QUESTIONS

1. What is the base interest rate?
2. Suppose the yield on a 10-year corporate bond is 6.2% and the yield on a similar-maturity Treasury security is 4.5%.
   a. What is the yield spread for this corporate bond?
   b. Why is there a yield spread between these two securities?
3. How does a conversion provision on a debt obligation provide an option to the investor?
4. If the yield on a Treasury security is 3% and that of a similar-maturity municipal bond is 2.5%, what is the muni-Treasury yield ratio for this municipal bond?
5. Explain the relation between a tax-exempt yield and a taxable yield for bonds with similar maturity and features.
6. What is a maturity spread?
7. If a three-year security has a yield of 5%, and a two-year Treasury security has a yield of 4.5%, what is the one-year forward rate two years from now?
8. What is the shape of the normal yield curve?
9. List the possible explanations for observed yield curves.
10. What is the relevance of the swap rate curve?
11. Typically, how do market participants gauge the credit risk associated with a bond issue?
12. What is the relationship between credit risk and the risk premium?
13. Suppose that the one-year spot rate is 4.1% and the two-year spot rate is 4.6%. What is the one-year forward rate one year from now?
14. Complete the following table:

2-Year Spot Rate	1-Year Spot Rate	1-Year Forward Rate
5%	4%	☐
4%	3.8%	☐
3.5%	3.25%	☐

15. Comment on the following statement: "Forward rates are good predictors of future interest rates."
16. Why can forward rates be viewed as hedgeable rates?
17. Consider the following yields to maturity:

Years to Maturity	Yield to Maturity
1	3.0%
2	3.5%
3	3.9%
4	4.4%
5	4.8%
6	5.2%

   a. Graph the yield to maturity against the time to maturity.
   b. Is this yield curve consistent with any of the yield curve theories? Explain.

18. A corporate treasurer is considering borrowing funds for 10 years. How can the corporate treasurer use forward rates in determining whether to borrow today or postpone borrowing?
19. Why are "biased" expectation theories of the term structure of interest rates biased?
20. Comment on the following: "There is no theory of the term structure of interest rates that would explain a yield curve in which interest rates increase with maturity for the first two years, decline with maturity until year 5, and then increase with maturity after year 5."

CHAPTER 19

Valuing Common Stock

During the 20th Century, the Dow advanced from 66 to 11,497. This gain, though it appears huge, shrinks to 5.3% when compounded annually. An investor who owned the Dow throughout the century would also have received generous dividends for much of the period, but only about 2% or so in the final years. It was a wonderful century.

—Warren Buffett, Letter to Shareholders of
Berkshire Hathaway, February 2008, p. 19

In this chapter, we discuss practical methods of valuing common stock using two methods: discounted cash flow models and relative valuation models. Both methods require strong assumptions and expectations about the future. No one single valuation model or method is perfect. All valuation estimates are subject to model error and estimation error. Nevertheless, investors use these models to help form their expectations about a fair market price.

DISCOUNTED CASH FLOW MODELS

If an investor buys a common stock, he or she has bought shares that represent an ownership interest in the corporation. Shares of common stock are a perpetual security—that is, there is no maturity. The investor who owns shares of common stock has the right to receive a certain portion of any

---

*The section on relative valuation is coauthored with Glen Larsen.

cash dividends—but dividends are not a sure thing. Whether or not a corporation pays dividends is up to its board of directors—the representatives of the common shareholders. Typically, we see some pattern in the dividends companies pay: Dividends are either constant or grow at a constant rate. But there is no guarantee that dividends will be paid in the future.

It is reasonable to figure that what an investor pays for a share of stock should reflect what he or she expects to receive from it—a return on the investor's investment. What an investor receives are cash dividends in the future. How can we relate that return to what a share of common stock is worth? Well, the value of a share of stock should be equal to the present value of all the future cash flows an investor expects to receive from that share. To value stock, therefore, an investor must project future cash flows, which, in turn, means projecting future dividends. This approach to the valuation of common stock is referred to the discounted cash flow approach.

There are various discounted cash flow (DCF) models that we can use to value common stock. We will not describe all of the models. Rather our primary focus is on models that are referred to as dividend discount models.

Dividend Discount Models

Most *dividend discount models* (DDM) use current dividends, some measure of historical or projected dividend growth, and an estimate of the required rate of return. Popular models include the basic dividend discount model that assumes a constant dividend growth and the multiple-phase models. Here we discuss these dividend discount models and their limitations, beginning with a review of the various ways to measure dividends. Then we look at how dividends and stock prices are related.

Dividend Measures Dividends are measured using three different metrics: dividends per share, dividend yield, and dividend payout ratio. The value of a share of stock today is the investors' assessment of today's worth of future cash flows for each share. Because future cash flows to shareholders are dividends, we need a measure of dividends for each share of stock to estimate future cash flows per share.

The *dividends per share* is the dollar amount of dividends paid out during the period per share of common stock:

$$\text{Dividends per share} = \frac{\text{Dividends paid to common shareholders}}{\text{Number of shares of common stock outstanding}}$$

If a company has paid $600,000 in dividends to common shareholders during the period and there are 1.5 million shares of common stock outstanding, then

$$\text{Dividends per share} = \frac{\$600,000}{1,500,000 \text{ shares}} = \$0.40 \text{ per share}$$

The company paid out 40 cents in dividends per common share during this period.

Another measure of dividends is the *dividend yield*, which is the ratio of dividends to the common stock's current price:

$$\text{Dividend yield} = \frac{\text{Annual cash dividends per common share}}{\text{Market price per common share}}$$

We also refer to the dividend yield as the *dividend-price ratio*.[1]

Still another way of describing dividends paid out during a period is to state the dividends as a portion of earnings for the period. This is the *dividend payout ratio*:

$$\text{Dividend payout ratio} = \frac{\text{Dividends paid to common shareholders}}{\text{Earnings available to common shareholders}}$$

If a company pays $360,000 in dividends to common shareholders and has earnings available to common shareholders of $1.2 million, the dividend payout ratio is 30%:

$$\text{Dividend payout ratio} = \frac{\$360,000}{\$1,200,000} = 0.30 \text{ or } 30\%$$

This means that the company paid out 30% of its earnings to common shareholders.[2]

The proportion of earnings paid out in dividends varies by company and industry. If the board of directors of a company focuses on maintaining a constant dividend per share or a constant growth in dividends per share in establishing their dividend policy, the dividend payout ratio will fluctuate along with earnings. We generally observe that corporate boards set the

---

[1] Historically, the dividend yield for U.S. stocks has been a little less than 5% according to a study by John Y. Campbell and Robert J. Shiller, "Valuation Ratios and the Long-Run Stock Market Outlook," *Journal of Portfolio Management* 24(1998): 11–26.

[2] The complement to the dividend payout ratio is the plowback ratio, which is the percentage of earnings retained by the company during the period.

dividend policy such that dividends per share grow at a relatively constant rate, resulting in dividend payouts that fluctuate from year to year.

What is the present value of the future dividend? The quoted price of the ordinary stock at the end of 1873 is the sale value. Is that the mathematical value? This value can only be estimated from prospective dividends, which will turn upon the difference between the income and the outgo through a series of years.

—William Farr, "On the Valuation of Railways Telegraphs, Water Companies, Canals, and other Commercial Concerns, with Prospective, Deferred, Increasing, Decreasing, or Terminating Profits," *Journal of the Royal Statistical Society,* 1876, p. 476

 TRY IT! DIVIDEND MEASURES

Calculate the:

1. Dividends per share
2. Dividend payout ratio, and
3. Dividend yield,

for each of the following companies:

Company	Cash Dividends to Common Shareholders	Number of Shares of Common Stock Outstanding	Earnings Available to Common Shareholders	Current Price per Share
P	$40,000	100,000	$200,000	$20
Q	$800,000	200,000	$4,000,000	$40
R	$250,000	250,000	$750,000	$15
S	$5,000	10,000	$25,000	$10

Basic Dividend Discount Models

As discussed, the basis for the dividend discount model is simply the application of present value analysis, which asserts that the fair price of an asset is the present value of the expected cash flows.[3] The cash flows are the expected dividends per share. We can express the basic DDM mathematically as:

$$P_0 = \frac{D_1}{(1+r_1)^1} + \frac{D_2}{(1+r_2)^2} + \frac{D_3}{(1+r_3)^3} + \cdots$$

or,

$$P_0 = \sum_{t=1}^{\infty} \frac{D_t}{(1+r_t)^t} \tag{19.1}$$

where: P_0 is the current price of the stock,
        D_t is the dividend per share in period t, and
        r_t is the discount rate appropriate for the cash flow in period t.

In this model, we expect to receive dividends. If investors never expected a dividend to be paid, this model implies that the stock would have no value. To reconcile the fact that stocks not paying a current dividend do, in fact, have a positive market value with this model, we must assume that investors expect that someday, at some time N, the company must pay out some cash, even if only a liquidating dividend.

The Finite-Life General Dividend Discount Model   We can modify the DDM given by equation (19.1) by assuming a finite life for the expected cash flows. In this case, the expected cash flows are the expected dividends per share and the expected sale price of the stock at some future date. We refer to this expected price in the future as the terminal price, and it captures the future value of all subsequent dividends. This model is the *finite-life general DDM* and which we can express mathematically as:

$$P_0 = \frac{D_1}{(1+r_1)^1} + \frac{D_2}{(1+r_2)^2} + \cdots + \frac{P_N}{(1+r_N)^N}$$

or

$$P_0 = \left[\sum_{t=1}^{N} \frac{D_t}{(1+r_t)^t} \right] + \frac{P_N}{(1+r_N)^N}$$

where P_N is the expected value of the stock at the end of period N.

---

[3]This model was first suggested by John Burr Williams, *The Theory of Investment Value* (Boston, MA: Harvard University Press, 1938).

Assuming a Constant Discount Rate A special case of the finite-life general DDM that is more commonly used in practice assumes that the discount rate is constant. That is, we assume each r_t is the same for all t. Denoting this constant discount rate by r, the value of a share of stock today becomes:

$$P_0 = \frac{D_1}{(1+r)^1} + \frac{D_2}{(1+r)^2} + \cdots + \frac{P_N}{(1+r)^N}$$

or

$$P_0 = \left[\sum_{t=1}^{N} \frac{D_t}{(1+r)^t} \right] + \frac{P_N}{(1+r)^N} \tag{19.2}$$

Equation (19.2) is the constant discount rate version of the finite-life general DDM, and is the more general form of the model.

Let's illustrate the finite life general DDM based on a constant discount rate, assuming each period is a year. Suppose that an investor makes the following estimates and assumptions for stock XYZ:

- Required rate of return of 10%.
- Current dividend of $2 per share.
- Growth in dividends of 4% per year.
- Expected price of the stock at the end of four years is $29.835.

Based on these data, the fair price of stock XYZ is

$$P_0 = \frac{\$2.08}{(1+0.10)^1} + \frac{\$2.16}{(1+0.10)^2} + \frac{\$2.25}{(1+0.10)^3} + \frac{\$2.34}{(1+0.10)^4} + \frac{\$29.835}{(1+0.10)^4}$$

$$= \$27.34$$

The expected price today, $27.34, is our estimate of the value of a share of the stock based on our estimates and assumptions.

If a little money does not go out, great money will not come in.
—Confucius, philosopher

Required Inputs The finite-life general DDM requires three sets of forecasts as inputs to calculate the fair value of a stock:

- Expected terminal price, P_N;
- Dividends up to the assumed horizon, D_1 to D_N, and
- Discount rates, r_1 to r_N, or r in the case of the constant discount rate version.

Thus, the relevant issue is how accurately these inputs can be forecasted.

The terminal price is the most difficult of the three forecasts. According to theory, P_N is the present value of all future dividends after N; that is, $D_{N+1}, D_{N+2}, \ldots, D_\infty$. Also, we must estimate the discount rate, r. In practice, we make forecasts of either dividends (D_N) or earnings (E_N) first, and then the price P_N based on an "appropriate" requirement for yield, price-earnings ratio, or capitalization rate. Note that the present value of the expected terminal price $P_N \div (1 + r)^N$ becomes very small if N is very large.

The forecasting of dividends is somewhat easier. Usually, information on past dividends is readily available and we can estimate cash flows for a given scenario. The discount rate r is the required rate of return, and forecasting this rate is more complex. In practice for a given company, we assume that r is constant for all periods, and typically estimate this rate from the capital asset pricing model (CAPM). We can use the CAPM to estimate the expected return for a company based on the expected risk-free rate, the expected market risk premium, and the stock's systematic risk, its beta.[4]

EXAMPLE 19.1: ESTIMATING THE DISCOUNT RATE

Consider three companies, A, B, and C. Suppose that

- The market risk premium is 5%, and
- The risk-free rate is 4.63%.

The beta estimate for each company is:

Company	Beta
A	0.9
B	1.0
C	1.2

The discount rate, r, for each company based on the CAPM is therefore:

Company	Beta	Calculation	Discount Rate
A	0.9	$0.0463 + (0.9 \times 0.05)$	9.13%
B	1.0	$0.0463 + (1.0 \times 0.05)$	9.63%
C	1.2	$0.0463 + (1.2 \times 0.05)$	10.63%

---

[4]Using the CAPM, the expected return is the sum of the risk-free rate of interest and a premium for bearing risk. The premium for bearing risk of a specific asset is the product of the asset's beta and the market's risk premium.

Assessing Relative Value Once we have an estimate of a stock's value from using the DDM, where do we go from there? We then compare our estimate of the stock's value with the observed price of the stock, if this price is readily available. If the market price is below the fair price derived from the model, the stock is undervalued or cheap. The opposite holds for a stock whose market price is greater than the model-derived price. In this case, the stock is said to be overvalued or expensive. A stock trading equal to or close to its fair price is fairly valued.

The use of the DDM tells us the relative value but does not tell us when the price of the stock should be expected to move to its fair price. That is, the model says that based on the inputs generated by the investor, the stock may be cheap, expensive, or fair. However, it does not tell us that if it is mispriced how long it will take before the market recognizes the mispricing and corrects it. As a result, an investor may hold onto a stock perceived to be cheap for an extended period of time and may underperform during that period.

While a stock may be mispriced, an investor must also consider how mispriced it is in order to take the appropriate action (that is, buy a cheap stock and expect to sell it when the price rises, or sell short an expensive stock expecting its price to decline). This will depend on by how much the stock is trading from its fair value and transaction costs. An investor should also consider that a stock may look as if it is mispriced (based on the estimates and the model), but this may be the result of estimates and the use of these estimates in the model may introduce error in the valuation.

Constant Growth Dividend Discount Model If we assume that future dividends grow at a constant rate, g, and we use a single discount rate, r, the finite-life general DDM assuming a constant growth rate given by equation (19.2) becomes:

$$P_0 = \frac{D_0(1+g)^1}{(1+r)^1} + \frac{D_0(1+g)^2}{(1+r)^2} + \cdots + \frac{D_0(1+g)^N}{(1+r)^N} + \frac{P_N}{(1+r)^N}$$

It can be shown that if N is assumed to approach infinity, this equation is equal to:

$$P_0 = \frac{D_0(1+g)}{r-g} \tag{19.3}$$

Equation (19.3) is the *constant growth dividend discount model*.[5] Therefore, the greater the expected growth rate of dividends, the greater the estimated value of a share of stock.

---

[5]Myron Gordon and Eli Shapiro, "Capital Equipment Analysis: The Required Rate of Profit," *Management Science* 3 (1956): 102–110.

How do we estimate g? If we believe that dividends will grow in the future at a similar rate as they grew in the past, we can estimate the dividend growth rate by using the compounded rate of growth of historical dividends. The compound growth rate, g, is found using the following formula:[6]

$$g = \left(\sqrt[\text{Number of years}]{\frac{\text{Last year's dividend}}{\text{First year's dividend}}} \right) - 1 \qquad (19.4)$$

Let's estimate the value of a stock, using the past growth as our best estimate of the future growth of dividends. Suppose a company paid $1.50 in dividends in 20X1 and paid $2.00 in dividends in 20X5. Using the time value of money mathematics, the 20X5 dividend is the future value, the starting dividend is the present value, and the number of years is the number of periods; solving for the interest rate produces the growth rate.

Substituting the values for the starting and ending dividend amounts and the number of periods into the formula, we get:

$$g = \left(\sqrt[4]{\frac{\$2.00}{\$1.50}} \right) - 1 = 7.457\%$$

If the discount rate, r, for this company's dividends is 15%, the value of a share of stock in 20X5 is:

$$P_0 = \frac{\$2.00(1 + 0.07457)}{0.15 - 0.07457} = \frac{\$2.14914}{0.07543} = \$28.49$$

Keep in mind that we are valuing this stock as of 20X5, which means that the numerator in this valuation equation is the expected dividend in 20X6, which is the 20X5 dividend multiplied by $1 + g$.

What if you estimate a stock's value and the estimated value is considerably off the mark when compared to the stock's actual price? The reasons for this discrepancy may include:

- The market's expectations of the company's dividend growth pattern may not be for constant growth; and
- The growth rate of dividends in the past may not be representative of what investors expect in the future.

---

[6]This formula is equivalent to calculating the geometric mean of 1 plus the percentage change over the number of years.

Another problem that arises in using the constant growth rate model is that the estimated growth rate of dividends may exceed the discount rate, r. Therefore, there are some cases in which it is inappropriate to use the constant rate DDM.

 TRY IT! THE CONSTANT GROWTH MODEL

Estimate the value of a share of stock for each of the following companies using the constant growth model and estimating the average annual growth rate of dividends from 20X1 through 20X6 as given below as the basis for estimated growth beyond 20X6:

Company	Dividends per Share, 20X1	Dividends per Share, 20X6	Discount Rate
1	$1.00	$1.20	8%
2	$2.00	$1.80	9%
3	$0.50	$0.60	7%
4	$0.25	$0.30	12%

Multiphase Dividend Discount Models   The assumption of constant growth may be unrealistic and can even be misleading. Instead, most practitioners modify the constant growth DDM by assuming that companies will go through different growth phases, but within a given phase, it is assumed that dividends grow at a constant rate.[7]

The most popular multiphase model employed by practitioners appears to be the *three-stage DDM*. This model assumes that all companies go through three phases, analogous to the concept of the product life cycle. In the growth phase, a company experiences rapid earnings growth as it produces new products and expands market share. In the transition phase

---

[7]For a pioneering work that modified the DDM to accommodate different growth rates, see Nicholas Molodovsky, Catherine May, and Sherman Chattiner, "Common Stock Valuation—Principles, Tables, and Applications," *Financial Analysts Journal* 21 (1965): 104–123.

the company's earnings begin to mature and decelerate to the rate of growth of the economy as a whole. At this point, the company is in the maturity phase in which earnings continue to grow at the rate of the general economy.

We can design a three-phase model to fit different growth patterns. For example, an emerging growth company would have a longer growth phase than a more mature company. Some companies are considered to have higher initial growth rates and hence longer growth and transition phases. Other companies may be considered to have lower current growth rates and hence shorter growth and transition phases.

Do you know how to mark tangible assets to their true market value or implement a multistage dividend discount model? Probably not. Why should you? Most people also don't know how to do a coronary bypass or operate a backhoe. That why you hire someone who does.

—Ken Gregory and Steve Savage, "Why We Prefer Funds," *Kiplinger's*, August 2002, p. 59

Expected Returns and Dividend Discount Models

Thus far, we have seen how to calculate the fair price of a stock given the estimates of dividends, discount rates, terminal prices, and growth rates.[8] We then compare the model-derived price to the actual price and the appropriate action is taken.

We can recast the model in terms of expected return. This is found by calculating the interest rate that will make the present value of the expected cash flows equal to the market price. Mathematically, we can express this as:

$$r = \frac{D_0(1+g)}{P_0} + g = \frac{D_1}{P_0} + g \qquad (19.5)$$

In other words, the expected return is the discount rate that equates the present value of the expected future cash flows with the present value

---

[8]The formula for this model can be found in Eric Sorensen and Williamson, "Some Evidence of the Value of Dividend Discount Models," *Financial Analysts Journal* 41 (1985): 60–69.

of the stock. The higher the expected return—for a given set of future cash flows—the lower the current value.

This rearrangement of the dividend discount model provides a perspective on the expected return: the expected return is the sum of the dividend yield (that is, D_1/P_0) and the expected rate of growth of dividends. The latter represents the appreciation (or depreciation, if negative) anticipated for the stock. Therefore, this is the expected capital gain or loss (or, simply, capital yield) on the stock.

Consider a company that currently pays a dividend of $1 per share, has a current share price of $20, and dividends are expected to grow at a rate of 5% per year. Using this information, we estimate the discount rate as 10.25%:

$$r = \frac{\$1(1+0.05)}{\$20} + 0.05 = \frac{\$1.05}{\$20} + 0.05 = 10.25\%$$

Given the expected return and the required return (that is, the value for r), any mispricing can be identified. If the expected return exceeds the required return, then the stock is undervalued; if it is less than the required return then the stock is overvalued. A stock is fairly valued if the expected return is equal to the required return.

With the same set of inputs, the identification of a stock being mispriced or fairly valued will be the same regardless of whether the fair value is determined and compared to the market price or the expected return is calculated and compared to the required return.

 TRY IT! ESTIMATING THE EXPECTED RETURN

Estimate the expected return for each of the following companies:

Company	Current Dividends per Share	Expected Growth Rate of Dividends	Current Value of the Stock
T	$1.00	2%	$25
U	$0.50	3%	$20
V	$1.25	1%	$10
W	$0.25	2%	$15

RELATIVE VALUATION METHODS

Although stock and company valuation is very strongly tilted toward the use of DCF methods, it is impossible to ignore the fact that many investors use other methods to value equity and entire companies. The primary alternative valuation method is the use of multiples (that is, ratios) that have price or value as the numerator and some form of earnings or cash flow generating performance measure for the denominator and that are observable for other similar or like-kind companies.

These multiples are sometimes called "price/X ratios," where the denominator "X" is the appropriate cash flow generating performance measure. For example, the price/earnings (P/E) ratio is a popular multiple used for relative valuation, where an earnings estimate is the cash flow generating performance measure. Keep in mind that the terms relative valuation and valuation by multiples are used interchangeably here as are the terms price and value.

The essence of valuation by multiples assumes that similar or comparable companies are fairly valued in the market. As a result, the scaled price or value (the present value of expected future cash flows) of similar companies should be much the same. That is, comparable companies should have similar price/X ratios. The key is to find the comparable companies that we can use for valuing a target company using valuation by multiples.

Valuation by multiples, or simply relative valuation, is quick and convenient. The simplicity and convenience of valuation by multiples, however, constitute both the appeal of this valuation method and the problems associated with its use. Simplicity, however, means that too many facts are swept under the carpet and too many questions remain unasked. Multiples should never be an investor's only valuation method and preferably not even the primary focus because no two companies, or even groups of companies, are exactly the same. The term "similar" entails just as much uncertainty as the concept of "expected future cash flows" in DCF valuation methods. Actually, when an investor has more than five minutes to value a company, the DCF method, which forces an investor to consider the many aspects of an ongoing concern, is the preferred valuation method and the use of multiples should be secondary.

Having said this, valuation by multiples can provide a valuable "sanity check." If an investor has completed a thorough valuation, he can compare his predicted multiples, such as the P/E ratio and market value to book value (MV/BV) ratio, to representative multiples of similar companies. In the MV/BV ratio, the book value of assets is the cash flow generating performance measure. That is, each dollar of book value of assets is assumed to generate cash flow for the company. If an investor's predicted multiples are comparable, he can, perhaps, feel more assured of the validity of his analysis. On the other hand, if an investor's predicted multiples are out of line with the representative multiples of the market, the investor should re-examine the assumptions, the appropriateness of the comparables, and the appropriateness of the multiple to the situation at hand.

When using relative valuation, an investor does not attempt to explain observed prices of companies. Instead, an investor uses the appropriately scaled average price of similar companies to estimate values without specifying why prices are what they are. That is, the average price of similar companies is scaled by the appropriate "price/X" ratio. In addition, there is nothing to say that multiple price/X ratios can be used or is appropriate for the situation and that each one will generally provide a different estimate of value. Hence, the trick in valuing with multiples is selecting truly comparable companies and choosing the appropriate scaling bases—the appropriate "X" measure.

The Basic Principles of Relative Valuation

To use the word "multiples" is to use a fancy name for market prices divided (or "scaled") by some measure of performance, a "Price/X" ratio where "X" is the measure of performance that is highly correlated with cash flow. In a typical valuation with multiples, the average multiple—the average price scaled (divided) by some measure of performance—is applied to a performance measure of the target company that an investor is attempting to value.

For example, suppose an investor chooses earnings as the scaling measure; that is, the investor chooses earnings to be the performance measure by which prices of similar companies will be scaled. To scale the observed prices of companies by their earnings, the investor computes for each company the ratio of its price to its earnings—its P/E ratio or its earnings multiple. He then averages the individual P/E ratios to estimate a "representative" P/E ratio, or a representative earnings multiple. To value a company, the investor multiplies the projected profits of the company being valued by the representative earnings multiple, the average P/E.

When valuing with multiples, the investor is agnostic regarding what determines prices. This means that there is no theory to guide the investor on how best to scale observed market prices by one of the following: net earnings, earnings before interest and taxes (EBIT), sales, or book value of assets. In practice, this means that valuation with multiples requires the use of several scaling factors or, in other words, several multiples.

Often the best multiples for one industry may not be the preferred multiples in another industry. This implies, for example, that the practice of comparing P/E ratios of companies in different industries is problematic

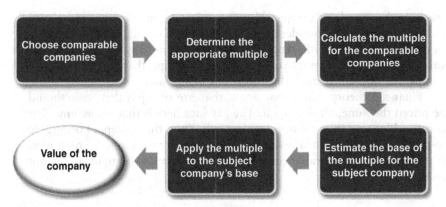

EXHIBIT 19.1   The Process of Relative Valuation

(and in many cases inappropriate altogether). This further implies that when the investor performs a multiple-based valuation, it is important first to find what the industry considers as the best measure of relative values.

Although valuation by multiples differs from valuation by discounting cash flows, its application entails a similar procedure—first projecting performance, and then converting projected performance to values using market prices, as we detail in Exhibit 19.1.

Specifically, if an investor believes, based on a study of comparable companies, that an appropriate forward-looking P/E (or any price/X ratio) for a subject company is 17 and expects earnings to be $3.00 per share in the next period, an estimate of a fair market price based on relative valuation assumptions is:

$$\frac{\text{Appropriate}}{\text{P/E ratio}} \times \frac{\text{Expected}}{\text{earnings}} = 17 \times \$3 = \$51 \text{ per share}$$

Choose Comparable Companies

The whole idea is to estimate a value of the subject company using the multiple implicit in the pricing of the comparable companies. Therefore, we want to select comparable companies that are as similar as possible to the company being valued. The flip side of this argument, however, is that by specifying too stringent criteria for similarity, the investor ends up with too few companies to compare. With a small sample of comparable companies, the idiosyncrasies of individual companies affect the average multiples too much so that the average multiple is no longer a representative multiple. In selecting the sample of comparable companies, the investor has to balance these two conflicting considerations. The idea is to obtain as large a sample as possible so that the idiosyncrasies of a single company do not affect the valuation by much, yet not to choose so large a sample that the "comparable companies" are not comparable to the one being valued.

Financial theory states that assets that are of equivalent risk should be priced the same, all else equal. The key idea here is that we assume that comparable companies are of equivalent risk. Thus, the concept of being able to find comparable companies is the foundation for valuation by multiples. If there are no comparable companies, then valuation by multiples is not an option.

Determine an Appropriate Multiple

To convert market prices of comparable companies to a value for the company being analyzed, an investor has to scale the valued company relative to the comparable companies. This is typically done by using several bases of comparison. Some generic measures of relative size often used in valuation by multiples are sales, gross profits, earnings, and book values.

Often, however, industry-specific multiples are more suitable than generic multiples. Examples of industry-specific multiples are price per restaurant for fast-food chains, paid miles flown for airlines, and price per square foot of floor space for retailers. In general, the higher-up that the scaling basis is in the income statement, the less it is subject to the vagaries of accounting principles. Thus, scaling basis of sales is much less dependent on accounting methods than earnings per share (EPS). For example, depreciation or treatment of convertible securities critically affect EPS calculations, but hardly affect sales. On the other hand, the higher-up that the scaling basis is in the income statement, the less it reflects differences in operating efficiency across companies—differences that critically affect the values of the comparable companies as well as the value of the company being analyzed.

Calculate the Multiple for the Comparable Companies

Once an investor has a sample of companies that he is considering similar to the company being valued, an average of the multiples provides a measure of what investors are willing to pay for comparable companies in order to estimate a "fair" price for the subject company. For example, after dividing each comparable company's share price by its EPS to get individual P/E ratios, the investor can average the P/E ratios of all comparable companies to estimate the earnings multiple that investors think is fair for companies with these characteristics. The same thing can be done for all the scaling bases chosen, calculating a "fair price" per dollar of sales, per restaurant, per square foot of retail space, per dollar of book value of equity, and so on.

Note that we put "fair price" in quotation marks: Because there is no market for either EPS or sales or any other scaling measure, the computation of average multiples is merely a scaling exercise and not an exercise in finding "how much the market is willing to pay for a dollar of earnings." Investors do not want to buy earnings; they only want cash flows (in the form of either dividends or capital gains). Earnings (or sales) are paid for only to the extent that they generate cash. In computing average ratios for various bases, we implicitly assume that the ability of companies to convert each basis (e.g., sales, book value, and earnings) to cash is the same. Keep in mind that this assumption is more tenable in some cases than in others and for some scaling factors than for others.

Realize that we use the term average to mean the appropriate value that is determined by the average company in the comparable group. It may not be the strict average. It may be a mean, median, or mode. The investor is also free to throw out outliers that do not seem to conform to the majority of companies in the group. Outliers are most likely so because the market has determined that they are different for any number of reasons.

Estimate to Base of the Multiple for the Subject Company

Once we have the multiple for the comparable, we apply it to the projected performance of the company that we are valuing. Therefore, the investor needs to project the same measures of the relative size used in scaling the prices of the comparable companies for the company being valued.

Consider an example in which we want to value Company X, using the comparables A, B, and C. And suppose we estimate the average P/E of companies A, B, and C to be 15. If we project earnings per share of Company X as $2, then applying the comparables' multiple of 15 gives us an estimate of the value per share for Company X of $30.

The simplest application of valuation with multiples is by projecting the scaling bases one year forward and applying the average multiple of comparable companies to these projections. For example, the comparable companies' average P/E ratio to the projected next year's earnings of the company being valued is applied. Clearly, by applying the average multiple to the next year's projections, an investor overemphasizes the immediate prospects of the company and gives no weight to more distant prospects.

To overcome this weakness of the one-step-ahead projections, we can use a more sophisticated approach, applying the average multiples to representative projections—projections that better represent the long-term prospects of the company. For example, instead of applying the average P/E ratio to next year's earnings, the comparable P/E ratio to the projected average EPS over the next five years can be projected. In this way, the representative earnings' projections can also capture some of the long-term prospects of the company, while next year's figures (with their idiosyncrasies) do not dominate valuations.

Apply the Multiple to the Subject Company's Base

In the final step, an investor combines the average multiples of comparable companies to the projected parameters of the subject company (i.e., the company to be valued) to obtain an estimated value. On the face of it, this is merely a simple technical step. Yet often it is not. The values that we obtain from various multiples (i.e., by using several scaling bases) are typically not the same; in fact, frequently they are quite different. This means that this step requires some analysis of its own—explaining why valuation by the average P/E ratio yields a lower value than the valuation by the sales multiple (e.g., the valued company has higher than normal selling, general, and administrative expenses) or why the MV/BV ratio yields a relatively

---

 TRY IT! RELATIVE VALUATION

Consider Company RV that has projected earnings per share of $2.5 and a projected book value per share of $20. Determine the estimated value of this Company RV, based on a relative value using:

- The price-earnings ratio, and
- The market value to book value ratio, and

using the average of the respective multiples of the comparables:

Comparable	Value per Share	Earnings per Share	Book Value per Share
X	$15	$1	$10
Y	$32	$2	$8
Z	$60	$5	$40

low value. The combination of several values into a final estimate of value, therefore, requires an economic analysis of both "appropriate" multiples and how multiple-based values should be adjusted to yield values that are economically reasonable.

THE BOTTOM LINE

- The basis for the dividend discount model is simply the application of present value analysis, which asserts that the fair price of an asset is the present value of its expected cash flows.
- Most dividend discount models use current dividends, some measure of historical or projected dividend growth, and an estimate of the required rate of return. The three most common dividend measures are dividends per share, dividend yield, and dividend payout.
- Variations of the dividend discount models allow the investor to vary assumptions regarding dividend growth to accommodate different patterns of dividends. Popular models include the finite-life general dividend discount model, the constant growth dividend discount model, and the multiphase dividend discount model.
- A dividend discount model can be recast in terms of expected return. The expected return is found by calculating the interest rate that will make the present value of the expected cash flows be equal to the market price.
- An alternative valuation method to the dividend discount model is the use of multiples that have price or value as the numerator and some form of earnings or cash flow generating performance measure for the denominator and that are observable for other similar or like-kind companies. These multiples are sometimes called "price/X ratios," where the denominator "X" is the appropriate cash flow generating performance measure.
- The essence of valuation by multiples assumes that similar or comparable companies are valued fairly in the market. When using relative valuation, no attempt is made by an investor to explain observed prices of companies. Rather, an investor employs suitably scaled average prices of similar companies to estimate values without specifying why prices are what they are.
- Despite the fact that valuation by multiples differs from valuation by discounting cash flows, the application entails a similar procedure, which involves first forecasting performance, and then converting projected performance to values using market prices.

SOLUTIONS TO TRY IT! PROBLEMS

Dividend Measures

Company	Dividends per Share	Dividend Payout Ratio	Dividend Yield
P	$1.00	20%	2.00%
Q	$1.00	20%	10.00%
R	$1.00	33%	6.67%
S	$1.00	20%	5.00%

The Constant Growth Model

Company	Dividends per Share, 20X1	Dividends per Share, 20X6	Discount Rate	Estimated Growth Rate	Estimate Value per Share
1	$1.00	$1.20	8%	3.71%	$29.036
2	$2.00	$1.80	9%	−2.09%	$15.899
3	$0.50	$0.60	7%	3.71%	$18.936
4	$0.25	$0.30	12%	3.71%	$3.755

Estimating the Expected Return

Company	Current Dividends per Share	Expected Growth Rate of Dividends	Current Value of the Stock	Discount Rate, r
T	$1.00	2%	$25	6.08%
U	$0.50	3%	$20	5.58%
V	$1.25	1%	$10	13.63%
W	$0.25	2%	$15	3.70%

Relative Valuation

Comparable	P/E	MV/BV
X	15.00	1.5
Y	16.00	4
Z	12.00	1.5
Average	14.33	2.33
Company RV's base	×$2.50	×$20
Estimated value per share	$35.83	$46.67

QUESTIONS

1. If a company maintains a constant rate of growth for the dividends per share that it pays, what is the likely effect on the company's dividend payout ratio?
2. What is the relationship between the discount rate applied to a stock's future cash flows and the value of a stock?
3. If the dividends per share of a stock are not expected to grow, what effect does this have on the valuation of the stock?
4. Suppose the dividends of a company are $2 in one year and $3 three years following. What is the average annual growth in dividends over these three years?
5. In the constant growth dividend discount model, what is the relationship between the required rate of return and the expected growth rate of dividends?
6. If a company's dividends are expected to decline, is it possible to still use the constant growth dividend discount model?
7. What is the relation between the expected return on a stock and the stock's dividend yield?
8. Concerning a dividend valuation model with multiple stages of growth,
   a. Why would an investor use a multiphase dividend discount model?
   b. In a three-phase dividend discount model, what are the three phases?
9. If the average P/E multiple for comparables is 15 and the company you want to value has expected earnings per share of $2, what is the estimate of this company's price per share of stock?
10. Why might you prefer to use a measure of cash flow generating ability such as earnings instead of sales in relative valuation?
11. If an analyst expects a company's dividend to be $2.50 next year, $3 in two years, and then constant at $3.25 forever, what is the value of the company's stock if investors require a return of 8%?
12. If investors expect a return of 12% on a stock that is expected to have a dividend yield of 4% next year, what is the expected growth rate on this stock?
13. Explain whether you agree or disagree with the following statement: "Unlike a dividend discount model, relative valuation seeks to explain the factors that determine the observed value of a share of common stock."
14. To what extent is the procedure similar for valuation based on discounting cash flows and valuation by multiples?
15. In seeking to establish comparable companies in relative valuation analysis, what is the problem with specifying too stringent criteria for companies to be included in the comparable group?

CHAPTER **20**

Valuing Bonds

Investing in junk bonds and investing in stocks are alike in certain ways: Both activities require us to make a price-value calculation and also to scan hundreds of securities to find the very few that have attractive reward/risk ratios. But there are important differences between the two disciplines as well. In stocks, we expect every commitment to work out well because we concentrate on conservatively financed businesses with strong competitive strengths, run by able and honest people. If we buy into these companies at sensible prices, losses should be rare. . . .

Purchasing junk bonds, we are dealing with enterprises that are far more marginal. These businesses are usually overloaded with debt and often operate in industries characterized by low returns on capital. Additionally, the quality of management is sometimes questionable. Management may even have interests that are directly counter to those of debtholders. Therefore, we expect that we will have occasional large losses in junk issues.

—Warren Buffett, Letter to Shareholders of
Berkshire Hathaway, February 21, 2003, p. 16

In this chapter we explain how to determine the price of a bond as well as the relationship between price and yield. Then we discuss various yield measures and their meaning for evaluating the potential performance over some investment horizon. In particular, we explain the various conventions for measuring the yield of a bond and why conventional yield measures fail to identify the potential return from investing in a bond over some investment horizon.

VALUING A BOND

The price of any financial instrument is equal to the present value of the expected cash flows from the financial instrument. Therefore, determining the price requires:

- An estimate of the expected cash flows.
- An estimate of the appropriate required yield.

The expected cash flows for some financial instruments are simple to compute; for others, the task is more difficult. The *required yield* reflects the yield for financial instruments with comparable risk.

The first step in determining the price of a bond is to estimate its cash flows. The cash flows for a bond that the issuer cannot retire prior to its stated maturity date (that is, an option-free bond) consists of:

- Periodic coupon interest payments to the maturity date.
- The par value at maturity.

Our illustrations of bond pricing use three assumptions to simplify the analysis:

- The coupon payments are made every six months. (For most U.S. bond issues, coupon interest is in fact paid semiannually.)
- The next coupon payment for the bond is received exactly six months from now.
- The coupon interest is fixed for the term of the bond.

While our focus in this chapter is on option-free bonds, later in this chapter we explain how to value bonds with embedded options.

Consequently, the cash flows for an option-free bond consist of an annuity of a fixed coupon interest payment paid semiannually and the maturity value. The *maturity value* is the lump-sum payment that represents the repayment of the loaned amount, which we also refer to as the par value or the face value of the bond. For example, a 20-year bond with a 10% coupon rate and a par, or maturity, value of $1,000 has the following cash flows from coupon interest:

$$\text{Annual coupon interest} = \$1,000 \times 0.10 = \$100$$
$$\text{Semiannual coupon interest} = \$100 \div 2 = \$50$$

Therefore, there are 40 semiannual cash flows of $50, and there is a $1,000 cash flow 40 six-month periods from now. Notice the treatment of the par value. It is not treated as if it is received 20 years from now. Instead, it is treated on a basis consistent with the coupon payments, which are semiannual.

The required yield is determined by investigating the yields offered on comparable bonds in the market. In this case, comparable investments would be option-free bonds with the same credit rating and the same maturity. The required yield typically is expressed as an annual interest rate. When the cash flows occur semiannually, the market convention is to use one-half the annual interest rate as the periodic interest rate with which to discount the cash flows.

Given the cash flows of a bond and the required yield, we have all the information needed to price a bond. Because the price of a bond is the present value of the expected cash flows, it is determined by adding these two present values:

- The present value of the semiannual coupon payments.
- The present value of the par, or maturity, value at the maturity date.

In general, we can estimate the value of a bond using the following formula:

$$P = \frac{C}{(1+r)^1} + \frac{C}{(1+r)^2} + \frac{C}{(1+r)^3} + \cdots + \frac{C}{(1+r)^n} + \frac{M}{(1+r)^n}$$

or

$$P = \left(\sum_{t=1}^{n} \frac{C}{(1+r)^t} \right) + \frac{M}{(1+r)^n} \qquad (20.1)$$

where: P is the price in dollars.
       n is the number of periods until maturity, which is the number of years × 2 for a bond that pays interest semiannually.
       C is the coupon payment in dollars per period.
       r is the periodic interest rate, which for a semiannual-pay bond is the required annual yield ÷ 2.
      M is the maturity value.
       t the time period when the cash flow is expected.

The coupon payments are equivalent to an ordinary annuity, so we can estimate the present value of the coupon payments as an ordinary annuity.

Financial calculators and spreadsheets permit us to value a bond in one single calculation, valuing both the annuity portion (i.e., the coupon payments) and the lump-sum payment (i.e., the maturity value) where:

The bond parameter of		In the calculator or spreadsheet as
Coupon payment in dollars per period	C	PMT
Periodic interest rate	i	i
Number of periods until maturity	n	N
Maturity value	M	FV

To illustrate how to compute the price of a bond, consider Bond A, a 20-year 10% coupon bond with a par value of $1,000 and interest paid semiannually.

$$P = \left(\sum_{t=1}^{40} \frac{\$50}{(1+0.055)^t}\right) + \frac{\$1,000}{(1+0.055)^{40}} = \$802.31$$

Let's suppose that the required yield on this bond is 11%. The inputs for a financial calculation to compute the price for this bond are as follows:

$C = 10\% \times \$1,000 \div 2 = \$50$ every six months
$M = \$1,000$
$r = 11\% \div 2 = 5.5\%$ per six-month period
$n = 20 \times 2 = 40$ six-month period

Suppose that instead of an 11% required yield, the required yield is 6.8% ($r = 3.4\%$). The price of the bond would then be $1,347.04, demonstrated as follows: The present value of the cash flows using a periodic interest rate of 3.4% (6.8%/2) is

$$P = \left(\sum_{t=1}^{40} \frac{\$50}{(1+0.034)^t}\right) + \frac{\$1,000}{(1+0.034)^{40}} = \$1,347.04$$

If the required yield is equal to the coupon rate of 10% ($r = 5\%$), the value of the bond would be its par value, $1,000:

$$P = \left(\sum_{t=1}^{40} \frac{\$50}{(1+0.05)^t}\right) + \frac{\$1,000}{(1+0.05)^{40}} = \$1,000$$

With *zero-coupon bonds*, issuers do not make any periodic coupon payments. Instead, the investor realizes interest as the difference between the maturity value and the purchase price. The price of a zero-coupon bond is calculated by substituting zero for C in equation (20.1):

$$P = \frac{M}{(1+r)^n} \qquad (20.2)$$

As we state in equation (20.2), the price of a zero-coupon bond is simply the present value of the maturity value. In the present value computation, however, the number of periods used for discounting is not the number of years to maturity of the bond, but rather, double the number of years. The discount rate is one-half the required annual yield.[1]

EXAMPLE 20.1: VALUING A ZERO-COUPON BOND

Consider a zero-coupon bond that has a maturity value of $1,000, matures in five years, and has a required annual yield of 8%. What is the price of this bond?

Solution

$$P = \frac{\$1,000}{(1+0.04)^{10}} = \$456.387$$

A fundamental property of a bond is that its price changes in the opposite direction from the change in the required yield. The reason is that the price of the bond is the present value of the cash flows. As the required yield increases, the present value of the cash flows decreases; hence, the price decreases. The opposite is true when the required yield decreases: The present value of the cash flows increases, and, therefore, the price of the bond increases. You can see this in Exhibit 20.1, where we show the price of Bond A for a range of required annual yields. Bond A is a 20-year, 10% coupon bond with a maturity value of $1,000. In Exhibit 20.2 we plot the price of the same bond for a range of annual required yields.

---

[1]This may seem counterintuitive because by definition a zero-coupon bond does not pay interest, so a semiannual period is meaningless. However, we use the same convention for zero-coupon bonds as coupon bonds so that the valuation and yields are consistent between the two types of bonds.

EXHIBIT 20.1 The Price-Yield Relationship for Bond A

For a bond with a $1,000 maturity value, 20 years remaining to maturity, and a coupon (paid semiannually) of 10%:

$$C = \$50$$
$$M = \$1,000$$
$$n = 40$$

and therefore:

Required Annual Yield	Price
9.0%	$1,092.01
9.5%	$1,044.41
10.0%	$1,000.00
10.5%	$958.53
11.0%	$919.77
11.5%	$883.50
12.0%	$849.54
12.5%	$817.70

As you can see in Exhibit 20.2, the relationship between the value of the bond and the yield is the bowed shape. In other words, this relationship is *convex*. The convexity of the price/yield relationship has important implications for the investment properties of a bond, as we explain later in this chapter.

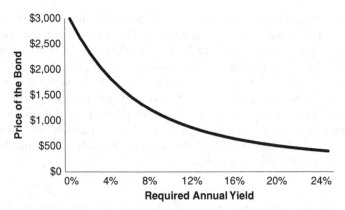

EXHIBIT 20.2 The Price-Yield Relationship over a Wide Range of Required Annual Yields for Bond A

TRY IT! BOND VALUES

For each of the following bonds, calculate the value of the bond. Each bond has a maturity value of $1,000 and pays interest semiannually.

Bond	Coupon Rate	Number of Years to Maturity	Required Annual Yield
A	5%	10	6%
B	6%	20	7%
C	5%	10	4%
D	8.5%	15	7%

Relationship Between Coupon Rate, Yield, and Price

As yields in the marketplace change, the only variable that can change to compensate an investor in an existing bond is the price of that bond. When the coupon rate is equal to the required yield, the price of the bond will be equal to its par value as we found earlier.

When yields in the marketplace rise above the coupon rate at a given point in time, the price of the bond adjusts so that the investor can realize some additional interest. This is accomplished by the price falling below its par value. The capital appreciation realized by holding the bond to maturity represents a form of interest income to the investor to compensate for a coupon rate that is lower than the required yield. When a bond sells below its par value, it is said to be selling at a *discount*. In our earlier calculation of bond price, we saw that when the required yield is greater than the coupon rate, the price of the bond is always lower than the par value ($1,000).

When the required yield in the market is below the coupon rate, the bond must sell above its par value. This is because investors who would have the opportunity to purchase the bond at par value would be getting a coupon rate in excess of what the market requires. As a result, investors would bid up the price of the bond because its yield is so attractive. The price would eventually be bid up to a level where the bond offers the required yield in the market. A bond whose price is above its par value is said to be selling at a *premium*.

The relationship between coupon rate, required yield, and price can be summarized as follows:

If	then	and we refer to this bond as a
Coupon rate < Required yield	Price < Par	discount bond
Coupon rate = Required yield	Price = Par	par bond
Coupon rate > Required rate	Price > Par	premium bond

Relationship Between a Bond's Price and Time

If the required yield does not change between the time the bond is purchased and the maturity date, what will happen to the price of the bond? For a bond selling at par value, the coupon rate is equal to the required yield. As the bond moves closer to maturity, the bond will continue to sell at par value. The price of a bond will not remain constant for a bond selling at a premium or a discount, however. A discount bond's price increases as it approaches maturity, assuming the required yield does not change. For a premium bond, the opposite occurs. For both bonds, the price will equal par value at the maturity date.

Consider Bond B, which has a par value of $1,000, a coupon rate of 5%, and 10 years remaining to maturity. Let's assume that the bond is currently priced by the market so that it has a yield of 8%, and if this yield remains until the bond matures. As we show in Exhibit 20.3, the bond is currently

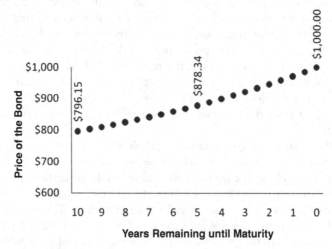

EXHIBIT 20.3   The Price-Time Relationship for a Discount Bond: Bond B (10-Year, 5% Coupon Bond with a Par Value of $1,000 Selling to Yield 8%)

priced at \$796.15. Bond B's price increases as it approaches maturity. If the yield is constant, this path is upward, with a slight curvature.

EXAMPLE 20.2: BOND PRICE OVER TIME

Consider a bond that has a coupon rate of 6% and is priced to yield 8%. If the bond's par value is \$1,000, what is the price of the bond if there is:

a. five years remaining to maturity?
b. 10 years remaining to maturity?
c. 20 years remaining to maturity?

Solution

Inputs:

$$C = \$60/2 = \$30$$
$$M = \$1,000$$
$$r = 8\%/2 = 4\%$$

a. \$918.89
b. \$864.10
c. \$902.07

A bond currently selling for a premium approaches its maturity value from above. Consider Bond C, which is similar to Bond B with a 5% annual coupon rate but is currently priced to yield 4%. In contrast to Bond B, which is a discount bond, Bond C is a premium bond. As you can see in Exhibit 20.4, the price of this premium bond will decline over time as the bond approaches its maturity.

Reasons for the Change in the Price of a Bond

The price of a bond will change for one or more of the following three reasons:

1. There is a change in the required yield due to changes in the credit quality of the issuer. That is, the required yield changes because the

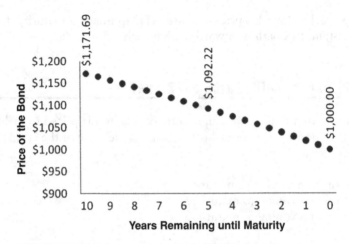

EXHIBIT 20.4   The Price-Time Relationship for a Premium Bond: Bond C (10-Year, 5% Coupon Bond with a Par Value of $1,000 Selling to Yield 4%)

market now compares the bond yield with yields from a different set of bonds with the same credit risk.

2. There is a change in the price of the bond selling at a premium or a discount without any change in the required yield, simply because the bond is moving toward maturity.

3. There is a change in the required yield due to a change in the yield on comparable bonds. That is, market interest rates change.

Different Discount Rates Apply to Each Cash Flow   So far, we've assumed that it is appropriate to discount each cash flow using the same discount rate. However, we can view a bond as a package of zero-coupon bonds, in which case a unique discount rate should be used to determine the present value of each cash flow. This means discounting each cash flow at the spot rate for the period when the cash flow is expected to be received. That is, we use the yield on a two-year zero-coupon bond to discount the cash flow that occurs two years from now, we use the yield on a three-year zero-coupon bond to discount the cash flows that occurs three years from now, and so on.

Consider Bond D that has a 5% semiannual coupon, three years remaining to maturity, and a par value of $1,000. And suppose we have the following set of spot rates for each six-month range of maturity:

Maturity	Spot Rate (Annualized)
6 months	4.5%
1 year	5.0%
1.5 years	5.5%
2 years	6.0%
2.5 years	6.5%
3 years	7.0%

If we apply these rates instead of a fixed discount yield, such as 6%, we arrive at a different value for the bond, as we show in Exhibit 20.5. In this exhibit, we show that that the price of the bond is higher using the spot rates from an upward-sloping yield curve, as compared to using the average of the rates (i.e., 6%) or the three-year spot rate of 7%.

Price Quotes We have assumed in our illustrations that the maturity, or par, value of a bond is $1,000. A bond may have a maturity, or par, value greater or less than $1,000. Consequently, when quoting bond prices, traders quote the price as a percentage of par value. A bond selling at par value is quoted as 100, meaning 100% of its par value. A bond selling at a discount will be selling for less than 100; a bond selling at a premium will be selling for more than 100.

The procedure for converting a price quote to a dollar price is as follows:

(Price per $100 of par value ÷ 100) × Par value

For example, if a bond is quoted at 96.5 and has a par value of $100,000, then the dollar price is

$$(96.5 \div 100) \times \$100,000 = \$96,500$$

EXHIBIT 20.5 Valuing a Bond Using Different Spot Rates: Bond D (3-Year, 10% Coupon Bond with a Par Value of $1,000)

Period	Cash Flow	Discounted at 6%	Discounted at 7%	Spot Rate (Annualized)	Discounted Using a Set of Spot Rates
6 months	$25	$24.27	$24.15	4.5%	$24.45
1 year	25	$23.56	$23.34	5.0%	$23.80
1.5 years	25	$22.88	$22.55	5.5%	$23.05
2 years	25	$22.21	$21.79	6.0%	$22.21
2.5 years	25	$21.57	$21.05	6.5%	$21.31
3 years	1,025	$858.42	$833.84	7.0%	$833.84
Value of Bond D		$972.91	$946.71		$948.65

If a bond is quoted at 103.59375 and has a par value of $1 million, then the dollar price is:

$$\text{Dollar value} = (103.59375 \div 100) \times \$1,000,000 = \$1,035,937.50$$

When an investor purchases a bond between coupon payments, the investor must compensate the seller for the accrued interest.[2]

CONVENTIONAL YIELD MEASURES

Related to the price of a bond is its yield. We calculate the price of a bond from the expected cash flows and the required yield. We calculate the yield of a bond from the expected cash flows and the market price plus accrued interest. In this section, we discuss various yield measures and their meaning for evaluating the relative attractiveness of a bond.

There are three bond yield measures commonly quoted by dealers and used by portfolio managers: (1) current yield, (2) yield to maturity, and (3) yield to call. In our illustrations below we assume that the next coupon payment is six months from now and therefore there is no accrued interest.

Current Yield The *current yield* relates the annual coupon interest to the market price. The formula for the current yield is:

$$\text{Current yield} = \frac{\text{Annual dollar coupon}}{\text{Price}}$$

For example, the current yield for a 15-year, 7% coupon bond with a par value of $1,000 selling for $769.40 is 9.1%:

$$\text{Current yield} = \frac{\$70}{\$769} = 9.1\%$$

The current yield calculation takes into account only the coupon interest and no other source of return that will affect an investor's yield. No consideration is given to the capital gain that the investor will realize when

---

[2]We do not delve into the nuances of valuing a bond with accrued interest. Fortunately, you can use specific spreadsheet functions and financial calculator functions to value bonds between interest payments.

a bond is purchased at a discount and held to maturity; nor is there any recognition of the capital loss that the investor will realize if a bond purchased at a premium is held to maturity. The time value of money is also ignored.

Yield to Maturity   The *yield to maturity* is the interest rate that will make the present value of a bond's remaining cash flows (if held to maturity) equal to the price (plus accrued interest, if any). Mathematically, we solve for the yield to maturity, YTM, using the same formula we used for the value of a bond—but this time we know the value and are solving for *r*. For a bond that pays interest semiannually and that has no accrued interest, we solve for *r* using:

$$P = \left(\sum_{t=1}^{n} \frac{C}{(1+r)^t} \right) + \frac{M}{(1+r)^n}$$

Because the cash flows are every six months, the rate that we solve for is *r*, which is a semiannual yield to maturity. Once we solve for *r*, we need to convert this into an annual yield. We have two choices for annualizing this yield: (1) doubling the semiannual yield or (2) compounding the yield. The market convention is to annualize the semiannual yield by simply doubling its value. The yield to maturity computed on the basis of this market convention of doubling the yield is the *bond-equivalent yield*. We also refer to it as the yield on a *bond-equivalent basis*.

There is not direct solution for *r*, so we need to resort to an iterative procedure. To illustrate the computation, consider Bond E, a 15-year, 7% coupon bond with a maturity value of $1,000. Using a financial calculator or a spreadsheet,

PMT = $35
N = 30
FV = $1,000
PV = $769.40

Solving for *r*, we get 5%. Therefore the yield to maturity is 5% × 2 = 10%.

We show the yield to maturity for different prices of Bond E in Exhibit 20.6. For example, if the price of Bond E is $1,000, the yield to maturity is the coupon rate, 7%, whereas if the price of Bond E is $1,200, the yield to maturity is 5.1%.

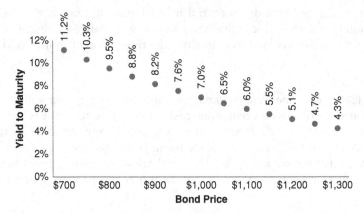

EXHIBIT 20.6 Yield to Maturity for Different Prices of Bond E (15-Year, 7% Coupon Bond with a Maturity Value of $1,000)

It is important to know the relation between the price and par value and the various yield measures discussed earlier we know:

A bond selling at:	therefore has:
Par	Coupon rate = Current yield = Yield to maturity
Discount	Coupon rate < Current yield < Yield to maturity
Premium	Coupon rate > Current yield > Yield to maturity

The yield-to-maturity calculation takes into account not only the current coupon income but also any capital gain or loss the investor will realize by holding the bond to maturity. In addition, the yield to maturity considers the timing of the cash flows. We show the relationship between the yield to maturity and the current yield for Bond E for different prices of the bond

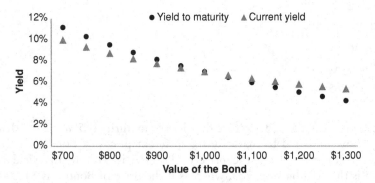

EXHIBIT 20.7 Yield to Maturity and Current Yield for Different Prices of Bond E

in Exhibit 20.7. Both the yield to maturity and the current yield decline for higher bond prices, but you can see the effects of the time value of money on the curvature of the yield-price relationship for the yield to maturity.

EXAMPLE 20.3: YIELDS

Consider a bond that has a coupon rate of 5%, with interest paid semi-annually, that matures in 10 years. If the current price of the bond is $975 and the maturity value of the bond is $1,000, what is the yield to maturity and current yield on this bond?

Solution

For the yield to maturity, solve the following for r and then multiply by 2:

$$\$975 = \left(\sum_{t=1}^{20} \frac{\$25}{(1+r)^t} \right) + \frac{\$1,000}{(1+r)^{20}}$$

$r = 2.663\%$. Therefore the yield to maturity is 5.326%.

For the current yield, the annual coupon is $50, which we divide by $975. Therefore, the current yield is 5.12%.

TRY IT! YIELDS

Calculate the yield to maturity and the current yield for each of the following bonds:

Bond	Coupon Rate	Number of Years to Maturity	Price
E	5.0%	5	$1,000
F	6.0%	10	$900
G	5.0%	15	$1,200
H	8.5%	20	$750

Yield to Call   The issuer may be entitled to call a bond prior to the stated maturity date. When the bond may be called and at what price is specified in the indenture. The price at which the issuer may call the bond is referred to as is the *call price*. For some issues, the call price is the same regardless of when the issue is called. For other callable issues, the call price depends on when the issue is called. That is, there is a *call schedule* that specifies a call price for each call date.

For callable issues, the practice has been to calculate a *yield to call* as well as a yield to maturity. The yield to call assumes that the issuer will call the bond at some assumed call date, and the call price is then the call price specified in the call schedule. Typically, investors calculate a *yield to first call* and a *yield to par call*. The yield to first call assumes that the issue will be called on the first call date. The yield to first par call assumes that the issue will be called the first time on the call schedule when the issuer is entitled to call the bond at par value.

The procedure for calculating the yield to any assumed call date is the same as for any yield calculation: Determine the interest rate that will make the present value of the expected cash flows equal to the price plus accrued interest. In the case of yield to first call, the expected cash flows are the coupon payments to the first call date and the corresponding call price. For the yield to first par call, the expected cash flows are the coupon payments to the first date at which the issuer may call the bond at par.

Mathematically, we can express the yield to call as:

$$P = \left(\sum_{t=1}^{n^*} \frac{C}{(1+r)^t} \right) + \frac{M^*}{(1+r)^{n^*}}$$

where M^* is the call price and n^* is the number of periods to the call date. If the coupon is paid semiannually, we first calculate r and then multiply this rate by 2 to arrive at the yield to call, YTC.

To illustrate the computation, consider Bond F, an 18-year, 11% coupon bond with a maturity value of $1,000 selling for $1,168.97. Suppose that the first call date is 13 years from now and that the call price is $1,055. The cash flows for this bond if it is called in 13 years consist of

- 26 coupon payments of $55 every six months and
- $1,055 due in 26 six-month periods from now.

We first solve for r that equates the current value of the bond with the expected cash flows, and then multiply this rate by 2:

$$\$1,168.97 = \left(\sum_{t=1}^{26} \frac{\$55}{(1+r)^t} \right) + \frac{\$1,055}{(1+r)^{26}}$$

Using a financial calculator or a spreadsheet, the inputs are:

PV = $1,168.97
FV = $1,055
PMT = $55
N = 26

In this case, that six-month rate is 4.5%. Therefore, the yield to first call on a bond-equivalent basis is 9%.

Investors typically compute both the yield to call and the yield to maturity for a callable bond selling at a premium. They then select the lower of the two as the yield measure. The lowest yield based on every possible call date and the yield to maturity is referred to as the *yield to worst*.

TRY IT! YIELD TO WORST

Estimate the yield to worst for the following callable bonds

Bond	Coupon Rate	Current Price	Number of Years to Maturity	Number of Years to First Call	Call Price at First Call
1	5%	$1,100	10	5	$1,000
2	6%	$1,000	20	10	$1,000
3	5%	$1,050	5	2	$1,010
4	7%	$1,100	15	5	$1,050

Potential Sources of a Bond's Dollar Return

An investor who purchases a bond can expect to receive a dollar return from one or more of these sources:

1. The periodic coupon interest payments made by the issuer.
2. Income from reinvestment of the periodic interest payments (the interest-on-interest component).
3. Any capital gain (or capital loss—negative dollar return) when the bond matures, is called, or is sold.

Any measure of a bond's potential yield should take into consideration each of these three potential sources of return. The current yield considers only the coupon interest payments. No consideration is given to any capital gain (or loss) or to interest-on-interest.

The yield to maturity takes into account coupon interest and any capital gain or loss. It also considers the interest-on-interest component; implicit in the yield-to-maturity computation, however, is the assumption that the coupon payments can be reinvested at the computed yield to maturity. The yield to maturity, therefore, is a promised yield; that is, it will be realized only if (1) the bond is held to maturity and (2) the coupon interest payments are reinvested at the yield to maturity. If either (1) or (2) does not occur, the actual yield realized by an investor can be greater than or less than the yield to maturity when the bond is purchased.

The yield to call also takes into account all three potential sources of return. In this case, the assumption is that the coupon payments can be reinvested at the computed yield to call. Therefore, the yield-to-call measure suffers from the same drawback inherent in the implicit assumption of the reinvestment rate for the coupon interest payments. Also, it assumes that the bond will be held until the assumed call date, at which time the bond will be called.

The Yield to Maturity and Reinvestment Risk

The yield-to-maturity measure assumes that the reinvestment rate is the yield to maturity. For example, let's consider Bond G, which has five years remaining to maturity and an 8% coupon. And let's further assume that Bond G has a maturity value of $1,000 and a current market price of $923. The yield to maturity for this bond is 10%.

Let's look at the potential total dollar return from holding this bond to maturity, which we detail in Exhibit 20.8. As mentioned earlier, the dollar return comes from three sources. In our example:

Cash flows from interest	$400
Capital gain	77
Interest on interest, from reinvesting the interest every six months at 10%	103
Dollar return	$580

The potential dollar return if the coupons can be reinvested at the yield to maturity of 10% is then $580. In other words, the investor invests $923

EXHIBIT 20.8 The Dollar Return on Bond G (5-Year, 8% Coupon, Selling at $923)

Assuming all cash flows are reinvested at 10% per year (or 5% every six months)

Six-Month Period	Cash Flow	Future Value of Cash Flow
1	$40	$62.05
2	$40	$59.10
3	$40	$56.28
4	$40	$53.60
5	$40	$51.05
6	$40	$48.62
7	$40	$46.31
8	$40	$44.10
9	$40	$42.00
10	$1,040	$1,040.00
	$1,400	$1,503.00
Present value of bond	$923	
Yield	10%	

and then has something worth $1,503 at the end of five years. The return on this investment, using the inputs:

$$PV = \$923$$
$$FV = \$1,503$$
$$N = 5$$

is 10% per year.

So an investor who invests $923 for five years at 10% per year (5% semiannually) expects to receive at the end of five years the initial investment plus $580. This is precisely what we found by breaking down the dollar return on the bond, assuming a reinvestment rate equal to the yield to maturity of 10%.

The investor will realize the yield to maturity at the time of purchase only if the bond is held to maturity and the coupon payments can be reinvested at the yield to maturity. The risk that the investor faces is that future reinvestment rates will be less than the yield to maturity at the time the bond is purchased. This risk is called *reinvestment risk*.

Two characteristics of a bond determine the importance of the interest-on-interest component and, therefore, the degree of reinvestment risk: the length of time to maturity and the coupon rate.

For a given yield to maturity and a given coupon rate, the longer the maturity, the more dependent the bond's total dollar return is on the interest-on-interest component in order to realize the yield to maturity at the time of purchase. In other words, the longer the maturity, the greater the reinvestment risk. The implication is that the yield-to-maturity measure for long-term coupon bonds tells little about the potential yield that an investor may realize if the bond is held to maturity. For long-term bonds, the interest-on-interest component may be as high as 80% of the bond's potential total dollar return.

Turning to the coupon rate, for a given maturity and a given yield to maturity, the higher the coupon rate, the more dependent the bond's total dollar return will be on the reinvestment of the coupon payments in order to produce the yield to maturity anticipated at the time of purchase. This means that when maturity and yield to maturity are held constant, premium bonds are more dependent on the interest-on-interest component than are bonds selling at par.

Discount bonds are less dependent on the interest-on-interest component than are bonds selling at par. For zero-coupon bonds, none of the bond's total dollar return is dependent on the interest-on-interest component. So a zero-coupon bond has no reinvestment risk if held to maturity. Thus, the yield earned on a zero-coupon bond held to maturity is equal to the promised yield to maturity.

VALUING BONDS THAT HAVE EMBEDDED OPTIONS

Our approach to valuation so far has focused on option-free bonds. That is, we've been dealing with bonds whose bond agreement provisions do not grant the issuer or the bondholder the option to alter the maturity date or exchange the bond for another type of financial instrument. Hence, assuming the issuer does not default, it is rather straightforward to estimate the cash flows.

Bond valuation becomes more difficult when either the issuer or bondholder has an option to either alter the maturity of the bond or to convert the bond into another security. We refer to bonds that have one or more such options as bonds with *embedded options*. These bonds include callable bonds, putable bonds, and convertible bonds.

- A *callable bond* is a bond issue that grants the issuer the right to retire (that is, call) the bond issue prior to the stated maturity date.
- A *putable bond* is a bond issue that grants the bondholder the right to have the issuer retire the bond issue prior to the stated maturity date.

- In the case of a *convertible bond*, the bondholder has the right to convert the bond issue into the issuer's common stock. Moreover, all convertible bonds are callable and some are putable.

There are sectors of the bond market that have even more complex structures that make valuation harder because it is difficult to estimate the bond's future cash flows. For example, a major sector of the bond market is the market for securities backed by residential mortgage loans, called *mortgage-backed securities*. The cash flows for these securities are monthly and include the interest payment, the scheduled principal repayment, and any amount in excess of the scheduled principal repayment. It is this last component of a mortgage-backed security's cash flows—the payment in excess of the regularly scheduled principal payment—that makes it difficult to project cash flows. This component of the cash flow is called a *prepayment*.

The right of homeowners whose mortgage loan is included in the pool of loans backing the mortgage-backed security to prepay their loan at any time in whole or in part is an option. That option is effectively equivalent to the option in a callable bond because the borrower will find it attractive to make prepayments when mortgage rates in the market decline below the borrower's loan rate.

In addition, there are securities that are backed by loans that are not residential mortgage loans. These securities are referred to as *asset-backed securities*. The structure of these securities is complex due to potential defaults, uncertain recovery rates, and potential prepayments, which cause uncertainty in the amount and timing of the cash flows. We won't go into the valuation of these securities here, but, needless to say, these valuations are complex.

A key factor determining whether the bond issuer in the case of a callable bond or the bondholder in the case of a putable bond would exercise an option to alter the maturity date is the prevailing level of interest rates relative to the bond's coupon rate. Specifically, for a callable bond, if the prevailing market rate that the issuer can realize by retiring the outstanding bond issue and issuing a new bond issue is sufficiently below the outstanding bond issue's coupon rate so as to justify the costs associated with refunding the issue, the issuer is likely to call the issue. For a putable bond, if the interest rate on comparable bonds in the market rises such that the value of the putable bond falls below the value at which it must be repurchased by the issuer (i.e., the put price), then the investor will put the issue.

What this means is that to properly estimate the cash flows of a bond with an embedded option, we need to incorporate into the analysis how interest rates can change in the future and how such changes affect the cash flows. This is done in more complicated bond valuation models. Practitioners commonly use two models in such cases: the lattice model and the Monte Carlo simulation model. The lattice model is used to value callable bonds and putable bonds.[3] The Monte Carlo simulation model is used to value mortgage-backed securities and certain types of asset-backed securities.

The lattice model and the Monte Carlo simulation model are beyond the scope of this book. What is important to understand is that these valuation models use the principles of valuation described earlier in this chapter. Basically, these models look at possible paths that interest rates can take in the future and what the bond's value would be on a given interest rate path. A bond's value is then an average of these possible interest rate path values.

Valuing Convertible Bonds

A convertible bond is a bond that can be converted into common stock at the option of the bondholder. The conversion provision of a convertible bond grants the bondholder the right to convert the bond into a predetermined number of shares of common stock of the issuer. A convertible bond is, therefore, a bond with an embedded call option to buy the common stock of the issuer.

In illustrating the calculation of the various concepts described next, we will use a convertible bond issue of Company H, which has a coupon of 5% and matures in 30 years. For this convertible bond issue, the market price of the bond is 80, or $800 for each $1,000 par value. Therefore, the yield to maturity on for this bond is 6.528%.

The *conversion ratio* is the number of shares of common stock that the bondholder will receive from exercising the call option of a convertible bond. The conversion privilege may extend for all or only some portion of the bond's life, and the stated conversion ratio may fall over time. For the Company H convertible issue, suppose the conversion ratio is 150 shares. This means that for each $1,000 of par value of this issue the bondholder exchanges for Company H common stock, 150 shares will be received.

At the time of issuance of a convertible bond, the issuer effectively grants the bondholder the right to purchase the common stock at a price equal to:

$$P = \frac{\text{Par value of the convertible bond}}{\text{Conversion ratio}}$$

---

[3]The lattice model for valuing bonds with embedded options was developed in Andrew J. Kalotay, George O. Williams, and Frank J. Fabozzi, "A Model for the Valuation of Bonds and Embedded Options," *Financial Analysts Journal* 49 (1993): 35–46.

In the prospectus, this price is referred to as the *stated conversion price*. The stated conversion price for the convertible issue of Company H per $1,000 par value is:

$$\text{Stated conversion price} = \frac{\$1,000}{150 \text{ shares}} = \$6.67 \text{ per share}$$

There are two approaches to valuation of convertible bonds: the traditional approach and the option-based approach. The latter approach uses the option pricing models to value a convertible bond and will not be discussed in this chapter. The traditional approach makes no attempt to value the option that the bondholder has been granted.

Traditional Value of Convertible Bonds The *conversion value*, or *parity value*, of a convertible bond is its value if it is converted immediately. That is,

$$\frac{\text{Conversion}}{\text{value}} = \frac{\text{Market price of}}{\text{common stock}} \times \frac{\text{Conversion}}{\text{ratio}}$$

The minimum price of a convertible bond is the greater of its:

- Conversion value, or
- Value as a bond without the conversion option—that is, based on the convertible bond's cash flows if not converted.

This second value is the bond's *straight value* or *investment value*. To estimate the straight value, we must determine the required yield on a nonconvertible bond with the same credit rating and similar investment characteristics. Given this estimated required yield, the straight value is then the present value of the bond's cash flows using this yield to discount the cash flows.

If the convertible bond does not sell for the greater of these two values, arbitrage profits could be realized. For example, suppose the conversion value is greater than the straight value, and the bond trades at its straight value. An investor can buy the convertible bond at the straight value and convert it. By doing so, the investor realizes a gain equal to the difference between the conversion value and the straight value. Suppose, instead, the straight value is greater than the conversion value, and the bond trades at its conversion value. By buying the convertible bond at the conversion value, the investor will realize a higher yield than a comparable straight bond.

Suppose Company H's stock price was $5. For the convertible issue, the conversion value per $1,000 of par value is therefore:

$$\text{Conversion value} = \$5 \times 150 = \$750$$

The straight value, using a discount rate of 6.53% for theoretical purposes only, is $800. Because the minimum value of the Bond H convertible issue is the greater of the conversion value and the straight value, the minimum value, or floor, is $800. We show this valuation graphically in Exhibit 20.9. The value of the bond as a straight bond is $800 for all values of Company H's stock. The conversion value of the bond follows the straight line upward, increasing as the price of the stock increases.

The price an investor effectively pays for the common stock if the convertible bond is purchased in the market and then converted into the common stock is the *market conversion price* (also called the *conversion parity price*):

$$\text{Market conversion price} = \frac{\text{Market price of the convertible bond}}{\text{Conversion ratio}}$$

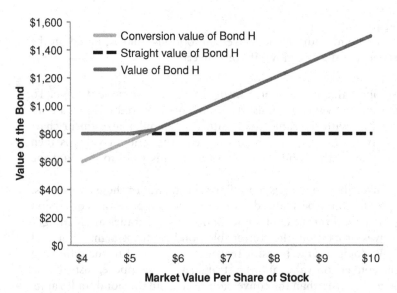

EXHIBIT 20.9   Value of the Convertible Bond of Company H for Different Market Prices of Company H Stock

In other words, if an investor bought Bond H for $800, he or she could exchange it for 150 shares worth $5 × 150 = $750. But the investor is not likely to convert the bond at this stock price and would therefore hold onto the bond that is worth $800. The market conversion price for Bond H, assuming the market price is its straight bond at $800, is $800 ÷ 150 = $5.333.

The value of the convertible bond, which is the greater of the conversion value or the straight value, follows the thicker line that begins at $800 and then increases once the price of the stock is beyond the market conversion price of $5.333, as we show in Exhibit 20.9.

The market conversion price is a useful benchmark because, once the actual market price of the stock rises above the market conversion price, any further stock price increase is certain to increase the value of the convertible bond by at least the same percentage. Therefore, the market conversion price can be viewed as a break-even point.

An investor who purchases a convertible bond rather than the underlying stock pays a premium over the current market price of the stock. This premium per share, which we refer to as the *market conversion premium per share*, is the difference between the market conversion price and the current market price of the common stock. That is,

$$\begin{array}{c}\text{Market conversion} \\ \text{premium per share}\end{array} = \begin{array}{c}\text{Market conversion} \\ \text{price}\end{array} - \begin{array}{c}\text{Current market} \\ \text{price}\end{array}$$

We usually express the market conversion premium per share as a percentage of the current market price:

$$\begin{array}{c}\text{Market conversion} \\ \text{premium ratio}\end{array} = \frac{\text{Market conversion premium per share}}{\text{Market price of common stock}}$$

EXAMPLE 20.4: CONVERTIBLE MEASURES FOR THE CONVERTIBLE BOND OF COMPANY H

$$\text{Market conversion price} = \frac{\$800}{150 \text{ shares}} = \$5.333 \text{ per share}$$

Market conversion premium per share = $5.333 − $5 = $0.333

$$\text{Market conversion premium ratio} = \frac{\$0.333}{\$5} = 6.66\%$$

Why would someone be willing to pay a premium to buy the stock? Recall that the minimum price of a convertible bond is the greater of its conversion value or its straight value. Thus, as the common stock price declines, the price of the convertible bond will not fall below its straight value. The straight value therefore acts as a floor for the convertible bond's price.

Viewed in this context, the market conversion premium per share can be seen as the price of a call option. The buyer of a call option—in this case, the investor in the convertible bond—limits the downside risk to the option price. The difference between the buyer of a call option and the buyer of a convertible bond is that the former knows precisely the dollar amount of the downside risk, while the latter knows only that the most that can be lost is the difference between the convertible bond's price and the straight value. The straight value at some future date, however, is unknown; the value will change as interest rates in the economy change.

The investment characteristics of a convertible bond depend on the common stock price. If the price is low, so that the straight value is considerably higher than the conversion value, the bond will trade much like a straight bond. The convertible bond in such instances is referred to as a *fixed income equivalent* or a *busted convertible*.

When the price of the stock is such that the conversion value is considerably higher than the straight value, then the convertible bond will trade as if it were an equity instrument; in this case, it is said to be a *common stock equivalent*. In such cases, the market conversion premium per share will be small.

Between these two cases, fixed income equivalent and common stock equivalent, the convertible bond trades as a *hybrid security*, having the characteristics of both a bond and common stock.

THE BOTTOM LINE

- The value of a bond is the present value of its expected coupon payments and the bond's maturity value, discounted at the bond's required yield.
- A fundamental property of a bond is that its price changes in the opposite direction from the change in the required yield. The value of a bond also changes with time, approaching its maturity value as the bond matures.
- Whether a bond trades at a discount or a premium to its maturity (par) value depends on the relationship between the coupon rate of the bond and the yield that the market requires on the bond. When the required yield in the market is below the coupon rate, the bond trades above its par value. When the required yield in the market is above the coupon rate, the bond trades below its par value. A bond trades at its par value when the coupon rate is equal to the yield required by the market.

- The three bond yield measures commonly quoted in the market are the current yield, yield to maturity, and yield to call.
- The dollar return from investing in a bond comes from one or more of the following three sources: (1) periodic coupon interest payments, (2) reinvestment income, and (3) any capital gain (or capital loss—negative dollar return) when the bond matures, is called, or is sold.
- A limitation of the yield-to-maturity measure is that it assumes that reinvestment income (interest on interest) will be generated by reinvesting the periodic coupon income at a yield equal to the computed yield to maturity. Reinvestment risk is the risk that coupon income will be reinvested at a lower rate than the computed yield to maturity.
- The valuation of a bond that has an embedded option, such as a callable, putable, or convertible bond, is more complex than an option-free bond because the option affects the bond's value.
- The value of a convertible bond is the greater of its straight value or its conversion value.

SOLUTIONS TO TRY IT! PROBLEMS

Bond Values

Bond	Value
A	$925.61
B	$893.22
C	$1,081.76
D	$1,137.94

Yields

Bond	Yield to Maturity	Current Yield
E	5.00%	5.00%
F	7.44%	6.67%
G	3.30%	4.17%
H	11.78%	11.33%

Yield to Worst

Bond	Yield to Maturity	Yield to Call	Yield to Worst
1	3.8%	2.8%	2.8%
2	6.0%	6.0%	6.0%
3	3.9%	2.9%	2.9%
4	6.0%	5.6%	5.6%

QUESTIONS

1. List the four inputs needed to value a bond.
2. When valuing a zero-coupon bond, why are semiannual periods used in discounting?
3. Describe the relationship between the price of a bond and the yield to maturity of the bond.
4. Suppose a bond has a coupon rate of 6% and a yield to maturity of 8%. Will this bond be priced as a discount bond or a premium bond? Explain.
5. Why may a bond's price change simply because of the passage of time?
6. What is the difference between a bond's current yield and its yield to maturity?
7. What is the yield to worst?
8. Concerning reinvestment of interest on a bond,
   a. What assumption is made about reinvestment of cash flows when using the yield to maturity?
   b. What characteristics of a bond affect its reinvestment risk?
9. If a bond is putable, what type of option does the investor in this bond have?
10. Suppose a bond has a market price of $90 and has five years remaining to maturity. If the bond is priced to yield 5%, is its coupon rate greater than, less than, or equal to 5%? Explain your reasoning.
11. Complete the following table, providing the dollar price of the following bonds:

Market Price	Par Value	Dollar Price
$94.0	$1,000	☐
$102.00	$100,000	☐
$75.50	$10,000	☐
$86.40	$1,000,000	☐

12. Consider a bond with coupon rate of 7% and a par value of $1,000. The maturity for this bond is greater than one year. Also assume that the required yield by the market for this bond is 8%. For the following three bond prices, explain why the bond may or may not trade at the respective price.
    a. $1,200
    b. $1,000
    c. $900

13. Suppose that two years ago a 10-year bond in your portfolio was selling for $1,100. Today, the same bond is selling for $1,050. You have researched the price of 10-year bonds of the same credit rating over the past two years and found that interest rates have declined. Explain why the bond's price declined despite the fact that 10-year interest rates have declined.

14. Which of the following two bonds has greater reinvestment risk: a 10-year 8% coupon bond or a 25-year zero-coupon bond? Why?

15. Why is it difficult to value a callable bond?

16. If a convertible bond has a value as a straight bond of $1,100 and a conversion value of $1,050, at what price will this bond trade? Why?

Solutions to End of Chapter Questions

CHAPTER 1

1. Financial management is the management of resources of a business entity, whereas investment management is the management of investments in a portfolio that is managed for an individual, an institution, or an entity.
2. The discount rate is the interest rate that translates future cash flows from an investment into a value today.
3. The responsibilities include managing the portfolio to be consistent with the beneficiary's investment objectives, constraints, and tax situation, while also considering legal constraints.
4. Capital budgeting is decision-making pertaining to long term investments, whereas capital structure is the mix of long-term sources of funding.
5. Current assets are assets of an entity that can reasonably be converted to cash within one operating cycle or one year, whichever is longer.
6.
   a. No. An investor cannot consistently earn abnormal profits in an efficient market.
   b. If a market is efficient, passive portfolio management is best.
7. The financing decision involves determining the form of the financing (debt or stock), the tenor (that is, the maturity) of the obligations the company wishes to take on, and the terms (e.g., the interest rate on the debt or the number of shares of stock).
8. Identify risk, assess it, and attempt to mitigate it and/or transfer it.
9. Enterprise risk management is the management of the risks for an entity as a whole.
10. Set objectives, establish investment policy, select an investment strategy, select specific assets, measure performance.

Solutions to End of Chapter Questions

CHAPTER 2

1. In the case of indebtedness, the borrower has a contractual commitment to repay the amount borrowed and interest. Equity is an ownership interest and the expectation of a return on the investment is in the form of dividends and any price appreciation.
2. Preferred stock is equity, but it is a fixed income security. Preferred stock may or may not have a fixed term.
3. Mutual funds take funds from investors and then invest these funds in a group of investments.
4. Maturity intermediation is the conversion of assets or securities with short-term maturities into assets or securities with longer-term maturities, or vice versa.
5. The Securities and Exchange Commission (SEC), Commodity Futures Trading Commission (CFTC), and Financial Industry Regulatory Authority (FINRA).
6. Examples: Commercial paper, Treasury bills, negotiable certificates of deposit, bankers' acceptance, repurchase agreements.
7. An exchange has a physical presence, whereas an over-the-counter market is a network of dealer or market makers.
8. Weak form (prices reflect past price information), semi-strong form (prices reflect public information), and strong form (prices reflect public and private information).
9. In a primary market, the issuer obtains funds from investors; in the secondary market, the issuer of the security is not involved in the transaction.
10. A spot market is a cash market, for an exchange today. A derivatives market involves trading in securities whose value depends on some asset's value of cash flows.

11. The money market is the market for securities with a maturity of one year or less. The capital market is the market for securities with maturities of greater than one year and for securities with no maturity (that is, perpetual securities, such as common stock).

12. An investor's strategy is affected by the degree of efficiency in the market because this dictates what is impounded in a security's price. If the market is only weak form efficient, then trading on the basic of publicly available information could generate abnormal profits; but if the market is semi-strong efficient, there would be no incentive to trade on publicly available information.

13.
   a. Information is asymmetric if there some market participants have more information than others that is relevant to the valuation of an asset.
   b. If market participants believe that some other participants have an unfair advantage in terms of relevant information, they may not trade, resulting in less liquidity in the market.
   c. As intermediaries, banks have served a role of providing information to market participants.
   d. Price discovery is the process of determining the value of an asset through the trading among buyers and sellers.
   e. Without the flow of information relevant to value an asset, there may not be ready buyers and sellers and, hence, trading leading to price discovery.

14.
   a. The information costs of financial assets are the costs of securing information necessary for the valuation of the assets.
   b. A market is liquid if there are buyers and sellers ready to trade an asset.
   c. Innovative products may involve complexities that are difficult to understand and may impose more information costs to properly value the products.

15.
   a. Standardization reduces the complexity of the various financial assets, and hence reduces information costs.
   b. Lowering information costs results in more participation by buyers and sellers, and hence more price discovery and liquidity.

Solutions to End of Chapter Questions

CHAPTER 3

1. The federal government, the state and local governments, government-sponsored enterprises, and government-owned corporations.
2. Government-owned corporations do not have publicly-traded stock and are operated as not-for-profit entities. GSEs are owned by shareholders and operate for a profit.
3. Both lend funds to individuals and businesses, but nondepository institutions do not accept deposits, whereas depository institutions do accept deposits.
4. Required reserves are the minimum reserves required to be held by banks, whereas excess reserves are the amount by which actual reserves exceed required reserves.
5. Life insurance, health insurance, property-casualty insurance, liability insurance, disability insurance, long-term care insurance, structured sellements, investment-oriented products, and financial guarantee insurance.
6. A mutual fund will accept additional funds for investment, whereas a closed-end fund does not.
7. Net asset value = ($1 − 0.2) ÷ 0.5 = $1.60.
8. Can trade throughout the trading day, prices have only small deviations from net asset value, and tax advantages.
9. In a defined benefit plan, the plan sponsor commits to a specific amount of benefit upon retirement. In a defined contribution plan, the plan sponsor commits to a specific contribution to the employee's retirement plan, but not to a specific benefit amount upon retirement.
10. Assist companies in raising funds, trading securities, advising in mergers and acquisitions (among other transactions), merchant banking, and providing brokerage services.

11. Depository institutions: commercial banks, savings and loan associations, savings banks, and credit unions.
12. Commercial banks obtain most of their funds by borrowing, including accepting deposits (e.g., checking accounts, savings accounts, time deposits, and money market accounts). These banks also obtain funds by issuing securities (debt and equity), and borrowing from the Federal Reserve.
13. Financial restructuring advising is guidance to company on its financing and capital structure, its operating structure, or its strategy. This advising may seek to simply improve the company's operations or, in the extreme, to forestall a bankruptcy.
14.
    a. Global banking is the area of finance that involves financing of entities, restructuring, and mergers and acquisitions. This is an area in which commercial banks and investment banks compete.
    b. Global wealth and investment management involves investment policies, investment strategies, selection of investments, and evaluating investments' performance.
15. Proprietary trading is trading for a company's own account. Financial intermediaries may generate income from commissions when they facilitate trades, but in proprietary trading these institutions do not generate commission income, but rather are investing on their own account in the expectation of generating gain (though losses are also possible).
16.
    a. Merchant banking is the investment by a financial institution in companies, typically involving an equity interest.
    b. The risks of merchant banking include the risk of loss of value, the difficulty in valuing investments (especially those of privately-held investments), and the lack of liquidity associated with some types of merchant banking activity.

Solutions to End of Chapter Questions

CHAPTER 4

1. Assets = Liabilities + Equity.
2. (1) transactions are recorded at historical cost; (2) the dollar is the appropriate unit of measure; (3) statements are prepared using the accrual basis and the matching principle; (4) the business will continue as a going concern; (5) there is full disclosure; and (6) the statements are prepared on the basis of conservatism.
3. Cash, marketable securities inventory, and accounts receivable.
4. The length of time it takes for an investment in inventory to return cash in the form of accounts collected from customers.
5. Accounts payable, wages payable, current portion of long-term debt, and short-term bank loans.
6. In the balance sheet, retained earnings are the accumulation of earnings that have not been paid out in the form of dividends to owners. In connection to the income statement, retained earnings are earnings, less dividends.
7. Neither. The minority interest is the equity in a company that represents the portion of the company not owned by the parent company. For reporting purposes, the minority interest appears in shareholders' equity.
8. Basic EPS is net income to common shareholders, divided by the average shares outstanding. Diluted EPS is net income to common shareholders, adjusted, dividend by the potential shares outstanding considering stock options and other dilutions, for example, from convertible shares.
9. Under MACRS, the tax liability is less than that reported in the financial statements, so the deferred tax liability represents the tax obligation in the future, which will be paid as MACRS depreciation becomes less than straight-line.

10. The sum is the change in the balance of cash from the previous fiscal period to the current fiscal period.

11. Historical costs are the actual expenditures made for an asset. For example, a building's value on the balance sheet in gross plant and equipment is its cost at the time of the company bought it or built it. Depreciation on the building is based on the original cost, so that the building's value in net plant and equipment reflects its original cost, less depreciation.

12. The footnotes that accompany the financial statements provide more information on deferred taxes. The footnote that is often entitled "Income taxes" provides information about the company's tax liability, tax expense, and, if relevant, deferred taxes.

13. All in millions
    a. Current assets = $6,076 + 25,371 + 11,192 + 717 + 2,213 + 3,711 = $49,280
    b. Total assets = $49,280 + 7,535 + 4,933 + 12,503 + 1,759 + 279 + 1,599 = $77,888
    c. Total liabilities = $3,324 + 2,000 + 3,156 + 725 + 13,003 + 1,684 + 3,142 + 3,746 + 1,281 + 6,269 =$38,330
    d. Stockholders' equity = $62,382 −22,824 = $39,558
    e. Total liabilities, plus stockholders' equity = $38,330 + 39,558 = $77,888
    Note:
    Assets = Liabilities + Stockholders' equity
    $77,888 = $38,330 + 39,558

14.
    a. Both Basic EPS and Diluted EPS are presented to provide information to investors regarding the earnings per share given the current shares outstanding (Basic EPS), and the earnings per share that would be if all potential shares (e.g., from exercise of executive stock options, any warrant exercise, and any convertible debt conversion) were issued (Diluted EPS). Diluted EPS is a "worst case scenario" EPS in terms of possible dilution from additional issuance of shares.
    b. Basic EPS means the earnings per share based on the current shares outstanding (using a weighted average of shares outstanding during the period the earnings were earned.
    c. Diluted EPS means the earnings per share based on the potential shares outstanding given all possible dilutions.
    d. The closeness of Basic EPS and Diluted EPS indicates that there is little potential for dilution.

15.
   a. The Financial Accounting Standards Board (FASB) is the standard-setting body for U.S. accounting.
   b. The International Financial Reporting Standards (IFRS) are the accounting standards accepted in many countries outside the U.S. These standards are promulgated by the International Accounting Standards Board (IASB). Eventually, the U.S. GAAP and IFRS will converge to one set of standards.
   c. Generally accepted accounting principles (GAAP) are a set of standards that are the accepted standards for accounting. U.S. GAAP is the set of standards promulgated by the Financial Accounting Standards Board (FASB).

Solutions to End of Chapter Questions

CHAPTER 5

1. Two primary differences: (1) A partnership is taxed only at the partner level, whereas the corporation is taxed at the corporate and shareholder levels; (2) A partnership has more limited access to funds than a corporation.
2. Limited liability is the legal situation in which the owners of a company are not liable for all of the debts of the business. In the case of a corporation or an LLC, which both have limited liability, the most owners can lose is their investment in the business.
3. (1) At the corporate level, and (2) At the shareholder level on distributed income in the form of cash dividends.
4. A corporation and an LLC may have perpetual lives.
5. Agency costs of costs borne by the agent, the principal, or both. For example, in the agency relationship in a corporation, the principals (the shareholders) bear the cost of excessive perquisite consumption by management.
6. The objective is to maximize the value of the shareholders' interest in the company.
7. Salary, bonus, options, performance shares.
8. Options are intended to encourage managers to be concerned about the value of the stock of the company because the greater the value of the stock, the greater the value of the executive stock options.
9. This provision represents the bonding costs; the manager bears a cost in terms of future benefit from working for the company's competitors following employment by the company.
10. If earnings are understated in one period, they are likely overstated. By moving expenses sooner, for example, the expenses in the following period(s) are less and, hence, earnings are more.

11. A company's market capitalization is the market value of its stock. This is the product of the current market price per share and the number of shares of stock outstanding.

12.
   a. With a C corporation, income is taxed at the corporate level (with the company's filing of its tax Form 1020), and then once again when it is distributed to shareholders in the form of dividends (if the shareholders are individuals, then the dividend income is reported on the individuals' tax Form 1040).
   b. The advantages are primarily the single level of taxation and the limited liability.

13.
   a. Agency costs are costs (explicit or implicit) that arise when the parties—the agent acting in the interests of the principal, and the principal—diverge.
   b. Principals can reduce agency costs by "bonding"; that is, making commitments that would be costly if interests diverge (e.g., a non-compete clause if the manager leaves the employment of the company).

14.
   a. Limited liability is the limit on the financial responsibility of a party to the obligations of an entity.
   b. Agree: The limited liability imposes a burden on the creditors because they may not receive the full amount that they are due if the fund is bankrupt. Disagree: Though the limited liability imposes a burden, the additional risk provides a potential for additional rewards, which would in that case offer more protection of the interests of the creditors.
   c. The seeking of short-term gains at the expense of long-term value and risks would be a form of agency costs. The motives of a fund manager to be "competitive" and perhaps even affect short-term compensation are self-serving motives.
   d. Stakeholders are any party affected by the actions of another. In the case of the management of funds, the stakeholders include not only the fund beneficiaries, but any party that becomes obligated to make up short-falls, anyone employed by the charity that may lose their job, anyone whose services are curtailed because of a lack of funds.

Solutions to End of Chapter Questions

CHAPTER 6

1. A strategy is the general direction a company takes for reaching an objective.
2. Comparative advantages relate to cost structure and product differentiation, whereas competitive advantages relate to market structure.
3. A strategic plan is the specific actions or roadmap a company intends to take to reach an objective.
4. A financial plan relates to the allocation of company resources and a plan of how the company will finance its investment decisions. A financial plan is one component in a company's strategic plan.
5. Regression analysis is a statistical approach to estimating the historical relation between two or more factors. It is useful to gauge general relationships that existed in the past, and is useful, to some extent, in forecasting.
6. A pro forma financial statement is a projected financial statement, based on sales and cash forecasting.
7. Economic value added is economic profit. Financial managers, who seek to maximize shareholder wealth, are interested in making decisions that enhance the value of the firm, and hence add economic value.
8. A balanced scorecard is a set of measures used to evaluate different aspects of a company's performance.
9. Significant profits and low barriers of entry will attract entrants. In terms of Porter's forces, the threat of entrants is high and, hence, there is significant rivalry.
10. Economic profits arise from a comparative or competitive advantage.

11.

   a. A strategic plan is designed to guide the company towards its objectives, assisting management in both the operational and the financial decision-making in a business entity.

   b. The strategic plan is useful in guiding decision-making, but conditions change, requiring adjustments in this plan. Financial decision-making is dynamic, and strategic plans must evolve through time.

12.

   a. Strategic planning is a plan to achieve a company's objectives. Financial planning is a component of strategic planning, used in conjunction with budgets and performance metrics.

   b. Financial planning involves budgeting (including sales projections and projections of financing needs) and performance measurement.

   c. Operational planning is the budgeting and evaluation of day-to-day operations, including a focus on management of operating expenses and short-term financing needs to support operations.

   d. Capital allocation refers to the long-term investment of a company in plant, property, and equipment.

   e. Agree: A financial plan is not meaningful without a strategy because you do not know the targets that help guide the decision-making.

13.

   a. EVA is economic value added, a measure of economic profit that considers not only revenues and expenditures, but also the cost of capital. Economic value added is calculated as revenues, less expenditures and taxes on a cash basis, less the dollar value of the cost of capital.

   b. EVA is a branded version of the economic construct of profit.

14.

   a. The balanced scorecard provides multiple dimensions for evaluating performance.

   b. The four new processes are: (1) understanding the strategy, (2) communicating and linking measures to the company's strategy, (3) planning, budgeting and target setting, and (4) providing feedback on performance.

Solutions to End of Chapter Questions

CHAPTER 7

1. The dividend payout ratio is the *proportion* of earnings paid to shareholders in the form of cash dividends. The dividend per share is the *amount* of dividend paid per share.
2. The retention rate $= 1 - 0.80 = 20\%$.
3. Dividend payout ratio $= \$2 \div \$8 = 25\%$.
4. Low or no transactions costs.
5. Technically, the difference is the accounting entry (shift from retained earnings to paid-in capital for a stock dividend, a memo entry for a stock split). Practically, the size: a stock split is generally used more often for larger distributions, a stock dividend for smaller distributions.
6. A reverse stock split is intended to increase the share price, possibly forestalling delisting from an exchange.
7. A stock split is expected to reduce a share price to a proportion of the predistribution price; a 2:1 should reduce the price to one-half, a 4:1 should reduce the price to 1/4, etc.
8. (1) Signal the future prospects of the company without a cash outlay; and (2) Reduce the price per share.
9. (1) Investors' preference for a stream of certain cash flows; (2) Signal future prospects of the company; (3) Force the company to seek external funds, resulting in increased monitoring of the company.
10. Tender offer & Dutch tender offer; open market repurchase; targeted block repurchase.

11.

Stock	Expected price per share after distribution	Number of shares outstanding after the distribution
ABC	$20 ÷ 2 = $10	1 million × 2 = 2 million
DEF	$40 × 5 = $200	0.5 million ÷ 5 = 0.1 million
GHI	$25 × 2.5 = $62.50	2 million × 2.5 = 5 million

12. Dividends = $50 million; Net income = $200 million; Shares outstanding = 3 million

    a. Dividend payout ratio = $50 million ÷ $200 million = 25%

    b. Dividend per share = $50 million ÷ 3 million = $16.67 per share

13. Retention ratio = 1 − ($2 ÷ $5) = 1 − 0.4 = 0.6 or 60%

14. Growing the dividend over time, when the dividend is based on a relatively fixed dividend payout, can be interpreted as the company's expectation that earnings from continuing operations (that is, before extraordinary and special items) will grow.

15.

    a. (1) A bird-in-the hand—that is, a dividend paid—is worth more than the expectation of an increasing share price. (2) A company paying dividends may be signaling that they are able to sustain the increased dividend payout in the future, and hence are signaling positive expectations about future earnings. (3) The payment of dividends uses funds that could be invested in long-term capital projects, which then forces the company to borrow—hence increasing the monitoring of the company by creditors and investors.

    b. Paying dividends affects only the financing decision, and companies paying dividends will simply need to borrow to fund profitable investment projects. Because the value of a company is the present value of all future cash flows that it generates, the value of the company is affected by the return on its capital projects, not how these projects are financed.

    c. Because dividends are typically taxed at rates higher than capital gains, shareholders who pay taxes should prefer to receive a return on their stock in the form of share appreciation, rather than through dividends.

    d. A perfect capital market is one in which there are no taxes, no transactions costs, no costs for information, and no flotation costs when issuing securities.

    e. The assumed investment policy is one in which the company invests in all profitable projects.

    f. Managers are perfect agents of shareholders if they act in shareholders' best interests, rather than their own. In other words, there are no agency costs.

The Basics of Finance by Pamela Peterson Drake and Frank J. Fabozzi

Solutions to End of Chapter Questions

CHAPTER 8

1. Financial leverage increases the sensitivity of the returns to equity to changes in operating earnings. The greater the financial leverage, the greater the return on equity for earnings beyond break-even, and the lower the return on equity for earnings below break-even earnings.
2. The interest tax shield is the amount of taxes that interest shields from taxation because of the deductibility of interest in determining taxable income.
3. If the marginal tax rate increases, the interest tax shield increases—and hence, the value of this tax shield to owners.
4. A 2% increase in operating earnings will result in a $2\% \times 2 = 4\%$ increase in earnings to owners.
5. Debt financing (1) reduces the funds available that may be wasted, and (2) provides additional monitoring from the market (evaluating a debt issue).
6. Because owners reap the benefits of gains, but do not share fully in the losses, limited liability encourages risk taking.
7. Costs to financial distress discourage debt financing, counterbalancing the benefit from interest deductibility at some point.
8. Interest on debt is tax deductible for the paying company, whereas dividends paid are not tax deductible.
9. The trade-off is between the benefit from interest deductibility and costs of financial distress.
10. The greater a company's operating risk, the sooner the company reaches an optimal capital structure in terms of the proportion of debt used to finance the company.
11. The pecking order theory of capital structure is the theory that states that companies have preference in the capital that they raise, with the

preference order of internal equity (that is, retained earnings), debt, and then new equity.

12. When there are taxes, the Modigliani-Miller theory implies that the optimal capital structure is the one with as much debt as possible—as long as there are no costs associated with financial distress.

13.
   a. Alternative C involves the greatest financial leverage.
   b. Alternative A involves the least financial leverage.

14. Costs associated with financial distress include direct costs, such as legal fees or consulting fees, and indirect costs, including foregone profitable opportunities, a loss of market share or competitive advantage, and the inability to secure long-term contracts.

15. Costs associated with bankruptcy include the direct costs, such as audit and legal fees, and indirect costs, including foregone profitable opportunities, the reduced value of intangibles because of an inability to fully exploit these assets, a loss of market share or competitive advantage, and the inability to secure long-term contracts.

16.
   a. Financial slack is the unused debt capacity of a company.
   b. Financial slack is created when the company intentionally manages its financing activity so that its capital structure is less than what the company can handle.
   c. Companies desire financial slack because it gives them flexibility, the ability to engage in investment opportunities that may come along for which financing is needed to make the investment.

Solutions to End of Chapter Questions

CHAPTER 9

1. Core risks are the business or operating risk that relate to the company's line of business. Non-core risks are those that are incidental to the company's line of business.
2. Portfolio theory focuses the attention on the risk of the whole, rather than on individual investments. Enterprise risk management focuses on the risk of the whole as well.
3. Sustainability risk is a broad spectrum of the risk of a business enterprise that includes social and environmental responsibilities.
4. Retain, neutralize, transfer.
5. A funded retained risk is one in which funds have been set aside to satisfy the potential loss, whereas an unfunded retained risk is one in which no provision has been made for the potential loss.
6. Insurance-linked notes and bonds transfer risk to the investor of the security.
7. Derivatives, insurance, structured finance, and alternative risk transfer (such as an insurance-linked note).
8. The core risk relates to a business's main enterprise, where a noncore risk is incidental to the business.
9. Derivatives can be used to transfer risk, such as using futures contracts to transfer the risk of a commodity's price to another party.
10. A cat bond, or catastrophe-linked bond, transfers the risk of the identified event from the business to investors.
11. Value stocks are generally viewed as those stocks that have market values that currently reflect lower expectations regarding future growth than other stocks in the market (and, hence, lower P/B ratios), and therefore as the P/B returns to normal or typically market levels, the price of the stock will rise.

12.
   a. This statement leaves out an important consideration: the risk of the portfolio (relative to that of the benchmark).
   b. Further evaluation of the return difference is necessary to attribute performance (e.g., to the style of selection).
   c. Leverage can exaggerate returns—both up and down—and must be considered as part of the investment policy.
13. Constraints may be imposed regarding risk, the asset allocation, and the cash flows from the investments.
14. Return = ($3,500 − 3,000 + 250) ÷ $3,000 = 25%
15. Time-weighted return = $[(1.05)(0.97)(1.04)(1.05)]^{0.25} = 1.112202^{0.25}$ − 1 = 2.6942%

Solutions to End of Chapter Questions

CHAPTER 10

1. The discounting is the reverse process of compounding. In compounding, we seek the future value of a lump-sum, whereas in discounting we seek the present value of a lump-sum.
2. Larger.
3. Smaller.
4. Continuous compounding. The greater the frequency of compounding, the greater the future value for a given annual percentage rate.
5. In an ordinary annuity, the first cash flow occurs one period from today (that is, end-of-period cash flows). In an annuity due, the first cash flow occurs today (that is, beginning-of-the-period cash flows).
6. In an ordinary annuity, the first cash flow occurs one period from today (that is, end-of-period cash flows). In a deferred annuity, the first cash flow occurs beyond one period from today.
7. This is a perpetuity. We calculate the present value by dividing the periodic cash flow by the discount rate.
8. The geometric average is most appropriate because it considers compounding. The arithmetic average does not.
9. A deferred annuity can be solved by first solving for the present value of an ordinary annuity, and then discounting this the present. The discounting in the second step may be a lump-sum or an annuity, depending on the nature of the problem.
10. The annuity due will have the higher present value, relative to the ordinary annuity, because each cash flow is received sooner than that of the ordinary cash flow.
11. In general, the investment with compound interest produces a greater value than the investment with the same interest rate but with simple interest. The only exception is in the case of annual compounding and

you are comparing the value of a one-year investment; in this case, the value would be the same.

12.

    a. As long as interest is compounded no more than a single time, at the end of the year, the EAR is equivalent to the APR.

    b. EAR and APR diverge as the frequency of compounding increases. The more frequent the compounding, the more EAR exceeds the APR.

13. For compound interest, $i = 0.04 \div 4 = 0.01$ or 1%; $N = 10 \times 4 = 40$

    a. Balance in the account $= FV = \$1,000 \, (1 + {}^{0.04}/_4)^{40} = \$1,000 \, (1 + 0.01)^{40} = \$1,488.86$.

    b. Interest on interest $= FV_{compound} - FV_{simple}$
$$= \$1,488.86 - [\$1,000 + (10 \times 0.04 \times \$1,000)]$$
$$= \$1,488.86 - 1,400 = \$88.86.$$

14. $PV = \$10,000 \div (1 + 0.06)^5 = \$10,000 \div 1.3382 = \$10,000 \times 0.747258 = \$7,472.58$

15. $PV = \$10,000$; $i = 3\% \div 12 = 0.0025$ or 0.25%

    a. $N = 24$; $PMT = \$429.81$ per month

    b. $N = 36$; $PMT = \$290.81$ per month

Solutions to End of Chapter Questions

CHAPTER 11

1. Both the current ratio and the quick ratio are liquidity measures. The quick ratio removes the least liquid current asset, inventory, from the numerator of the current ratio, providing a more stringent liquidity measure. Numerically, the current ratio is always greater than or equal to the quick ratio at a given point in time.
2. The longer the cash conversion cycle, the greater a company's need for liquidity.
3. A cash conversion cycle may be negative if the company receives more generous credit terms from its suppliers than it provides its customers.
4. The inventory turnover, multiplied by the number of days in inventory, is equal to the number of days in the period.
5. The total asset turnover must be 2.0, based on the Du Pont relationship: net profit margin × total asset turnover = return on assets.
6. If debt ÷ assets = 0.35, this means that equity is 65% of assets, or the debt equity ratio is 0.35 ÷ 0.65 = 0.5385.
7. If the use of debt increases, vis-à-vis equity, then equity multiplier increases and the return on equity increases.
8. If the company does not have any debt, the return on assets is equal to the return on debt.
9. The basic earning power allows you to compare companies without regard to how they chose to finance their operations. This is useful when comparing companies that operate in the same line of business, in which they should experience the same level of business risk.
10. If debt-to-assets is 50%, this means that the equity multiplier is 2 and therefore the return on equity is 20%.
11. Because Company B's quick ratio is greater than Company A's, we can conclude that Company A has relatively more inventory than Company

B. We conclude this because the current ratios are the same, yet Company A's quick ratio is less than Company's B, which indicates that the numerator of the quick ratio has a larger subtraction for inventory in the case of Company A.

12. Company D has a longer operating cycle, and therefore most likely has a greater need for liquidity than Company C. However, Company D does not have more liquidity than Company C, and therefore has more risk of not satisfying its near-term obligations.

13. A return on fixed assets would be a ratio of net income or operating income to fixed assets. You could break this into two components, a fixed asset turnover and a profit margin.

14. It would be useful to have information on the trend in the company's asset turnover, operating profit margin, interest burden, and tax burden. It would also be useful to see if the company's lines of business changed over this period (for example, through acquisitions), that may suggest changes in the company's underlying fundamental relationships.

15.
  a. Current ratio = $2,000 \div $500 = 4$
  b. Quick ratio = $1,000 \div $500 = 2$
  c. Inventory turnover ratio = $10,800 \div $1,000 = 10.8$ times
  d. Total asset turnover ratio = $12,000 \div $6,000 = 2$ times
  e. Gross profit margin = $1,200 \div $12,000 = 10\%$
  f. Operating profit margin = $1,050 \div $12,000 = 8.75\%$
  g. Net profit margin = $600 \div $12,000 = 5\%$
  h. Debt-to-assets ratio = $1,000 \div $6,000 = 0.1667$
  i. Debt-to-equity ratio = $1,000 \div $5,000 = 0.2$
  j. Return on assets, basic earning power = $1,050 \div $6,000 = 17.5\%$
  k. Return on equity = $600 \div $5,000 = 12\%$

16. Company Y has more leverage. Its equity multiplier (that is, total assets divided by shareholders' equity) is 2.0, whereas Company X's equity multiplier is 1.5.

17.

Cash	13.89%	Current liabilities	8.33%
Accounts receivable	8.33%	Long-term debt	25.00%
Inventory	22.22%	Equity	66.67%
Plant & equipment	55.56%		
Total assets	100.00%	Total liabilities and equity	100.00%

Solutions to End of Chapter Questions

CHAPTER 12

1. Depreciation is not a a cash outflow, but rather is a noncash expense that reduced net income. Therefore, depreciation is added back to net income in the calculation of cash flow.
2. The financial statements prepared using accrual accounting reflects non-cash items in income, such as sales on credit. The adjustment for changes in working capital account is done to convert net income based on accrual accounting into cash flow.
3. Net income is $3 million less $2 million, or $1 million.
4. The changes in working capital accounts are used in determining cash flow from operations. The sum of the cash flows from operating, financing, and investment activities is the change in the cash account from one year to the next.
5. Net income from the income statement is the starting point for the cash flow from operations statement of cash flows.
6. Yes, if the depreciation expense, the amortization expense, or the changes in working capital accounts are sufficiently large.
7. Two items: after-tax interest expense and capital expenditures.
8. EBITDA and cash flow from operations differ due to the changes in working capital accounts, interest expense, and taxes.
9. A negative free cash flow indicates that there are no funds that can be invested in value destroying investments.
10. A positive free cash flow indicates that there are funds available that could be invested in value destroying investments.

11. FCFE = $100 million; FCFF = $125 million; Interest after tax = $10.
    From the basic formulas for free cash flow:
    Definition 2: FCFF = CFO − adjusted interest − capital expenditures
    Definition 3: FCFE = CFO − capital expenditures + borrowings − debt repayments
    Therefore, FCFE = FCFF − adjusted interest + borrowings − debt repayments
    $100 million = $125 million − 10 million + borrowings − debt repayments
    Borrowings − debt repayments = −$15
    or, in other words, net debt repayment of $15 million

12. Free cash flow to equity (FCFE) = $200 million − 50 million = $150 million
    Free cash flow to the firm (FCFF) = $200 million − 50 million = $150 million

13. CFO = Net income + depreciation − change in working capital.
    $35 million = $30 million + $3 million − change in working capital
    Change in working capital = −$2 million, which means that working capital investment declined during the period.

14. For fiscal year 20X2, Cash flow = net income + depreciation and amortization − increase in working capital = $290.
    a. Cash flow to capital expenditures = $290 ÷ $100 = 2.9
    b. Using total liabilities as the measure of debt,
       Cash flow to debt ratio = $290 ÷ ($130 + 163) = $290 ÷ $293 = 0.9898

Solutions to End of Chapter Questions

CHAPTER 13

1. By reducing expenses, it increases a company's cash flows. Reducing expenses will increase taxes, but there will be a net benefit from the reduction in expenditures.
2. The depreciation tax shield is the amount of taxes reduced by deducting depreciation. The depreciation tax shield increases available cash flow, and hence makes the project more attractive.
3. If the facility had no other use, this would be a sunk cost and this cost does not affect the investment decision. If the facility could have been used (e.g., rented out), then this forgone rent should be considered in the investment decision.
4. Mathematically, if the project has a positive net present value, it must pay back in terms of undiscounted and discounted cash flows.
5. The difference is a recapture of depreciation, and is taxed as ordinary income.
6. Straight-line depreciation will result in lower depreciation in the earlier years, and hence lower depreciation tax shields, vis-à-vis MACRS depreciation. The lower cash flows earlier in the project's life will reduce its net present value.
7. In the case of mutually exclusive projects, the NPV and PI methods can be used.
8. This means that the discount rate is less than the cross-over rate.
9. If there is a limit to the capital budget, the net present value method is most appropriate.
10. The differing reinvestment assumptions: the NPV method assumes reinvestment at the cost of capital; the IRR method assumes reinvestment at the IRR.

11.

Opening a retail outlet	New market
Introducing a new line of dolls	New product
Introducing a new action figure in an existing line of action figures	New product
Adding pollution control equipment to avoid environmental fines	Mandated
Computerizing the doll molding equipment	Replacement
Introducing a child's version of an existing adult board game	New product

12. Expected sales of the new boots, as well as the potential loss of sales from the existing line of boots.

13. The book value at the end of the 10th year is zero for both machines, so the sales price is equivalent to the gain.

		Machine 1	Machine 2
a.	Acquisition		
	Initial cost	$100,000	$80,000
	Set-up cost	$20,000	$30,000
	Total acquisition cash flow	−$120,000	−$110,000
b.	Disposition		
	Cash from sale	$20,000	$10,000
	Tax on gain	7,000	3,500
	Cash flow from disposition	$13,000	$6,500

14. See the table below for details.

   a. $40.2 million

   b. $11.4 million, $13.320 million, and $12.456 million

   c. $15.984 million

   d. −$40.2 initially, and then $15.4 million, $20.52 million, and $42.632 million

	Year			
	0	1	2	3
Initial cost	−$40,000,000			
Change in working capital	−200,000			$ 200,000
Sale price				25,000,000
Tax on gain on sale				−784,000
Investment cash flows	−$40,200,000	$ 0	$ 0	$24,416,000
Change in revenues		$20,000,000	$20,000,000	$20,000,000
Change in operating costs		5,000,000	5,000,000	5,000,000
Change in depreciation		4,000,000	7,200,000	5,760,000
Change in taxable income		$19,000,000	$22,200,000	$20,760,000
Change in taxes		7,600,000	8,880,000	8,304,000
Change in income after taxes		$11,400,000	$13,320,000	$12,456,000
Add: depreciation		4,000,000	7,200,000	5,760,000
Operating cash flows		$15,400,000	$20,520,000	$18,216,000
Net cash flows	−$40,200,000	$15,400,000	$20,520,000	$42,632,000

Note:

	Year		
	1	2	3
Book value of the jet, end of period	$36,000,000	$28,800,000	$23,040,000
Tax on gain on sale			
Sales price			$25,000,000
Book value			23,040,000
Gain			$ 1,960,000
Tax rate			40%
Tax on gain			$ 784,000

15. This means that if you invest in the project, you expect to increase the value of the company by $10 million.
16. This means that (1) the ratio of the present value of the cash inflows to the present value of the cash outflows is 1.3, and (2) the project has a positive net present value.

17. The profitability index is ($30 + 100) ÷ $100 = 1.3

18.

a.	Payback	= 3 years
b.	Discounted payback at 10%	= 4 years
c.	Discounted payback at 16%	= Does not payback
d.	Net present value at 10%	= $10,945.29
e.	Net present value at 16%	= −$2,063.68
f.	Profitability index at 10%	= 1.11
g.	Profitability index at 16%	= 0.98
h.	Internal rate of return	= 15%
i.	Modified internal rate of return with reinvestment at 0%	
[Terminal value = $140,000]		= 8.8%
j.	Modified internal rate of return with reinvestment at 10%	
[Terminal value = $162,435]		= 12.9%

19.

a. At a cost of capital of 5%, $NPV_{Thing\ 1}$ = $1,677 and $NPV_{Thing\ 2}$ = $2,045. Prefer Thing 2.

b. At a cost of capital of 8%, $NPV_{Thing\ 1}$ = $907 and $NPV_{Thing\ 2}$ = $762. Prefer Thing 1.

c. At a cost of capital of 11%, $NPV_{Thing\ 1}$ = $216 and $NPV_{Thing\ 2}$ = −$356. Prefer Thing 1.

d. At a cost of capital of 14%, $NPV_{Thing\ 1}$ = −$405 and $NPV_{Thing\ 2}$ = −$1,331. Reject both.

e. Cross-over discount rate is 7.09%

f.

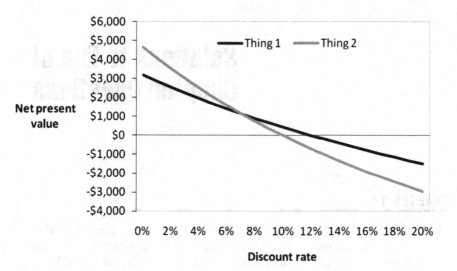

Solutions to End of Chapter Questions

CHAPTER 14

1. In the cash and carry trade, the investor sells futures, buys the asset, financing it, and then delivers it at the end of the contract. In a reverse cash and carry trade, the investor buys futures, sells the asset, and lends the proceeds, taking delivery of the asset at the end of the contract.
2. The profit is zero.
3. Futures and forwards are similar, but futures are standardized contracts and trading involves a clearinghouse, whereas forwards are not standardized and are traded over-the-counter, subject to counterparty risk.
4. The option is out-of-the-money because the underlying's value is less than the exercise price.
5. The payoff is −$5.
6. The greater the time to expiration, the greater the call and the put option—because there is more time remaining for the option to become valuable.
7. The more volatility of the underlying's value, the more valuable both the call and the put option.
8. You could buy a put option or you could sell a call option.
9. You could buy a call option or you could sell a put option.
10. Interest rate swap.
11. In the case of derivatives, there is some underlying that is involved in a potential transaction in the future. For example, in the case of an interest rate swap, there is a future exchange of the net cash flows at each agreed-upon future date. There is risk that one of the parties—the other party, the counterparty—will not comply with the agree-upon exchange at one of the future dates.
12. The manufacturer could enter into a futures contract now to lock in the price of the lumber three months from now. The manufacturer would

be the buyer, with a commitment to take delivery of the lumber at a future point at time at a specified price.

13.

  a. Forward contracts do have the advantage that they can be customized, but unlike futures contracts, there is counterparty risk—the risk that the other party to the transaction does not carry out their obligations under the contract.

  b. A factor to consider is that by tailoring it to the corporation's needs, there must be another party willing to take the other side of the transaction, as tailored as it is.

14. A put option is an option to sell the underlying. A call option is an option to buy the underlying.

15. An American option may be exercised at any time prior to the expiration date. A European option may be exercised only at the expiration date.

16. Disagree. In the case of an option, the buyer of the option has a choice whether to exercise the option. In the case of futures, the buyer is committed to a transaction unless an offsetting transaction is made.

17.

  a. A call option: an option to buy the underlying at a specified price.

  b. A put option: an option to sell the underlying at a specified price.

18. The payoff (that is, profit) for a call option is the price of the underlying − exercise price − option premium; the greater the option premium, the more that the underlying's price must exceed the exercise price for a profit. The payoff (that is, profit) for a put option is the price exercise price − price of the underlying − option premium; the greater the option premium, the more that the price of the underlying must be less than the price of the underlying to be profitable.

19.

  a. intrinsic value = $42 − 40 = $2; time value = $5 − 2 = $3

  b. intrinsic value = $40 − 50 = −$10 → $0; time value = $5 − 0 = $5

20.

  a. Interest rate swap

  b. Orono pays 7% × $75 million = $5,250,000; Portland pays 4% × $75 million = $3,000,000. The net payment (Orono to Portland) is $2,250,000, or 3% of $75 million.

Solutions to End of Chapter Questions

CHAPTER 15

1. Equity; Bonds; Real estate; cash equivalents.
2. Policy asset allocation focuses on the long-term objective, seeking the greatest return for the level of risk consistent with the investment objective. The dynamic asset allocation is the adjustment of the asset mix of a portfolio in response to anticipated market conditions.
3. Market cap is market capitalization, the market value of equity outstanding of a corporation. Some advocate that the returns to stocks of companies with small versus large capitalization are different, and select common stocks appropriate with this belief.
4. An active portfolio strategy involves changing the investments in the portfolio to seek better portfolio returns. A passive portfolio strategy focuses on the initial construction of the portfolio, rather than altering investments. A passive portfolio is consistent with the belief that the markets are efficient, whereas an active portfolio strategy seeks abnormal returns that arise from pricing inefficiencies.
5. A price-efficient market is one in which the current prices of assets reflect all publicly available information.
6. The arithmetic average return ignores compounding of returns from one subperiod to the next.
7. The time-weighted return is better for evaluating a portfolio manager because it is not affected by the contributions and withdrawals of the fund.
8. $R_{TW} = (0.95 \times 1.1 \times 1.1)^{1/3} - 1 = 4.754\%$.
9. PV = $1; FV = $1 × 0.95 × 1.1 × 1.1 = $1.1495; N = 3; IRR = 4.754%.
10. The purpose of performance attribution models is to assess the performance of an investment or fund associated with the selection of investments and the allocation among investments.

11.

    a. Structured insurance is a form of risk transfer that combines traditional insurance with securities, in which investors in the securities bear some of the risk.

    b. Another name for structured insurance is "insurance-linked securities".

    c. An example of structured insurance is the catastrophe-linked bond (or "cat bond").

Solutions to End of Chapter Questions

CHAPTER 16

1. A utility function is a theoretical description of the tradeoff an individual economic agent has between return and risk.
2. If the correlation is positive, the covariance between the two assets' returns is also positive.
3. Diversification is achieved by combining investments whose returns are not perfectly positively correlated. Greater diversification is achieved the lower the correlation.
4. The efficient portfolio is one of the feasible portfolios. It is the feasible portfolio with the highest return for a given level of risk.
5. The semivariance provides information on the dispersion below the mean or expected value, whereas the variance provides information on the dispersion above and below the mean.
6. A safety-first rule is a decision rule that minimizes the probability of falling below a specified value.
7. Prospect theory is a theory of individuals' behavior such that decision-making depends on how a problem is framed, that the focus is on how values change, rather than the values themselves, and that the decision weight given to gains is different than that given to losses.
8. Framing is the situation. Some behavioral theories argue that investors are influenced by the situation or how an investment is presented, rather than simply on an investment's expected return and variance.
9. Classical safety-first, value at risk, conditional value at risk, lower partial moment.
10. A cognitive bias is a bias in decision-making that results from errors in judgment. These errors include framing and overconfidence.

11.
  a. If the covariance is negative, the correlation is negative.
  b. The portfolio's risk will be less than the weighted average of the risks of Asset A and Asset B.

12.
  a. B: same return, lower risk
  b. C: same return, lower risk
  c. C: higher return, lower risk

13.
  a. Expected return is 5%
  b. Standard deviation is 12.247%

Calculations

Scenario	Probability	Possible outcome	Probability weighted outcome	Deviation from the expected value	Squared deviation	Probability weighted squared deviation
Recovers	40%	0.20000	0.08000	0.15000	0.02250	0.00900
Does not recover	60%	−0.05000	−0.03000	−0.10000	0.01000	0.00600
Expected value =		0.05000	0.05000	Variance =	0.01500	
			Standard deviation =		0.12247	

14.
  a. Expected value = 0%
  b. Standard deviation = 15%

Calculations

Scenario	Probability	Possible outcome	Probability weighted outcome	Deviation from the expected value	Squared deviation	Probability weighted squared deviation
Recovers	50%	0.15000	0.07500	0.15000	0.02250	0.01125
Does not recover	50%	−0.15000	−0.07500	−0.15000	0.02250	0.01125
Expected value =		0.00000		Variance =	0.02250	
			Standard deviation =		0.15000	

15. Altering the weights of the securities will change the portfolio risk, similar to Exhibit 16.5, because the weights of the two securities are used in calculation of the variance of the portfolio [see Equation 16.6].

Solutions to End of Chapter Questions

CHAPTER 17

1. Diversifiable risk is the risk that an investor can reduce or eliminate by combining assets in a portfolio such that these assets' returns are not perfectly positively correlated among themselves.

2. In the CAPM, we assume that investors will seek the most return for these least amount of risk. A large component of this is holding a well-diversified portfolio. Therefore, proponents of the CAPM model argue that assets are priced such that investors are only compensated for the risk that they cannot diversify away.

3. This choice cannot be determined without addressing the individual investor's utility function because neither stock dominates the other in terms of risk and return.

4. In pricing assets, only the nondiversifiable risk is compensated.

5. This is the market risk premium. This is the expected risk premium for the market as a whole.

6. Beta is the sensitivity (a.k.a. elasticity) of a stock's return to changes in the return on the market.

7. It means that Asset A has more systematic risk than Asset B. However, it does not mean that Asset A necessarily has more risk (systematic plus unsystematic) than Asset B.

8. The capital market line is the relation between expected return and risk, as measured by variance. The security market line is the relation between expected return and systematic risk, as represented by beta.

9. Plotting above the security market line means that the stock is undervalued: bidding up the stock's price will reduce its return, forcing it on the SML.

10. Expected return $= 0.02 + 1.2(0.10 - 0.02) = 0.02 + 0.096 = 11.6\%$.

11. An efficient portfolio in the presence of a risk free asset is formed by combining an investment in the market portfolio with either an investment in the risk-free asset or borrowing at the risk-free rate.

12. The CAPM cannot be tested unless we specify the correct market portfolio, which is the value-weighted portfolio of all risky assets.

13. The assumption regarding borrowing and lending at the risk-free rate of interest is questionable because investors cannot borrow at the risk free rate.

14. The homogeneous assumption in the CAPM is the assumption that all investors perceive the same expected return and risk associated with the assets.

15. The law of one price implies that assets that have similar payoffs, both in terms of expected returns and risk, should be priced the same; if they are not priced the same, there is an arbitrage opportunity.

16. The fundamental principles of the APT model are that asset prices are determined by one or more factors and that returns on assets are driven by unanticipated changes in these factors.

17. The APT is more general because it allows for the possibility of more than one factor to affect asset prices (that is, it is a multifactor model), and the APT does not require specifying a market portfolio.

18. The APT factors are unknown, and therefore cannot be adequately tested.

19.

   a. Disagree: Unsystematic risk is nearly eliminated in a diversified portfolio, whereas the unsystematic risk of an individual asset in the portfolio may be significant.

   b. Disagree: Investors are compensated only for the risk that they cannot get rid of; investors are not compensated for diversifiable (that is, unsystematic) risk because they could reduce it if they wished to by diversifying.

20. Disagree. As with the CAPM, investors are not compensated for risk that they could remove but choose not to.

Solutions to End of Chapter Questions

CHAPTER 18

1. The sum of the real interest rate and the expected rate of inflation.
2. The yield spread is 170 basis points. This spread is the additional premium for bearing credit risk.
3. The investor has the option to exchange the debt for another security at a specified exchange rate.
4. The muni-Treasury yield ratio $= 0.025 - 0.03 = 0.83$.
5. The rate on a taxable security that is equivalent, on an after-tax basis, to that of a non-taxable security.
6. The difference in yields, expressed in basis points, between Treasury securities of different maturities.
7. $(1 + 0.05)^3 = (1 + 0.045)^2 (1 + f)$; $1.157625 = 1.092025 (1 + f)$; $f = 6.01\%$.
8. The normal yield curve is upward sloping.
9. Expectations regarding future interest rates; liquidity premiums for longer maturities; preferred habitat among investors; market segmentation.
10. Used as a set of benchmark interest rates for loans and bonds.
11. Market participants generally gauge the credit risk of a bond issue by relying on the credit ratings by the rating agencies.
12. The greater the credit risk of a bond, the greater the risk premium on the bond (and, hence, the greater the bond's yield).
13. Solve for r in the following:
    $(1 + 0.046)^2 = (1 + 0.041) \times (1 + r)$
    $1.094116 = 1.041 \times (1 + r)$
    $(1+r) = 1.094116 \div 1.041$
    $r = 5.1024\%$

14.

2-year spot rate	1-year spot rate	1-year forward rate	
5%	4%	$(1.1025 \div 1.04) - 1$	= 6.0096%
4%	3.8%	$(1.0816 \div 1.038) - 1$	= 4.2%
3.5%	3.25%	$(1.071225 \div 1.0325) - 1$	= 3.7506%

15. Forward rates are not a perfect predictor of future rates because if they were, then we would know what bond prices would be in the future. Further, empirical evidence indicates that forward rates are not good predictors.
16. Forward rates are referred to as hedgeable rates because they indicate how an investor's expectations must differ from the market consensus to make a correct decision. The forward rates are a hedgeable measure of future rates.
17. This is an upward-sloping yield curve.

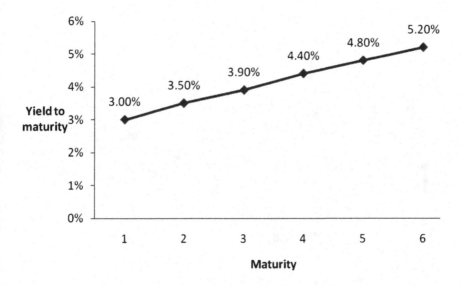

18. By calculating the forward rates, based on today's rates for various maturities, he/she can derive the slope of the yield curve, which suggests the expectations for interest rates in the future.
19. The "bias" in biased expectations theories is the belief that interest rates include premiums for liquidity preference (that is, risk) and to induce investors from their preferred habitat.

20. What is described in the quote is a humped yield curve. A humped yield curve is not consistent with the liquidity preference theory and the market segmentation theory. However, a humped yield curve may be consistent with the preferred habitat theory, in which interest rates are determined by the supply and demand for securities at the different maturities.

Solutions to End of Chapter Questions

CHAPTER 19

1. If earnings grow at a rate similar to the dividends, the dividend payout will remain constant. However, if earnings fluctuate, this will have the effect of a varying dividend payout ratio.
2. The greater the discount rate, the lower the present value of the stock. The discount rate should reflect the uncertainty associated with the amount and timing of dividends.
3. The value of the stock will be based on a perpetual stream of cash flows. Using the dividend discount model, this means that the growth rate, g, will be zero.
4. The average annual growth is $g = (\sqrt[3]{\$3/\$2}) - 1 = 14.47\%$.
5. The required rate of return must be greater than the expected growth rate; otherwise, the result does not make sense (that is, a negative value for the stock).
6. Yes. A negative growth rate still works in the dividend discount model.
7. The expected return on the stock is the sum of the expected dividend yield and the expected capital yield of the stock.
8.
   a. Assuming a constant growth rate ad infinitum may not be appropriate. Companies tend to experience growth phases throughout their life cycles, and the expected growth rates should change accordingly.
   b. Growth, transition, and maturity.
9. The estimate is $\$2 \times 15 = \$30$ per share.
10. Earnings captures the results of both operations and financing decisions, whereas sales does not reflect operating efficiency or financial leverage.

11. Value of the stock = $39.7162

Year	Expected Dividend	Expected Terminal Value	Total Cash Flow	Present Value
(Cash flow discounted at 8%)				
1	$2.50		$2.5000	$2.3148
2	$3.00	$40.6250	$43.6250	$37.4014
3	$3.25			
			Value =	$39.7162

Note: Terminal value (end of Year 2) = $3.25 ÷ 0.08 = $40.6250 [valued as a perpetuity]

12. Required rate of return = dividend yield + growth rate

12% = 4% + growth rate Therefore, the growth rate is 8%

13. Agree. Relative valuation focuses more on the fundamental factors behind the growth, rather than strictly dealing with dividends and expected growth in dividends.

Disagree: The dividend discount model can be evaluated in terms of fundamental factors by restated dividends in terms of dividend payouts and retention rate, multiples, etc.

14. Both the dividend discount models and the relative valuation models use proxies for the market's expectations (dividends and growth with the dividend discount models; comparable companies' multiples for the relative valuation models).

15. If you are too stringent, you will have a limited number of observations/estimations of the market's valuation.

Solutions to End of Chapter Questions

CHAPTER 20

1. Maturity value (FV), yield to maturity (r × 2), number of periods to maturity (n), periodic cash flow (the interest, or PMT).
2. The use of semiannual periods is to put the zero-coupon bond valuation on the same basis as the typical semiannual coupon bond.
3. There is a negative relation between the yield on a bond and the bond's value: the greater the yield to maturity, the lower the value of the bond.
4. When the yield to maturity is higher than the coupon rate, the bond will sell at a discount from its face value. This is because the market is demanding the higher yield than what the bond produces through the coupon; the remainder of the yield is from the appreciation in the bond from its discounted value to its face value.
5. If the bond is selling at a discount from its face value, the bond's value will rise until it reaches its face value. If the bond is selling at a premium to its face value, the bond's value will decline until it reaches its face value.
6. The current yield is a rough approximation of the bond's true return, ignoring the time value of money. The yield to maturity considers the time value of money, and assumes that any coupons on the bond are reinvested in a similar yielding investment.
7. The yield to worst is the lower of the yield to maturity and the yield to call for a callable bond.
8.
   a. We are assuming that each cash from is reinvested immediately in a similar yield investment.
   b. Coupon rate and maturity.
9. The investor has an option to sell the bond back to the issuer if the bond is putable.

10. The coupon rate is less than the yield to maturity because the bond is selling at a discount from its face value.

11.

Market Price	Dollar Price
94.0	$940.00
102.0	$102,000
75.0	$7,500
86.4	$864,000

12. PMT $= 3.5$; FV $= 100$; i $= 4\%$
   a. Not. PV $= 120 \to$ N would be negative (using a calculator)—in other words, it does not make sense. Therefore, the bond will not trade for 120 if its maturity is more than one year based on the given yield.
   b. Not. PV $= 100 \to$ N would be 0, which is not plausible if the maturity is actually more than one year.
   c. Possible. PV $= 90 \to$ N is 41.035, which is slightly more than twenty years.

13. As a premium the bond approaches maturity, its value converges toward the bond's maturity value.

14. The 10-year coupon bond has more reinvestment rate risk because (1) it has a coupon, which requires reinvestment each period, and (2) it matures sooner than the zero-coupon bond.

15. A callable bond is difficult to value because it is not possible to specify precisely if and when the bonds will be called from the investors. The issuer's decision is based on both interest rates on any refunding and the costs of issuing new bonds.

16. The convertible bond will trade at the greater of its value as a straight bond and its conversion value, and therefore will trade at $1,100.

Glossary

AA rated yield curve See *Swap rate yield curve.*

Abnormal return A return on an asset in excess of that expected for the asset's risk.

Absolute return Realized return on an investment.

Accelerated depreciation Depreciation in which more depreciation is deducted early in the asset's life, relative to straight-line depreciation.

Accounting identity The relationship among accounts such that assets are equal to the sum of liabilities and equity.

Accounts payable Amounts due to supplies for purchases on credit.

Accounts receivable Amounts owed by customers.

Accounts receivable turnover The number of times, on average, that a credit account is created for a customer and this account is then paid.

Accumulated comprehensive income or loss The total amount of income or loss that arises from transactions that result in income or losses, yet are not reported through the income statement.

Acid-test ratio See *Quick ratio.*

Active portfolio strategy A process of managing a portfolio that involves altering the portfolio to take advantage of market conditions and mispricings.

Active strategy An investment strategy that seeks to "beat the market" through actively trading securities.

Activity ratios Ratios that provide information on the effectiveness of putting a company's assets to use.

Actual reserve Average amount of reserves held by a bank at the close of business at the Federal Reserve.

Additional paid-in capital The amount paid by shareholders for stock at issuance in excess of par value.

Agency costs Costs that arise from conflicts of interest between the agent and the principals in an agency relationship.

Agent The party who acts in the interest of the principal in an agency relationship.

Alternative risk transfer A combination of an insurance contract and a capital market instruments used to transfer risk to another party.

American option An option that can be exercised any time on or before the expiration date.

Annual percentage return The return for a year, determined as the product of the interest rate per compounding period and the number of compounding periods in a year.

Annuity due An even series of cash flows occurring at even intervals of time, with cash flows occurring at the beginning of each period.

APR See *Annual Percentage Rate.*

Arithmetic rate of return The arithmetic average of subperiod rates of return.

ART See *Alternative risk transfer.*

Articles of incorporation A legal document that specifies the name of the corporation, its place of business, and the nature of its business.

Asset allocation The mix of investments from different asset classes in a portfolio.

Asset management See *Investment management.*

Asset management companies See *Investment company.*

Asset manager See *Portfolio manager.*

Asset pricing model A theoretical model of how investors price assets in the market.

Asset retirement liability Contractual or statutory obligation to retire or decommission an asset.

Asset turnover See *Total asset turnover.*

Asset-backed securities Debt obligations that are backed by assets other than residential mortgages.

Assets Resources of a business enterprise, which may consist of cash, inventory, property, and equipment.

Asymmetric information Uneven possession or access to information necessary to value assets.

Atlantic option See *Bermuda option.*

At-the-money option The situation in which a call option's exercise price is equal to the underlying's value or a put option's exercise price is equal to the underlying's value.

Average credit sales per day The credit sales for a period, divided by the number of days in the period.

Average day's cost of goods sold The cost of goods sold over a period, divided by the number of days in the period.

Average purchases per day The purchases over a period, divided by the number of days in the period.

Balance sheet A report of assets, liabilities, and equity of a company at a point in time.

Balanced scorecard A set of measures of performance that address different aspects of a company's strategic plan.

Bankers' acceptance Short-term loan that is backed by a bank's promise to pay. Generally used in import and export transactions.

Bankruptcy A legal process of settling the claims of creditors and owners for a company in financial distress.

Bankruptcy costs The direct and indirect costs associated with a company in Chapter 11 bankruptcy.

Base interest rate The interest rate for an investment without any default risk, which is the sum of the real interest rate and the expected rate of inflation.

Basic earnings per share Net earnings to common shareholders over a fiscal period, divided by the weighted average shares outstanding during the fiscal period.

Bermuda option An option that can be exercised before the expiration date, but only on specified dates.

Best-efforts underwriting An underwriting arrangement whereby the investment bank does not buy the issue from the issuer, but rather sells the security to the public, earning a profit on those shares it sells.

Beta A measure of the sensitivity of the returns on an asset to changes in the returns in the market.

Biased expectations theory The theory that purports that forward rates represent both expected future rates, as well as other factors.

Black-Scholes option pricing model An option pricing model of a European option, that values an option based on the price of the underlying, the exercise price, the risk free rate of interest, the time remaining to expiration, and the volatility of the underlying asset's value.

Bond Indebtedness that has an indenture agreement. In general use, a debt with an original maturity greater than 10 years.

Bond Indebtedness in the form of a security.

Bonding costs Costs incurred by the agent in an agency relationship to insure that the agent acts in the principal's best interest.

Bonus A cash reward based on some performance measure.

Book value The value of an asset at a point in time according to financial reporting standards.

Budget A company's investment and financing plans, expressed in monetary terms.

Budgeting The mapping out of the sources and uses of funds for future periods.

Business finance See *Financial management.*

Business risk The uncertainty associated with the sales and operating profit of a business, determined in large part by the business enterprise's line of business.

Business risk The risk associated with the uncertainty of operating earnings; the combination of sales and operating risk.

Busted convertible See *Fixed income equivalent.*

Bylaws Rules of governance of a corporation.

Call provision A provision of a security that allows the issuer of the security to buy the security from investors at a specified price, the call price.

Call schedule A schedule of call prices corresponding to different dates on which a callable security can be bought back by the issuer.

Callable bond   A debt obligation that may be bought back by the issuer at a specified price.

Capital   Long-term sources of financing, which include interest-bearing debt and equity.

Capital asset pricing model   An asset pricing model that allows for only one risk factor (market risk) to affect the prices of assets.

Capital budgeting   The decision process of allocating a company's funds to long-term investments.

Capital budgeting   The process of identifying and selecting investments in long-lived assets; that is, selecting assets expected to produce benefits over more than one year.

Capital lease   Rental obligations that are long-term, fixed obligations.

Capital market   The market for long-term financial instruments.

Capital market line   The line depicting the relation between the return on a portfolio and risk, where risk is measured in terms of the variance of the returns of the portfolio.

Capital structure   A company's mixture of debt and equity that is used to support the operating and investing activities of a company.

Capital structure   The mix of debt and equity used to finance a company.

Capital yield   The return on a share of stock from the change in the value of the share of stock.

CAPM   See *Capital asset pricing model.*

Carrying value   See *Book value.*

Cash-and-carry trade   A futures position in which the investor sell futures and borrows to buy the underlying asset, and then delivers this asset and pays off the loan at the end of the contract.

Cash conversion cycle   The length of time a business enterprise ties up cash, on average, in net working capital.

Cash flow   The flow of funds of a company within a period of time.

Cash flow from financing activities   The cash flow associated with borrowing, debt repayment, issuance of stock, the payment of dividends, and repurchasing stock.

Cash flow from investing activities   The cash flow associated with capital expenditures, asset retirement, or other changes in long-term investments.

Cash flow from operating activities   The sum of net income, noncash expenses, less any decrease in working capital accounts.

Cash flow from operations   See *Cash flow from operating activities.*

Cash flow interest coverage ratio   The number of times that a period's interest expenses could be paid by the company's cash flow before interest and taxes for that period; a measure of a company to satisfy its debt obligations.

Cash flow to capital expenditures coverage ratio   The ratio of cash flow of a company over a period to the company's capital expenditures for the period.

Cash flow to debt ratio   The ratio of cash flow to the sum of a company's debt obligations.

Cash market   The exchange of an asset for cash.

Cash settlement contracts   Futures contracts that are settled in cash, instead of taking an offsetting position.

Cat bond   See *Insurance-linked note.*

Catastrophe-linked bond   See *Insurance-linked note.*

Catastrophic risk management   The planning intended to minimize the impact of potential catastrophic events.

CD   See *Certificate of deposit.*

CDS   See *Credit default swap.*

Certificate of deposit   A promissory note of a bank to pay a depositor.

Characteristic line   The empirical model such that the excess returns on a stock are a linear function of the excess return on the market portfolio.

Classical safety-first rules   Decision rules that focus on the minimization of the probability of loss.

Close corporation   See *Closely held corporation.*

Closed-end fund   A regulated investment company invests in a portfolio of investments, but which does not issue additional shares or redeem shares.

Closely held corporation   A corporation that has a few owners who exert complete control over the decisions of the corporation.

CML   See *Capital market line.*

Cognitive biases   Systematic bias in decision making.

Commercial bank   Depository institution, which accepts deposits from savers and lends or invests these deposits.

Commercial paper   A promissory note issued by a large, creditworthy company or municipality.

Commodity swap   An agreement in which two parties agree to exchange payments based on the value of a specified commodity.

Common stock   The security that represents the residual ownership in a corporation.

Common-size analysis   An analysis of the financial accounts of a company that requires comparing an account to a benchmark.

Comparative advantage   The advantage a company has over other companies in terms of the cost of producing or distributing goods and services.

Competitive advantage   The advantage a company has over other companies as a result of the market's structure.

Complementary projects   Projects in which the investment in one enhances the cash flows of one or more other projects.

Compound interest   An arrangement in which interest is paid on both the principal amount and the accumulated interest.

Compounding   The process of interest being paid on both the principal and the interest already earned on this principal.

Conditional value at risk   A safety-first rule that focuses on expected value of a portfolio's returns, given that the value at risk has been exceeded.

Contingent projects   Projects that are dependent on the acceptance of another project.

Continuous compounding   Interest that is compounded instantaneously.

Contracting costs   The costs associated with creating and enforcing contractual agreements, such as a loan.

Conversion parity price   See *Market conversion price.*

Conversion provision   A provision of a security that allows the investor to exchange the security for another security.

Conversion ratio   The number of shares of common stock that the investor in a convertible security receives if the investor chooses to convert the security into stock.

Conversion value   The value of the stock that an investor in a convertible receives in exchange for the convertible security; the product of the conversion ratio and the market price of the stock.

Convertible bond   An indebtedness that may be converted into ownership units of the issuer at the option of the investor at a specified rate.

Convertible bond   A debt obligation that permits the investor to exchange the bond for another security, such as the common stock of the bond issuer.

Convertible note   See *Convertible bond.*

Core risk   Risks that a business enterprise is in the business to bear.

Corporate finance   See *Financial management.*

Corporation   An entity granted its existence by a state, operated to the benefit of the owners (the shareholders), who have limited liability.

Correlation   A standardized measure of how the outcomes of two assets co-vary, which ranges from −1 to +1; the result of the covariance of two assets' possible outcomes divided by the product of the two assets' standard deviations.

Cost of capital   The return that providers of capital (creditors and owners) expect for the use of their funds; the marginal cost of raising an additional dollar of capital.

Counterparty   The other party to an exchange.

Counterparty   The party on the opposite side of the transaction.

Counterparty risk   The uncertainty regarding the ability of the counterparty to perform in a transaction.

Covariance of a random variable   A measure of how two assets' returns vary together for a given probability distribution.

Credit default swap   An agreement for credit protection against specified events that affect the credit quality of a bond.

Credit protection buyer   The party to a credit default swap that pays for protection from specific events that affect the credit quality of a security.

Credit protection seller   The party to a credit default swap that agrees to insure against the impairment of the credit quality of a security.

Credit spread   The risk premium between the yields on Treasury securities and non–Treasury securities.

Creditor   The lender of funds.

Crossover rate   The discount rate at which the net present values of two projects are equal.

Currency swap   An agreement in which two parties agree to swap cash flows in different currencies.

Current assets   Assets that can reasonably be converted into cash within one operating cycle or one year, whichever is longer.

Current liability   An obligation that is due within one year or one operating cycle, whichever is longer.

Current ratio   A liquidity ratio that measures the company's ability to meets its current obligations, calculated as is the ratio of current assets divided by current liabilities.

Current yield   The ratio of the annual coupon on a bond to its market value.

CVaR   See *Conditional value at risk.*

Date of record   The date that determines which investors receive a particular distribution.

Days purchases outstanding   On average, the number of days of purchases outstanding at the end of the period.

Days sales in inventory   The number days of inventory on hand at a point in time, considering the average days' sales.

Days sales outstanding   The number of days of credit sales that are represented by the account balance in accounts receivable.

DDM   See *Dividend discount models*

Debt   A promise to repay the amount borrowed, plus interest, at a specified point of time in the future.

Debt instrument   See *Debt.*

Debt ratio   The ratio of debt to equity.

Debt-equity ratio   See *Debt-to-equity ratio.*

Debt-to-assets ratio   The proportion of the assets of a company that are financed by debt obligations; the ratio of debt to total assets.

Debt-to-capital ratio   The ratio of interest-bearing debt to total capital.

Debt-to-equity ratio   The ratio of debt to equity of a company.

Declaration date   The date the board of directors declares a distribution.

Declining balance method   Depreciation method in which a constant rate is applied against a declining carrying value of an asset.

Default risk   The risk that the issuer of a security will be unable to make timely payment of interest or principal when due.

Deferred annuity   An even series of cash flows occurring at even intervals of time, with the first cash flow occurring beyond one period from today.

Deferred tax liability   An account that represents the expected tax obligation.

Defined benefit plan   A pension plan in which the plan sponsor promised to make specified payments to qualifying employees at retirement.

Defined contribution plan   A pension plan in which the plan sponsor commits to a specified contribution, but the amount upon retirement is not guaranteed.

Degree of financial leverage   A measure of the sensitivity of earnings to owners to changes in operating earnings, attributed to the use of debt financing.

Delivery date   See *Settlement date*

Demand deposit   Funds deposited with a bank that can be withdrawn upon demand of the depositor.

Depository institutions   An entity that accepts deposits and loans funds.

Depreciation tax shield   The amount of the reduction in taxes resulting from the depreciation deduction.

Derivative   A security whose value depends on the value of an underlying asset, such as a stock.

Derivative instrument   See *Derivative.*

DFL   See *Degree of financial leverage.*

Diluted earnings per share   Adjusted net earnings to common shareholders over a fiscal period, divided by the weighted average shares potentially outstanding during the fiscal period, where potential shares reflect convertible securities and executive stock options.

Discount rate   The rate of interest that Federal Reserve Bank charges banks who borrow using the Fed discount window.

Discount rate   Rate of interest used to translate future cash flows into a value today.

Discounted payback period   The time it takes for a project's discounted cash inflows to add up to the initial cash outflow.

Discounting   The process of determining a present value of some future value or set of cash flows.

Diversifiable risk factors   See *Unsystematic risk factors.*

Diversification   The reduction of risk from investing in assets whose returns are not perfectly correlated with one another.

Diversification   The reduction of risk, without sacrificing return, by investing in assets whose returns are not perfectly, positively correlated.

Diversify   The application of diversification principles to reduce the risk of a portfolio.

Dividend   A distribution to share owners.

Dividend   A distribution to the owners of a corporation.

Dividend discount models   Models for valuing stock that uses an estimate of current dividends, expected growth in dividends, and a required rate of return.

Dividend payout ratio   The proportion of earnings paid in the form of cash dividends during a period.

Dividend payout ratio   The proportion of earnings paid out in the form of cash dividends to shareholders.

Dividend per share   The monetary amount of dividend paid per share of stock.

Dividend reinvestment plan   A program that allows shareholders to reinvest cash dividends in shares of the company.

Dividend yield   The return on a share of stock in the form of dividends; the ratio of dividend per share to the share price.

Dividend yield   The ratio of dividends on a share of stock to the market value of the stock.

Dividend–price ratio   See *Dividend yield.*

Dividends per share   A monetary amount of dividends that are paid per share of stock.

Dividends received deduction   A deduction available to corporations of a portion of the dividends received from another corporation.

Dollar return   The sum of the change in the market value of a portfolio and any capital or income distributions from the portfolio.

Dollar-weighted rate of return   The internal rate of return of an investment.

Domestic market   Market in which issuers domiciled in a country issue securities and in which these securities are traded.

Downside risk   See *Lower partial moment risk measure.*

DPO   See *Days payables outstanding.*

DRP   See *Dividend reinvestment plan.*

DSI   See *Days sales in inventory.*

DSO   See *Days sales outstanding.*

DuPont system   A method of decomposing a return ratio into its components, such as profit margins and turnovers, to facilitate understanding of change in the return ratio.

Dutch auction   An offer to buy that specifies a range of prices, with those willing to sell specifying a price within the range. Once offers are made, the buyer pays that price (based on bids) necessary to purchase the desired quantity.

Dynamic asset allocation   An process of altering the mix of assets in a portfolio from the portfolio's long-term mix in response to changing market conditions.

EAR   See *Effective annual rate.*

Earnings before interest, depreciation, and amortization   Operating income of a company before the deduction for depreciation expense and amortization.

EBITDA   See *Earnings before interest, depreciation, and amortization.*

Economic agents   Entities that make investment decisions in financial markets.

Economic life   The length of time that the investment provides economic profits.

Economic value added   A measure of a company's economic profit.

Effective annual rate   The rate of interest for an annual period that takes into account the compounding of interest within the year.

Effective rate of interest   See *Effective annual rate.*

Efficient frontier   The set of efficient portfolios for a set of assets.

Efficient portfolio   A portfolio that provides the highest expected return for a given level of risk.

Employee stock ownership plan   A defined contribution pension plan that is designed to invest in the employer stock on the behalf of the employee.

Enterprise risk management   The management of the risk of a business enterprise that is inclusive of the different operations, segments, and subsidiaries of a business entity, which views risk of the entire enterprise.

Equity   The ownership interest in a business enterprise.

Equity instrument   A security or unit of ownership in a company.

Equity investment style   A process of classifying equity securities based on a dimension or characteristic, such as size or a multiple, with expectation of taking advantage of superior returns that are attributed to the dimension or characteristic.

Equivalent taxable yield   The yield on a taxable security that is equivalent, after tax, to the return on a similar maturity, features, and risk to a municipal, nontaxable security.

ERM   See *Enterprise risk management.*

ESOP   See *Employee stock ownership plan.*

ETF   See *Exchange-traded fund.*

Euromarket   See *External market.*

European option   An option that can only be exercised at the end of the expiration period.

EVA   See *Economic value added.*

Excess reserve   The amount by which actual reserves exceed required reserves of a bank.

Exchange   A market with a physical location for the trading of assets.

Exchange-traded fund   A fund, similar to an open-end fund or a closed-end fund, with units representing shares of this fund traded much like stocks.

Ex-date   See *ex-dividend date.*

Ex-dividend date   The date determined by the exchanges to identify which investors are owners as of the declared date of record.

Exercise price   See *Strike price.*

Expansion project   A project that enlarges the company's established market or product line.

Expectations theory   A theory that states that the observed structure of interest rates reflects investors' expectations regarding future interest rates.

Expected shortfall   See *Conditional value at risk.*

Expected tail loss   See *Conditional value at risk.*

Expense ratio   An annual operating expense associated with a regulated investment company.

External market   A market in which securities are offered at issuance simultaneously to investors in a number of countries and issued outside the jurisdiction of any single country.

Face value   See *Maturity value.*

Feasible portfolio   Any portfolio that can be constructed with available assets.

Fed discount window   The lending of funds to banks by the Federal Reserve to meet banks liquidity needs.

Federal funds market   The market that banks use to manage any shortage in the required reserve.

Federal funds rate   The rate of interest charged to banks on borrowed funds.

Fiduciary duty   The legal responsibility to make decisions or to see that decisions are made that are in the best interest of a party.

FIFO   See *First-in, First-out.*

Finance   The application of economic principles to decision making that involves the allocation of money under conditions of uncertainty.

Financial analysis   The analysis of the financial performance and financial condition of a company.

Financial asset   Intangible asset that represents a claim on future cash flows.

Financial distress   Situation in which a company makes decisions under pressure to satisfy its legal obligations to creditors.

Financial economics   Another term used to identify finance, which emphasizes the role of economics in financial decision making.

Financial instrument   Evidence of ownership to a claim on future cash flows, such as a stock or a bond.

Financial intermediary   An entity that facilitates the flow of funds from those with excess funds to those in need of funds for investment purposes.

Financial leverage   The use of debt to finance a business enterprise.

Financial management   The financial decision making of a business entity. Also referred to as business finance and corporate finance.

Financial planning   The allocation of a company's financial resources to achieve a company's investment objectives.

Financial restructuring   A significant alteration of a company's capital structure.

Financial risk   Uncertainty associated with a party's reliance on debt financing, relative to equity financing.

Financial risk   The uncertainty associated with the earnings to the owners of a business due to the use of debt, which generally has a fixed cost and commits the business to a legal obligation to repay the debt.

Financial risk   The uncertainty regarding the outcome in terms of a financial measure, such as earnings.

Finite life general DDM A specific dividend discount model that uses a terminal or expected future price of the stock at some future period in place of a set of dividends beyond that point in time.

Firm commitment offering An underwriting arrangement whereby the investment bank buys the securities from the issuer and then sells these securities to investors.

First-in, first-out Inventory method in which the oldest costs of inventory are used in calculating costs of goods sold.

Fixed asset A long-term asset that has a physical existence, such as equipment or a building.

Fixed income equivalent The value of a convertible security as a straight bond, which results from the value in conversion being significantly below the security's straight value.

Fixed income instrument Financial assets whose cash flows are specified contractually, such as a bond or a note.

Flat yield curve A yield curve in which the rates of higher- and shorter-maturity securities are similar.

Foreign market Market in which issuers not domiciled in a country issue securities and the securities are traded.

Foreign market The market for securities that are issued by issuers who are not domiciled in the country.

Forward rate The interest rate that is expected to exist in the future.

Forward stock split See *Stock split*.

Framing Decision making that is influenced by the situation or the manner in which the situation is presented.

Free cash flow The cash flow of a company in excess of the expenditures for profitable investments.

Free cash flow to equity Cash flow from operations, less capital expenditures, plus net borrowings.

Free cash flow to the firm Cash flow from operations, adjusted for the after-tax interest expense, less capital expenditures.

Funded retained risk An assumed risk in which funds are set aside to absorb potential losses.

Futures contract A legal agreement between a buyer and seller such that the seller agrees to make a delivery and the buyer agrees to take delivery of something at a specified price at the end of a specified period of time.

Futures price The price agreed to in a futures contract for a specific transaction.

GAAP See *Generally accepted accounting principles*.

General partnership A partnership in which the partners share in the management of the business, share in its profits and losses, and are responsible for the liabilities of the business.

Generally accepted accounting principles In the United States, accounting methods that are codified by the Financial Accounting Standards Board.

Government-owned corporation   Corporate entities funded by the federal government for specific projects.

Government-sponsored enterprise   A corporations created by the federal government.

Gross plant and equipment   The total cost of physical assets.

Gross profit margin   The ratio of gross profit to revenues.

Gross property, plant, and equipment   See *Gross plant and equipment.*

Growth rate   The rate at which a value appreciates or depreciates.

GSE   See *Government-sponsored enterprise.*

Hedge fund   A pool of investment funds that are not regulated and are available for investment only to accredited investors.

Hedgeable rate   See *Forward rate.*

Heuristic   A rule of thumb or guide that reduces decision time.

Holding period return   The yield on an asset over a specified period, considering the change in the value of the asset and any cash flows, such as interest or dividends.

Horizontal common-size analysis   The restatement and comparison of accounts relative to a benchmark, where that benchmark is that accounts value in a selected base year.

Humped yield curve   A yield curve in which the rates of longer-maturity securities are similar to those of shorter-maturity securities, but less than the rates on intermediate-maturity securities.

Illegal insider trading   The trading of the stock of a company based on non-public, material information by an insider of the company.

Income statement   A summary of operating performance of a business entity over a period of time.

Incremental cash flows   The change in a company's cash flows related to a specific project.

Independent directors   See *Outside directors.*

Independent projects   Projects whose cash flow are not related to those of another project.

Indexed funds   A regulated investment company that invests funds in a portfolio that is intended to replicate an index.

Individually managed account   See *Separately managed account.*

Individually sponsored plan   A pension plan that is for a specific individual.

Information asymmetry   The situation in which a party or parties to a transaction have more information than the other party or parties to the transaction.

Initial margin   The minimum amount deposited per contract at the inception of a position.

Inside directors   Members of the board of directors who are employees of the corporation.

Insurance premium   The payment made for insurance protection.

Insurance-linked note   Synthetically insurance in the form of a capital market debt obligation, often used for insurance large losses, such as catastrophe losses.

Intangible asset   An asset that has no physical existence.

Intangible asset   A nonfinancial asset that does not have a physical existence, but creates future cash flows for a company.

Interbank yield curve   See *Swap rate yield curve.*

Interest coverage ratio   The number of times that a period's interest expenses could be paid by the company's earnings before interest and taxes for that period; a measure of a company to satisfy its debt obligations.

Interest rate swap   An agreement in which two parties agree to swap cash flows based on interest rates.

Interest tax shield   The amount of tax savings due to the deductibility of interest to arrive at taxable income, computed as the product of the marginal tax rate and the interest expense.

Internal market   The domestic and foreign markets for securities issued in the domestic market.

Internal rate of return   The yield on an investment, assuming that all intermediate cash flows are reinvested at this yield; the discount rate at which the present value of all cash flows of an investment is equal to zero.

In-the-money option   The situation in which a call option's exercise price is less than the underlying's value or a put option's exercise price is greater than the underlying's value.

Intrinsic value   The value of an option if exercised immediately.

Inventories   Investments in raw material, work in process, and finished goods, which are expected to be sold to customers.

Inventory turnover   The number of times, on average, that inventory flows into and out of a company.

Inverted yield curve   A yield curve in which the rates of longer-maturity securities are lower than those of shorter-maturity securities.

Investment company   An entity that manage the funds of individuals, businesses, and state and local governments.

Investment management   The decision making regarding individual and institutional funds. Also referred to as asset management, portfolio management, money management, and wealth management.

Investment manager   See *Portfolio manager.*

Investment profile   An graph of a capital project's net present value as a function of its cost of capital.

Investment value   See *Straight value.*

Investor   A party that buys an asset, such as a security, with the anticipation of a return in the form of future cash flows.

Investor's equity   The value of an investment position reduced by any borrowed amount.

IRR See *Internal rate of return.*

Issuer An entity that provides a security, such as a stock or a bond, in exchange for funds.

Joint venture A business entity formed as either a corporation or a partnership, generally for a specific business purpose and life.

Key performance indicators Measures used in a balanced scorecard.

Last-in, first-out Inventory method in which the most recent costs of inventory are used in calculating costs of goods sold.

Leveraged portfolio A portfolio in which the investor borrows funds to purchase some of the assets in the portfolio.

Liabilities Obligations to repay the amount owed, in some cases with interest.

LIBOR See *London Interbank Offered Rate.*

LIFO See *Last-in, First-out.*

Limited liability The presence of a limit on owners' liability for obligations of the business enterprise.

Limited liability company A form of business in which the owners have limited liability, but the business may elect to be taxed as a partnership.

Limited liability partnership A form of business in which the owners have limited liability.

Limited partnership A partnership that has at least one general partner and one limited partner, where the business is conducted by the general partner and the limited partner or partners have a limited interest in the profits and losses of the business.

Liquidity In the context of a market, the presence of buyers and sellers ready to trade. In the context of a business enterprise, the ability of a business enterprise to satisfy its short-term obligations.

Liquidity premium The additional compensation for the risk associated with being able to sell a security for close to its true value.

Liquidity risk The risk associated with the ability to sell a security at a value close to its true value.

Liquidity theory The theory that purports that the higher rates for longer-maturity securities in an upward-sloping yield curve represents compensation for liquidity and, therefore, the forward rates derived from the yield curve are not unbiased estimates of future interest rates.

Listed The situation in which an issuer of securities has selected to have its securities traded in the market.

LLC See *Limited liability company.*

LLP See *Limited liability partnership.*

Loan amortization An arrangement in which the principal amount of a loan is paid off over time, with more principal repaid in each successive payment.

London Interbank Offered Rate The rate major international banks are willing to offer on Eurodollar deposits to each other.

Long call position An investment position that involves buying call options.

Long futures See *Long position in futures.*

Long position in futures The investment position in which the investor buys a futures contract.

Long put position An investment position that involves buying put options.

Long-run planning See *Long-term planning.*

Long-term liability Obligations due beyond one year.

Long-term planning Financial planning for future periods, usually three to five years in the future.

Lower partial moment risk measure A safety-first rule that uses both the investor's risk aversion and a target rate of return.

MACRS See *Modified Cost Recovery System.*

MAD See *Mean-absolute deviation.*

Maintenance margin The minimum level that an investor's equity may fall from adverse price movements before the investor is required to deposit additional funds.

Mandated project A project that is required by an outside party, such as a government agency.

Marginal tax rate The tax rate on the next dollar of taxable income.

Market anomaly A strategy that can generate abnormal returns.

Market cap See *Market capitalization.*

Market capitalization The total value of stock outstanding, which is calculated as the product of the market price per share and the number of shares outstanding.

Market conversion premium per share The difference between the market conversion price for a convertible security and the current market price of the stock that can be obtained through conversion.

Market conversion premium ratio The market conversion premium, stated as a percentage of the market value of the stock for which a convertible security can be exchanged.

Market conversion price The effective value per share of stock in conversion of a convertible security; the ratio of the market price of a convertible bond to the conversion ratio.

Market risk The risk related to the overall movement of the market.

Market segmentation theory The theory that purports that the shape of the yield curve is due to preferred maturities of investors.

Market structure The mechanism in which buyers and sellers interact to determine the price and quantity in an exchange.

Market value added A measure of the difference between the market value of capital and the amount of invested capital.

Marketable securities Securities that can be some quickly.

Markowitz diversification See *Diversification.*

Master limited partnership A limited partnership with limited partner interests traded on a public exchange.

Maturity intermediation The transformation of longer-term assets into shorter-term assets.

Maturity spread The spread between any two maturities in a sector of a market.

Maturity value The amount of a loan due at the end of the loan period.

Mean-absolute deviation A measure of dispersion that is based on the absolute value of deviations from the mean.

Mean-standard deviation See *Standard deviation.*

Mean-variance analysis See *Mean-variance portfolio analysis.*

Mean-variance efficient portfolio See *Efficient portfolio.*

Mean-variance portfolio analysis The theory proposed by Harry Markowitz that focuses on assets' mean and variance as criteria for portfolio selection.

Merchant banking An investment bank that commits its own capital in lending or taking an equity stake in a business entity.

Minority interest In a balance sheet, the proportion of a company's assets not owned by the parent company. In an income statement, the earnings of a company representing the interest not owned by the parent company.

MLP See *Master limited partnership.*

Modern portfolio theory The theory developed by Harry Markowitz that focuses on the role of diversification within a portfolio in affecting the risk and return of a portfolio of invested assets.

Modified Accelerated Cost Recovery System A depreciation system used for U.S. taxes that is based on an accelerated method of depreciation.

Modified Cost Recovery System A system of depreciation prescribed by the U.S. Tax Code.

Modified internal rate of return The return on an investment, considering a specific reinvestment rate.

Money management See *Investment management.*

Money management See *Portfolio management.*

Money manager See *Portfolio manager.*

Money market The market for short-term securities.

Money market demand account An account in which funds are deposited and earn interest, though restrictions may be placed on withdrawals.

Money-weighted rate of return See *Dollar-weighted rate of return.*

Monitoring costs Costs associated with monitoring or limiting the actions of an agent in an agency relationship.

Mortgage-backed securities Securities that are backed, or secured with mortgages.

MPT See *Modern portfolio theory.*

Municipal yield ratio The ratio of the municipal bond yield to a comparable-maturity Treasury security.

Muni-Treasury yield ratio See *Municipal yield ratio*

Mutual fund A regulated investment company that solicits funds from investors and then invests these funds in a portfolio of investments, with the opportunity for investors to redeem shares and to invest additional funds.

Mutually exclusive projects Projects for which the acceptance of one precludes the acceptance of the other(s).

MVA See *Market value added.*

National market See *Internal market.*

NCF See *Net cash flow.*

Nearby futures contract The futures contract with the closest settlement date to the particular contract.

Negotiable CD See *Negotiable certificate of deposit.*

Negotiable certificate of deposit A promissory note of a bank that can be bought and sold by investors.

Net cash flow The sum of operating and investment cash flows in a given period of an investment's economic life.

Net operating cycle See *Cash conversion cycle.*

Net plant and equipment Cost of physical assets, less accumulated depreciation.

Net present value The value today of all cash flows of a project, discounted at the project's cost of capital.

Net present value profile See *Investment profile.*

Net profit margin The ratio of net income to revenues.

Net property, plant, and equipment See *Net plant and equipment.*

Net working capital The short-term assets that would remain if current liabilities are satisfied; the difference between current assets and current liabilities.

Net working capital to sales ratio The current assets available, after meeting current obligations, per dollar of sales.

Next futures contract The futures contract with a settlement date just after a particular contract's settlement date.

Noncore risk Risks that are incidental to the operations of a business.

Nondiversifiable risk factors See *Systematic risk factors.*

Nonlinear payoff A payoff on an investment such that the downside risk is different than the upside potential.

Nonsystematic risk The risk that can be diversified away.

Note Indebtedness that does not have an indenture agreement. In general use, a debt with an original maturity less than or equal to 10 years.

Notes payable Indebtedness in the firm of a security.

Notional amount See *Notional principal amount.*

Notional principal amount Principal amount that serves as the basis for the determination of cash flows in a swap agreement.

NPV See *Net present value.*

Number of days of credit See *Days sales outstanding.*

Number of days of inventory See *Days sales in inventory.*

Number of days of purchases   See *Days payables outstanding.*

OCF   See *Operating cash flows.*

Offshore market   See *External market.*

Open interest   The number of contracts entered into but not yet liquidated.

Open-end fund   See *Mutual fund.*

Operating cash flows   The cash flows related to the revenues, expenses, and depreciation of assets involved in a capital project.

Operating cycle   The length of time it takes to turn the investment of cash into goods and services for sale back into cash in the form of collections from customers.

Operating profit margin   The ratio of operating profit to revenues.

Operating risk   The degree of uncertainty concerning operating cash flows that arises from the particular mix of fixed and variable operating costs.

Operational budgeting   Short-term financial planning.

Optimal capital structure   The mix of debt and equity financing the company that maximizes the value of the company.

Optimal portfolio   The best portfolio of the set of portfolios on the efficient frontier; the point of tangency of the efficient frontier and an investor's utility curve.

Option premium   The cost of an option.

Option price   See *Option premium.*

Option writer   The seller of an option.

Order-driven market structure   A market in which centralized bid-matching matches the orders of the buyers and sellers.

Ordinary annuity   An even series of cash flows occurring at even intervals of time, with cash flows occurring at the end of each period.

OTC   See *Over-the-counter market.*

Out-of-the-money option   The situation in which a call option's exercise price is greater than the underlying's value or a put option's exercise price is less than the underlying's value.

Outside directors   Members of the board of directors who are not employees of the corporation.

Over-the-counter market   A market that does not have a physical existence, but which trades securities or other assets through a network of dealers.

Owners' equity   See *Equity.*

Par value   A stated amount of a security. In the case of a bond, the par value is the bond's maturity value.

Parity value   See *Conversion value.*

Partnership   A business owned by more than one party.

Partnership share   Ownership unit in a partnership.

Passive funds   See *Indexed funds.*

Passive portfolio strategy   A process of managing a portfolio that is focused on the construction of a portfolio that is consistent with the portfolio objectives, but without significant management of investments after the construction of the portfolio.

Passive strategy An investment strategy that does not involve active management of a portfolio, and involves minimal trading of securities in the portfolio.

Payback period The time it takes for the cash inflows from a project to add up to the initial cash outflow.

Payment date The date, determined by the board of directors, on which a dividend distribution is made.

Performance evaluation The measurement of the return on a portfolio, considering the portfolio's benchmark's return and the portfolio's risk.

Performance shares Share of stock given to employees, based on some measure of operating performance.

Perpetuity A uniform series of cash flows occurring at even intervals of time forever.

PI See *Profitability index.*

Plan sponsor An entity that establishes a pension plan, such as a business or a union.

Plowback ratio See *Retention ratio.*

Policy asset allocation The long-term asset mix of a portfolio.

Porter's Five Forces Forces that affect the ability of companies in an industry to generate economic profits: bargaining power of suppliers, bargaining power of buyers, threat of new entrants, threat of substitute products, and rivalry.

Portfolio Set of investments that are managed for the benefit of the client or clients.

Portfolio management The process of managing investments.

Portfolio manager The person who manages a portfolio by selecting investments, monitoring the portfolio's performance, and measuring and evaluating the portfolio's performance.

Positively sloped yield curve See *Upward-sloping yield curve.*

Postpayback duration The economic life of a project beyond its payback period.

Preferred habitat theory The theory that purports that yields in a yield curve represent both future interest rates, but also a premium for risk.

Preferred stock An ownership interest in a corporation that has a superior claim to the income and assets of a company relative to common stock owners, which may have a fixed maturity or may be a perpetual security.

Premium In the context of insurance, the amount paid to receive protection against an occurrence of an event.

Prepayment The option that a borrower has to prepay a portion or all of the loan prior to maturity.

Price discovery The process of determining a price of an asset by the interactions of buyers and sellers.

Price efficiency A characteristic of markets which describes asset prices as reflecting available information, such that it is not possible to earn returns in excess of that considering the asset's future cash flows and risk.

Primary market The market in which an issuer first issues a security to investor, receiving funds in exchange for the security.

Principal The person or group of persons the agent represents in an agency relationship.

Private plan A pension plan sponsored by a business entity for its employees.

Pro forma balance sheet A projected balance sheet, which summarizes expected amounts of assets, liabilities, and equity.

Pro forma income statement A projected income statement which summarizes expected income and expenses.

Probability distribution A set of probabilities for each possible outcome for a random variable.

Professional corporation A form of business in which owners have unlimited liability, but which is treated as a partnership for tax purposes.

Profitability index The ratio of the present value of the cash inflows to the present value of cash outflows of a project.

Profitability ratios Ratios that provide information on what is left of revenues after expenses.

Prospect theory A theory of decision making under uncertainty, describing behavior as involving a heuristic: first, individuals consider the possible investments and decide which ones are similar and which ones are different; second, the individuals then evaluate the possible outcomes and probabilities, selecting the investment that has the highest utility.

Public corporation See *Publicly held corporation.*

Publicly held corporation A corporation with ownership interests sold outside of a close group.

Pure expectations theory The theory that purports that forward rates are expected future interest rates.

Put provision A provision of a security that allows the investor to sell the security back to the issuer at a specified price.

Putable bond A debt obligation that may be sold back to the issuer at a specified price.

Quick ratio A liquidity ratio that measures the company's ability to meet its current obligations, calculated as the ratio of current assets, less inventory, divided by current liabilities.

Quote-driven market structure A market in which intermediaries, such as market makers, provide quotes for purchase and sales, and stand ready to buy or sell at these quotes.

Rate of return The dollar return on an investment, expressed as a percentage of the initial investment.

Rating agencies Companies that evaluate and rate the default risk of debt obligations.

Real interest rate The rate of interest that would exist in the economy in the absence of inflation.

Record date See *Date of record.*

Regression analysis The application of statistical techniques to gauge the relation between two of more variables.

Regression line A statistical depiction of the average relationship between two (or more) variables.

Regulated investment company A financial intermediary that sells shares to the public and invests those proceeds in a diversified portfolio of securities.

Reinvestment risk The risk that the investor may face yields on reinvested cash flows that are lower than the yield to maturity of a security.

Relative return Difference between the realized return and the expected return.

Relative valuation A method of valuing a stock or a company that requires using multiples of similar or comparable companies, and applying these multiples to the stock or company.

Reoffering price The price at which an investment bank offers securities that it is underwriting to investors.

Replacement project A project that involves the maintenance of existing assets to continue the current level of operating activity.

Repo See *Repurchase agreement.*

Repo rate The interest rate charged in a repurchase agreement.

Repurchase agreement A short-term loan backed by specific collateral.

Required rate of return The return expected by the suppliers of capital for the risk of the investment.

Required reserve Dollar amount of funds required to be maintained on hand, based on the reserve ratio.

Required yield The return that investors demand, which relates to the time value of money and the uncertainty of the security's cash flows.

Reserve ratio Percentage of deposits that a bank must maintain on hand.

Residual loss The agency costs other than monitoring costs and bonding costs.

Restricted stock grant The grant of shares of stock to the employee at low or no cost, conditional on the shares not being sold for a specified time.

Retained earnings The accumulation of earnings over time, less dividends paid over time.

Retention ratio The proportion of earnings retained by the company during a period.

Return See *Rate of return.*

Reverse cash-and-carry trade A futures position in which the investor buys futures, sells the asset, and lends funds at the inception of the contract, and then buys the asset and has the loan paid off at the end of the contract.

Reverse stock split A reduction of the number of shares of stock, specified as the number of shares post-split to the number of shares presplit, e.g., 1:4.

RIC See *Regulated investment company.*

Risk   Uncertainty regarding a future outcome.

Risk appetite   The amount of risk that an entity is willing to accept or retain.

Risk control   The process of identifying, evaluating, monitoring, and managing the risk of an business enterprise.

Risk finance   The management of the retained risk of an enterprise.

Risk management   The process of identifying risks and managing those risks through acceptance, mitigation, and transference.

Risk management culture   The environment in which the entity has an approach to dealing with risks and that approach is part of the business's management culture.

Risk neutralization   A risk management policy in which the management of an entity pursues a risk management policy to mitigate an expected loss without transferring the associated risk to another party.

Risk premium   Additional compensation required by investors for bearing risk.

Risk retention   The amount of risk an enterprise is willing to assume.

Risk tolerance   The amount of risk that is tolerated, with any risk exceeding this tolerance triggering action to reduce risk.

Risk transfer management   The transfer of risk by management to a third party via insurance, derivatives, structured financial products, or some other means.

Risk-free asset   An asset whose expected return is known with certainty.

Riskless asset   See *Risk-free asset.*

Safety-first rules   Decision rules that seek to maximize the probabilities of producing returns above some benchmark return.

Salary   A direct payment of cash of a fixed amount per period.

Sales risk   The degree of uncertainty related to the number of units that will be sold and the price of the good or service.

Salvage value   The expected value of an asset at the end of its economic life.

Savings deposit   Funds deposited with a bank that earn interest and can generally be withdrawn by the depositor upon demand.

Secondary market   The market in which investors trade securities or other assets.

Securities finance   The borrowing or lending of securities.

Securities lending transaction   The lending of securities by one party to an investor in need of those securities on a temporary basis.

Security   A financial asset that represents a claim on future cash flows, such as a bond or a stock.

Security market line   The line depicting the relation between the return on a stock to its market risk.

Selling group   A group of investment banks and others that market a security issue.

Semi-strong form of market efficiency   The degree of market efficiency in which current prices reflect all available public information.

Semivariance A measure of dispersion that considers only the possible outcomes below the expected value.

Separately managed account A professionally managed portfolio tailored to the investor's objectives.

Settlement date The designated date of the transaction in a futures contract.

Share Ownership interest in a corporation.

Shareholder Owner of an interest in a corporation.

Shareholders' equity The ownership interest in a corporation.

Short call position An investment position that involves selling or writing call options.

Short futures See *Short position in futures*.

Short position in futures The investment position in which the investor sells a futures contract.

Short put position An investment position that involves selling or writing put options.

Silo structure The structure of a business enterprise in which each part of the business is operated independently of the other parts of the business.

Simple interest An arrangement in which interest is paid only on the principal amount.

SML See *Security market line*.

Sole proprietorship A business owned by a single individual.

Spot market See *Cash market*.

Spread The difference in interest rates or yields, generally expressed in terms of basis points.

Standard deviation of a random variable A measure of dispersion or possible outcomes around the expected value, calculated as the square root of the variance.

Stated conversion price The ratio of the par value of a convertible bond to the conversion ratio.

Stated value See *Par value*.

Stock appreciation right A cash payment based on the amount by which the value of a specified number of shares has increased over a specified period of time.

Stock dividend Distribution of additional shares of stock to shareholders, generally specified in terms of the proportion of new shares to the number of existing shares, e.g., 25%.

Stock option The right to buy a specified number of shares of stock in the company at a stated price—referred to as an exercise price at some time in the future. The exercise price may be above, at, or below the current market price of the stock.

Stock split Distribution of additional shares of stock to shareholders, generally specified in terms of the ratio of shares after the distribution to the number of existing shares, e.g., 2:1.

Straight value   The value of a bond without considering the value of any embedded option.

Straight-line depreciation   Depreciation in which the same proportion of an asset's cost is depreciated each period.

Strategic plan   The path that the company intends to follow to achieve its objective.

Strategy   A direction the company intends to take to reach an objective.

Strike price   The price at which the option buyer can buy the underlying asset, in the case of a call option, or sell the underlying asset, in the case of a put option.

Strong form of market efficiency   The degree of market efficiency in which current prices reflect all public and private information.

Structure of interest rates   The relationship among interest rates of debt instruments based on a number of factors, including risk and maturity.

Structured finance   Securities created for specific risk and return profiles, such as asset securitization and structured notes.

Style box   A method developed by Morningstar to characterize securities based on two dimensions; for stocks these dimensions are market capitalization and style, whereas for bonds they are credit quality and maturity.

Sum-of-year's digits method   A depreciation method that uses a declining rate applied to the asset's depreciable basis, with this rate as ratio of the remaining years divided by the sum of the years.

Supranational   An organization that extends beyond a single country's boundaries, which shares in decision making of the organization.

Sustainability risk   A broad spectrum of the risk of a business enterprise that includes social and environmental responsibilities.

Swap   An agreement whereby two parties (called *counterparties*) agree to exchange periodic payments.

Swap curve   See *Swap rate yield curve*.

Swap rate   The fixed rate paid by the fixed-rate counterparty in a swap.

Swap rate yield curve   The rates for different maturities that reflect the average credit risk of banks that provide interest rate swaps.

Syndicated bank loan   A bank loan in which a group of banks lends funds to a borrower.

Systematic risk   See *Market risk*.

Systematic risk factors   Factors that affect the risk of an investment that cannot be diversified away.

Tactical asset allocation   A form of dynamic asset allocation that is based on opportunities to capture abnormal returns.

Taft-Hartley plan   A pension plan sponsored by a union on the behalf of its members.

Tangible asset   An asset with physical properties, such as a machine or inventory.

Tender offer   An offer, made directly to shareholders, to purchase shares of a company.

Three-stage dividend discount model   A multiphase dividend discount model that assumes that there are three distinct phases of growth in a stock's dividends in the future.

Time deposit   Funds deposited with a financial institution that have a fixed maturity date and earn interest. More commonly referred to as *certificates of deposit.*

Time premium   The difference between an option's price and the intrinsic value; the value of an option attributed to the possibility that the option may become more valuable in the time remaining to expiration.

Time value of an option   See *Time premium.*

Time-weighted rate of return   The geometric mean of subperiod rates of return.

Total asset turnover   The ratio of revenues to assets; a measure of the effectiveness of putting assets to use to generate revenues.

Treasury bill   A short-term security issued by a government. In the United States, these bills have maturities of four weeks, three months, and six months.

Treasury securities   Securities issued by a government.

Treasury spot rates   The theoretical rates that would exist for a given yield curve that represent what the U.S. Treasury would have to pay if the securities are zero-coupon securities.

Treasury stock   Stock of a company that is bought back by the company for use in executive stock options and other purposes.

Two-parameter model   See *Mean-variance portfolio analysis.*

Underlying   See *Underlying asset.*

Underlying   The basis of a derivative contract, which may be a stock, a bond, or any other asset.

Underlying asset   The asset or security specified in a derivative instrument, such that the value and or cash flows of the derivative instrument depend on the specified asset or security.

Underwriting syndicate   A group of investment banks that underwrite an issue.

Unfunded retained risk   An assumed risk for which losses are not financed until they occur.

Unit investment trust   A regulated investment that has a finite life and a fixed portfolio of investments.

Unsystematic risk factors   Risks that can be reduced or eliminated through diversification.

Unvalued contract   An insurance arrangement in which the value of the insured property is not fixed.

Upward-sloping yield curve   A yield curve in which the rates of longer-maturity securities are higher than those of shorter-maturity securities.

Useful life   See *Economic life.*

Utility function   A series of values assigned to possible choices that an entity faces.

Value at risk   A safety-first rule that focuses on the maximum loss at a specified probability level over a specified time horizon.

Valued contract   An insurance arrangement in which the value of the insured property is fixed.

VaR   See *Value at risk.*

Variance of a random variable   A measure of dispersion or possible outcomes around the expected value.

Variation margin   The amount of margin beyond the initial margin, generally required in cash.

Vertical common-size analysis   The restatement and comparison of accounts relative to a benchmark account's value for that period; for a balance sheet, this benchmark is total assets, and for an income statement this benchmark is revenues.

Weak form of market efficiency   The degree of market efficiency in which current prices reflect all of the information available in past prices.

Wealth management   See *Investment management.*

Working capital   Current assets, which serve to meet the needs of the day-to-day operations of a business.

Yankee market   The foreign market in the United States.

Yield curve   The yields on Treasury securities at a point in time for securities with different maturities.

Yield curve spread   See *Maturity spread.*

Yield-to-first call   The yield on a callable security, assuming that the security will be called by the issuer at the first available call date.

Yield to maturity   The expected return on a security, based on the security's current value, maturity value, and expected cash flows, such as coupon payments.

Yield-to-par call   See *Yield-to-first call.*

Yield to worst   The lower of a callable security's yield to maturity and yield to call.

Zero-coupon bond   A bond that does not pay interest; rather, the investor receives a return from buying the security at a discount from the bond's face value.

About the Authors

Frank J. Fabozzi, PH.D., CFA, CPA, is a Professor in the Practice of Finance and Becton Fellow at Yale University's School of Management, Editor of the Journal of Portfolio Management, and Associate Editor of the Journal of Structured Finance and the Journal of Fixed Income. Frank's writing spans the gamut from the basics of corporate finance to complex structured products and financial econometrics.

Pamela Peterson Drake, PH.D., CFA, is the J. Gray Ferguson Professor of Finance and Department Head of Finance and Business Law at James Madison University. Prior to joining James Madison University, she was a Professor of Finance at Florida State University, and an Associate Dean and Professor of Finance at Florida Atlantic University. Pam has collaborated with Frank in a number of books, including books on the basics of finance, financial analysis, and financial management. At James Madison University, Pam teaches financial analysis, analytical methods in finance, and advanced financial policy.

Index

Printed in the United States
by Bookmasters

Printed in the United States
By Bookmasters